GOD WITH US

God with Us

A Theological Introduction to the Old Testament

Christoph Barth

edited by
Geoffrey W. Bromiley

WILLIAM B. EERDMANS PUBLISHING COMPANY
GRAND RAPIDS, MICHIGAN

Library of Congress Cataloging-in-Publication Data

Barth, Christoph, 1917-1986.
God with us: a theological introduction to the Old Testament / Christoph Barth;
edited by Geoffrey W. Bromiley.
p.   cm.
Translated and condensed from the Indonesian ed.
Includes index.
ISBN 0-8028-3680-1
1. Bible. O.T.—Theology.   I. Bromiley, Geoffrey William.   II. Title.
BS1192.5.B375   1991
221.6—dc20   90-22473
                                                                  CIP

Contents

CONTENTS

[vii]

Foreword

THIS BOOK IS THE SHORTENED FORM of a work originally written in Indonesian for the use of lay Christians and their pastors within the Indonesian churches. It was written by a man who shared the decisive years of access to independence and nation building. The first draft served as lectures at institutions of higher learning in Jakarta and Ambon. The book itself was written in Europe as Christoph Barth had accepted a professorship at Mainz, Germany, in order to have access to international scholarship.

It was Christoph Barth's conviction that God always speaks and acts in specific historical conditions and that the witness given to these deeds remains meaningful to coming generations. In listening to the word of old, they hear God speaking in their own situation. Therefore, Christoph Barth included many elements of "introduction" (which have been left out in the English version as other literature is readily available in this field) and expounded each of the main themes of Israel's faith throughout the centuries in a polyphonic manner.

He intended to write a textbook sharpening his student's ears, so that in listening to what God had said and done in the past, they would be open to what God's Spirit says and does now. As a foreigner and as a scholar he refrained from actualizations, yet, being the first author to write an Old Testament theology in Indonesia, he carefully chose words and concepts that might resonate in a society struggling to be a community where people of different backgrounds may live in peace and justice.

After twelve years of teaching in Germany, Christoph Barth again devoted his energy to theological education in Indonesia. In annual visits he tested his material and learned of new developments. Unfortunately, cancer prevented him from finishing his life's work, and he entrusted the very last prophets to his wife (i.e., Nahum and Zephaniah, and from Haggai to the end) and asked her to close with "Him who has been sent to give his Life."

This textbook is widely used in Indonesia (where it was published in successive volumes between 1970 and 1990). From the beginning the author hoped that it would also become available to other Christians in Asia, in Africa, and in the West. Thanks to Mr. William B. Eerdmans, Jr., who published it, and to Dr. Geoffrey Bromiley, who prepared the shortened English edition, this hope has now become true, and we are grateful for it.

Marie-Claire Barth, M.Th. Prof. Dr. Ihromi
Basel *Jakarta*

Editor's Preface

PRIOR TO HIS DEATH Professor Christoph Barth left in typescript an English version of his Indonesian Old Testament theology. Unfortunately, this was much too long and unbalanced to be viable for publication as it stood, and with the consent of his widow it is now being made available in a greatly condensed form.

Although much excision has had to be made to achieve a suitable length and to bring the parts into proportion, every effort has been made to preserve both the essential theological content of the original and the exact wording, apart from alterations necessary to make transitions or occasional stylistic improvements.

One of the distinctive qualities of this Old Testament theology is the attempt to expound the message of the Old Testament in a manner that is generally more faithful to the Old Testament itself, namely, as an account of the mighty acts of God rather than a series of abstract doctrines. In keeping with this overall plan the titles of the later sections have been slightly modified to bring them into line with the earlier ones. One or two missing section theses have also been supplied so as not to break the common pattern.

The biblical quotations are normally taken from the New English Bible (NEB). Where the Revised Standard Version is followed, "RSV" is added. In some instances, Barth used his own translation (cited as CB). Where necessary (e.g., when a Hebrew term is discussed), the difference in versification between the Masoretic text (MT; the Hebrew text of the OT) and the English has been noted; otherwise, the English versification has been followed. The Hebrew and Greek transliterations follow a standard modern scheme.

Regrettable though the condensation may be, it is hoped that the work in this form will have a wider impact and make a more solid contribution to the study of biblical theology than would otherwise have been possible.

Pasadena, Pentecost 1990   Geoffrey W. Bromiley

Introduction

1. The Old Testament, Israel's Holy Scripture

THE CHURCH HAS ALWAYS CONSIDERED the OT part of holy scripture. Yet although the OT constitutes the older and larger part of the Bible, it has not always been fully valued in the church's life. In general Christians read and enjoy Genesis, parts of the Prophets, a few Psalms, and no more. They prefer the NT books, which are shorter and, they feel, more readily understood. This situation is anomalous.

The NT writers themselves had a different opinion and attitude. First, they did not know any part of scripture as the "Old Testament." They simply spoke of the scriptures, the holy scriptures, Moses and the Prophets, and the like. Second, they did not know their own books as the "New Testament." Both terms, "Old Testament" and "New Testament," meant something different to them. Paul spoke of the "old testament" when he had in mind all God's acts and revelation before Christ's advent. He used "new testament" to describe God's revelation in Christ (1 Cor. 3:14-18; 5:18-21).

The earliest Christians knew only one holy scripture, that of Israel, the collection of books that the Jews recognized as authoritative testimony to God's revelation. With the Jews, the apostles and first Christians read this scripture as witness to God's deeds and self-revelation in the context of his covenant with Israel. The disciples of Christ did not write a new holy book but simply an application of the one holy book to the person and life of their Master. On the ground and authority of that one book they knew Jesus as God's Son, Messiah, Lord, Shepherd, and Savior. Without that book they could not have understood who he was nor become his messengers by word, deed, and writing. From that book they learned that he was not dead but lives and reigns, sitting "at the right hand of God the Father Almighty" from now to the world's end.

[1]

God's gift through Israel's scripture, then, was witness to Jesus, to the mission of Israel and God's new people, to God's coming kingdom. The apostolic writings simply confirm that what scripture announces has really occurred, and that a new community has thus been born consisting of both Jews and Gentiles. God himself by the power of the Spirit brings about this birth. But he draws on the testimony of scripture in so doing (cf. Luke 24:44-47; John 5:39; Acts 2:14-36; 3:12-26; 7:1-53; Heb. 11; etc.).

Israel's holy scripture, then, was God's chief instrument when he created his new people of all nations. But its function did not end there. The witness is always needed because God's people must be born anew in every age. If we view the OT as an ancient document, telling of a remote era, having significance only as a prelude to the gospel that is more fully and accessibly presented in the NT, the NT authors themselves invite us to read and search the OT, not just to find extra knowledge or spiritual treasure, but to know who Jesus is and to find pointers to God's will and salvation in our own day. In this sense the old scripture is still a treasury of new revelation that the church everywhere needs.

2. Meaning of the Expression "Theology of the Old Testament"

THE WORD *theologia* is of Greek derivation. The early church adopted it when penetrating the western world. Originally it had been used for stories and teaching about the western gods. The church applied it to the God of Israel who is finally revealed in Jesus Christ. For Christians "theology" means teaching about God. OT theology, then, is teaching about God in Israel's scripture. But we need to qualify this general definition for a more accurate understanding.

First, we must guard against the over-narrow view that an OT theology simply summarizes OT teaching about *God* and nothing more. All religions agree that "God" is inseparable from other contents of belief. Teaching about God subsumes teaching about the world and humanity, about life and death, about origin, nature, and destiny. This is especially true in the case of the OT. In one sense Israel's God stands aloof as sovereign over all creatures. Yet in another sense he associates himself intimately with their fate in a way far beyond what we find in other religious thinking. In the OT, theology means teaching about God *and* humanity, God *and* the world. God constitutes himself the very essence of the OT testimony, yet the OT also teaches us about Israel and the nations, about sin and redemption, an old world in disorder, a new world that comes. OT theology is a summary of the whole OT message and witness.

Second, OT theology might seem to be concerned only with the thirty-nine canonical books of the OT to the exclusion of the twenty-seven books of the NT. But the terms "OT" and "NT," as we have seen, are incorrect. Israel's scripture was an open collection. In many decisive respects its witness was set forth in the apostolic writings later known as the NT. We should thus speak of only one holy scripture. Across the centuries the church has recognized the NT as having equal authority with the OT, and this conviction is right. Yet on the testimony of the authors themselves the authority of the NT derives from that of the OT. OT theology, then, must allow for the fact that the NT witnesses to the fulfilment of what is written in Israel's scripture, and is thus part of it.

Third, an OT theology must be written in the context of theological science as a whole. Theology is a kind of workshop or storehouse at the church's disposal. Called to witness to God in the world, the church needs continually to rethink its message and reassess its tools. Theology has to recover what is lost, put right what is wrong, mend what is broken, seek what is needful, and even test what seems to be right. OT theology is one branch of this critical and constructive activity. It stands closely related to OT exegesis and interpretation. Exegesis of particular texts needs its guidance, but it, too, depends upon an exegetical basis. OT theology has also a close relation to systematic theology, which is heavily dependent upon it but which also gives it invaluable assistance and guidance. Even practical theology is closely allied as it helps OT theology to present the biblical message clearly and relevantly but also feeds upon increasing knowledge of the true content and meaning of the message.

3. Old Testament Theology in the Past

CHRISTIAN THEOLOGY IS AS OLD as the church itself. Reading and interpreting scripture, systematically pondering and presenting its message, and applying it to contemporary situations have always been considered requisite to the church's life. If OT theology as we now know it is a comparatively younger discipline, it has an old and venerable forerunner. The NT writings are a kind of OT theology, offering as it were a summary of the Law, the Prophets, and the Writings, and reflection upon their message in the light of Christ's coming.

In the first centuries of the church and the Middle Ages many attempts were made to explain the church's message to both Jews and Gentiles. Unfortunately, Christians were too much inclined to take for granted the essential harmony between church doctrine and scriptural witness, especially as regards the Israelite background of the latter. The Alexandrian allegorical method of interpreting the OT gradually prevailed over the more historical method of Antioch, and as a result Christian authors could not respect the OT as an even relatively independent entity with its own message. No wonder they did not feel the need for an OT theology that could correct the church's message and not just confirm it.

A big step forward came with the 16th-century Reformation and the rediscovery of the authority and independence of scripture, and not least the OT, vis-à-vis the church. This period saw a remarkable development of biblical studies. New translations and commentaries appeared, many of them based on the Hebrew, so that the unique voice of the OT was heard in a new way. Genesis, Isaiah, and the Psalms in particular played a part in the associated renewal of the church.

Nevertheless, OT study as we now know it could come to birth only with further developments. The Renaissance, the Enlightenment, and rationalism did much to change readers' attitudes. They now saw the Hebrew Bible not as essential to Christian doctrine, life, and culture but as belonging to a world of its own. Early 19th-century Romanticism, with its new sensitivity to ancient cultures, opened the way to a new understanding of the OT as the library of Israel and the Jews which must be read "objectively" and not with the presuppositions of Christian dogmatics.

With the end of the Christian consensus even more radical views were advanced. The theory of evolution asserted that religion in general, and that of Israel in particular, moved from primitive beginnings to increasing stages of maturity. Sociologists of religion argued that religion is a function and reflection of the social life of a nation or tribe. Pan-Babylonianism claimed Sumero-Babylonian roots for almost every element of Israel's religion. As we now see, these assumptions did little to promote true objectivity. Yet undeniably the historico-critical method made real progress in OT study possible.

The 19th century saw the first serious efforts in biblical theology. Theological faculties gradually brought this new subject into their curricula, and textbooks on OT and NT theology appeared, often under such titles as "The Religion of the OT." Conservative scholars tried to present this religion as a coherent system, while more critical colleagues focused on the historical development of religious ideas in the OT literature.

Not surprisingly, not all church people appreciated the new independence of biblical study. Many resented the publication of OT and NT theologies alongside traditional dogmatics. They suspected biblical interpretation that might diverge from church doctrine and even contradict it. Only a minority welcomed what they saw as the rediscovery of the Bible's true message.

It is true that many basic problems remain unsolved. Yet the efforts made in the field of biblical theology have not been in vain. At least a consensus on the primary task of the discipline has been reached. So far as possible OT theology must let scripture speak for itself. It must survey the main topics of faith which the books express. It must allow the essential message to go out to our own time.

NORMATIVE

4. God Acts—The Heart of the Matter

IF, HOWEVER, WE TRY to unfold the central message, the question arises: What is the essence of the OT? Where is the heart of this heterogeneous library to be found? Research on the origins and literary forms of the OT has produced a new awareness of the fundamental significance of God's mighty acts in history. In 1952 G. Ernest Wright published a famous study *God Who Acts* (Studies in Biblical Theology 1/8), and Gerhard von Rad's *Old Testament Theology* followed in 1957 (volume I, Eng. tr. 1962) and 1960 (volume II, Eng. tr. 1965). OT theology as Wright sees it "is a recital or proclamation of the redemptive acts of God, together with the inferences drawn therefrom" (p. 11). In von Rad's book OT theology unfolds as a dynamic story instead of a static system of religious ideas. This is in line with Israel's own understanding. Of the many indications of the decisive role of God's redemptive acts in the OT, we may mention the most obvious that form-critical study has brought to light.

First, we note the thematic structure of the Pentateuch. This tells of God's first acts, how he created heaven and earth, chose the ancestors of Israel, brought Israel out of Egypt, led his people in the desert, revealed himself at Sinai, and finally gave Israel the land of Canaan. The Pentateuch, of course, has other aspects. It witnesses to Israel's beliefs: the transcendence and unity of God, human nature and destiny, the calling and salvation of the people. It also presents the command of God embodied in the law. Yet the doctrinal and legal elements are integrated into the structure of the story of Israel's origins in the mighty acts of God.

Second, we note the hymns and the prayers of national or congregational lament in the Psalms. An element common to both types of psalm is commemoration of God's redemptive acts. The hymns recite the acts as praise and confession (Pss. 66, 81, 111, 114, 135, and 136). The laments seek God's intervention as in past salvific deeds (Pss. 74, 80, and 89). The acts are the same as in the Pentateuch. This congruity can hardly be accidental.

Third, we note the many confessional summaries of history in the OT, as in Deut. 26:5-9 (cf. 6:21-23). In von Rad's view these are ancient cultic creedal formulas that are basic to the present structure of the pentateuchal

[5]

story. We find similar summaries in the prophets (Jer. 2:6-7; Ezek. 20; Isa. 63:7-14), in Neh. 9:6-31, and in 2 Chron. 20:6-8, 9-10.

Fourth, we note that when the apostles first proclaimed Jesus as Christ to the Jews they often began by recalling the great acts of God (Greek *ta megaleia tou theou,* Latin *magnalia Dei;* cf. Acts 2:11). The apostles realized that only the most evident and essential witness of scripture could "prove" Jesus to be the promised Messiah. They thus made this their starting point, as in Acts 7:2-50, Rom. 9:4-5, or Col. 1:13. The first Christian creeds (cf. 1 Cor. 15:3-4) were also summaries of God's acts "according to the scriptures."

It would be an exaggeration, of course, to argue that every OT book, or every part of every OT book, was consciously written as witness to God's historical acts. Cultic prescriptions in Exodus and Leviticus and the wisdom literature represented by Job, Proverbs, and Ecclesiastes prove the contrary. Nevertheless, no part of Israel's scripture does not at least presuppose God's mighty acts in word and deed to bring in his kingdom. God's dynamic initiative, not timeless religious truth, is the main theme of biblical testimony.

5. The Nine Chapters of This Book

A GLANCE AT THE TABLE OF CONTENTS will show that this book falls into nine chapters, each of which deals with one of the divine acts that are the essential subject matter of the OT. This division is unusual as regards the selection, number, and order of the topics as well as the method of presenting them. It thus requires explanation.

a. The Ninefold Division Calls for Justification

We can adduce no direct biblical basis for it. Clearly many more than nine acts of God in history might be considered as important themes of biblical witness, e.g., the raising up of the judges, the institution of the priesthood, or the many deliverances from national peril. A selection has been made according to a twofold criterion.

First, acts have been chosen that had a significant resonance in the OT literature. The broader their resonance, the surer one can be of their authority as fundamentals of Israel's faith. Creation, the patriarchs, the exodus, the desert wandering, the Sinai revelation, the gift of Canaan, the election of David, the election of Zion, and the sending of the prophets— these acts of God all meet the first criterion.

[6]

Second, acts have been chosen that appear as items in the summaries mentioned in § 4 above. True, the sending of the prophets occurs only sporadically, e.g., in Amos 2:11 and Mic. 6:4. Yet the OT witness sufficiently backs the choice and the NT summaries confirm it.

b. The Problem of Order

Finding the best order in which to arrange the acts poses a delicate problem. No central idea, guiding principle, or system of doctrine can solve this problem of finding the best order to arrange the acts. One might try to arrange the material according to the position of the subject matter within the canon. Or one might attempt a chronological order according to the approximate time of the acts. Or one might try to fix the age of each hypothetical tradition in Israel's faith. Or finally one might try to build on a presumed salvation history in the OT, giving each part its proper place in it. None of these approaches, however, can be applied consistently.

The first is impossible because the texts relating to God's various acts are spread over the whole canon, e.g., creation texts in Genesis, Prophets, and Psalms. The second cannot succeed because most of the acts pertain to more than one moment in history, e.g., prophets continuing down the ages. The difficulty with the third is that many traditions might seem to be the oldest, e.g., creation in Gen. 1–2, exodus in Hos. 11, desert wandering in Jer. 3:2, or the gift of Canaan in Isa. 5:1-7. As for salvation history, it is doubtful whether any of the OT writers had such a thing in mind. The summaries of God's acts simply compile outstanding instances, each item is an independent salvation history, and there is no continuous historical scheme.

The chapters of this book, then, are like beads on a string. No pretense is made of historical or systematic order. The order simply follows the traditional sequence, i.e., that of the biblical summaries. The titles, too, follow those that the Bible itself uses for the great acts of God.

c. Presentation of the Topics

The chapters are divided into four or more sections, each devoted to one main aspect of the topic: the manner and aim of God's action; how he reveals himself by it; what is said about God's people—its election, failure, misery, salvation, revival, and mission; the function of individuals who are chosen as instruments or mediators of God's action; and the light in which the nations appear. These aspects are not equally represented in every chapter. Each of the topics, however, has a theological aspect (in the strict sense), an anthropological, a soteriological, and an eschatological aspect, so that each contains an OT theology on its own.

A tenth chapter was originally planned that would unfold the fulfilment according to the NT. But it seemed impracticable to do this within the limits of a closing chapter. Nothing less than an abridged NT theology would have been needed—a fresh undertaking beginning with the insight that the NT is essentially nothing other than the application of scripture to the person and life of Jesus of Nazareth. Others with greater competence must shoulder this task, stimulated, it is hoped, by the nine chapters of the present book.

Chapter I

God Created Heaven and Earth

1. The Witness of Scripture

The Lord, the God of Israel, created the world and all its creatures, and still reigns over it and preserves it. This is one of the themes of Israel's faith and therefore of OT scripture. Israel apprehended it when God revealed himself from Mt. Sinai as Creator and Governor of the universe and Savior from Egypt. Creation ranks first as a topic of Israel's faith but with a complementary function to other topics.

"IN THE BEGINNING, God created heaven and earth" (CB). These are the first words of Genesis and of all scripture. For Israel creation is a salvific fact, an event that evokes thankful joy and confession of faith. It is not just an objective general truth. It provides an unshakable and everlasting foundation for Israel's very existence even in periods when everything seems in collapse and all hope futile. One would think it should have a leading place among the topics of Israel's faith, but the evidence is against this. Few biblical texts deal with creation, and even those that do are not typical expressions of Israel's faith.

The list of genuine creation texts is amazingly short. We have the two well-known creation stories in Gen. 1 and 2. There is a reference in Gen. 14:18-22. Creedal summaries in Jer. 32:17, Neh. 9:6, and Ps. 136 put it first. Many Psalms extol the Creator's power and wisdom (Pss. 9, 19, 24, 29, 33, 36, 74, 90, 93, 96–99, 104, 139, 147, 149). Wisdom texts include Prov. 3:19-20 and 8:22-31, while Job 38–41 might pass for a poetic treatise on the miracles of God's creation. Isaiah shows a deep interest in creation in 40:12-26; 42:5; 43:1; 44:24-28; 48:13; 51:9-10; 54:5. Jeremiah seems to speak in the name of the Creator of the land (4:23-28; 5:21-25) who is also the Creator of world history (18:1-12; 27:5-6). There are also short creation hymns in Amos 4:13; 5:8; 9:5-6 (cf. also Isa. 37:16; Jer. 51:15-19).

Only in later passages is creation integrated into the series of God's saving acts. For long periods Israel does not seem to have been compelled unanimously to confess the Lord its God as Creator of heaven and earth. Only by the time of the exile did the topic become a generally accepted element of Israel's faith at the very beginning of creedal summaries. Early summaries (e.g., Deut. 26:5-9; 6:21-23) focus on Israelite topics: the election of the patriarchs, the redemption from Egypt, and the gift of Canaan. They do not deal with creation and preservation, which concern all creatures and humanity as a whole.

In this sense creation is secondary or complementary. We do not detract from its importance by giving it this modest place and function. Nevertheless, witness to creation is definitely not the primary element in Israel's faith. It is not a key to understanding the OT in its entirety. The acts of God that brought Israel into existence have theological priority. Creation passages clarify, confirm, and complement the witness to these basic acts, putting them in their universal context. In this role they have their own importance and urgency.

In proof we might refer first to many Psalms that praise God as Creator and Preserver. Israel learned to praise the Lord as Creator of heaven and earth in temple worship. Creation here preludes, undergirds, and crowns God's acts for Israel. The God who called Israel into being created and governs the universe (Ps. 74:12-17; 77:12-21; 89:6-13; 134:4-12; 136:5-26; 148:1-14). Even the most cosmos-oriented creation hymns show in some way their rooting in Israel's faith (cf. 8:2; 29:2, 11; 19:8-14; 104:1, 24, 31).

In Isa. 40–55 there are frequent allusions to creation at the center of the message. The key words here are *bārā'* ("create," 11 times), *yāṣar* ("shape," 10 times), and *'āśāh* ("make," 8 times)—always with the Lord as subject. What did the Lord create? In half the passages heaven and earth, in the other half Jacob or Israel. Both are the work of the one Creator. Both are created with one intention. Heaven and earth were created with Israel in view, and should Israel face extinction, the whole universe would be in jeopardy!

The two creation stories in Gen. 1 and 2 proclaim the creation of human beings as God's ultimate intention in creating the world. Man comes first in Gen. 2, while male and female are the crown of creation in 1:27. The common point is that humanity is created and called to live in community with its Creator, as caretaker in God's garden (2:15) or steward over all created things (1:28). God did not need fellowship (cf. 1:26), but human beings do, and with freedom and kindness God calls them into relationship with himself. Creation is thus a first step toward the creation of Israel as a people that will listen to God's commands (2:16-17) and participate in his rest (2:1-4a).

The wisdom texts, while extolling God's power and wisdom as Creator, do not so plainly state that this Creator is Israel's God, Savior, and Redeemer. Yet they tell us that wisdom begins with the "fear of the Lord" (Prov. 1:7; 9:10; 15:33; Job

28:28), and a passage like Jer. 10:12-16 (cf. 51:15-19) clearly equates the Creator of heaven and earth with Israel's Creator.

Our survey thus supports the thesis that creation as an act of God is a complementary topic in Israel's creed. In this regard the church's creeds followed a similar course. The early creeds had no reference to creation, just as the oldest NT summaries (e.g., 1 Cor. 12:3; 15:3-4; Phil. 2:11) were exclusively christological. Creation became a creedal topic only from around A.D. 150, and received additional stress only at Nicea in 325. The development of the church's creed thus paralleled that of Israel's creed.

2. Creation as Miracle

Many nations around Israel praised their gods as powerful creators that laid a durable foundation for world order and prevailing political and social systems. Israel viewed creation as an innovative act that from the very first was part of the story of God's saving intervention on the world's behalf. OT scripture exalts creation (a) as a miraculous deed performed by God's powerful Word alone, (b) as God's victory over the forces of chaos and annihilation that inevitably endanger all creatures, and (c) as a perfect work by which God made all things for their ultimate destination.

CREATION IS A WORK that evokes praise. Israel knew many reasons for praise of the Creator. A survey of these motifs might begin with a study of the words most often used for God's activity as Creator. The Bible uses terms with very concrete, down-to-earth meanings. Like a craftsman, God is said to have "formed," "shaped," or "made" heaven and earth. Taking raw materials, he "produced" what he planned out of them, thereby showing his "know-how" or "wisdom" (*ḥokmāh,* originally "craftsmanship"). Only one Hebrew word is equivalent to our abstract idea of "creating."

The word *yāṣar* (Gen. 2:7, 8, 19) means "to form, shape," e.g., like a potter or sculptor. The verbs *bānāh* ("to build," Gen. 2:22; Amos 9:6), *yāsad* ("to ground," Isa. 51:13), and *kônēn* ("to erect," Isa. 45:18) are all building terms. Tent building is the model for *nāṭāh* ("to stretch out," Isa. 44:24; Ps. 104:2; Job 9:8). Work done with the hands or fingers is denoted by *'āśāh* ("to make," Gen. 1:7, 16, 25, 26; cf. Ps. 19:2). It is not known whether *qānāh* ("to create," Gen. 14:19, 22; Deut. 32:6; Ps. 104:24) also had at one time a concrete meaning connected with craftsmanship.

The one word that does not fit the picture is *bārā'* (Gen. 1:1, 21, 27; 5:1, 2;

6:7, and several times in Isa. 40ff.). Many attempts have been made to fix its precise meaning. It seems to denote "creating" as an absolutely miraculous and unheard-of activity, not to be compared with anything that we might do. Does it mean creating out of nothing? We find this understanding in 2 Macc. 7:28, which reflects the time when Judaism came under Greek influence. P. Humbert ("Emploi et portée du verbe bârâ [créer] dans l'AT," *Theologische Zeitschrift* 3 [1947] 401-22) prefers the idea of producing something *new*. As he sees it, newness rather than existence out of nonexistence captures the decisive character of the Creator's act.

None of the verbs seems to mark the Creator's work as miraculous in itself. We must look elsewhere to find the miracle of creation. Why was Israel amazed and even overwhelmed, yet also full of joy and gratitude, in the face of creation? Why does the heavenly host praise its Creator, and why are all creatures invited to join in the hymn? The answer lies in the miracles of creation: how numerous and manifold are God's creatures, how high the heaven, how vast the earth, how deep the sea, how immeasurable the power of him who creates and preserves them all, how unfathomable his wisdom, how innumerable the marks of his fatherly love and kindness! Of such reasons for praising the Creator there seems to be no end.

Israel was not alone in its praise of the Creator. Mythological texts excavated at Ugarit (15th century B.C., modern Ras Shamra) on the Mediterranean coast of Syria show that the high god El was worshiped there as Father of humankind, Creator of all creatures, and Creator of the earth. Enlil, Marduk, and other Mesopotamian deities also bear the title *bānū/bānāt šamû û erṣeti*, "creator/creatrix of heaven and earth." Amon-Re, at one time called Aton or Atom, the sun-god of Egypt, was also glorified as creator of the universe and humanity. One might adduce similar beliefs from many periods of history, and research on tribal religions in many continents has brought to light a widespread motif of adoration. Note should be taken of the cultic purpose of this praise. The most commonly used hymns and epic or mythological texts formed an integral part of important community ceremonies, e.g., New Year or coronation day, and had in view the establishment or restoration of the social order by recitation or reenactment of the creation story.

Formally, then, Israel was much in line with its neighbors near and far. Did it then conform to a general pattern? Was it saying and intending virtually the same thing as other socioreligious communities? Insofar as it was itself a socioreligious community, we may accept this conclusion. But Israel was also unique and had something distinctive to say. We shall try to see what this was by examining creation first as creation by the Word, second as a victory over chaos, and third as a work of incomparable perfection.

a. Creation by the Word

God created the world by his powerful Word and command. Only three statements in the OT expressly say this. Yet these three represent the biblical witness. The best known is in Gen. 1:3: "God said, 'Let there be light,' and there was light." The same scheme of command and accomplishment recurs (with variations) seven times in Gen. 1. We might also refer to Ps. 33: "The Lord's word made the heavens, all the host of heaven was made by his command. . . . For he spoke, and it was; he commanded, and it stood firm" (vv. 6, 9). Finally Ps. 148, summoning all creatures to praise the Lord, gives as the reason: "For he spoke the word and they were created; he established them for ever and ever by an ordinance which shall never pass away" (vv. 5-6). To these, of course, we should add the NT witness from John 1: "Through him [the Word] all things came to be; no single thing was created without him" (vv. 3-4).

The point of all these texts is that creation is a miracle inasmuch as God performed it simply by his Word, i.e., by an amazingly simple yet powerful instrument of action.

Various theories have been suggested in elucidation. Some interpreters find here the mark of a refined religious imagination that thinks of God as able to do anything by simple command. Others see evidence of a more advanced stage of imagery that seeks to reduce anthropomorphism by spiritualizing. Others suggest that "Word" has here the quality of a personal power proceeding from God but essentially one with him. If there are elements of truth in these proposals, there are also weaknesses. The first suffers from the fact that creation was by Word *and deed* in juxtaposition. The problem with the second is that word and work are equally anthropomorphic. The difficulty with the third is that the stress in the OT passages is on the miraculous power of God's creative Word, not on its hypostatic or personal character.

The achievement of creation by just a Word is indeed a tremendous miracle (cf. the saying of the centurion to Jesus in Matt. 8:8). Yet the power exerted by the divine command is not the deepest reason for Israel's astonishment in the face of creation. The heart of the matter lies in the identity of him who created everything by his Word. For Israel God's Word was not just an instrument of divine power. By it God reveals himself as Lord, as Israel's God. His Word is closely associated with his incomparable name. All his mighty deeds in history, including creation, are demonstrations of his deep involvement with this tiny community of Israel. God's creating Word is the Word of his unfailing love for his chosen people (Ps. 33:4, 10-12, 18, 21-22). This was Israel's unique reason for praising creation by the Word.

b. God's Victory over Chaos

A further reason for Israel's glorifying of the Creator's work was that it had and has the character of a victorious deed. The story of creation extols God's struggle against the dark powers of chaos and destruction, and his victory over them. Creation is good news in the full biblical sense of the term.

When God created heaven and earth he had to meet an enemy, depicted in Ps. 74:12-17 as an atrocious monster (cf. also Ps. 89:8-11; Job 26:12-13). It is true that the references to this enemy are few and poetic, yet they are still an integral part of the OT tradition (cf. Isa. 51:9-10). Thus in Gen. 1:2-3 the creation of light brought to an end the reign of darkness over the face of the abyss. But who was the enemy? Poetic texts use mythological names like Leviathan (cf. Isa. 27:1; Ps. 74:14) or Rahab (Isa. 30:7; Ps. 87:4; Job 26:12), apparently dragons or sea-monsters (cf. Job 7:12; Ezek. 32:2; Ps. 74:13). Others use decoded terms, e.g., *tᵉhôm*, the primeval ocean or abyss (Gen. 1:2; 7:11; Exod. 15:5, 8; Ps. 33:7), or *ḥōšek*, darkness as the power inimical to light and life (Gen. 1:2; 1 Sam. 2:9; Job 10:21), or *tōhû wābōhû*, without form or void, i.e., chaos (Gen. 1:2; Isa. 34:11; Jer. 4:23).

The point here is that Israel had a deep awareness of evil powers which from the very beginning of the world menaced all beings but God. No one had seen these powers in the form of actual monsters. Rahab and Leviathan were symbols, but symbols indicate realities. Three cosmic phenomena clearly manifested the activity of these superhuman, demoniacal, and destructive forces: the ocean with its unfathomable depth and terrific waves, the desert with its pitiless heat and drought, and night with its engulfing of all life in absolute darkness.

The existence of hostile powers, though not denied, was not an article of Israel's faith. What God's people believed and proclaimed was that God defeated chaos once and for all when he created heaven and earth. Once crushed by his mighty arm, the monster may no longer rage wantonly nor the ocean overflow its fixed borders (Gen. 1:2; 7:11; 8:2). By virtue of this first victory the earth stands immovable and firm in spite of the sea's pounding waves (Ps. 93:2-4). The initial victory is reason for confidence and hope in the world's future.

How did Israel know this? No direct witness could endorse it. No one was present when the world's foundations were laid. Ancient tales might have provided a basis, but the sacral poetry shows clearly that primeval events were later known to be rooted in Israel's historical experience. The allusion in Ps. 74:14-15 is to the victory over Pharaoh at the Red Sea as well as to that over Leviathan. We find the same juxtaposition in Isa. 51:9-10. Primeval and historical events are here interwoven and seen as a unity. Tales about the Creator's victory express what Israel knew as God's saving act at the beginning of its own history. Pharaoh and his army were for Israel a terrible incarnation of chaotic forces. Not by chance, but by virtue of the Lord's victory, Israel escaped them. The Red Sea victory was thus a solid basis for belief in the Creator's initial victory over all the forces of chaos and evil.

c. God's Perfect Work

The obvious perfection of God's creative achievement was a third reason for glorifying it. So perfect are God's creatures that only awe and admiration are appropriate. But by what criterion does Israel reach this conclusion?

Some passages refer to the witness of creation itself, e.g., Ps. 19:1 (cf. Paul in Rom. 1:20). Others stress the wisdom that is evident in created things, e.g., Ps. 104:24; Jer. 10:12. In Gen. 1:3, 13, 18, 21, 25, God himself, knowing the destiny of his creatures, calls his work good, i.e., fit or suitable for the end or venture of perfect encounter and togetherness between his creatures and himself. Gen. 2 agrees by showing that all things are created in harmony for the sake of God's relationship with the human race.

The more Israel reflected on the perfection of God's creation, the more it perceived his salvific purpose. Intrinsic characteristics of creation lost importance and God's ultimate design became increasingly central. This took place with the gradual integration of creation into the Israelite elements of OT witness. Creation was perfect because it was suitable to God's purpose in world history and supremely in Israel's history. The upshot may be seen expressly in the Testament of Moses, an Essene writing of the 1st century B.C.: "God, the Lord of hosts, . . . created the world for the sake of his people, but he did not reveal the purpose of creation from the very beginning" (1:11-12).

Other nations were conscious of the perfection of the world. They deeply admired its beauty and richness, the unfailing function of its natural laws, and the equilibrium of forces that guarantees the constancy of the established order both cosmic and social. Israel, too, appreciated these qualities and praised God for them. Yet Israel also praised the Creator for a perfection of heaven and earth that is not yet apparent but still to be revealed in fulness. The next three sections will try to show this from the OT.

3. God Created Heaven and Earth

In the Bible "heaven and earth" is a concise formula for all that God created: (a) the firmament, the celestial ocean, the celestial bodies and stars, God's celestial abode and angels, all summed up as heaven;

(b) mountains, valleys, rivers, forests, deserts, habitable lands, seas, plants, animals, humans, also death and the underworld, all summed up as earth; (c) heaven, though also created, with relative priority over earth, so that it may be a symbol and even a representative of God, yet both in their togetherness reflecting the free relationship and community between Creator and creature that is the ultimate purpose of God's creative action.

"IN THE BEGINNING God created the heavens and the earth" (Gen. 1:1 RSV). This formula was by no means Israel's own invention. We find it in the sacral language of many nations long before Israel made it its own. The patriarchs already knew God as the Creator of heaven and earth (cf. Gen. 14). The formula then came into the worship of Israel (cf. Ps. 124:8), and especially into creeds and creedal summaries (cf. Neh. 9:6; Jer. 32:17). It was from Israel rather than from other nations that it then made its way into the Christian Apostles' Creed: "I believe in God the Father Almighty, maker of heaven and earth," and then in expanded form into the Nicene Creed: "We believe in one God, the Father Almighty, Maker of heaven and earth, and of all things visible and invisible."

a. The Creation of Heaven

In trying to clarify what the Bible means by the creation of heaven, we should note that heaven in the sense of classical antiquity has little in common with what we now know as the sky or outer space. Heaven is what is above our heads from birds and clouds to celestial bodies. In this regard the OT uses the language of the time to express what it has to say. The content is what demands our attention and acceptance.

Heaven was also the sphere of supraterrestrial power. In it resided the authorities that control rain and drought, blessing and curse, life and death. From this standpoint it might be a source of fear and despair. Hence the biblical proclamation that God is the Creator of heaven (cf. Ps. 96:6) comes as a liberating message. With this knowledge heaven can be extolled as a perfect creation that reflects God's wisdom both as a whole and in detail.

Most evident to the human eye is the firmament, the vault of heaven. The sun, moon, and stars, while they might be harmful to humans (Ps. 121:6), were created to be a blessing, in particular to give light, to measure time, to "govern" day and night (Gen. 1:14-18). The winds, the clouds, the rain, and the rainbow that seems to bridge heaven and earth—all these phenomena reflect the Creator's beneficent wisdom. "He alone created them" means that "he owns them." They are not independent forces but living instruments of his hands. He made them to serve spontaneously his will and purpose for his earthly creatures.

High above the visible sky God made his own invisible "heaven" and there established his "throne" (Ps. 23:10; 103:19). From there he governs his entire kingdom and descends from time to time to reveal himself by his presence, word, and deed. Little is said about this divine dwelling, God's council of heavenly sons, or his messengers (angels). God's "heavenly host" may be the sun, moon, and stars (Deut. 4:19; 17:3) or it may be an army ready to intervene on earth (Josh. 5:14-15). "Sons of God" is an archaic expression for the divine assembly (Ps. 82:1; 1 Kgs. 22:19; Job 1:6; 2:1), though in Gen. 6:1-4 it seems to be used for fallen angels.

Although creation passages refer to God's creation of the sky (Ps. 96:5), for some reason they do not say that he created heaven as his own abode. God is "clothed in majesty and splendour" (104:1-2). He laid the beams of his "pavilion" (104:3). He "established his throne in heaven" (103:19). But no details are given about the creation of the higher heaven, of angels, of the "sons of God," or of other celestial powers. We simply read in Prov. 8:22-31 that wisdom, itself the first of God's creatures, was the chosen instrument by which God created all things. For the rest, the celestial forces all do humble service as instruments of God's mighty acts. They are not God's equals; he has taken them into his service as "messengers."

There is ample reason, therefore, why the heavens *(šāmayim)* should be a subject of joyful admiration. The OT witness is not interested in cosmology for its own sake. It gratefully praises the Creator who made heaven according to his wisdom. Earthly beings owe it to the divine wisdom that the upper powers do not crush our world. Instead, heaven is "on duty" as a source of blessing and hope.

b. The Creation of Earth

Along with the heavens God created the earth. What does the Bible mean by "the earth"? Earth is the lower part of the cosmos that can be seen, touched, and trodden upon. Humans can to some extent own and control it, but all the power they have is power on earth.

A close relation exists between human power and the extent of earth. A nation's power grows with the land it controls. The greater the number of nations, the wider the known earth. We see this from the list of nations in Gen. 10 and Daniel's visions of the kingdoms of earth.

Many biblical passages praise God as Creator of the earth. Ps. 104, which is parallel to older Egyptian models, is typical. It expresses the admiration of Israel for the number of earth's inhabitants, the abundant provision the

Creator has made for them, and the striking beauty and perfection of all terrestrial creatures.

Yet Israel is aware also of the frightening aspects of life on earth. God's people do not close their eyes to these negative features. In hymns and liturgies they find in such features a reason for praising God the Creator. The ocean constantly assaults the earth. The desert, a terrible desolation of sand, stone, heat, darkness, and death, unceasingly beleaguers the habitable land. Catastrophes such as storms, earthquakes, and locusts continually afflict the dwellers on earth. These shocking realities might seem to be a reason for questioning the perfection of God's work. It might seem that hostile powers, demons, or deities share control with God. Yet in OT scripture these negative features in no way lessen the perfection of God's creation. In this context the perfection is a gracious gift that the Creator himself freely grants (cf. Ps. 104:29-30) rather than an inherent quality of earth itself.

Lamenting over the negative realities of ocean, desert, catastrophe, and death can turn into glorifying of the Creator because God took measures to repulse, to dam up, and therefore to control whatever might or did endanger his earthly creatures. He set the ocean within fixed boundaries, gave the desert its allotted place, and established the earth on solid foundations to safeguard it against inundation. The OT witness does not seem to present God as the actual Creator of the evils. They arose with the creation of creatures distinct from himself. If he can "create" evil by bringing disaster upon a sinful people in judgment (Isa. 45:7; 54:16), his true creative work was to make the earth "a place to dwell in" (Isa. 45:18).

God's precautionary measures when creating the earth appear the more miraculous when we remember his intention to "give" the earth as a gratuitous fief to humanity. Even his special gift of a country to his chosen people is set in a fresh light in this regard. Humanity dwells in a land that is created and protected by the Lord. Individuals and nations may have to secure their own territory, but their ultimate and authentic security depends on him who is alone the Creator and Proprietor.

c. Heaven and Earth as a Whole

The expression "heaven and earth" appears in many biblical passages and creedal formulations. In this regard Israel simply took over an established phrase for the universe, the totality of created things (cf. Hebrew *kōl* in Ps. 8:7 [Eng. 6] and Greek *ta pánta* in Col. 1:6). Yet if the confession of God as Creator of heaven and earth was not formally original, the biblical passages show characteristic divergences from the common usage.

First, they clearly set the Creator above the universe. He is not an element in the created world, e.g., its spirit, soul, or totality. The universe is a mere creature. No divine nature, quality, or power can be attributed to it. The Lord involves himself deeply in it. He chooses heaven as his abode and earth as the theater of his action. But if his involvement was so deep at times that his deity might seem to be sacrificed, the OT never dishonors God as a creature or reveres creatures as if they were God.

Even nations outside Israel did not always confuse Creator and creatures. The power to create was a divine privilege. Yet the distinction was never consistently respected. In some cases it seems to be deliberately ambiguous. Thus the Babylonian creation story has Marduk create, but he does so out of the body of the slain Tiamat. The world's divine origin and substance is thus starkly asserted. An ancient Egyptian creation story describes a primeval pyramidal hill as the beginning of heaven and earth, and it appears as either creature or creator (cf. H. Frankfort, et al., *Before Philosophy: The Intellectual Adventure of Ancient Man* [repr. 1973], pp. 59-61). As we know them from OT texts and the Ras Shamra tablets, the gods of Canaan represent natural forces, so that no clear distinction between creature and creator is discernible. The creator-gods of the nations can boast of natural evidences of their power, so that Israel could be tempted to worship them, only a small minority refusing to "bend the knee to Baal" in Elijah's time (1 Kgs. 19:18). Yet the OT witness is that heaven and earth are not divine. They are not their own creators. The Lord made them and reigns over them.

Second, heaven and earth together are God's one creation (Ps. 115:15; cf. 148:13). The visible sky and the invisible heaven and its host are no less creatures than earth. Heaven has a clear, if limited, priority over earth. It is usually mentioned first. Yet the creation stories in Gen. 1 and 2 show a primary concern for earth. There is no absolute distinction. The two complement one another. Heaven was not created to exist for itself alone, but for its role on behalf of earth. Similarly, earth was not meant to exist for its own sake. As heaven gives leadership, e.g., by worshiping God (Isa. 6:3), separating light and darkness (Gen. 1:3), and obeying God's commandments (Ps. 103:21), earth is called to follow its initiative. In this sense heaven precedes and has a governing position, so that divine titles can sometimes be given to heavenly powers, e.g., *'elōhîm* in Ps. 8:6 (Eng. 5) or *benê 'ēl* in Deut. 32:8 (cf. the Septuagint, the Greek version of the OT, hereafter abbreviated LXX). In relation to earth these powers, as it were, represent God. Yet they are no more than instruments of his authority and are not to be worshiped. Their power is for service; it is not to be revered.

Third, many OT passages portray heaven and earth in a common solidarity of dependence on God. Both are in constant need of his protection and preservation. Heaven might be nearer to God and have extraordinary power as his eternal abode and instrument of government. Postexilic Judaism can use *šāmayim* ("heavens") as a substitute for the divine name or even for

God himself, as in swearing by heaven (cf. Matt. 5:34). Nevertheless, heaven is not above the danger of annihilation. Even the heavenly council can contain elements that oppose the wise government of God. Together with earth, and no less fervently, angels, too, await the establishment of God's kingdom. Awareness of the common need of salvation lies behind the prophetic expectation of "new heavens and a new earth" (Isa. 65:17) which finds an echo in NT prophecy: "Then I saw a new heaven and a new earth, for the first heaven and the first earth had vanished, and there was no longer any sea" (Rev. 21:1).

4. God Created Humanity

Among all heavenly and earthly creatures humanity was granted a special place. God called it to partnership and community with himself, as shown in his covenant with Israel. He created it (a) a unity of soul and body held together by the spirit of life, the soul leading (like heaven), the body following (like earth), the spirit representing divinely given life; (b) in two sexes as man and woman, thereby establishing a free partnership and communion analogous to his covenant, in which man calls and engages himself (like God) and woman freely answers (like Israel); (c) as a race of lords with dominion over fellow creatures, yet also as a race of servants working for its own and others' interests, and thus in both respects imitating its Creator; (d) as the crown of creation, God's vice-gerent and image, in virtue of the above features and functions.

Is HUMANITY REALLY the crown of creation, the most important of all God's creatures? As a human judgment, this statement sounds presumptuous. The biblical witness is not insensitive to the danger of human complacency. It thus avoids direct statements that might lead to it. As God's chosen people Israel learned to know human defects more intensely than human qualities. If scripture assigns outstanding importance to humanity, it did not find proof of this in experience. The Creator himself is the one decisive witness in its favor.

In Gen. 2 *'ādām* (human being), formed from the dust of the ground, is God's primary concern; all other creatures are satellites, as it were. In Gen. 1 humanity came into being on the sixth day, concluding or "crowning" the whole process of creation (1:26-27). Ps. 8 describes man as "master over all thy creatures" (v. 6). In Deut. 4:32 the revelation of God on Mt. Sinai is the greatest of miracles, equaled only by that of the creation of humanity.

Why is humanity granted this outstanding position? It is not because of any theory of human priority in natural history, nor because of optimistic views of humanity. It is because of God's plan, purpose, and intention for humanity. It pleases God that humanity should be his partner in an adventure of voluntary obligation and relationship. From this standpoint humanity can be described as "very good" (Gen. 1:31). It has surpassing excellence as God's perfect creation in its nature as soul and body, its differentiation as man and woman, its twofold function as lord and servant, and its calling as God's chosen trustee and image.

a. Soul, Body, and Spirit of Life

A miraculous feature of every human being is twofold existence as soul and body. Two different natures coexist, an invisible and spiritual, a visible and material. They are inseparably united yet exist independently. Human beings are both at the same time; they cannot exist in one of the two ways alone. They are entirely body, yet animated body, and entirely soul, yet embodied soul.

(1) Every human being is an animated body (Hebrew *bāśār,* "flesh"). Flesh, visible and palpable, stands for all the bodily parts. Biblical poetry extols the body as God's skillful achievement (Job 10:8-11; Ps. 139:13-16). It is praised for its strength and beauty. The young Joseph is "handsome and good-looking" (Gen. 39:6). David is "handsome, with ruddy cheeks and bright eyes" (1 Sam. 16:12). Ps. 45:2-4 exults in the all-surpassing beauty of the king, and the Song of Songs in the beauty of the bride and bridegroom.

There is also a sense, however, of the body's weakness and limited duration. This is not the pessimism of a dualistic disdain. It is realism. The prophets hammer home the folly of dependence on human physical strength. "The Egyptians are men, not gods" (Isa. 31:3 NEB margin). "A curse on the man who . . . leans for support on human kind [RSV flesh]" (Jer. 17:5). "All flesh is grass, and all its beauty is like the flower of the field" (Isa. 40:6 RSV). "Flesh," then, means transitoriness and moral corruption. "All flesh" can have a negative ring (Gen. 6–9). Finitude alone might be tolerable, but sin associates it with guilt and judgment. Materiality in itself is no cause for regret (Gen. 1:31). The negative aspect of death emerges only with the fall: "Dust you are, to dust you shall return" (3:19).

The OT teaches us to praise the body as a good and even perfect creation. Israel had no reason to despise human corporeality nor to try to suppress it. Even as regards the body's weakness and temporality, while human beings vainly boast of their health and beauty, and sin brings corruption and judgment, there is still good cause to trust in the Creator. He himself answers for the body, for "he knows how we were made" (Ps. 103:14), remembers that we are only mortals (Ps. 78:39), and "gives vigour to the weary, new strength to the exhausted" (Isa. 40:29).

(2) Adam is also created as an invisible, incorporeal being, as soul (*nepeš*). He became a living creature as God "breathed into his nostrils the breath of life" (Gen. 2:7). He does not *have* a soul; he *is* a soul. To be a soul as well as a body is the distinctive manner of human life. By the union of soul and body, we are individual persons.

A question arises whether we are also spirit. The OT tends to resist this view. Unlike soul and body, the spirit of life is given or lent by the Creator. It is creative power. When God takes it away, we die and return to dust (Ps. 104:29-30), and "the spirit returns to God who gave it" (Eccl. 12:7; cf. Ezek. 37:4ff.). The soul is not itself immortal. When a person dies, the soul dies, and a corpse is a *nepeš mēt,* literally "dead soul" (Num. 6:6; cf. Josh. 2:14; 1 Kgs. 19:4; Job 36:14). Biblical usage can be flexible, however, and is thus confusing. Elijah prayed for the child's "soul" (RSV; cf. NEB "breath of life") to come into him again (1 Kgs. 17:21). "Spirit" (Hebrew *rûah*), which is usually the breath of life, can also denote what we would call a person's "heart" (cf. Gen. 41:8 [NEB "mind"]; 1 Sam. 30:12; Ezek. 3:14; Ps. 51:14 [Eng. 12]). Yet in the main it is true that we *are* soul, but we *have* spirit.

Although the OT might often put body first, as in Gen. 2, in general it grants a relative priority to soul, as in the phrase "soul and body" (Isa. 10:18 RSV). The soul has a leading function. It is as soul that we are living individuals with spontaneous feelings, hopes, intentions, desires, love and hate, joy and distress. The invitation goes out to the soul: "Bless the Lord, my soul" (Ps. 103:1). The soul, our spiritual nature, takes the initiative, for good or for bad. The body has no separate feelings or desires. It feels and desires what it expresses as living soul. Here is confirmation of the unity of soul and body, but also of the priority of soul.

Nevertheless, this priority is only relative. The soul is not divine, celestial, or everlasting, the body alone human, earthly, and perishing. Location of the soul (*nepeš,* NEB, RSV "life") in the blood (Gen. 9:4; Lev. 17:11) emphasizes that it participates fully in the body's quality as earthly creature. The body points down to the earth from which it is taken. Yet by its union with living soul it participates in the soul's quality as invisible creature which points up to the Creator who called it into being. The difference between the two aspects is that we live on earth but also under heaven, and we *know* it. As creatures of double nature we are called and qualified to play our part in God's design. Is humanity God's perfect creation? Israel had good cause to extol the Creator of our human race. Our mode of existence as both body and soul was one of the reasons.

b. Men and Women as Partners

Another mystery of humanity as God's perfect creation is its creation in two sexes, male and female. As in the case of the comparable mystery of existence in soul and body, humanity exists inseparably in two complementary modes. Here is another reason for Israel's admiring and exalting of the Creator's work.

Few scriptural passages refer to this aspect. If there are many incidental references to the destiny and function of man and woman, not many reflect on their essential togetherness as God's creation.

In Gen. 2 God formed humankind (*hā'ādām*, v. 7) as his first and foremost creature, with no initial mention of sexual differentiation. The first human being is evidently "man" (NEB, RSV). God then makes provision for man in the garden, of which he is the caretaker and tenant (vv. 15ff.). To remedy man's loneliness God brings to him animals and birds, but only his close kin, one of his own flesh and blood, can be a true partner for him. Hence God takes "one of his ribs" and makes woman from it, "bone from my bones, flesh from my flesh" (vv. 21-23) With the arrival of this authentic partner he achieves his true humanity.

The point of the account in Gen. 1 is the same. "God created man [*hā'ādām*] in his own image, in the image of God he created him; male and female he created them" (v. 27). No account is given here of the manner of the creation, but creation in the image of God and in the two sexes is essential to human existence. The complementary togetherness of men and women is a decisive feature of what it means to be truly human. Gen. 1 also displays an interest in continuous progeny. God created human beings both male and female because it pleased him to let human offspring be produced by the mating of men and women. The partnership of husband and wife and their complementary functions as father and mother belong to the perfect creation that is the object of Israel's praise.

Animals as well as humans are created male and female. Why does Gen. 2 make no mention of this simple biological fact? Gen. 1 takes a vivid interest in it (cf. vv. 20-22). The same blessing as enables humble creatures to produce progeny is later conferred on humanity as male and female (vv. 27-28). The point of the omission in Gen. 2 is that here personal encounter and partnership, not progeny, are the decisive feature and mystery of our existence as male and female. Since this is the typically human feature, animal sexuality can be ignored.

Men and women are human beings on the basis of perfect equality. They complement each other. Neither could live as a truly human being while denying the other's existence and function. Yet they are different. Their disparity is what enables each to be the other's complement. But wherein lies the difference, the distinctiveness of each?

In Gen. 1 men and women are summoned to be fruitful and thus to become fathers and mothers. They perform this highly creative act together by equal participation. But in and by it fatherhood becomes the peculiar calling of men, motherhood of women. This distinction is not limited to the family sphere. Responsible leadership is generally associated with fatherhood, loyal attendance with motherhood. This is not an iron rule. Leadership is not tied to men nor service to women. Men might be entrusted with the motherly function and women might be leaders by the grace of God. Moses must care for God's people like a mother or nurse (Num. 11:11-12), and Deborah, a "mother in Israel" (Judg. 5:7), took the lead in place of the timid Barak (4:4ff.).

Discussion of the function of the sexes must also take Gen. 2 into account. Here woman is created as a "helper," to be in man's presence (2:18 RSV). But "partner" (NEB) is perhaps a better rendering to express what the passage has in mind.

The Hebrew term used here is *'ēzer.* The sense is "help" or "helper," as in names like Eliezer ("God is helper") or Ebenezer ("stone of help"). But the help in question is help out of a situation of distress or despair. The helper is not a mere assistant or servant. Had the woman been created as no more than a servant, the text would surely have chosen an ordinary word for this (e.g., *'ebed*).

Woman is to be with man (literally "in his presence"). Availability might suggest being in attendance, but in the context it denotes relief from loneliness and therefore true and unfailing companionship. The NEB thus offers a faithful if not a literal rendering: "I will provide a partner for him." Partnership, of course, includes service, but not in the sense of inferiority and subjection.

God created humanity in two sexes, but he did so in a distinct order and sequence. As in the case of heaven and earth or soul and body, the order is not accidental. As symbolized by the fact that in Israel fathers and sons are counted first, and men alone sit at the gate to discuss and decide town problems, partnership does not mean identity. Man enjoys priority. But this priority is relative, not absolute.

The biblical message plainly upholds a relative precedence of man over woman. Yet Gen. 2 shows that this is not the absolute precedence of traditional patriarchalism. The initiative is that man discovers and chooses woman, but he discovers and chooses her as an equal partner. The sequence reflects man's precedence as potential father, and in terms of the initiative it lies behind the depiction of God's relationship with Israel as husband and father (cf. Hos. 2–3; Jer. 2–3; Ezek. 23), or Christ's relationship with the church as bridegroom (Eph. 5:32; Rev. 19:9; 21:9). Along these lines woman's part is to react to the initiative, to answer the courtship, to follow the proposal, to accept a way of life in togetherness and trust.

In the case of woman, however, the response can be genuine only on the basis of equality and in terms of true partnership. It cannot mean passive submission to man's responsible leadership. Man cannot be allowed to abuse his precedence, to decide and act alone, not to grant his partner an active role. As man's helper out of his loneliness, woman cannot leave him to himself. Indispensable sharing in responsible leadership is a vital element in biblical togetherness. We neglect this only to our detriment.

c. Responsible Lords and Willing Servants

A third feature of human existence now calls for notice. Many biblical passages seem to express astonishment that humanity has the responsibility of both humble work and commanding authority. Contradictory though they may appear to be, both functions belong to the nature of humanity as male and female. Here is another mystery of human creation and destiny that causes Israel to magnify the Creator's wisdom and goodness. Why are human beings both so lowly and yet so exalted and powerful?

According to Gen. 2 God put man in the garden (vv. 8, 15). With his wife he was not only to enjoy its fruits but also to tend it responsibly (v. 15). There is no suggestion of a burden here. The context shows plainly that everything is so arranged as to make life smooth and enjoyable. Responsible service does not have to be servitude. It gives life a purpose and meaning. It ennobles it.

In Gen. 1 man and woman, made in God's image, are to rule (vv. 26ff.). They may perform this noble task without concern for food, since plants and trees abundantly provide for their needs (vv. 29-30). They constitute a race of sovereign lords over all animals and plants, though with no right to kill animals. This royal function undoubtedly involves serious work, but the stress undeniably falls here on the aspect of rule.

Other biblical passages confirm the points made by the two creation stories. Wisdom writings extol the just person who earns a living by honest and skillful work (Prov. 22:29). Idleness is one of the most dangerous of enemies (18:9). A capable wife merits special praise (31:10ff.). Even if lifelong labor has no ultimate value (Eccl. 5:10ff.), there is still "nothing better than that a man should enjoy his work, since that is his lot" (3:22).

But wisdom writings are also aware of the amazing power of human beings. Whether they be princes or commoners, if they conform to the rules of wisdom, then riches, honors, and influence may be theirs. This is in accordance with our created nature and destiny (Prov. 8:15ff.). As Ps. 8 says of man, "thou hast made him little less than a god, crowning him with glory and honour. Thou makest him master of all thy creatures; thou hast put everything under his feet" (vv. 5ff.).

A creature of earth, a dependent leaseholder earning a living by labor, yet also little less than a god, a sovereign lord enjoying freedom, wealth, and honor? There seems to be an irreconcilable contradiction here. Biblical Israel realized that it did in fact face one of the mysteries of human existence at this point, and that to achieve an appropriate attitude one must avoid several misunderstandings and perversions of God's true intention.

Thus one might think that lordship and power are good in themselves—a blessing—as distinct from labor and service—a curse. By long experience Israel learned that this is not so. Lordship may turn into tyranny as labor can turn into slavery. Both governing and serving functions become inhuman when they are polarized as good and bad within a dualistic ideology.

Again, a sexist society might discriminate between one sex— usually men—as lords, and the other as subjects and servants. Biblical Israel accepted the relative priority of men over women, but it also taught that in consequence of true partnership both sexes are equally engaged in both responsible lordship and dedicated service. Exclusive lordship of the one is no less inhuman than exclusive servitude of the other.

Discrimination might also arise between ruling and working classes: aristocrats and commoners, higher castes and lower, rich and poor, colonizers and colonized. Israel, after long experience of subjugation by foreign nations, was tempted to think of itself as a race of lords awaiting leisurely enjoyment of power. But such tendencies were intercepted by its calling to lead humanity in a very different direction. Creation established no discrimination between lords and servants.

By creation all are meant to be lords and all servants. As Luther put it in his challenging *Freedom of a Christian,* believers are sovereign lords over all things but also humble servants of everything and everybody. The Creator had good reason to give humanity this twofold and apparently contradictory destiny. The one side of it complements the other. We are put to work, but precisely as voluntary workers we share in nobility and lordship. We are sovereign lords, but as such we are responsibly engaged and active for the common good. Responsible labor and service are the secret of true lordship. True lordship verifies itself in dedicated work.

Here is one of the outstanding aspects of creation in God's image. God himself works and involves himself with unrivaled dedication, thereby risking his eternal glory but also proving himself the world's true Lord and God. He is also the One who rules the world with eternal omnipotence, but who thereby predestinates himself to the service and salvation of the world. In God alone are lordship and service truly and fully united and complementary. The calling of humanity is to follow this unique example. In this calling lies another ground for praise of the Creator.

d. Created in the Image of God

Among all creatures humans alone are said to have been created in God's image and likeness (Gen. 1:26; cf. Ps. 8:5). Jews and Christians generally find in isolated statements of this kind the very essence of biblical anthropology. What is meant by the saying in Gen. 1:26 in its own context and against its Near Eastern background? In answering this question we will have to take into account what we have already said about soul and body, man and woman, and lord and servant. If our creaturely weakness and misery are all too apparent, yet we are made in the image of God. Perhaps no other saying states so clearly what it meant for Israel to be called the "people of God."

God decided on the sixth day to create man, male and female, in his own image, because he wanted them to rule over his whole creation in sea and air and on the land (Gen. 1:26-27). They were to have a royal function. But such a function was beyond the competence of human beings that are creatures themselves. They needed special authorization. God thus delegated his authority in order to equip them for their task of rule. He blessed them—not only to be fruitful and to fill the earth, but also to subdue it (1:28).

Humanity has a function of rule as God's delegate or mandatory. On the one hand, this means that human rule is not absolute or unlimited. If we may utilize the power and riches of earth, we may not exploit them. On the other hand, God's mandatory is to some extent similar or comparable to God himself. This is why Ps. 8 may say that God created man as "little less than God" (RSV; NEB "a god").

What Gen. 1 means, then, by saying that we are made in God's image is that we are made God's mandatory in the task of ruling the earth. If we cannot prove this beyond question, the context supports it, and so does the extrabiblical evidence.

Ancient Sumerian, Babylonian, and Egyptian texts speak of kings being shaped in the image of their gods. Mesopotamian kings are hailed as the image of Bel or Shamash, Egyptian kings may boast of being the holy image of Re. Less frequently human beings in general are said to be created as a likeness or image of the gods. In the more common usage it is to be noted that the image is rooted in creation and that it comprises the power to rule on earth. In Egypt, by the way, "image of God" is often an equivalent of "son of God."

[27]

If "in the image of God" denotes creation as God's steward and mandatory on earth, we may discard some of the familiar interpretations of the saying. Thus there is no point in arguing for a literal meaning, as though human beings had a bodily resemblance to God, or at least to angels or other divine beings. Gen. 1 specifically stresses God's transcendence over his creatures, so that the idea of a similarity of outward appearance is highly unlikely.

Again, there is no need for a figurative interpretation, i.e., spiritual similarity, as though human intelligence, rationality, will, sentiment, etc., were of divine essence and the life of God a model of human personality. Speculative theories of this kind have little basis in the text itself.

Finally, there is no need to seek divine-human resemblance in the sphere of social relations. True, God does not live alone. True also, he desires partnership with us. Man and woman, too, need community and partnership both with one another and with God. There is truth, no doubt, in the analogy, yet it hardly seems to be found directly in the text itself.

In the context of the passage and against the background of contemporary culture, "in the image of God" signifies the creation, endowment, and appointment of humanity to be God's mandatory, commissioner, or vice-gerent with far-reaching authority over the animals and also over earth's powers and riches. This is a trusteeship. It involves power but also labor, lordship but also service, privilege but also duty. It can never be taken for granted. The quality of the "image" is based, and continually depends, on God himself and his faithful endorsement and renewal of his commitment. We are all meant to be kings and queens by God's grace, but we may never enjoy the privilege nor do the duty without a knowledge and acknowledgment of God's commissioning for it. Among all creatures we are those whom God has engaged in partnership in his kingship and who are thus especially responsible to him. The fact that we are his responsible commissioners lies at the heart of the biblical witness to our nature and destiny and is a final reason for Israel's praise of the Creator.

5. God Preserves His Creatures

The biblical witness to the Creator's work does not overlook what has become of the world but records God's gracious acts of preservation and renewal. (a) The stories of primeval history astonish us by their candid acknowledgment of human guilt. Although created perfect, given a noble task, and granted amazing development in numbers, culture, and power, humanity revolted against its Creator. (b) Pain and frustration, and finally death, vitiated human life in consequence, and give testimony to God's final judgment. Even the earthly environment was drawn into the turmoil of destruction. (c) Nevertheless, God kept faith with his creatures. He preserves them from final judgment. He continues his work, leading it on to the achievement of a new and perfect world that will manifest his victory over all rebellious powers.

WHEN GOD CREATED heaven and earth "in the beginning," everything was done perfectly according to his wisdom, and was suitable for his purpose. He "saw all that he had made, and it was very good" (Gen. 1:31). "Thus heaven and earth were completed" (2:1), and he "ceased from all the work he had set himself to do" (2:3).

Creation might thus seem to be a finished work. Yet the OT never puts God's creative activity solely in the past. "In the beginning" is not just the starting point of world history. It refers also to God's eternal priority and initiative. God created the world long ago but he is also at every time the world's Creator. He long ago began to reveal himself as such, but he also does so continually, offering fresh evidence of his creative and innovative activity by preservation and development. This continuous aspect of creation now calls for our attention.

Scripture often links creation to preservation. In Gen. 1 creation is also an act of protection against chaos, in Gen. 2 against drought, famine, and loneliness. Praise of creation in Ps. 104 or 145 is also praise of God's providence on behalf of his creatures. Isaiah's message of comfort is a message of continuous creation in God's care for his handiwork.

This aspect of creation perhaps comes out most clearly in Gen. 3–11. We have here the expulsion from Eden (ch. 3), the murder of Abel (4:1-16), the genealogy of Cain's descendants (4:17-24), the genealogy of Adam's descendants to Noah (5:1-32), the flood (chs. 6–9), the nations descended from Noah (10:1-32), the tower of Babel (11:1-9), and a table of Noah's descendants to Abram (11:10-32). These stories are all in sequence with that of creation, so that chs. 1–11 form a single unit. Creation and preservation belong together, as we see liturgically in the General Thanksgiving of the Book of Common Prayer: "Almighty, God, Father of all mercies . . . we thank thee for our creation, preservation, and all the blessings of this life." The world's Creator is also its Preserver, and indeed its Redeemer.

a. Creative Development

In primeval history as recorded in Gen. 3–11 we come up against two seemingly irreconcilable facts. First, we have manifold evidence of God's abundant blessing in the expansion of the race. Second, the race has revolted against its Creator, not here and there, but from the outset and consistently. The thorough confession of human guilt, strange though it might seem to be in the context, is characteristic of Israel's praise of the Creator. There was ample reason to magnify the wonders of divine blessing and preservation. Even surrounding nations felt compelled to praise their gods as benign shepherds and preservers of the world. For Israel, however, preservation merited supreme praise as a triumph over human rebellion. With this in mind, we turn to what the Bible says about God as the Preserver of his creatures.

God's continuous care for the world is evident in the development of humanity. He lets it make progress in vital respects. Its numbers increase. It discovers and occupies one country and continent after another. Its living space rapidly expands. Farming and cattle breeding are the first of an increasing diversity of professions and crafts. Family, clan, tribe, and nation develop new forms of social order. Solitary dwellings turn into villages. Wooden and stone houses replace primitive shelters. The rise of kingdoms, commerce, and law paves the way for urban settlement. Religious devotion, cultic rites, and sanctuaries go hand in hand with cultural development in every form.

Such advances did not come alone. The OT shows that the Creator himself encourages human creativity in accordance with humanity's destiny as God's image and mandatory.

Some examples will serve to illustrate the development. Humanity increases in numbers (Gen. 6:1; 10:5). People live as farmers (4:2), shepherds (4:2), hunters (10:9), nomads (4:12), craftsmen (4:22), musicians (4:21), and winegrowers (9:20). Tools are made of copper and iron (4:22). Brick is used in building towers (11:3), and pitch in shipbuilding (6:14). Laws protect society (4:15). Many tribes and nations populate the earth (4:21-22; 10:1-32). God is worshiped (4:3-4; 5:22; 7:1; 8:20).

In spite of their weakness, human beings are also creative in an unbelievably direct way, i.e., by the procreation of sons and daughters. What happens between man and wife is a creative act analogous to that of the Creator himself.

Do they really create by their own will and potency? Two passages show notable sensitivity on this point. In Gen. 4:1, when Cain was born, Eve exclaimed triumphantly: "With the help of the Lord I have brought a man into being." The word for "to bring into being" (Hebrew *qānāh*) was often used for God's own creative activity (e.g., Gen. 14:19, 22). It resembles Cain (Hebrew *qayin*) phonetically. Cain is the first man "created" by his parents. Yet the help of the Lord is needed.

In Gen. 5 we then have a list of Adam's descendants through Seth. V. 3 tells us that Adam "begot a son in his likeness and image." There is an unmistakable allusion here to 1:26-27: the creation of man in *God's* image and likeness. The obvious difference between divine and human creation is that only by God's special permission and blessing can humans do what the Creator initially and constantly does. Yet man and woman undoubtedly are allowed to participate here in God's own creative act.

To these two passages we might add Ps. 139:13-16, which in a meditation on human generation admirably expresses Israel's glorifying of God creating and preserving work. It is God who knits us together, but in continuous preservation and renewal of the world he permits us to cooperate in this creative activity.

As for human achievements, the Bible notes them with pride yet also with astonishment and even stupefaction. How strange that God should undertake so risky a venture, abandon so much of his power, and entrust creatures with such authority! What is humanity, indeed, that God should appoint it his partner (Ps. 8)? The amazement is due to the apparent littleness and weakness of humans. Especially in Gen. 3–11 we see the impact of human guilt. Overshadowed by humanity's failure to meet its destiny, God's providence is the more paradoxical and miraculous. To humanity's fall we must now direct our attention.

b. The Scandal of Human Rebellion

Preservation of the world means the preservation of a world distorted and depraved by human rebellion. God created everything perfectly. He endowed humanity with power and blessing. There was no reason for it to revolt against its Creator. Yet it did. It revolted at the very outset. To praise God's goodness without frank admission of humanity's scheming to destroy the world would be dishonest. The record in Gen. 3–11 thus interweaves confessions of sin into the story of achievement.

The most familiar account of human rebellion is the story of the fall in Gen. 3, which must be read with the paradise story in ch. 2. Nowhere does the confession of human wickedness belong more closely together with glorification of the Creator's goodness. Rebellion here is a bold attempt to regard God's commandment as a means of repression. Eating the fruit of the forbidden tree, the man and his wife obtain "knowledge of good and evil," and feel as if they were like God, no longer subject to his supremacy.

The story of Cain and Abel in Gen. 4:1-16 is also a record of human rebellion. Rebellion here takes the form of fratricide motivated by jealousy about divine favor (4:4). Like Adam and Eve in ch. 3, Cain feels that he is repressed by God. But this time the rebellion takes the form of violence against his brother.

The flood story in Gen. 6–9 is another account of humanity's revolt against the Creator. In 6:5 we read: "The Lord saw that man had done much evil on earth and that his thoughts and inclinations were always evil" (cf. 8:21). Human corruption, with Noah as the exception (6:8-9), had infected the whole world.

The story of the tower of Babel (Gen. 11) is another record of revolt. This time the revolt is disguised as human progress. No charge is made of violence or apostasy. A giant city is built with a skyscraper tower. The intention is to preserve unity and identity. To God, however, this striving reveals overweening ambition: "Henceforward nothing they have in mind to do will be beyond their reach" (11:6).

Yet another biblical tradition that reflects early human rebellion is the Sodom story in Gen. 13 and 18–19. Sodom lay on the fertile plain of Jordan, which was like "the Garden of the Lord" (13:10). But the people of Sodom "were wicked, great sinners against the Lord" (13:13; cf. 18:20). The incognito visit of divine messengers confirmed the report and the destruction of the city followed (cf. 19:1ff.). Violence and sexual perversion gave evidence of the incurable decay of humanity.

A survey of the stories of revolt yields the following results.

(1) Each story has its own way of indicating the revolt without actually using the term. Even a theological key word like "sin" is rare (cf. Gen. 4:7; 18:20). Nor is there any reference to a fall. In Gen. 3 the theme is distrust of God's intentions and the breaking of his commandment. Jealousy and fratricide are the form of rebellion in ch. 4. Limitless expansion and self-help are the emphasis in ch. 11. General charges are made in the flood story. Evil thoughts and acts, and brutal violence, have become the way of life that humanity has chosen.

(2) The stories follow a sequence from creation to the flood, to the dispersion of humanity, and to the generation of Abram, who marks a new beginning. In the sequence the human story is one of a constant series of revolts. God can handle the revolts, but the human story as such is one of constant rebellion with no human hope of improvement.

We have no reason to conclude that in Gen. 1–11 there is a dramatic rise in rebellion as regards both scope and seriousness. It is true that at first we have only individual acts, then the revolt of all humanity. It is also true that the first offense seems relatively inoffensive, while later we have violence and perversion. Yet a crescendo is hardly the point of the stories. They are not interested in a transition from individual to collective sin, since Adam and Cain are representative figures. Nor do they contend for an increasing gravity of sin, since the first offense is by no means "light" when compared with what follows. The point of the stories is that human rebellion is a lamentable fact that has been with the race always and everywhere from the very first.

(3) The human revolt against God does in fact occur at once. The Bible does not depict a golden age of harmony with God and neighbor. No sooner are Adam and Eve put on the earth to live as responsible beings than they begin to revolt. Humanity as God's perfect creation is the only reality that precedes—and outlives—the state of siege that human rebellion creates.

The first recorded act of the first pair, for example, is to eat the forbidden fruit. Sin is thus original sin, i.e., sin from the very origin of the human race. The race as well as the individual sins from "youth upwards" (Gen. 8:21).

(4) Human rebellion is a baffling event. Generations have sought its cause in vain. Myths have tried to solve the so-called problem of evil (Latin *unde malum,* whence evil?). But the biblical accounts do not try to explain it. Rebellion against the Creator will always be unexpected, unfounded, unreasonable, inexcusable, and unjustifiable. If God created all things perfectly, there can be no explanation, no acceptable reason, for sin.

The OT itself does not say that rebellion against God recurs continually because our first parents fell into disobedience. Tertullian (ca. A.D. 200) and Augustine (ca. A.D. 400) tried to explain ongoing sin as a kind of contagious disease that we inherit from Adam and that has damaged our previously innocent nature. Adam and Eve thus caused humanity to become a race of sinners. But the Bible does not specifically say this. In fact, Gen. 3 condemns the attempt to throw the blame on anyone else: Adam on Eve (3:12), Eve on the serpent (3:13), and both implicitly on God, who created both serpent and woman. Neither Adam, nor Eve, nor any of us can escape personal responsibility for what we do. To blame Adam is ultimately to rationalize and excuse evil. No "cause" can exonerate us from individual blame.

One might ask whether the Creator could not have prevented this fiasco of human revolt. Why did he not create humanity infallible? To ask this kind of question, however, is again to try to clear humanity of guilt. It is also to miss the real purpose of Israel's God, namely, to create voluntary partners and not robots that must respond automatically to his will and command.

c. Suffering and Preservation

God preserves what he created. He does not forsake the work of his hands. This is a comforting message. Yet it is also a surprising message. Why should God keep faith with a rebellious humanity? Preservation is no doubt a continuation of creation, yet God's acts of preservation are so amazing that it seems each time as if a new revelation takes place.

As we look again at the stories of preservation, we note the following aspects. First comes God's never-ceasing interest and engagement in the world. Then come punishments and judgments. Finally we see God's healing compassion. If humanity holds an outstanding place in the drama, all creatures are involved, and that not merely in a passive way.

(1) The OT records with astonishment that instead of turning from the world God constantly busies himself with it. There seems to be no reason for his care for creation. In view of human sin it would be natural for him to

show no further interest in it. Yet it pleased him to attend to his creatures, to keep his eyes and ears open to what was happening to them. He accompanied his world, taking trouble to scrutinize it personally, closely, and repeatedly, as if its cause were always his.

We find plain and concrete illustration of this concern. God walks in the garden, meets Adam and Eve, and finds out about their trespass (Gen. 3:8ff.). Abel's blood cries out to him from the earth (4:10). Not content with second-hand information, God "came down" to see what was happening (11:5; cf. 6:5). As Ps. 14:2 puts it, "The Lord looks down from heaven on all mankind" (cf. 33:15; 102:19; Jer. 32:19; Jon. 1:2).

There is nothing extraordinary, perhaps, about God's seeing and hearing what happens on earth. But that is hardly true of his "feeling" about what he saw and heard. God is sensitive, almost vulnerable. He can be startled, alarmed, upset, disturbed. He suffers from disappointment. He is "grieved at heart" (Gen. 6:6). He so deeply regrets human corruption that he feels "sorry that he had made man on earth" (6:6-7).

That God is sorry does not simply mean that he is angry. He has suffered what seems to be a painful defeat or setback. He has spent his love on humanity to win it as a voluntary partner, but it has rejected his offer and refused his love. He has taken the risk of true love and seems to have lost. He suffers "love's expense" (cf. W. H. Vanstone, *The Risk of Love* [repr. 1978]). Although sorry that he has been thwarted, however, he will not hesitate to try again, like the potter in Jer. 18:1-11. In creating humanity (or Israel) out of ordinary clay, God risks failure in spite of his own perfect workmanship, but he will not abandon his project.

Sorrow, grief, pain, and anger are God's first response to humanity's revolt. They carry serious consequences for creation. While God is in anguish, the world's foundations shake. When he no longer rejoices in his works (Ps. 104:31), the world that depends on him so utterly cannot escape involvement in his sorrow. Yet his sorrow is also comforting and promising. There is hope for the world so long as he refuses to accept rebellion as a final reality and takes responsibility for it.

(2) Rebellion has consequences for humanity and all creation. God does not simply watch human deeds and regret them. He takes active measures to give humanity some sense of his displeasure and disappointment. The time comes for reprimands and judgments. Many of these may be relatively lenient and disciplinary. None is mere retaliation. Rather than avenging humanity's refusal to return his love, God for a time simply withholds his blessings, so that the race falls easy prey to death. In Gen. 1–11 no final rejection is intended by even the severest measures. The negative measures easily turn out to be tokens of unceasing love and care.

One such measure involves the deterioration and diminution of human life on earth. Life is made hard for Adam and Eve. Childbirth becomes a terrible strain for woman, and the more she longs for her husband, the greater her dependence (Gen. 3:14-16). Man finds himself in an infertile region and has to pay a heavy toll of sweat and tears to earn his living (3:17-19). Cain and his descendants must survive as vagrants and nomads, dogged by constant fear (4:11-16). After Babel the race suffers from diversity of language and the resultant misunderstandings and tensions, with eventual dispersion (11:9). A successive diminution of life expectancy to seventy years also seems to be a consequence of human revolt (5:1-32; 6:1-3; Ps. 90:10).

Is death also a consequence? "The wages of sin is death" (Rom. 6:23 RSV). Death indeed suddenly strikes the generation of the flood and the citizens of Sodom, as it would later strike those of Nineveh and Babylon, Samaria and Jerusalem. But expulsion rather than death is Cain's punishment. Similarly, although Adam and Eve are told that in the day they eat the fruit they will die (Gen. 2:17; 3:3), physical death does not immediately strike them. Death is the consequence of sin, but is this death in the general sense of creaturely finitude and mortality, or is it natural death turned into final judgment? In the last analysis it would seem that death as viewed in this negative perspective might well be the most serious consequence of human rebellion.

Disease also needs to be considered in this connection. Why is there no mention in Gen. 1–11 of the sicknesses and plagues that are such a notorious symptom of life's deterioration and diminution? Israel and other nations tended to link disease to both human sin and divine anger. Many biblical prayers connect healing from illness with forgiveness of sin (Pss. 6, 13, 22, 31; Isa. 38:10-20; etc.). Here, however, death is perhaps subsumed under human frailty and mortality. Death includes these as its precursors. At the same time, the OT does not see a specific disease as in itself, in every case, a consequence of sin (Job).

In different ways, then, God opposes and impedes the revolt against him. He makes life more difficult. He expels and destroys, so that the stories come down as stern warnings. Yet we are not told that he actually rejects the work of his hands. The curse that is mentioned (Gen. 3:14, 17; 4:11) involves a worsening of life's conditions, not total annihilation. Expulsion proves to be a protective measure that guards humanity against final extermination (Gen. 3, 4).

Humanity and other creatures have to undergo setbacks. They suffer pain, hardships, social tensions, and death. In a limited way they share in the Creator's own disappointment and pain. This is all true, yet God also bears with his creatures. If primeval history is a series of setbacks, it is also a sequence of demonstrations of God's wondrous patience and unceasing preservation.

(3) We now turn to the third aspect of preservation, which reveals the Creator's goodness much more directly. It is his healing compassion. If God's love accompanies the world with constant presence, care, and vigilance, and discourages rebellion by disciplinary measures, it also helps the world positively to overcome the consequences of revolt.

It should be noted that God's acts of healing and reconstruction are an aspect of preservation, not a separate activity. We must not misconstrue the different aspects as separate acts in a sequence: observation, angry reaction, and finally loving attention. If we put the healing activity last, it is because it is so unexpected and wonderful when considered in conjunction with divine punishment.

Although humanity and other creatures must suffer the consequences of rebellion, there are limits and even an end to suffering. In neither severity nor length is suffering unlimited. Nobody is left alone totally or forever. Sooner or later the Creator himself will alleviate and put an end to suffering. Many proofs of his merciful activity may be found in Gen. 1–11.

Cain cries out in despair in Gen. 4:13 (cf. Job, or Paul in Rom. 7:24), but complaints of this kind are groundless. Death itself prevents further misdeeds that might eternalize Adam's misery (Gen. 3:19). Cain would finally build a city (4:17). The flood did not last forever (8:2).

The Creator's loving concern for his chastened creatures is apparent also in his alleviating of suffering. Punishments often turn out to be easier than expected, creative and not merely negative. Merciful commutations may be seen even in the midst of cruel punishments.

Adam and Cain, for example, would continue to live, enjoy marital love, and produce offspring (Gen. 4:1-2; 5:1ff.; 4:17). Among Adam's descendants there would be Enoch, whom God took (5:24), and Noah, whom Lamech hailed with the words "This boy will bring us relief from our work" (5:29).

Perhaps the most striking evidence of the Creator's loving involvement is the emergence of a new type of humanity, rare in primeval history, always exceptional, yet casting light on a dark picture. The stories in Gen. 1–11 show that what accounts for this miracle is primarily God's providential care, and only secondarily goodwill on the human side.

Abel is a first instance of this new humanity. No exceptional merit is ascribed to him as a recipient of God's favor. He dies an innocent victim of his brother's jealousy. Yet his blood cries out to God. Enoch walked with God for three hundred years, but apart from that he is not described as a moral hero. Noah, too, was blameless and walked with God (6:9), though in the last analysis what counts in his case, too, is not religious or moral heroism but the divine favor. Finally, at the end of primeval history, there is Abram, who, although intimately linked to the postdiluvian development of the race, is a key person in a new era of God's dealings, so that he stands at a turning point between two periods of God's actions in the world and on its behalf.

The series of extraordinary people, of whom Abram is the last, marks God's gracious dealings with the race. Preservation finally means no less than the creation of a new humanity, not merely the maintaining of the humanity that remains after the revolt. The emergence of these persons does not account for the preservation of the world. On the contrary, God's saving purpose comes to light in their appearance.

Human weakness and pride cause trouble and suffering down the ages. But "while the earth lasts seedtime and harvest, cold and heat, summer and winter, day and night, shall never cease" (Gen. 8:22). God will preserve his creatures. He will accomplish his eternal purpose. Here is reason enough to praise the Creator. He will not abandon his work or leave it unfinished (Ps. 138:8).

Chapter II

God Chose the Fathers of Israel

1. The Witness of Scripture

God chose Abraham, Isaac, and Jacob, revealed himself to them, granted a covenant to Abraham, extended it to Isaac, Jacob, and their children, and promised them protection, blessing, offspring, and land; therefore Israel has continually praised the Lord and believed in him. In Israel's creed this topic introduces the topics of the exodus and the gift of Canaan, linking the creation of heaven and earth to all that follows, and forming the basis of what God did on Mt. Sinai.

"THE GOD OF THIS PEOPLE of Israel chose our fathers." This is how Paul began his exhortation in the synagogue at Pisidian Antioch while preaching the gospel in Asia Minor. He took as his basis the tenets of faith to which the Jews had adhered for centuries, commencing with the election of the fathers (Acts 13:17-22).

The OT confirms that this topic was a basic article of Israel's creed. The article describes a past event that is worthy to be remembered, namely, that God chose, called, and established Abraham, Isaac, and Jacob, revealed himself to them, granted them a covenant, and promised them posterity and land. But this event is meaningful only because it is God who acted in it. It does not belong to the past alone. It retains its validity and explains and modifies the present. As God acted toward the patriarchs, so he has the power to act at all times. The situation of the patriarchs is thus the basis of Israel's trust in God. Because God chose the fathers, their children can ask his help today and tomorrow. If God did not confirm what he then started, that past event would be meaningless, and broadcasting it would make no sense.

In the OT only Genesis has the election of the fathers as its main subject. Chs. 11–50 tell the stories of Abraham, Isaac, and Jacob with a view to showing what God did for the fathers. Little is said about the fathers in other books. Their names occur, but there is only brief allusion to their story.

The three names are mentioned in Exod. 2:24; 6:3, 8; 32:13; 33:1; Lev. 26:42; Num. 32:11; Deut. 1:8; 6:10; 9:5, 27; 29:12; 30:20; 34:4; 2 Kgs. 13:23. Summaries of the story occur in Josh. 24:2ff. and Ps. 105:8-23. Israel is often called "the descendants of Abraham, Isaac and Jacob" (Jer. 33:26). Isaac may be omitted (Mic. 7:20), or Isaac and Jacob (Ps. 47:9; Neh. 9:7-8; Isa. 41:8), or Abraham and Isaac (Hos. 12:3-8; Deut. 26:5; 1 Sam. 12:8; Ps. 22:24). No names are given in Deut. 6:23; Jer. 32:22; cf. Acts 13:17.

The OT creeds show that the election of the fathers is an article of Israel's faith. In many creeds this election precedes the exodus and the gift of the land (Deut. 26:5-9; Josh. 24:2-13). Creation comes before it once (Neh. 9:6-31). It is sometimes an introduction to the gift of Canaan (Deut. 6:21ff.; Jer. 32:17-23). A few creeds omit the fathers altogether (Ps. 135:1; Deut. 32:6-14; Ps. 78).

Where does this topic belong in Israel's faith? The relevant events obviously took place at the beginning of Israel's history. If the creation story tells us where humanity as a whole comes from, the story of Abraham tells us where Israel comes from. It would thus seem that the story of the fathers is the very basis of Israel and therefore the main article of its faith. But this view does not survive examination. The first chapter is not necessarily the most important.

The fathers apparently lived between 2000 and 1500 B.C., long before Israel came on the scene as a community or people. They were nomads in the Fertile Crescent between Babylonia, Syria, Canaan, and Egypt. This region, unlike Egypt, had been under the domination of different powers from south, north, and east. Semitic tribes came into it from the steppes or Arabia around 2000 B.C. The Amorites settled in fertile areas, built towns, and set up kingdoms like Ugarit and Haran (cf. Gen. 11:31). Their way of life was very close to that described in Gen. 11–50. Added credibility is thus given to the stories of the patriarchs, which some scholars had been tempted to classify as mere folktales.

The aim of the OT is not to write a history of Israel. In history a people's origin plays a basic role. But the OT does not weigh events according to their sequence in history. Earlier events do not necessarily determine what came later. In the OT God's essential revelation was given in the liberation from Egypt and the gift of Canaan. Neither creation nor the election of the fathers has the same priority.

The topic of the fathers' election is thus complementary to the main articles. Israel's first affirmation is that it came out of Egypt (Hos. 11:1; Amos 3:1; Ezek. 20:5-6; etc.). Only then does it acknowledge its descent from the fathers. This is the right sequence for modern readers, too.

Thus many creeds and hymns make no reference to the story of the fathers. A few others that take it up do not make the fathers a topic in their own right. They mention them simply as an introduction to the exodus (Deut. 26:5; Josh. 24:2-4). At times their importance is that Canaan was promised to them (Deut. 6:13; Ps. 105:5-11). They attracted fresh attention only after the exile (Neh. 9:7-8), and in later writings like Wisdom of Solomon or Jubilees could even begin to be viewed as the most important of all the topics.

According to the main thread in the stories of the fathers, God deals with them directly. What are these divine acts that arouse the people's astonishment and gratitude and thus become objects of their faith and praise? Four aspects command our attention: God chose the fathers, revealed himself to them, granted a covenant to them, and gave them a promise. We noted the same four actions—election, revelation, covenant, and promise—in relation to creation, and we will come across them again later. But they have particular meaning as related to Abraham, Isaac, and Jacob.

2. God Chose His People

God revealed himself to Abraham, Isaac, and Jacob because he willed to elect them (a) according to his own free will and pleasure, not because of any right, merit, or value of theirs; (b) to give them a role in his plan as forerunners of his people, not just as recipients of his blessing; (c) moving them to respond to his summons to be his servants, prophets, and witnesses; (d) and leaving aside for a while, without forgetting or rejecting them forever, Lot, Ishmael, Esau, and their descendants.

FROM GOD AS CREATOR of heaven and earth we now turn to God in his dealings with a few individuals. Whereas his action was previously as wide as the universe itself, it is now in the narrow space occupied by a few people. Yet the two actions are closely linked. The Creator lays a foundation for the covenant with Israel, and the election of the fathers aims at the human race as a whole.

God *elects* a few individuals. The verb adequately describes the free and wonderful decision that is involved in the action. But what are the motive, authority, and purpose of him who performs it?

The stories of the patriarchs in Gen. 11–50 do not use the word "elect." They simply say that God reveals himself, that his voice is heard, that he speaks, that he gives the fathers a message, revelation, or promise. He does not favor others in the same way.

The special treatment of Abraham comes out clearly in Abraham's confession: "The Lord the God of heaven who *took* me from my father's house and the land of my birth, the Lord who swore to me" (Gen. 24:7). We find the same verb in Josh. 24:3: "I *took* your father Abraham from beside the Euphrates." Similarly, God deals kindly with Jacob; he is with him, protects him, cares for him, and blesses him. All these verbs indicate what will later be described as choice or election (cf. Deut. 4:37; 7:6; Neh. 9:7). While, then, we would do violence to the text by viewing God's action toward the fathers under the sole heading of election, we may justifiably use the term "election" as a key to their understanding.

a. Election without Prejudice

God chooses as he likes. Why did he elect Abram rather than Haran (Gen. 11:27), or Isaac and Jacob rather than Ishmael and Esau? The stories prompt such questions but never answer them. God does not have to give reasons for his decisions. He chooses freely. His motivations are his own, as in the stories of preservation in the first chapters of Genesis.

Strictly, of course, God does have reasons for acting as he does. His free choosing is not arbitrary choosing. He does not act partially, showing favor to one and withholding it from another as we do. He chooses out of free compassion. The grounds are not in the chosen person but in his own will and plan. Abraham, his descendants, and Israel as a whole will not know, and cannot know, why they among so many others have been elected. They can only accept the fact without understanding the mystery.

The mystery is clearly felt in the stories. No reason is given for Abram's election in Gen. 12. Abram certainly is not cast in the role of a hero (cf. 12:10-20). When it comes to inheriting his calling and promise, prevailing custom, which would point to the first son, is overridden no less than five times. Ishmael loses the inheritance to Isaac (ch. 16; 17:15-27; 21:1-21), Esau, through the machinations of his twin and his mother, to Jacob (27:1-40), Reuben to Judah (29:31-35), Manasseh to Ephraim (48:17-22), and Perez to Zerah (38:27-30; Ruth 4:18-22).

Israel always tended to magnify the fathers as heroes yet never succeeded in doing so. The OT describes them as very ordinary mortals who often fell and sinned. No people on earth knows its ancestors as Israel does. Confronting the people of the northern kingdom, who esteemed Jacob highly, Hosea boldly calls him one who cheated others from his mother's womb (12:4-8). Isaiah reminds the exiles that "your first father sinned" (43:27 RSV). Understandably, no monuments could be erected to them.

The fathers are also too closely linked to the nation to be exalted. We can distinguish patriarchs and nation, but we cannot separate them. In choosing the fathers God elected Israel. Why Israel rather than Edom or Egypt? Whoever knows Israel cannot explain the mystery, and the OT does not try. Instead of glorifying Israel, it praises God for his free and unforeseeable decision.

The NT takes the same course. It tells us that Jesus simply "called the men he wanted" (Mark 3:13). At Corinth God chose "low and contemptible" people, thus leaving no place for pride (1 Cor. 1:25-31; cf. Jer. 9:23). As we read in Eph. 1:5: "According to his own will and pleasure God destined us to be his children through Jesus Christ" (CB).

b. Forerunners of the People of God

In, with, and through the fathers God elected the whole people of Israel. Jacob became Israel (Gen. 32:28; 35:11), the people of Israel is Jacob (49:7, 24). The fathers achieve their greatest significance as forerunners and representatives of the people. The calling, the role, and the greatness and weakness of the people can nowhere be more clearly described than in Gen. 11–50. Yet the closeness of the relation does not rob the fathers of their own identity.

Abraham, Isaac, and Jacob are men of flesh and blood. They are not just symbols of sainthood. Nor are they merely representatives of the people that God elects. God did not first choose a people. He first chose individuals with their own name, sex, character, face, role, and history. The fathers are not just numbers one, two, and three in a long list of generations. Their portraits still have a specific print and color. Abraham differs from Jacob, Leah from Rachel. The fathers are living people. More clearly perhaps than in other parts of scripture, election is here related to specific persons who, for all their limitations, are set in the light of God's glory.

c. Election as a Personal Challenge

God chooses individuals. He calls them, taking them out of the common mass. What does this special treatment mean? It means, of course, that the fathers are singled out, as Israel will be later, and crowned "with glory and honour" (Ps. 8:5). God can even call Abraham "my friend" (Isa. 41:8). But that is not the end of the divine purpose in election. The fathers are not chosen merely to enjoy the gifts of God in their own family circle. In choosing them, God sets them on the move, both physically and spiritually. They are so pushed and challenged that they are always en route.

First, God's Word challenges and requires the fathers to listen, obey, and believe. They may not always meet the demand. Nevertheless, whether they respond in obedience and faith or disobedience and disbelief, they are elected and called to set out on their journey and to become new.

Abraham, Isaac, and Jacob seldom had the chance to settle in a single place or situation. From the day that Abram left Ur they were wanderers. True, Abram lived for a time in Haran (Gen. 11:31), but he had to leave Haran, too (12:4). The amazing thing is that with the call God aroused a willingness to obey: "Abram set out as the Lord had bidden him" (12:4). This willingness survived even the test of Gen. 22. He "put his faith in the Lord" even when the Lord's promise seemed to be wholly incredible (15:6). He might laugh, like Sarah (cf. 17:17; 18:12). He was not the hero of faith that we might suppose. Yet God awoke in him a faith that was wonderful and strong, as he did also in Jacob in connection with the vow of Gen. 28:20ff. (cf. 31:7, 11, 13; 35:1-3).

Second, God's Word challenges and requires the fathers to take a new attitude to others. They are not set on a journey merely to put their trust in God's promises and obey his words. They are not to be servants of the Lord (Gen. 26:24) merely in the sense of having a special relationship with him. This very relationship implies also a responsibility to those among whom they will reside as aliens (17:8).

Abraham, Isaac, Jacob, and their descendants had contacts with the peoples of Mesopotamia, Syria, Canaan, and Egypt, and also with the nomads in the neighboring deserts. As "Hebrews" (14:13), they were foreigners, newcomers, aliens. Their attitudes and deeds were critically appraised. Did they live as models of peace-loving, just, and truthful people? This was their responsibility. They were called "to conform to the way of the Lord and to do what is right and just" (18:19), to "practise loyalty and justice and wait always upon your God" (Hos. 12:6).

Rarely in Genesis do the fathers emerge as examples of truth and justice. They are feared in Egypt and Philistia less because of their character than because of God's blessing (Gen. 12:10-20; 20; 26). They are seldom respected for their good deeds (cf. 21:22-34). If the OT had wanted to portray them as genuine witnesses to justice, it could hardly have recorded the treacherous acts of Jacob's sons at Shechem. Only God, in the end, can bear such witness.

The Joseph stories are to some extent an exception in this regard. They tend to focus on the one character of Joseph as a model of wisdom. Yet even Joseph and his brothers have to undergo many trials and confess their faults in a conversion which exemplifies God's aim in calling his chosen ones (cf. Gen. 44:33).

God did not choose the fathers because they were good and faithful. On the contrary, he chose ordinary people and challenged them "to follow the way of the Lord" so that they in turn could become a challenge to those among whom they lived as aliens. Only on a few occasions and in a limited way were they able to fulfil this responsibility. As the stories of the fathers remind us, praise belongs to God alone and not to us (50:20).

d. God's Purpose for the Non-Elect

God chose flesh-and-blood people and moved them to become his servants and witnesses. But what happened to the many who were not chosen and whom God did not challenge to become new creatures? If the elect are privileged, then obviously the non-elect do not enjoy the same privileges. Yet the stories of the fathers devote much attention to them. They have their own roles and responsibilities. They are just as good as the elect, and sometimes better. They are not put in an especially bad light. God has not necessarily refused, rejected, or cursed them. They have a place in his plan.

3. God Revealed Himself

God's most important act toward the fathers was his revelation. He showed himself to them, spoke so that they heard his voice, disclosed his name, and made known his presence at holy places in Canaan. The God who thus revealed himself was no family, tribal, or local deity but the Lord God of Israel, the Most High, Creator of heaven and earth. He revealed himself before Israel became his people or Canaan its country.

GOD CHOSE THE FATHERS. His action was also his self-disclosure. Two separate acts were not involved, like acts in a play. What we have here are two facets of the same action. The story of the deeds of God is one, but the stress falls now on a different dimension.

God revealed himself to the fathers. When he called and moved them, he did not remain hidden. His action was one of election but also of revelation. Rightly, then, we turn our attention from the action to him who acted. God showed himself. He let himself be heard. He disclosed his presence. He revealed who he is. He made known his name.

Revelation occurs in other parts of the OT as well. God revealed himself in the exodus and at Sinai. All the deeds of God to which the OT bears witness reveal who God is either directly or indirectly. Yet as each act has its own character, so his revelation, like creation or election, has different facets and emphases. This is not to deny the oneness of God in his deeds and self-revelations. It is simply to stress his richness, which opens up wonderfully new aspects every time he acts.

a. Revelation in Canaan

We note first the places where God revealed himself to the fathers. Abraham experienced his disclosures (Gen. 12:1, 7; 15:1; 18:1; 22:14), and so, too, did Isaac (26:2) and Jacob (28:13; 35:9; 48:3). Mostly Genesis gives us the locations: Beersheba and Beer-lahai-roi in the Negeb; Moriah, Mamre, Bethel, and Shechem in central Canaan; and Mahanaim and Peniel beyond the Jordan. Two features attract our attention.

First, all these places are in Canaan, i.e., the land that Israel will occupy. God's good pleasure is to reveal himself there, and only occasionally elsewhere, e.g., later on Mt. Sinai. Why? Historians might reply that Israel's religion is rooted in the soil of Canaan, so that it naturally follows that God is said to be present there. Yet Genesis does not assume that God was inevitably or naturally present in Canaan. The fathers were always astonished when they became aware of God's presence: "Truly the Lord is in this place, and I did not know it" (Gen. 28:16). God does not belong to any particular place. It is his good pleasure to reveal himself at one place or another. This free pleasure of God is what astonishes the fathers. His coming is as unexpected as his choosing. The fathers built altars at the places of his revelation (12:7-8; 13:18; 22:9; 26:25; 35:1, 3, 7) because they were astonished, startled, and afraid, yet also grateful for the wonderful ways of God.

Second, nearly all the places where God revealed himself were holy places. We are all familiar with names like Beersheba, Shechem, and Bethel, and we know that Israel worshiped there for generations. Not so well known is that the Canaanites worshiped at these places before the fathers came. Yet any former "holiness" the places might have had was irrelevant, as we see later from the prophets. Why, then, did God choose these places to reveal himself? A partial answer will be given below (see § c).

The Hebrew word for "place" (12:6; 13:3-4; etc.), i.e., *māqôm,* can also mean "sanctuary" or "holy place." Hence the NEB correctly has "sanctuary at Shechem" in 12:6.

Israel praises the God who revealed himself, not in outer space nor in the universe at large, but in particular places as it pleased him. These places *became* holy places because he revealed himself at them. Canaan *became* the holy land because it pleased God to make his presence known there. But can we really say that these places are holy only because Abraham, Isaac, and Jacob met God there? As places where God would reveal himself, did they not have a holiness that reached back to an earlier time? Do we not have to say, perhaps, that instead of sanctifying them with their own practices, the Canaanites had unconsciously venerated them as places where the God of Israel planned to reveal himself?

b. Ways and Means of Revelation

We come now to the manner of God's revelation. No single teaching, model, or dogma regarding this revelation dominates the OT. God reveals himself in many ways and the text also describes his self-revelation in many ways. It may be direct and concrete. It may take the form of indirect and abstract speech. Various expressions are used, but all tell of the same wonderful acts of God.

Instead of saying that God revealed himself, we should perhaps say that he "appeared" (12:7; 17:1; 18:1; 26:2, 24; 35:1, 9; 48:3). The appearance is one that can be seen, felt, and heard. It is not just an intangible spiritual presence. God did not merely grant a vision; truly, if temporarily, he offered himself. How? Sometimes he appeared and spoke. Sometimes he appeared by night. Sometimes he appeared as a man, and only at the end did it become evident that the angel of the Lord or the Lord himself had been the visitor. Sometimes nothing was seen, but his presence was felt and his voice, or that of an angel, was heard. Sometimes a voice came first and only then an awareness that God had revealed himself.

To take an example, three men came to Abraham and Sarah near the holy tree of Mamre by Hebron (18:1-16a). They came in the heat of the day. They acted as one in their coming, going, washing, resting, eating, and speaking. Were they three angels? Or God with two angels? Or the one God in three persons? We cannot say for sure, since the text does not say. What it does say is that "the Lord appeared to Abraham."

Again, in 19:1ff. two men came to Lot to tell him to leave the accursed town of Sodom. They introduced themselves as men sent by the Lord (v. 13). They are also called angels (vv. 1, 15). Both speak first, then only one, and finally God himself (vv. 2, 12, 17, 24, 29).

Between the above examples is the connecting story of Abraham's intercession for Sodom. The three who had visited him at Mamre set out for Sodom, and Abraham, who at first accompanied them, stopped with the third, conscious of being in God's presence (18:16ff.).

Other stories of God or an angel appearing include the appearance to Hagar in 16:7ff., where God comes as the angel and Hagar herself is certain that she has seen God. We might also refer to the angels of God that met Jacob in 32:1-2, and later to the experience of Joshua in Josh. 3:13-15. Judg. 13 contains references to the angel of the Lord in vv. 3 and 21, to a man of God or a prophet in v. 6, and to God himself in v. 22.

One of the best-known appearances in a dream was that to Jacob at Bethel in Gen. 28:10-22. Here Jacob saw the Lord himself standing beside him (vv. 10, 11a, 13-16), but he also saw the angels of God going up and down the ladder to heaven. Other appearances in dreams were to Abimelech of Gerar (20:3), to Isaac (26:24), and to Laban (31:24); cf. later to Solomon (1 Kgs. 3:5). In these stories God needs no angels as go-betweens. He himself comes to whom he wills (20:3; 31:24). An angel mediates when Abraham offers his son at Moriah (22:11, 15), but this time he does not appear; he simply calls from heaven.

No matter how God's presence is described, one thing is clear. Interest focuses on the presence, not the form or appearance, on the word, not the coming. The OT wants us to know that God was there and to listen to what he said. To listen to God's Word is to listen to God himself. Neither a mute appearance nor a word from a distant heaven would have helped the fathers. It was because God was present that his Word carried meaning. His Word had power because he was there. This was why Israel praised the God who appeared to the fathers.

c. The Name Conveying God's Identity

In appearing, God made himself known. Abraham, Isaac, and Jacob were Israel's forerunners. Yet at first they did not and could not know him who appeared to them. They were no doubt religious men. They would be familiar with the idea of "God." But they did not yet know him who was calling them.

When people want to be known, they introduce themselves by name. God did the same when he appeared. In following this custom he was not merely showing courtesy or civility, though that probably played a role. Yet we have to remember that in the OT God is not the guest or newcomer who has to be introduced. The fathers are the newcomers to God's house (Bethel) and land. God made known his name, then, because this was his good pleasure and plan. He wanted those whom he had chosen to know him by name.

What is this name of God? The stories tend to bewilder us because they give many answers to this question. God does not have just one name but many. In the OT as a whole God's name is YHWH (Yahweh). All Jews know this, although because they must not use the blessed name in vain, they customarily use a title: the Lord (Adonai). Strangely, however, the common witness of the OT does not apply uniformly in the stories of the fathers.

"I am Yahweh"—with these words God does introduce himself once to Abraham (Gen. 15:7 CB) and once to Jacob (28:13). He also appears under this name to Abraham (12:7; 18:1) and Isaac (26:2, 24). Hagar (16:13), Abraham (12:8; 13:4; 21:33), and Isaac (26:25) call upon him under this name. God uses this name when speaking to Adam (2:16). Cain and Abel made offerings to Yahweh (4:3), and Enoch began to invoke Yahweh by name (4:26). This is one part of the witness that opens with creation and the fathers. Elsewhere, however, revelation of the true name of God comes only with the exodus (Exod. 3–4). In the stories of the fathers, then, we also find the general term "God" (Elohim), e.g., in Gen. 20:1-18; 22:1-19; 18:17-18; 20–22; 35:1ff.; and cf. 17:1ff.; 27:41–28:5; 33:9-13; Exod. 6:2.

God revealed his name to the fathers, yet he allowed himself to be known by other names as well. The one God revealed himself, but he used various provisional appellations and titles by which to make himself known. This alternation between "Yahweh" and more general titles indicates, perhaps, the provisional position of the fathers as "already" but "not yet" within Israel. At the same time it is the one God who under the name of Yahweh or any other elects and calls them, and makes himself known to them.

Altogether Genesis presents us with over twelve divine names. We may put them under three heads according to their characteristics. The first group contains those that use the name El. The people of Canaan had already used this name before Israel came. Israel took it over along with Elohim. (Both names have to be translated "God," so that when we read ancient or modern renderings we cannot know which the Hebrew is using.) God told Jacob: "I am El, the God of your father" (Gen. 46:2-3 CB), Jacob set up an altar at Shechem to "El, the God of Israel" (33:20 CB). At Bethel, too, he built an altar to El (35:1, 3). The name recurs dozens of times in the OT, especially in Psalms and Job.

Like other peoples that used the name El, Israel commonly added a qualification. As the Shechemites invoked Baal-berith or El-berith (Judg. 9:4, 46), so Abraham addressed God as El-Olam (Gen. 21:33, "the everlasting God"), Hagar called him El-Roi (16:13), and God introduced himself to Jacob as El-Bethel (31:13). The best-known combination, perhaps, is El-Shaddai ("God Almighty," e.g., 17:1; 28:3; 35:11), and Melchizedek taught Abraham to worship the Lord under the name El-Elyon ("God Most High," 14:18-22).

In the second group we find names that use Elohim. This is a general concept rather than a name. The people of Canaan and Syria used to call their deities *ilani* (the plural of *ilu*), which may denote the totality of divine beings, single deities, or representatives of the divine world. In the OT Elohim is always a general designation, not a name. Only when compounded with other words (in the form Elohe) can it be used as a divine name, e.g., the "God of heaven." Most important for us are combinations with names of persons, e.g., one of the fathers. Thus God revealed himself to Jacob as Elohe-Abraham ("the God of your father Abraham," Gen. 26:24) and Elohe-Isaac ("the God of Isaac," 28:13). Similarly the sons of Jacob served Elohe-Abika ("your father's God," i.e., the God of Jacob, 50:17). Later we read of "the God of your forefathers, the God of Abraham, the God of Isaac, the God of Jacob" (Exod. 3:6; cf. 1 Kgs. 18:36; Matt. 22:32). The original distinction between El and Elohim seems to have been that El was used for the local God and Elohim for the tribal God, with different gods according to place or tribe. It is the one God, however, who makes himself known to the fathers as either El or Elohim.

To the third group belong divine names that contain only the fathers' own names. Thus we find Pahad-Isaac in Gen. 31:42, 53 ("Fear of Isaac") and Abir-Jacob in 49:24 ("Strong One of Jacob"); cf. Ps. 132:2, 5 ("Mighty One of Jacob"). The translations, by the way, are far from certain. Since names of this kind seem to have come originally from tribal groups, this category is plainly very close to the second.

We conclude that in their pluralistic religious world the fathers already knew Yahweh, the God of Israel, because he revealed himself to them. Yet they still invoked him by divine names that originated in the religious life of the surrounding nations. Yahweh himself let them do so. He was not identifying himself with the pagan deities. Instead, he was taking over their names and making them his own, just as he confiscated their holy places for his own worship. The pagan background of the names did not prevent his using them as instruments of revelation to the fathers. It pleased God to do this in order to manifest himself as the one God. The Genesis stories show a remarkable breadth of vision in this regard. Though elements of foreign religion are usually portrayed negatively, at this point they are allowed a positive aspect as mirrors or reflections of God's presence. A mirror is dark in itself but it can reflect light that falls upon it. This actually happened when God graciously revealed himself in the pluralistic religious world of the fathers.

4. God Made a Covenant

Having chosen and called the fathers, God made a covenant with them, solemnly swearing fidelity to Abraham, renewing his promise to Isaac and Jacob, and giving them an earnest of his covenant with Israel at the exodus. The covenant is essentially one. In Abraham all Israel became God's people. Showing favor to Abraham, God manifested himself once and for all as Israel's God.

GOD HAD A SPECIFIC PURPOSE in choosing the fathers and revealing himself to them. The stories make this clear. Many of them culminate in a saying that discloses God's intention and plan. The Word of God is the act of God. This comes out most clearly when God is said to have made a covenant with the fathers.

Once when Israel was overwhelmed by the armies of Benhadad of Syria and might justly have been destroyed, we read that God took pity on Israel "because of his covenant with Abraham, Isaac, and Jacob" (2 Kgs. 13:23). The covenant is seen here as a central element in the stories of the fathers. The same holds good in Exod. 2:24 and Neh. 9:8. The reference might be to one covenant with all three fathers (Exod. 2:24; 6:4-5), or to three covenants, one with each of them (Lev. 26:42).

In the stories themselves we read only twice that God made a covenant, both times with Abraham (Gen. 15 and 17). Gen. 15 tells of a vision that came to Abram by night (vv. 1-6), then of a revelation that took place by day but became manifest only after dark (vv. 11-17). The making of the covenant involved a strange ceremony. Abram killed five animals as an offering, cut three in half, and arranged them so as to leave a way open between the pieces. Then "a trance came over Abram and a great fear came upon him" (v. 12), and "there appeared a smoking brazier and a flaming torch passing between the divided pieces. That very day the Lord made a covenant with Abram" (vv. 17-18). He solemnly promised to give the land of Canaan to Abraham and his descendants (vv. 7, 18b; cf. ch. 12).

The second story, Gen. 17:1-14, limits itself to two facts: God appears and God speaks. It gives more attention, however, to the content and conditions of the covenant. God speaks three times. He first states the aim (v. 1b), then explains his gifts to Abraham (vv. 3-8), then spells out Abraham's obligation, i.e., male circumcision (vv. 9-14). Circumcision, of course, is a covenant sign, namely, a sign of willingness to obey God. Abraham must "walk in God's presence" (v. 1 CB) step by step as God makes his will known to him.

There are obvious differences between the accounts. The one refers to a ceremony with sacrifice, the other to circumcision. The one describes the land as a gift, the other posterity and God's presence as well. In the one, God reveals himself as Yahweh, in the other as El-Shaddai. The one refers to the covenant only once, the other thirteen times. In the one, the covenant confirms the promise, in the other it initiates it. Yet in both God makes a covenant with Abraham that is valid for all his descendants. This covenant is the beginning of the shared covenantal history of God and his people. When God made it, Israel was born. All God's future acts at the exodus, at Sinai, and at the conquest of the land are simply a fulfilment of what happened when God made a covenant with Abraham.

What does it mean that God "made a covenant"? The expression has a legal background. Religious language speaks about the relationship between heaven and earth, between Creator and creatures. Law deals with relations between people. It thus uses the concept of the covenant. When people buy or sell, when they marry, when they make wills or inherit, legal agreements are drawn up to define their rights and duties. Contracts of this kind are necessary both in social and international relations.

The Genesis stories offer many examples of agreements or covenants among both individuals and nations in which each party agrees to the rights and duties of the other and a common meal is shared as a sign of the community that has been established. Along these lines covenants were made between Abraham and Abimelech (27:27-32), Isaac and Abimelech (26:26-31), and Jacob and Laban (39:46ff.). Often witnesses were present to confirm the agreement, e.g., the Hittites when Abraham bought the cave of Machpelah (23:16, 18). Both sides might swear loyalty and invoke God as witness, monuments or cairns being set up as a memorial to the divine presence (31:46).

God's covenant with Abraham is a legal institution in spite of the fact that it does not regulate relations between human partners. Israel seems to have been the first religious community to dare to speak of a covenant in which God becomes the partner of a human group and binds himself in alliance with it. We are so accustomed to this today that we fail to understand how utterly strange it is that God and people should become partners in a legal agreement that is binding on both sides. Must not God lower himself and humanity be exalted if partners of such unequal standing are to meet?

Recent excavations in Asia Minor have brought to light some clay tablets containing covenant texts between the Hittites (an important people in the patriarchal period) and other nations. In some of these the Hittite high king made agreements with lesser kings and their peoples. These minor rulers swore allegiance to the high king and promised to respect the rights of other vassals. In return they gratefully received the high king's protection and leadership. The high king himself did not take an oath, which would be unfitting. He simply stated his readiness to protect his vassals.

These texts throw light on God's covenant with Abraham inasmuch as they involve partners of different status. Does this mean that God's covenant with Abraham is to be understood in terms of the vassal treaties? There may be signs of familiarity with these treaties, but the striking thing is that Genesis turns the conditions upside down. It is God, not Abraham, who binds himself with an oath (24:7; 26:3; 50:24), and he makes no specific demands upon Abraham but grants a favor to which his partner is in no way entitled. Comparison with the political covenants simply shows how strange and wonderful the covenant with Abraham truly is.

Israel boldly called the relation between God and Abraham a covenant. God's dealings with the fathers were so different from those of pagan deities with their followers that an unusual term had to be used. In choosing Abraham God did not show him an isolated kindness which he might withdraw at his pleasure. He entered into a lasting and regulated relationship that could be understood only in legal terms because it was founded on God's own justice.

We might note some other OT terms that are rooted in the covenant as a legal institution. Justice ($ṣ^e dāqāh$) is a virtue that all ages have praised. Understandably, then, all nations see their deities as just and even as the source of justice. But what is meant by the justice of the Lord God of Israel? Is it that of the supreme judge who vindicates the good and punishes the bad but shows favor to none, simply applying a law that is permanent and universal? Distributive justice of this kind is indeed included whenever the God of Abraham, Isaac, and Jacob is said to be just. We must add immediately, however, that only his own law, the law of his faithfulness to Abraham, can be meant. This is the law of him who "raises the lowly from the dust" (1 Sam. 2:8 CB). Often in the Bible, then, God's $ṣ^e dāqāh$ (or $ṣedeq$) is his deliverance or salvation ("victories, triumphs," Judg. 5:11; "victories," 1 Sam. 12:7; "justice," Ps. 48:11 [Eng. 10]; "righteous," 103:6).

This fact must be taken into account in our rendering of the word *ḥesed*. The older translation (e.g., King James) was usually "mercy," which is often seen as opposed to justice. A judge who takes pity on the accused and shows mercy is not likely to be legally just. But when God performs *hesed,* he acts according to his covenant law. To express this, the NEB uses the verbal form "to keep faith with" (e.g., Gen. 24:12, 14, 27, 49) or nouns such as "unfailing love" (e.g., Ps. 31:8, 17 [Eng. 7, 16]) or "true love" (e.g., Ps. 13:6 [Eng. 5]; 51:3 [Eng. 1]). Faithful love is the very heart of God's justice. The Greek translators of the patriarchal stories sensed this and used *dikaiosýnē,* "justice, uprightness, righteousness," in Gen. 19:19; 24:27; 32:10 (MT 11).

"I am not worthy of all the true and steadfast love which thou hast shown to me" was Jacob's confession in Gen. 32:10. According to God's covenant Jacob had a "right" to this love. A legal agreement sets rights and duties for both parties. Yet God does not *owe* help to Jacob nor has Jacob any *claim* to it. In making a covenant God has bound himself, but he has not become the prisoner of his own act, still less of his human partner. He keeps faith freely by his own decision. Because of this very freedom he can be trusted.

When the OT portrays God as "submitting" to the legal agreement that he has set up, it is speaking figuratively. After all, the covenant is simply God's Word to Abraham when he promised him his blessing. Through the covenant God laid bare his heart to Abraham and declared his firm intention to keep his Word. His plan and intention is described by the OT as an eternal covenant in the legal sense. God's faithfulness to it may be trusted. His Word is to be trusted. He himself in his revelation is to be trusted. The covenant is not a legal precedent. It is not a document that has authority apart from God himself. We see how impossible that is from the affirmation: "By my own self I swear" (22:16; cf. Heb. 6:13-18).

The tension that we noted between the "already" and the "not yet" of the revelation to the fathers applies also to the covenant with them. The "already" of the covenant as an eternal institution is the point of Gen. 17, the "not yet" of the covenant as a provisional agreement comes out in Gen. 15. In both cases God obviously intends the covenant with Abraham to be his covenant with Israel. He has already made this covenant with the fathers but it has yet to come into full effect for Israel.

5. God Grants His Promises

Swearing his covenant with the fathers, God has them (and Israel) look ahead to the great things that he will do for them. This hope is described in many ways: God promises the fathers and their offspring blessing, land, and descendants; he promises that the fathers' descen-

dants will be a blessing to all nations; he grants some fulfilment of the promises, but the true fulfilment is constantly thwarted, endangered, and postponed.

THE PATRIARCHAL STORIES refer so often to the promises, and give them such prominence, that it might be asked why we did not open this part with them. The fact that we end with them does not belittle their significance. Indeed, they constitute the central testimony that the OT gives concerning the fathers. They answer three questions: Why did God choose the fathers? Why did he reveal himself to them? Why did he grant them a covenant? We understand God's purpose in doing these things only when we look at the promises.

A promise relates to the future. The intimated fulfilment and gift are still to come. The promise has been given. Giving a promise is no less important than fulfilling it. For as soon as God promises, he begins to fulfil. Nevertheless, the main orientation of a promise is to the future.

Among God's mighty acts the OT accords an important place to his promises. Strangely, it has no specific word for "promise." God says: I *shall* give, I *shall* bless, you *will* become, you *will* receive. His declaration of what is going to happen, strengthened at times by his oath, is his promise. The word "promise" comes in only tentatively and occasionally with the Greek translation, which uses *epangelía* ("announcement of what is to come"; cf. *euangélion,* "good news"). The NT picks up the term *epangelía* with particular reference to Abraham and the other fathers (Acts 7:5, 17; Rom. 4:13, 16; Gal. 3:16-18; Heb. 6:13; 7:6; 11:17). In the NT the promise is the decisive means by which God reveals himself both in Genesis and throughout scripture. Moses and the prophets received the promises *(epangelíai)* and the apostles' task was to witness their fulfilment *(euangélion).* We shall follow the apostles' example and use "promise" for an utterance that reveals what God will give in the future.

God granted wonderful promises to Abraham, Isaac, and Jacob. Canaan was to be their lasting possession. Their descendants would be as innumerable as "the stars in the skies and the sand on the shore." A community of nations would spring from them. They would enjoy fertility and the divine presence and protection. God took an oath that he would do these things according to his plan.

Different passages stress different aspects. From one angle God's blessing is like a shining light in which the fathers stand but which they also reflect. From another angle the blessing consists not merely of material or spiritual gifts but of God himself: "I will be your God, yours and your descendants after you."

Many stories refer to the promises of land, progeny, and blessing, though not always in the same order, nor all together. Important texts are Gen. 12:1-3; 13:14-16; 15:5, 7,

18; 27:4-8; 28:3-4, 30:15; 32:13; 35:11-12; 50:24; Exod. 6:4-7; 32:13. Land alone is listed in Gen. 12:7; 15:7, 18; 24:7; 50:24; Exod. 13:5; 33:1; Num. 10:29; 14:23; 32:11; etc. The promise of Isaac's birth is a special form of the promise of posterity.

The promise of a transmission of blessing to the nations occurs in the famous words in Gen. 12:3: "In thee shall all the families of the earth be blessed" (cf. 12:2-3 CB; 18:18; 22:18; 26:4; 28:14; Acts 3:25; Gal. 3:8). The point seems initially to be that in Abram God's activity of blessing begins as opposed to the primeval diminution of human existence. Accurate translation is a problem, since the form translated "shall be blessed" might also be reflexive: "shall bless themselves," and this might have the sense that they will wish to be blessed like Abram and his descendants (NEB "will pray to be blessed as you are blessed"). Another possible rendering is "will get blessed," i.e., will have the opportunity of blessing rather than being involuntarily blessed.

God promises himself in Gen. 17:7-8 and Exod. 6:7: "I will be your God." The Exodus text adds: "You will become my people" (CB). The NEB has here: "I will adopt you as my people," using the adoption formula that we find in Ps. 2:7; cf. also the marriage formula of Hos. 2:23.

The promises are the very center of the patriarchal stories. For Israel the time of the fathers was the time of promise, expectation, and hope. The stories all incline toward the future. This shared orientation is the more astonishing in view of the different individual aims and themes that may be detected in them.

Many of the stories as such have little to do with the giving of the promises. They relate to holy places such as Mamre or Bethel and show why Israel worships there (Gen. 12:6-7; 16:7ff.; 18:1ff.; 22:1ff.). They explain why animal offerings are made (22:1ff.), or circumcision is practiced (17:9ff.), or the sinew of the nerve in the hollow of the thigh is not eaten (32:22-32). They have to do with relations between the fathers and the inhabitants of the land (14:1-24; 20:1-18; 21:22; 24:1-67; 26:1-33). They tell about the blessing and protection that God has already granted the fathers (12:10-12; 13:1-5; 14:8-24). They refer to past events (14:1-17; 19:24-29). They record the purchase of land (23:1-20; 33:18-19). They tell why the fathers were given particular names (Abraham in 17:1-8, Isaac in 17:13-22 and 18:1-5, Jacob in 24ff., his children in 29:31–30:24, and Israel in 32:22-32).

Clearly, then, many stories have no primary or specific interest in the granting of promises or in blessings that are yet to be conferred. None of the above stories is inherently oriented to the future. Some even focus on past events.

Thus we read that God had already given the land of Canaan to the fathers (Gen. 28:4; 35:12). Apart from Isaac, Abraham already had numerous progeny (25:1-3). The fathers built altars and made offerings to the Lord; he was already their God. God "had blessed him [Abraham] in all that he did" (24:1), and he was similarly present with Isaac and

Jacob (21:22; 28:20). Jacob had many children (chs. 29–30), great riches (chs. 30–33), and sure possession of land (48:22).

Nevertheless, although the fathers had already received and enjoyed God's blessings, the stories, for all their individual aims and themes, all have also a common emphasis: the promises of God, and orientation to their future fulfilment. They could have this emphasis because of the interrelationship of Abraham, Isaac, and Jacob, the strategic occurrence of the element of promise in the different stories, the obvious delays in the fulfilment of the blessings, the role of the patriarchs as the forefathers of Israel, and finally the link to the exodus at the end of the Joseph narrative.

Chapter III

God Brought Israel out of Egypt

1. The Witness of Scripture

The Lord liberated Israel from oppression in Egypt with mighty signs and wonders, and brought it through the Red Sea. This act is a subject of praise and the very foundation of Israel's faith on which all other elements in its creed rest.

"I AM THE LORD YOUR GOD who brought you out of Egypt, out of the land of slavery" (Exod. 20:2). These familiar words introduce the Ten Commandments. With them we come to another part of our study. Though we treat the topic third, it is first in importance. It occurs almost everywhere in the OT. In every period it was the article of confession that most united and inspired the people of Israel.

We stand again before an event that God wonderfully brought about. What kind of event was it? The OT calls it a victory. The Egyptian army suffered an unexpected defeat that allowed the Israelites to escape from their pursuit and hence from bondage. Obviously the powerful Egyptian empire was not shattered by this loss on its borders. Yet the victory has come down to us as a pivotal event, the exodus from Egypt.

Israel celebrated it as a wonderful event because it could not find for it any natural reasons. We cannot explain what happened either by the strength of the Israelites, the weakness or stupidity of the Egyptians, or the configuration of the terrain that might favor Israel rather than Egypt.

Instead of taking pride in their own bravery or tactics, instead of mocking the Egyptians for foolish self-confidence or carelessness, Israel praised God as the true warrior-hero. "With his right hand he shattered the enemy" (Exod. 15:6ff. CB; cf. v. 21b). In every account this note of praise is

[56]

sounded. The community remembers the event with joy, singing, clapping of hands, and dancing.

The title of the Book of Exodus reflects the contents of the first fifteen chapters. Just as the OT witness to creation centers in Gen. 1–2, and its witness to the call of the fathers in Gen. 12–50, so most of the stories relating to the deliverance of Israel from Egypt may be found in Exod. 1–15. An important factor in the recounting of what took place, apart from that of preserving the record of a decisive event, was the answering of a need in the life of the community of Israel: the celebration of the Passover.

No event was celebrated by Israel with more attention and joy than the Passover (Hebrew *pesah*), the coming out of Egypt. In its commemoration, texts were needed that could be read, sung, or told. Hence Exod. 1–15 serve also as Passover readings, with rules for the celebration in chs. 12–13, and a hymn at the climax of the feast in ch. 15. A fresh light comes on the chapters when we see them as a great thanksgiving and not merely as a record of past events.

The liberation from Egypt is a theme of praise at Israel's worship in general and not merely in Passover celebration (cf. Ps. 66:6; 136:10-15; 114). We see this from its role in the creeds, which normally take the form of hymns of praise. Virtually every confession of Israel's faith mentions it. The God in whom Israel believes is "the Lord who brought Israel out of Egypt." From this formula, which not by chance appears more than 120 times in the OT, we learn who God is and how he has manifested himself. By the liberation from Egypt God established the ground on which Israel stands. Through it Israel came into being as God's own people. Other topics might also be seen as the basis of Israel's existence as God's people: the election of the fathers, the revelation at Sinai, preservation in the wilderness, the gift of the land, indirectly even creation itself. Yet none of these is described so specifically as the beginning of Israel. The exodus, then, undeniably enjoys priority, and it influences in some way the OT witness to all the other great deeds of God, in all of which we find a parallel intention, a similar note, and a common aim.

The election of the fathers took place with the exodus in mind and as an introduction to it. The formula in Gen. 15:7 is similar to that in Exod. 20:2 or Deut. 6:23. Abram's experiences in Egypt foreshadow those of Israel later. Vocation, revelation, covenant, and blessing were all given to the fathers, and yet all were still promise. Similarly, the events at Sinai, in the wilderness, and at the occupation all presuppose the liberation from Egypt. As the earlier deeds of God look ahead to the key event, the later deeds depend upon it.

Why is the exodus of such decisive importance for Israel? We shall answer this question by describing each of the main emphases that the OT witness puts upon it.

2. God Liberated His People

(a) In bringing his people out of Egypt, God grants them freedom from slavery and adopts them as his own people. Treating Israel as his firstborn child and chosen people, he evokes faith and praise from a people who serve and worship him of their own free will. (b) As the Lord's servant, Israel is free both from imposed slavery and from dependence upon the forces that other nations worship. God gives the people his law to preserve this freedom for the whole people and for each of its members.

EXODUS PRAISES GOD because he won a battle. Since the Egyptian army was destroyed and Israel escaped without loss, this was a notable victory. Yet although the victory was so decisive, its true importance does not lie in the military realm. Israel praised God for a triumph of much broader and deeper consequence. Thanks to it, Israel could leave the land of slavery. It was liberated.

a. Liberation and Redemption

Even as he won the victory "with the right hand," hurling horse and rider into the sea, God brought his people out of Egypt. He acted in a way that made it possible for them to walk out, to leave the place of oppression. "To bring out," "to let somebody go out"—this is the key verb for an understanding of God's intention.

Hebrew has in fact two verbs to express this. The first, *yāṣā'*, means "to go out" with no thought of destination. It simply means going out, i.e., not being where one was before. The second, *'ālāh*, means "to go up," to leave a lower place for a higher. English, however, has to use "to go out" for both, or, in the causative, "to bring out." The verbs are parallel in the original. Sometimes there is no difference at all between them. At other times the emphasis varies as Egypt or Canaan is in view (cf. Gen. 15:14 and 1 Sam. 15:2, 6).

We read that God "brought out" or "brought up." But this does not mean that the people were passive. They for their part "came out" or "went out" (cf. Gen. 15:14; Josh. 2:10; 5:4-6; 2 Kgs. 8:9; Mic. 7:15) or "came up" (Exod. 13:18; Judg. 11:13), just as the fathers went when God called them to move. It is God, of course, who enabled the people to go out of Egypt and up to the land of promise. God set the people on the move and accompanied them. Statistically, we find the expression "God brought out" 21 times in Exodus (e.g., 3:10; 6:5), 4 times in Numbers, and 22 times in Deuteronomy. "God brought up" (e.g., Exod. 3:8, 17) is twice as common as "Israel went out" (cf., e.g., Gen. 15:14) or "went up" (cf. Exod. 13:8-9). The people of Israel rose up to leave Egypt, but it was God who moved them to do so.

"Out of Egypt" does not mean only that Israel left the land of Egypt and moved to another country. The OT describes Egypt as the land of slavery. In leaving it Israel left not only a geographical area but a condition of life. God not only brought his people from one country to another; he brought them out of bondage into freedom. A number of verbs show this very clearly. "To bring out or up" means also "to free," "to save," "to rescue," "to release," or even "to redeem" from Egypt, the land, likened to a house, where Israel had suffered oppression and slavery.

In Exod. 6:6 we read: "I will release you from your labours in Egypt. I will rescue you from slavery there." The Hebrew verb *nāṣal* ("rescue") is common in this connection (cf. 3:8; 5:23; "save," 18:4, 8-10; "deliver," Judg. 6:9; 1 Sam. 10:18). Another verb with the same meaning, *yāšaʿ*, occurs only once but the case is significant: "That day the Lord saved [freed, delivered] Israel from the power of Egypt" (Exod. 14:30). Israel is seen as a people in chains, groaning in bondage. God's intervention is portrayed as the storming of a prison, the breaking of chains, the freeing of captives.

Two verbs that are usually translated "redeem" sound a different note. This word is used today in connection with the pawnshop. The pawned object has to be "redeemed" within a certain time by a redemption payment. In the same sense one might think of the compensation paid to the government by a person wanting to leave a position before the period of obligatory service is over, e.g., by someone who received a scholarship or grant for study on the condition of certain years of service after qualification. In ancient Israel a redemption sacrifice could be made to God to redeem what belonged to him by right (Exod. 13:11-13). There might also be redemption of a slave or bond servant by the payment of a fixed price. The Hebrew verb *gā'al* is used when a wealthy member of the family is under obligation to redeem a relative who is in prison for debt or who has been made a prisoner of war. This is the first verb. The other verb, *pādāh*, has a broader meaning. It can be used not only for the redeeming of a slave or a lawful possession or inheritance (Exod. 13:13), but also for the rescuing of a person out of trouble or danger ("rescue," 2 Sam. 4:9; "save," Ps. 78:42; "set free," 119:134). The original use of this verb seems to have been for the redemption of a slave when the slave was not related to the redeemer, so that the latter acted voluntarily and not under customary obligation.

The difference between obligatory redemption (e.g., Boaz and Ruth in Ruth 3:9; cf. 3:12; 4:1-12) and voluntary redemption is no longer apparent when God is said to redeem his people from the power of the Egyptians. Whether his action be expressed by *gā'al* (Exod. 6:5; 15:13; cf. Isa. 41:1; 48:20) or by *pādāh* (Deut. 7:8; 9:26; 13:5; 15:15; 21:8; 24:18; 2 Sam. 7:23; Mic. 6:4), it is always of his own free will that he redeems Israel.

God clearly liberated his people by what he did in Egypt. But how? If Israel was "redeemed," what price did God pay for the liberation of this slave? The OT says nothing about any payment. God did indeed redeem Israel, but he paid nothing. "You were sold but no price was paid, and without payment you shall be ransomed [redeemed]" (Isa. 52:3). As Peter would put it later, "you know that it was no perishable stuff, like gold or silver, that bought your freedom" (1 Pet. 1:18).

God redeemed his people legitimately according to his own law. The exodus story often stresses the legal aspect. Israel belonged by law to God. It had been arbitrarily oppressed by Pharaoh. In freeing his people God simply restored its legitimate position, which Egypt had for generations disregarded.

A verb rooted in the law of slavery describes the liberation of Israel. This is the verb *šalaḥ*, "to let go." A slave may go away free when the years of service have been completed or if for some reason there is no longer any entitlement to hold the slave (Exod. 21:2-11). Since Pharaoh had no rights, God required him to "let my people go" (4:23; 5:1; 7:16; 8:21; 9:1, 13; 10:3, 7). This term is an important one in the story; it occurs no less than forty times. Though Pharaoh many times hardened his heart and broke his word, he finally had to yield to a power much greater than his own. Forced by a strong hand and outstretched arm, "in the end Pharaoh will let them go" (6:1). In this case the slave will go out free without any payment (21:11).

The liberation of Israel also accords with the law of slavery in that freed slaves had to be given a present: "When you set him free, do not let him go empty-handed. Give to him lavishly from your flock, from your threshing-floor and your wine-press" (Deut. 15:13-14). The point is that slaves must be treated with respect according to their humanity, for Israel was itself a slave in Egypt before the Lord redeemed it (15:15). A model for the giving of a present to liberated slaves may be found in Exod. 3:21-22; 11:2-3; 12:35-36, where God gives Israel such favor with the Egyptians that "you will not go empty- handed. Every woman shall ask . . . for jewellery of silver and gold and for clothing" (cf. Exod. 12:35 and Deut. 15:13). Possibly the Egyptians wanted to put Israel under an obligation with these presents, but by giving them they unwittingly granted legal freedom to Israel. In this sense they were indeed "plundered" by the Israelites.

A further factor is that Israel was freed in such a way that it left an illegal service for a legal service. It moved from an abnormal to a normal situation. Former slaves were set free to live as free persons (Exod. 21:2; Deut. 15:12). But free persons have both rights and obligations. To be free is not to be one's own master and to do as one pleases. Pharaoh was requested to free Israel, not to enjoy an indeterminate liberty, but to serve the Lord: "Let my son go, so that he may worship me" (Exod. 4:23; 8:1, 20; 9:1, 13; 10:3, 7). The Israelites go out free from Egypt. They are rid of the labor illegally forced upon them by the Egyptians. But this freedom is a freedom to serve and worship God. To serve God, to work for him, to care for him, to worship him—all these are aspects of the verb *'abad*. This verb describes the normal status of Israel. The Israelites are "servants of the Lord" (cf. Lev. 25:42), and they are set free to take up this service. Does this mean exchanging one form of slavery for another? Certainly not! Those who serve the Lord—his "slaves"—are truly free because they are liberated from every kind of illegal slavery.

By a valid act God liberated Israel from slavery in Egypt. This liberation took place. It is an undeniable fact. God himself acted. He thus guaranteed that Israel would remain free. Hence Israel never tires of praising God for this action. It believes in its divine liberation and prays for its actualization in every period of history.

b. Liberation and the Birth of God's People

To become the servant of the Lord is to be truly free, and conversely to become truly free is to be the servant of the Lord. The title of the chapter covers both aspects. If the stress is first on the action of the liberating God, i.e., on the verbs of action, it falls secondly on the people, the object of the act of liberation.

Who is this people which is the Lord's people? The expression "people of the Lord" appears suddenly in the exodus story. Abraham, Isaac, and Jacob knew the Lord because he had elected and called them. Each of the fathers, with his house, is called a "people" ('am, Gen. 32:7; 35:6). Yet the expression "people of the Lord" is not applied to them. It is in the exodus story that those who were previously "the house of Jacob," "Jacob's sons," "the children of Israel," "the Hebrews," "the Israelites," or "the people of Israel," acquire a new title. They are henceforth "the people of the Lord."

We are not told in Exod. 1–15 exactly when Israel was first called "the people of the Lord." We do not know the circumstances of the giving or accepting of the title. There is a hint, however, in the story of the call of Moses when with face covered he hears God's words: "I have indeed seen the misery of *my people* in Egypt. . . . Come now; I will send you to Pharaoh and you shall bring *my people* Israel out of Egypt" (Exod. 3:7, 10). The liberation carries with it the promise: "I will redeem you with arm outstretched. . . . I will *adopt* you as *my people,* and I will become your God" (Exod. 6:6-7). God has already marked this people as his own, and with the liberation its adoption as such takes place.

God liberated Israel because it was the people of the Lord, descending from Abraham, Isaac, and Jacob, to whom he had given the promise. At the same time Israel became the people of the Lord because it was the people whom God freed from slavery in Egypt. These complementary statements agree that God's mighty act in Egypt constituted Israel officially and authentically the people of the Lord. Many OT texts confirm this conclusion.

On the one hand are passages that sing of the exodus as the foundation on which Israel stands and the beginning of its history (Ps. 66:5-6; 74:12-15; 77:11-20; 78:12-13; 80:8; 103:7; 106:7-12; 136:10-15). On the other hand are passages that relate the Red Sea triumph to God's victory at the beginning of time (Ps. 74:12-15; 89:9-12; Isa. 51:9-10).

The prophets for the most part find the beginning of Israel in the exodus (Amos 2:10; Hos. 11:1; Mic. 6:3-4; Jer. 31:32; Ezek. 20:5-6). In Isa. 43:14ff. the Creator of Israel, who will give it a new exodus, is extolled as the God "who opened a way in the sea . . . who drew on chariot and horse to their destruction." The liberation from Egypt and the birth of the people are one and the same act. In Ezek. 20:5-6 the adoption of Israel is related to God's oath that he "would bring them out of Egypt."

Since the liberation from Egypt is the birth of the people, the act of God also involves action on the part of the people. To be sure, Israel cannot give birth to itself. God alone can bring this people into being as his own people. Nevertheless, the divine act does not leave the Israelites as passive spectators. God so acts that they become conscious of his purposes, that they themselves begin to move, that they take up his purposes into their own attitudes and actions. This was what was involved as the people of the Lord came into being. They were freed by God, but they were freed to live, move, and act as *his* people.

The people of Israel left their Egyptian slavery. This is the good news of Israel's liberation. It is a gospel that must be told again and again from generation to generation. But God's action is not just an extraordinary past event. It is also a powerful appeal that still has authority today. To hear the good news of liberation is to hear a call and a command. The news is this: "You have already become free." But the news carries the command: "Live now as free men and women." The liberating message of freedom from slavery in Egypt can be heard only as an urgent injunction: "Now serve the Lord." The news of liberation initiated a movement the power of which can be felt throughout the OT.

Like the OT, the NT unceasingly portrays the acts of God as acts of liberation. The apostles describe God's work in Jesus Christ as liberation from slavery to sin and death. "Everyone who commits sin is a slave," but if "the Son sets you free, you will indeed be free" (John 8:34, 36). "But now, freed from the commands of sin, [you are] bound to the service of God" (Rom. 6:22). "Christ set us free . . . refuse to be tied to the yoke of slavery again" (Gal. 5:1; cf. Jas. 2:12; Eph. 2:19).

God's mighty deed brought Israel into being as his people. The stories describe the birth as follows. The Israelites were anxious and afraid. They "looked up and saw the Egyptians close behind. In their terror they clamoured to the Lord for help" (Exod. 14:10). But with the victory they suddenly began to believe: "When Israel saw the great power which the Lord had put forth against Egypt, all the people feared the Lord, and they put their faith in him and in Moses his servant" (14:31; Ps. 106:12). Confidence in God is a characteristic of this newborn people. God's acts all have the aim that the people should believe in him. The freedom he granted was not complete if it was only an outward liberation. There had to be inner freedom as well. Israel had suffered from fear as well as oppression. They achieved true freedom, and came into being as God's people, as they shed their awe of the Egyptians and put their trust in the Lord.

It is no accident that the birth of faith comes last in the exodus story. Moses worked miracles in Egypt primarily to bring Israel to belief in God, but we read many times that Israel did not believe (cf. Exod. 4:1, 5, 8, 9, 13; 6:9). The new attitude came unexpectedly. God called upon the people to "have no fear . . . stand firm and see the deliverance that the Lord will bring you this day . . . hold your peace" (14:13). Israel had only to believe; God would do everything else. And as the people, helpless to do anything themselves, did in fact see the mighty act of divine liberation, they believed in God, and being freed from fear, they achieved true freedom as the Lord's people.

This truth regarding real freedom found acknowledgment in the 1942 Declaration of Human Rights when it stated that human freedom is finally "freedom from fear."

The mighty deed of God freed Israel from fear of other humans for fear of God. The exodus thus became the foundation of Israel's freedom and would remain so in all the difficulties, troubles, and new forms of oppression that the people would experience. The exodus brought Israel into being as a believing people.

The freedom of the people is the freedom also of each of its members. It prescribes the attitude that they must all show toward one another. In liberating his people God created a community in which all its members would live as free persons, respecting the freedom of others and thus accepting the implications of God's act of liberation. As a people that gave each of its members the right to live as a free person, Israel was truly free and lived as the people of the Lord.

This aspect of God's deed finds expression in Deuteronomy. Certain of its laws are of special interest in this regard. The law of God protects the rights of slaves, cares for resident aliens, and defends the interests of the poor, orphans, and widows. Why? The answer is always the same: "Remember that you were slaves in Egypt and the Lord your God redeemed you; that is why I am giving you this command today" (Deut. 15:15). "You too must love the alien, for you once lived as aliens in Egypt" (10:19; cf. 23:7; 24:18).

The laws in Exod. 22:21-27 and 23:9 are similarly grounded upon God's act of liberation. So are those in Lev. 17–26. The command, "You shall not do as they do in Egypt where you once dwelt" (Lev. 18:3), introduces a whole series of moral laws which closes with the words: "I am the Lord your God who brought you out of Egypt" (19:36b). God's redeeming act inspires not only concern for the poor but a general concern for all others: "You shall love your neighbour as a man like yourself" (19:18; cf. Deut. 10:19: "You too must love the alien").

God's aim was that his people should be a community to serve him. They could not serve him while groaning under oppression. They could do so only as a liberated people. Their willingness to serve the Lord was a sign that they had come into being as his people. So, too, was their readiness to believe in God. So, too, was their readiness for mutual love. Of themselves, of course, the Israelites had no wish to serve the Lord. But God, their mighty Liberator, moved them to do so.

This service of the Lord is *worship*. To serve has a broader meaning than to worship. It means living in God's service. Yet it also includes the liturgical aspect. Indeed, stress is laid upon this aspect, so that the NEB has good reason to translate *'ābad* (literally "serve") as "worship": "The Lord the God of the Hebrews sent me to bid you let his people go in order to worship him" (Exod. 7:16; cf. 4:23; 5:3, 8, 17; 8:1, 20). This is the initial limited request of Moses to Pharaoh (5:1). Refusal of this religious freedom is proof that Pharaoh's was an unjust and cruel government that was unworthy of obedience. The demand for limited freedom thus became a demand for total liberty. When Pharaoh finally had to let the people go to worship, this could mean only that they would go never to return.

Ultimately Pharaoh's attitude was of little account. Newborn Israel would celebrate a feast to the Lord. In fact, the celebration began on the very night of Israel's leaving Egypt. The Israelites were to take a lamb or kid for each household, slaughter it, smear blood on the doorposts, and prepare and serve a hasty sacrificial meal, and to do it all with belts fastened, sandals on their feet, and staff in hand (Exod. 12:3ff.). The point was that in smiting the Egyptians the Lord would "pass over" their doors (12:13, 23, 27, Hebrew *pāsaḥ;* cf. the noun *pesaḥ*, Greek *páscha*). Even while preparing to depart, Israel was already celebrating, worshiping God (cf. 12:25). That they should be a worshiping people was God's purpose in giving them this distinctive life-sign.

As noted already, the whole exodus story might be seen as Passover instruction. The events leading up to Israel's liberation, and especially the events of the first Passover night, are told in such a way as to show how the Passover was first celebrated in Israel. From one angle this celebration seems to be the whole aim of God's intervention.

By his act of liberation God did indeed intend to call into being a people that would serve and worship him. Not by chance is Israel called the "assembled community" (*qᵉhal 'ᵃdat*) for the first time in Exod. 12:6. The story is not told, of course, merely to give us information about the religious customs of the people. It is told as the story of the ongoing people of God at worship. The continuing celebration is indisputable evidence of God's act in Egypt. In that place, at that time, and in those circumstances lies the people's origin. What God did then and there is the only reason why Israel worships him. Attention focuses not on the rite as such but on the act of God that it commemorates.

The scope of this kind of confession can be appreciated only if we compare it with the celebration of the holy days in Israel. The sabbath and the Feasts of Weeks and Tabernacles are next in importance to the Passover (cf. Exod. 24; Deut. 16; Lev. 23). The OT shows some awareness that there were parallels for feasts of this kind in the nomadic and agricultural communities around Israel. But Israel, chosen to be the people of the Lord who is sovereign over natural forces, could not imitate the religious observances of other nations. Israel's celebrations had their real meaning "since the days of Egypt." The sabbath, which might have been simply a rest day in the lunar calendar, was the day on which Israel remembered its liberation from Egyptian bondage (Exod. 12:14-17). Weeks and Tabernacles also acquired a specific basis and content (Deut. 16:9-15; Lev. 23:33-43). Pentecost itself bore special meaning both as regards the lamb, which was slaughtered to protect the firstborn, and the unleavened bread, which was necessary because of the haste: "They had been driven out of Egypt and allowed no time even to get food ready for themselves" (Exod. 12:39). Two elements that were intrinsically unrelated thus came together in the one celebration which became a celebration of praise to God for his mighty act of liberation.

At the heart of the worship for which Israel was freed we find a *remembrance* (Exod. 12:14) of the mighty acts of God on his people's behalf and a *meal* that the family enjoys (12:8ff.) on leaving the house of oppression for "the place of rest" (cf. Deut. 12:9). This act of worship could be celebrated only with joy and thanksgiving. It gives expression to the distinctive life of this people of the Lord that had just come into being.

In the interests of clarity, let us close by stressing three aspects of the liturgical act.

First, the Lord *himself* set his people free. He took up Israel into his own action and motivated the people to do his will. The Israelites put their faith in the Lord. When ready to depart, they slaughtered a lamb for protection. Yet their participation did not liberate the people, nor did the blood of the Passover lamb. God accepted the offerings, but he alone redeemed the people (Heb. 11:28-29).

Second, the Lord liberated his people from *slavery in Egypt*. Where and when he pleases, he is willing to free his people from other slaveries too, e.g., slavery to sin. Through the liberation from Egypt, he showed himself to be the Redeemer from all bondage and the Victor over every worldly power. He rescued Israel from only one type of slavery, but this liberation has meaning for all generations.

Third, the Lord sets his people *truly free*. It might be said that by his act God awakens ideals of freedom and social justice among the Israelites, who in turn make them possible for other nations. Yet God did not tell Israel to "hang her ideals among the stars." He gave true freedom. He gave a limited but concrete freedom which people could feel both body and soul on this 14th Nisan/Abib of the year of the exodus. All our ideals would evaporate had not Israel then been set truly free.

3. God Revealed His Name

God both manifested himself to the fathers by provisional names and also made known his own name to them. (a) It was chiefly in Egypt, however, that he revealed his own name and nature, first through his word proclaimed by his servant Moses the prophet, then through his mighty act of liberation, so that Israel, Pharaoh, and all nations might know, see, and experience it. (b) Even though the origin and meaning of the name YHWH remain obscure, Israel has always viewed it as an expression of his own nature in the light of his revelation through the liberation from Egypt.

WITH THE ACTS that are the objects of Israel's praise and OT witness, God fulfils his plan for humanity. We have looked at God's liberation of his people. Yet the exodus has to be considered from many angles, of which the liberation of Israel is only one. To put this aspect first is not to rank it as the most important. We began with it because it is the aspect that can serve as the key to an understanding of the others.

God's acts always take place between God and human beings who experience them as miracles, as totally unexpected developments. In the case of the exodus God hears the Israelites' cries, sees their suffering as slaves, responds, and comes down to manifest himself. We have already met God's self-revelation in regard to both creation and the fathers, and we shall come across it repeatedly. But as the exodus has an outstanding role in the witness of scripture, so in relation to it revelation has a special meaning that influences the whole OT understanding of God. Here, indeed, lies the primary revelation of God. All other revelations have here their material starting point. In this event God revealed his name.

God revealed his name to Moses and through him to Israel. He commissioned Moses in Midian (Exod. 3:7ff.), initiated his mission in Egypt (6:1-13), and sent him to Pharaoh and the Israelites (3:10ff.). Central at each point is the revelation of the Lord's name to Moses with a command to make it known to his people: "You must tell the Israelites this, that it is Jehovah [Yahweh] the God of their forefathers, . . . who has sent you to them" (3:15). "Go . . . and tell them that Jehovah [Yahweh] the God of their forefathers . . . has appeared to you" (3:16). "God spoke to Moses and said, 'I am the Lord [Yahweh]. I appeared to Abraham, Isaac, and Jacob as God Almighty. But I did not let myself be known to them by my name Jehovah [Yahweh]'" (6:2-3).

There is agreement here that while the name *Yahweh* might have been known earlier, yet before the exodus God was not really known by this name. The former acts and revelations thus find their real meaning in the acts and revelations of the exodus. This event is the decisive revelation that is the key to all revelations both before and after.

Many passages in addition to Exod. 3 and 6 support the conclusion that God's deed in Egypt was the central revelation. Exod. 7:5 tells us that God acts so that "Egypt will know that I am the Lord [Yahweh]" and 9:14 that he does so in order that "you may know that there is none like me in all the earth." The formula "that you/they may know" recurs in 5:2; 7:12; 8:6, 18; 9:14, 29; 10:2; 11:7. Jethro, Moses' father-in-law, concludes: "Now I know that the Lord [Yahweh] is the greatest of all gods, because he has delivered the people from the power of the Egyptians" (18:10-11). As Deut. 4:34-35 puts it: "You have had sure proof that the Lord [Yahweh] is God; there is no other" in heaven above and on earth below (cf. 7:6-7).

The creeds, too, mention the exodus as the time when God revealed himself decisively: "In Egypt . . . thou hast won for thyself a name that lives to his day" (Jer. 32:20; cf. Neh. 9:10; Isa. 63:12). Psalms praise the Lord similarly (cf. 103:7; 77:14-15; 106:8-9). So does Ezekiel: "I bound myself by oath to the race of Jacob and revealed myself to them in Egypt . . . and declared: I am the Lord [Yahweh] your God" (Ezek. 20:5).

The revelation of God's name is a matter for praise. Israel is proud because it alone among the nations has the privilege of knowing the name, and also the responsibility of glorifying it in the world. The OT attaches such importance to this revelation that it can sometimes present it as the beginning and end of all the wonderful deeds that God does for his name's sake, and in order that his name may be known. If Israel is grateful and rejoices that it knows God's name, it is because of the special relation of the revelation of the name to the exodus. To this relation we must now turn.

a. Meeting None Other than God Himself

It is no accident that the revelation of the name of God has a special place in the story of the liberation from Egypt. That story would not be complete, nor would it adequately reflect what it seeks to report, if it told only of the great miracles with which God brought Israel out of Egypt. The story is true to the events only as it accords a place to the revelation of God's name. Only thus does it properly speak of the exodus as the focus of Israel's faith and praise.

It was the God whose name is Yahweh that freed his people. He and no other did this wonderful deed. How do we know this? The story of the revelation of God's name answers this question. God himself revealed his name. He was present himself among his oppressed people.

The texts tell us that God revealed his name so that it might be known or remembered. He did not simply give information about what to call him; he also granted his presence. Moses was asked to tell the elders of Israel "that Jehovah [Yahweh] . . . has appeared to you" (Exod. 3:16). The angel of Yahweh had appeared to him in the burning bush

(3:2). The elders would then tell Pharaoh that "the Lord [Yahweh] the God of the Hebrews met us" (3:18). God himself, the God of the fathers, had appeared to Moses when he called him.

God did not just make known his name. He did not simply grant a measure of illumination concerning himself. As the many OT phrases put it, he himself came, came down, visited, stood in front, appeared, and met those to whom he chose to reveal himself. He might do this in the form of the angel of the Lord (cf. 2 Sam. 24:16). He might be heard but not seen (1 Sam. 3:1-14). No matter how his presence was felt, however, Yahweh met men and women himself. In revealing himself and his name, he met his chosen ones face to face. He did not make his name known by way of the intellect alone but by experience of his presence. This presence was felt as a mystery and wonder, yet it was also concrete. God came, as it were, in the form of "a man" (cf. Josh. 5; Judg. 6; 13).

It was God himself, whose name is Yahweh, who freed his people. He was present among the Israelites, felt their plight, and responded to their cry (Exod. 2:25). His presence was what gave the liberation the character of an event that was worthy to be an object of faith and praise to all generations.

In revealing his name God not only made his presence felt in Egypt in a historical event but also unveiled the mystery of his being, his uniqueness, his otherness. Knowing the name of God we can identify him. Among all the forces "in the heavens above, or on the earth below, or in the waters under the earth" (Exod. 20:4), he alone bears the name Yahweh. The uniqueness of the name is a sign of the uniqueness of God himself. His deity cannot be likened to anything else.

The OT does not hesitate to speak of divine beings below or even beside God. The Song of Moses in Deut. 32 can even say that when God "laid down the boundaries of every people according to the number of the sons of God, . . . the Lord's [Yahweh's] share was his own people" (vv. 8-9). In other words, God gave each "son of God" power over one nation, but made Israel his own heritage. Ps. 82:1 also speaks of God taking his stand "in the court of heaven to deliver judgement among the gods them- selves." Far from occupying a lonely throne, God is seated among the gods (cf. Ps. 58:1 RSV, NEB margin), or the sons of God (Job 1:6 RSV), or the holy ones (Ps. 89:5). These divine beings make up the "host of heaven."

Israel knew of the existence of divine forces and experienced their power. The God of Israel was one of these forces. He was worshiped with titles that might be applied to others as well: God, Lord, King, Most High, Creator, Shepherd. How, then, did Israel also know that Yahweh is "above all gods" (Ps. 135:5), "a great king over all gods" (95:3), the "God of gods" and "Lord of lords" (136:2-3; cf. 86:8; 89:6-8; 95:3; 96:4; 97:7, 9)?

Clearly it was important to know the name of the Lord in order to distinguish between the Lord and the lords, between God and the gods. Of themselves the Israelites could not know who had done the wonderful deeds which liberated them from Egypt. The acts themselves could not tell them who is truly God and King. Just as a warrant becomes valid only when it is signed by the one who issues it, so the events of the exodus were validated as the ground of Israel's existence only when God revealed his name: "I am Yahweh."

Without the revelation of God's name the story of the exodus would be a soulless story. It would be like a sentence without a subject. The liberation of Israel from bondage in Egypt is a historical event like all the others to which the OT bears witness. But the event in itself is not the object of the witness. The object is the event as it was enacted by the God who bears the name Yahweh. This is why Israel recorded the event in concert with the revelation of the name of the God who is worthy to be praised forever and ever.

The account of the revelation of the name of God reaches a climax when God gives a command and commission to those to whom he makes it known. Moses had to go and tell. He could not keep the knowledge to himself. He had to pass it on to Aaron, the elders, all Israel, Pharaoh and his court and subjects, and finally all nations.

God reveals his name to all humanity. He commissioned ordinary people like Moses, Aaron, the elders, and all the Israelites to bear witness to the event that they experienced. His name was to be published, noised abroad, and extolled, so that all the world would know it. This was Israel's task. This was why God set this people apart from every other nation. Israel was to go out to the world proclaiming: "Know that the Lord [Yahweh] is God" (Ps. 100:3).

Inasmuch as God differs from the gods his name must be proclaimed in a specific way. Israel praises the name (Hebrew *hālal*), remembers it (Hebrew *zākar*), and calls upon it (Hebrew *qārā'*). In so doing it confesses that there is no other God besides Yahweh. At the same time Israel diverges from other peoples by avoiding the frequent repetition of the name that would supposedly add prestige to it (cf. the function of *lā ilāha illā allāh* according to mystic Muslim understanding, Allah being the very name of God and not merely an appellation).

From the general standpoint of world history Israel's liberation from Egypt was not an event of great importance. In virtue of the revelation of God's name, however, it was an event of lasting dynamic power. It motivated Israel to confess and praise "the greatest of all gods" (Exod. 18:10-11). It thus brought the people of God into being and gave them their mission in and to the world. For this reason the revelation of the name rightly has a central place in our treatment of this aspect of the biblical witness.

b. A Name Unspeakable yet Meaningful

"I am Yahweh—this is my name," said God to Moses, to the elders, and to all Israel. Why Yahweh? What is the meaning of this name? What is its origin? These questions have often been asked both by Jews and by all who have listened to the OT witness. But even after much serious study we are not in a position to offer much by way of an answer to them. We do not know with any certainty the original form of the name, nor how it should be pronounced, nor where it came from, nor what it originally meant. Lacking scientific certainty, we must be content to survey the problems and the more convincing suggestions.

What do we know about the form of the name? It occurs some 6,800 times in the Hebrew text of the OT. In Hebrew, as in other Semitic languages, only the consonants are written. It is assumed that the vowels are known and need be indicated only where misunderstanding might arise. God's name is thus written *YHWH* and readers are expected to know how to pronounce it. Misunderstandings would not arise so long as the name was in daily use, but after the exile the situation changed with the use of Aramaic and the dwindling numbers of those who could understand or read Hebrew. By the 5th century A.D. the scribes began to add vowels to the Hebrew text, but they gave special treatment to the name *YHWH,* the tetragrammaton (or name with four letters).

The point was that from the days of Ezra and Nehemiah such stress had been laid on the holiness of God's name that it was used only at worship, and even there it slowly disappeared and the pronunciation was forgotten. The scribes did not write it out fully, either because they revered it too much or because the vowels had been forgotten. In time, however, they began to add other vowels so that in reading it would be replaced by other words meaning "the lord" or "the name," the aim being to avoid taking the name of the Lord in vain (Exod. 20:7). We conclude, then, that the original sound of God's name has been lost, disappointing though this may be to many readers of the Bible. In the 15th century Christian scholars began to read the tetragrammaton with the vowels of the Hebrew text, namely, as YeHoWaH, and many Christians still use this form as the name of God (which became "Jehovah" through Latin influence). It can hardly be correct, however, since it is based on an inadequate knowledge of the Hebrew.

Scholarly research has suggested that the proper pronunciation is perhaps YaHWeH. Theodoret, a 5th-century Christian theologian, reports that the Samaritans in his day still used Yabe or Yawe as God's name. Clement in the 3rd century and Epiphanius in the 4th had also noted this. Many biblical proper names consist of a verb, adjective, or noun linked with the divine name. Thus in the case of El we have Eliakim, Eliezer, Elnathan, Nathanel, Elhanan, or Hananel. In the case of YHWH the corresponding names are Hezekiah (Hiskiyahu, or, in shortened form, Hiskiyah), Jeremiah (Yirmeyahu or Yirmeyah), Elijah (Eliyahu or Eliyah), and these give us the form Yahu or Yah, which is very like Yahweh. The explanation of the name in Exod. 3:14 also suggests Yahweh.

[70]

Another possibility, however, is Yao, Yaho, or Yahwo; cf. names like Jehoiakim (Yehoyakim), Jonathan (Yahonatan), or Jehohanan (Yehohanan). Many ancient Christian texts give evidence of the use of pronunciation. In adopting the more commonly accepted form Yahweh we realize that it is at best only a well-founded hypothesis.

What do we know about the origin of the name? Where does it come from? Who used it first? It did not come down from heaven; it was God himself who came down. Revealing himself to Israel, he adopted Israel's language. His name is rooted in this language. It is taken from words and names in the daily speech of the Hebrews. Possibly it was known already to tribes in the area between Egypt and Canaan before God chose to make himself known to Israel under it. The area comprising the desert of Zin, the steppes of Paran and Sinai, and the mountain of Seir was the special dwelling place of YHWH, and Sinai, Horeb, or Paran was his holy mountain (Deut. 33:2 LXX; Judg. 5:4-5; Hab. 3:3, 7). In this regard special note should be taken of Moses' father-in-law Reuel (also called Hobab or Jethro), who was both head of the Kenites and priest of the Midianites (also a Cushite). It was perhaps through him, a priest at the mountain of God, that Moses first heard the divine name. At the same time, God undoubtedly revealed himself directly to Moses. In this revelation he chose to make himself known to Moses and to Israel by this name.

What is the meaning of the name? Innumerable attempts have been made to answer this question. Perhaps too much importance has been attached to the issue, though it is true that a link is seen in the OT between the name of a person and who that person is. Thus Solomon (Hebrew $š^e l\bar{o}m\bar{o}h$) means "king of peace" (Hebrew $š\bar{a}l\hat{o}m$; cf. 1 Kgs. 5:4 [Eng. 4:24]) and Nabal means a churlish man (cf. 1 Sam. 25:25). In the case of YHWH, the account of the call of Moses supplies a clue to the significance of the revealed name of God. If the Israelites ask Moses about the name of God, he is to say: "I AM WHO I AM," or: "I AM has sent me to you" (Exod. 3:14 RSV).

The Hebrew shows us what is the relation between these words and the name YHWH, for the Hebrew word for "I am" (*'ehyeh*) is very similar to the name (*yahwēh*). The similarity suggests that both have a similar meaning and that both are perhaps forms of the verb *hāyāh* (Aramaic and Arabic *hawā*). If *'ehyeh* means "I am," *yahwēh* obviously means "he is." But both forms may also be translated by a future tense: "I shall be" and "he will be."

Even in its ambiguous form as either present or future, the explanation is a pointer to what is probably the true significance. Moses is to tell Israel that it will see the liberation that YHWH will grant. As God is, so he will be. God is "he who is and who was and who is to come" (Rev. 1:4, 8; 4:8). Naturally we do not have here an abstract concept of the divine eternity. The French rendering of YHWH as *l'Eternel* is not, then, a happy one. "I Am" or "I Shall Be" draws attention to what God plans to do and therefore will do among the Egyptians when he comes to his oppressed people. The name of God is a promise of God's presence and help. Whenever Israel calls upon him it can be certain that he will be with it as its God and Redeemer. What the name denotes is the faithfulness of God.

Other parts of the OT do not repeat the explanation. The Book of Hosea may allude to it, however, when the prophet is told to call his second son Lo-ammi ("Not my people") with the divine warning: "For you are not my people, and *I will* not *be* [Hebrew *lō' 'ehyeh*] your God" (1:9). In other words, the promise is temporarily revoked. Israel is no more to enjoy the promise contained in the name YHWH. For the most part, however, Israel has no need of constant repetition of the explanation, since it has the ongoing fact of the divine fulfilment. It knows that YHWH has been its God "since Egypt," and it can thus invoke and praise him without inquiry into the specific meaning of the name as such.

Why did Israel read and pronounce YHWH as "the Lord"? It was perhaps Ezekiel who introduced this way of reading, since he commonly placed "the Lord" next to YHWH by way of explanation (*'adōnāy YHWH*, e.g., 2:4; 3:11). By the time the OT was translated into Greek (ca. 3rd century B.C.) the Jewish community had begun to read "the Lord" either with YHWH or in place of it. The LXX, then, adopted *Kýrios* ("the Lord") for YHWH. Readers of the LXX, whether in Palestine or abroad, whether Jews or Gentiles, were thus taught to know God by the name "the Lord." Only Israelites worshiped God by the name YHWH; all peoples could worship him as "the Lord." In substituting "the Lord" for YHWH the LXX provided an ecumenical name for God, but it also endangered the specific witness of the OT by removing from it the very name of God as God himself revealed it. The danger becomes even more obvious as the holy book of Israel is adopted as the holy book of nations who no longer know God by his original name.

Jewish scholars, while taking great care to prevent anyone from pronouncing the holy name audibly, have also taken great care to prevent the tetragrammaton from disappearing from the holy text. Thus YHWH remains in the Hebrew Bible. For it readers use "the Lord" or "the name." If "the Lord" is added in the original, as in Ezekiel, they use "the Lord God" to avoid the infelicitous "the Lord Lord." Modern translations follow Jewish practice and also use "the Lord" for YHWH. Older renderings have "Jehovah," which, even if inaccurate, at least preserves the proper name. Some new translations use "the LORD" (capital and small capitals) when the original has YHWH. The NEB has "the LORD" for YHWH alone (Gen. 4:1; Exod. 3:16), "the Lord" for *'adōnāy* (Ps. 2:4), "the LORD God" for *YHWH 'elōhîm* (Gen. 2–3), and "the Lord GOD" for *'adōnāy YHWH* (Gen. 15:2, 8; Deut. 3:24).

"LORD" is not the name of the God of Israel. It is a title, one title among others such as King, Father, Shepherd, Redeemer, or Savior. Yet LORD has been singled out for use instead of God's name. This is not because we must suppress the name. It is because we need to explain it so that in every generation Israel and all peoples may come to know the God to whom the OT bears witness as "our God since Egypt."

God revealed his name. He granted to Israel the favor of knowing, invoking, confessing, honoring, and praising this name and believing in him. The form, origin, and meaning of the name do not finally matter. The mysterious tetragrammaton has only the importance of a name. Israel does not praise the name as such, but the name as a pointer to the wonder-working God. The deeds of God, and especially the liberation from Egypt, ensure that his name is the name above all names. On the one hand, apart from the deeds, the name would be just one word among others. On the other hand, without the revelation of the name of him who did the deed, the wonderful events would have remained mute. In revealing his name, God speaks. It is by both word and deed that God calls his people into being, whether in Israel or in any other time or place.

4. God Defeated Egypt

In liberating Israel from slavery God defeated Pharaoh and Egypt because they hardened their hearts. He thus established a sign for Israel and for every nation. (a) Israel praises God because he defeated Rahab (Egypt), the symbol of abused power and of the destruction that it brings. (b) Israel praises God because of his righteous judgments on human pride and hardness of heart. (c) Israel acknowledges its own hardness of heart and thus expects that in time God will extend his mercy to Egypt, too.

THE OT EXALTS THE DEED OF GOD as a victory. God was victorious over Pharaoh, his armies, and his gods (Exod. 12:12). He smote and shattered the nation that had for so long oppressed his people. In virtue of God's victory and Egypt's defeat, Israel was freed from oppression and free to serve its God. By the same victory God came to be known as the Lord, the God who has the power and the purpose to liberate humanity.

If the event of the exodus primarily concerns God and Israel, the Egyptians were also affected in a way that demands our attention. At a first glance Egypt's role was purely negative. What other role is there for a nation that oppressed another, that violated its freedom and rights, that stubbornly resisted the will of God, and that was punished with plagues and defeat in consequence? We might be inclined to ignore such a nation, thinking that God had condemned and discarded it. Yet we have to recognize that the Egyptians played an important part in the exodus story, whether negative or positive. Egypt and its king were forever imprinted on Israel's confession of faith, just as Pontius Pilate is remembered as the representative of Rome in the creed of the NT people of God.

Even outside the exodus, Egypt played an important role. As noted already, many elements in Israel's confession of faith depend directly or indirectly on the exodus. Not surprisingly, then, the name of Egypt recurs throughout the OT. Not the name of the original Canaanites, nor that of neighboring peoples, nor that of other nations that defeated Israel and sent it into exile, but the name Egypt occurs most frequently (about 680 times) in

Israel's scripture. Egypt was the prototype and most important representative of foreign nations *(gōyim),* of those that were not God's people. Why? Did Israel choose it as such? Did Israel pass the nations in review and decide that Egypt best symbolized them? No, Israel simply reflected upon events. Its life as the people of God among foreign nations had begun in Egypt.

We recall Rom. 9–11, in which Paul sets Moses, the representative of Israel, over against Pharaoh, the representative of Egypt. Why did Paul introduce Egypt in that context? In one sense his whole epistle is a discussion of the relation between Israel and the nations. The good news of the freedom offered in Jesus Christ comes as a challenge to both Jews and Greeks. Notwithstanding the differences between them, Paul invites both of them to believe the good news (Rom. 1:16). In this context Pharaoh stands for the nations outside Israel. The choice is not arbitrary. Paul makes it as a student of Israel's scripture.

a. A Victory

God defeated the Egyptians. This statement summarizes all that the OT tells us about the event of Israel's liberation. The Lord forced Pharaoh to let his people go, and when an attempt was made to stop the people he hurled the Egyptians into the sea.

The Lord's victory came in two stages which are recorded in the two main strands of the narrative in Exod. 1ff. First we have the plagues, which culminate in the Passover celebration, the slaying of the firstborn, and the release of the people. Then we have the pursuit, the plight of the people, and the miraculous deliverance from Pharaoh and his armies at the *yam sûp* (Sea of Reeds). Several later OT passages similarly commemorate these two stages of the victory, e.g., Ps. 136:10-15; Neh. 9:9-11; Josh. 24:2-13. The same combination may be found also in Stephen's speech in Acts 7:36 (cf. Heb. 11:28-29).

The story of the plagues tells how Moses, Aaron, and the elders of Israel persistently asked Pharaoh to let their people go. To add force to their plea God through Moses and Aaron brought the pressure of the plagues on the Egyptians: blood, frogs, maggots, flies, boils, hail, hailstorm, locusts, and darkness. In spite of promises that he would accede to Israel's request, Pharaoh constantly went back on his word, hardening his heart and refusing to liberate the people. If, however, the earlier plagues had served only as signs, portents, or warnings, the final plague, the slaying of the firstborn, forced the release of the people. The slaying of the firstborn broke down the resistance of Egypt and opened the way to Israel's freedom. In the light of this final plague we see that God condemns in order to liberate, that he puts to death in order to secure the victory of life, that he defeats the Egyptians in order that his name may be known, first in Israel, then through Israel in Egypt itself and in every nation.

Pharaoh released Israel as a result of the final plague, but then had a change of heart yet again, assembled his troops, and pursued the Israelites as they journeyed out of Egypt, drawing close to them as they were "beside the sea by Pi-hahiroth to the east of Baal-zephon" (Exod. 14:9-10). When the Israelites saw the Egyptians behind them and the sea in front, they were very afraid (v. 10b), but Moses exhorted them to stand firm in faith and to wait for the Lord's deliverance (vv. 13-14). Keeping the Egyptians at a distance (vv. 19-20), God drove back the sea with a strong east wind as Moses raised his staff over it (v. 21). Israel then passed "through the sea on the dry ground," but when the Egyptians followed, the waters returned, they were thrown into a panic, and horse and rider perished in the sea (vv. 23ff.). Having released his people by the final plague, God secured their definitive liberation and sealed his victory over Egypt by thwarting the attempt of Pharaoh to reverse the decision, and by inflicting a crushing defeat on the force that was sent out to intercept the liberated people.

b. The Obstinate Oppressor

God defeated Egypt. The Egyptians are the object of the verb "to defeat." Who were the Egyptians, the people represented by Pharaoh, his court, his ministers, his magicians, and his civil servants? What has the OT to say about them?

Israel's liberation from Egypt was liberation from the "house of slavery." Israel experienced the Egyptians as a people that exploited and oppressed them, that did not respect the rights or need of minorities or weaker groups in society. For the Israelites, Egypt became the very name and symbol of human exploitation.

Egypt misused its power to exploit the poor and to oppress Israel. Other nations—the Amalekites, the Philistines, the Syrians, the Edomites, the Assyrians, the Babylonians, the Persians, and the Romans—would similarly use their power to subjugate and oppress Israel. Israel's history might be described as a three-thousand-year passion. The Israelites suffered perpetually from hate, treachery, persecution, oppression, and destruction. Egypt was the first of the nations to treat them in this way, thereby launching, as it were, the anti-Semitism that remains virulent to this very day. From the days in Egypt Israel has been the Lord's people, and from that same time it has also suffered oppression!

This negative aspect of Egypt, however, is not the only one to emerge

[75]

from Exod. 1–15 or from the OT as a whole. Positive aspects may also be discerned. Only the apocryphal Wisdom of Solomon describes Egypt as altogether a nation of oppressors (10:15). The OT itself makes no such generalization.

Descended from Ham according to Gen. 10, Egypt dealt justly with Abram on his stay there, the fault in the relation being on Abram's side when he failed to present Sarai as his wife (Gen. 12:10-20). Later, Egypt granted asylum to the family of Joseph, who had himself been rewarded by Pharaoh for his talents (cf. Gen. 37; 39–50; Exod. 1). Later still, Solomon had friendly relations with Egypt (1 Kgs. 3:1; 7:8; 9:16), and Egypt gave protection to Jeroboam, Solomon's divinely chosen successor, when the king planned to kill him (11:40). In the NT Jesus and his parents would seek refuge from Herod in Egypt (Matt. 2:14-15).

In Egypt Israel came into contact for the first time with a great world power. It had there its first experience of a mature state with a civil service, army, and laws. Israel itself would never develop a theory of state that would apply to all nations in every time and place. It observed how other nations organized society, secured their wealth, established law and order within their boundaries, and defended these boundaries against foreign incursion. It did not consider any state to be theoretically just or unjust, but looked at each state pragmatically according to its own experience with that state.

When Israel itself later became a state under Saul, it no longer viewed Egypt as an overwhelming power, but regarded it as a neighboring, if stronger, nation. This new relationship brought with it a great danger. Israel was tempted to betray its calling as the Lord's people and to become a state like other states. Allowing itself to be drawn into the field of international politics, Israel disregarded God's plan not only for itself but also for other nations. It was thus inevitably bound for trouble. The mistake came first in the relations with Egypt. The prophets not only condemned Egypt (Isa. 19:1-17; Jer. 43:8-13; Ezek. 29– 32) but also condemned the kings of Israel who sought to secure their power by taking Egypt as an ally (Isa. 30–31).

The condemnation of Egypt itself was not God's last word. Beyond judgment there was hope for Egypt. The prophets proclaimed God's mercy along with his judgment. They were authorized to say what God would do after judgment had fallen. A clear example occurs in Isa. 19:18-25: "The Lord will strike down Egypt, healing as he strikes; then they will turn back to him and he will hear their prayers and heal them" (v. 22). As the message of salvation in Isa. 40ff. complements the prior message of condemnation, so that of 19:18ff. is the necessary complement of 19:1-17.

Nevertheless, Egypt represents the nations that are not God's people. It stands for states that do not acknowledge God's name and that rebel against the King of kings. For such states in such a situation there can be no hope. Pharaoh will obviously oppress Israel, and other nations will do the same.

Their dealings with the Lord's people follow from their attitude to the Lord himself. If Egypt had the chance to carry through its purposes to the end, Israel would be destroyed and all humanity with it. The one hope of the world is that God will frustrate the plan of Egypt and the nations. In fact, God does not let those in power do as they wish. He sets them limits according to his own time. Even nuclear destruction—a truly apocalyptic menace to the world today—cannot cross these limits.

God will not let humanity destroy itself even though that might be the natural consequence of its rebellion against him. He erects dams against the flood. This is why Israel praises him as Creator and Preserver. He will let no tower of Babel rise to heaven. He will let no earthly kingdom attain everlasting dominion (cf. Nebuchadnezzar's vision in Dan. 2). His will to preserve the world is rooted in his creative work and always stands. Creation itself was a victory over the powers of darkness and destruction, which are compared to wild beasts. At the end of time God will again win a victory over the great dragon (Revelation). Egypt, too, can be seen as a dangerous "dragon" (*rāhāb*, Isa. 51:9; Ps. 89:10; cf. 87:4; Isa. 30:7).

In what sense is Egypt a dragon, a personification of the powers of darkness and destruction? Does not this image overemphasize the evil aspect of Egypt and contradict the good side that Israel also experienced? Israel, however, does not measure Egypt by its deeds in this or that situation. Instead, it bears witness to its liberation from the house of slavery. It could attain freedom only because God wonderfully defeated Egypt. For this reason Egypt became the foremost representative of the powers of darkness. At the very moment when Egypt was about to destroy the Lord's people, God stripped it of its power. This defeat of Egypt was God's victory. The dark colors used to depict Egypt must be set against the light colors used to describe God's victory and Israel's liberation. Egypt is wholly dark, not in and of itself, but in contrast to God's work of liberation and preservation.

But what is the evil of Egypt that God exposed, condemned, and defeated? The Egyptians were not guilty of any unusual wickedness. Only in later Jewish literature, not in the OT, are they berated as a conceited, faithless, and inordinately wicked nation. Exodus makes only one charge, and it makes it only against Pharaoh. He is obstinate, obdurate, and unwilling to listen.

In its history Israel met various types of pharaohs: good ones who were open to advice and who worked for justice and the well-being of their people, and bad ones who, conceited and arrogant, aimed only to increase their power even at the expense of the bodies and souls of their subjects (cf. Exod. 1:8; 2:23). The pharaoh of the Exodus was one of the bad pharaohs. He "knew nothing of Joseph." He forgot what Joseph had done for his country. He knew only the interests of the state as he saw them. The Israelites had to serve these interests. He built new towns and dealt harshly with the labor force. Seeking security, he fixed stern rules for resident aliens and immigrants, as we learn from a papyrus dating from 1200 B.C. He not only used the Israelites as a labor force—a common practice relative to aliens—but imposed on them intolerably harsh conditions.

When the request came for liberation from this situation, Pharaoh, viewing the Israelites as his own property, refused point-blank to let them go. In so doing he came into conflict with God's will. He recognized this, but "hardened his heart," "stiffened his neck," unwilling to accede to a demand whose authority he did not acknowledge. Who was this "Lord the God of Israel," who supposedly presented him with this demand? A shepherd-tribe of slaves might worship its own deity, whoever he might be, but that deity had no right to intervene in the internal affairs of the kingdom (Exod. 5:1-2).

In a sense this attitude was understandable. Pharaoh could not be expected to know the Lord. Yet when the Lord acted to make his name known, even if Pharaoh did not understand who this God of the Hebrews was, his refusal to listen brought him into confrontation with the will and command of God as this was made clear to him not only by words ("Let my people go") but also by wonders and plagues as God's servants explained their meaning. Pharaoh now had no excuse; he knew God's will and commandment.

Why did Pharaoh reject God's demand? It was not simply because of ignorance. It was because of hardness of heart. This is the charge that is brought against Pharaoh. His hardness of heart is the cause of the suffering of Israel, and indeed of all Egypt. But it is also an occasion for praise of God, for the hardness of Pharaoh's heart is the cause of the explosion that brings about Israel's freedom.

Pharaoh's hardness of heart meant that he would not abandon his position. He was unwilling to move (Exod. 7:14; 9:7). He was rigid. He was not necessarily hard of heart by nature. We read indeed that he made his heart hard (8:19; 9:12; 10:7). At times the courtiers and magicians showed signs of yielding (8:19; 10:7). Even Pharaoh could promise to let the people go (8:8, 28; 9:28; 10:8, 17, 24; 12:31-32). But he quickly withdrew his promise. He was merely acting out a play with alternating offers and withdrawals.

God also had something to do with Pharaoh's hardness of heart. As he hardened his own heart, so the Lord also hardened it (cf. Exod. 9:12; 10:20, 27; 11:10; 14:4, 8, 17). If the Lord knew that the king of Egypt would not give the people leave (3:19), he also made this Pharaoh obstinate so that he would not let the people go (4:21). God directed events to delay Israel's departure. This does not mean, of course, that God was responsible for the obstinacy of the Egyptians and its unhappy consequences. Pharaoh was responsible, but God freely disposed of his character, disclosing its true nature in such a way as to bring to light its meaninglessness and to bring to pass God's own will.

There is a connection here with the revelation of the Lord's name. God defeated Egypt and liberated his people in order to reveal his name, so that they all acknowledge that he is Yahweh. This was his aim in all that he did in Egypt. He did not make Pharaoh worse than he was. He simply set him in a situation in which he could give free rein to his obstinacy. In this way he made his own name better and more clearly known (9:15-16). He did so by means of "sign after sign and portent after portent in the land of Egypt" (7:3). The relation between Pharaoh's obstinacy and the portents comes out plainly in 11:9: "Pharaoh will not listen to you; I will therefore show still more portents in the land of Egypt." The longer the obstinacy, the more numerous and powerful the signs, and the greater the praise of Israel and the renown of God's name throughout the world.

Six times in Exod. 7–9 the plagues are set in relation to Pharaoh's refusal to listen to Moses and Aaron (7:13, 22; 8:15, 19; 9:12, 35). The obduracy can even be an occasion for ridicule. God makes sport of the Egyptians (10:2). They think that they are masters of the situation, but it is the Lord's will that is really shaping events. God had stated from the very start what would happen, and the longer Pharaoh kept Israel back, the more vividly would the truth of this declaration be displayed. The more clearly, too, would God's glory shine! "I will make Pharaoh obstinate, and he will pursue them, so that I may win glory for myself at the expense of Pharaoh and all his army; and the Egyptians shall know that I am the Lord" (14:4; cf. vv. 17-18). God uses Egyptian obstinacy to manifest his strength, to prove the validity of his word, and to manifest his glory.

Paul made the same point in Rom. 9. The fact that God made Pharaoh stubborn did not mean that he could excuse himself (9:18-21). God did not treat Egypt unfairly any more than he granted special favors to Israel. He dealt with both justly, using both to fulfil his purpose: Israel as an instrument of mercy, Egypt as an instrument of wrath (9:22-23). The dealings were complementary. God did not exclude the instrument of wrath from mercy nor that of mercy from wrath. He set both mercy and wrath before us and made the two parties models of the destruction that applies to all and the grace that applies to all. Paul closed by quoting from Hosea and Isaiah to show that as the vessel of wrath is not without hope, so that of mercy has no reason for pride (9:24-29).

c. Israel's Obstinacy

Were the Israelites themselves any less obstinate than the Egyptians? If not, why were the Egyptians finally defeated and destroyed whereas the Israelites were made to listen and believe and were thus finally rescued from the danger that threatened them?

If it is often said that Pharaoh "will not listen" to the Lord's command that has "come to his ear" (CB Exod. 7:4, 13, 16, 22; 8:15, 19; 9:12; 11:9), the same can be said of the Israelites; they seem to be just as deaf (4:1, 8, 9; 6:9, 12; cf. 16:20). Again, if Pharaoh is said to be hard of heart, and to have hardened his heart still further, obduracy seems to be the characteristic condition of the Israelites (32:9; 33:3, 5; Deut. 9:6; 10:16; 2 Kgs. 17:14; Jer. 7:26; Ps. 95:8; Neh. 9:16, 20).

Obviously the Egyptians were not alone in their fault. Both the Egyptians and the Israelites were stubborn, obdurate, blind to God's miracles, and deaf to his commands, whether in conceit or in despair (Exod. 6:9). What we have here is the human condition in its alienation from God.

If Israel can praise God, then, it is not solely because he brought judgment on the obstinate Egyptians but because in grace he brought deliverance to equally obstinate Israel. The judgment of Egypt is the negative deed that stands alongside the positive deed of the saving of Israel. This twofold nature of God's dealings with us is the kernel of Israel's confession of faith. As God's firstborn son, Israel is granted life and salvation while the firstborn of Egypt are slain (Exod. 4:22). God's people rejoice, not merely because their enemies are conquered, but even more so because they have themselves been granted life. Israel was not redeemed, of course, through the death of the Egyptians. But the Egyptians were involved in the redemption of Israel. In this sense even the vessel of wrath can be a vessel of grace in God's plan of salvation.

5. God Sent Moses and Aaron

When God brought Israel out of Egypt, he called, sent, and empowered leaders for his people. The Lord himself brought his people out, but he gave individuals a share in his work as the people's Leader and Liberator: first the elders of Israel; then Moses with the task of making God known, working miracles, leading the people to freedom, representing God, and establishing true worship; and finally Aaron and Miriam as Moses' assistants.

A FURTHER ASPECT of the OT witness to God's liberation of his people is that God raised up human leaders for the people. Moses played the main role, but Aaron and Miriam shared the leadership with him along with Israel's elders. In telling the story of the exodus we have to give these leaders their due place. As Pharaoh and his ministers represented Egypt, so Moses, Aaron, and the elders represented Israel. Moses and Aaron also represented God inasmuch as they acted as his servants and instruments in carrying out his purpose. In a sense Moses represented Egypt, too, as the adopted son of an Egyptian princess who gave him an Egyptian name and education (Exod. 2:10). Not without his own obduracy (Exod. 3–5), Moses stood over against Pharaoh. The two played complementary roles as instruments in God's hands.

Moses and Aaron stood in relation to Israel, to God, and to Egypt. In a special way Moses was linked to all three, opposing God's will like Pharaoh, clamoring for help with Israel, and acting with the power and authority of God. Particular attention must be paid, therefore, to the part that he played.

Who were Israel's leaders? Moses and Aaron were obviously the most prominent. We see this from the later summaries. "I sent Moses and Aaron, and I struck the Egyptians with plagues" (Josh. 24:5). "He sent his servant Moses and Aaron whom he had chosen. They were his mouthpiece to announce his signs, his portents in the land of Ham" (Ps. 105:26-27). "He sent Moses and Aaron, who brought them out of Egypt" (1 Sam. 12:8). In Exod. 15:20, however, we learn that Miriam, too, was a prophetess alongside Moses, and Mic. 6:4 can mention her as also a leader of Israel: "I sent Moses and Aaron and Miriam to lead you." Finally, the elders of Israel had a part. Most of their names have been forgotten, but Nadab and Abihu are mentioned in Exod. 24:1, 9, and Hur in 17:8-16.

Moses, Aaron, Miriam, and the elders all played leading roles. Why is it, then, that they are seldom mentioned all together? The material reason is that the Lord himself was the supreme Leader and Liberator. Only in this light can we understand what is said about the role of those whom he sent to be human leaders.

Thus the basic form of Israel's creed is that "the Lord brought us out of Egypt with a strong hand and outstretched arm" (Deut. 26:8). "Thou didst bring thy people Israel out of Egypt," says Jeremiah in 32:21. "I brought them out of Egypt," says God himself in Ezek. 20:10 (cf. Neh. 9:9-11; Acts 13:17). If Exod. 1–15 as a whole might leave the impression that the exodus was the work of Moses and Aaron, in 3:8 we read that God has come down to rescue the people, in 3:17 that God has resolved to bring them up out of their misery in Egypt, and in 7:25 that the Lord himself struck Egypt with plagues.

The Lord himself did it all. He did not need ambassadors, or spokesmen, or executors of his will, or servants to assist him. All he needed was his arm, his hand, or even his finger (Exod. 8:19). The liberation of Israel was not the result of divine-human cooperation. It was God's own work. No matter how important might be the role and contribution of Moses and others, they were no more than instruments in God's hands. He used them but did not depend on them. The kernel of the story ignores the role of Israel's leaders.

With this in view, we look first at the part that was actually played by Israel's elders. They appear initially in Exod. 3:16, 18, where Moses is asked to assemble and address them, and told that "they will listen to you." Moses and Aaron did this, and performed the signs before the people. How did the elders react? With the people, they obviously believed and "bowed themselves to the ground in worship" (4:31), having listened to God's word through Aaron and witnessed what he did (v. 30).

The elders as well as Moses had to go to Pharaoh (3:18). They did this in 5:15: "The chief men came and appealed to Pharaoh" (CB). If Moses sometimes conducted discussions with Pharaoh alone (8:1, 20; 9:1, 13; 10:1; 11:8), or in company only with Aaron (8:12; 9:10; 10:3, 16), on this occasion the chief men met Pharaoh as Israel's representatives, and Moses and Aaron waited for them (5:20). Negotiations at this point were primarily in the hands of the elders, since there is every reason to suppose that the chief men, those whom Pharaoh's overseers recognized to be responsible, were in fact the elders. The people itself was acting here through its legal representatives. If the initiative then passed to Moses and Aaron, the elders still had their own part to play in the decisive event.

The elders were never given the title of prophets. Nevertheless, they had at this point a prophetic role inasmuch as God both sent them (Exod. 3:18) and called upon them to suffer for his name's sake (5:14). In a sense even the more prominent Moses and Aaron still stood on the same level as the elders and worked together with them. One might almost say that the sending of Moses and Aaron sums up that of the elders. Only on the basis of this "lay" sending can we understand what is meant later by God's sending of the prophets.

At the same time Moses was clearly the one whom God sent supremely to lead Israel. No other was his equal. Yet in inquiring into his role we must not forget what was just said about the Lord as Israel's only Leader and Liberator, and also about the elders and their contribution to Israel's liberation.

Our present question does not concern Moses' role in the OT as a whole but only his role in the event of the exodus. It would obviously be artificial to distinguish between Moses in Egypt and Moses at Sinai or in the desert. Everywhere we find him in the role of leader. Yet his role was not the same in Egypt, at Sinai, and in the desert. In Egypt he was not the giver of God's laws, nor the one who suffered under the burden of a prophetic vocation, nor the mirror of God's presence with his shining face (Exod. 34:30). In the exodus story he was the instrument that God used specifically to liberate his people.

Moses was sent by God. God told him in Exod. 3:10ff.: "Come now; I will send you to Pharaoh and you shall bring my people out of Egypt. . . . I am with you." At first Moses was shocked: "No, Lord, send whom thou wilt" (4:13). When he failed to secure Pharaoh's assent, he complained: "Why, O Lord, . . . didst thou ever send me?" (5:22). But again God sent him to Pharaoh (6:10-11) with the repeated demand that Pharaoh let God's people go.

What does the verb *šālaḥ*, "to send," mean in this context? It often occurs when someone is raised to the status of a prophet, with God as subject and the person involved as object (e.g., Isa. 6:8; Jer. 1:7). Moses, then, was sent as the Lord's prophet. He was sent to speak the word of the Lord that he had heard (3:15; 4:28; 6:5, 10). As the typical prophet, he had to struggle with the refusal of those to whom he was sent (the Israelites in 6:9, Pharaoh in 5:2; 7:14; etc.). He made intercession for those whom God punished (8:30; 9:25ff.). He also worked signs (4:1-9).

Yet Moses was clearly not just one prophet among others. He was a prophet in a unique way. His calling went far beyond that of other prophets. Although the Lord himself freed Israel from Egypt, Moses, as the Lord's ambassador, also "brought the people out of Egypt" (3:12). Born into a laborer's family and narrowly escaping death, he had been adopted and elevated by a royal princess, and had a garment of nobility that was unusual in a prophet. Was Moses similar, then, to the just kings of other nations (e.g., Sargon, king of Akkad, ca. 2600 B.C.) who dispossessed tyrannical and cruel rulers? He certainly defeated a despotic pharaoh and saved his people. He had a liberating and redeeming role. God granted him a share in his own glory as Savior by giving him a part in the working of the divine signs and wonders. He thus placed him much higher than all other prophets. At the same time, the OT also insists on the humility of Moses, on the fact that he did not have of himself the qualifications for his special role.

Moses was called and sent in both Midian (Exod. 3:1–4:17) and Egypt (6:1-6), but he was only too conscious of being ill-equipped for his prophetic task. He said: "I have never been a man of ready speech; . . . I am slow and hesitant of speech" (4:10). He was a "halting speaker" (6:30). Was he just making excuses when he made these admissions? Was it false modesty? Was it lack of faith? God at any rate accepted his objections. Moses was not qualified. He had to have someone else as his "mouthpiece" (4:16, literally "mouth") or "spokesman" (7:1, literally "prophet"). If on the one hand he was highly exalted as God's representative, on the other hand he was so humbled as to seem almost useless.

God chose Moses as his instrument, yet he did not depend on him. On three occasions, indeed, Moses might well have been killed (2:1-10, 11-12; 4:24-26). If he had been, God would still have liberated Israel. As it was, God decided to act through Moses, and for this reason, ill-qualified though he was, and knew himself to be, for his exalted role, Moses acted as Israel's preeminent leader under God in the formative event of the exodus.

The second of Israel's individual leaders was Aaron. He, too, was sent "to bring the people of Israel out of Egypt" (Exod. 4:14ff., 27ff.). What, then, was his specific role in the event?

Aaron (Hebrew *'ah^arôn*) might well have been one of Israel's elders like Nadab and Abihu (cf. Exod. 17:1-13; 18:12; 24:1, 9, 14). Yet he also acted as a prophet and spokesman second only to Moses, whom he complemented (4:14, 30; 7:1-2). He was also Moses' helpmate in the working of signs (7:9-10, 19-20; 8:3-6, 16-17). With Moses he gave instructions for the Passover celebration (12:1ff.). Finally, Pharaoh summoned him along with Moses to tell them to lead the people out of Egypt, and although Moses plainly had the major role in chs. 13–14, we read in 12:50 that the people did as Moses and Aaron commanded them.

Like Moses (2:1), Aaron was a Levite (4:14). This meant literally that he was of the tribe of Levi. But the word took on special significance in Aaron's case because he would be the forefather of Israel's priests (cf. Ezra 7:1-5). Aaron was Moses' elder brother (Exod. 6:20) and Miriam was their sister (15:20). He was not yet a priest at the time of the exodus; his appointment and anointing as such still lay ahead. In a sense, indeed, there was a certain ambivalence about his role at this juncture. As a prophet, he was secondary to Moses. As future head of the priesthood, he was not yet a priest. He was a leader, but he had little opportunity to show his leadership.

God chose and sent Aaron alongside Moses to liberate his people from the house of slavery. He accepted these two as his instruments. He made both of them witnesses of his work and representatives of the whole people in this function. In sending them he made it clear that the function of a witness is a supreme favor and a lasting reason to give God the praise.

We turn finally to the third of Israel's leaders, Miriam. The OT tells us little about this prophetess. We are not even told about her commissioning. What we do read is that Miriam, the sister of Moses and Aaron, was an accomplished singer who sang the Lord's praises. Her short and joyful song is an early witness to the Reed Sea triumph and to the whole event of the exodus. She "took a tambourine in her hand," and all the women followed her "dancing to the sound of tambourines" (Exod. 15:20). She then struck up a song ("sang them this refrain," NEB), and the women and perhaps all Israel took up the chorus: "Sing to the Lord, for he has risen up in triumph; the horse and his rider he has hurled into the sea!"

Chapter IV

God Led His People through the Wilderness

1. The Witness of Scripture

God led Israel on the way from Egypt, the house of slavery, through the desert to Canaan, the promised land. He took care of a grumbling and unbelieving people and granted it signs of his presence when it faced danger and destruction. For these deeds Israel praised God when it settled in Canaan. In the biblical account this topic links the liberation from Egypt to the gift of Canaan and thus reminds Israel that by its very nature it is a people of the way.

"THE GOD OF THIS PEOPLE of Israel . . . bore them for some forty years in the desert" (CB). So said Paul in his sermon at Pisidian Antioch (Acts 13:17ff.). He was referring to the wilderness wandering which is dealt with extensively in Exodus, Leviticus, Numbers, and Deuteronomy. Numbers begins in Hebrew with the words *b*e*midbar* ("in the wilderness") and is thus known traditionally by Jews as "The Book of the Wilderness." The main elements of the desert story are in Exod. 15:22–18:27; Num. 9:15–17:13; 20:1–26:65. Foreshadowing the story are the fathers' Negev wanderings. Prophets like Amos, Hosea, Jeremiah, and Ezekiel refer back to the wilderness period (cf. Amos 2:10; Hos. 9:10; Jer. 2:4, 6; Ezek. 20). Many psalms (cf. 78, 81, 95, 105, 106) also recall it, and some NT texts allude to it as well (cf. Matt. 3:1; 4:1; Mark 1:12-13).

Why does this topic of Israel in the wilderness occupy so important a place in the OT witness? It is hardly enough to say merely that this people once lived nomadically in the desert. That can hardly tell us why the experience was worth remembering after many centuries of more sedentary life. The real reason is that those who had the experience obviously viewed it as crucial. Israel did not choose the topic as a central tenet of its faith. It received it as such from the wilderness generation.

What did the people actually experience in the wilderness? The shortest and most pregnant answer lies in the creedal summaries. All of them mention the experience except Deut. 6 and 26, Jer. 32, 1 Sam. 12, and Ps. 135, where there are special reasons for the omission.

God led his people through the wilderness. "It was I who . . . led you in the wilderness forty years, to take possession of the land of the Amorites" (Amos 2:10). "Where is the Lord, who . . . led us through the wilderness, through a country of deserts and shifting sands, a country barren and ill-omened, where no man ever trod, no man made his home?" (Jer. 2:6). "He led his people through the wilderness" (Ps. 136:16). "Forty years long thou didst sustain them in the wilderness" (Neh. 9:21; cf. Acts 13:18).

From the textual evidence we draw three conclusions. First, Israel saw God's own deeds in its wilderness experience. The confessions and the narratives all refer to miracles. The Lord accompanied and preserved his people by wonderful acts when it faced danger and destruction.

Second, God's deeds in the wilderness invite Israel to give thanks to the Lord (Pss. 78, 105, 106, 136) and to confess its faith in him. The acts of God in the desert became an article of Israel's faith.

Third, God's deeds in the wilderness are among the basic events that brought Israel into being. We need not be surprised, then, that texts like Deut. 32:10 or Jer. 3:2 can present them as the true beginning of Israel.

The topic of the wilderness is closely connected with that of the exodus on the one hand and that of the gift of the land on the other. It deals with events that took place between the two. Israel was no more in Egypt. It had *already* left the house of slavery, the "smelting-furnace" (Deut. 4:20; 1 Kgs. 8:51). But it had *not yet* reached Canaan, the "place of rest," the promised patrimony (Deut. 12:9). Though dependent on the two main topics, the wilderness topic has its own distinctive character. During this time of transition events took place that determined Israel's way throughout its history.

Familiar to all readers of the OT are the Lord's wonderful presence, Israel's stubbornness and lack of faith, the Lord's own faithfulness, and the acts of mercy and judgment by which he brought it to the promised land. Our present task is simply to bring to light the main aspects of the topic (apart from the Sinai revelation) as it is recorded in the biblical texts.

2. God Chose a Stubborn People

Facing scarcity of water and food, exposed to many dangers, Israel
soon began to complain, accused its leaders and even God himself,

rebelled against the Lord, did not believe in him, and even tempted him. While confessing its own lack of trust, however, Israel praised God for faithfully sustaining the people. Israel could also remember the wilderness period as a happy time of youth when it responded to the love of God and cherished him.

ISRAEL SPENT MANY YEARS in the desert. It no longer lived beyond the Euphrates like its first father (Josh. 24:2-3), nor did it struggle under the yoke of the Egyptians, but it had not yet settled in the land that God had promised to the fathers. It wandered in the wilderness. We perhaps have difficulty today in imagining what the desert meant to people in the past. It was a place not fit to be called a "land." It did not provide the bare necessities of life. The very fact that Israel "lived for a long time in the wilderness" (Josh. 24:5) was thus a wonder in itself.

Israel and other nations of the Middle East had bad memories of the desert. When the sun shone on the sand the heat became intolerable. At night the temperature fell quickly and it was very cold. People could not long survive under these extreme conditions. They were bound to perish. "Some lost their way in desert wastes . . . hungry and thirsty, their spirit sank within them" (Ps. 107:4-5). The desert was accursed. Evil spirits reigned there and destroyed all living creatures. It was the exact opposite of habitable, fertile country.

Many of the stories from the time of the desert wandering tell how Israel was wonderfully saved from the clutches of destruction. We grasp the true meaning of these stories only if we see them in the light of the witness to Israel's salvation through God's faithfulness to his covenant people.

The wilderness stories bear witness to the fact that God chose Israel and cared for it as his own people. Against the wilderness background Israel's election is seen in a new light. Whom did God choose as his people? Not merely a group of foreign laborers who were suffering under the Egyptian rod and for whom election meant liberation, but also a nomadic people who wandered in the desert and for whom election meant preservation. From this standpoint we must examine three aspects of election: God chose his people in the desert; he thereby made them willing to live as his people; and yet they proved to be a stubborn people.

a. Election in the Desert

God chose Israel as his people. He chose it in the days of the fathers. He chose it when he freed his people from Egypt, met it at Sinai, and gave it Canaan as its patrimony. He also chose it in the desert. He did not choose Israel only once. He chose it time after time in an ongoing series of acts in history.

"I have been the Lord your God since your days in Egypt, when you knew no other saviour. . . . I cared for you in the wilderness, in a land of burning heat, as if you were in pasture. So they were filled, and, being filled, . . . forgot me" (Hos. 13:4-6). In this passage the word "cared" might also be translated "knew" (so RSV), but the Hebrew (*yāda'*) is often used also in the sense of "choose," especially in older texts like Amos 3:2: "For you alone have I chosen among all the nations of the world; therefore I will punish you for all your iniquities" (CB).

Texts which plainly speak of Israel's birth in the wilderness include Hos. 2:2-3: "Plead my cause with your mother . . . to forswear those wanton looks, to banish the lovers from her bosom. Or I will strip her and expose her naked as the day she was born; I will make her bare as the wilderness, parched as the desert, and leave her to die of thirst." We might also refer to the Song of Moses in Deut. 32:9-12: "The Lord's share was his own people. . . . He found him in a desert land, in a waste and howling void. He protected and trained him, he guarded him as the apple of his eye. . . . The Lord alone led him." Another passage is Jer. 2:2-3: "I remember the unfailing devotion of your youth, the love of your bridal days, when you followed me in the wilderness. . . . Israel was then holy to the Lord . . . no one who devoured her went unpunished." In Jer. 31:2-3, too, we read that "a people . . . found favour in the wilderness," and God gives the promise: "I have dearly loved you from of old, and still maintain my unfailing care for you."

The number of texts is impressive. There is strong testimony to Israel's origin in the wilderness. Yet the witness is not equally distributed among the different books. Although represented in certain prophetic books and the Song of Moses, it does not actually feature in the wilderness stories themselves. The parable of God's adoption of the desert foundling in Ezek. 16:4ff. undoubtedly reflects Israel's wilderness election, but the narratives of Exodus and Numbers do not specifically refer to an election of Israel in the desert. Their focus is on the preceding history. Israel was already God's people when it came into the desert. God had chosen it in Egypt. Now in the desert, as the people of his choice, it was the object of his care and preservation.

b. Initial Obedience

God chose Israel. In so doing he moved the hearts of the Israelites and made them willing to respond and to live up to their vocation. They could not pride themselves on this. They could only praise the God who gave them a readiness to believe his promises, to unite as the one people of God, and to acknowledge his name as he had revealed it to them. Part of the OT witness to the deeds of

God is the description of the way in which God takes the people that he chooses and equips and moves it to fulfil its vocation.

We saw this already when studying the exodus. God took measures then to free Israel objectively. But he did not wait to see if the people would understand their new status and realize their freedom subjectively. The human reaction to God's liberation also came within the scope of his act and gift. This was true in relation to creation and the calling of the fathers insofar as these, too, carry a reference to the birth or origin of the people of God both objectively and subjectively.

Plainly the wilderness narratives largely ignore the fact that God had awakened Israel to be his faithful and willing people. They stress instead the complaining and grumbling of the people, their stubbornness and rebellion, their inability to show either patience or faith. Yet the weight of the negative tales cannot crush the positive side. If the emphasis is on the fall of "the virgin Israel" (Amos 5:2), the story of Israel's fall presupposes that it was first made to stand. Israel stood before it fell. This is a less prominent but no less significant aspect of the work of God for Israel.

In the case of Jer. 2, it is interesting that stress is laid on the love and trust and devotion of Israel in the wilderness days. Usually it may be the people's grumbling and unbelief that catch our attention (cf. Ps. 81:13: "If my people would but listen to me, if Israel would only conform to my ways!"). From one angle, however, the days of want in the desert were sunlit days. It was not that Israel first trusted and then rebelled. Even as the people kicked against Moses and the Lord, they still had a basic belief in God which enabled them to persevere in spite of the hardships and the disappointments.

The point is that God had not only met and chosen Israel. He had not only adopted this foundling as his legal child. In choosing it, he also lifted it out of its hopeless state and enabled it to become a faithful servant, an obedient child, a loving wife, a responsive army, a loyal people. In making it his people by adoption, God gave it the capacity to be what it now was.

Several texts call for notice in this regard. The prophets appealed to Israel in the desert to show what kind of child, wife, servant, ox, vine, or fruit tree God chose. Israel was like a bride showing true love to her husband (Jer. 2:2), like a dear friend from the days of youth (3:4), like a heifer that is broken in (Hos. 10:11), like grapes or ripe figs that are precious in the wilderness (9:10), like a rapidly growing and fruitful vine (10:1), like a lovingly brought-up boy (11:1ff.), like the firstfruits of the harvest, holy to the Lord (Jer. 2:3), like a bride adorned with robes and jewels (Ezek. 16:8ff.), like a possession so valuable that it must be guarded like the apple of the eye (Deut. 32:10). It was a people ready to follow God in the wilderness (Jer. 2:2).

If Israel is not presented here as a pack of rebels, but highly esteemed as the Lord's people, it is not, of course, by reason of any merits of its own. Israel neither did remarkable deeds nor displayed an attitude worthy of special credit. Praise could be given only to the Lord who met and chose and adopted Israel as his own people. God did not elect it to be a gang of rebels. He did not make it free in the sense of being free to decide whether to be his people or not. This idea of freedom runs contrary to the whole biblical understanding of freedom. God took up Israel in order that it might live and move and stand firm as his people. If it trusted and obeyed and followed him, if it did "what is right and just" (Gen. 18:19), if it practiced "loyalty and justice" (Hos. 12:6) relative to both God and neighbor, it did not merit a reward but simply lived up to the standard for which God had created it. God had set his people on the way to follow him. When it left this way, it did not merely offend against God; it denied its own nature. By emphasizing that Israel followed God's way in the wilderness, the prophets had the sole aim of calling the people back to its true nature and inviting it to praise God by living up to that nature.

c. Complaining and Revolting

God chose and adopted his people. He made it willing to fulfil its vocation in this new period of its history even as it wandered through the wilderness. Having looked first at the positive aspect in the prophets, since this is frequently ignored, we must now examine the more negative wilderness stories as we have them in Exodus and Numbers. We properly understand these stories, however, only against the background of the positive prophetic witness.

What, then, did the Israelites do for the most part in the desert? The answer of the desert stories, especially in Exod. 15–17 and Num. 14–17, is that they *complained.* From the day that they came into the desert until the day they left it for Canaan, they did little else but complain. Many of the stories have complaint as their focus, e.g., Israel at Marah (Exod. 15:22ff.), the gift of manna (16:1ff.), Israel at Massah and Meribah (17:1ff.), the episode of the scouts (Num. 13–14), the rebellion of the sons of Korah (ch. 16), the revolt of Dathan and Abiram (ch. 16), and Aaron's blooming staff (17:1ff.). The word "to complain" (Hebrew *lûn*) occurs no fewer than 20 times in Exodus (15:24; 16:2, 7, 8, 9, 12; 17:3) and Numbers (14:2, 14, 27, 29, 36; 16:11; 17:6, 20, 25). It belongs so fully to the desert stories that there is only one other OT occurrence (Josh. 9:18). The complaints express dissatisfaction, impatience, and ignorance: "What are we to drink?" (Exod. 15:25); "Why have you brought us out of Egypt . . . to let us all die of thirst?" (17:3); "If only we had died at the Lord's hand" (16:3). Complaint is totally different from groaning and crying for help. When people cry out in pain and appeal for relief, God hears them (Exod. 2:22-23; Ps. 5:2-3; etc.). In complaint, however, people do not simply cry out in pain. They accuse someone of treating them unjustly, and they ask for what they consider to be their right.

The Israelites complained. They were angry. They accused those whom they deemed responsible for their sufferings. They complained against Moses (Exod. 15:24; 17:3), against Moses and Aaron (16:2; Num. 14:2), and even against God (Exod. 16:7-8; Num. 14:2). Directly or indirectly Israel claimed its due from God. The Israelites found fault with him. They rebelled openly against him. They disputed with Moses and God and challenged them (Exod. 17:2; Num. 20:13). They were apparently calling God to account. In Num. 20:10 we read specifically that they were called "rebels" against God. The related verb (Hebrew *mārāh*) occurs in Deut. 1:26, 43; 9:7, 23-24; 31:27; Ps. 78:17, 40, 56; 106:7, 33, 43. The Israelites are called (literally) "children of rebellion" (Num. 17:25 [Eng. 10], NEB, RSV "rebels"). Israel is a "race of rebels" (Isa. 30:9) or the "house of rebellion" (e.g., Ezek. 2:5 RSV; NEB "rebels").

We read also that the Israelites "tried" God or "provoked" him. They "grieved" him in the desert. They "tried God's patience and provoked the Holy One of Israel" (Ps. 78:40-41). God himself may test his servants (Gen. 22:1; Exod. 15:25), but it is a totally different matter for Israel to test God (Exod. 17:2; Num. 14:22; Deut. 6:16; Ps. 95:9; cf. Matt. 4:7; 1 Cor. 10:9; Heb. 3:9).

Israel's accusing of God was in fact a self-accusation. It had just been liberated from Egypt. It had been elected, adopted, and set on its way as the people of God. But it was obviously unable and unwilling to live up to its new position. It stood in contradiction to its own true being. Even as God's people it was a house of rebellion. This was not a temporary contradiction. Nor was it a contradiction limited to certain groups or certain spheres of life. Israel rebelled from the very first and in its whole existence. No single individual was exempt.

Even Israel's leaders were guilty of rebellion. Aaron and Miriam revolted against Moses; "they blamed him for his Cushite wife" (Num. 12:1-15). Moses had in fact married one of the daughters of a priest of Midian (Exod. 2:15-22), a woman not of Cush but of the tribe of Cushan, which was akin to Midian (cf. Hab. 3:7). Aaron and Miriam apparently disapproved of the marriage and made it an occasion for attacks on Moses. But in opposing Moses they opposed the Lord himself, who trusted Moses (Num. 12:6-8).

Even Moses himself was not consistently faithful. A fault is recorded in Num. 20:1-13, where we read that "the Lord said to Moses and Aaron, 'You did not trust me so far as to uphold my holiness in the sight of the Israelites.'" What the specific fault was we are not told, but the story shows plainly that Moses, too, belonged to the house of rebellion.

It is astonishing that Israel frankly bears witness to the utter failure of the fathers to live up to their glorious calling as God's people. In bearing this witness it confesses its own sins and accuses itself of evil. To blame others is easy. To agree that we all have a part in original sin is also easy. Not so easy is to admit to one's own failure. The OT writers do not follow the example of other nations and make the story of the fathers into one of blameless heroes. If they paint the cruelty and obstinacy of Egypt in dark colors, they also tell the desert stories of Israel's rebellion against God. They accuse Israel of being no less bad and even worse than other nations.

Confessing their sins, the Israelites did something that we all find hard to do. They acknowledged that they were totally unable to fulfil their calling. Were they taking too pessimistic a view? Were they perhaps soiling their own nest? No, for we must never forget that confession of sin is closely linked to confession of faith. The two confessions glorify God and extol his deeds in a single witness. God chose a stubborn people. The covenant rested on the love of God, not on the fidelity of his people. The Israelites did not look primarily at themselves and their alternating arrogance and despair. They looked at him who alone is worthy of praise.

3. God Carried His People in the Wilderness

Although Israel rebelled again and again, God kept the covenant that he had made with them. (a) He showed signs of love in wonderfully helping and protecting them. (b) He also showed signs of wrath in punishing them and withdrawing his helping hand. Yet if the wilderness generation, including Moses, was not allowed to enter the promised land, God did not give up his covenant. On the contrary, he confirmed it by this judgment.

AS WE HAVE SEEN, God moved his people to follow him of their own volition and with full trust, yet also as a stubborn people who denied their calling. We now turn to the OT witness to the way in which God acted toward his people in the wilderness with deeds of both love and judgment. The stories and hymns that deal with the desert wanderings pay much attention to this aspect. God protected the people. He gave them food and drink in the wilderness. He rescued them from danger. He also inflicted judgments to arouse their conscience.

The deeds reveal the meaning of Israel's preservation. They show concretely and colorfully what God's purpose was when he said: "I chose you in the wilderness." They were visible and tangible experiences of the Word, just as the Word told what was happening through the signs. The signs and the Word were two aspects of the one action of God.

God chose his people. He set them free. Liberated from Egypt, they wandered in the desert. In the desert election meant preservation. God protected his people. He guarded them "as the apple of his eye" (Deut. 32:10). He led them in "constant love" (Exod. 15:13). He brought or carried them "on eagles' wings" (19:4).

A common biblical expression is that God "carried" his people in the wilderness. "You saw there how the Lord your God carried you all the way to this place, as a father carries his son" (Deut. 1:31). Moses confessed that he himself was unable to carry the burden of the people (Num. 11:11-18). Even the help of the elders did not suffice. The burden had to be God's own burden (cf. Isa. 46:3-4). "It was no envoy, no angel, but he himself . . . lifted them up and carried them through all the years gone by" (63:9). Like a shepherd, God tended his flock, gathered them together with his arm, and carried the lambs in his bosom (Isa. 40:11). The wilderness experience might well have been the basis of the shepherd metaphor.

a. Miracles of Merciful Protection

God carried the people by performing wonderful deeds to protect them. He guarded and preserved Israel from the menace of death. The people would certainly have died if left to their own devices. But the Lord did not forsake Israel. He did not abandon them to their fate. He was true to his covenant with them. In what way was this a miracle?

No doubt a people living in a fertile country, with "a city to live in" (Ps. 107:7), can easily confess: "The Lord is my shepherd; I shall want nothing" (23:1). But it is not so easy for a people that has lost its way "in desert wastes" (107:4), that is stripped "of every prop and stay, all stay of bread and all stay of water" (Isa. 3:1 NEB margin). The desert strips wanderers naked and leaves them at a loss. They have no shelter against the heat of day or the chill of night. They have no fence to protect them against wild animals or hostile marauders. They do not know which way to go. Their supplies of food and water run low. Their pride is brought low and their loftiness humbled, and the Lord alone is exalted (Isa. 2:11, 17). The wilderness days taught Israel to exalt the preservation that God granted them by his wonderful acts.

The gift of drinking water was decisive in this regard. All who live on the edge of the desert face the problem of securing water—the primary need of all living creatures. In general there is no lack of water in the desert, but it is hidden in the depths. It seldom comes to the surface, and when it does, it often tastes bitter or salty. An absolute necessity, then, is to know where to find pure water. Lucky are those who come across a source (Hebrew *ʿayin*) or spring (*māqôr*) in a valley at the foot of a stony mountain! Happy are those who by digging find a subterranean stream and can thus build a well (*beʾēr* or *bôr*)!

It is always a wonder for desert dwellers when they find drinking water. The site of a spring or well would often be regarded as sacred. Stories of springs tell of ancestors who found water long ago. Israel in fact spent only a limited time in the desert. Among the tribes Judah alone lived close to a desert (Josh. 15:1-4). But through its desert experience Israel may be regarded as a wilderness nation, and its tradition includes stories of springs of water (Marah in Exod. 15:22-26, Massah and Meribah near Kadesh in Num. 20:1-13, the springs at Elim in Exod. 15:27, the wells of Abraham and Isaac in Gen. 26:15ff., the well of Moses in Beer in Num. 21:16-18; and cf. John 4:5-15). Stories of water flowing from the rock are also remembered (Deut. 8:15; 32:8; 33:8; Ps. 74:15; 78:15, 20; 105:41; 114:7).

God gave the Israelites water when they were dying of thirst. He so led his people that they always found water when they would have perished without it. We are not told how the Israelites themselves planned always to have water at their disposal. They made no provision for the future. They depended totally on God's mercy. They were refreshed by water, but then they thirsted again. Again and again God showed his mercy by providing this basic necessity of life. Israel thus learned to confess that in the last resort no human planning can grant human security—only the Lord himself.

God not only gave water to his people; he also gave food. Bread and meat had been available in Egypt (Num. 11:5) and would again be plentiful in Canaan, the land flowing with milk and honey (Exod. 3:8). But they were lacking in the desert, and Israel's leaders did not take measures to provide the people with them. Israel's life was preserved in the desert, not by provisions brought from Egypt, nor by bought or grown supplies, but by the food that God himself gave. God gave his people "flesh . . . and bread" (Exod. 16:11-15) or "meat" and "manna" (Num. 11:4-9).

True, the Israelites did not leave Egypt empty-handed. They "picked up their dough before it was leavened, wrapped their kneading-troughs in their cloaks, and slung them on their shoulders" (Exod. 12:34). They also took with them "cattle in great numbers, both flocks and herds" (v. 38). They also received gifts of jewels and clothes from the Egyptians. But the unleavened bread was part of the Passover celebration. Some of the flocks and herds were used for sacrifice. The jewels hardly provided the people with adequate resources to buy food in the desert even had food been available. God himself had to make provision for Israel.

God made provision by giving the people manna ("bread from heaven," Exod. 16:4; Ps. 78:24; 105:40; John 6:31) and quails. Like all no-madic people, Israel was not totally without resources. In addition to its remaining flocks it could have bought food at accessible oases (Exod. 15:27). On its own, however, it did not have the means to ensure its survival in the desert, the "vile place, where nothing will grow" (Num. 20:4-5), the "waste and howling void" (Deut. 32:10). It had to have the help that God himself provided in the form of manna and quails.

. Manna is still known today in the desert of Sin. The bedouins who live there often collect small egg-white pearls and use them as honey to sweeten their food. In fact these pearls fall from a shrub when a louse has sucked its sap. They have to be collected early, before the sun melts them, or ants will feed on them. They have saved many people from death both before and after the Israelites. Nomads in the desert are also familiar with quails. Good runners but poor fliers, these birds are often the victims of winds (Num. 11:31; Ps. 78:26). They are then an easy prey and provide a tasty meal that can often help to keep people alive in the desert. For Israel, however, the quails, like the manna, came as the Lord's totally unexpected provision without which it could not have survived the wilderness journey.

The wonderful gift of food, like that of water, answered Israel's question whether the Lord was really its shepherd. Israel did not praise God for the availability of food and water alone. It praised him because by these gifts he manifested himself as Israel's shepherd at the very moment when Israel could no longer provide for itself and was about to perish. On the basis of the desert experience Israel could confess faith in the Lord from whom its help came: "Then he gave orders to the skies above and threw open heaven's doors. . . . he sent them food to their heart's desire" (Ps. 78:23ff.). A manifestation of God himself preceded the giving of the manna (Exod. 16:6ff.). It was granted so that "you shall know that I the Lord am your God" (v. 12; Deut. 29:6).

It may be noted that the wonderful gift of food and drink often accompanies Israel's complaints and disputes and lack of faith and patience (Exod. 16:2-3; Num. 11:4-7). Even when God gave the Israelites proof of his faithfulness by providing water, "they sinned against him yet again . . . they tried God's patience wilfully, demanding food to satisfy their hunger. They vented their grievance against God and said, 'Can God spread a table in the wilderness? . . . can he provide meat for his people?' . . . because they put no trust in God, and had no faith in his power to save" (Ps. 78:17ff.). At times God's protection may be recorded as an example of grace with no reference to Israel's complaining, but whenever the people's attitude is mentioned, it is one of rebellion. God's mercy is all the greater, all the more wonderful, because it is a sign of his faithfulness to a stubborn people.

The manna was also a continuing sign of God's protection. It was not given once only. Every day God provided his people with food. Whenever it was needed, the manna was there (cf. Exod. 16:4; Josh. 5:12; Neh. 9:21). The Israelites were living "from hand to mouth," from God's hand! They could not provide for themselves. They could not even keep the manna from one day to the next. Each day they depended on God and his ongoing provision for his people.

Exodus 16 also relates the heavenly bread to the sabbath. God had laid a foundation for the sabbath when he rested on the seventh day at creation (Gen. 2:1ff.). But now the sabbath was instituted as a day of rest for the Lord's people. "Tomorrow is a day of sacred rest, a sabbath holy to the Lord" (Exod. 16:23). A special supply of manna would thus be given the previous day (v. 29). Israel was to sanctify the sabbath, but it was not meant to be a burden. Saved every day from famine, on the seventh day Israel did not even need to look for food. God took the burden upon himself. He gave an additional supply which he did not allow to spoil (16:5, 19ff.). In want and danger, the people had the gift of perfect freedom. For this they gave God thanks and praise.

In other ways, too, God saw that Israel went "short of nothing" in their march through the desert. Clothes and sandals did not wear out (Deut. 2:7). Feet did not swell (8:4; Neh. 9:21). There was protection against enemy attack. When the Amalekites attacked Israel at Rephidim, Moses sent out picked men to fight them, but Israel won because the Lord was "at war with Amalek" (Exod. 17:16) as he had been at war with Egypt at the Reed Sea (Exod. 14:14, 25).

The Israelites did not go out into the desert unarmed. They had simple weapons which they used to defend themselves against assailants. But the OT has no interest in their equipment or battle experience. The people might be arranged in hosts (cf. Exod. 13:18), but they could hardly be regarded as an army ready for battle. Moses might select warriors for the battle in Exod. 17, but the outcome lay with the raised or lowered hands of Moses (17:11). When Aaron and Hur held up Moses' hands, "Joshua defeated Amalek and put its people to the sword" (17:13). We may not be told specifically what was the role of Moses' "holy hands" or of the staff of God that he held in them (17:9). Nor can we be sure what precisely is meant by the name of the altar that Moses built, "The Lord is my banner" (RSV), along with the mysterious words that follow: "A hand upon the banner of the Lord" (RSV). What is clear is that Israel's army could not have withstood the Amalekite attack had not the Lord fought for Israel as he did against the Egyptians and as he would do again in the days of Midian (Num. 31). Praise belonged to the God "who guarded us [Israel] on all our wanderings among the many peoples through whose lands we passed" (Josh. 24:17).

b. Miracles of Curative Inflictions

Thus far we have looked only at the stories of God's mercy, how he provided his people with nourishment and security irrespective of Israel's belief or unbelief. We must now turn to accounts that tell of God's judgments upon his stubborn people. An unavoidable question is whether the Lord is still a good shepherd for Israel when he not only provides for it but also executes his sentences upon it. The answer of the OT witness is that Israel in the wilderness knew judgments as well as mercies and praised God equally for both.

Most of the judgment stories occur in Numbers: the fire of Taberah in 11:1-3, the plague at Kibroth-hattaavah in 11:31-35, the penalty of forty years' wandering after the return of the scouts in 14:26-35, 39, the death sentence on the scouts in 14:36-38, the death sentence on the children of Korah and on Dathan and Abiram in 16:1-35, the plague in 16:41-50, the judgment on Moses and Aaron at Meribah in 20:1-13, the poisonous snakes in 21:4-9, the judgment on Zimri and Cozbi in 25:8, and the judgment on the whole people in 25:5, 9. The sentences take the form of plague, snakebite, sudden death, or swallowing up, though some people are killed by the Levites and others simply die in the wilderness.

As we look at Exodus and Numbers, an astonishing difference is that the stories in Numbers are mostly judgment stories whereas those in Exodus, apart from the story of the golden calf, are for the most part mercy stories. It is not, of course, that we have a more pessimistic view in Numbers and a more optimistic view in Exodus. The point is that the aim in Numbers is to emphasize the judgment of God upon his wilderness people, while that in Exodus is to put the stress on his mercy toward them. Yet judgment and mercy are not to be set in contradiction with one another. They relate to one another and complement one another as the two sides of God's dealings with his people. God's mercy does not cancel out his judgment nor does his judgment repeal his mercy. The different emphases do not denote any material difference.

There is also no reason to suppose that the difference is chronological, since the themes of mercy and judgment occur at every stage and throughout the OT witness. In the story of the desert wandering acts of mercy do not precede or follow those of judgment, and in the OT record one age does not stress the acts of mercy and another the acts of judgment. Thus in Ps. 105 the emphasis falls on mercy, in Ps. 106 on judgment, but the difference has nothing whatever to do with the age of the composition of the two psalms. It springs from the difference in intention. Ps. 105 seeks to give thanks to God, Ps. 106 to confess the sins of the people.

Either way, the attitude of Israel is basically the same, as is also the attitude of God. In Exodus no less than Numbers, God faces a faithless, stubborn, and complaining people, and to this people he shows both mercy in judgment and judgment in mercy.

A new feature in the judgment stories of Numbers, of course, is the prominence that is given to the anger of God at Israel's attitude. Except in ch. 32, Exodus never speaks of this. Numbers, however, refers to it constantly (11:1-10; 12:9; 16:46; 25:4; cf. Ps.

95:11; 78:21, 31, 38). Moses, too, became "very angry" when he faced the stubborn people (Num. 16:15; cf. Exod. 32:19, 22). Yet the anger of God in no way contradicts his mercy, his fidelity, his patience, or his willingness to forgive. It is the same God who shows amazing patience in Exodus and who reaches the limit of his patience in Numbers. In showing mercy, he does not let Israel do as it wants, as if its rebellion were not an occasion for anger. In showing anger and condemning his rebellious people, he has not totally exhausted his patience, nor is he about to sever all relation with Israel. The complaints of Moses (Num. 11:11-14) and of the Lord himself (14:11, 27) show clearly that the Lord has always a heavy burden to carry. He is angry at his people's stubbornness, not merely when condemning it, but even when showing mercy and bearing his anger patiently.

God did not give up his people. He kept faith with them even in judgment. This is evident from the way in which he punished. Though angry, he did not let his anger break loose. The whole people deserved to perish, but only a part did so. The number might be impressive, but God's merciful restraint of his wrath was even more impressive.

All the Israelites complained, and all ought to have been condemned (cf. Num. 14:12; 16:21; Deut. 9:14, 19, 25; Ezek. 20:13, 21). Yet only a limited number was in fact condemned (Num. 11:1-3, 31-35; 14:37; 21:6-9; 25:4, 7-9). Once Moses and Aaron alone suffered on the people's behalf (Num. 20:1-13; Ps. 106:32). At times those who incited the people to revolt were punished, e.g., Aaron in Exod. 32:1-10, or Korah, Dathan, and Abiram in Num. 16:26. Even when a dreadful judgment of fire or plague struck, it was soon arrested. At times Moses interceded, even offering his own life for that of the people (Exod. 32:32). At times the plague might stop with the death of those who instigated the rebellion (Exod. 32:25-29; Num. 14:37; 25:4-5, 6-11, 13), or when expiation had been made (Num. 16:41-50). No matter how many might be stricken, the focus was always on the fact that God restrained his anger (cf. Ps. 78:38): "I pitied them too much to destroy them and did not make an end of them in the wilderness" (Ezek. 20:17).

Several OT texts bear witness to the truth that God's wrath and condemnation are "just for a moment" and of little consequence compared to the loving mercy that he bestows on his people from generation to generation. For all the terrible judgments, the wilderness story as a whole does not allow us to conclude that Israel's God is alternately merciful and angry, now the good shepherd, now the stern judge. God does not balance acts of wrath against acts of mercy. In all his deeds he leads and preserves his people in the desert. He does so, however, according to his free will as the holy God.

"His anger is but for a moment, and his favor is for a lifetime" (Ps. 30:5 RSV). "In sudden anger I hid my face from you for a moment; but now have I pitied you with a love which never fails" (Isa. 54:8). Though not referring directly to Israel in the wilderness, these familiar verses apply to that period, too. In both Exod. 34:6-7 and Num. 14:18 we read that the Lord is "a God merciful and gracious, slow to anger, and abounding in steadfast love and faithfulness, . . . forgiving iniquity and transgression and sin, but who will by no means clear the guilty" (RSV). In condemning, God does not contradict his mercy but shows how wonderful his mercy truly is. Knowing his judgments (Num. 14:34), Israel knows his mercy. It is because the Lord cares that he punishes (Amos 3:2). The stories of God's mercies and judgments are testimonies to his glory and holiness. The glory that manifests itself as a cloud when God acts as a shepherd (Exod. 16:9-10) is also the glory that displays his holiness when he must apply mercy by judgments (Num. 20:12-13).

Psalm 99 summons Israel to praise God for his holiness (vv. 3, 9), recalling that in the days of Moses and Aaron God was a forgiving God to them but an avenger of their wrongdoings. Israel thus praises God for acts of judgment as well as mercy. As Ps. 119:75 says: "I know, O Lord, that thy decrees are just, and even in punishing thou keepest faith with me." To be sure, such verses are rare, and none praises God's judgments directly. Nevertheless, acts of punishment are inseparable from acts of faithfulness and mercy. In the desert stories we cannot tear mercy and judgment apart. Israel remembers both. Realizing that it should have been totally cast off as a rebellious people, it sees that God's mercy is no cheap grace but a wonderful and precious grace that is worthy of increasing praise. The desert stories are never simple tales of divine forgiveness. They cannot be, for they bear witness to the mystery of God's own burden as he carried Israel. How great that burden was may be seen when Israel had to bear it itself if only for a moment. All the more reason did it have, therefore, to praise the Lord who himself took up the burden of the people.

4. God Was Present among His People

Throughout the wilderness journey the Lord himself went with his people, leading them as a good shepherd guides his flock. The wilderness story points to the mystery of God's presence (a) as an everlasting presence by day and by night (in the cloud or fire, as the angel of the Lord, in the holy tent with the ark as his throne), the emphasis being on God's constant faithfulness; (b) as an occasional presence (in the tent or in meetings with Moses), the emphasis being on his sovereignty and holiness; and (c) as a presence in the holy tent, the emphasis being on the ministry of selected persons: Moses, Aaron, and Aaron's descendants.

GOD COULD SHOW MERCY and pass judgment only when present. Hence he had to come down from heaven or come from his earthly dwelling (e.g., Sinai), be with the people on their wanderings, and remain with them when they settled at this or that place in the desert. Had the Lord not been with his people they would have disappeared in the "waste and howling void" (Deut. 32:10). God might, of course, have kept Israel alive from afar, yet it pleased him to come among his people, to let them feel his nearness. Even as God dwells in a high and holy place far from his creatures, he wills to draw near to his people at decisive times and to be present with them. It is thus that he manifests himself as the Lord, the God of Israel, and does the wonders that are the object of Israel's praise.

God's presence plays an important role throughout scripture. God does not create heaven and earth and then leave his creatures to their fate. He helps them. Preservation is the first blessing of his presence. The stories of the fathers praise God because he was with these chosen forerunners of his people. The revelation of his name in the story of the exodus also manifests his presence. It is because of his genuine presence with the people that the events of the exodus gain the meaning of a constant liberation.

God's presence takes on special significance, however, in the context of Israel in the wilderness. God's deeds are always wonderful and mysterious, but in the desert an even sharper light falls upon them. His readiness to go with his people in the wasteland arouses a special sense of wonder and amazement that rings through all the witnesses to it.

There is amazement, of course, at the desert itself. The later Israelites viewed God's presence in it from the standpoint of dwellers in villages and cities. The wilderness is no less a part of God's creation than the vault of heaven or the ocean depths or the world of the dead. But like the ocean or Sheol, the wilderness is a form of the world that God neither desires nor likes and that is thus uninhabitable. Its very barrenness and sterility show that God abandons it. The Creator may certainly act wherever he wishes, but he is surely not likely to choose a place that he has forsaken.

Then there is amazement that God goes with Israel. Naked in the desert, Israel might be called a son or bride or beloved wife, but it had no merit or attractiveness of its own. Only by God's astonishing decision did the people become precious. Again and again they behaved as a stubborn people. How, then, could the holy God accompany such a pack of rebels? His encounter with them could surely mean only their destruction. If Israel were ever tempted to regard God's presence with them as a natural and permanent state, the desert stories reminded them time and again that this was an impossible assumption.

No act of God in setting up his people points so clearly to the wonderful character of his presence as does the protection that he granted Israel in the wilderness. Going into the desert, Israel experienced loneliness and helplessness. In this very situation of despair they learned to confess: "The Lord is my shepherd; I shall want nothing. He makes me lie down . . . he leads . . . he renews . . . guides. Even though I walk through a valley dark as death I fear no evil, for thou art with me" (Ps. 23:1-4). This confession held true in every generation. Israel's witness to the wilderness period opened up a concrete historical understanding.

a. Forms of Presence

In great compassion the Lord "didst not forsake them in the wilderness" (Neh. 9:17, 19). Israel was the people among whom God dwelt (Num. 11:20; 14:14). Yet they could not take this presence for granted. At times they had to ask anxiously: "Is the Lord in our midst or not?" (Exod. 17:7). At times Moses might issue the threat: "You will not have the Lord with you" (Num. 14:42). How did God manifest his presence in the wilderness?

"God made them go round by way of the wilderness towards the Red Sea" (Exod. 13:18). Here God acted as guide. His leading was constant: "All the time the Lord went before them, by day a pillar of cloud to guide them on their journey, by night a pillar of fire to give them light, so that they could travel night and day" (v. 21; cf. Deut. 1:30-33). Only once did the pillar move behind them to throw the Egyptians into a panic (14:24). By the pillar and fire God told the people when to remain and when to move (Num. 9:15ff.; cf. Exod. 40:36-38). The pillar and fire were symbols of his own presence as leader and guide.

The Lord was also present and guided his people by his angel. In Exod. 14:19 the angel as well as the pillar moved to the rear to keep the Egyptians at bay. This guiding by the angel may not be as familiar to us as that by the cloud and fire, but many important texts refer to it. At the end of the story of the golden calf, the Lord tells Moses to lead the people away and gives him the assurance: "My angel shall go ahead of you" (Exod. 32:34). The same guidance is promised in 33:2, and even earlier in 23:20-21: "I send an angel before you to guard you on your way and to bring you to the place I have prepared. Take heed of him and listen to his voice. Do not defy him." Ps. 34:7 takes up the same motif of the angel that goes ahead and provides protection for the people on their way, bringing them to the land of promise.

God also led the people by means of the ark. In Num. 10:33, 35-36; 14:14 it was the ark that showed the people where to go and where to stay: "Then they moved off from the mountain of the Lord and journeyed for three days, and the Ark of the Covenant of the Lord kept a day's journey ahead of them to find them a place to rest. . . . Whenever the Ark began to move, Moses said, 'Up, Lord, and may thy enemies be scattered. . . .' When it halted, he said, 'Rest, Lord of the countless thousands of Israel.' " At the end of the story of the scouts, when in spite of Moses' warning the people set off for the high land of Canaan, "neither the Ark of the Covenant of the Lord nor Moses moved with them out of the camp" (Num. 14:44), and disaster followed. How the ark was carried we are not told specifically. What counts is that God led Israel by means of it.

An interesting point in Num. 10:29-36 is that Hobab the Midianite, who was used to the desert, was invited by Moses to join Israel and guide them on their way. When he refused, Moses pressed him, and it would seem from Judg. 1:16 and 4:11 that Hobab's clan did in fact join Israel. Yet the story does not say that Hobab acted as guide. Neither Hobab nor any other human being was to lead Israel through the wilderness. God himself was present with his people to guide them.

The cloud and fire, the angel, and the ark—these were the three means by which the Lord led his people. Relating the three modes to one another may be difficult, but all three denote God's constant presence, the wonderful nature of this presence, and the freedom of the presence, which meant that no one could control or guarantee its mode.

The freedom of the presence came out expressly only when the people proudly set forth and God manifestly did not go with it (Num. 14:39ff.). The wonder of the presence is everywhere apparent. The stress is not on the mode but on the everlasting presence itself. The pillars of cloud and fire never leave their place in front of the people. The same may not be said specifically about the angel and the ark, but it is to be presupposed. As the summaries of faith tell us, God led, guided, and carried his people the whole forty years in the wilderness. Irrespective of the mode, the guiding presence of God was an abiding presence.

b. The Tent of the Presence

Israel also knew another form of the presence that was too distinct from the first three to be parallel with them. Exodus and Numbers refer continually to the tent of the presence, the tent of tokens, or the tabernacle, which plays so important a role in the faith of Israel. The account in Exod. 33 merits special attention.

This chapter is closely related to ch. 32, the story of the golden calf, and ch. 34, the renewal of the covenant. Around these three chapters are sections telling how the tabernacle is to be built, furnished, and maintained (chs. 25–31, 35–40). The whole unit chs. 25–40 has to do with God's revelation on Mt. Sinai. At the end of the events there, the glory of God came down in a cloud for the first time (24:15b-17). The tabernacle was thus to be built, and it was to be consecrated when the cloud covered it and God's glory filled it (40:34-35). Chs. 32–34 are also closely related to the events on Mt. Sinai. The incident of the golden calf followed those events immediately, and its upshot was the renewing of the covenant that the people had just broken. The meeting of Moses with God in ch. 32 formed a bridge between the golden calf and the covenant renewal. The whole section Exod. 25–40 is thus to be seen in the light of the Sinai revelation.

At the same time most of the elements of the section relate closely to Israel in the wilderness. The texts that deal with the tabernacle answer the question how Israel was to worship God in the desert, not how it was to live in Canaan. The three sections of ch. 33 also have to do with God's presence in the wilderness, and when Moses received the tablets of the law in ch. 34, he said: "May the Lord go in our company" (34:8-9).

As we look more closely at ch. 33, we first see in v. 7 that already during the wilderness journey Moses used to "take a tent and pitch it at a distance outside the camp." In this tent the Lord met Moses, and it was thus called the "Tent of the Presence" (NEB) or the "tent of meeting" (RSV). Whenever the Lord wished to speak to Moses, or Moses wished to hear the Lord's mind and to receive his instructions, or one of the people "sought the Lord," Moses entered this tent, and "the pillar of cloud came down, and stayed at the entrance to the tent while the Lord spoke with Moses. . . . face to face, as one man speaks to another" (vv. 8-11). Here, then, we have an occasional presence, not the abiding presence of God's leading of his people through the wilderness.

Verses 1-6 deal more specifically with the desert journey. After the incident of the golden calf, Moses was told to lead the people to the place that God had named in 32:34. But the order was now given in a harsher and more terrible form, for God said: "I will not journey in your company, for fear that I annihilate you on the way; for you are a stubborn people" (33:3, echoing 32:9; cf. 34:9). This was a hard sentence. Was it comfort enough that God would send an envoy or angel to guide the people, or that he would not destroy it on the journey? Might it be that the Lord would go back on his decision as the Israelites put away their ornaments in token of penitence and mourning (33:4ff.)? It was surely bad news that Israel must journey on without God's presence, but Moses himself was not satisfied, and he interceded for the people. As he saw it, Israel would no longer be "the Lord's own people" if the Lord did not go with them. Boldly and insistently, then, he asked God to amend his decision (33:12-13, 15-16, 18).

In reply God first gave the promise: "My face will go in front of you" (33:14 CB). What did this mean? The NEB translates "I . . . in person," the RSV "my presence." But Moses was still not satisfied. The face might be no more than a representation or a vision. Next, then, God assured him that his face meant no less than himself in person. Yet Moses was insistent. He wanted to see what he had heard (v. 18). But to see God's face is to see his person, and to see his person is to see his glory, which means death for sinners. God, therefore, allowed Moses to see his glory, but only as he was hidden in a crevice, as God's hand covered him, and he could see only the Lord's back (vv. 22-23) or see him in a cloud (34:5). Even so, the experience was so tremendous for Moses that "the skin of his face" (RSV) shone so brightly that the Israelites were afraid to approach him (34:29-35).

The witness of these chapters is that a serious crisis arose in the relation between God and his people. This crisis endangered God's promise to accompany Israel and threw its whole existence into jeopardy. It is in the context of this story that we read of the tent of the presence where the Lord met with Moses. Here the Lord was pleased to be present with his people in a way that emphasized his freedom. The tent was pitched outside the camp (33:7). Why? Because the Lord could not be too directly present with a stubborn people. His own holiness and the welfare of a people that could not stand his presence forbade it. He went with the people, but not in its midst. He was near, but also at some remove. He kept contact, but stayed outside the camp. His tent was not among Israel's tents.

We note also that God was present according to his own free will at the time and place of his own choosing. If elsewhere there is stress on his constant presence, the emphasis here is on his freedom. The tent of the presence might be a lasting institution, but God met Moses only when he wished to do so. Even then he came down in a cloud and stayed at the entrance. Only as he himself pleased did the tent truly become a tent of meeting or the tent of the presence.

At this tent it was Moses that the Lord met. Moses had here a decisive role. It pleased God to speak to him "face to face" (33:11). Moses himself had no authority to lead the people but he had "found favour with" the Lord (33:12). It was with Moses as his intermediary, then, that the Lord accompanied his people.

Note, too, that at this tent the Lord chose to manifest his glory. The emphasis may fall on God's freedom, but this freedom does not mean only that the presence was a rare or unusual favor. God's presence at the tent involved an abundant manifestation of his grace. Where God's presence is rare, unusual, and wonderful, there he manifests himself in all his glory. For this reason the free presence is no less significant than the constant presence.

Exodus 33:7-11 closes with a short remark that deserves notice: Moses' "young assistant, Joshua son of Nun, never moved from inside the tent." Joshua was Moses' servant (24:13) and the military leader of Israel (17:8-16), but he was also the guardian of the tent of the presence. He was not a priest or a Levite, yet it was he who guarded the tent. Here was another manifestation of the freedom of God. The priests would also have a role in the wilderness journey. God would manifest his presence by means of their service. Yet he was also free to manifest it without that service.

c. The Priestly Tabernacle

We now look at the tent or tabernacle as it was constructed and used during the wilderness journey under the direction of the priests and Levites. Several names are used for what is generally known as the tabernacle. Some of these are clear and simple like "tent" (*'ōhel*, e.g., Exod. 33:7; Num. 9:17), "dwelling" or "tabernacle" (*mišqān*, e.g., Exod. 26:1; Num. 1:50), or "sanctuary," "Holy Place" (*miqdāš*, e.g., Exod. 25:8; Num. 3:38; *qōdeš*, e.g., Exod. 28:43). Tents were the usual dwellings of nomadic peoples, and God himself would decide to dwell in a tent among us, so that we saw his glory (John 1:14). The Hebrew word for "tabernacle" could denote any kind of dwelling. "Sanctuary," too, had the more general sense of a holy place or temple; it did not necessarily mean a tent.

To make it clear that no ordinary tent or dwelling was at issue, other nouns were used with *'ōhel* or *mišqān*. One such noun was *mô'ēd*, which probably means "meeting." The expression "tent of meeting" could denote either the place where Moses met the Lord or the place where the congregation assembled for worship. Another noun, *'ēdût*, seems to have the sense of "testimony." We thus read of the tent or tabernacle of the testimony (cf. Num. 9:15 RSV; Exod. 38:21 RSV) or Tent (or Tabernacle) of the Tokens (NEB). The word *'ēdût* was often used for the tablets on which the laws were inscribed, and the ark where these were kept was called the "ark of the testimony" (Exod. 25:22 RSV; NEB "Ark of the Tokens"). The tent of the testimony would thus be the tent where the ark, which indicated God's own presence, was kept.

The tabernacle differed from Moses' tent of meeting in various ways. Whereas the latter was pitched outside the camp, the tabernacle stood in the midst of the Israelites' tents (Num. 2:2). The latter also seems to have been empty, but the tabernacle was divided into two parts: first the holy place with the altar of incense, the table for the bread of the presence (or showbread), and the lampstand with seven branches, then the most holy place with the ark and its "cover" or "mercy seat" (RSV). A veil separated the "most holy place" (RSV; NEB "Holy of Holies") from the holy place, and another veil separated the holy place from the court with its altar of whole-offerings and the basin for ablutions. In the case of the original tent of meeting, Moses alone entered it and Joshua was its guardian. In the case of the tabernacle, however, Aaron replaced Moses, and he entered the tabernacle not to listen to God's word but to bring the annual atonement offering for the people (Lev. 16:34), his sons assisting him (Num. 3:4) along with three clans of Levites who cared for the tabernacle (3:4).

The tabernacle, too, can be called the tent of the presence, but it was not the same as the original tent. It was the place where Israel worshiped God on its wilderness journey. It served already as the temple, albeit in a temporary and mobile form corresponding to the needs of a congregation that had not yet come to its rest. The ark with the tablets, the cover as the seat of divine mercy, the altar of whole-offerings for the sacrifice of reconciliation, the priests and Levites as representatives of the people for the celebration of the liturgy—all these would be elements in Israel's worship when a stone temple was built on the rock of Zion that God would choose as his dwelling. All that Israel needed for worship was present already. Amid the dangers of the desert journey Israel was granted the favor of living as God's people in the fullest sense.

Exodus 35–40 tells how the tabernacle was built. In the introduction absolute rest was commanded on the sabbath (35:1-3). A contribution of gold, silver, or kind was required from each member of the people to provide what was needed for the tabernacle and its contents (vv. 4-19). Skilled craftsmen were set aside to supervise the work (35:30–36:7). Hangings and coverings were made of linen, goats' hair, leather, and hides (36:8-19). Planks were cut and silver sockets prepared (vv. 20-34). The linen and embroidered veil and screen were made with the necessary posts and hangings (36:35-38). The ark was constructed (37:1-9), as were the table (vv. 10-16), the golden lamp (vv. 17-24), the altar of incense (vv. 25-28), the altar of whole-offerings (38:1-7), and the basin of ablutions (v. 8). The court was then equipped (vv. 9-20). We are next told how the metals were collected (vv. 21-31) and the priestly vestments made (39:1-31). Finally, Moses inspected the work, approved it, and consecrated the tabernacle (39:32– 40:33). Everything was done according to the instructions given to Moses in Exod. 25–31.

The real point of the tabernacle, of course, does not lie in the details but in God's readiness to come and stay among his people. The splendor of the tabernacle reflects the wonder of God's presence in the wilderness. With the ark, the mercy seat, the altar, and the priests and Levites to minister in it, the tabernacle serves as the central manifestation of the divine presence. The basic miracle of God's coming to meet his people occurred not when the temple was built but with the construction of the tabernacle in the wilderness. The miracle of the wilderness presence anticipates the miracle of the divine presence in every age. The presence in the tabernacle is so meaningful that the presence at other times is simply a repetition or actualization of it. The later temple could be understood as the Lord's dwelling only on the basis of the holy tent that preceded it.

An important aspect of the Lord's presence to which the tabernacle testifies is that God dwells here in a way that manifests his freedom. The presence is a meeting: "It is there that I shall meet you" (Exod. 25:22; 29:42-43). Only when the Lord comes down in a cloud that covers it does the tent become God's dwelling (40:34-35; Lev. 16:2). The presence is an event, not an ongoing institution. The climax of the presence is when God speaks his Word: "From above the cover . . . I shall deliver to you all my commands for the Israelites" (Exod. 25:22; 29:42; cf. Num. 14:10-11). An expression that occurs over fifty times from Exod. 25 to Num. 27 shows that God is not bound to his dwelling: God meets his people "at the entrance to the Tent" (Exod. 29:4, 11, 42, etc.).

The tabernacle, as noted, was set in the middle of the camp in accordance with God's promise that he "would dwell among them" (NEB) or "dwell in their midst" (RSV; cf. Exod. 25:8; 29:45; Lev. 26:11-12). This does not contradict the original siting of Moses' tent outside the camp, for between the tabernacle and the Israelite tents the tents of Moses, the Aaronic priests, and the three Levite families of Gershon, Kohath, and Merari (Num. 3:23, 29, 35, 38) shielded the holy tent from too close a contact with the tribes and kept the people at a safe distance from the place where the glory of God came down (Exod. 40:34-35; Lev. 9:6, 23; Num. 14:10, 21). Even though dwelling in the midst of the people, the Lord remained holy and at a distance from the camp.

We note also that the altar of whole-offerings stood before the holy tent (Exod. 27:1-8; 38:1-7). The Lord's presence among his people was inconceivable without "blood from the sin-offering of the yearly Expiation" (30:10). The priests "make expiation for them [the Israelites], and then no calamity will befall them when they come close to the sanctuary" (Num. 8:19). Here again we see that the Lord's presence was something precious and extraordinary that no one should take for granted.

The tabernacle prefigured the temple where the Lord would dwell among his people when they settled in the land. Yet it did so as a place where God freely met his people as he himself willed. It kept alive an awareness of the mystery of the divine presence and of the constant crisis in the relation between God and his people which caused Israel to walk on the verge of destruction, not only in specially dangerous situations, but throughout their desert journey, then in the land in which they would find rest, and later in exile and among strangers. The Lord's presence among his people was always a miracle and an occasion for praise and thanksgiving.

In this connection it is significant that the Aaronic blessing occurs in the account of preparations for the journey in Num. 1–10. Aaron and his sons are to "put [the Lord's] name upon the people of Israel" (6:22ff. RSV). God himself will bless them. The fact that God himself blesses and protects the people, that he makes his face to shine upon them, is both an object of prayer in Israel and also a gracious gift that God grants as it pleases him.

5. God Brought His People to Their Rest

God led his pilgrim people through the wilderness with Egypt, the land of oppression, behind it, and Canaan, the land of promised rest, ahead. Israel had no dwelling, no land, no source of income. It could not defend itself against aggression. Its only recourse was to God himself, who would complete what he had begun in Egypt. In its indigence Israel discovered the secret of its strength in every age, the strength of a people living by God's Word alone.

WE HAVE THUS FAR CONSIDERED three aspects of Israel's wilderness journey: God chose, led, and accompanied his people through the desert. We must not omit, however, a further aspect according to the OT witness: God brought his people to a goal. He gave it a future. The desert journey was a journey to Canaan, the land of divine promise. We must now look at the journey from this angle.

God chose, led, and accompanied the people with a goal in mind. Israel had to live a nomadic life for many years, yet the journey would have an end and a destination would be reached. God did not turn Israel into a nomadic people. He carried them and protected them, but did not intend them to stay forever in the desert. If he was with his people in the wilderness, it was not because of any preference for this forlorn place. His purpose was always to bring his people to the land of Canaan and to give this land to Israel (Josh. 24:8; Amos 2:10). We must now look at the journey in the light of this single aim.

Many of the wilderness stories—the finding of springs, the securing of food, and the fending off of snakes—are common to nomadic tribes and do not stand in any necessary relation to the topic of the promised land. Nevertheless, Israel enjoyed the protection of the Lord who had liberated them from Egypt, and who led them through the desert, in order that they might enter the promised land. With their constant complaints and distrust of God's Word, Israel enjoyed God's protection in a special way, and their experiences were distinctive in their orientation to a specific future.

God *brought* his people to the land of rest. He *conducted* it. This expression needs some explanation. It does not simply mean that God guided the people as one who knew the way. Nor does it mean that he carried it. What it denotes is that he brought it to its destination. The people would come to the place it was aiming for. In the Hebrew we have the verb *bô'*, "to come," in its causative form, "to make somebody come in," "to let somebody enter." We still have here an aspect of God's leading the people, but we now see that it was with this aim in mind from the very first that God set out to lead Israel.

In leading and protecting his people in the wilderness, God purposed to bring them into the land that he gave them as a patrimony. At times the verb *bô'* may be used in connection with the gift of the land, but frequently it occurs in the context of the wilderness journey (Exod. 15:17; Josh. 24:8; Deut. 26:9; Jer. 2:7). God brought his people to their rest. From the standpoint of the desert, Canaan was a place of rest *(m^enûḥāh)*. It was peaceful, safe, and secure. It had the very qualities that the desert lacked. The bitter experiences of wilderness life taught the Israelites to give their country that extraordinarily appreciative name: the "place of rest."

We find it in Deut. 12:9: "For till now you have not reached the place of rest, the patrimony which the Lord your God is giving you." Only in Canaan would the Lord grant his people safety (RSV) or security (NEB) (v. 10). The promise finds fulfilment in Josh. 1:13, 15; 21:44; 22:4; 23:1; cf. 2 Sam. 7:1, 11; 1 Kgs. 8:56. In Ps. 95:11 the Lord swears in his wrath that "they shall never enter my rest." The reference is to the story of the scouts, though "patrimony" or "country" is the term used in the accounts in Num. 14:23-24 and Deut. 1:34-39. In Ps. 23:2 the Shepherd Lord "leads me beside the waters of rest" (CB). The promise in Exod. 33:14 is that "my face will go in front (of you) to give you rest" (CB). Moses will have his mind set at rest (NEB), but under his leadership the whole people will also be given rest (RSV) (cf. Jer. 6:16: "You will find rest for yourselves").

Israel was God's people on its way to the place of rest that God had already promised. As a pilgrim people it differed from every other nation. It was marked by its wilderness experience. Was this a mark of poverty and weakness or a mark of wealth and strength? Both aspects may be found in the OT witness.

a. Israel Was on Its Way

Israel had not yet reached its destination. This simple but meaningful negation characterizes its whole forty-year journey. As a number takes on a negative value when we put a minus sign in front of it, so Israel's life in the desert stands under this sign of "not yet." The desert period was a minus period. It was a period of lack and want. Yet the biblical witness is not subject to mathematical rules. The weakness did not negate Israel's strength during this period. As a pilgrim people Israel lived with no security, "a vagrant and a wanderer on earth" (cf. Gen. 4:14). In this very misery, however, it was no less rich.

We see the positive aspect when we recall the blessings that Israel had already received. God had already chosen and adopted them as his own people. He had already provided them with the necessities of life for the journey. He was already going with them by day and by night. He had already promised them the land. The people were blessed already, as Balaam said when they were about to enter Canaan (Num. 22–24). From the very beginning of the journey we thus catch a note of confidence, gratitude, and praise (Exod. 13:21-22).

Nevertheless, we cannot ignore the negative side. The blessings were real but provisional. They were no more than signs of a coming reality. They were "advances" on a future inheritance. The pilgrim people did not yet have the blessings in their fulness. The wonderful life of promise was still a mystery. It still lay under the shadow of curse and death. The glory of Israel as the "people of the Lord" (Deut. 32:15; Isa. 44:2) could not shine forth in the desert as it would do later. Manna nourished the people but it was poor food in comparison with the rich produce of the promised land (cf. Josh. 5:10-12). God gave the people water, but they had to wait for it patiently while suffering from thirst. The Lord went with his pilgrim people, but they did not always feel his presence, for it was a free presence. The people were obviously poor in spite of their strength as God's own people. To enjoy food and water in the midst of hunger and thirst, to know protection in the midst of danger, to experience abundant life in the midst of want, the people had to be a people of patience, of trust, and of hope.

This attitude made up the very life of Israel as God's people. It was born as a people that trusted the Lord. Daily events might show it to be an unbelieving pilgrim people. Yet it was also a people that was constantly called and invited to turn from its unbelief and to return to its first trust as the people that had seen the deeds of God and heard his Word. It was the people that was asked to acknowledge its lack of confidence and to come to a new faith. The confession of Ps. 23:4: "Even though I walk through a valley dark as death I fear no evil, for thou art with me," casts vivid light both on the poverty of a people that is richly blessed and on the abundant riches of a miserable pilgrim people.

b. Forty Years—Through Death to Life

Israel was on their way as a pilgrim people. They had not yet reached their destination. The people had to wander in the desert for forty years. Could a people who were nomadic for so long really be a pilgrim people? They were a people on their way. They had not yet arrived. They were still suffering and struggling in the desert. They still had to hope for the land that they did not yet see. But was there any certainty that they would really reach the destination? Could we still call them a pilgrim people if it was clear that they would not in fact do so?

This dreadful possibility became a reality in the story of the scouts (Num. 13–14; Deut. 1:19-46; Ps. 106:24-27; 78:32-41). The people were already on the very threshold of Canaan. No major obstacle blocked their entry. The Lord summoned them to go forward. But they had doubts. They wanted the land to be explored first. At the Lord's command Moses granted the request. The results were mixed. The land was a good land but there were also dangers. Frightened by the dangers, the Israelites "muttered treason in [their] tents" (Deut. 1:27) and "cried out in dismay; . . . they wept" (Num. 14:1b). The pilgrim people showed here none of the endurance that should have become its very character. Caleb (Num. 13:30) and Joshua (14:6) failed in their efforts to rouse the people from this "spiritual death." Israel's attitude was the more reprehensible because by way of the scouts they had already "seen" the land of rest that previously had been only a matter of promise. As a judgment, therefore, the scouts who had given a bad report died of the plague (Num. 14:37) and those who would not hearken to the Lord, but murmured against him, were forbidden to enter the promised land, this blessing being now reserved for their children (14:26ff.; Deut. 1:35).

First-generation Israel was a pilgrim people that would not enter the land of its rest. It would live on as a wandering people. It would always be on the run. Its journey would have no end. Its only limit would be the death that awaits every creature. Its desert journey had no aim. It could only wait for the forty years to end (Num. 26:63-65). It thus lost all hope and comfort. Preservation continued, but the period of preservation was now also a period of judgment. Instead of entering the land after two years in the desert, the people had to spend another thirty-eight years of wandering. Strangely, we learn little about this protracted period. From its beginning in Num. 14 to its end with the death of Aaron in 20:22-29, we have the record of only three incidents. It was a period of waiting for the whole of the first generation, apart from Caleb and Joshua, to die. Whereas judgment had previously been passed only on a part, it now fell upon the whole. The Israelites were not destroyed. Many of them might live to a good age. But the verdict "entrance forbidden" had been handed down, and this generation would never know anything but a nomadic life. The children, too, had to be nomads until their parents perished (Num. 14:33). Israel had become a pilgrim people with no more reason for hope.

Yet the judgment did not apply to the younger generation. A sharp line was drawn between the old Israel and the new, between those who were adults and those who were minors at the time of the rejection of the report of the scouts (Num. 14:22ff.). The point of the distinction is clear. The first Israel rebelled against the Lord's command. This Israel, then, would not enter the land of its rest. Rebels cannot enter the promised land. Yet God did not withdraw his promise. The land that he had pledged to the Israel of the parents he would give to their children. The *old* Israel would have no place in the land. A *new* Israel, a people renewed by the Lord, would enter into the patrimony.

The story of the passing of one Israel and the rise of another is one of the strangest in the wilderness witness. As we are told in Josh. 5:6-8, "the Israelites travelled in the wilderness for forty years, until the whole nation . . . had passed away," but then "the whole nation" was circumcised with Joshua. Two different nations are mentioned. The one dies, the other lives. The one stays outside the land, the other enters it. Yet the two nations are both Israel: disobedient Israel on the one side, believing Israel on the other; one generation the instrument of wrath, the other the instrument of mercy.

In fact, then, the pilgrim people of God does have hope. It *will* enter into its rest. But it must first die and then be born anew. This is the message of the change of generations. Yet the death of the old Israel and the birth of the new are not just a timeless call to renewal. They are historical events. Because of the radical renewal, the pilgrim people of the desert still had a real future. It became strong in the midst of want.

The change of generations and the renewal of Israel are reflected also in the transfer of leadership from Moses to Joshua. Moses was buried "in the land of Moab," "in a valley in Moab opposite Beth-peor" (Deut. 34:6; cf. 3:29). He was obviously not allowed to enter the promised land. This was his own fault (Num. 20:1-13). When Aaron, who also sinned at Meribah, died soon afterward (Num. 20:22ff.), Moses was told that he would die shortly after his brother (27:12ff.). Joshua then replaced him as head of the community, i.e., as the man who would receive and transmit the Lord's commands (Num. 27:16-21; Deut. 34:9). Joshua, "the servant of the Lord," would enter the land of rest.

The replacement of Moses by Joshua stands related to the replacement of one generation by another. Moses had to die because he was under God's wrath with all his generation. Joshua could enter as the forerunner of the new Israel. Why did they have such different fates? Moses bore the wrath of God, not merely for himself, but "because of you" (Deut. 3:26; cf. 1:37). It pleased God to count him among the generation of the old Israel. He stood together with them under the divine anger. He shared their fate in solidarity with them. Joshua instead received mercy. This was not in virtue of his merits. Even in the incident of the scouts Caleb played the leading part (Deut. 1:19-46). God had mercy on Joshua by his own decision (Exod. 33:19). Here again, then, we stand before the mystery of the wisdom of God as he set one person to be the instrument of his wrath and another the instrument of his mercy. Moses and Joshua, the two servants of the Lord, were the vanguard of the pilgrim people. In their complementary roles and service for this people they foreshadowed another servant of the Lord who would one day accomplish by his death and resurrection what Moses humbly suffered and Joshua triumphantly obtained.

c. Pilgrims Even in Canaan

Israel was a pilgrim people on its way. It had not yet reached its destination. Did this truth apply to Israel only on its journey from Egypt to Canaan? Many texts of scripture state that this manner of living did not totally end with the occupation of the promised land. From one standpoint Israel always remained a pilgrim people, always short of its destination, always expecting a blissful future. We can understand this point of view when we remember Israel's history as an exiled and scattered people which felt again both its pressing poverty and its hidden strength. Strangely, however, Israel still felt itself to be in some ways a pilgrim people even when it had settled in the promised land.

In Jeremiah's days, when the northern kingdom of Israel had collapsed and Judah was under increasing pressure from Nebuchadnezzar, the Rechabites stood out in Israel, living among the people yet not conforming to the customary lifestyle. The Rechabites descended from the Kenites, who were vagrants and wanderers on earth (1 Chron. 2:55). Their forefather Jonadab had commanded them: "You shall never drink wine. . . . You shall not build houses or sow seed or plant vineyards. . . . Instead you shall remain tent-dwellers all your lives, so that you may live long in the land where you are sojourners" (Jer. 35:6-7). What was Jonadab's point? He was certainly not denying the general right of Israel to enjoy the produce of Canaan. By making a vow for himself and his family to live only as sojourners in the land that God had given Israel as a patrimony, he was setting up a sign to remind Israel of its pilgrim status, which was now, as it were, submerged, but which might reemerge at any time. When we note the attitude of the people of Judah to the Rechabites, we see how much it needed this sign. Though the Rechabites were few in number, the rest regarded their lifestyle as a threat to the established bourgeois life of the people at large.

The sermons of Deuteronomy also bear witness to the fact that even when it settled in Canaan Israel would still be a pilgrim people. Its entry into the land did not mean entry into the place of rest (12:9; 25:19). It did not really possess its patrimony. It would have to become a people of children again, as in the days of Joshua, leaving the dead behind, and entering on the new life that was ahead (cf. 30:15-20).

When Israel settled in the land, it also celebrated holy days at special times (Exod. 23:14-17; 34:22-23; Lev. 23; Deut. 16:1-17). The festivals might be agrarian by nature, but Israel used them to worship God and to acknowledge his great deeds in the creation of the world and the liberation of his people. The community, however, did not merely remember past events. It actually went back in time and shared in them. It, too, went out of Egypt (cf. the "our" of Exod. 12:27). It, too, was present at Sinai (Deut. 5:3, 22). It, too, wandered through the wilderness. This is why Ps. 95:8 could issue the challenge: "Harden not your hearts, as at Meribah, as on the day at Massah in the wilderness" (RSV). The community had settled already in the place of its rest, but it was still "the people of his pasture, and the sheep of his hand," and it had not yet entered fully into its rest (95:7, 11).

By chance or intentionally the important wilderness word $m^enûhāh$ ("rest") was also used several times in connection with the sabbath. The seventh day of each week was not only to be sanctified negatively in the sense "to stop" (šābat), i.e., to stop working, but also positively in the sense "to rest," to enjoy peace, quietness, and security (cf. the positive term nûah in Exod. 20:11; 23:12; Deut. 5:14). The sabbath rest corresponded to rest in the land that God would grant. Sanctifying the day of rest went hand in hand with the land of rest. Neglecting the day of rest could easily lead to losing the place of rest. As a pilgrim people Israel was on the way to the place of rest that God had promised. It would finally enter it. But even in Canaan it was still on its way. For six days each week it would work and struggle. But it would also be looking ahead to the promised rest of the seventh day. By this sign, too, the people of God remembered its lasting character as a pilgrim people.

A familiar NT passage (Heb. 4:1-11) shows that even the NT people of God, gathered from Jews and all nations, lives on earth as a pilgrim people. But its hope of entering the place of rest is even more secure. For its trust is in Jesus, the servant of the Lord, who finally accomplished what both Moses and Joshua could only prefigure.

Chapter V

God Revealed Himself at Sinai

1. The Witness of Scripture

An article of Israel's faith, and the nucleus of its witness to God's saving acts, is that the Lord himself was present on his mountain in the wilderness and that he shaped a unique and everlasting relation between himself and his people. On Mt. Sinai (or Horeb) God concluded a covenant with Israel, revealed his law, and established Israel's worship as a way of forgiveness of sins. He did so through his servant Moses as an intermediary.

"THOU DIDST DESCEND upon Mount Sinai and speak with them from heaven" (Neh. 9:13). This statement tells us that wonderful events took place on Mt. Sinai. God revealed himself there. This revelation was of fundamental importance, for in it God fully disclosed his permanently authoritative Word and will. On Sinai or Horeb, the mountain of God, he gave his people "right judgements and true laws, and statutes and commandments which were good."

We thus come to a new topic in Israel's witness, the revelation on Mt. Sinai. The events that took place on the summit and at the foot of this mountain are so important that they call for serious study. God revealed himself, of course, in and through all his wonderful acts: the electing of the fathers, the bringing of his people out of Egypt, and his leading of this people through the wilderness. On Sinai, however, he himself appeared and revealed his will. The revelation itself was his act.

Unlike those that precede, this topic does not primarily take the form of stories but of laws, ordinances, statements, commandments, exhortations, and explanations. These cannot be "told"; they have to be "taught."

The second half of Exodus and most of Leviticus, Numbers, and Deuteronomy deal with the Sinai revelation, and the bulk of the material consists of laws and expositions. Thus we have the Ten Commandments in Exod. 20:1-17, the covenant law in 20:22–23:33, commandments relating to the tabernacle and priesthood in chs. 25–31, the so-called second decalogue in 34:10-26, ordinances relating to sacrifice in Lev. 1–7, laws of purification in chs. 11–15, the law of holiness in chs. 17–26, laws relating to special offerings in ch. 27, various ordinances in Num. 3–6 and 8:1ff., and the laws of Sinai as promulgated in Moab in Deut. 4:44–30:20.

Yet the Sinai material did not consist of laws alone. The laws came in a package. Before and after them were accounts of the way in which the revelation came about and the laws were received and promulgated. The legal texts contain references to the revelation of the laws concerned. For the OT, the Sinai revelation was an event. It was God's act.

The event is narrated only briefly and with much repetition in Exod. 19:1-25; 20:1, 18-21; 24:1-18; and Deut. 5:2-5, 22-33. Complementary events accompanied the main event. The incident of the golden calf was the occasion of the second revelation of the law (Exod. 32–34; Deut. 9:7–10:11). The ordination of the priests introduced the ritual laws (Lev. 8–10). The tribal offerings for the tabernacle played a similar role (Num. 7). We might also refer to the construction of the holy tent (Exod. 35–41) and the first celebration of the atonement ceremony (Lev. 16). Closely related to the mountain, though not strictly to the revelation, were the call of Moses (Exod. 3:1-4, 17), Jethro's visit (ch. 18), and later in Israel's history the pilgrimage of the prophet Elijah (1 Kgs. 19:1-18). As already noted, the holy tent stood in close relation to Israel's desert wandering.

Although it is true that God's laws cannot be told but have to be taught, it is also true that the static legal material is handed down to us in a frame of dynamic stories, so that the laws themselves take on a narrative character. The laws do not stand alone. They belong to the event of God's meeting with his people.

God spoke in order to make known his will. He did so at a specific time and place and before known witnesses. The Sinai revelation was a historical event. Yet it is not enough to say merely that the law was revealed. The revelation of the law can be understood only in connection with other events at Sinai. The Lord met his people there. He came down. He manifested his presence in a cloud. The Israelites were told to sanctify themselves and to assemble at the sound of trumpets. The Lord spoke to them through his intermediary Moses. The encounter ended with the offering of sacrifices and a common meal (Exod. 19; 20; 24). A full service of worship took place which would be a model for worship in every age. The meeting at Sinai laid the foundation for all further meetings. The Lord revealed himself there as the

"God of the Israelites" and met the people of Israel as "the people of the Lord." He awakened there a willingness on the part of the people to accept their vocation and to live according to the covenant that he made with them. All this is signified by the Sinai event.

As part of his encounter with the people the Lord gave the Torah. It is a misunderstanding to think of the Torah merely as a book of laws. It was the instrument by means of which God carried out his plan to turn Israel into his people and to preserve it in its new status. Two-thirds of the Sinai material report God's words, but through his words God works.

The Sinai revelation was the rock on which Israel stood. It was its birth as the people of God. It was thus an object of faith and praise in every generation. As such it stands alongside the other topics that deal with the foundation of Israel's existence: the fathers, the exodus, the wilderness. Since all these topics witness to the very beginning of Israel's life as God's people, it is hard to say which was the more decisive, or when and where Israel actually came into existence. Each topic deals with the true origin of Israel, but from a different angle.

The Sinai topic occupies a strange position relative to the others. From one standpoint none of the others is as important. The first five books of the OT could be called "The Book of the Torah." In this book Sinai has a key position, and the gift of the Torah is the climax or core of all God's acts. This book was the first to be received as holy scripture. When Jeremiah contrasted God's coming new covenant with the old covenant, he was obviously referring to the Sinai covenant (Jer. 31:31-34). The NT Epistles understand the Sinai event as the very heart of God's revelation to Israel (2 Cor. 3; cf. Matt. 5–7).

Israel became the Lord's people through the covenant that God made with it at Sinai. If the covenant had been made only at Sinai, the Sinai revelation would obviously be the basic OT topic. The liberation from Egypt and the initial leading in the wilderness would be with a view to bringing the people to Sinai. The leading to Canaan and the gift of the land would be on the basis of the Sinai covenant. But other parts of the OT witness warn us against too hastily drawing this kind of conclusion.

Even in the Book of the Torah two creedal passages (Deut. 26:5-9; 6:21b-23) confess the election of the fathers, the liberation from Egypt, and the gift of Canaan, but do not mention at all the event at Sinai. In the creed in Josh. 24:2-13, too, we look in vain for the Sinai revelation. The same is true when we turn to the confession in Jer. 32:17-23a or the short creeds in Amos 2:10, Judg. 6:8b-10, 1 Sam. 12:8, and Jer. 2:6-7. Sinai is missing again in the extolling of God's acts of old in Pss. 78, 105, 111, 114, 135, and 136. The witness of the prophets is even more astonishing. Though they would seem to be challenging the people for breaking the laws that God gave at Sinai, the prophets hardly ever refer specifically to Sinai. Amos, Hosea, and Isaiah totally ignore it. Jeremiah (31:31ff.) and Ezekiel (20:11) allude to it but do not specifically mention Sinai. Of the OT creeds, that in Neh. 9 alone actually has the order of the Book of the Torah. Oddly enough, even the NT creeds do not refer to Sinai. In Acts 7:38 we read of the living utterances that Moses received, but in Acts 13 there is no reference to the Sinai event.

We thus face two diverging facts. On the one hand, the Sinai topic plays a dominant role. On the other, it is almost completely absent from Israel's confessions of faith and hymns of praise. The Sinai topic obviously determines Israel's understanding of its existence no less and perhaps even more than the other topics. Yet it cannot be placed on the same level as the others. The Sinai revelation is an "extraordinary" act of God.

Three main aspects of the Sinai revelation call for attention. First, God concluded a covenant with Israel. Second, he gave his laws to his people. Third, he established a mode by which his people's sins could be atoned. The role of Moses also calls for discussion, but it will be dealt with in the section on the giving of the laws.

2. God Concluded His Covenant with Israel

In its account of the Sinai event the OT records a solemn ceremony at which God acted among his people and concluded a covenant with them. (a) He revealed himself in his glory as the God of Israel. (b) He spoke and revealed his will in the form of laws to shape the life of his people. (c) He aroused Israel to willing acceptance of its status and responsibility as his people.

AT SINAI GOD CREATED ISRAEL and made it his people. He had chosen Abraham, Isaac, and Jacob. He had freed the people from oppression. He had carried them thus far through the desert. Now he concluded an eternal covenant with them. Here is where we begin.

God concluded a covenant or an alliance with the people. Human groups, when entering into relations with one another, have always made covenants, alliances, or agreements to establish orderly and safe relations. God used this legal form to fulfil his plan for humanity when he made a covenant with Abraham. In private and public, law covenants are drawn up to regulate relations between those with common interests. When God made a covenant, however, he acted "from above." He for his part did not need us, but we have absolute need of him, for without him his creatures cannot live. It was of his own free will and purpose that God concluded his covenant. It pleased him to choose one nation from among all nations. He wanted Israel consciously to become his people and to live in communion with him before all neighboring nations.

The covenant that God made with Israel differs widely from all private or public human covenants. Strictly speaking, we cannot compare it with any other. It is as incomparable as all God's acts. Israel itself realized that God's covenant with it had a unique character and was to be understood as a wonder. The events at Sinai could be told, but the mystery behind them could not be explained. It could be only acknowledged in awe and astonishment that God had been pleased to make this covenant and thus to assemble Israel as his people from generation to generation.

In making a covenant with Israel, God acted toward his people. But he now acted in a different way. He acted in a ceremony, in a service of worship. He himself was the main actor. He led the service. The congregation that assembled at his call played a subsidiary role. God himself set it in motion to participate willingly in a ceremony that took place by God's own will and power.

The service of worship at which the covenant was concluded stands in total contrast to what religions normally consider to be proper worship. Normally the worshipers take the initiative. They come together, sanctify themselves, offer prayers and praises, bring sacrifices, and do whatever else belongs to the worship of gods or spirits. Normally the divinity is expected to respond to the human initiative. The god's help or blessing is sought. Prayers are made in the hope that the god will come to grant what is expected or to receive what is offered. The order of the covenant service, however, differed completely. God himself took the initiative. He himself acted. At first, Israel could not even respond. They could not yet act as the people of God before God made his covenant with them.

The Sinai ceremony at the concluding of the covenant had three main parts. First, God manifested himself and made his presence felt. Second, God spoke and made known his intention to make a covenant. Third, God roused his people to accept his plan and to fulfil their own role in the covenant. All three parts are equally important. The first and third parts describe the partners who enter into the covenant, the second states the conditions.

From the OT material we might gather that a more elaborate order was in fact followed. First came (1) the preamble in which God introduced himself by name and declared his intention to conclude the covenant. Then followed (2) a historical introduction recalling the facts that led to the making of the covenant and validating God's right to make it. Next came (3) the declaration of principle in which God stated his will that the people should enter into communion with him and become his partner as a people

[119]

dedicated to God and obeying him. (4) Special instructions then expounded the laws, ordinances, and prohibitions that followed from the covenant as described in the declaration of principle. (5) By an oath the assembly then promised to conform to the instructions. Customarily a witness would be needed, which might take the form of a stone inscription (cf. the description of the tablets of the law as tokens). At the end came (6) a blessing and a curse to remind the people of the benefits that accrue to those who keep the covenant and the disasters that threaten those who break it.

An order of this kind seems to have been followed at covenant ceremonies when the rulers of mighty kingdoms like Sumer, Hatti, or Egypt made alliances with satellite states. If so, what took place at Sinai accorded with familiar patterns as regards its structure. At the same time, it must be stressed that in the records we do not have more than hints of this contemporary pattern, helpful though the various elements may be for an understanding of the Sinai event.

The Sinai covenant was obviously not the only one that God made with his people. God had already concluded a covenant with the fathers, especially with Abraham. He would later make a covenant with Israel when it conquered Canaan (Josh. 24). Is it necessary or even possible for an "everlasting" covenant to be constantly renewed? Fundamentally Israel can only once become God's people, yet the stories of its birth as such relate this to different episodes. The episodes do not at root involve different events. Basically there is only the one event of the conclusion of the unique covenant and the once-for-all birth of Israel as the Lord's own people. The birth, however, took place over a period of time. The one covenant applied in different ways to the fathers, to liberated Israel, and later to Israel in the land of promise. Different aspects of Israel's beginning had thus to be described, and the one covenant called for reaffirmations at the successive stages.

a. God Revealed His Glory

The first main element in the covenant liturgy is God's self-revelation. God himself came and made his presence felt with a view to concluding the covenant. Theophany is the usual word for this divine coming and self-manifestation. As we have seen, it pleased God to be near his people. He was totally and really present with it at decisive moments. He came, or came down, to play a part in its history. His coming or theophany, then, opened the ceremony. It was also the heart of the ceremony and its culmination. God himself was Lord of the ceremony. It was he who took the initiative. In every Sinai record, the crux is that the Lord appeared.

From one standpoint it could be said that the Lord was already on Mt. Sinai (cf. Gen. 28:16; Exod. 3). Thus when the Israelites had pitched their tents before the mountain, Moses "went up to God" (Exod. 19:3 RSV), who had brought him there to himself (v. 4). Moses, Aaron, Nadab, and Abihu, with the seventy elders, were all called upon to "come up to the Lord," though Moses alone was to come near (Exod. 24:1-2, 9-12). Already present on Sinai, God called them to a meeting with himself.

From another standpoint, however, the Lord came down on Mt. Sinai. It was not his permanent home. He "will descend upon Mount Sinai in the sight of all the people" (Exod. 19:11; cf. v. 20). As he stated, "I am now coming to you in a thick cloud, so that I may speak to you in the hearing of the people" (v. 9). Mt. Sinai was smoking because the Lord had "descended upon it in fire" (v. 18 RSV; cf. the flaming torch of Gen. 15:17 and the burning bush of Exod. 3:2). "He let you see his great fire, and out of the fire you heard his words" (Deut. 4:35-36).

Naturally, God was not literally in the cloud or fire any more than he was literally on the mountain. The cloud and fire were signs of his presence. Nor were they the only signs. We read also that "the whole mountain quaked greatly" (RSV), that "there were peals of thunder and flashes of lightning, dense cloud . . . and a loud trumpet blast" that even "grew ever louder" (Exod. 19:16, 18-19; cf. 1 Kgs. 19:11-12; Ps. 50:3 RSV; 97:2-5 RSV). All these phenomena, which remind us of a volcanic eruption, were signs of God's presence, as was also in its own way the warning that the people should not touch the mountain lest they be "stoned or shot dead" (Exod. 19:13).

Whether Moses went up to the Lord or the Lord descended, whether the signs were cloud and fire or volcanic phenomena, the essential thing was the mystery of the divine presence. Why should God want to be present in the midst of a people that was unworthy to meet him and could not stand before him?

On the one side, the theophany implies rejection of the people that had pitched its tents before the mountain. All the signs of God's presence expressed his wrath and enmity. Catastrophe threatened the people. A dangerous eruption was God's reaction to those who had come to adore him in solemn worship and with pious praises, prayers, and offerings. Was this really the Lord, the God of Israel, whom the people knew and in whom it had put its trust? Or was it a mountain-god, a wilderness demon, a dangerous force, that "met Moses, meaning to kill him" (Exod. 4:24)? No, it was the Lord who had already manifested himself as Israel's God. Throughout all ages Israel would know God as the one who draws near to his people but who also remains distant, foreign, terrible, and holy.

A mysterious feature among the signs was the sounding trumpet. The trumpet was usually sounded either to warn the people in time of war or to request the Lord's presence at the celebration of holy days (Num. 10:1-10). At Sinai, however, we do not read that the Israelites blew the trumpet. The sounding of the trumpet seems rather to be a sign of the advent of the Lord in power, as at the second coming of Christ (cf. Matt. 24:31; 1 Thess. 4:15, 17; 1 Cor. 15:52; cf. also the seven trumpets of Rev. 8–11).

Other elements in the Sinai account also suggest rejection. Thus Moses was to sanctify the mountain by putting barriers around it to keep the people at a distance (Exod. 19:12-13, 21-23). The people must not "force their way through to the Lord to see him." The Israelites had also to purify themselves before coming to the Lord, showing their readiness by washing their clothes and refraining from sexual intercourse (19:10, 14, 15, 22). The preparations had all to be made in two days, for the tremendous event of God's coming would take place at dawn on the third day. On that day, "when the ram's horn sounds, they may go up the mountain" (19:13c).

Could they really go up to the Lord? Had the barrier of death been torn down? Was their impurity cleansed? Had a meeting become possible? In fact only the elders, with Moses, Aaron, Nadab, and Abihu, were allowed to go, and within this group Moses was the only one who was allowed to go on every occasion (19:3, etc.), once with Aaron (19:24) and once with Joshua (24:13). As to the people at large, the order is that they "shall not come up with him" (24:2 RSV).

The negative side of God's presence among his people implies a positive side as well. If God rejected an impure and corrupt people (Exod. 32:7), he also came to receive them. He rejected all, but he also accepted all. The trumpet sounded wrath and destruction, but it also blew to announce the opening of a ceremony at which the covenant would be concluded. Moses went down to warn the people (Exod. 19:14, 21, 24; 32:15), but he also went down to declare God's Word to them (19:7ff., 25; 24:3; 34:32). The theophany, then, was the opening scene in the drama of the making of the covenant. It enclosed the core of the covenant within itself. For the content of the covenant, however, we must turn to the revelation of the Word that Moses proclaimed.

b. God Proclaimed His Law

The revelation of God's Word is the second main element in the conclusion of the covenant. Fundamentally the covenant became a fact when it pleased God to come and be present among his people. In so doing he acted, appeared, and manifested himself as Israel's God who had chosen this people as his own and was treating it as such. But he had still to complete his action. He did so in the form of his Word. The proclaiming of the Word was not another action but another aspect of the same action. God had concluded the covenant with his presence, but the event of his presence entailed a revelation in the form of words. The presence did not conclude the covenant without the words. The words were more than exposition of the covenant. Both presence and words were act or event. God concluded his covenant by both.

As a main element in the covenant ceremony, the revelation of God's Word was not just the promulgation of law. It included also the preamble, the historical introduction, the declaration of principle, the explanation, and the blessing and curse. It was not simply a part of the ceremony, but a dimension of it. The whole conclusion of the covenant had the character of revelation of God's Word. The revealed word in its totality has thus to be understood in its relation to the conclusion of the covenant.

God's Word at Sinai aimed at the conclusion of the covenant with Israel, and in fact achieved it. If the Word consisted of the promulgation of laws, commandments, ordinances, and admonitions, these had here an authority and creative power far beyond anything that they normally have.

(1) In speaking his Word, God revealed himself. The Lord was the acting subject. He was now concluding the covenant by means of words as he had already done so by the theophany with its visible, audible, and palpable signs. He was not just fulfilling a legal requirement in revealing himself. He was establishing a hitherto nonexistent fact. The formula "I am the Lord" by which God usually introduced himself in the relevant texts implies all that God did on behalf of his chosen people.

The self-introduction formula often stands in sentences that form a preamble to important texts. The Ten Commandments begin: "God spoke, and these were his words: I am the Lord your God" (Exod. 20:1-2; cf. Deut. 5:6). The decisive words at the conclusion of the Shechem covenant are introduced thus: "This is the word of the Lord the God of Israel," and the people answered: "The Lord our God we will worship and his voice we will obey" (Josh. 24:2, 24; cf. Ps. 50:7; 81:10-11). The words "I am the Lord your God" also introduce the important chapters 18–19 in the Holiness Code of Leviticus, and similar formulas recur throughout the chapters (18:2, 5, 6, 19, 30; 19:3, 4, 10, 12, 14, 16, 18, 25, 28, 30, 31, 34, 36, 37). By thus revealing himself, God announced his name as a partner in the covenant.

In this revelation God also acted by acknowledging his people: "I am the Lord *your* God," i.e., the God of Israel. God made the covenant in order "to be your God" (Gen. 17:7-8; cf. Exod. 6:6; Ezek. 20:5). In stating who he is, God also proclaimed himself Israel's God and thus made Israel his people. He acted by speaking these words.

By revealing his name God also revealed his attributes as "a god compassionate and gracious, long-suffering, ever constant and true" (Exod. 34:6), as the "Jealous God" (34:14), as "righteous in his acts" (Ps. 103:6), as "holy" (Lev. 19:2) and "inspiring awe" (Ps. 111:9). The attributes are listed in order that we might know God's character. He did not simply possess these attributes. They tell us how he acts. He put the attributes into practice by concluding the covenant. Declaring who and how he is, he created new facts.

Furthermore, in making the covenant with Israel God did not simply reveal his name. He also reminded his people of the prehistory, of the great deeds that he had already done on their behalf. After the words "I am the Lord your God" at the beginning of the Decalogue, we read: "who brought you out of Egypt, out of the land of slavery" (Exod. 20:2; Deut. 5:6). Similar summary statements may be found in Exod. 19:4; Josh. 24:2-13; Deut. 8:2-10; Lev. 11:45; 19:36. Concluding the covenant with Israel, God did not act arbitrarily. He followed his own logic. He had already done great things for this people: the election of the fathers, the liberation from Egypt, their preservation in the wilderness, the promise of the land. These acts belonged to past history, but their full validity came to light when God revealed himself with his name and attributes at the conclusion of the covenant.

(2) God spoke and revealed his will. Most of the words at Sinai have the form of laws and ordinances. The revelation of the covenant law is the second main aspect of God's speaking on Mt. Sinai. The form, content, and intention of these laws will call for notice later. We must now consider them as God's Word at the conclusion of the covenant.

As God acted in revealing his name, he also acted through the Word by which he gave his laws. The laws were not just conditions under which God was ready to conclude a covenant if the people accepted them. God is so mighty that in revealing his will in the form of laws he also accomplished his will. The promulgation of the laws is another aspect of the divine action. With it he laid the foundation on which Israel would stand as the covenant people.

"The covenant I make with you and with Israel is in these words" (Exod. 34:27). "Behold the blood of the covenant which the Lord has made with you in accordance with all these words" (24:8 RSV). "These words" were obviously the instrument by which God acted, and the instrument was so important that the whole action was summarized in it. The Hebrew word for "covenant" *(berît)* is sometimes used in the sense of "covenant laws" (cf. Hos. 8:1; Ps. 50:16; 78:10; Deut. 33:9; Exod. 31:16). To "keep my covenant" (Exod. 19:5) means the same as to "listen to my word" or to "obey my laws," and the same applies to expressions like "the tablets of the covenant" (Deut. 9:9), "the Ark of the Covenant" (Num. 10:33), "the book of the covenant" (Exod. 24:7), and "the words of the covenant" (Exod. 34:28; Deut. 29:8; Jer. 11:2).

In revealing his laws God concluded the covenant, and in concluding the covenant he revealed his laws. The two things are inseparable. The fact that the revealing of God's will is an act comes out clearly in the words of Sinai, which have the character of a declaration of principle. By the covenant God adopted Israel as his people. This nation or ethnic group became the people of the Lord. They thus had access to a new reality. God spoke and addressed Israel. He did not first reveal his name and will and laws, and then invite or summon Israel to enter into a covenant with him on that basis. Being pleased to call himself the God of Israel, God was pleased to make of Israel his own people. He took a unilateral action in adopting Israel as his people. He did it unconditionally because it pleased him to do it. He said to Lo-ammi (not my people): "You are my people" (Hos. 2:23).

Naturally, this unilateral decision did not leave Israel passive. When God decides, we must decide too. God's words call us again and again to make a decision and to act accordingly. The Sinai revelation challenged Israel to make up its mind. At times, then, we almost have the impression that the concluding of the covenant depended on Israel's attitude: "If only you will now listen to me and keep my covenant, then out of all peoples you shall become my special possession" (Exod. 19:5; cf. Deut. 11:13-15, 22-24; 28:1-14).

Nevertheless, important though the human attitude may be, God never waits for it, or lets the making of the covenant depend upon it. His decision to adopt Israel came first. On this basis Israel *could* make up its mind. "Here and now I make a covenant. . . . Observe all I command you this day" (Exod. 34:10-11). "The covenant is to constitute you his people this day" (Deut. 29:13). Israel was to be "my kingdom of priests, my holy nation" (Exod. 19:6), God's "special possession" (Deut. 7:6), the object of his unique care (Amos 3:2). This fact did not rest primarily on a common agreement, but on God's own decision.

God's Word in the forms of laws and ordinances not only revealed God's will but also began to fulfil it. Israel was not simply told to become the Lord's people, a "holy nation" (Exod. 19:6; cf. Jer. 2:3), liberated from oppression to be a "kingdom of priests" (Exod. 19:6). God's Word freely elevated Israel to this status. Each of the laws and ordinances contributed to the realization of God's will for his people.

Since God wanted Israel to be "his special possession," he made it his people by his Word in the form of laws and ordinances, many of which singled out Israel and so marked it that the nations could recognize it to be the Lord's people and Israel could see itself as such.

Since God wanted Israel to be a "holy people," he purified and sanctified it by his Word in the form of laws and ordinances, many of which aimed at Israel's holiness, offered a definition of purity, and had the power to sanctify the people.

Since God wanted Israel to be free, he liberated it by his Word in the form of laws and ordinances, many of which were instruments of liberation and had the power to defend Israel's freedom against the forces of physical and spiritual oppression and slavery.

Since God wanted Israel to be a united people among the nations, worshiping the Lord as the only God, he challenged and moved it to unity by the Word in the form of laws and ordinances, many of which aimed at gathering the people together to worship the Lord.

The aim, content, and authority of the Sinai laws allow us to say that their gift was legitimately Israel's pride. Israel had no less reason to praise God for giving it his laws than for his other mighty deeds. This fact helps us to understand why Israel never regarded the Torah as a constant burden but viewed it as "good news" upon which it should meditate day and night (Ps. 1:2). By his Word in this form God invited his people to live in communion with himself and to share in his uniqueness, his authority, his holiness, his freedom, and his dedication and fidelity to all his creatures.

The evangelical aspect of the Torah is often missed. Many view the law as an exacting burden that God laid on his people. It should be seen instead as God's perfect gift, not merely because its form and content are good, but because it shaped Israel into the Lord's own people. God built up Israel as his people by his Word in the Torah.

(3) God spoke and addressed the people with counsel, teaching, and admonition. If it is undeniable that the revelation reached its climax with the promulgation of the law, other aspects of the promulgation call for notice in addition to the laws and ordinances. Divine words introduced, accompanied, and concluded the revelation of the actual laws and ordinances.

Two misunderstandings must be avoided. First, we are not to see the exhortations as a mere frame for the laws. They are really part of the revelation. They display its very heart. Second, we are not to see the exhortations as additions, as if the laws alone were the original revelation. The Word of God that introduces the laws and comments on them is no less important than the laws themselves.

As already noted, God carried out his will through his Word in the form of laws. The execution of his will was the main point of the exhortations that accompanied the laws. He had not yet fulfilled his will for Israel so long as the people that he had adopted for holiness and freedom remained passive. The people had to be motivated. They had to be made willing. They had to be challenged and set going. They had to accept God's gift freely. They had to be ready to enter of their own volition into the covenant that God had made with them. The Word that went along with the law spoke to the heart of the people (Hos. 2:14).

Israel was reminded time and again that it must behave in accordance with the new status that God had given it. The Lord had already revealed himself as Israel's God. He had already adopted Israel as his people. He now summoned them to awareness of the implications of his wonderful gift. "If only you will now listen to me" is how the summons ran in Exod. 19:5. This saying has a conditional form, but we are to construe it as an invitation and a challenge (cf. Ps. 81:8; Exod. 34:11). Parallel exhortations often begin with the words "But now" or "Now therefore": "Now therefore fear the Lord . . ." (Josh. 24:14 RSV); "Hold the Lord in awe then . . ." (Josh. 24:14 NEB); "O that today you would hearken to his voice" (Ps. 95:7 RSV). The call follows directly upon the confession: "For he is our God, and we are the people of his pasture" (Ps. 95:7 RSV). Exhortations of this type abound in Deuteronomy (cf. 7:6, 11), and we might also refer to Lev. 18:4-5 (RSV): "I am the Lord your God. You shall therefore keep my statutes and my ordinances."

If the declaration of principle assumed that Israel would be ready to listen to the Lord and obey him on the basis of the covenant, the blessing and curse confronted all Israelites with their own responsibility. They had to make their own decision in the light of what God had already done for them. The Lord had already declared: "I am your God." He had already adopted them as his people and given them his law. They now had to acknowledge his election. They now had to follow up on what he himself had done. They did not have to take the initiative. As Jesus would later say to his disciples: "You did not choose me: I chose you" (John 15:16). But they did have to have their own share in the fulfilment of God's choice: "Choose here and now whom you will worship" (Josh. 24:15). The decision they had to make was heavy with consequences. Before them stood blessing and curse, life and death (Deut. 27:15). This challenge was the point of the element in the covenant service that closed the ceremony.

As a companion to the laws, this Word of God moved Israel toward its free decision to enter into the covenant relation. God used different means to achieve this ultimate goal. He invited, solicited, wooed, and coaxed. He also demanded, required, claimed, and threatened. Yet Israel's God did not really need to induce with blessings or compel with threats. Had he not adopted Israel as his people? Had he not already declared himself to be its God? He had, in fact, already decided upon the covenant. The only missing feature was the arousing of Israel to take up God's Word and to say for itself: The Lord is our God and we are his people (cf. Ps. 100:3). Israel had to be ready to repeat the blessing and rejoice in the full communion of the two covenant partners. But it also had to be willing to repeat the curse and to recognize that God hates all who break the covenant and deny communion. It had to acknowledge its new status by sharing the Lord's zeal which pours down blessing when love is answered but curse when holiness is threatened. The will of God was fulfilled herewith. God's Word had power to build up the community. This is the witness of Sinai, as of all the OT.

c. God Awakened Israel's Readiness

Finally, Israel declared its readiness to enter into the covenantal relation and took an oath upon the covenant. The third main part of the ceremony stressed the element of human participation in the making of the covenant. Here too, of course, God was the main actor. He did not stand back and wait for Israel to act. His Word moved the hearts of the Israelites to make them ready to share fellowship with God. The Word reached its goal. Israel's action showed its power (cf. Isa. 55:11).

As we look at Israel's part, we see that it did not come only at the end of the ceremony. Israel participated at every point. It prepared itself for the Lord's coming. It was involved in the promulgation of the laws. It swore an oath and offered sacrifices. Its action was parallel throughout to God's action. Yet because its answer depended totally on God's Word and deed, we can consider it only at the end. God spoke first, then Israel answered. God called first, then Israel was moved to reply.

To see human action as the consequence of God's action is not to deny that the people had to make a free choice. They did not echo or repeat automatically what God told them. Falling in with God's decision, they made their own voluntary decision. Later generations might not be able to extol this decision as an act of moral heroism, but they could rightly praise the Lord who at Sinai gave the people the freedom to decide for him. If the Sinai generation had only a limited part in the making of the covenant, it certainly played that part.

First, it spoke "all the words of the covenant" after God. The people listened to the words, kept silence (Deut. 7:9), then opened their ears and hearts—a miracle indeed for a people of "fat heart" and "deaf ears" (Isa. 6:10 CB). By themselves speaking the words of the covenant, the Israelites showed that they had truly and wonderfully heard God's words and made them their own words. They thus became speakers for God in the world, his witnesses. Saying "Amen" to God's liberating and sanctifying Word, Israel began to live as the Lord's own people.

According to the accounts in Exod. 19:7-8 and 24:3, the people expressed its agreement by acclamation: "The people all answered together"; "The whole people answered with one voice." In the case of the blessings and curses, however, half the tribes were set on Mt. Gerizim and half on Mt. Ebal, the former pronouncing the blessings, the latter the curses (preserved in Deut. 27:15-26). In the initial reading Moses and the priests, Moses and the elders, and Moses alone took the lead (cf. Deut. 27:1, 9-10), as Joshua would later do at Shechem (Josh. 8:34-35; 24:25). Yet when prominence is given to Moses, we have to remember that the role of Moses was simply to represent the people. Indeed, in Deut. 5:23ff. we learn that the tribal heads and the elders asked Moses to "go near and listen to all that the Lord our God says." The whole people had to hear the covenant words, but how could Israel stand before God (Exod. 24:3) and respond to him? Would not mere mortals (RSV "flesh," Deut. 5:26) be swallowed up by the fire of the glory and might of the living God (cf. Josh. 24:19)? Yet God showed his compassion to Moses (Exod. 33:12), and Moses could thus pass on God's words to the people and elicit their own acceptance and repetition.

Second, Israel took part in the making of the covenant by demonstrating in deeds what it had expressed already in words. By various acts Israel stood openly to its decision and clearly bound itself to the covenant. As God backed up his Word by deeds that revealed its meaning, so Israel performed meaningful actions in confirmation of its verbal acceptance of all that God had said.

Thus the Israelites sanctified themselves as the Lord commanded them (Exod. 19:10-11). They had to do this for themselves. They did it first by washing their clothes. Washing clothes is an ordinary necessity of life, but the Israelites did it here as a sign of their readiness for renewal. They were putting off the old life of impurity. They were putting on the new life. They thus arrayed themselves in clean clothes (cf. Gen. 35:2). In this regard they adopted a common sign of spiritual renewal that is found among many peoples, e.g., among Indonesians when they wear new clothes after the month-long Muslim fast is ended.

Israelites also solemnly threw away any idols that were still among them (cf. Gen. 35:4; Josh. 24:33). At Sinai, on the occasion of the golden calf, Moses burnt and ground the calf to powder. The expulsion and destruction of idols symbolized the turning from all the gods of the nations to the Lord as the one God with whom the people was now in everlasting covenant.

The Israelites also "stripped off their ornaments" (Exod. 33:6). Possibly they made of them a voluntary offering in order to express their gratitude for the covenant blessings. Previously they had stripped off their earrings and brought them to Aaron (Exod. 32:3), possibly with a sacrifice of thanksgiving in view.

The people had two days in which to prepare; the ceremony would take place on the third day (cf. Amos 4:4 RSV; Hos. 6:2). Part of the preparation included the renunciation of sexual intercourse (Exod. 19:5) and fasting. Moses himself, the representative of the people, engaged in a prolonged fast: "forty days and forty nights, neither eating nor drinking" (Exod. 34:28).

A sacrifice was also offered. Moses "built an altar at the foot of the mountain" and then sent twelve young men who "sacrificed bulls to the Lord as whole-offerings and shared-offerings" (Exod. 24:4-5). The aim of the sacrifice became apparent when Moses flung half the blood over the altar and half over the people, thereby symbolizing blood kinship between God (represented by the altar) and Israel.

The ceremony reached its climax in a joyful communion meal (cf. Gen. 26:30). Already the elders of Israel who had been invited to come up to Sinai, when they "beheld God, and ate and drank" in his presence (Exod. 24:11

RSV). With the conclusion of the covenant, the time for abstinence had gone and the time of rejoicing had come.

After the ceremony a memorial needed to be set up in confirmation and witness. It was probably for this reason that Moses "put up twelve sacred pillars, one for each of the twelve tribes," near or around the altar at the foot of Mt. Sinai (Exod. 24:4, 8). Lest the repeated words and promises should be forgotten, the laws were also carved on stone tablets and written in a book as well. This was done "in the presence of all the Israelites" (cf. Exod. 24:4; Josh. 8:32; 24:26), thus testifying that the Israelites as a whole had taken the words to heart and intended to follow them, acknowledging God's laws as the foundation of their life as his people. God himself had already written the basic laws (cf. Exod. 24:12; 31:18). As the people repeated the words that God had spoken, so they followed God in giving written form to his laws.

Finally, the Israelites swore an oath expressing their resolve to stand by the covenant decision: "All that the Lord has spoken we will do" (24:7 RSV). In taking an oath before the tablets and the book of the covenant of the law as witnesses (24:7; Deut. 31:26), Israel was doing what was customarily done at the making of agreements (cf. Gen. 26:31). The oath constituted a final act of ratification by which the people bound itself as the Lord's people.

By word and act, therefore, God moved the people to play their part in the making of the covenant in response to his own primary part. In this regard the Sinai ceremony had significance for all succeeding generations in Israel. It was not merely remembered as a past event by which Israel had responded to God and pledged themselves to be his people. It also formed an ongoing liturgy for the renewal of the covenant whenever God's people met to deepen their sense of divine vocation.

3. God Granted the Torah

The divine commandments collected in the books of the Torah draw their meaning from the fact that God used them as instruments to confirm his covenant. (a) The legal material is always set in relation to accounts of God's wonderful deeds. (b) All the laws, though very different in character, command equal respect. (c) God granted all the laws in order to sanctify, liberate, and unite Israel as his own people.

AS NOTED ALREADY, the second main element at Sinai was the promulgation of God's laws. God granted the laws within the covenant ceremony, so that they are an intrinsic part of the conclusion of the covenant. With that in mind, we now turn to the form, content, and aim of the laws. The Holiness Code, one of the legal documents, closes with the words: "These are the statutes, the judgements, and the laws which the Lord established between himself and the Israelites on Mount Sinai through Moses" (Lev. 26:46). No statement could better bring out the relation between the laws and the covenant.

Misunderstandings of the laws make this reminder urgently necessary. The Jews themselves call the laws *Torah*. This word (Heb. *tôrāh*) first meant a single pronouncement of God's will. It could then mean a collection or book of laws. It next came to denote the first five books of scripture which contain God's laws. All scripture finally came to be known as Torah (cf. 1 Cor. 14:21; Rom. 3:19; Gal. 4:21; John 10:34; 15:25; etc.). The implicit danger is that one may then wrongly view the OT as a book of law which the NT, as gospel, has now replaced. The misunderstanding is contrary to the true content of scripture, for the OT contains good news of God's wonderful deeds and the NT is full of clear and authoritative commands, e.g., in the Sermon on the Mount and the apostolic admonitions. To overcome the misconception we need to know the true role and content of the Torah and to gain a proper understanding of the covenant laws.

a. Instrument of God's Action

The legal material of the OT is found in the first five books and makes up about half of their content. But the laws are not presented in isolation. They are integrated into the story of God's making of a covenant with his people. They explain what God is doing by his revelation. They belong integrally to the record of the conclusion, confirmation, or renewal of the covenant.

The so-called covenant law of Exod. 20:2–23:19 begins with the words: "These are the laws you shall set before them" (21:1). It takes its name from the remark that Moses "took the book of the covenant and read it aloud for all the people to hear" (24:7). Exhortations closed the collection (23:20-33).

The so-called law of holiness or Holiness Code (Lev. 17–26) begins in 17:1, or perhaps with "my laws and . . . my institutions" in 18:4, and closes with 26:46. It derives its name from its stress on the holiness of God and the people.

The so-called Deuteronomic law (Deut. 12–26) begins with the words: "These are the statutes and laws that you shall be careful to observe" (12:1) and closes with a similar formulation (26:16). The term "Deuteronomy" means "second law" and rests on a misunderstanding of 17:18 by the Greek translators; the true reference is to a copy of the same law.

We also find smaller codes. In many cases these are summaries consisting of only ten or twelve commandments. These summaries could be easily read in worship and memorized by the people.

The most famous summary is the Decalogue, the ten words or Ten Commandments. This occurs first in Exod. 20:2-17, which relates the sabbath commandment to creation, then in Deut. 5:6-21, which advances a further reason for the commandment. Quotations from the Decalogue (Hos. 4:2; Jer. 7:9; Ezek. 18:5ff.; 1 Tim. 1:8-11) give evidence of its importance throughout Israel's history. Similar groups of commands and prohibitions may be detected within the laws of Exod. 22–23, but they did not have the same influence as the Decalogue.

Deuteronomy 27 forms a frame for the Deuteronomic law of chs. 12–26. It has the pattern of a ceremony of covenant renewal such as we later find at Shechem. The climax comes with a series of laws in the form of curses to which the people respond with an Amen (27:15-26). The twelve words there lay strong emphasis on human rights. Lev. 19 also enshrines elements of the Decalogue, although in this case with considerable expansion.

These general summaries all stress the rights of God, the rules of worship, and human rights and duties. They are designed for solemn reading and acceptance as part of the liturgy. All are connected with the covenant that God made with his people at Sinai.

The Sinai legislation also includes a number of legal collections relating to specific problems. Lev. 1–5 and 6–7 present the rules for the five main categories of offerings and sacrifices. Other collections that deal with this theme are found in Num. 15:1-31; 28–29; also Exod. 29:38–30:38.

For the laws of purification we turn to Lev. 11–15 (the Law of Purification). Similar stipulations, partly more detailed, are offered in Num. 5:11-31 and 19:1-22. Several groups of rules regulate the priestly ministry: the relations between priests and Levites in Num. 18:1-7, the ordination of priests in Exod. 29:1-37, necessary qualifications of the high priest in Lev. 21:10-15, the purification of priests in Lev. 21:1-9, their vestments in Exod. 28 and Num. 15:37-41, their income in Num. 18:8-25, the altar in Exod. 20:22-26.

Many laws deal with feasts and the relevant worship. Rules for the Passover occur in Exod. 12:43-49 and Num. 9:10-14, for the sabbath in Exod. 31:12-17 and 35:1-3, and for the day of expiation or atonement in Lev. 16. The rules for circumcision had already been given in Gen. 17:9-14, and rules for vows may be found in Num. 6.

The laws regulating daily life are grouped according to subject. In Deut. 27:15-26 we find four sexual prohibitions (cf. Lev. 18:6-23). The covenant law contains laws of safekeeping in Exod. 22:4-14 and of legal proceedings in 23:1ff. Lev. 25:1ff. regulates the sale of patrimony land and its return in sabbath and jubilee years. Lev. 25:35-55 governs the redemption of Israelites who might sell themselves in payment of debt. The rules of inheritance may be found in Num. 27:8-11.

Many laws dealing with single themes form groups of ten, e.g., Exod. 21:2-11; 22:4-14; Lev. 21:1-9. By counting on the fingers of both hands the people could easily remember the general and special laws that followed this pattern.

In general the laws were all heard and spoken aloud by the whole community at the covenant ceremony. Some of them, e.g., the laws relating to qualifications for the priesthood or proceedings at law, might be too specialized to be of interest to any but the priests, elders, judges, and officials concerned. Yet these special groups held office only as representatives of the whole people, so that even the most specialized laws were of indirect concern to every Israelite.

A word might be said about the terms that the OT uses for laws. In passages like Ps. 19 or Ps. 119 we find no less than eight different designations. God, we read, granted laws (singular form: *tôrāh*), instructions (*ʿēdût*), precepts (*piqqûd*), statutes (*ḥōq*), commandments (*miṣwāh*), decrees (*mišpāṭ*), words (*dābār*), and promises (*ʾimrāh*). Obviously some of these terms have their own specific meaning. One might be used for a command, another for a prohibition, one for an absolute order, another for a conditional rule, one to forbid an action, another to prescribe a punishment, one for a basic law of general application, another for a special rule applying only to an official group. But the OT does not neatly categorize them. It uses the terms interchangeably, so that we cannot make clear-cut distinctions or classify the laws according to different degrees of authority or importance. In our view, moral laws and liturgical rules might seem to differ in quality, but in the OT all are equally God's Word.

b. The Torah as a Unity

God's laws are not only equal; they also form a unity. They might differ in form, content, and character, but all had been proclaimed at the Sinai revelation, all proclaimed by the meditation of Moses, and all issued with the same authority as God's own eternal revelation and Word. Furthermore, all had the same aim: the creation, preservation, and renewal of Israel as God's own people.

The laws of God are a closely interwoven unity, a single, God-given charter. This is the common witness of the OT. The NT agrees, for it speaks of the one Torah (Greek *nómos*), which it also calls "the Law of Moses" (e.g., Luke 2:22), or simply "Moses" (e.g., Luke 16:29). Confession of the one law is closely related to confession of the one God.

The unity of the Torah has different aspects which demand brief consideration. The first point that the OT stresses is that the whole Torah was *given* during the basic revelation at Mt. Sinai. It was at Sinai that God made his covenant with Israel and called his people into being. As he granted his covenant at this one place, so he revealed his covenant law (cf. Exod. 34:28) at this one place. Only the laws promulgated at Sinai, either directly or indirectly, had authority in Israel.

It is true that God also gave the people a statute and ordinance at Marah (Exod. 15:25-26), that Moses declared God's statutes and laws in the wilderness near Sinai (18:16, 20), that he later proclaimed precepts, statutes, and laws in Transjordan (Deut.

4:4), and that Joshua drew up a statute and ordinance at Shechem (Josh. 24:25-26), but these anticipations and repetitions do not alter the fact that Sinai was the place where Israel received its law from God.

Second, God granted the whole Torah through the mediation of the one man Moses. Moses was the channel through which God revealed his will. We may read at places of laws that were revealed differently, either directly to Israel or through other intermediaries, yet the laws thus revealed would always be the same as laws that either would be or already had been made known through the mediation of Moses, God's chosen servant. All the books of both the OT and the NT acknowledge that only the Mosaic law had authority in Israel.

God himself might take the initiative. Thus in Exod. 20 and Deut. 5 God gave the Decalogue directly to the assembly (Exod. 20:22; Deut. 5:22). But even here Moses had a subsidiary role. He received the stone tablets on which the ten words were inscribed and handed them to the people. Fearing the glory of God, the frightened people then asked Moses to approach the Lord and to tell them his remaining laws and ordinances. Earlier God had made known his law to Abraham and Isaac (Gen. 18:19; 25:5), and later he would make it known through Joshua and prophets like Samuel. Nevertheless, it was Moses in particular through whom God chose to promulgate his law to Israel.

This choice, of course, was not based on any special merit or glory of Moses himself. He had a servant role. He was also a representative of the people. He thus stood for the covenant of God with his people and of the people with their God.

Third, God granted Israel the whole Torah as his revelation, as his own Word. Many Sinai texts insist that God himself, and he alone, is the author of the law. It was transmitted, of course, in human wording. But even though human intelligence and knowledge might play a role in its making, the human participants were instruments of God's own mighty act. Since the Torah was the charter of God's covenant with Israel, none but God himself could be its author.

God's authorship comes out plainly in the story of the stone tablets that Moses brought down from the mountain. Written with the finger of God, and handed over directly to Moses, these bear impressive witness to the origin of the whole Torah. This resolute affirmation of the divine origin did not exclude the fact that it pleased God to engage Moses, too, in the promulgation of the Torah. The second time Moses himself wrote the commandments upon the tablets (Exod. 34:27-28). Moses also passed on to the people the many detailed laws that he had received from the Lord on Sinai (31:12; 35:1ff.). The law did not fall from heaven. It was not promulgated directly by God's voice from Sinai. God gave it to the people by means of Moses. The divine authorship did not exclude human service. It included it. Yet even though God chose to reveal his law through Moses, he gave it as his own revelation, as his own Word.

Fourth, the whole Torah, given at the one time, has lasting authority. God gave Israel what Israel believed to be a perfect law (Ps. 119). The Torah so dealt with all important matters that it needed no later revision or addition. The laws might be scattered across the five books in a rather confusing way, but they constituted a closely knit body of law which was complete in itself and relevant for all generations in Israel.

The Torah was eternally valid for Israel because it was covenant law. God concluded the covenant once and for all. The people might need to confirm or renew it in critical situations, but God concluded it once and for all. It was thus unique, complete, sufficient, and eternal. It had permanent authority. It might take on different meanings in different ages: one at the foot of Sinai, another during the later desert wanderings, another on the brink of the invasion of Canaan, another after Israel's settlement in the land. There was need for repetition of the original hearing. The people had to take part again and again in the primal event at Sinai. The laws were living laws. Even within the Torah itself there might be modifications for particular circumstances, e.g., laws of manslaughter as well as the general prohibition of murder, or exceptions to the law of the central sanctuary. Laws of kingship did not have immediate relevance at Sinai or in the first days in Canaan. Each generation had to hear the law afresh and see its application to changing circumstances. The Torah itself, however, was closed, for God himself had spoken once and for all. This very fact was the reason why there had to be constant rehearsing.

Fifth, the Torah was promulgated as an eternal law for the chosen people of the Lord, for Israel. Many of its laws might have equivalents in the legislation of other nations. Most countries had their own legal systems regulating religious and social relations between the inhabitants themselves and also between the people and their deities. Israel was not the only nation to worship God by set regulations or to prohibit blasphemy, murder, adultery, robbery, and lying. It is easy to see, then, why many people view the Torah as simply the national law of Israel on the same level as the similar laws of other ethnic groups. Yet Israel was not just one nation among others. Its identity was defined by its coming into existence as God's people at Sinai, and it lived ever after on the basis of this unheard-of deed of God. The Torah had authority over Israel as covenant law. It was not customary law or national law; it was divinely given law.

Paul in Rom. 9 described the spiritual privileges that distinguish the Israelites from all other peoples: the adoption, the promises, the covenant, covenant law, and true worship.

For Paul as for every believing Jew, the Torah was God's special gift to Israel that marked it off as a people. It was the covenant charter.

The Torah was granted to a limited community, the people of Israel, smaller in one sense than the nation, yet broader in another sense, since others might belong to the people by residence or filiation. This community was the Lord's people because its members confessed the Lord as their only God. When some of the great legal collections or summaries begin with the words: "I am the Lord your God" (Exod. 20:2; cf. Lev. 19:2), this is not merely an introductory formula but a reminder of the basic relation. The laws of the Torah bind and challenge those who confess God and his mighty deeds. The community is not an ethnic group, a tribe, or a nation in the natural sense of these terms. It is a "congregation" (Mic. 2:5 CB; Deut. 23:1-8), a *qāhāl*, which may in fact mean a "levy for service."

The Torah was granted to a community that would live in Canaan. Many of the laws refer to specific situations in that land. Fields and vineyards, flocks and herds, daily relations, even slavery—all had to be catered for. Yet the Torah was not the law for a Canaanite society. It was the law not of a nation but of an immigrant community. It was a law for a people who came to live in that country because the Lord their God gave them the land (Deut. 6:20-25).

We arrive at the same conclusion when we consider that the Torah was addressed to a people who were called the Lord's people in virtue of their liberation from Egypt. The Holiness Code and the law of Deuteronomy stress repeatedly that the liberation from Egypt was the event that united the people, the foundation on which Israel stood. The laws in these sections were expressly said to be valid for those who confessed that the Lord is the God "who brought you out of Egypt" (cf. Lev. 18:3; 19:34; 22:32-33; 25:38, 42, 55; 26:13; Deut. 6:12; 13:6; 15:15; 20:1; 24:8, 9, 18; 25:17; also Exod. 20:2).

The Torah was addressed also to the community of tribes that was called Israel. Not all the sections mention this name, but the Holiness Code and the law of Deuteronomy refer to it whenever possible. "Hear, O Israel" is the well-known introductory sentence in Deut. 6:4; 4:1; 5:1; 9:1; 20:3. Wickedness (Deut. 17:12), outrage (22:21), and abomination (17:4) were not to occur "among the Israelites."

Several times the Israelites would establish a state under the name of Israel or Judah, but they never tried to use the Torah as the constitutional law of such a state. Israel might live as a nation like other nations, or as a religious community like other religious communities. But Israel in the biblical sense was not really a nation or a religious community. It had a character of its own. Oriented to this people of the Lord, and having the task of preserving God's covenant with his people, the Torah was unique, and it was valid for this distinctive community alone.

Sixth, and finally, the whole Torah upholds the community. God granted it with a view to keeping the people within the covenant that he had made with them. The promulgation of the laws was at the core of the making of the covenant and it revealed a fundamental aspect of God's dealings with the people. With his Word in the form of laws, God blessed the people. He gave them a free and unconditional gift. He requested this and forbade that in order to confirm Israel's position as his own holy people. The Torah is rightly praised, therefore, as the very heart of the grace and blessing that God abundantly poured upon his people.

Is it permissible, however, to speak here only of grace and blessing? We recall that the Torah also threatens and even curses those who will not "listen to all the words of these laws." Undeniably the Torah has a negative aspect inasmuch as it opposes, condemns, and curses those that rebel against the Lord. Israel accepted both aspects of the law, recognizing that the one aspect does not cancel the other. As God swears by his own name that he will always stand by his covenant with Israel, by the same oath he rejects all that might endanger the continuity of the covenant. Israel cherished the Torah as the Word of the God who is "compassionate and gracious" (Exod. 34:6) but also "jealous" and "holy" (Exod. 20:5; Josh. 24:19); of the God of free grace whose grace the people could never use at their own whim as though it were their own possession.

The Torah has often been misunderstood. People have seen in its laws hundreds of oppressive rules and ordinances, or prided themselves on having within it an independent way of salvation. The mistake has been to separate the law from God himself and to seek to follow it independently of God. What we really have to obey is the will of God under the guidance of the laws that he has given. Israel was moved to "serve" (RSV) or "worship" (NEB) the Lord (Josh. 24:14-24). Could they do this? Obviously not! "You cannot worship the Lord, for he is a holy God, a jealous God" (v. 19 CB). The Torah is threat as well as blessing. "Hold the Lord in awe then, and worship him in loyalty and truth" (v. 14). But doing this removes all possibility of regarding the law as a burden. He who challenges, invites, and moves the people to worship him is the compassionate and merciful God himself (cf. vv. 2-13).

c. The Aim and Authority of the Laws

Looking at their content, we have seen that the laws regulate different domains of life: trade (just weights and measures, loans), agriculture and animal husbandry (including land ownership), marriage (including prohibited sex relations), justice (law suits, judges, and witnesses), protection of life (homicide), physical integrity (wounds), property (kidnapping, theft, custody, inheritance), honor (one's good name), parental rights and human relations (with Israelites and aliens), war, feasts, rest periods, offerings, worship (temple, altar, sacral objects), purification, priests, prophets, etc. In all these areas what the laws aimed to do was to establish *order* and to give everything its proper place in the overarching unity. But what was the order that the laws were designed to establish and maintain?

Thus far we have given only the general answer that the laws were meant to set up the order that corresponds to Israel's status as the Lord's people. We must now look at this order in greater detail. God did not command Israel to do this or not to do that merely to teach Israel that he is the Lord and thus to enforce blind obedience to all that he might request. Nor is it enough to say that by the laws Israel was to be kept apart from all the nations around it.

God's laws ordered the life of the Israelites for a specific purpose. God revealed his will, and Israel accepted and recorded it, in a manner that brings to light this purpose. If the first couple in Eden had been forbidden to eat of the fruit of the tree in the midst of the garden, the aim was neither to limit their freedom nor to test their readiness to obey. The prohibition was in the couple's own interest. God alone knows good and evil, and he alone can grant this knowledge. To respect God's right is thus to be sure of one's own. God wanted Israel to know good and evil. For this reason he granted his laws. The Israelites lived in good order when they acknowledged this right of God. Respect for God's right meant respect for human rights. The point of each law was to reveal and secure God's right in the relevant field of Israel's life and in this way to establish human rights as well.

The reason is not set forth expressly in every ordinance. Many prohibitions are bluntly stated: "You shall not make a carved image. . . . You shall not commit murder. You shall not commit adultery . . ." (Exod. 20:4ff.). "You shall not boil a kid in its mother's milk" (23:19). "You shall not eat meat with the blood in it" (Lev. 19:26a). "You shall not sow your vineyard with a second crop. . . . You shall not wear clothes woven with two kinds of yarn" (Deut. 22:9ff.). So are many positive orders: "Every first birth of the womb belongs to me" (Exod. 34:19). "Three times a year you shall keep a pilgrim-feast to me" (23:14). "A charge must be established on the evidence of two or of three witnesses" (Deut. 19:15). But in many cases the reason or intention is also given. Explanations are given for the three main festivals: Passover, Weeks, and Tabernacles. Reasons are offered for the sabbath rest, including the needs of people and animals (Exod. 23:12). The firstborn belong to the Lord because God spared the firstborn of Israel when he slew the firstborn of Egypt. Sexual intercourse among close relatives is forbidden in order to avoid the abominable practices that are common in Canaan.

Promulgating his laws, God thus expressed his will and purpose. But the laws did not merely reveal God's will. They also realized it. If God called his people to live in good order, he also sanctified them (Lev. 20:8; 22:32; 21:8; Exod. 31:13). If he called upon the Israelites to be holy, he also redeemed them to be his servants. If he summoned them to live as free men and women, he also freed them. If he called upon them to live as brothers and sisters, he also united them as a community or congregation. God's Word in the form of laws had the power to realize its intention, and it made full use of this power.

It is important to emphasize that God's laws have power because we all too easily view them as perfect rules that gain power only as they are obeyed. They did indeed require obedience, but they also had the strength to move the Israelites to obey them. The laws of God give what they demand. When the Israelites did not obey them, they simply showed that they had not listened to them or opened their hearts to their power. When anyone is in fact moved to obey them, however, praise is due to the might of God's Word alone. As it is a miracle that Israel came into being at all as God's people, so it is a miracle when men and women both past and present keep God's laws.

God's laws sanctify, free, and unite his people. In this way they establish and preserve the order by which Israel is moved to live. We will now look more closely at these three aspects.

We recognize, of course, that Israel itself did not arrange the Torah under these three heads, but stressed always the unity rather than the diversity of God's laws. Thus holiness is the one guiding principle of the whole law in Lev. 17–26. In Deut. 12–26 all the laws are summed up under such concepts as the right and good (6:18; 12:2), love of God (6:5; 11:1), and fear of God (10:12, 20). Thankfulness figures prominently in opening and closing exhortations of Deuteronomy (6:10ff.; 9:4ff.). The only legal differentiation is between laws dealing with God's rights (worship) and those dealing with human rights. The Decalogue in Exod. 20 (Deut. 6) is the best-known example. The first part forbids the worship of other gods, the making of images, misuse of the divine name, and desecration of the sabbath. The second part enjoins respect for the rights of others by demanding the honoring of parents and forbidding murder, adultery, theft, false witness, and covetousness. Other summaries follow a similar pattern (Deut. 27:15-26; Lev. 19:3-14; Exod. 22:18-31). Even here, however, although the laws setting forth God's rights enjoy a certain autonomy and priority, they cannot be separated from those that protect human rights. It may well be that the one set was on one of the tablets that God gave to Moses and the other set on the other, although the two tablets might just as well have been two copies. But in any case the two sets supplement one another. Since God bound himself to his people, his own rights cannot be respected if human rights are ignored, and human rights cannot be respected independently of God's rights. Israel did not have sacral law on the one side and secular law on the other. It acknowledged only one law, covenant law, which regulated every area of life.

The three aspects of the work of the law—sanctifying, freeing, and uniting—are three aspects of one and the same divine work. Hence we are not to divide the laws into three categories according to the aspect to which they give emphasis. Some laws do, of course, lay particular stress on one aspect. Thus the sabbath law underscores sanctification, slavery laws insist on freedom, and the law of worship may give prominence to unity. Implicitly, however, each of the three aspects is always present. Indeed, we might have chosen other aspects. Not the concept but the content is what is significant.

(1) The law of God sanctifies or hallows the people. The whole Torah can be viewed under this aspect. Sacral and social laws alike have sanctifying as their aim. God hallows the people because he himself is holy. The Holy One of Israel (see Isa. 1:4; etc.) cannot but wish his people to be holy too. But what does the word "holy" (*qādōš*) mean?

In its original sense it means what is different, estranged, or separated from what is profane. Holiness, otherness, and numinous power are basic religious ideas in all cultures. All languages have words for them. Israel's ideas of holiness resembled those of other peoples. But the reason Israel gave for holiness differed. The Lord was holy, i.e., different from all other beings, because of what he did. His covenant was the reason for his holiness. Not a concept of his almightiness or mystery but the mystery of his intervention in history brought Israel to the confession that God is holy. The Lord had adopted Israel as his own people. By this action he alienated or separated himself from all the powers that are usually called gods. Therewith he estranged Israel, too, from all other peoples.

"You shall be holy, because I, the Lord your God, am holy" (Lev. 19:2; 20:26; 11:44; cf. Exod. 22:31). "I am the Lord who hallows you" (Lev. 20:8; 21:8; 22:32; Ezek. 20:12; 37:28). God both hallowed his people and demanded that they be holy. He invited them to share in his own work. He revealed his holiness (Ezek. 20:4; 28:25). He also commanded the people to acknowledge and respect it (Lev. 22:32).

The whole Torah is basically oriented to holiness. The Holiness Code makes this explicit. All the laws that God promulgated were laws of the covenant that God made with Israel. All of them thus helped to set Israel apart, to isolate it, as the one people of God.

Israel was hallowed when the people respected their holy God. Many of the laws establish God's "holiness right," especially those that deal with worship. The first three prohibitions of the Decalogue are the core: "You shall have no other god. . . . You shall not make a carved image. . . . You shall not make wrong use of the name of the Lord your God" (Exod. 20:3-7).

Worship of other gods was everywhere forbidden in the law (Exod. 20:3, 5; Deut. 5:7, 9; Exod. 34:14; Lev. 19:4a), whether by legal maxim: "Whoever sacrifices to any god but the Lord shall be put to death under solemn ban" (Exod. 22:20; cf. Deut. 17:2ff.), or by commandment: "You shall fear the Lord your God, serve him alone" (Deut. 6:13; cf. Josh. 24:14, 23). Other nations normally worshiped one god along with others. Israel could not do this. But why not?

A common answer is that Israel adhered to monotheism as we find it classically stated in the Muslim *shahadat: lā ilāha illā allāh* ("there is no god but Allah"). Monotheism is viewed as the common teaching of the three great religions, Judaism, Christianity, and Islam. God's law, however, did not rest on a doctrine or principle. It did not rest on an abstract monotheism. God did not forbid the worship of other gods on the ground that there are no other gods. The issue was not the *existence* of other gods but the *worship* of other gods in Israel. Israel was not to "bow down to any foreign god" (Ps. 81:9).

But again, why not? Why must not the Israelites even "speak the name" of other gods, much less "invoke" them or sacrifice to them (Exod. 23:13; 22:20)? The resolute OT answer is that "I, the Lord your God, am a jealous god" (Exod. 20:5; Deut. 5:9). The Lord had declared himself to be Israel's God. He had adopted this people. How, then, could he step back and disavow his action? The point of his jealousy was that he had a passionate desire to keep his possession. He refused to share it with other powers. Having bound himself unconditionally and unrestrictedly to Israel, he asked for no less total dedication on Israel's part.

This burning desire and strong intention could also be called holiness. Thus the adjectives "holy" and "jealous" are parallel in Josh. 24:19. By prohibiting the worship of other gods, the Lord was hallowing his people and inviting them to share in the work of sanctification.

The law also prohibited carved images. This prohibition is the second commandment of the Decalogue, so closely related to the first that Luther could combine the two (cf. Exod. 34:14-17; Lev. 19:4). It is a commandment in its own right, however, in Deut. 27:15 and can even be put first in Exod. 20:23: "You shall not make gods of silver to be worshipped as well as me, nor shall you make yourselves gods of gold." Israel was not even to make images of the Lord himself, as we see from the story of the golden bull-calf, which was obviously meant to be a symbol of the presence of God: "These are your gods, O Israel, that brought you up from Egypt" (Exod. 32:4). In its worship of the Lord Israel was not to try to guarantee his presence by any visible representation.

Why was it unacceptable for Israel to do this? A common explanation is that the Lord, being invisible, cannot be likened to any object, animal, or person. As the first commandment did not rest on an abstract monotheism, however, the second did not rest on an abstract concept of God's invisibility. In fact God could manifest himself in any form that he chose. The real reason for the forbidding of images was again the Lord's jealousy (Exod. 20:5; Deut. 5:9). As his holiness excluded the worship of other gods, it also ruled out all carved images. It ruled out carved images of God himself that would enable the people to control him, to guarantee his presence. God retained his freedom to manifest himself as it pleased him, e.g., from heaven (Exod. 20:22), or from the fire (Deut. 4:12). This was why the covenant people were forbidden to make images as instruments of worship.

The prohibition of misuse of the name of the Lord is the third commandment in the Decalogue (Exod. 20:7; Deut. 5:11: Luther's second). It, too, was designed to secure God's holiness, in this case the holiness of his name. Detailed laws prohibited the cursing or blaspheming of the name (Exod. 22:28a; Lev. 24:16 RSV). Other laws forbade its misuse in fraudulent oaths (Lev. 19:12a) or perjury (Lev. 6:3, 5; cf. Jer. 5:2; Ps. 15:4). Others again forbade misuse of the name in magic or sorcery. The name of the Lord was misused, too, when the Israelites adopted sacred prostitution (Amos 2:7) or human sacrifice (Lev. 18:21), or when they offered impure gifts to God (Lev. 22:2), or transgressed God's laws in other ways (Ezek. 36:20-23).

Why were such things forbidden? Was God's name like a consuming fire that would burn up those who toyed with it? Was God like a king who avenges the dishonoring of his name? Explanations of this kind see God's name as a holy and divine reality that endangers those that do not respect it. But if there is truth in this, another explanation also suggests itself when we look at the role that the name of God played in the concluding of the covenant which underlies all the laws. An essential part of the making of the covenant was that God revealed his name. God was at work. He was adopting Israel as his people. To misuse his name was to interfere in the action by which he revealed the core of his holiness. God forbade any act that expressed contempt for his name because he was sanctifying his people and moving it to sanctify itself; cf. Lev. 22:31-33.

We must also view the prohibition of sabbath work in its relation to the sanctifying of Israel. This prohibition is the fourth commandment (Exod. 20; Deut. 5: Luther's third). The most important reason that is given for this law is that the sabbath is holy. God set it aside as his own day (Exod. 20:10) and hallowed it. He declared it to be a *holi*day (holy day), a day of rest. By hallowing the sabbath the people sanctified itself: "The sabbath is a sign . . . that you may know that I am the Lord who hallows you" (Exod. 31:13). The three annual feasts served a similar purpose (23:14ff.; 34:12-24; Deut. 16:1-17). They were pilgrim feasts for the Lord, holy days that would serve to hallow the Lord's people.

"You shall be my own possession . . . my kingdom of priests, my holy nation" (Exod. 19:5-6 CB). These famous words sum up what the Torah has to say about the purity of Israel. The laws of purity are found in Lev. 11–15, though cf. also Exod. 22:31 and Deut. 14:3-22. The word "pure" *(ṭāhōr)* means "clean," "genuine," "holy." It is first used literally, then also spiritually. Purity is obviously very close to holiness. "Purify" and "hallow" are used indiscriminately in Lev. 16:19. In Lev. 11–15 purity has to do first with Israel's physical life. Clean and unclean animals are listed in ch. 11. Purification after childbirth is the theme in ch. 12. Rules about skin disease are given in chs. 13–14. Discharges are regulated in ch. 15.

As regards clean and unclean animals, the question arises why some are clean and others are not. It is obviously not a matter of mere health or taste. Physical distinctions play a part (Lev. 14), but another criterion seems to be whether the animal might be offered as a sacrifice to the Lord. Thus wild boars and pigs were holy animals in the religion of the Canaanites and other surrounding peoples. To offer or eat pork was thus to share in the ritual of nations from which God had separated his people (cf. 1 Cor. 8; 10:14–11:1; Acts 15:20, 29). The food regulations, then, were a permanent sign of Israel's otherness as the Lord's people.

The Torah sanctified the whole field of sex. It pronounced unclean such phenomena as emissions or bleeding at menstruation and after childbirth (cf. Lev. 12; 15:16-18; Deut. 23:9-14). Sex between those of close kinship is an "abomination to the Lord" (Lev. 18:6-17; Deut. 27:20, 22-23; cf. v. 15 RSV). So is sex with the wife of a fellow Israelite (Deut. 24:1-4; Lev. 18:20). Also included as abominations are intercourse with animals (Deut. 27:21; Lev. 18:23; Exod. 22:19) and homosexual intercourse (Lev. 18:22). Why are such relations unclean? Why do they contradict God's holiness? Why are they so totally prohibited? We are not given any specific explanation, but a possible reason is that sex had a sacral role among many of the nations in and around Canaan, as, for example, in the worship of fertility goddesses, or male and female temple prostitution. The Torah desacralized sex, and in so doing hallowed it for the Lord and sanctified his people in this important area of their life.

The Torah also hallowed the field of disease and death. Leprosy, other skin diseases, and possibly mental illnesses resulted in contradiction of God's holiness. So did death. To touch a corpse (Num. 19:10b-22) meant uncleanness, as did eating an animal killed by wild beasts (Exod. 22:31). The mourning customs of the Canaanites were forbidden (Deut. 14:1-2). No attempt was to be made to contact the spirits of the deceased (26:14). The bodies of people murdered or executed defiled the land and its inhabitants (21:1). These laws were designed to keep the people clean and healthy. Parallel rules concerned the cleanliness of the camp in times of war and the frequent washing of both the Israelites and their clothing (Exod. 29–40; Lev. 1–22; Num. 18–19; Deut. 21:6). Purification rites of this kind were a visible acknowledgment of the purity that God had given his people and enabled them to participate, as it were, in his work of sanctification.

Purity was especially important for the priests. The priests were representatives of the community that God had chosen to be "a people holy to the Lord," a "kingdom of priests" (Deut. 7:6; Exod. 19:6). Their office was to teach Israel to distinguish between holy and unholy, pure and impure, and to offer holy sacrifices to the Lord. The laws relating to them were meant to ensure that they lived and acted as examples of holiness. As the community was called to serve God perfectly and to worship him wholeheartedly (tāmîm, Josh. 24:14), and the sacrifices were to be perfect and without blemish (tāmîm, e.g., Lev. 1:3, 10), so the priests had to be pure and holy (Lev. 21:1-9, 10-15, 16-24), without physical defect, lest in entering the holy place they might trespass upon God's holiness.

All Israel's firstborn belonged to the Lord. Included were the firstfruits of herd and field, which were to be brought to the Lord to show that all was really his. In the case of firstborn sons, since God wanted his people to live and not die, a kid or a lamb was to be given in redemption. The Levites too, being holy to the Lord, took the place of all firstborn sons in Israel. Indeed, they represented the people as a whole, for all Israel was God's firstborn son.

If the purpose of the Torah was to sanctify or hallow the people, this applied no less in the field of social relations than in that of worship. The laws of the Holiness Code (Lev. 17–26) do not concern only what might be called the religious life. Human rights are also at issue. Parents must be honored (Lev. 19:3, 32). Life, property, and honor must be protected (19:11, 13, 16, 18). There must be fairness in judicial and commercial transactions (19:15, 36). Ordinary folk must be respected (19:13ff.). Rules relating to sex and the sabbath also have obvious implications for human relations. In every case the laws stress the otherness of Israel as a people who belong to God alone. The sanctifying of the people is thus of primary importance.

(2) Through his laws God granted freedom to his people. The whole Torah can be considered from this standpoint, too. The Lord had chosen and adopted Israel as his own people. This gave Israel a new status. They did not just exchange one owner for another. They were the Lord's people. God was their legitimate Lord, King, Shepherd, and Husband. He alone had a claim to their service. Yet being put in the Lord's service was a promotion. Israel had found grace in God's eyes. Israel had been lifted out of the dust and crowned with honor (cf. Deut. 28:13). Israel had been granted a name and position and rights corresponding to their status as a people loved by God. God had set their life in order. He had put them on their feet so that they could step out on the way of righteousness. He had done this by his Word and covenant. His law did not merely require a new way of living; it created a new attitude. This creative power of the Torah finds expression in Ps. 19:7-8. God renewed his people. In this sense he gave them a freedom which is the very core of the new life that his Word created for them.

But how did the law make Israel free? Freedom is not so obviously a theme of the law as holiness is. In fact, Hebrew has no express words for "free" and "freedom." The lack of terms, however, does not mean that the thing itself is not present. The story of the exodus magnifies God as the Liberator of his people. God brought his people out of slavery in Egypt. The aspect of freedom may not everywhere receive equal stress in the law, but if holiness is often to the fore, so, too, is freedom.

Freedom is prominent not only in laws based upon the liberation from Egypt but wherever commands or prohibitions have as their aim the securing, protecting, or restoring of human rights in the community of Israel. It is illuminating in this regard to ask how far a given law pursues this aim not only in the case of social laws but also in the case of liturgical laws.

In the NT, we recall, God's law is called "the law that sets you free" or "a law of freedom" (cf. Jas. 1:25; 2:12; Rom. 8:2). The Greek words are *eleútheros, eleuthería,* and *eleuteróō.* The point is that to become God's servant is to become a free man or woman, liberated from every form of slavery (1 Pet. 2:16). God's servants are his children. They have entered upon their promised "liberty and splendour" (Rom. 8:21). In the NT it is Jesus Christ, the Word of God, who is the great Liberator (John 8:32). The NT uses the Greek terms to sum up the aim and intention of the Word of God. In so doing it offers a valid explanation of the Torah's own witness.

Certain liturgical laws show what we mean by saying that God's law granted freedom to Israel. The law against worshiping any God but the Lord undoubtedly safeguarded God's holiness but it also set Israel free from any need to take part in the religious ceremonies of other nations. Israel could not bow down to other gods or make covenant with the nations and their gods (Exod. 23:32; 34:12; Deut. 12:29-31). It could not split its allegiance between the Lord and alien gods. Israel's weakness made a strict prohibition necessary, but the law was a release as well as a prohibition. "You shall not" meant that Israel was free from the obligation to worship other gods or to follow the evil ways of other nations.

The forbidding of carved images also meant freedom for Israel. It bound Israel to the mystery of God's presence wherever and whenever he chose. But it also freed Israel from futile bondage to a god trapped in an idol. An imprisoned god of this kind could only imprison those who worship it.

The law against misuse of the Lord's name not only condemned those who violated God's holiness but also protected the people against enslavement to the fear associated with the practice of magic and sorcery: "pursuing empty phantoms and themselves becoming empty" (Jer. 2:5). The Israelites were free to abstain from this path because they had no need to take it. In committing them to hallowing of God's name, the commandment also freed them.

The forbidding of work on the sabbath protected God's right by sanctifying the day that was holy to him, but God's right was also in the interests of human rights and welfare. No family member, servant, alien, or even animal could be made to work on this day. Forbidding work, the commandment permitted rest. On this day God's people were relieved of the burden of daily toil and could live freely and find refreshment (Exod. 23:12).

As regards social laws, we may turn again to the Decalogue. The honor of parents was protected by the fifth commandment (Exod. 20:12) and the corresponding prohibition: "You shall not revile your father and mother" (cf. 21:17). Aged parents were one of the weaker groups in earlier Israelite society. Their rights were not automatically protected. Younger adults, then, were commanded not to strike (21:15), browbeat and vex (Prov. 19:26), or mock their parents (Prov. 30:17). Freedom was thus secured for parents by commandment of the law.

The sixth commandment erected a dam against all arbitrary killing. The Hebrew verb *(rāṣaḥ)* means murder. It is never used for killing in war or for the killing of a tyrant, and only once for the execution of a death sentence (Num. 35:30). Israelites were to have the right to live securely. God's law offered them protection against death at the hands of murderers. God claimed the blood of murderers (Gen. 9:6). At this point again divine right guaranteed human rights. As Creator, God owns the life of all those who are made in his image. This divine right offered the security against murder that is a basic human right. The divine righteousness that guaranteed this freedom also formed an example for the anointed king: "May he redeem them from oppression and violence and may their blood be precious in his eyes" (Ps. 72:14).

The seventh commandment, by forbidding adultery, set up a fence to protect married life from outside interference. The verb *nā'ap* applies in the first instance to the male trespasser; *zānāh* was the usual verb for adultery on the woman's side. A man was not to have intercourse with another man's wife, nor a woman with a man who was not her husband or not yet ready to marry her. The question of monogamy or polygamy was not primarily at issue here. The prohibition simply protected the dignity of Israelites as members of the people of God. The marriage bond was for them a symbol of the covenant bond of the Lord with Israel. Adultery signified breaking the bond and destroying the freedom for which the people were redeemed (Hos. 2–3; Jer. 2–3; Prov. 6:32).

[145]

The eighth commandment: "You shall not steal," is usually viewed as protecting the right of property. The original intention, however, is not so evident, for the verb (gānab) has no object and property rights are safeguarded in the tenth commandment. Originally the law perhaps had a very specific form of theft in mind, not the stealing of mobile or immobile property, but kidnapping (cf. Gen. 40:15; 2 Sam. 19:42; 2 Kgs. 11:2). If so, God was protecting personal freedom by this commandment. As the specific offense became less common, the law could, of course, take on a broader reference, but in what may well be its original form it still has relevance, protecting the person against, e.g., the slave trade, the exploitation of the poor and weak, and the organized "disappearance" of political opponents, as well as the holding of children or others to ransom.

The ninth commandment, which forbids false witness, applies more narrowly to court testimony. Not false slander but lying to mislead a judge was at issue. The Torah demanded that a charge must be established on the evidence of two or three witnesses (Num. 35:30; Deut. 19:20). This placed a heavy burden on witnesses. If they lied, an innocent person might be condemned to death (like Naboth in 1 Kgs. 21:9-14). The tongue was not a weapon to be used to bring down others. Nor, of course, should it be used to defile the good name of another (cf. Lev. 19:16; also Ps. 27:12; 35:11; 41:5; 54:3). Here again the law defended a basic human freedom, protecting the Israelites against false charges that might be brought against them.

The tenth commandment, which prohibits coveting, is often thought to be aimed against the inner desire in an intensification of the commandment against stealing (cf. Matt. 5:17ff.). But if the eighth commandment was primarily protecting the freedom of the person, it was the tenth that protected the free right to private property. New studies of the verb "to covet" (hāmad) indicate that it covered more than desire, just as the verb in Deut. 5:21 meant taking in one's hand and not just setting one's heart upon. "To covet" was usually followed by "to take." House, wife, patrimony, servants, and cattle were protected against the covetousness that leads to an invasion of freedom. It should be stressed that God's law does not guarantee the right to any property, but only to such as is necessary to making a living.

In addition to the general social laws, three groups of specific laws clearly reflect the liberating purpose of the Torah. First, we have those dealing with the rights of slaves. Once the Israelites settled in the land they would adopt the bondage system whereby servants and laborers, whether captured in war, bought, or born in the master's house, "belonged" to free Israelites (cf. Exod. 21:4; Lev. 22:11; Deut. 21:10). In some cases even free Israelites might be sold in payment of debts they could not otherwise settle (Deut. 15:12). The law of God did not abolish slavery of this kind, but neither did it simply legalize or justify it. Instead it insisted that foreign slaves be treated humanely (Exod. 21:26-27) and provided for the release of Israelite slaves after a set period, and in any case by the year of jubilee (cf. Exod. 21:2; Deut. 15:12ff.; Lev. 25:39ff.). The intention of the law was clearly to promote freedom, as may be seen also from the ordinance relating to runaway slaves.

A second group of specific laws protects the rights of the weak: widows, orphans, aliens, hired laborers, and the poor. The law expressly prohibited the oppression or exploitation of weak or humble people. The strong had not to use the weakness of others to increase their own wealth and power (Exod. 22:21ff.; 23:9; Deut. 27:18-19; Lev. 19:13-14). The weak had to have a share in the people's privileges (Exod. 12:48). Prophets like Amos, Hosea, Isaiah, and Micah gave special emphasis to this aspect of the Torah, which distinguished it from the known codes of neighboring nations. The right of the weak could even extend to other creatures, especially oxen and other domestic animals (cf. Exod. 23:4-5; Deut. 22:1-4, 6-7; 24:4).

A third group protects the rights of those charged with offenses. Many laws gave emphasis to the prohibition of false witness (cf. Exod. 23:1; Lev. 19:16; Deut. 19:15-21). Judges in particular were to be fair, since otherwise they might be more dangerous to society than criminals (cf. Ps. 26:9-10). They were not to "side with the majority to pervert justice" (Exod. 23:2), or to be partial (v. 3), or to deprive the poor of justice (v. 6), or to pervert justice by subservience to the great (Lev. 19:15), or to accept bribes (Exod. 23:8). Persons who might commit homicide accidentally were granted sanctuary (Deut. 19:1-13). Sentences had to be executed in a just and honorable manner (Deut. 24:16; 25:1-4; 21:22-23), not merely for the sake of the weak, but in the interests of justice itself.

(3) God's laws united the people. They brought the Israelites together in a community that would consciously seek to live up to its vocation as the Lord's people. All Israelites and not just the nation as a whole were given this new status. But they could not live up to their position as the Lord's holy and free people if they tried to do so only individually or in families. By respecting the rights of neighbors they shared in God's work of uniting a free people that would be holy to him. God's laws had both the aim and the effect of uniting the people. This is true of the Torah as a whole, and since it is an aspect that is often neglected, we must give special attention to it.

The Torah, of course, has no collection that one might call the law of unity. Nor are there any specific words to express the idea of unity or unifying. At most one might say that the Deuteronomic law clearly intends to bring the Israelites together as a community. At the same time, the Torah as a whole is addressed to a *people,* to a *community.* In addressing the people in this way, the law of God institutes and establishes and confirms them as a community.

Certain liturgical laws make this point. Forbidden to serve other gods, the Israelites were called upon to worship the one Lord (Deut. 6:4). Having been pleased to become their God, the Lord made Israel his people. Previously Israel had not been a people (ʿam), congregation (ʿēdāh), or community (qāhāl) in this sense. Nor could they be so if they served other gods or made carved images. Those who did such things had already left the community. The death penalty for this kind of offense had the basic aim of bringing home to Israel the conditions of its own life or death. The ordinances might frighten, but their purpose was to preserve the people's unity as a community that worships the Lord alone.

Israel had also to celebrate three pilgrim feasts a year to the Lord (Exod. 23:14, 17; 34:23; Deut. 16:16). The men were to come into the Lord's presence, representing the whole community. All Israel was then to join in the feast; even slaves and aliens were not excluded (Deut. 16:1ff.). It was not by chance that the Lord summoned his people to come together in this way. In such gatherings, as in its gatherings on the sabbath, Israel was a "sacred assembly" (Lev. 23). When it met for sacrifice and thanksgiving, and for common eating and drinking, remembering the great deeds of the Lord, Israel was knit together in unity and deepened its fellowship as the Lord's people.

The social laws also strengthened the bond of unity. They put a difference between Israelites and aliens. In protecting basic human rights, they focused primarily on the rights of free fellow Israelites. Their first aim was to promote the solidarity of the people. Israel was called upon to unite as a legal community in which all enjoyed their own rights but also recognized the rights of others, assisting one another (Deut. 22:1ff.), settling disputes openly to avoid strife and feuds, overcoming hatred against fellow citizens (Lev. 19:17-18), and thus forming a close-knit community on the principles of equality, all of them, and not merely members of the same clan (mišpāḥāh) or tribe (šēbeṭ or maṭṭeh), treating one another as brothers and sisters in the one family.

This familylike relation was limited. Neither the original Canaanites nor the Egyptians, Edomites, or Moabites could belong to the community. They stood outside. They were not members. They did not participate in the making of the covenant. They were not at the assemblies for its renewal. They had their own ethnic, linguistic, religious, social, and political unity, but they did not have the unity of Israel as the people of God. The Lord himself, present in Israel, had brought this people together as his own community.

Although separate, however, Israel was not meant to be a closed community whose members sought only their own interests. The social laws covered dealings with aliens as well as compatriots. In trading with either the one or the other, one weight was to be used (Deut. 25:13-16). The principle of Exod. 12:49 that resident aliens should count as "native-born" applied not only to the Passover but to other fields as well. Aliens did not live in ghettos. The laws stressed the rights of outsiders. They were to be loved no less than Israelites (Lev. 19:34), who had themselves been resident aliens in Egypt. If the laws set Israel in a limited community, God himself fixed the limits as he chose.

As we close this consideration of the aim and content of the Torah, we see that Israel had every reason to give thanks to the God who spoke on Sinai, as in the familiar Pss. 19 and 119. Nor were the benefits of the law for Israel alone. Aliens who settled in the land shared the common life and experienced something of the holiness and freedom that the Torah granted. Through the small and weak community of Israel, all nations are and shall indeed be blessed (Gen. 12:3; 22:18; 26:4).

4. God Granted Reconciliation

The events on Mt. Sinai culminated in the institution of worship, in which God opened up a way of expiation and reconciliation. (a) The tabernacle was the site of the ministry of reconciliation and all the other elements of worship. (b) God designated priests to serve and mediate in Israel's worship. (c) God instituted Israel's worship by accepting the first offerings of sacrifices.

GOD'S REVELATION ON MT. SINAI involved more than the actual concluding of the covenant. The concluding of the covenant came to fulfilment with the institution of a ministry of reconciliation. God not only showed by his Word how this ministry should be performed. He also took an active part in it, working out the reconciliation by his glory whenever offerings were presented in accordance with his will.

The ministry of the reconciliation was granted to the people of the Lord that had come into being with Abraham. Reconciliation would be meaningless without the covenant. Conversely, the covenant itself is grounded in the sacrifices (Ps. 50:5). An account of the ministry of reconciliation is thus essential if the conclusion of the covenant at Sinai is to be properly presented.

a. Hallowing the Tent as the Place of Worship

As we have noted already, the tent of the presence was constructed at Sinai, and the glory of the Lord came down and consecrated it. We must now ask what was the specific meaning and role of the tent in relation to the Sinai event. God was present in the tent, but to what end did he graciously wish to be present?

Various answers might be given to the question of the meaning of the tent. One answer might simply be that God dwells there. He lets his name dwell there. The tent becomes a dwelling for his name (Deut. 12:5, 11). God reveals himself there. People can invoke him by name there, calling on the name of the Lord (cf. Gen. 13:4; 1 Kgs. 18:24). His name can be remembered there (cf. the use of the word *zikkārôn*, "remembrance" or "reminder," in worship, e.g., Num. 5:15 RSV; 10:9-10; Lev. 23:24; Exod. 28:12, 29). People may seek him there (cf. Gen. 25:22; Exod. 18:15) and also find him (Isa. 55:6 RSV). They may confess or praise his name there (1 Kgs. 8:33; also 60 times in the Psalms, and often in Chronicles). They ask for blessing and receive it there (Exod. 20:24). They come into God's presence there (Exod. 23:14, 17). It is there that God was pleased to meet with his people as their God (Exod. 29:45; Lev. 26:12), and true worship could thus be offered to him.

A more precise answer is that the tent was consecrated by the descending of God's glory upon it in order that it might be a place of reconciliation. Worship in the temple is primarily the ministry of expiation or reconciliation. The Israelites may also offer prayers and praises, fall down before God, confirm the covenant, and celebrate joyful feasts. Nevertheless, the ministry of reconciliation is at the core of the worship to which the tent was dedicated.

(1) We see this first from the terms that are used. Dominant are words for expiation and atonement, or, as the NT would say, forgiveness and reconciliation. These words do not merely refer to specific ceremonies. They are key words to describe Israel's worship in general.

If we look at the statistics for Exod. 25–40, Leviticus, and Numbers, we see that words derived from the roots *kpr* and *ht'* are of supreme importance. Verbal forms of the first root *(kipper)* occur 72 times. The noun *kappōret* ("cover") is found 25 times and *kippurîm* ("expiation" or "atonement") 8 times. Verbal forms of the second root ("to purify from sin") occur 15 times, and the noun *ḥaṭṭāt* ("sin-offering") is found no less than 100 times.

"Atonement," "expiation," and "reconciliation" are only tentative renderings of the Hebrew terms in question. The root *kpr* seems to involve covering up something so that it can no longer be seen (cf. Gen. 6:14). The verb *kipper* was used for covering somebody's face with a present, i.e., appeasing. The noun *kappōret* denoted the cover placed over the ark, but with the implication that here God covers sins, i.e., grants forgiveness of sins; hence the Greek *hilastḗrion* and the RSV rendering "seat of mercy."

Originally the root *ht'* carried the sense of missing the mark, i.e., sinning. The noun *ḥaṭṭāt* then denoted the offering that does away with sin. Verbal forms of the same root thus came to be used for doing away with sin. "To purify from sin" is a free but not incorrect rendering.

We do not know precisely how the ceremonies of expiation or purification were performed nor how they differed from one another. There was no doubt some overlapping, as we see from Exod. 30:10, in which the terms for expiation, atonement, sin-offering, and reconciliation are used together. What is apparent is that the need for reconciliation lay at the heart of Israel's worship.

(2) Supporting this conclusion is the description of the sanctuary, which shows clearly for what kind of worship it was used. The sanctuary was divided into three parts: the holy of holies, the holy place, and the court. Veils separated the parts. First and foremost, then, the sanctuary was not the place where the people could come to praise the Lord, to find refreshment, to listen to God's Word, to be taught his laws, or to celebrate his feasts. It was first and foremost the place where the central event of Israel's worship took place, the service of expiation and reconciliation.

The pattern of the sanctuary was very similar to that of pagan sanctuaries of the period — a court for burnt offerings, a holy place with priestly furnishings, and a holy of holies for worship of the deity (in paganism by way of statues). For all the similarities, however, Israel had its own reasons for worship in a holy tent and its own reasons also for separating the tent into the three parts. Israel worshiped in the tent because God had appointed it the place of his presence, and it set the holy place between the court and the holy of holies as a bridge between the unholy people and the most holy God. The priests, sinful like all the people, yet consecrated, had the role of mediators between God and the people.

When we look at the furniture and utensils of the tent we see that these, too, served the making of reconciliation or expiation. The holy of holies contained only the ark and the tokens, the tablets of the law. The function of the ark was simply that of containing the tablets. It was not strictly the seat of God or the symbol of his presence. Over it was the cover, which was of pure gold and as long and wide as the ark. This was not a lid but an independent cover with the two cherubim of gold on top (Exod. 40:20-21). God, we are told, appeared in a cloud above the cover (Lev. 16:2; cf. Exod. 25:22). Inasmuch as the cover denoted also the covering of sins, it stood in close relation to the ministry of expiation and reconciliation.

In the holy place the table with the bread of the presence or the showbread stood to the north (Exod. 25:23ff.; Lev. 24:5), the lampstand with seven lamps to the south (Exod. 25:31ff.), and the altar of incense in the middle in front of the veil separating the holy place from the holy of holies (Exod. 30:1ff.). The incense altar was used in preparation for the ceremony of reconciliation or expiation (Exod. 30:10).

In the court, at the entrance and before the screen for the door that prevented people from looking into the holy place (Exod. 26:36; cf. 29:42), stood the big altar for "whole-offerings" (NEB) or "burnt offerings" (RSV) (Exod. 27:1-8; 38:1-7), which again played a central role in connection with the ministry of expiation or reconciliation. The bronze basin for ablution between the altar and the veil (Exod. 30:17-22) was also used mainly in relation to the same ministry. The other objects in the court (Exod. 35:17-18) were all connected with the main ones that we have just listed.

(3) The holy tent (later the temple) was the place where the Lord revealed himself in the granting of forgiveness of sins when the people requested it through the ceremony of "covering" that we call expiation, reconciliation, or atonement. The worship of the sanctuary revolved around this ceremony. The OT, although not denying the legitimate role of other aspects of worship, says little about them.

The tabernacle contained no pulpit. Does this mean that there was no place for teaching or preaching God's Word? No, the tent was the tent of the presence. The tablets were at the point above which God manifested his presence. The "cover" was not a substitute for God's Word but an expression of its very core.

There was also no specific place for prayer in the tabernacle. Yet we read in Isa. 56:7: "My house shall be called a house of prayer for all nations." We find in Deut. 21:1-9 that prayer was in fact an integral part of the ceremony of reconciliation (v. 8). All that could be asked of God was finally summed up in the short request that God would accept expiation for Israel.

We like to see the holy tent as the center of Israel's religious life and the source of its every blessing. If the Torah says little about this, it shows clearly enough that blessing came to Israel through the ceremony of reconciliation. Moses emphatically blessed all those who contributed to the construction of the tabernacle (Exod. 39:43). Aaron (or Aaron and Moses) blessed the people when the first whole-offering had just been burnt on the altar before the newly consecrated tent (cf. 1 Chron. 23:13). Finally, we recall the familiar Aaronic blessing and its connection with the Nazirite vow in the context of the ceremony of reconciliation.

The mood in the description of the sanctuary and its function and furnishings tends to be one of seriousness rather than thanksgiving. Nevertheless, at the decisive moment, when the Lord comes in the fire of his glory, when the offering for the covering of sin is set aflame, and when it is seen that God accepts the people's sacrifice—then there is an explosion of pent up feeling which reminds us of the joy of the feasts: "All the people saw, and they shouted and fell on their faces" (Lev. 9:24).

b. Installing Priests for the Ministry of Reconciliation

The designation and consecration of priests, the nomination of priestly families and clans—in short, the beginning of the elected priesthood—is the second main element in the inauguration of the worship of the tabernacle at Sinai. Its importance may be seen from the wealth of relevant material between Exod. 25 and Num. 9. We have here another aspect of Israel's election by the free historical act of God.

The laws deal with the priestly garments (Exod. 28:39; 39:1-31; Lev. 8:1-13), consecration (Exod. 29:1-37; 40:12-16; Lev. 8), and ministry (Lev. 1–7; 11–15; 17; 21–22; 27), with the first offerings (Lev. 9–10; 16), and with the registration, ministry, and consecration of the Levites (Num. 1:40-53; 3–4; 7–8). Stories may also be found relating to the ministry of the priests (Num. 15:1-31; 28–29), the rebellion of the sons of Korah (Levites) against the priests (Num. 16–17), the naming of Phinehas as high priest (Num. 25:6-18), and the census of the Levites (Num. 26:57-62).

By instituting the priesthood God fulfilled the promise that he made to Abraham (Gen. 17:7-8) and repeated to Moses: "I will adopt you as my people, and I will become your God" (Exod. 6:6). In the holy tent Israel fashioned a place to meet with God. The Lord sanctified this place, but the meeting itself was possible only through the institution of the priesthood. The priesthood was instituted because God had adopted Israel. It existed for the sake of the people. Many of the ordinances relating to it were in fact addressed to the assembly as a whole (cf. Lev. 1:1-2; 11:1; 12:1; 15:1-2; 17:2; 27:2; Num. 5:2; 6:2; 15:2; 16:16; 28:2). All Israel had to come together to witness the ordination of the priests and to take part in it (Lev. 8:3).

All Israel was adopted, but it had the priests as its representatives. What was the authority and power of these representatives? What was their function in the life of the Lord's people? These are the questions that the material relating to the priests answers. We begin with their institution or installation.

(1) God himself installed priests to serve him. As we read in Exod. 28:1, Aaron and his sons were summoned before Moses "to serve as my priests." In every account we see how important was the act of consecration. It had three main aspects: God himself took action, he did so at a certain time and place, and he did so in a special ceremony.

No human being but the Lord, the God of Israel, and he alone installed the priests. Installation by the people could only acknowledge and confirm God's prior installation. The original installation took place at a specific point. It coincided with God's adoption of Israel as his people at Sinai. Adopting the people, God constituted the only legitimate priesthood. God separated the priests, or set them apart (Num. 8:14). He took them (3:12), chose them (16:5, 7), and consecrated them (Exod. 31:13), as he also did Israel as a whole. Installation was not set over against adoption. God separated, took, chose, and consecrated both the larger circle of the whole people and the smaller circle of the priesthood, with himself at the center of both circles. The priests might be described as especially holy, but their purer holiness was only a symbol of the holiness of all God's people. There might also be special covenants with the priests and Levites (Num. 25:12-13), but these special covenants can be understood only within the context of the general covenant that God made with all Israel.

For descriptions of the ceremony of priestly installation and consecration we turn to Exodus (chs. 28–29; 40) and Leviticus (ch. 8). The candidates were to be washed, clad in the sacred garments, and anointed (Exod. 28:4; 29:4ff.; 40:12-15; Lev. 8:6-13). An important sacrifice followed. Moses offered a bull as a sin-offering, a ram as a whole-offering, and another ram as an installation-offering. The candidates laid their hands on the heads of the animals that were offered in expiation of their sins, and they were sprinkled with the covenant blood (Exod. 29:20-21; Lev. 8:23-24). Though washed in pure water, clad in sacred vestments, and anointed with the finest oil, the candidates could not be priests for God before their sins were covered (expiated) with blood. This expiation had to be repeated annually (Lev. 16).

Only the priests, Aaron's descendants, were ordained in this way. Distinct from the priests were the Levites, who like the Aaronic priests were descendants of Levi, but not by Amram and Aaron. The Levites participated in the priestly ministry, but as assistants and under the guidance of the Aaronic priests. The priests needed the Levites, but the Levites could not act alone. A separate account is thus given of their election, installation, and consecration.

Numbers 8 contains a brief account of the consecration of the Levites. Moses, Aaron, and the whole community took part. Moses set the Levites apart and sprinkled them with "lustral water" (v. 7; literally, water for the washing away of their sins). The Levites then shaved their whole bodies and washed their clothes so as to be declared pure. Next, the people assembled before the holy tent and an astonishing rite followed. The Israelites laid their hands on their heads as if to present a sin-offering for themselves. Aaron presented the Levites "before the Lord as a special gift from the Israelites" (v. 11). The Levites then laid their hands "on the heads of the bulls" which Moses offered, one as a sin-offering and the other as a whole-offering "to make expiation for the Levites" (v. 12; cf. Num. 8:5-12, 20-22).

According to Num. 3:9-13 and 8:16-19 the Levites were given or dedicated to the Lord. The Israelites gave them in exchange for the firstborn, who had belonged to God since the night of liberation from Egypt. They also gave them to Aaron and his sons. It might also be said (8:18-19) that the Lord himself took them and gave them to Aaron and his sons. In other words, Israel dedicated them to the service of God, and God dedicated them to the service of Israel.

(2) God called and consecrated both priests and Levites to his own service. This service consisted primarily of the offering of sacrifices, but it might take many other forms as well. Thus the priests could speak a word from the Lord, perhaps when wearing or carrying the ephod, the form and ornaments of which are carefully described in Exod. 28 and 39. As the Lord himself spoke through the mouth of the priest, the priest had a function very close to that of the prophet.

Wearing the breastpiece of judgment, the priest could also act as a judge. This breastpiece, too, is described in Exod. 28 and 39, but we are not told what was its exact significance. From Exod. 28:30 and Lev. 8:8 it would seem to have been the place where the priest kept the Urim and Thummim, i.e., lots by which to obtain decisions from the Lord. The priest would act as a judge especially in cases which could not be settled except by a decision from God (cf. Deut. 17:8ff.; 21:5).

A statement in Deuteronomy reminds us that the priest or Levite also acted as a teacher: the Levites "observe thy word . . . they teach thy precepts to Jacob, thy law to Israel" (33:9-10). It was the priests' duty "to make a distinction between sacred and profane, between clean and unclean, and to teach the Israelites all the decrees which the Lord has spoken to them through Moses" (Lev. 10:10-11). Knowledge and understanding of God's laws *(da'at)* and the ability and authority to teach and guide *(tôrāh)* the people were essential if the priest was fully to discharge his function (cf. Lev. 14:57; Hos. 4:1-2; Mic. 3:11; Ezek. 7:26). Ezra would later be a model in this regard (Ezra 7:10).

The priest had also a healing function in God's service. This ministry of healing extended to the physical as well as the spiritual realm. Separating the clean from the unclean seems to have been, in part at least, for checking the spread of contagious diseases (cf. Matt. 8:4). If God himself was Israel's supreme Healer (Exod. 15:26), the priest, too, had to bind up the people's wounds.

At the same time, the primary function of the priest was to offer sacrifices. Prior to Sinai, nonpriestly persons had also offered sacrifices, e.g., Cain and Abel, Abraham, and probably Isaac and Jacob. Even at and after Sinai, they might still do so, e.g., the young men in Exod. 24:5, Gideon (Judg. 6:19ff.), Manoah (Judg. 13:2), the family of David (1 Sam. 20:29), Saul (13:10), Adonijah (1 Kgs. 1:9), and Solomon (8:62; 9:25). Nevertheless, it was especially to the priests that the Lord committed the ministry of reconciliation or expiation.

The laws relating to the priestly ministry focus on the sacrificial aspect. Even vestments that remind us of other functions were worn so that the priests might be "acceptable to the Lord" (Exod. 28:38) and therefore able to perform the offering. The ephod (Exod. 28:11) and the breastpiece of judgment (28:21, 29) bore the names of the twelve tribes engraved on precious stones so that the priests might "bear . . . the sons of Israel" (RSV) before the Lord. In addition, most of the laws relate directly to sacrifice (Lev. 1–7; 14–17; 21–23; Num. 5–6; 8; 18–19; 28–29). What nonpriestly persons had formerly done would now be the primary responsibility of the priests, acting, of course, as representatives of the whole community.

The concentration on sacrifice is most evident in the ordinances dealing with the ministry of the high priest, originally Aaron, the ancestor of all legitimate priests. The relevant regulations (Lev. 8:7-9; 12; 16:11-28; 21:10-15; Exod. 30:7-10; Num. 35:25, 28) describe the vestments, installation, and specific ministry of the high priest. A turban and gold rosette (cf. the royal crown in 2 Sam. 1:10) distinguished Aaron and his successors (Exod. 28:37; 29:6; Lev. 8:9). He alone might enter the sanctuary within the veil where the Lord was present above the *kappōret* (Lev. 16:2). Representing the priests and the whole assembly, he was to enter the holy tent alone and "make expiation for himself, his household, and the whole assembly of Israel" (Lev. 16:17). This act on the day of expiation (or atonement) was the climax and center of the ministry both of the high priest himself and of the whole priesthood.

All priestly responsibilities were included in this ministry of reconciliation. When the priests fulfilled this ministry, they implicitly discharged all the other functions of their ministry. In making reconciliation they were also prophets, judges, teachers, and healers. Placing expiation at the heart of their ministry, they laid the foundation for the successful performance of all their other duties.

The Levites, too, as we have seen, were set aside when Israel prepared to leave Sinai. They were not to be numbered with the other Israelites (Num. 1:48; 2:33). They were assigned a special place to pitch their tents. They were given a specific ministry, distinct from that of the priests but related to it. What was this ministry?

The main function of the Levites was to serve. As all Israel was chosen and moved to serve the Lord, to discharge a ministry or *diakonia,* and as service was the essence of the function of the priests for all their glory, so the Levites of the three clans of Gershon, Kohath, and Merari were to serve. But the Levites were to do so in a very concrete sense. They were entrusted with manual tasks.

They were to carry the tabernacle. They alone were to be "its attendants" and "pitch their tents round it" (Num. 1:50). The Kohathites, pitching their tents to the south, had responsibility for the holy of holies. The Gershonites, pitching their tents to the west, were responsible for the hangings, coverings, and screens. The Merarites, pitching their tents to the north, took care of the heavier equipment: planks, bars, posts, and sockets. Among the Levites the Merarites ranked lower than the Gershonites and the Gershonites than the Kohathites, but all the Levites had a clearly subsidiary role to that of the priests.

The lowly estate of the Levites had a positive side as well. The Levites had the privilege of serving in the holy tent (and later the temple). They did so as representatives of the whole people. The Israelites as a whole gave them to the Lord and made provision for all their needs (Num. 7) as a sign of thanksgiving to God. Their service was the people's service, rendered in the name of the whole people (3:8; 8:19). Pitching their tents around the tabernacle, the Levites were very close to the priests. Albeit in a lesser role, they shared with them in the task of mediating between the holy Lord and his unholy people. Their ministry was closely interwoven with that of the priests. If it was meaningless apart from the priestly ministry, the latter was impossible without it. To serve in the ministry of the sanctuary was a humble and lowly task for all concerned, but in this very lowliness and humility there was honor and glory for the Levites no less than the priests.

Participation in a common ministry, and membership in a common tribe, meant that the distinction between priests and Levites could sometimes be disregarded. Thus the terms "the priests," "the Levites," "the levitical priests," and "the tribe of Levi" could be used as equivalents in Josh. 3 and 6, and Deuteronomy could stress the fact that the Levites give the blessing (10:8) and teach and explain the law (27:9, 10, 14; 31:9-13). The priests might be higher than the Levites, but the link between them also received emphasis. When the temple replaced the tabernacle and there was no further need to carry the tent and its equipment, the Levites were to "stand every morning, thanking and praising the Lord, and likewise at evening, and whenever burnt offerings are offered" (1 Chron. 23:24-32 RSV). They were thus engaged in the supreme ministry of praise along with teaching and preaching God's Word (cf. 2 Chron. 17:7-9; 20:14-17; Neh. 8:7-8).

(3) God chose, commissioned, and installed the priests and Levites by name. The names show that God's deeds at Sinai concerned specific persons at specific times and in specific situations. The best known of the priestly persons are, of course, Aaron and his sons Nadab and Abihu, Eleazar and Ithamar. We also recall Levi, father of the Levites, and his sons Gershon, Kohath, and Merari. Nor can we forget Phinehas, son of Eleazar. Not much is reported about most of these persons. Perhaps the main point of including the names is to show the continuity of the legitimate priesthood, as may be seen from the inclusion of genealogies of the priests and Levites in Exod. 6:15-24; Num. 3:17-20; 1 Chron. 5:27–6:38; and Ezra 7:1-5. All the names have a place in the history of the one priesthood that began at Sinai, and from that fact the ministry of individuals and groups in Israel's worship drew its legitimacy.

God himself selected and installed a legitimate priesthood, a group of men who had the right and task of performing the ministry of reconciliation on the people's behalf. Moses and Levi also had an important place in this ministry. Their relation to the priesthood is not contested. Nevertheless, Aaron and his sons were the ones whom God chose specifically for this ministry. Moses belonged to the tribe of Levi and could be called a priest in Ps. 99:6. His descendants also played a priestly role (Judg. 18:30). Yet God did not elect Moses to the priestly office in the strict sense. He might have had more ability, experience, and claim than Aaron. But God chose as he himself willed.

In this regard it is worth noting that the origin of the tribe of Levi stood under a dark cloud. Because of the dishonor brought on their sister Dinah, Simeon and Levi (Gen. 34) acted treacherously toward the Hivites who lived at Shechem. This act endangered not only their own families but the whole family of Israel that was still few in number and attempting to settle peacefully in Canaan. Simeon and Levi were thus cursed for their cruelty and their tribes were later scattered in Israel (49:7). The Levites had no patrimony of their own but lived among the other tribes as "aliens" in dependence and poverty. Yet they also had the advantage of their disadvantage. Their wealth was that of devotion to the will of the Lord. They kept the words and laws of the Lord and strengthened Israel in its unity as the Lord's people (cf. Exod. 32:25-29).

Within Israel no group was better qualified for the priesthood than the Levites. Even so, not every individual Levite could be a priest. Levites served the Lord both within and outside the priesthood in the stricter sense. Their ministry was both broader and narrower than the specific priestly ministry. All Levites might be called priests, and all priests Levites (Deut. 18:1-8). Only some Levites, however, were set apart for the priesthood. This was not an arbitrary restriction insofar as the priestly ministry was essentially a ministry of reconciliation. Why, then, was the family of Aaron singled out for the priesthood in its specific sense?

In the last resort we cannot say. God chose his servants as he pleased. None dares summon God to give an account for his choice. The election of Aaron and his descendants is a given fact. It is not based on any obvious ability or merit. Indeed, it is astonishing and almost unbelievable. The story of the golden bull-calf puts Aaron in a very poor light. He first advised the people to make an idol, proclaiming a feast in Moses' absence (Exod. 24:14). He then tried to shift responsibility for the sin upon the "evil people" (32:22 RSV). Yet God chose this very dubious character to be the head of Israel's priesthood.

The point is clear. Even the priests whom God elects to discharge the ministry of reconciliation are themselves sinners. The expiation or covering of sins has to take place first on their own behalf. Even so, two of Aaron's sons, Nadab and Abihu, had to be eliminated because of serious transgression, and Eleazar and Ithamar narrowly escaped a similar fate (Lev. 10:2ff.). The death of Nadab and Abihu was a constant reminder to Israel that the Aaronites were not really worthy of their lofty position. If Eleazar and Ithamar lived on and fathered sons, including Phinehas, they did so as signs of the Lord's mercy upon Aaron in spite of his own lack of right or merit.

Indeed, Aaron himself, like Moses, had finally to die before reaching the land of promise. As Joshua succeeded Moses, so Eleazar succeeded Aaron. As Aaron represented all the priests insofar as they are unworthy before God, Eleazar represented them insofar as they are newly born and therefore acceptable to God.

All the same, it was with Aaron that God dealt at Sinai. He alone of all the Levites became the ancestor of all legitimate priests. If to be a true priest was not merely to be a descendant of Aaron but to serve before the Lord, it was still to Aaron and his family alone that the ministry of expiation was committed: expiation for the sins of all Israel, people and priests alike. God established the Aaronic priesthood to discharge this vital and central ministry.

c. Instituting Worship through Acceptance of Israel's Offerings

The beginning of the ministry of reconciliation with the first offerings is a further central element in the Sinai story. This element is no less important than the construction of the holy tent and the installation of the priesthood.

God initiated the ministry of reconciliation when he revealed himself at Sinai. Initiating this ministry was the core and culmination of the revelation. The covenant that God made with Israel at Sinai took effect with the acceptance of Israel's first offering. God was now the God of Israel and Israel was the people of God. When Aaron performed "the rites of the sin-offering, the whole-offering, and the shared-offerings," "the glory of the Lord appeared to all the people" and "fire came out from before the Lord and consumed the whole-offering," so that the people "shouted and fell on their faces" (Lev. 9:22-24).

At Sinai God made known his laws (Exod. 31:18) and told the people how to offer acceptable worship (chs. 25–31). His Word in the form of commandments had also the power to attain its purpose. The tent was made and consecrated. The priests put on their vestments and were installed. They then brought the first offerings and the Lord accepted them in a manifestation of his glory to the whole people. The commandments that God had given were carried out and the Lord accepted the performance of them. God had engaged the Israelites to share in his own work and deed. Stress must fall, however, on the primacy of God's own act, this time in the initiation of acceptable worship.

We may begin by surveying the material relating to the bringing of offerings. Some of it would be fully applicable only with the entry into the land (Num. 15:2), but the OT relates all of it to the events at Sinai and connects it with the worship that God initiated there. It consists of rules for the altar of whole-offering (Exod. 27:1-8; 38:1-8), for the altar of incense and the making of incense (30:1-10, 34-38), for daily offerings (29:38-42), for offerings at priestly consecration (29:1-27; Lev. 8), for the first offering of Aaron and his sons (Lev. 9), for purification-offerings (ch. 12), and for offerings on the Day of Atonement (ch. 16), also regarding the role of blood (ch. 17), the flawlessness of animals (22:17-30), food-offerings (24:4-9; Num. 15:1-21), the lustration-offerings for Nazirites (Num. 6:1-21), Passover offerings (9:1-14), offerings in expiation of inadvertent offenses (15:22-31), sin-offerings to prepare the water of ritual purification (ch. 19), offerings on the installation of Levites (8:5-13, 20-22), and offerings for the days of pilgrim feasts (chs. 28–29).

Although much of this material is in the form of rules, note should be taken of the narrative context. We have here the story of the time when Israel first brought offerings to God in worship. But we also have the primary story of God's own initiation of this worship. The accent is on what God himself did at Sinai, and what he alone could do.

Three aspects of God's action are given prominence. First, he favorably received the offerings that Israel brought. Second, he guided Israel in the regulation of its worship. Third, he graciously bestowed forgiveness of sins on Israel. The third point brings us to the innermost aim of all Israel's worship.

First, God favorably received Israel's offerings. Lev. 8 tells of God's favorable acceptance of the initial offerings. Moses himself in fact made the first offerings at the installation of Aaron and his sons as priests. But the story focuses attention on the installation itself and then on the first offerings that the priests themselves made (ch. 9). The first point to be noted as regards these offerings is that everything was done as the Lord commanded. Lawful observance was essential. Yet this was not the decisive aspect. The climax came with the revelation of the Lord's glory (9:23) that was hoped for at the outset (v. 6). By manifesting his glory to the whole people, God showed that he accepted its offerings. With this acceptance Israel came into being as the community that worships the Lord.

We do not know how the people could distinguish between offerings that the Lord accepted and those that he rejected. In Gen. 4:4-5 we simply read that he received Abel and his gifts with favor but not Cain's. The Aaronic priests might decide whether an offering was "accepted . . . to make expiation" (Lev. 1:3-4), but it was finally the Lord himself who decided (cf. Ezek. 20:40-41; Jer. 6:20; Amos 5:22; Hos. 8:13; Mal. 1:10). Numerous or unblemished offerings could not secure God's favor. Those who brought the offerings might pray that God would accept them, for basically the offering itself was a prayer. By accepting the first offerings at Sinai God gave no guarantee that he would always accept all offerings. The Lord's acceptance was a unique and wonderful event. Yet it was also an invitation to Israel to bring offerings as the law prescribed, and it carried the promise that God would in fact receive them favorably when they were offered with humble supplication.

Second, God guided Israel in the regulation of its worship. As already noted, much of the Sinai material consists of rules and ordinances relating to offerings. God revealed all these laws through the mediation of Moses, who transmitted them to the Aaronic priests and to the community that they represented. The rules were all of divine origin and the people praised God for the guidance that he granted it by means of them. Only their divine origin, even if it was by way of Moses, could invest the regulations with unquestionable and lasting authority. In fact, God would not have received the first offerings had it not been plain that they were offered in accordance with his word and will.

In this regard we intentionally use the term "guidance" for God's action because the word *tôrāh* had at one time the force of "divine guidance," and it is often used in connection with the cultic ordinances (Lev. 1–7). Often, indeed, guidance is a more appropriate concept than commandment. God did not actually command Israel to bring him offerings. The material specifies the right time, place, manner, and intention for each type of offering, but nowhere do we find a command that the offerings must be brought. Instead of commanding that the offerings be made, God granted guidance as to the way in which offerings that were already known should be made. The renewal and the condensation and simplification of customary forms was the issue.

The Sinai regulations were a call for renewal. God was summoning the people to start again from the very beginning as his people. Nothing less than a total rethinking of Israel's worship was needed. The offerings might be the same as those already known, but they were now to be offered in a new way and with a new purpose.

The Sinai regulations also involved condensation and simplification. We read of many different kinds of offerings: whole-offerings (NEB) or burnt offerings (RSV) (*'ōlāh* or *kālîl*), grain-offerings (NEB) or cereal offerings (RSV) *(minḥāh)*, incense offerings *(qᵉṭōret)*, offerings by fire *('iššeh)*, shared-offerings (NEB) or peace offerings (RSV) *(šelem)*, votive offerings *(neder)*, thank-offerings (NEB) or offerings for thanksgiving (RSV) *(tôdāh)*, sin-offerings *(ḥaṭṭāt)*, guilt-offerings *('āšām)*, Passover offerings *(pesaḥ)*, and offerings of firstfruits *(rē'šît)*. But though a distinction might be made between blood offerings *(zebaḥ)* and cereal or fruit offerings *(minḥāh)*, all might be described as *qorbān*, which means "gift" or "offering."

Furthermore, God's Word at Sinai in fact acknowledges only five types of offerings: whole-offerings, cereal-offerings, peace-offerings, sin-offerings, and guilt-offerings (Lev. 1–7). God might not refuse other kinds, but all offerings could be reduced to these five types and presented accordingly. It might seem, indeed, that the five could be reduced to three: votive offerings, community offerings, and reconciliation offerings. The text itself mentions five. But different kinds would often merge into a single ceremony, a full ceremony resulting only when each had been successively presented. Thus at the installation of the priests (Lev. 8), at their first offerings (ch. 9), and on the Day of Atonement or expiation (ch. 16; cf. Num. 28–29), we find different types of offerings, e.g., whole-offerings, sin-offerings, and peace-offerings. Evident here is the tendency to associate the various offerings in single common ceremony.

There was also standardization in the manner of presenting offerings. Each offering involved five consecutive steps or acts: presentation of the gift; laying one's hand on the head of the animal presented; the slaughtering of the animal; pouring out of the blood; the burning of the offering. This was the pattern, of course, for blood offerings. But these formed the core of Israel's worship; unbloody offerings were complementary.

Everything in the prescribed order related to the ministry of reconciliation. Did someone make an offering to express thanks or fulfil a vow? Did someone wish to deepen communion with God, or to strengthen national unity, or to make a covenant treaty? Did someone want to avert punishment for uncleanness or sin? Whatever the concern, without reconciliation no offering could hope to reach its goal. All God's guiding rules for worship point straight in this one direction, from which alone a decisive renewal of Israel's worship can be expected.

This brings us to the third important aspect of God's deed at Sinai. He not only received the offerings that Israel brought and guided Israel in the regulation of worship. He also graciously bestowed forgiveness of sins on Israel. The offerings were offerings of reconciliation.

The terms that we use in this regard, with no clear distinction among them, are reconciliation, expiation, and atonement. The problem here is that Hebrew has no precise equivalents for "to reconcile," "to expiate," or "to atone," or for the corresponding nouns. Most of our renderings are necessarily approximations. They are admittedly tentative. Yet fortunately, in the end, they express much the same idea as the Hebrew. Reconciliation is perhaps the most comprehensive term. It sums up what the others also denote. It is the act of making good, of making amends, of compensating for damage, guilt, or injustice. Paul admirably expressed what is in view in Pom. 5:10-11 and 2 Cor. 5:18-19 when he spoke of God reconciling the world to himself.

God himself granted reconciliation. He did so by instituting a special ministry of reconciliation. He alone had the power to make good the damage done by human sin. The emphasis on God's own action relative to the Sinai ministry shows this clearly. Nevertheless, the texts do not expressly say that God reconciles. They do not seem to be written in order to exalt God's deed. They tell us only what the people must do, whether the whole community, the individual, or the priest. It almost seems as if an offering in due form will automatically be acceptable to God (cf. Lev. 1:9, 13, 17). The priest "shall make expiation for their guilt [or for them, or for him] so that they [or he] shall be forgiven" (CB Lev. 4:20, 26, 31, 35; 5:10, 13, 16, 18, 26; 19:22). The impression is thus left that reconciliation is a human action. Even if it is the ceremony of reconciliation that the priest is making, the same impression is left.

All religions and cultures are familiar with the idea that offerings might be made in an attempt to bring redemption from evil forces. Israel, too, would fall at times into the mistake of thinking that offerings work automatically (ex opere operato). God alone redeems, it was thought, but the people can make expiation by bringing effective offerings. The prophets would sharply attack this notion (Amos 5; Hos. 6; Isa. 1; Jer. 7). So would Pss. 40, 50, and 51. Might it be, however, that the Sinai material offered some basis for the misunderstanding, as some modern scholars suppose?

Naturally, the people had to present the offerings, not God himself. In this sense they "made" expiation. But what did they really "make"? What did they accomplish by their acts? We have noted already the five steps involved in the presentation of an offering. But what did each of these liturgical acts mean?

In the first liturgical act believers brought their gifts, the fruits of field or garden, fowl or cattle, to "the entrance of the Tent of the Presence before the Lord" (Lev. 1:3; 3:1, 12; 4:4). The meaning is clear. They were bringing gifts near to the Lord (Hebrew *hiqrîb*, "to bring near to," whence *qorbān*, "offering") and offering them to him. To be acceptable the gifts had to be without blemish or defect (Lev. 22). They had also to be of value to the givers, according to their economic status, as an expression of their intention to offer true gifts to God.

The second act took place only in the case of blood offerings. Those who brought the offering, whether priests (Exod. 29:10, 15, 19) or not (Lev. 1:4; 3:2), laid their hand on the head of the animal, sometimes confessing their sins while so doing (Lev. 5:5; 16:21). The laying on of hands is usually thought to signify the transfer of sins to the animal and hence the death of the animal as a substitute for the sinner (cf. Gen. 22:13; Deut. 3:26; Isa. 53:12). A possible objection to this view is that the transfer of sin would make the animal unclean and therefore unsuitable as an offering. Another suggested interpretation of the laying on of hands is that it signifies the wish to make an offering and the acknowledgment of a need for reconciliation. Naturally the laying on of the hand could not of itself effect expiation.

Special rules applied to the Day of Atonement or expiation. In this case a bull was to be presented as a sin-offering to make expiation for the priesthood (Lev. 16:11, 14). Then a goat was presented to make expiation for all Israel (vv. 15, 17). Another goat had then to be presented on which Aaron would lay both hands, confessing all Israel's sins, and thus laying them upon the head of the goat, which would then be chased off into the wilderness to "carry all their iniquities upon itself into some barren waste" (vv. 20-22). Here the symbolic act of transferring sins was part of a special ritual that did not apply to ordinary offerings, since the so-called scapegoat was not slaughtered but driven away.

The third liturgical act was the slaughtering. Normally this was done by those who brought the animals (Lev. 1:4, 11; 3:2, 8, 13; 4:14, 24). On occasion the priests might do it (1:15), or the high priest (4:3). Why had the animal to be slaughtered? As noted, the generally accepted view is that it suffered the penalty for sin as a substitute. A possible problem with this interpretation is that the decisive word *kipper* occurs only in connection with the last two steps (4:20; 5:26; 8:15; 16:16, 18; 17:11).

The fourth and fifth acts, the pouring or sprinkling of the blood and the burning, belong together, blood and flesh being closely related. The blood, however, is dealt with in a distinctive way and always comes first. Aaron and his sons alone were to perform these acts, by which the plea for reconciliation was presented to the Lord. The blood was to be sprinkled on the surface of the cover or in front of the veil and on the horns of the altar. What was left was to be poured at the base of the altar of whole-offering (Lev. 16:14-15; 4:5ff., 18, 25, 30, 34). The other parts of the animal were to be presented to the priests and burnt either as a whole (1:9, 13, 17) or in part (3:9-11, 14-17;

4:8-10, 19, 26, 35; Exod. 29:13). In the case of peace-offerings part could be eaten by those who brought the offering, and in the case of expiation-offerings part had to be eaten by the priests (Lev. 6:24-30). An obscure text (10:17) seems to imply that eating by the priests has something to do with the making of expiation. Anything neither burnt on the altar nor eaten had to be burnt to ashes outside the camp (4:11-12).

The precise relation between the total offering of the animals and the making of expiation is unclear. Did the smearing of the blood or the burning of the flesh in some way effect reconciliation? Was there reconciling power in the blood, which is the life? Or did the whole ceremony have the force of a request for reconciliation by God himself as the worshipers brought their gifts in an act of confession and thanksgiving?

We are certainly not to think that the ceremony itself could automatically effect expiation for sin and reconciliation of the sinner with God. Nor are we to imagine that the offering to God was meant as a gift that would win God's favor and therefore result in the gift of reconciliation in return. Behind the symbolism stands a request for atonement and the presentation of this request in the celebration of a ceremony of reconciliation. But only God himself can grant reconciliation or make expiation. The decisive act in the whole ceremony is that of God himself.

What does the divine action involve? One aspect is the forgiveness of sins. This is expressed by the word *sālaḥ*. Those for whom the priests made expiation according to the established rules would be forgiven (Lev. 4:20, 26, 31, 35; 5:10, 13, 16, 18, 26; 19:22). God himself is the subject of the verb. He it is who forgives the people's iniquity and sin (Exod. 34:9; Num. 14:19; Jer. 31:34; Ps. 25:11; 103:3). He does so by covering it up (*kissāh* and *kipper*), or carrying it away *(nāśā'),* or not remembering it any more *(lō' zākar).*

Hebrew has many different words for sin, the most important being *ḥēt', ḥaṭṭā'āh,* and *ḥaṭṭāt* (from *ḥaṭṭāh,* "to miss the mark"), *'āwōn* (from *'āwāh,* "to go on crooked ways, pervert"), *peša'* (from *pāša',* "to act unfaithfully, rebel"), and *šegāgāh* (from *šāgag,* "to commit an error"). All these different forms of sin bring the people into danger so that they can no longer stand before the Lord. The terms denote the consequences of sin as well as the actual transgression. Since these consequences cannot be avoided, expiation is needed. Forgiveness, or atonement, does not simply wipe out the sinful act. It also stops, or at least delays or reduces, the consequences. One of the worst consequences is the endangering not only of the self but also of the family, clan, or nation (cf. the sin of Achan in Josh. 7). All the more reason, therefore, for the divine forgiveness if the people were not to be betrayed to ultimate destruction.

Specific sins for which there might be expiation are not listed. The witness of the OT is that in spite of the sinfulness of the people God set up a sacrificial ritual in which the Israelites could present their request for reconciliation, which would also in some sense symbolize it, and which God would favorably accept, willingly forgiving offenses so long as restitution was made wherever possible (Lev. 6:4-6). This is the Sinai gospel.

God's favorable acceptance of the Sinai offerings did not mean that he would automatically receive all future offerings that were presented in the duly prescribed form. The initial acceptance, however, carried the promise and the hope of future acceptance, assurance of which might come through the word of a priest (1 Sam. 1), through individual blessing (Ps. 41:12), or through the feeling that God "has granted all my desire" (Ps. 13:6). At Sinai God displayed his freedom to grant reconciliation and he established the hope that he would mercifully answer the request of his people by himself making reconciliation.

Chapter VI

God Granted Israel the Land of Canaan

Introduction

GOD ACTS IN HISTORY. He intervenes in the world. He manifests the power of his love. He initiates the new, just, and good world that we call his kingdom.

God acted in the countries between Syria and Mesopotamia, calling Israel's forebears from that region. God acted in Egypt, challenging the mighty kingdom of the Nile, and freeing his people from the clutches of Pharaoh. God acted in the desert, leading Israel through it, revealing himself, and making his will known in the form of laws on Mt. Sinai.

God also acted in Canaan, the holy land, bringing his people into this country and granting it to Israel. According to the biblical witness, his own kingdom began to take root in this part of the world that lies between Egypt and Mesopotamia. It had its first center in Canaan, from which it would expand to the whole world.

It is easy enough to locate Canaan geographically but not so easy to define its frontiers. At times it might be simply the long and narrow stretch of hill country west of the Jordan (Judah, Samaria, and Galilee). At other times it might include the lowlands toward the Mediterranean and the mountainous area east of the Jordan. In the promise of Gen. 15:18 it would apparently comprise the whole territory between the Mediterranean and the desert of Arabia and from the border of Egypt to the Euphrates. The OT never fixes permanent frontiers. It simply describes the borders that existed at various times, e.g., under David, Hezekiah, or Nehemiah. What matters is that there is this land, large or small, fertile or arid, that God himself gave to Israel and that became its legitimate possession.

The gift of the land was a historical event. It created a new situation. It took place at a specific time and place under unique circumstances. Israel always regarded Canaan as its home, yet it also remembered a time when its forebears were aliens there. Other nations had lived in Canaan and owned it. They had come in waves centuries before Israel ever reached it. The Israelites were constantly aware of being newcomers in Canaan. It had not always been theirs. The OT witness kept this awareness alive.

Israel had to occupy Canaan. Prior to its coming the land had already been invaded many times, especially after the 20th century B.C. Powerful nations like the Hittites and the Egyptians had held it. Ethnic groups in search of land, e.g., the Horites and Amorites, had moved into it. Around 1500 B.C. it was composed of several small kingdoms, most of which had fortified towns as centers. It stood under the cultural influence of Egypt. Outside the fertile areas, however, there were still hills, mountains, and forests that were empty and unsafe. These were the areas that Israel could first invade and conquer at a time when Egyptian control had slackened.

Historical research confirms the conquest and gradual occupation of the whole land by Israel. But scripture bears witness to a further fact. The Lord himself, the God of heaven and earth, granted this land to his people. The divine gift rather than the occupation of the land as such is what lies at the core of Israel's faith and confession.

1. The Witness of Scripture

God granted the Israelites the land of Canaan as their dwelling place and patrimony. For this reason Israel praised God, trusted him, and hoped in him. But the gift also invited Israel to live a holy life in this land that belongs to the Lord.

THE FACT THAT THE GIFT OF CANAAN is an essential article in the creed of Israel needs little corroboration. Any Bible concordance shows that the gift is a common topic. We find it 13 times in Genesis (12:7; 13:15, 17; 15:7, 18; 17:8; 24:7; 26:3; 28:4, 13; 35:12; 48:4), 7 times in Exodus (6:4, 8; 12:25; 13:5, 11; 32:13; 33:1), 5 times in Leviticus (14:34; 20:24; 23:10; 25:2, 28), 10 times in Numbers (13:2; 15:2; 16:14; 20:12, 24; 27:12; 32:7, 9; 33:53; 36:2), no less than 76 times in Deuteronomy (1:8; etc.), 17 times in Joshua (1:2; etc.), 6 times in 1 Kings (8:34, 36, 40, 48; 9:7; 14:15), 12 times in Jeremiah (3:19; 7:7, 14; 11:5; 16:15; 17:4; 22:39; 24:10; 25:5; 30:3; 32:22; 35:15), 6 times in Ezekiel (11:17; 20:15, 28, 42; 36:28; 37:25), 8 times in Psalms (78:54-55; 105:11, 44; 106:24; 111:6; 135:12, 21; 136:21), and a few times in other OT books (cf. Judg. 6:9; Amos 9:15; Neh. 9:8, 36; 1 Chron. 16:18).

The affirmation takes different forms but always includes four elements. First, *the Lord* is the subject. It is he who gives the land. If Moses is also said to do so (Josh. 9:24), it is only in execution of the Lord's will. Second, God *gives* it. The Hebrew verb *(nātan)* implies a legally valid act of bestowal. It is usually found in the past tense ("has given") but may also take the present form ("is giving") or even the future ("will give"). Third, *the land* is the direct object of the giving. No doubt exists as to what land or earth (*'ereṣ* or *'ᵃdāmāh*) is meant. It is Canaan, the land "which he swore to our forefathers," or "flowing with milk and honey." Fourth, the indirect object is *Israel*. At times one of the fathers (Abraham or Israel) or one of the tribes (Reuben or Ephraim) may represent Israel, but the final point is always that the land is given to Israel.

Why do we find so many references to the gift of the land? One obvious answer is that Israel's possession of the land was never sure or self-evident. It had to be constantly reminded of the gift and taught its implications afresh. Thus the affirmation occurs in exhortations (e.g., in Deuteronomy), in prophecy (e.g., in Jeremiah and Ezekiel), in creedal summaries, and, of course, in stories of the conquest (e.g., in Joshua and Judg. 1). In every case it serves as an expression of Israel's faith. The gift of the land was an article of faith no less than the liberation from Egypt or the revelation at Sinai, as von Rad rightly discerns in volume I of his *Old Testament Theology*.

As an article of faith the gift of the land stood in an especially close relation to the liberation from Egypt. The verbs "to bring out" *(yāṣā')* and "to bring in" *(bô')* are complementary. Liberating his people, God brought them out of the land of slavery. But he completed the act of liberation by bringing them into the place of rest which he had promised to their ancestors. "Exodus" and "eisodus" go together.

The gift of the land is also closely related to the election of the fathers. The fathers themselves had been brought first into the land, and God had sworn or promised it to them. The gift was thus a fulfilment of the promise, though we must add at once that it was always a matter of promise and never of totally secure possession, as we shall see later.

The gift of the land is related, too, to the wilderness wandering. The two topics are opposite but complementary sides of the same event. The time of expectation in the desert corresponds to the time of fulfilment in the land. In the desert Israel stood constantly under the menace of death; in the land they prospered "in the land of the living" (Ps. 27:13).

Is there a relation also between the gift of the land and the creation of the world? Few biblical texts imply it, but the parallelism is obvious between the garden of Eden and the land flowing with milk and honey. As our first parents were set in the garden and made responsible for it, so Israel was given the land and made responsible for a life in it in obedience to the revealed will and law of God.

At a first glance there might seem to be total opposition between the Sinai revelation and the gift of the land. At Sinai God commanded; in Canaan he gave. Yet the two aspects belong together. At Sinai God gave Israel the laws that would rule its life in the promised land. He granted Canaan to Israel in order that it might live there as a holy nation in observance of his commands.

When we come later to the institution of the monarchy, the election of Zion, and the sending of the prophets, we shall have to consider how far the biblical witness sets these topics as well in the light of the gift of the land, and what their relation to this gift is.

Taken as a whole, the witness of the OT cannot be understood in isolation from the fact that God gave the land of Canaan to his people. How he did so we must now examine.

2. God Gave Israel the Land by Conquest

God gave Israel the land (a) by a miraculous act in which (b) Israel acted together (c) under a common leader and (d) with a common mind, (e-f) judgment being executed on the Canaanites, and (g) the land distributed to the tribes and families.

To SEE HOW ISRAEL ENTERED the land of promise we have to investigate the materials found primarily in Joshua but also scattered across Genesis, Numbers, Deuteronomy, and especially Judges. Systematic consideration brings to light the following elements in the story: The conquest was a miracle; it came about by concerted action; Joshua led it; the Israelites were all of one mind; the original inhabitants of the land were corrupt; they were thus to be exterminated; the land was divided among the tribes.

a. The Conquest Was a Miracle

Many of the most familiar accounts of the conquest and occupation of Canaan describe it as a miracle. Strong nations in so difficult a country could be defeated only by divine intervention. The wonderful victories were God's work. Israel could not take a single step on its own. Against well-equipped armies and fortified towns, it did not have the necessary resources.

How could Israel possibly cross the Jordan (Josh. 3–4), take Jericho (ch. 6) and Ai (ch. 8), and then defeat five Amorite kings (ch. 10) and Jabin king of Hazor (ch. 11)? How could it drive out and destroy such powerful enemies? This was not a human achievement. The Lord himself "fought for

Israel" (10:14; 23:3; Deut. 1:30). *God* delivered the Canaanites "into the hands of the Israelites" (CB Josh. 2:24; 6:2; 8:1). *God* "drove them out in front of Israel" (CB Exod. 23:28; 33:2; Deut. 33:27; Josh. 24:18). The success was not Israel's but God's. This was the truth that Israel must always remember lest it glory in its own strength (cf. Ps. 44:2-3) or lose hope when pressed by mighty enemies.

The Israelites, of course, played their part. They fought courageously. They used clever strategy. They made alliances as needed, they were not just onlookers watching the Lord at work. Nevertheless, it was the Lord alone who granted them the victory. The glory finally belonged to God.

b. The Conquest Was a Concerted Action

In the conquest the Israelites acted together as a single army made up of all twelve tribes. They crossed the Jordan together. They took towns and defeated Canaanite armies together. They shared both the dangers and the victories. No tribe ever withdrew either for lack of interest or for fear. Even Reuben, Gad, and the half tribe of Manasseh did not settle in their own territories east of the Jordan before participating in the common campaign (Num. 23; Deut. 3; Josh. 22).

A careful study of scripture shows, of course, that once the country had been taken over and divided, the tribes still had much to do individually to complete the occupation. In some cases this was a very slow and lengthy process, as we see from Josh. 15:63; 16:10; 17:12-13; Judg. 1:1; 17–18. The land was given to all Israel, and all Israel had to take it. But it was then divided among the Israelites, and individual Israelites in the tribes had the task of taking over possession. There was first a time for united action when effective entry had to be made into the land. Only then could the time come for the longer and often imperfect task of total occupation in which tribes and families would have to act on their own.

c. Joshua Led the Conquest

The conquest of Canaan took place under the leadership of a single commander, Joshua. Acting in unity, the Israelites were united under this one leader. As Moses led Israel in the liberation from Egypt, at Sinai, and throughout the wilderness wandering, Joshua led it in its thrust into Canaan.

Why did Joshua have this outstanding role? He was certainly one of Israel's great heroes, like Moses, David, or Elijah. Deut. 34:9 describes him as a man "filled with the spirit of wisdom." His main feature, however, was that he succeeded Moses as "the servant of the Lord" (Josh. 24:29; cf. 1:7; 3:7; 4:14). He represented the new generation that escaped the fate of the wilderness generation and at last entered the land of rest. He completed the work of salvation that Moses had initiated.

The preeminence of Joshua did not mean that there were no other leaders. Caleb was obviously another of Israel's chiefs. He, too, had played a positive role in scouting the land, and like Joshua he was allowed to take part in the conquest. Plural references in Josh. 3:1; 4:13; and 9:15-16 show that Joshua had other supporting captains as well. Eventually he would focus his activity on his own tribal area of Ephraim (17:14ff.), where he would later be buried (24:30). At the same time, supreme command at the conquest, especially in its earlier stages, rested on the one man Joshua.

d. The Israelites Were of One Mind

At the time of the conquest, the Israelites were of one mind in their devotion to God. They "served the Lord during the lifetime of Joshua and the elders that outlived him" (Josh. 24:31; Judg. 2:7). Their loyal obedience corresponds to the pledge that some of the tribes vicariously took before entering on their patrimony (Josh. 1:16-18). To obey Joshua's commands was equivalent to serving the Lord himself.

Loyalty of this kind on Israel's part was unusual and no merit attached to it. Rather, it was seen as a wonderful gift from God in contrast to the attitude of the people earlier in the wilderness and later after the death of Joshua (Judg. 2:2, 10-12; 3:5-6). Praise belonged to God alone for enabling the people to show such loyalty to the exceptional leader that he had given them in Joshua. This extraordinary devotion was what made effective entry into Canaan possible.

Naturally, the OT does not portray the conquest generation as ideal. The fiasco at Ai was a sharp reminder of human frailty. In the completing of the occupation, too, many tribes showed unexpected timidity when faced by solidly entrenched enemy pockets (Judg. 1:21, 27-36). It would not be until the time of David that Israel finally wrested Jerusalem from the Jebusites. In the initial stages of the conquest, however, the people achieved a commitment that brought rapid success and made the eventual occupation of the whole of Canaan possible.

e. The Canaanites Were Corrupt

In the process of occupying the promised land, judgment fell on the prior inhabitants of Canaan. They were condemned as stubborn idolaters of bad character and immoral habits, guilty of the very worst of sins. Like the people of Sodom and Gomorrah in Gen. 13:13; 18:20 and the Moabites and Ammonites in 19:30-38, the Canaanites defiled the land by their abominations, so that finally the land would spit them out (Lev. 18:17-18) and the Lord would push them back and drive them out (Josh. 23:5; 1 Kgs. 14:24). There was every reason, indeed, for God to take away the land from them and give it to the newborn people of Israel.

At the same time, the condemnation was not total. Whenever Canaanites were ready to accept Israel, coexistence was possible, as with the Gibeonites, or those with whom Israel was able to dwell peacefully according to Judg. 1:27-36. Coexistence, of course, brought tensions, especially with intermarriage. Syncretism became an acute danger, as may be seen later from the desperate struggle of Elijah to preserve the very identity of Israel as the Lord's people. The condemnations of the Canaanites in Deuteronomy and Joshua were directed more against their corrupting influence on Israel than against the people as such. Were Israel to fall into the Canaanite ways of idolatry and immorality, it might gain the land but it would lose its own true self in the process.

f. The Canaanites Were to Be Exterminated

Hand in hand with condemnation of the Canaanite world and its lifestyle went destruction of the Canaanite population. Wholesale extirpation was especially a feature of the first stages of the conquest. Thus the reports of Israel's victories in Josh. 1–12 repeatedly tell us that defeated kings were "slain with the sword" (CB), that their towns were set aflame, and that the Israelites "put every living soul to the sword until they had destroyed every one" (Josh. 11:12-14). If we ask why there had to be this mass annihilation, three considerations might be helpful.

First, this was a time of existential emergency. Israel was forced to use violence because the kings decided to resist their entry (Josh. 10:3-6; 11:1-5). The only options were either to give up, to retreat, perhaps to be enslaved again, or to take up the challenge and fight back. The Israelites themselves were inclined to surrender, but the Lord commanded them to resist. This was a unique "holy war" in which the very existence of Israel in the fulfilment of the divine purpose was at stake.

Second, the Canaanites, as already noted, represented an acute spiritual danger to Israel. Later decades would show that living at peace with them meant living in agreement with their idolatry and serving both the Lord and Baal, as under Ahab in Elijah's day. With this kind of peace Israel could quickly lose its true raison d'être. It was thus commanded to demolish pagan altars and do away with those who worshiped at them (cf. Exod. 23:20-33; 34:10-16; Num. 33:50-56; Deut. 7:1-6; 12:3; Judg. 2:2). The command to exterminate the Canaanites should be read in this context.

Third, the extermination was not as total as might be supposed from the initial reports. As we have seen, Israel did in fact make peace with many of the original inhabitants in its more gradual completion of the occupation. In so doing, it missed its chance of removing the Canaanite danger once and for all and brought upon itself a protracted battle for its own survival. Nevertheless, Israel had neither the strength nor the will to engage in total extirpation of the original population. Nor did it need to do so. Once it gained control in a given area, total suppression of idolatrous and immoral practices and their replacement by the worship and lifestyle of the covenant would have sufficed.

g. The Land Was Divided among the Tribes

The first stage of the conquest reached its climax with the distribution of the land (Josh. 13–21). From one standpoint this was a single action under Joshua, the supreme leader. The allotments already made to Reuben, Gad, and the half tribe of Manasseh were ratified, portions for Judah and Joseph (Ephraim and the other half tribe of Manasseh) were agreed upon, and arrangements were made for the division of the rest of the land among the remaining tribes. In fact, of course, Eleazar, the tribal heads, and the people as a whole all had a part, with Joshua, in the distribution (cf. Josh. 14:5; 18:1; 19:51), and the process extended over a lengthy period, beginning with the action taken already by Moses, continuing with the arrangements made for the tribes of Judah and Joseph, and concluding with the mapping of the country and the prolonged efforts of the tribes to occupy the territory assigned to them. At the same time, it was important that there should be the concerted action under Joshua when prior allotments were confirmed, new arrangements were accepted, and provision made for all further assignments. Why?

First, the formal distribution made it plain that the Lord had given this one land to this one people. Second, it made it no less plain that in this one land each tribe and family would have its own patrimony, which it held not merely by right of conquest but by divine gift. Later political and economic developments would severely test this sense of unity and continuity (cf. already Josh. 22:10ff.), but it was a cardinal article of Israel's faith according to the OT witness that this was the one land of the one people and that God had given all Israelites a divinely assigned status and possession in this one land and people.

3. God Gave Israel a Pleasant Land and a Fair Patrimony

(a) On the one hand, Canaan was called Israel's possession and patrimony; (b) on the other hand, it was called the Lord's possession, the right to the land being linked to the Word of God, (c) the promise that constantly points to future fulfilment.

a. Israel's Own Land

THIS EXPRESSION and the reality that it denotes are familiar to all readers of the Bible. Does it need further explanation? The difficulty is that the exact meaning of the relevant Hebrew terms is by no means clear.

A common term for Canaan is *nahⁱlāh,* "inheritance," "heritage" (RSV) or "patrimony" (NEB) (e.g., Josh. 11:23; Judg. 20:6; Deut. 4:21, 38; 12:9; 15:4; 1 Kgs. 8:36; Ps. 135:12; 136:21). Canaan is also called *'ᵃhuzzāh,* "possession" (Gen. 17:8; Lev. 14:34; Num. 35:8; Deut. 32:49; Josh. 21:41), *môrāšāh,* "possession," "property" (Exod. 6:8; Deut. 33:4; Ezek. 11:15; 36:5), *yᵉrušāh,* "land of (their) possession," "territory" (Deut. 2:12; Josh. 12:7), or *ḥēleq,* "portion" (Mic. 2:4 RSV). Sometimes it is simply *'ereṣ yiśrā'ēl,* "land of Israel" (1 Sam. 13:19; 2 Kgs. 5:2, 4; Ezek. 40:2; 1 Chron. 22:2), or *'admat yiśrā'ēl,* "soil of Israel" (25 times in Ezekiel). The word *nahⁱlāh* is often used also for the patrimony of a single tribe (Josh. 16:8), clan (14:14), or individual (Naboth in 1 Kgs. 21:3-4).

This survey shows that God gave Israel a right to the land. The expressions clearly have property rights in view. But were these rights the same as in Western law, which stands under the influence of the Roman right to use and abuse? Care must be taken not to misinterpret the original biblical meaning of the terms or to do violence to them.

In this regard many Asian and African languages use words deriving from the Arabic root *milk,* "property," "holding," "estate." The corresponding verb means "to have power over" and the personal noun *(malik)* means "owner." This family of words plainly implies full rights to property whether in the form of land, objects, animals, or persons. The owner can freely dispose of it so long as no harm is done to others.

The desire to have full and absolute control over one's property was certainly not alien to an Israelite. Even today Israelis tend to think of Canaan as a possession that they may use as "private property." They have come to regard the stories of the Lord's gifts of the land as permanently valid documents of land tenure. But recent studies (especially G. Gerleman, "Nutzrecht und Wohnrecht. Zur Bedeutung von *nhlh,* " *Zeitschrift für die alttestamentliche Wissenschaft* 89 [1977] 313-25) show a need to reexamine the biblical terms in question.

"Inheritance" or "patrimony" is the usual rendering of the Hebrew word *naḥᵃlāh,* which occurs 46 times in Numbers, 25 times in Deuteronomy, and 50 times in Joshua. Translations and dictionaries tend to agree that it denotes ongoing, inherited possession. But this sense is by no means certain. We never find the term relative to the taking over of a property by the heirs of a deceased father, nor does it mean "patrimony" in other West Semitic languages. It occurs in expressions that have the sense of returning. "To go back to one's tent" in Judg. 7:8 (RSV) is virtually synonymous with "to go back to one's *naḥᵃlāh*" in Josh. 24:28 (CB). The meaning here is obviously much closer to "dwelling place" than to "patrimony" (NEB). Along similar lines the sanctuary or dwelling place of the Lord is his *naḥᵃlāh* in Exod. 15:17 and Ps. 29:1. If property is at issue, one's dwelling place is the property.

The correct translation of *'ᵃḥuzzāh,* which occurs 20 times in Leviticus, 9 times in Numbers, 6 times in Joshua, and 15 times in Ezekiel, is just as debatable. It is generally thought to denote "possession" in the sense of "legal property." It certainly includes this, as does *naḥᵃlāh.* The noun *'ᵃḥuzzāh* comes from the same root as the verb *'āḥaz,* "to take," "to hold." The noun, then, denotes an object that one holds. But the verb is hardly ever used for "to take in possession," so that one may doubt whether *'ᵃḥuzzāh* really means "possession." Thus when Jacob was given an *'ᵃḥuzzāh* in Egypt (Gen. 47:11), this was not a "possession" (RSV) but a "place to settle," i.e., land for pasture and cultivation. The same may well apply to the field of Machpelah which Abraham acquired as a plot in which to bury his wife (Gen. 23). Did this really become his "possession" (vv. 4, 9, 20 RSV and NEB), or did he simply acquire the right to use it? A similar question arises about the land that Jacob bought at Shechem (Gen. 33:19; cf. 2 Chron. 11:14; Num. 35:2).

Hebrew *môrāšāh* and *yᵉrušāh* are also important terms. They are not very common, and are nearly always used in relation to Canaan. They stem from the verb *yāraš,* "to inherit," "to occupy," "to own," as in the expression "to take a country or stretch of land in possession" (6 times in Numbers, 45 times in Deuteronomy, 11 in Joshua, 4 in Judges). The root is also found in other Semitic languages such as Arabic. Is this the biblical word family for the everlastingly valid possession of the land that the Lord gave Israel? The verb *yāraš* often does mean "to inherit" (e.g., 2 Sam. 14:7), but this is not the sense in the phrase "to take in possession," which refers to de facto occupation (often by force) rather than to inheriting. Thus many invaders were said to have taken possession of Canaan (cf. *yāraš* for "plunderers" [NEB; RSV "spoilers"] in 2 Kgs. 17:20), and the idea of valid and permanent possession is hardly relevant in such cases.

Great care is thus needed in interpreting expressions that describe Canaan as Israel's possession. Unquestionably the Lord gave the land to Israel. But in what sense and to what end? Did he give Israel and its tribes and clans title to the land forever? Did he grant them a permanent right to it? Did he give them the right to use it as they wished or needed?

The common renderings of the relevant biblical terms suggest that he did, but linguistic findings do not support this. The crucial terms do not carry the legal sense of a lasting private property right. The more probable meaning is that Canaan was to be a *naḥᵃlāh* for Israel. It was to be its dwelling, its place of residence, the homeland which it occupies, where it has right of domicile, and where it also has land use, the right to farm its fields and pasture its flocks. As the words *môrāšāh* and *yerušāh* seem to imply, what is at issue is not so much rightful ownership as factual occupation. This understanding enhances rather than lessens the significance of God's gift. God did not simply give away the land. He gave it with a long-term plan. He would himself stay with his people. He would help them to live in it.

b. The Lord's Own Land

The Song of Moses (Exod. 15:1ff.) calls Mt. Zion the Lord's "dwelling place," or "the mount that is thy possession" (v. 17). Israel obviously extolled Zion as the Lord's possession in a special sense (cf. Ps. 24:3; Isa. 2:3). But Zion was the center of a larger surrounding territory which was also God's property. The holy land as a whole was his. With its conviction that Canaan was the Lord's possession, Israel was taking a step that had far-reaching implications.

"Grant rain upon thy land, which thou hast given to thy people as an inheritance" (1 Kgs. 8:36 RSV). This petition in Solomon's prayer at the consecration of the temple self-evidently describes Canaan as God's own land. Similarly Ps. 85:1 recalls the days of old when the Lord had been gracious to *his* land. Ps. 10:16 thanks the Lord that "the nations have vanished from *his* land." The Lord claims Canaan as his land in Ezek. 36:5 and 39:16, and it is called "the land of the Lord" in Isa. 14:2; Joel 3:2; Zech. 9:16; and 2 Chron. 7:20. We might also quote the prophet Hosea, who warns an unfaithful Israel: "They shall not dwell in the Lord's land" (9:3). Canaan can also be described as the Lord's vineyard (Isa. 5:1ff.). Jeremiah records God's lamentation over the land— "my own land" (CB, Hebrew *naha̱lāh*), "the beloved of my soul," "my vineyard," "my portion" (RSV) or "my field" (NEB)—upon which the people's wickedness has brought calamities (Jer. 12:7ff.; cf. 2:7; 16:18). To be ousted from the land meant to be "far from (the presence of) the Lord," "to have no share in the Lord's inheritance" (CB 1 Sam. 26:19-20; 2 Sam. 14:16). All these references show that Canaan was the Lord's own land.

It was, of course, as "the lord of all the earth" that God had title to Canaan (cf. Josh. 3:11, 13; Ps. 97:5; Zech. 4:14; 6:5). The question as to how Canaan came into his possession never arose. Canaan, too, belonged to the Creator of heaven and earth. He had sovereign rights over all lands and could give them to whom he pleased. But his claim to Canaan had to be asserted against local deities that might also be called "prince lord of the land" *(zbl bᶜl 'rṣ)* and that might also claim Canaan as the land of their possession (cf. *'rṣ nḥl* on stone tablets found at Ugarit dating from the 15th century B.C.). Neither these deities nor the forces of nature owned the land. It belonged to the Lord, who had demonstrated his all-surpassing power and sovereignty. He could give it to Israel because it was his and would always be his.

Individual Israelites might question this act in the course of Israel's history. Other peoples also lived in Canaan and assigned it to other gods like Baal. The crown and landowners staked claims that seemed to leave no place for God's ownership. The loss of the land at the exile suggested that the Lord, too, had lost it to foreign deities. But notwithstanding the evidence of changing historical situations, the true confession of Israel's faith, rooted in the Word of the Lord who reveals what truly is, confidently proclaimed that the land was God's.

We recall that even the fathers who had wandered in Canaan had been conscious that God was there. Manifesting himself to them at Shechem, Bethel, Mamre, and Beersheba, he had promised to give them the land. The Lord did not need to compete with other gods. He did not have to drive these gods out. In the last resort, did not he alone dwell there? He could give them the land because it already belonged to him.

Some passages in Joshua stress the prominent role of the ark when Israel crossed the Jordan and entered Canaan. In these early days the ark was a symbol of God's presence, and as such it made the advance of the Israelites possible. Where the Lord was present, Israel triumphed (e.g., at Jericho, Josh. 6). If he was absent, Israel suffered defeat (e.g., at Hormah, Num. 14:39ff.). The Lord entered first, Israel followed, and striking victories were achieved. Before the Lord of all the earth, no rival could remain in power. This would be demonstrated again in the dreadful consequences to the Philistines when the ark of God was present among them (1 Sam. 5).

It might be said at times that God comes from afar, e.g., from Sinai or Seir or Paran (Deut. 33:2; Hab. 3:3; Judg. 5:4). The point here is that the people cannot take his presence for granted. Each time it is an event, a new experience. His coming, however, still denotes his authoritative possession of the land. The reverse side of this possession, of course, is that God, having given the people the land, can also take it away. As his presence cannot be taken for granted, neither can the people's own possession. As the prophets warn Israel, if it does not remain faithful to the covenant, God's message to it is the stern one: "I will uproot you from my land which I gave you" (2 Chron. 7:20).

The Lord seized hold upon Canaan as his special property, his residence, the base from which to act among his people. It is understandable, then, that the expression *naḥᵃlat YHWH* ("the Lord's possession or dwelling place") could apply not only to the land but also to its people (Deut. 4:20; 9:26, 29; 1 Sam. 10:1; 2 Sam. 20:19; 1 Kgs. 8:51, 53; 2 Kgs. 21:14). It is also understandable that this land that the Lord took to himself could be no ordinary land. It was the *holy land*. As such, it was not to be abused. Its inhabitants could not arbitrarily dispose of it or defile it. The land was given to Israel, but by reason of the gift it did not cease to be the Lord's own land.

c. The Promised Land

The gift of the land was an event. In the records, however, the promise always accompanied the gift. Israel could not receive the gift without the promise that precedes, accompanies, and follows it. We can understand the intention of God in making the gift of the land only in terms of his Word in the form of the promise. This is the specific witness of the OT.

THE PROMISE WAS GIVEN first to the fathers: "To you and to your descendants I will give all these lands" (Gen. 26:3; cf. 12:7; 13:15, 17; 15:7, 18; 17:8; 24:7; 28:4, 13; 35:12). The promise then recurs in the context of the liberation from Egypt (Exod. 3:8, 17; 6:4; 13:5; 15:17; 23:20; 33:2-3; cf. Lev. 20:24). God will bring the people out of Egypt and bring them into Canaan, the land flowing with milk and honey in which various nations still live. Then there are references back to the promise in the common formula (with slight variations): "The land which he promised on oath to Abraham, Isaac, and Jacob" (cf. Gen. 50:24; Exod. 13:5; 33:1; Num. 11:12; 14:16; 32:11; Deut. 1:8; etc.; Josh. 1:6; 21:43; Judg. 2:1; Jer. 11:5; 32:22; etc.).

The reference of the promise is not always to the gift of Canaan. Sometimes a son or numerous descendants might be promised (Gen. 15:1ff.; 16:17; 18:1ff.). Blessing is also promised. The fathers will be richly blessed themselves and they will also be a blessing to all nations (Gen. 12:2-3; 18:18; 26:4; 28:14; cf. Exod. 12:32). Above all other gifts, and comprehending them, God promises himself: "I will be your God. . . . I will be God to your descendants" (Gen. 17:7-8; Exod. 6:7).

It will be seen that God promises his grace in many different forms: the land, progeny, abundant blessing, and his own presence as Israel's God. The different aspects belong together and complement one another. Yet in a certain sense the promise of the land holds a central position. It would be on the land that Israel would multiply, that it would be showered with temporal and spiritual blessings, and that God himself would be pleased to be present with it as its God.

What does the word "promise" actually imply? A statement is a promise of a person's readiness to do something. It precedes a deed in favor of another. A space of time, determined by the one who makes the promises, elapses between the word and the deed. Biblical Hebrew, however, has no specific word for "promise." In Hebrew a person simply says or tells someone that he or she will do something for others. This applies to God, too. Even when he makes a declaration of that kind, no specific term is used. An announcement is made in words, no immediate consequence is apparent, and everything depends on a later fulfilment for which the person to whom the announcement is made has to wait. God's promise thus seems to share in the weakness of comparable human assurances. Nevertheless, God's Word is a Word of power. Unlike a human promise, it is totally trustworthy and reliable. It secretly creates a new reality. It calls for faith; it also generates it. Jewish thinkers were right, then, to introduce a special term exclusively for God's promises. The word *habṭāḥāh* carries the sense of assurance. In the NT it becomes *epangelía* in Greek, *promissio* in Latin, "promise" in English. In this form it is a key word of biblical theology.

God confirmed his promise of the land in two ways. The first was in the form of blood in Gen. 15. The second was in the form of an oath (26:3). By the ceremony of ch. 15 God set his seal on the promise. By the oath he bound himself, pledged his own name, identified himself with the promise of the land. The OT can think of no more valid confirmation. God's promises were true; they would thus be fulfilled. He would do what he said he would do.

In a sense, of course, the fulfilment came with the conquest and occupation of the land. This was a palpable fact and the promise might seem to have no further relevance. God had given Israel the land. Yet that is not the end of the matter. In Genesis the promise of God is sometimes expressed in a way that suggests fulfilment already (cf. the perfect tense in Gen. 15:18; 35:12). Fulfilment came also at the conquest: "The Lord gave us this land." Yet even then the complete fulfilment still lay with God. Israel had achieved only partial occupation. Definitive fulfilment seemed to have come with the kingdom of David. But then the promise acquired new and painful relevance with the dissolution of the twin kingdoms, the banishing of the people, and the subjugation of the land of promise to foreign rulers. Had God withdrawn the promise? Could he no longer keep it? What Israel had to realize was that the promise and the gift were never meant to be a simple transfer. What God did was a venture. It was a challenge that awaited a response. It could succeed only if Israel responded freely and loyally to the divine challenge (cf. Deut. 4:1; 30:15-20). The promise had been fulfilled already. It could be fulfilled again (Amos 9:15; Jer. 32:41; Ezek. 20:45). It was the basis of commitment and hope.

The gift of Canaan was a historical fact. This fact, however, was intrinsically connected with God's sovereign promise, challenge, and decision. Israel had a "spiritual" right to the land but not a historical or legal claim. Apart from God's Word no attempt to secure or protect it could make this land

Israel's own. Nevertheless, no turn in world events could undo God's promise. For Israel, and through Israel for all nations, Canaan was always the promised land.

An implication of the promise that seldom attracts attention is that it brought blessing not only to the people but also to the land itself. Through the promise Canaan became more than it naturally was. It became a new Canaan prefiguring a new world in which "love and fidelity come together, justice and peace join hands" (Ps. 85:11). It was for Israel a "good land," a patrimony fairer than that of any nation (Jer. 3:19; cf. Ezek. 20:6), the *menûhāh,* the place of rest or security (Exod. 33:14; Deut. 3:20; Josh. 1:13; 21:44). Does this mean that Canaan was already like paradise, like the new earth of Isa. 65:17, like the coming kingdom of God (Ps. 145:11-12)? No, perfection was never found in Canaan, either before or after the Israelite settlement. But the promise of the Lord opened the people's eyes to see the land as the good gift of God and to give God thanks for it. It did not need to think of the new Canaan as a heavenly homeland. God's kingdom was to come on earth, and the little country of Palestine was the place chosen for its beginning. The Israelites, then, were not just to dream of the kingdom. They were to share in its realization. The promised land was given them for this purpose.

4. God Gave Israel a Land in Which to Grow Up

God gave Israel the land in order that it might grow up there as a people that was (a) called to worship the Lord alone, (b) called to live as a community, and (c) called to be a witness to the nations.

THE AIM OF GOD in giving the land to Israel was that it might live there in peace, free from oppression and slavery, exempt from hunger, unconstrained by fear or danger, "each man dwelling under his own vine, under his own fig-tree, undisturbed" (Mic. 4:4 CB). Many songs of thanksgiving praise the Lord for the blessings that came to the people with the gift of the land (Ps. 65; 67; 85; 104; 107:35-38; 135:12-14; 145). Part of the rejoicing at the first Passovers after the conquest was that the people could eat "what had grown in the land of Canaan" (Josh. 5:10-12).

Nevertheless, God had more in view with this gift than that Israel should eat the produce of Canaan (Josh. 5:12), enjoy its fruit (Jer. 2:7), and live long in the land (Exod. 20:12). God bestowed all these blessings upon Israel in order that it might live as his people. He gave the people a land in which to live happily but he also gave them a land in which to live in his presence, worshiping him alone, growing up as his people, and becoming his witness to the nations. Canaan was the nursery in which Israel was to grow up like a young tree and in due time to bear fruit.

Concretely, although Israel was born much earlier, it first became the Lord's people in Canaan. It began here to live consciously as such. Now came its definitive emergence, not as the "large company" (NEB) or "mixed multitude" (RSV; Exod. 12:38) that had come out of Egypt, but as Israel, the Lord's people. It had been born and consecrated and led, but it reached maturity only in Canaan. God took it like a vine out of Egypt and planted it in Canaan to grow up there (Isa. 5:1ff.; Jer. 2:21; Ps. 80:8). He adopted Israel as a son in Egypt (Hos. 11:1), gave it this land, and expected it to call him Father here and never to cease to follow him (Jer. 3:19). He met Israel, his bride, in a state of utter destitution and lavished good gifts upon her in the hope that she would prove to be a faithful wife (Jer. 3:30; Hos. 2:11; Ezek. 16:1ff.).

From all the above comparisons we see that God expected a response to his goodness: fruit from the vine, obedience from the son, love and faithfulness from the wife. This does not mean that, having made the gift, he himself was passive, simply awaiting Israel's reaction. No, he was still active, moving his people to responsive action. He used Canaan as an instrument, not to threaten or force the Israelites, but "to harness them in leading-strings, to lead them with bonds of love" (Hos. 11:4 CB). God's wish was that Israel should be aware of its calling, true to its task, faithful in its community, and active in its role as God's people among the nations—and that it should be so voluntarily and of a responsible adult will. Only with this kind of awareness and maturity could Israel live up to the blessing that the Lord graciously bestowed upon it.

The Torah confirms this view. Though the laws and commandments were revealed at Sinai, they were to be fully observed in Canaan. Many of the collections begin with the formula: "When the Lord has brought you into the country . . . then you must observe" (Exod. 13:5; Lev. 14:34; Num. 15:8; Deut. 12:29). The prophets, too, interpret the gift of the land as the main inducement to Israel to live as God's people lest it be expelled from the land (cf. Amos, Hosea, Micah, Jeremiah, and Ezekiel). The historical books share the same view.

a. Called to Worship the Lord Alone

When the aged Joshua summoned the tribes to Shechem, in an act that would have far-reaching consequences he called upon the assembly to worship the Lord "in loyalty and truth" (Josh. 24:14). But he gave the people a choice: "If it does not please you to worship the Lord, choose here and now whom you will worship" (v. 14). When the people reiterated their promise to be true to the Lord, Joshua accepted it, and the day ended with a confirmation of the covenant on the part of the assembly (vv. 16-28).

Israel's declaration at Shechem was this: "The Lord our God we will worship" (v. 24). It took this decision freely. The Shechem generation was now in the land of promise. This fact influenced its faith. The promise had become a reality. Israel had occupied the land. It was living with its fruits. The changed situation had brought a closer relation to the Lord. Israel recognized that indeed he alone is the Lord. Him alone, then, Israel would worship.

The repeated affirmation "We will worship the Lord" (Josh. 24:18, 21, 24) might have the implication that Israel would always worship the Lord. Yet Joshua knew better. Human beings cannot keep a vow of this kind faithfully for generation after generation. What happened at Shechem was only a beginning. Time and again Israel would in fact forget, violate, and deny the Shechem oath. Israel had to be reminded and rebuked by divine judgments. God would not himself forget. He would keep, lead, call, and teach Israel, repeatedly reminding it of its commitment. Thus the tribes would meet again and again at Shechem (Deut. 11:29), Shiloh (Josh. 18:1), or Gilgal (Josh. 5:10ff.; 1 Sam. 11:14-15) in recommitment. Israel met in this way, not because its sense of being God's people was now part of its flesh and blood, but because God again and again reminded it of what it was constantly in danger of forgetting.

Israel needed continual nurture. It had to be reminded and exhorted. Canaan was the place where it could develop an awareness of being the Lord's people. This land was a school where it could learn to worship the Lord. Yet why Canaan? Was not this the home of nations that did not worship the Lord? In answering this question we must consider first how Canaan challenged Israel, second how Israel learned to worship the Lord with such Canaanite elements as it could adopt, and third how it could profit from elements that it had to reject.

(1) By entering Canaan Israel faced a tremendous challenge. It was deeply impressed by the space, beauty, and fertility of the country. It was affected even more by the superiority of the inhabitants in both numbers and power. Canaanite culture was more advanced. Religious ceremonies abounded. Many aspects of Canaanite civilization were most attractive, others strange and even horrible. The generation of the conquest had to learn to live among people that did not recognize the Lord God.

As newcomers they had not imagined the greatness of the challenge. But God knew. He wanted his people to be exposed to this challenge, to be tested, and to learn to stand on their own amidst the Canaanites (cf. Deut. 8:2; 13:4; Judg. 2:22). The trial was risky. Israel could easily fall into temptation. Yet the Lord wanted his people to go through this trial so as to learn from it consciously to choose him. The test, as Israel would learn, was to its own advantage (Deut. 8:16).

(2) As the Israelites came to have closer relations with the urban inhabitants of the fertile lowlands of Canaan, they could not help being impressed by the temples and religious ceremonies that they now found. Far from flatly rejecting the religious life of Canaan, they took over certain elements.

Israel saw, for example, that Yahweh could rightly be called by the Canaanite titles El (Akkadian *ilu,* Arabic *Allah*), Baal, Adon, and Milk, as may be seen from proper names from this period, e.g., Eliyahu or Elijah (Yahweh is God), Adoniyahu or Adonijah (Yahweh is Lord), Malkiyahu or Malchiah (Yahweh is King), and Jerubbaal (Yahweh is Lord, Judg. 9:1), though with the later struggle against Baal, names of the latter type were changed, Jerubbaal becoming Jerubbesheth (2 Sam. 11:21). The ideas of the court of heaven (Ps. 82:1) or of God riding on the clouds (Ps. 68:4 RSV) might also derive from Canaan, and the Canaanite story of Baal's victory over the deity of death could be applied to the Lord in Ps. 74:12ff.; 98:9ff. Possibly a hymn to the Canaanite weather-god served as a model for Ps. 29 as well.

Furthermore, it is not impossible that Israelite sanctuaries such as Mamre, Bethel, and Shechem as well as Carmel, Tabor, Shiloh, and Jerusalem had all been places of worship for the original inhabitants. Local custom also seems to have been wrongly followed when God was worshiped in the form of a carved image (Judg. 3:19; 6:25), and the teraphim (a divine mask? cf. Judg. 17:5; 1 Sam. 22:18) might also be of Canaanite origin.

Some of these items of religious belief and observance no doubt helped Israel truly to worship God, but with others Israel simply slipped into worship according to Canaanite models. This leads us to our third consideration: How did Israel profit from what it had to reject?

(3) The process of assimilation, of Canaanization, became dangerous the moment the Lord's identity was at stake and the specific character of Israel's worship either became obscure or was totally lost, Israel being no longer fully conscious of the difference between the worship of the Lord and the worship of Baal. Would Israel fall prey to what seemed to be a reasonable amalgamation? At the crucial point would it know how to distinguish between the Lord, its Liberator from Egypt, and Baal, the guarantor of rain, fertility, and other natural benefits?

The OT thankfully makes it plain that God continuously watched over his people. Repeatedly he made them aware of the perils of syncretism. He reminded them by sending a prophet (1 Kgs. 16:1; 17:1), a Nazirite (Judg. 13:5), the Levites (Exod. 36:26), or the Rechabites (Jer. 35:6). Rare and unpopular as these voices were, they could not finally be silenced. Sacral assemblies discussed the issues and sought ways out of the syncretistic deadlock that would be in accordance with the divine will.

In the matter of appellations, Israel could accept these only so long as they did not equate the Lord with foreign deities. The neighbors of Israel had to realize that Israel's Lord differed from their own gods, and Israel, too, had to be prevented even unconsciously from worshiping alien gods. For example, Baal could not be used at all as a name for the Lord. The Lord might be called El, the name of the supreme God of Canaan, and Elohim became the common term for God, but even so clarifying additions were found to be helpful, e.g., Elohe Israel, "God of Israel," and the like.

Israel had also to make clear both to itself and to others that the gods of the nations are lower and less powerful entities than the Lord, so that they could not be proper objects of worship. Slowly in Canaan the Israelites had to learn the meaning and relevance of the first two commandments: "You shall have no other God," and "You shall not make a carved image." But Israel had to learn as well how harmful many of the religious practices of Canaan might be, e.g., sacred prostitution, divination, human sacrifice, and the deification of the souls of the deceased. Sacred objects that became a snare or trap to Israel were better destroyed: "You shall tear down all their images and smash their sacred pillars" (Exod. 23:24). Along these lines Gideon radically cleansed a Canaanite sanctuary (Judg. 6), and Elijah and others resolutely contested the destructive influence of Baal worship. The people at large were obviously slow to appreciate the dangers of Canaanization. Again and again they had to be made aware of them and to take appropriate measures against them.

In some sense one might argue that in spite of God's constant attention Israel did not achieve full spiritual maturity by means of its training in Canaan. It was never able truly to worship the Lord and love him with a whole heart. As a result God canceled the gift of the land, permanently so far as the northern tribes were concerned (2 Kgs. 17:20), for seventy years in the case of Judah (Jer. 29:10). Nevertheless, the Lord kept his word to Israel. He still called it and led it. He always had a minority, a remnant that did not bend the knee to Baal (1 Kgs. 19:18). This faithful community might be found only in isolated times and places, but even in its weakness it represented the whole people. Thanks to the Lord's promise, Israel survived and the divine purpose was in fact achieved.

b. Called to Live as a Community

As noted, Canaan was the Lord's instrument to train Israel in worship, by which it would find the very mystery of its own happiness and experience the core of the divine blessing. In experiencing this blessing, it would also find a new dimension of life opening up, for it would grow into a worshiping *community.* God wanted the Israelites to join together as individuals, clans, and tribes. He did not want them to live apart without deeper relations to one another. Israel was to grow into a living community in which each cared for all as in a family. The English term "community" comes from the Latin *communio* and has the sense of having things in common, but behind the biblical use stands the Hebrew *'am,* which denotes people with blood ties. *'am Yhwh* is one of the oldest and most common appellations for Israel.

It was in Canaan that Israel grew into a settled community. The tribes had certainly lived and struggled together in the wilderness, at Sinai, and in Egypt. But they still had to come together step by step when they had divided the land and taken up their separate inheritances. They did not do this automatically. Divergent interests and differences in size and power pulled them apart. Their common ancestry alone was not enough to bring them into authentic community. The Lord himself took the initiative to unify them as a worshiping community, training and teaching them and thus inculcating in them the will and the wish to be a real fellowship and to live as such. Canaan again was an instrument in the process.

(1) In itself Canaan was hardly a fit tool in God's hand. Because of the great variety in its geographical configuration, population, culture, and social and religious practices it invited the tribes to live in isolation. How different was the dry hill country to the east from the fruitful lowlands in the valleys of the Jordan and Jezreel, or the mountainous area in the west from the coastal plains inhabited by the Philistines! How different in origin and culture were the Amorites, Hittites, Jebusites, etc., that we now call Canaanites! How varied was the social pattern of small farmers on the one hand, townsfolk on the other with their officials, soldiers, landlords, craftsmen, traders, and slaves! How varied, too, were the deities and the forms of worship!

This diversity did not favor the development of close fellowship. In this sense Canaan dangerously challenged Israel. Meeting different circumstances and cultures, each tribe tended to develop differently and progress at different paces. The variety could be an advantage, but it increased the difficulty of any growth of the tribes into a single community.

(2) In the early stages Israel undoubtedly underwent to some extent a process of Canaanization. It had to learn how to live a sedentary life, applying its laws to the new situations and adapting itself to individual circumstances. For a period the result was that the individual tribes tended to take on the appearance almost of separate nations that had no very cohesive relations. How different was Judah in the hill country from Issachar, or the powerful Joseph tribe, or the less settled Benjamin and Dan! The Song of Deborah offers a realistic picture of the difficulty of forming a common front to face what did not seem to be in the more immediate sense a common danger.

(3) Within the process of Canaanization, however, we may note also a process of Israelization. If Canaanite influences were driving the tribes apart, they were also giving birth to a desire to find and strengthen the identity of the tribes as a single community, the federation of Israel. Local cooperation

favored the process as tribes in the north found a center in Mt. Tabor, those in the center at Shechem or Gilgal, and those in the south at Mamre or Hebron.

(4) Yet the common wish or intent of the tribes to unity was not enough. The Lord himself also took the initiative, from time to time sending leaders endowed with the power and authority of his Spirit, protecting the people against the danger of total assimilation, and helping tribes that came under special threat either from within or without. Defeats followed by foreign oppression constantly reminded the people that they had in God alone their one God and Savior. When they cried to him for help, he heard their cry and raised up leaders, the judges, who could liberate the people from their enemies. These interventions strengthened in Israel an awareness that the kin-tribes belonged together as the one people of the Lord (Judg. 5:13).

Although a given judge might deliver only his own tribe (Judah in the case of Othniel in Judg. 3:9, Benjamin in that of Ehud in 4:6; etc.), an appeal was made to neighboring tribes for help (5:13ff.; 6:35; 7:23-24). The level of cooperation might vary, but slowly and steadfastly mutual fidelity grew as the tribes gained the mastery in their separate areas but also saw their common exposure to external assault. Realizing their dependence on the one Lord, the tribes also came to see more clearly their dependence on one another in a common community.

(5) God encouraged cooperation in times of peace as well as war. Assemblies of the whole people took place according to Josh. 24:1; Judg. 20:1; 1 Sam. 10:19; etc. These assemblies were for common worship but they also strengthened the relations among the tribes. They fostered a mature feeling of common responsibility, averting estrangement, overcoming conflict, clearly stating individual rights and duties in concrete situations, and explaining God's will with greater clarity so that it could be followed in the problems that faced the people. In the legislation that governed the conduct of the tribes, it came to be seen that behind every distinction the basic reality was that every member of every tribe, i.e., of the whole community, was a brother or sister with an equal right to the love and respect of all others (Lev. 19:17-19). For all the tensions, the people thus came together as the one people of the one Lord who guided and trained it in Canaan.

c. Called to Be a Forerunner of the Nations

As we try to understand theologically the purpose of God in giving Canaan to his people, we note also that by this gift God did not favor Israel to the detriment of other nations. What he did for his own small people had significance for all peoples. They, too, were granted a gift, a blessing, and a responsibility. The people whom God trained in Canaan were to be a model for the nations, their forerunner. They were to open up a way that all nations could follow and on which they also could find blessing.

At the conquest, of course, the nations were adversaries that had to be defeated. In most of the OT, indeed, the stress falls on the Lord's dealings with his chosen people. Less prominence is given to God's purpose for other nations and his actions on their behalf. Yet if this aspect of the witness is limited, it is no less unequivocal.

At least three times in their history as residents of Canaan the Israelites had important encounters with other nations. The first was during the occupation. In this case the first period of forcible entry gave way to an attempt at peaceable coexistence, though with ultimate reaction lest Israel lose its real identity, suffer total assimilation into Canaanite society, and miss its divine calling. The second encounter was under the reigns of David and Solomon, when for a brief period many foreign peoples were subject to Israel and alliances were forged with the other great powers of the area. The third encounter was during the exile when the kingdoms had been shattered, the leading citizens led away, and those who were left in the land subjected to foreign occupation.

From these encounters Israel learned many lessons. The first, perhaps, was that it could not fulfil the divine purpose unless it preserved its individual identity as the Lord's people. The second, learned under David and Solomon, was that it had the opportunity of sharing the blessings of the kingdom with other peoples. The third, learned when Israel itself became a subject people, was that Israel is really the servant of the Lord, not of other nations, and that the Lord has entrusted it, not with the task of exacting vengeance (cf. Ps. 137), nor of merely achieving its own restoration, but of being a divinely commissioned witness to every nation (Isa. 40–55).

Exile and emigration! (Even today far more Jews live outside their homeland than in it.) But we do not have here a punishment alone. The Lord transformed what was originally condemnation into a blessing and a sending. Scattered throughout the world, the members of God's people could be witnesses, forerunners, and motivators among all peoples and nations. The Lord's people old and new are called upon to share in the worldwide work of God until the final consummation of his kingdom.

Chapter VII

God Raised Up Kings in Israel

Introduction

GOD ACTS IN HISTORY. He created heaven and earth, elected Israel's ancestors, liberated his people from Egypt, led them through the wilderness, revealed his laws at Sinai, and gave them Canaan as a home. He never ceased to work. He came to carry out the plan of inaugurating a new world of justice, the kingdom of God.

The core of the NT witness tells us that the kingdom began to be realized in Jesus Christ. At the same time, is not the kingdom at the heart of the OT witness? True, there was hardly a mention of it in Chapters I–VI above. The first reminder of it comes in the many stories of human kings and kingdoms. Most of the nations of antiquity had kings. Israel lived for centuries under monarchical rule. A close relation exists, however, between human kingdoms and God's kingdom. Human kings are God's deputies. Their kingdoms are related to God's kingdom.

In the OT we are astonished to find that the noun "king" (Hebrew *melek*) occurs over 2,500 times, the verb "to rule as king" or "to become king" *(mālak)* over 340 times, and the noun "kingdom" *(mamlākāh, malkût,* etc.) over 200 times. The noun *melek* is the noun that is most often used in the OT apart from *ben* ("son") and *'elōhîm* ("God"). The idea of kingship is plainly one of the most common and the most important in the OT.

Why is there this interest in kings? History and sociology might suggest that as most nations adopted monarchy, and this form of government deeply influenced the whole social system, it was natural that Israel should come under the same influence. For Israel, however, monarchy as a political and social system also had a theological dimension, for the Israelites were in relation to the eternal kingdom in which God rules in love and justice. The interest of Israel lay not so much in the institution of kingship as such but in

God's use of the institution as Ruler over his people and humanity. The Lord, the God of Israel, wants just government. It is to this end that he acts, raising up kings here and overthrowing them there.

God's decisive steps in ruling the nations will culminate one day in his raising up a king that will fully do his will on earth. The prophets expressed and kindled this developing hope that we usually call messianic expectation. Meantime God allowed the institution of kingship in Israel which began with the anointing of Saul ca. 1020 B.C. and ended with the death of Jehoiachin in Babylonian exile ca. 550 B.C. We must now consider what happened during this period.

(1) Israel came into being as a community that had no king, that had no centralized government, that gathered only to face a common enemy or to engage in common worship. The tribes at first felt no need for a strong central government and were jealous of their independence no less from one another than from foreign powers.

(2) In Canaan, however, Israel found that nearly all the existing inhabitants had kings. Through relations with the Canaanites an awareness of the lack of effective government began to develop. Gradually a wish arose to have a king "like other nations" (1 Sam. 8:5), though it was understood that this form of rule might deprive the people of many of the liberties they had previously enjoyed.

(3) The perilous situation of the tribes gave greater urgency to the wish. In addition to internal strife Israel found itself under pressure from the Amalekites and Midianites to the south, the Midianites and Ammonites to the east, the Arameans to the north, and the Philistines to the west. Remnants of the city-kingdoms of Canaan increased the danger.

(4) Philistine pressure finally became so strong that the tribes agreed to accept Saul as their first king. Judah abstained, but later became a kingdom of its own with David as its first ruler (2 Sam. 2:1ff.). The union of the two states gave birth to greater Israel under David and Solomon. This kingdom included several foreign territories but lasted only about 70 years (1000-930 B.C.). The two kingdoms then separated again, Israel comprising northern and central Palestine (930-722 B.C.), Judah the south (930-586 B.C.).

(5) Monarchy brought with it revolutionary changes in Israelite society. Outward security and inward law and order increased. Yet the price was high. Tribal autonomy decreased and the central state exacted burdensome taxes and levies. The authority of the king and civil service expanded at the expense of inherited landed property. A professional army replaced the tribal militia and foreign alliances and power politics became the order of the day.

(6) In many ways the full development of the new system was hampered by the inherited customs of Israel as the people of God. Israel's kings never enjoyed absolute authority. They could never impose their will as

the kingdom's supreme law. They could ascend the throne only as they were divinely designated and anointed. They were God's servants. They might try to imitate foreign rulers, but they could never break entirely with Israel's distinctiveness.

(7) As monarchy began in Israel, so it ended when Judah fell in 586 B.C. and its territory became a Babylonian province. From that time onward Israel was under foreign rule. In spite of heroic efforts, the people could never permanently reestablish Israel's sovereignty. Israel's share in politics and civil government did not end, for the Israelites would still have public responsibilities. But they would no longer discharge these in the form of monarchy.

1. The Witness of Scripture

By raising up kings in Israel, God associated human personages with his own government of his chosen people. All kings and governments receive their power from God and are responsible to God. Israel's kings were also to bear witness to God's coming kingdom. By enthronement they were commissioned to defend right and justice and to establish and uphold peace, primarily among their own people. David and Solomon were examples of both success and failure, but Israel's other kings were judged according to their own attitudes and actions. God in his own time will call his Servant, the messianic King, who by his suffering will turn failure into victory and bring salvation, justice, and peace to the earth.

KINGSHIP IS NOT USUALLY REGARDED as a basic theme of Israel's faith. Only rarely did Israel praise the Lord for raising up its kings (cf. Ps. 78:65ff.; Neh. 9:27). Nevertheless, the main historical books all deal with the leaders whom God gave to his people, the judges first, and then the kings. Psalms, too, gives an important place to the kings, especially to David. The prophetic books include visions of the coming righteous king. In the NT Paul at Pisidian Antioch, in his summary of God's dealings with Israel, recalls that God appointed judges (Acts 13:20), then kings (vv. 21-22), and finally Jesus of the posterity of David (v. 23). The thesis of monarchy is in fact a basic one in salvation history.

The monarchy might often take an ambivalent form. It brought hardships to the people and involved them in harmful secular entanglements. Having a theological dimension, however, it has an inalienable place in Israel's faith and the OT witness.

Kingship in the OT stands in a reciprocal relationship to other OT topics. As regards creation, the OT does not support the Egyptian belief that monarchy is rooted in the very order of nature. Kingship was not essential. Ezekiel could ridicule the king of Tyre for dreaming of being a king at the world's center (Ezek. 28:11-18). A king, being also human, could be no more than a first among equals. Only by grace could he have a part in the creation of God's new world, i.e., by delivering the people through whom God was working out his purpose.

There are interesting points of contact between the kings and the patriarchs. David fulfilled the promises given to Abraham (Gen. 15:18-21) when he became king of Judah (2 Sam. 2:1-4) and then of all Israel (5:1-3). By his enthronement David also fulfilled Jacob's blessing of Judah (Gen. 49:8-12). The climax of the story of Ruth is the truth that God's dealings with the patriarchs come to fulfilment in her great-grandson David (Ruth 4:11, 17). An allusion to the northern kingdom of Israel may be found in Jacob's blessing of Joseph, "the prince among his brothers" (Gen. 49:26; cf. Deut. 33:16-17). The divine promise to Abraham and Sarah, the father and mother of the nations, was that "kings shall spring" from them (Gen. 17:6, 16).

No direct relation seems to exist between the monarchy and the liberation from Egypt, the journey through the wilderness, and the revelation at Sinai. At most one might recall that Israel was itself to be a kingdom of priests (Exod. 19:6) and that David founded his kingdom on ancient Israelite traditions, bringing up the ark to Jerusalem and thus placing this basic symbol at the very center of his kingdom. Solomon, too, in his famous prayer in 1 Kgs. 8, stated his willingness to lead the people according to the laws that Moses gave them (vv. 57-61). The building of the temple, of course, stands closely related to the construction of the wilderness tabernacle.

A two-way relation exists between kingship and the gift of the land. God granted the land in order that the people might be one people under one leader. Conversely, kings who violated the land came under sharp censure.

A close link exists between the raising up of kings and the election of Jerusalem, the theme in Chapter VIII below. It would be hard to understand the central role of Jerusalem apart from David, who captured the city from the Jebusites (2 Sam. 5:6-12) and made it his capital. The act by which God chose Zion as his own dwelling cannot be distinguished from that by which he raised up David as king over his people (Ps. 78:68-72; 132:11-14). Both acts serve the same aim: the life of Israel as God's chosen people (2 Sam. 7:8, 24).

The sending of the prophets (see Chapter IX below) is also linked to the raising up of the kings. How tense were the relations between prophets and kings! Yet also how close were the responsibilities of these two categories of servants of the Lord!

2. God Enthroned Israel's Kings

Israel praises God, gives thanks, confesses its faith, and seeks God's help—because God acted and spoke. Among God's deeds we now look at his raising up of kings. Why did the Lord, the God of Israel, do this? How did he do it? What does it mean that he did it?

a. The Lord's Own Initiative

KINGS ARE RAISED UP by an act of state that officially and legally entrusts given members of the community with the office. Elders, tribal heads, priests, prophets, and other leaders attend the solemn ceremony, participating as either actors or witnesses. Recording such ceremonies, the OT allows that Israel's representatives could legitimately enthrone kings.

Nevertheless, the OT also bears witness that God himself took the initiative in this matter. Before the leaders installed a king, God had already chosen him and raised him up in his own way and with his own aim. God's act did not rival the act of state nor make it superfluous or invalid. It laid the foundation for it.

What did the Lord do when he raised up a judge or king? The Hebrew verbs are clear enough. Thus we find the causative of the verb *mālak;* God made Saul or Solomon king (1 Sam. 15:11, 35; 1 Kgs. 3:7). We also read that God had already chosen *(bāhar)* the king (1 Sam. 10:24; 16:8-10). The people are told to "appoint as king the man whom the Lord your God will choose" (Deut. 17:15). God's "chosen one" *(bāhîr)* can be a royal title (2 Sam. 21:6; Ps. 89:4). Alternatively God appoints *(ṣiwwāh)* David king (1 Sam. 25:30; 2 Sam. 6:21).

Another common term is *hēqîm,* "to raise up," from *qûm,* "to stand." Later this word would be used for raising up from the dead (Hos. 6:2). It stresses the divine initiative. God raises up judges and saviors (Judg. 2:16), or kings of David's house (1 Kgs. 15:4), or the just king of David's line (Jer. 23:4-5; Ezek. 34:23). David is "the man whom the High God raised up" (2 Sam. 23:1).

Commonly, too, the Lord "anoints" *(māšaḥ)* a man to be king (1 Sam. 10:1; etc.). Kings thus go by the title of *mᵉšîaḥ YHWH,* "the Lord's anointed" (cf. 1 Sam. 2:10; Ps. 2:2). Less frequent terms are "to enthrone" *(nāsak* in Ps. 2:6, though the meaning of this verb is not quite certain), "to appoint as prince" *(nātan nāgîd,* 1 Kgs. 14:7; Isa. 55:4), and "to elevate" *(hērîm,* from *rûm,* "be high") (CB 1 Sam. 2:10; 1 Kgs. 14:7; Ps. 89:19).

Has God alone the right to appoint kings in Israel? No, the representatives of the people may also do so (2 Sam. 2:4; 1 Kgs. 8:1). Indeed, "all the people" invested Saul as king (1 Sam. 11:15 RSV). "All Israel" made

Rehoboam king (1 Kgs. 12:1). The tribal heads, too, had authority to anoint a king (Judg. 9:8), as did the men of Judah (2 Sam. 2:4), the men of the northern tribes (19:10), and even the "people of the land" (2 Kgs. 23:30).

As a rule, however, God through one of his prophets took the lead, acting before Israel's representatives could do anything. God alone raised up a judge, savior, king, or shepherd by a creative act beyond the range of human possibility (cf. Judg. 2:16; 1 Kgs. 14:14; Jer. 23:4-5; Ezek. 34:23). Independent action on Israel's part could only bring disaster (Deut. 28:36). God alone could choose. Choice by Israel violated the Lord's prerogative, and in consequence God said: "I gave you a king in my anger" (Hos. 13:11). Since God alone could elevate a man to be king, any who elevated themselves could only fall (cf. the king of Babel in Isa. 14:13-14).

Why did the choice belong to the Lord alone? The answer lies in the role of the Spirit of God relative to Israel's leaders and kings. The Spirit was imparted to many judges (e.g., Gideon) and especially to David and Solomon. They were constituted leaders by this extraordinary gift. As von Rad points out in his *Old Testament Theology*, charismatic leaders of this type were unique to Israel. Other countries enthroned their kings with splendid ceremonies but did not see the need for divine inspiration if they were to be able to rule. The role of the Spirit is a distinctive feature of kingship in Israel.

When Gideon, for example, was called to lead the people against the Midianites, "the Spirit of the Lord took possession" of him and with only 300 soldiers he won a total victory (Judg. 6:33ff.; 7:1–8:3). From the Spirit he received authority, courage, wisdom, and above all the divine presence. The story of Jephthah, the "great warrior," is to the same effect. When the elders fetched Jephthah to fight the Ammonites, the Spirit came upon him and he assembled volunteer forces and gained a great victory, enjoying both the authority of command and the help of the Lord (Judg. 11:1ff.).

Of Samson, too, we read that "the Spirit of the Lord began to drive him hard" (Judg. 13:25). His great strength alone did not guarantee him success against the Philistines (16:19). But when the Spirit "seized" him (14:6, 19; 15:14) he saved his people as God had planned (14:14). The Lord alone may and must choose because it is only by the Spirit's power that judges and kings can discharge their functions.

Endowment with the Spirit, of course, was not institutional. If the Spirit came upon Othniel (Judg. 3:7-11) we are not told of any descent of the Spirit on Ehud or Deborah and Barak. At the same time, great stress is laid on the Spirit's role in the case of the two military leaders who became the first two kings in Israel, Saul and David. Saul's anointing by Samuel (1 Sam. 9–10:16) was followed at once by his meeting with a group of prophets, and then "the spirit of God suddenly took possession of him, so that he too was filled with prophetic rapture" (10:10; cf. v. 6). Again at Gibeah, when news came of the Ammonite attack, "the spirit of God suddenly seized him" (11:6) and he mustered the people, crossed the Jordan, and victoriously attacked and routed the enemy (11:7-11). Similarly, the anointing of David by Samuel (1 Sam.

16:1-13) had as its climax the descent of the Spirit: "The spirit of the Lord came upon David and was with him from that day onwards." If the same is not specifically said of Solomon, the "depth of wisdom and insight" that he received from God (1 Kgs. 4:29) might well be regarded as a gift of the Spirit, not now for military leadership, but for peacetime government.

Inasmuch as it is the Spirit who equips Israel's leaders, the initiative in appointing kings plainly lies with God. Official acts by the people or their representatives are secondary. They are not irrelevant, but they have no basis except in God's act. No leader can either grasp or possess God's gracious presence. Neither civil or religious ceremonies on the one hand, nor human enthusiasm, courage, or strength on the other, can enable a ruler to play his proper part. Only the Lord's free decision to grant him the Spirit makes him a true leader. This basis of authority proved to be a strong bulwark against abuses of the monarchy as an institution.

The dramatic event by which the Spirit came upon persons totally changed them. In Saul's case, for example, the Spirit "turned him into another man" (cf. 1 Sam. 10:6 RSV). What does this mean? The point is not that Saul became a prophet, or that he merely received great strength, or that he came to know states of ecstasy or rapture. The real truth is that by the Spirit Saul became the Lord's possession and stood under the authority of Israel's true Savior. He received the grace, then, that enabled him to share in God's work of government, leadership, and liberation.

God granted his Spirit at times when his people were in extreme danger and would have been destroyed had not God intervened. God himself acted to save, but he did so by taking chosen persons into partnership in his work of salvation. Can human beings really be saviors? Is not the Lord alone the Savior of Israel (cf. 1 Sam. 10:1 and Hos. 13:4)? Yes, but this only Savior raises up simple people to be instruments of his action. To save Israel in God's strength is the core of the task that Israel's leaders and rulers had to perform. By choosing kings and giving them such saving tasks, God took a great risk, yet no more so than in adopting Israel as his people, sending prophets to speak his Word, or establishing priests to offer worship and to be mediators between his people and himself.

The extent of the risk may be seen from the many failures of those whom God endowed with his Spirit. We think of Gideon, Jephthah, Samson, and Saul. We think of the sorry reigns of many of the kings of Israel and Judah. We think of the disasters that finally terminated the monarchy. The kings whom God selected were not free from faults and they had to bear the consequences of their misdeeds. Was kingship, then, a total failure? Did God have to put a complete end to it? No, for God keeps his promise to David and stands by the commission that he gave to Israel's rulers, namely, to be models for the governments of the nations. God does not give up the initiative or the promise to grant his Spirit. Israel's kings might vanish, but Israel was and is still waiting for the final King and Savior in whom God's promise will come to definitive fulfilment.

b. Raising Up, Anointing, and Enthronement of the King

When God raises up someone to kingship, the first steps are hidden. It is all a mystery when God sees the man, sends a prophet to anoint him, and confers his Spirit upon him. The next steps, however, must be public. The official representatives of the people must have a part in giving the king authority and bearing witness to his legitimate accession. The official ceremony was the enthronement.

With the enthronement, do we leave the spiritual field and enter the political field? We may distinguish these fields, but not separate them. When God raised up a man to kingship, his action had a political dimension. Public enthronement was also a ceremony with spiritual dimensions. It is a mistake to see Israel only as a religious community with no political or social responsibilities. With the ceremony of enthronement Israel acted like any other nation, but in so doing it accepted a challenge from God. Several biblical texts call for notice in this regard.

The first enthronement story occurs in Judg. 9:6. When Abimelech, a son of Gideon, seized power, the citizens of Shechem and Beth-millo met and made him king at Shechem. From the parable of Jotham that follows (9:7-15) we may deduce that Abimelech was anointed (v. 8). The ceremony took place at a sanctuary with all the people as witnesses.

A feature of Saul's installation as king was the participation of the people in the ceremony: "They all acclaimed him, shouting, 'Long live the king'" at Mizpah (1 Sam. 10:24), and then "all went to Gilgal and invested Saul there as king" (11:15).

As regards David, we read that the men of Judah came to Hebron, "and there they anointed David king over the house of Judah" (2 Sam. 2:4). Seven and a half years later "all the elders of Israel came to the king at Hebron; there David made a covenant with them before the Lord, and they anointed David king over Israel" (2 Sam. 5:3). It should be noted here that the elders presided over the ceremony of anointing.

In relation to David's successor the OT reports three attempted coups d'état: by Absalom (2 Sam. 15:10-12), by Sheba (20:1-2), and by Adonijah (1 Kgs. 1:5-10, 25-27). All failed by a narrow margin. Finally Solomon,

David's son by Bathsheba, became king (1 Kgs. 1:32-40, 43-48). He was anointed by the Zadokite priest and the prophet Nathan (1:34ff.) and acclaimed by the whole people: "Long live King Solomon" (1:34, 39).

Later the revolt of Jehu led to his anointing by a prophet and acclamation by his soldiers (2 Kgs. 9–10). Athaliah's abortive coup ended with the enthronement of Joash (11:1-20). The priest Jehoiada "put the crown" on the head of Joash and "handed him the warrant" (NEB), and the people "proclaimed him king, and anointed him; and they clapped their hands, and said, 'Long live the king'" (11:12 RSV). The people then escorted the young king to the royal palace and seated him on the throne (11:19).

On the basis of these texts R. de Vaux, the French historian, in his book *Ancient Israel: Its Life and Institutions* (Eng. tr. 1961), pp. 100-107, proposed the following reconstruction of the ceremonial. The candidate took his place on an estrade in the temple court. A diadem or crown was placed on his head, perhaps with other emblems. A warrant was given him with his name and titles, his rights and duties, and the divine commission and promise. He was anointed and thereby recognized by the people's representatives. The people acclaimed and greeted him. He was escorted to the palace and seated on the throne. The people's representatives and leaders pledged their loyalty.

Israel's neighbors, of course, had similar ceremonies, but the three acts of anointing the king, giving him a warrant, and enthroning him show clearly how distinctive was Israel's concept and practice of kingship.

(1) Anointing. By tradition, oil was used to cleanse and strengthen. Because it supposedly strengthened, many nations used it to anoint their kings. Pouring oil on their heads was thought to endow them with miraculous power and divine authority and glory. Later oil was used as a symbol. The Hittites anointed their kings from the 14th century B.C. Perhaps the Israelites were directly or indirectly influenced by them (cf. Judg. 9:8, 15), but in adopting the rite they saw in it a new meaning.

It should be noted that anointing continued throughout the monarchy, i.e., from Saul (1 Sam. 10:1) to Jehoahaz (2 Kgs. 23:30). David, Absalom, and Solomon were all anointed, as was Joash. Though we have few references from the northern kingdom of Israel, there can be little doubt that the practice was continually observed there, too.

The anointing always had a political dimension. The elders, tribal heads, and people all took part in the ceremony. They did so, of course, as members of the Lord's people. The anointing took place before the Lord with offerings and prayers for God's blessing on the newly invested king, the Lord's anointed. Nevertheless, the Israelites were also investing the king as head of state and head of the civil government, with responsibility for the general welfare of society.

We note, too, that anointing rested on an agreement stating the conditions under which the king might rule. This gave his government a legal basis. The people's representatives delegated power to the king, but not without making sure that he could be trusted. The limits of the monarchy and the associated institutions had to be clearly defined. The candidate had to take an oath of office (cf. David's covenant in 2 Sam. 5:3 and the vow in Ps. 101). The people's representatives also swore that they would discharge their own duties according to the agreed rules of the kingdom (cf. 1 Sam. 10:25).

The people's rights were often violated. Abner, Saul's commander, arbitrarily brought Saul's son Ishbosheth to Mahanaim "and made him king" over the northern tribes (2 Sam. 2:9). David designated his successor on his own authority (1 Kgs. 1:33-35). Officers of the palace and temple imposed candidates by force (2 Kgs. 12:20; 21:23). Usurpers also took power by force, e.g., Abimelech, or the last northern kings (15:18-31). Twice foreign kings decided who would sit on the throne of Judah (23:24; 24:17). The OT viewed such practices as abnormal. It deplored the division of Israel after Solomon's death, though recognizing Rehoboam's fault (1 Kgs. 12:1-10). The arbitrary investiture of a king contradicted the dignity and maturity of the people.

We note again that the people's right to anoint a king did not infringe on the Lord's right to take the initiative in anointing whom he wished. The Lord himself anointed Saul (1 Sam. 9:16), David (16:12-13), and Jehu (2 Kgs. 9:3) to deliver Israel either from the Philistines or from domestic peril. He also raised up Cyrus to destroy Babylon and to make possible the rebuilding of Jerusalem and the temple (Isa. 44:28). There was no rivalry between divine and human anointing. Like the gift of the Spirit, the divine anointing was a promise of the Lord's presence which the civil ceremony could not give. Only in a few instances, however, was this hidden promise given.

(2) Warrant. There can be no absolute certainty regarding the warrant of investiture. Everything depends on how we construe the ʿēdût that was given to Joash along with the crown in 2 Kgs. 11:12. The RSV renders the term "testimony," and many exegetes think it might have been a copy of the Torah. The NEB, however, has the translation "warrant," and von Rad (*Old Testament Theology*, I, 319) saw here a ceremony similar to that at Egyptian coronations, when Pharaoh received a warrant from Amon-Re, the Egyptian high god. Ps. 2 possibly alludes to a warrant of this kind when it refers to the Lord's decree (*ḥōq*) in vv. 7-9. A quotation from the warrant is sometimes seen in Ps. 110:1-4.

A central element in the warrant was that the king was declared to be God's son. The Egyptian king was the son of Re; the kings of Sumer and Babylon were lauded as sons of God, and many Assyrian kings bore the same title; Keret, a hero of Ugaritic myth, was called son of El; Mesha of Moab (ca. 900 B.C.) styled himself son of Chemosh (or Kemosh); and Alexander the Great and Augustus were both called sons of God. The king was viewed as the meeting place of heaven and earth, charged to keep the balance of the universe, but able to do so only if he was by nature both human and divine.

The OT could hardly espouse the common concept, though individual Israelites might accept it. Hence, while the king in Israel may also be addressed as God's son, we find distinctive features. In the Egyptian warrant, for example, the newly enthroned king was said to be the son of God by birth, but in Ps. 2:7 sonship dates only from the day of investiture (cf. 1 Sam. 7:14). It is by the Word of the Lord that the king becomes God's son (Ps. 89:27). He had been born a human child, but the Lord as it were adopted, acknowledged, and proclaimed him his son.

Again, Israel's kings were sons of God only in the light of David's election. The saying in 2 Sam. 7:14: "I will be his father, and he shall be my son," was addressed to David. It carried the promise that the close relation between the Lord and this servant of his would obtain for all the kings of his house. The stress, however, was not on divine origin but on filial relation. The kings might do evil and need correction, but they could be certain that the love which God had for David would be shown to them. They needed this fatherly love if they were to be strong and to be able to rule, though it might be also the love that meant discipline and correction.

A further point is that not the king alone but the whole people is called God's son in the OT. The kings could not boast of being different from the people in this regard. God had adopted Israel. His word to Pharaoh at the liberation from Egypt was this: "Israel is my first-born son. . . . Let my son go, so that he may worship me" (Exod. 4:22). His word in Hos. 11:1 is to the same effect: "When Israel was a boy, I loved him; I called my son out of Egypt." Sonship is the basis of the laws: "You are the sons of the Lord your God" (Deut. 14:1). In all his majesty, the king was no more than a representative of the people at large (cf. 2 Sam. 5:12; 2 Chron. 9:8).

(3) Enthronement. After the anointing in the temple court, the king was escorted with joyous shouts to the palace and seated on the throne in symbol of taking up the task of government. This act confirmed publicly what had just taken place in the holy court.

Since enthronement, too, was by no means restricted to Israel, the question of its specific significance in OT theology obviously arises. The OT shows no great interest in thrones as such. Saul simply sat in his house in Gibeah (now Tel el-Ful, just north of Jerusalem). Nothing is said about a throne either in his case or David's except that Solomon took his seat on the throne of his father David (1 Kgs. 1:46-48). In his great wealth Solomon himself made a great ivory throne overlaid with fine gold (10:18-20), but nothing like it had ever been made before. The point about the throne was that its ascent meant assuming the task of government, and the first responsibility of government was to make a copy of the law (Deut. 17:18).

A most important truth in the OT is that the Lord himself, the King of heaven, sits on the throne, seated above the cherubim, or on his heavenly throne, actively engaged in the government of the world, so that his people need not fear the dangers that threaten them (cf. Pss. 47; 93; 96–99). God's deeds in history might suggest at times that he has only just been enthroned, and Israel hopes for his future enthronement when his kingdom seems to be hidden or invalidated by present disorders. Yet he never ceases to sit on the throne and to rule the world.

In contrast to neighboring states that exalted their thrones, supposedly upheld by the gods, the OT exalts only the throne of David. Solomon and Ahab might make magnificent thrones, but the kings of Judah were all said to sit on the throne of David (Jer. 13:13; etc.). This did not mean an exalting of David but an emphasis on the divine promise in virtue of which alone the throne of David lasted. The throne of David was also the throne of Israel, since God keeps faith with David and his house for Israel's sake. The people, then, were not subjects or dependents. The throne was theirs. They were the Lord's people. They shared the majesty and responsibility of government.

Enthronement meant that Israel's kings were allowed a remarkable place "at the right hand of the Lord." This expression belongs to the investiture ceremony (cf. Ps. 110:1; 80:17). Though uncommon, it was the origin of an important tradition that greatly influenced the NT and won an eminent place in the Christian creed. The place at the right hand was the place of honor (1 Kgs. 2:19) and power (Ps. 80:17-18). Though Israel's king was a simple human being like all others, and even as a ruler was the head of only a comparatively insignificant state, he had the authority and responsibility of an officer of God. His rule, then, had a share in the divine rule and was under a specific obligation to conform to it.

The OT speaks of the throne or kingdom of the Lord as well as the throne of David or Israel. Thus David "chose Solomon to sit upon the throne of the Lord's sovereignty over Israel" (1 Chron. 28:5), and "Solomon sat on the Lord's throne as king in place of his father David" (29:23). The Queen of Sheba on her visit to Jerusalem, speaking to Solomon, praised "the Lord your God who has delighted in you and has set you on his throne as his king" (2 Chron. 9:8). Reference is also made to "the kingdom of the Lord as ruled by David's sons" (13:8). All Israel under David and Solomon and their successors was called the kingdom of the Lord, and its kings sat on the throne of the Lord. The kingdom of the Lord, of course, surpassed the narrow limits of the kingdom of Judah (cf. Ps. 145:8-13). The throne of God was infinitely more splendid than Solomon's pretentious throne of ivory and gold (cf. Ps. 93:2; 103:19; Isa. 6:1). Nevertheless, the Lord and his kingdom were closely involved in the raising up of David to kingship, and the Lord would not leave his work unfinished (Ps. 138:8 NEB).

David's throne would not last as such. Its glory would never come up to that of the Egyptian, Assyrian, or Persian thrones. Its uniqueness, however, was that the Lord's name rested upon it. For this reason Israel's kings also had a unique function. Being given so glorious a throne, they also had an extraordinary office and task.

c. Office and Task

The Lord, the King of kings, raised up kings in Israel (1 Sam. 9:15-16). What office and task did he entrust to these kings? A king must obviously rule with justice and wisdom. Even a pagan king like Hammurabi recognized this in his famous Code. But Israel's king ruled neither in his own name nor solely in the name of his people. He held his office from God and received his task from God, for was he not the son of God sitting at the right hand of God? What, then, was his distinctive office and task?

Of the OT terms for "king," *melek* is the most common. An older term applied to Saul (1 Sam. 9:16) and David (13:14) is *nāgîd,* possibly meaning leader (cf. also Solomon in 1 Kgs. 1:35 and other kings in 14:7; 16:2). *nāśî',* a chief, is another older term (1 Kgs. 11:34; Ezek. 46:8). *śar,* meaning prince, might also be used for "king," as in the phrase *sar šālôm,* "Prince of peace" (Isa. 9:5 [Eng. 6]).

In many ways the office and task of Israel's kings resembled that of the kings of other nations. When hard pressed by the Philistines, the Israelites specifically asked for "a king to govern us, like other nations" (1 Sam. 8:5, 20). These other nations might have lofty views of kingship. Hammurabi's Code refers to a "devout, god-fearing prince" who will "cause justice to prevail in the land" and "destroy the wicked and the evil." A true king will be a "shepherd whose scepter is righteous," who will govern the peoples in peace, and grant justice "to the orphan (and) the widow" (J. B. Pritchard, ed., *Ancient Near Eastern Texts Relating to the Old Testament,* 3rd ed. [1969], pp. 164, 178).

(1) If we seek the distinctive features of the OT king, the first point is that the king was to be a liberator or savior. Saul came into office at a time of emergency under foreign pressure. He was anointed to "deliver my people from the Philistines" (1 Sam. 9:16; 10:1). David was appointed to fight the Lord's wars (1 Sam. 25:28). Later a king was raised up as "a deliverer for Israel, who rescued them from the power of Aram" (2 Kgs. 13:5). Egyptian and Mesopotamian rulers also had the task of saving the people, but this was not their primary raison d'être. The primary character of the king in Israel influenced the whole biblical witness, for the ultimate messianic King would be a true deliverer, a savior.

Yet what does this office of Israel's kings imply? First, we must recall that Israel really had no savior apart from God himself. The prophetic saying: "You knew no other saviour than me" (Hos. 13:4), sums up this article of faith. Or we might quote Isa. 43:11: "I am the Lord . . . and none but I can deliver." No foreign god could deliver Israel, but neither could any human being, whether inside Israel, lest the people should say: "My own hand has delivered me" (Judg. 7:2 RSV), or outside (Isa. 31:1-3). Israel's whole existence, its life and death, depended on the one King who again and again rescued it from oppression and extermination. Psalms that extol the Lord as King (47; 93; 96–99) underscore a basic truth that cannot be called into question by the fact that men, too, delivered Israel.

Second, the Lord chose specific individuals as saviors *(môšîaʿ)* of his people, namely, the judges, Saul, and David (1 Sam. 12:11; Neh. 9:27). The long list of saviors who delivered Israel includes Othniel, Ehud, Shamgar, Gideon, Tola, and Samson, also Barak, Jephthah, and Samuel, and finally Saul and David. But could any human being really save others? The Bible leaves no room for misunderstanding. The Lord himself saves. But he does so through chosen leaders whom he allows to share in his saving work.

Third, by accepting human participation the Lord took a great risk. It seemed as if he was raising up saviors besides himself. He was apparently stepping into the background and letting his human officers work out deliverance before the people's eyes. The danger arose that the officers would be praised and that the people would forget that he alone is Israel's Savior. This danger did not become acute in the days of the judges, but it did so once Israel asked for a king (Judg. 8:22; 1 Sam. 8:5). Obviously the royal office breeds pride. People are tempted to glorify their king for his own strength and virtue, and to forget their only King and Savior (1 Sam. 8:7; 12:12). Gideon refused the crown for this reason (Judg. 8:23). Samuel first rejected the people's request for the same reason (1 Sam. 8:6). The prophets issued similar warnings (cf. Hos. 13:10).

Fourth, the OT hesitates to say that a king really delivered Israel (1 Sam. 12:11). Saul began and failed (1 Sam. 31). David alone succeeded (2 Sam. 5:17-25). Yet even this famous king was vulnerable at the very peak of his reign. He needed the Lord to save him: "The Lord has delivered you this day from the power of all those who rose up against you" (2 Sam. 18:31 RSV). In the Psalms David constantly cries out for help or gives thanks for deliverance (Ps. 3:7-8; 7:1-2; 31:1-3; etc.; cf. 2 Sam. 22:3-4). This human savior was no less dependent on God than any other creature.

Fifth and finally, David, for all his weakness, was a forerunner and model for all his successors in both North and South. All had the task of delivering the people and all received their office from God (cf. Rom. 13:1-7), though most of them might not be aware of it (cf. Ps. 82). In fact these kings failed to live up to the hopes placed upon them. They did not carry out their vocation. Kingship ended with disasters that brought the people under the rule of foreign kings. Nevertheless, the hope persisted that God would raise up a savior and king from the house of David. Indeed, even a foreign ruler could be called by God to deliver his people (cf. Cyrus in Isa. 45:1, 13). In the end God would inaugurate his kingdom on earth, saving his own people first, then all nations. A king of the Jews (Mark 15:2) of David's stock (Rom. 1:2-4) would accomplish this salvation in a way that exceeded every hope. The authority of all kings and rulers depends on this central act of divine liberation. Guilty of overturning justice day by day (cf. Pilate in John 19:11), they nevertheless enjoy the patience of God and receive from him the power to rule the nations as his agents.

(2) Israel's king was also to be a just ruler and judge. The same might be said of all kings. They should not act arbitrarily or cruelly but with wisdom and justice. They should not seek their own advantage but work for the common good so that all people might live in peace and prosperity. Israel's king in particular had not only to save the people from outward threats but also to check dangers from within, protecting the rights of the poor and securing what we now call social justice.

The Hebrew term *mālak*, "to rule as a king," naturally carries with it the sense of dispensing justice. The verb *šāpaṭ*, with the derived noun *šōpēṭ*, has the basic meaning "to act as judge"; cf. Moses in Exod. 18:13, Deborah in Judg. 9:4-5, Samuel in 1 Sam. 7:15, Absalom in 2 Sam. 15:4, and Solomon in 1 Kgs. 3:9 RSV. On a national scale, to judge is to rule, so that "ruler" rather than "judge" is often the correct rendering of *šōpēṭ* (e.g., Mic. 4:14; Ps. 2:10; Isa. 40:23; Dan. 9:12). At the same time, when the idea is that of helping orphans, widows, aliens, prisoners, slaves, or debtors, *šāpaṭ* means "to secure justice for someone," or even "to liberate," and the *šōpēṭ* is a helper or liberator rather than a neutral judge or ruler. Thus the Lord acts as judge between David and Saul when he acquits or delivers David (1 Sam. 24:15). In the prayer: "Give me justice, O Lord" (Ps. 26:1), "justice" clearly has the sense of deliverance or liberation. The king, and indeed the whole people, is expected to exercise justice in this specific sense (Ps. 72:4; Isa. 1:17, 23; Jer. 5:28; Prov. 29:14).

As regards the so-called judges, Deborah (Judg. 4:5) and Samuel (1 Sam. 7:16f.) dispensed justice, but the others are not specifically said to judge or rule. The word *šāpaṭ* can be applied to them because they secured justice by delivering the people. With the kings the emphasis shifted. They, too, helped Israel to its right by delivering the people, but distributing justice now played a larger part. The kings had the wider duty of promoting law and justice in the community (cf. Judg. 19:1; 21:25). This had the following implications.

First, the kings received this office from the Lord, the one King,

Judge, and Ruler of the earth. He alone establishes perfect justice with unfailing authority. "God is a just judge" (Ps. 7:11). He is "the judge of all the earth" (Gen. 18:25). But first he is the Judge of his own people (Ps. 50:4; Deut. 32:36). Israel's kings were thus called upon to be good defenders of the people's rights. They did not control justice. None could be so bold as to set up a code of laws for Israel as Hammurabi did for his state. Justice had to be "given" them. The more bitter the people's experiences with their kings, the more they prayed to God: "Endow the king with thy own justice, and give thy righteousness to a king's son" (Ps. 72:1).

Second, Israel's kings came to office in a society ruled by constitutional law. Legal institutions with courts and officers from the village to the tribal level preceded the monarchy. Judges had exercised a measure of authority over Israel as a whole. If the kings and their courts became the supreme judicial authority during the royal period, they did so by delegation. The people entrusted to them the rights formerly held by local and tribal officers. The king did not receive his office directly from the Lord. His mandate as the highest judge came from the people acting as a constitutional community in responsibility to God. And when the royal office was abolished, the people took back the judicial office. This link between the king's office and the people's constitutional responsibility is unique to Israel.

Third, the kings were guilty of serious abuses in the discharge of their office. A sense of their high responsibility might be present (cf. Ps. 45:6-7; 101:1-8). The people prayed that the king would "judge thy people rightly and deal out justice to the poor and suffering" (Ps. 72:2). David "maintained law and justice among all his people" (2 Sam. 8:15), and so, too, did Solomon (1 Kgs. 3:28). Yet even these great kings were guilty of acts of cruelty and lawlessness, and during the whole period of the monarchy the prophets fiercely accused the royal successors of unrighteousness (Amos 2:6-8; Hos. 5:11; Mic. 3:1-3; Isa. 1:21-23; Jer. 5:28; Ezek. 22:6-7). Criticism of this kind was unique in antiquity. It prevented the rulers from using the ideal of social justice as mere propaganda to cloak their acts of injustice.

Fourth, in spite of negative experiences with unjust rulers, Israel clung to its hope that a king would come to fulfil the divine commission. This hope was founded on God's promise. The Lord would not let his people live under oppression forever. He would raise up a just king on David's throne. This king would truly dispense justice. When would this rule of justice come? Would it be delayed until the last days? That was not the point. God would inaugurate the kingdom of justice in his own time, but with that sure and certain hope in view his people was to struggle here and now for a just society, accepting responsibility on the basis of the divine promise and with the divine help: "Pursue justice and champion the oppressed" (Isa. 1:17). When king and people took this prophetic call to heart, and acted accordingly, the promise of a just king began to find fulfilment even if it did not yet find the full and perfect realization that God himself would finally bring.

(3) If the king was a liberator and a just ruler and judge, he was a bringer of *šālôm*. Not by accident the just king who is finally to come was given the title "prince of *šālôm*" (Isa. 9:5 [Eng. 6]). But what precisely does the term *šālôm* imply? It comprises both deliverance on the one hand and the health and prosperity associated with justice on the other.

Hebrew *šālôm* denotes the order and security that Israel, like all other nations, needed and desired. God met this basic need by giving his people the land of Canaan as *menûhāh* or "place of rest." Under the judges, security would last only for a few decades (cf. Judg. 3:11; 5:31; 8:28), but under the kings it was meant to be the normal situation. It was so under David (2 Sam. 7:1) and especially under Solomon (1 Kgs. 4:24), whose name could be taken to mean "man of peace" (1 Chron. 22:9). "Peace for the people" (Ps. 72:3 CB; cf. Luke 2:14) was the expected fruit of wise government, the peace at issue being that of physical security, freedom from both external war and oppression on the one hand and internal strife and exploitation on the other.

But just government would also result in the general well-being of the people. *šālom* meant prosperity and well-being as well as security. If the land enjoyed peace under Solomon, this meant enjoyment of the fruit of the land without disturbance: "Every man under his own vine and fig-tree, from Dan to Beersheba" (1 Kgs. 4:24-25). Ps. 72:16 gives us the picture: "May there be abundance of corn in the land . . . may the crops flourish like Lebanon, and the sheaves be numberless as blades of grass." We are reminded of the promise of a land flowing with milk and honey (Exod. 3:8; etc.) and many similar promises (Deut. 33:28; Amos 9:13-15). The people that enjoyed *šālôm* in this sense had no more to fear from enemies (2 Sam. 7:20) nor had it any need to be afraid of hunger or thirst or any other material lack.

In English we tend to think of peace as the opposite of strife, especially in international relations, and *šālôm* could also have this sense. Israel hoped that a just ruler would improve relations with neighboring nations (cf. 1 Sam. 7:14). Under Solomon Israel "enjoyed peace on all sides" (1 Kgs. 4:24). At peace with other nations, David could also be their "prince and instructor" (Isa. 55:4), and in this way Israel could channel blessing to the nations according to the basic promise of Gen. 12:2-3. The coming just king is to "speak peaceably to every nation" (Zech. 9:11; cf. Isa. 11:10). The government of a just king has universal significance.

In achieving *šālôm*, then, Israel's kings were to ensure security from foreign and domestic oppression, prosperity in a fertile land, and peace and openness in dealing with other nations. But do not all kings and governments seek *šālôm* in this threefold sense? Peace on earth is unquestionably a basic human need. The OT, however, bears witness to some specific aspects of this need.

First, Israel's king is commissioned to bring the peace and prosperity that come from the Lord, the heavenly King. Because the God of Israel differs from all the gods, the *šālôm* that he gives will be different as well. The gods represent natural forces. Their concern is with cosmic harmony. They commission rulers to maintain the existing order irrespective of its quality. God, however, requests a different kind of *šālôm*. He demands the overthrow, not the preservation, of the existing order. He has a plan of salvation that will destroy every unjust order. The courts at Jerusalem and Samaria might be conservatively minded, but they would be constantly challenged by the prophets, who proclaimed the peace and prosperity that God himself desires and promises.

Second, because the Lord himself gives the people peace and prosperity according to his own plan (cf. Ps. 29:11; 85:8-13; 147:14), no king of Israel could pride himself on being the prince of peace. Obsequious court prophets might promise peace even at times when the very existence of the kingdom was at stake (Jer. 6:14), but the prophets castigated this arrogance. Of what avail to cry peace and prosperity when there was neither peace nor prosperity? The only ultimate result could be ruin. Set in the light of God's own gift of *šālôm*, all human government falls under criticism unless it adopts a wise, realistic, and modest policy. Recognition of this truth is one of Israel's great contributions to the task of achieving true peace and prosperity in the world.

Third, the divine promise of a coming prince of peace was not meant simply as a comforting vision to excuse actual failure. It was also a sharp reminder to societies and governments that neglect their own responsibility for achieving peace and prosperity. Granting new hope to his people, the Lord also called and moved them to new awareness and activity. This was the final goal that God had set and would reach. It was the goal, then, toward which the king and his people should constantly strive. The challenge of the Lord's promise motivates his people to work for *šālôm* in its comprehensive sense.

In sum, the OT king, invested with a secular office, has the task of delivering the people, ruling with justice, and working for *šālôm*. He must do this in obedience to God and with the help of the Lord who raises up rulers of his own choice. A just government is linked to God's own purpose and work in bringing about his kingdom on earth.

3. God Assessed Israel's Kings

God made his own assessment of Israel's kings. They are seen (a) in the light of his grace, (b) in the shadow of his wrath, and (c) in relation to the fulfilment of his own purpose.

Introduction

THE OT DOES NOT GIVE equal attention to all Israel's kings. Many are dismissed briefly with short references to their name, age at enthronement, length of reign, and death and burial. A short evaluation may accompany the factual information. Kings are often said to have done "what is wrong in the eyes of the Lord." This judgment stands over nearly all the kings of Israel and twelve out of the twenty kings of Judah.

Other kings merit more attention and receive positive evaluations. Eight kings of Judah are in this group. Long descriptions are given of the reigns of Hezekiah and Josiah. The reigns of Asa, Jehoshaphat, Joash, Amaziah, Azariah, and Jotham are also seen in a positive light. They all did "what is right in the eyes of the Lord."

Three kings stand out above all others: Saul, David, and Solomon. The material relating to these three kings of the united monarchy is both more abundant and of a different quality. In it we feel the heartbeat of Israel's love for its kings. Because of these three men kingship became a topic of Israel's faith. The story of their reigns is the key to an understanding of the two categories of kings mentioned above.

It is unnecessary to explain how important David's reign was. Every reader of the Bible knows its meaning for the faith of Israel and of the new people that God has called together from all nations. David is the most famous of Israel's kings. He is the model. He also has a unique role in connection with the coming messianic King.

Saul, too, has his place as king before and next to David. The two lived in close relation to one another. What would Saul be had not David succeeded where he failed? But what would David be had not the Lord raised up Saul to open up the way for him? These two kings complement one another. We can understand David's reign only when we have knowledge of that of Saul.

Solomon also has his place next to David, his father and predecessor. For all its greatness, David's reign would be incomplete had not his son by Bathsheba succeeded him. By the grace of God David achieved great things, yet only the acts of Solomon brought God's promise through Nathan to fulfilment. David and Solomon complete each other. The brightest picture of David would be out of focus were not a place made for Solomon his son.

The reign of David, then, must be understood in its double relationship to that of Saul his predecessor and that of Solomon his successor. The reigns of Saul and Solomon stand in sharp contrast to one another, but the Bible views them in the same way. Saul is not one-sidedly rejected as the evil king nor Solomon one-sidedly praised as the good king. God showed grace to both. God also rejected both inasmuch as both became arrogant. For this reason we must evaluate their reigns, like that of David and the other kings, from two standpoints. We see them first in the light of God's grace and blessing, then in the light of their sin and condemnation. We finally consider the implications of their twofold depiction.

a. The Kings in the Light of God's Grace

(1) Although the Lord through Samuel opposed Israel's desire for a king (1 Sam. 8:8), he also acceded to it (8:7, 9) and chose Saul as Israel's first monarch (9:1ff.; 10:17ff.; 11:1ff.). The general impression of Saul's reign is that of failure with a dramatic end. But the early days were bright. The accounts of his election show that his rise to kingship was the work of God. He and his son Jonathan played a heroic role in the war against the Philistines (1 Sam. 13–14). The victory over the Amalekites, for all the negative features, was a striking success. Enjoying the gift of the Spirit, Saul was a king by divine grace. Five aspects of this positive evaluation call for notice.

First, Saul did not scheme to become king. He did not court popularity among the people. He became king by divine initiative. He was first anointed by Samuel when in search of his father's asses, then chosen by lot in answer to the people's demand. No human machinations were involved.

Second, although Saul was tall and handsome (1 Sam. 9:2), his physical advantages and strength played no decisive role. It was his endowment with the Spirit that enabled him to deliver his people (10:1). He was a God-given savior in the chain of deliverers raised up by God for Israel.

Third, although Saul was a gallant king, the accounts do not magnify his qualities as such, but trace his success to his obedience to the Lord. Both he and Jonathan consulted God before taking action (14:10, 18, 37). They realized that they were dependent on God's help (11:3). Saul was at first a faithful servant of God. He banished witchcraft (28:3) and kept God's paths even to his own disadvantage (14:36ff.).

Fourth, all Israel, including Samuel and David, recognized Saul as the Lord's anointed (10:7; 24:7). Samuel had no doubt that God had entrusted him with a definite mission: "God will be with you" (10:7). He mourned deeply when disaster finally came upon Saul (15:35).

Fifth and finally, in spite of his jealousy and pursuit of David, Saul was not a cruel or vindictive man. There is no record of his oppressing or exploiting the people as many later kings did. Though little is said about his government, we know nothing to his discredit. Dark and dreadful though his final end would be, the light of God's grace shone over Saul and his house at first, so that the total picture is not one of unrelieved darkness and tragedy.

(2) In contrast to Saul, David and his reign stand predominantly in the light. God loved David, and the brightness of his grace shone fully upon

him. Nevertheless, as there is a more positive side to Saul, so there is a more negative side to David. Notwithstanding the greatness and splendor of his reign, many factors show it to have been far less than ideal.

David began life in lowly conditions as a small farmer's youngest son. Bright and handsome, but with small prospects, he was anointed by Samuel when Israel already had a king, so that the choice was secret, and for years he could not be more than second to Saul, with whom he was closely linked. His humble origin and modest status help to explain his strong sense of dependence on God. David also had to suffer. Promised a great future, enjoying initial success at court and in battle (1 Sam. 16:14ff.; 17:1ff.), married into the royal family, he incurred the jealousy of Saul, was forced to take refuge in the wilderness and abroad, and narrowly escaped with his life (18:6ff.; 19:1ff.; 21–23; 26–27). The way of suffering was the divinely appointed way to kingship.

An interesting point is that David honored, respected, and obeyed Saul. Later, when Jehu was anointed king, he would quickly eliminate the family of Ahab so as to attain to the throne without delay. David, however, recognized Saul as the legal king. He neither hatched plots against him nor engaged in open revolt. He neither killed nor captured Saul when he had the chance to do so (1 Sam. 24; 26). His loyalty was manifested in his close friendship with Jonathan (chs. 18–20) and the steps he took when king to protect the life and honor of Saul's family (2 Sam. 1; 4; 9). He never treated Saul as a wicked king who had to be overthrown.

The secret of David's attitude is to be found in his relation to the Lord. He did not lead a particularly holy life. He was not a prophet. He hardly set a good example for religious people. His qualities did not include exemplary piety (1 Sam. 16:18). But God took the initiative and was ready to be always with David (18:12, 14; 20:13). This being so, David sought God's will in difficult situations (20:22; 23:2, 4; 2 Sam. 2:1). To speak with God, either crying for help or giving thanks, was as important for David as his daily food or the air he breathed. A good musician, he initiated the singing of psalms to God (cf. 1 Sam. 16:14-23). In contrast to the arrogance of many rulers, he showed humility before God and a readiness to suffer for his sake.

A warrior and military commander, David won great victories, yet with different methods from those of most heroes. He came against Goliath, the Philistine champion, not with sword, spear, and dagger, but "in the name of the Lord of Hosts" (1 Sam. 17:45). The secret of his victories lay in the presence of God. This and not the merit of David and his comrades, the ability of Joab, or the courage of the Israelite army, was the decisive factor (2 Sam. 8:6).

The reign of David and the city of Jerusalem are closely related. Shortly after he became king of all Israel David took this town from the

Jebusites and gave it the name "City of David" (2 Sam. 5:7, 9). He then brought the ark there from its provisional abode. An incident on the way, however, showed that the Lord himself cannot be moved around as clever statesmen decide (2 Sam. 6:6ff.). The Lord came, but only because he had "chosen Zion and desired it for his home" (Ps. 132:13). The city of David became important only because God himself had chosen it.

Surprisingly, the OT does not describe at length the results of David's glorious reign. It simply states that he "ruled over the whole of Israel and maintained law and justice among all his people" (2 Sam. 8:15). Indirectly the OT shows that Israel truly enjoyed security, prosperity, *šālôm* in all its dimensions under this king. But the grace of God was to be praised for this, not the merits of the king.

(3) God also took delight in Solomon, David's son by Bathsheba (1 Kgs. 10:9): Bathsheba "gave birth to a son and called him Solomon," and "the Lord loved him" (2 Sam. 12:24). This love was so great that Solomon would become a symbol of all-surpassing happiness and splendor, rightly named Solomon, for the name implies *šālôm* (1 Chron. 22:9). The wealth of biblical material devoted to him in the historical books and wisdom literature testifies to the importance of his reign.

It should be noted, however, that Solomon does not stand alone. David is always next to him. The link that binds them is closer than that of father and son. Solomon was important only as David's son and successor in whom God's promise by Nathan was to be fulfilled. He had full royal authority, yet he sat on the throne of David. Israel enjoyed peace under his rule, but his father had established this state of security and prosperity. He built the temple, but only because his father had taken Jerusalem, brought the ark there, found "a sanctuary for the Lord" (Ps. 132:5), prepared the materials, and even instructed the workers (1 Chron. 22; 23–26; 28:1–29:19). Solomon's achievements rested on the prior achievements of David.

Nevertheless, if David was superior to Solomon in some respects, Solomon was superior to David in others. He achieved what David could not achieve. The splendor of his reign and the respect he enjoyed abroad, as shown in the visit of the Queen of Sheba, were a new and unprecedented reality. He amassed great wealth, especially in the form of gold (1 Kgs. 10:10-11, 14-23). He lived in luxury (4:22-23, 26-28; 10:4-6). He promoted trade (10:27-29). He built strongholds and store cities (9:16-19). He organized a strong civil service (4:2-19). He improved the administration of justice (3:28). He advanced national prosperity (4:20). His policy was a peaceful one of development. His achievement was complementary to that of David, but by no means smaller.

The secret of Solomon's successes lay in his wisdom. Wisdom was his predominant gift (1 Kgs. 3–10). What sort of wisdom was it? It included "a heart with skill to listen, so that he may govern thy people" (3:9, 28; 10:9), an understanding of life "as wide as the sand of the sea-shore" and expressed in proverbs and songs (4:29-31), and the ability to govern, plan, administer, and develop (5:12; 10:4-8, 24). It also included a knowledge of nature (4:33) and above all a recognition that the fear of the Lord is the beginning of wisdom (Prov. 1:7). The Lord himself gave Solomon this "heart so wise and so understanding" (1 Kgs. 3:12). He did so because he loved him and delighted in him (2 Sam. 12:24; 1 Kgs. 10:9). The glory belongs, not to the ability of the king, but to the grace that God abundantly bestowed upon him.

Solomon's supreme achievement was the building of the temple, a permanent house for God alongside the royal palace: "Here have I built thee a lofty house, a habitation for thee to occupy for ever" (1 Kgs. 8:13). The legitimate pride of the builder and the pleasure in the people's compliments may still be felt. Yet again the greatness of the achievement does not obscure the fact that the glory is not Solomon's but God's. It pleased the Lord in his mercy to let his name dwell in the midst of his people in this hand-made house (ch. 5; 6:11-19). Solomon could not have brought the project to success had not God allowed and enabled him to undertake it.

(4) Among the later kings of Judah who did what was right in God's eyes none was as great as Saul, David, or Solomon. After Israel broke up ca. 926 B.C., the two kingdoms were both too small to play an independent role in international politics. The northern kingdom of Israel existed for two centuries, Judah for more than three, but even though the Lord anointed their kings, they had little influence. They never amounted to much more than petty kingdoms living at the mercy of the great powers.

The kings of these two kingdoms are evaluated by the model of David, the "man after God's own heart" (1 Sam. 13:14 CB). In comparison, they fall far short. Even the most famous of them, Hezekiah and Josiah, are no match for David. Yet these petty kings were still David's heirs and successors. Some of the light of God's mercy shone on them and raised them above mediocrity. The light of divine grace did not overshadow them but made them lights in dark places. Precisely because of the high model of David they have their own importance and command respect.

Asa, son of Abijam, who reigned from 908 to 868 B.C., was the first of Judah's kings said to have done "what was right in the eyes of the Lord, like his ancestor David" (1 Kgs. 15:11). He did away with sacred prostitution, destroyed idols, and repelled the attack of Israel, although at great cost, for he restored Judah only with the help of Ben-hadad of Aram, whose army he bought with gold and silver from the temple and palace treasuries (15:12-24). At first a man of deep faith, Asa incurs criticism later for his lack of faith (2 Chron. 16). Only by grace and not by merit is he listed among the good kings.

Jehoshaphat, son of Asa, who reigned from 868 to 851 B.C., "followed in the footsteps of Asa, his father," though still permitting worship at the hill-shrines outside Jerusalem. Unlike Asa, he lived at peace with Israel. He reorganized and decentralized the administration of justice and ordered the judges to be honest (2 Chron. 19:4-11). His wonderful victory over the allied Moabites and Ammonites (20:1-30) teaches us that God's people can be saved from any danger if they will keep faith and wait on the Lord. Yet the abortive enterprise of trading by ship with Tarshish (2 Chron. 20:35-37; 1 Kgs. 22:48-49) shows that even good kings could make serious mistakes.

Joash, son of Ahaziah, who reigned from 840 to 801 B.C., "did what was right in the eyes of the Lord all his days" (2 Kgs. 12:2). He was anointed king as a child of seven, having barely escaped an attempted extermination of all David's posterity (ch. 11). Carefully educated by Jehoiada the priest, he later repaired and improved the Lord's house. At the last minute he saved Judah from the attack of Hazael of Aram by giving him court and temple gold. He was finally killed in a palace revolt, having betrayed his faith after the death of Jehoiada, and having thus brought judgment on himself and his kingdom (2 Chron. 24).

Amaziah, son of Joash, who reigned from 800 to 785 B.C., "did what was right in the eyes of the Lord, yet not as his forefather David had done; he followed his father Joash in everything" (2 Kgs. 14:3). This ambivalent judgment reflects the facts. Amaziah showed signs of faith in his victory over Edom, but he later fell victim to arrogance, was defeated by Israel, and met his death in a conspiracy (14:7, 8-22; cf. 2 Chron. 25).

Azariah or Uzziah, son of Amaziah, who ruled from 792 to 747 B.C. (fully perhaps only from 785), also "did what was right in the eyes of the Lord, as Amaziah his father had done." He later became a leper and died in isolation (2 Kgs. 15:1-7). But early in his reign, with the help of a priest called Zechariah, he defeated the Philistines, improved fortifications, and promoted the building of wells, agriculture, and cattle husbandry. Unfortunately, these achievements made him arrogant and hence the judgment of leprosy and a solitary death (2 Chron. 24).

Jotham, son of Uzziah, who reigned from 757 to 742 B.C., was a good king who followed in the footsteps of the younger Uzziah. His main achievement was to make improvements in the temple (2 Kgs. 15:34).

Hezekiah, son of Ahaz, who reigned from 725 to 697 B.C., was one of the most remarkable of Judah's kings. His reign might almost be compared to that of David (2 Kgs. 18:3) or Solomon (2 Chron. 30:26). "There was nobody like him among all the kings of Judah who succeeded him or among those who had gone before him" (2 Kgs. 18:5). He is so highly praised because he was the only king who was able to stop sacrifices outside Jerusalem, working with great energy to achieve this goal (18:4; cf. 2 Chron. 29–31). He also "rebelled against the king of Assyria" (2 Kgs. 18:7), though this hardly worked to the country's good. Jerusalem enjoyed a wonderful deliverance from the Assyrian army (1 Kgs. 18:17-19, 37; Isa. 36–37; 2 Chron. 32:9-22), but much of the land was occupied (2 Kgs. 18:13-16) and Hezekiah had to pay a heavy fine to Assyria for his attempt at complete independence.

Josiah, son of Amon, who reigned from 639 to 609 B.C., was the last of Judah's kings to be praised. He "followed closely in the footsteps of his forefather David, swerving neither right nor left" (2 Kgs. 22:2). Josiah ordered a total reformation after masons found the book of the Torah, possibly Deut. 12–26, while engaged in temple repairs. He eliminated old and new pagan elements that had crept into religious life, not only from Jerusalem but from all Judah, and even from Bethel. He reconsecrated the Lord's house in Jerusalem as the only legitimate place of worship (2 Kgs. 22:3–23:27). For all his merits, however, Josiah lacked wisdom and embarked on a war in which he lost his life (23:29-30). In himself he would have been of little account, but the Torah and the words of the prophetess Huldah moved him to turn to the Lord "with all his heart and soul and strength" (23:25).

In Israel Jeroboam, son of Nebat, reigned from 926 to 907 B.C. He was chosen by God in spite of his many faults. He was a "young man" "of great energy" to whom Solomon entrusted an important office (1 Kgs. 11:28). A prophet spoke to him this word from God: "I will appoint you to rule over all that you can desire, and to be king over Israel. . . . I will be with you. I will establish your family for ever" (11:37-38). Obliged to flee to Egypt and to live for a time as a refugee, he was finally anointed at the people's assembly at Shechem. He then rebuilt this town as his capital (12:20, 25). Before he fell into sin (14:16; 15:30; 16:31) he was respected by both people and prophets.

A flash of light falls on Baasha, who reigned from 905 to 882 B.C., when the Lord says to him: "I raised you from the dust and made you a prince over my people Israel" (1 Kgs. 16:2). The same applies to Jehu (845-818 B.C.), who enjoyed divine support even though he abused his calling. The negative aspects of these kings could not eliminate their divine election or the glimmer of light in which they reigned.

b. The Kings in the Shadow of the Lord's Anger

Although the OT offers examples of good or passable kings who brought true religion and a measure of peace and prosperity to Judah and Israel, it does not disguise the negative side of kingship. In fact the bad kings outnumber the good. How often we read of them: "He did what was wrong in the eyes of the Lord" (30 times in 1 and 2 Kings). This judgment falls on all the kings of Israel and most of those of Judah. A king is often said to have done evil "as his forefathers had done" (2 Kgs. 23:32, 37), leaving the impression that all

David's successors fell under the condemnation. The good kings are a happy exception to the general rule.

Some kings began well but then denied their faith and did wrong. Even Solomon's reign, which stood under God's blessing, was suddenly overshadowed by a dark cloud (cf. 1 Kgs. 3–10 with ch. 11). A similar brusque change came in the case of Jeroboam (chs. 11–14). Only two kings properly discharged their office to the very end.

The monarchy as a whole is indeed cast in a negative light. God opposed it at the outset, and it ended with the exile and the destruction of Jerusalem and the temple. Why, then, did God permit it? Why did he tolerate it so long? "For the sake of our father David" is the OT's answer to the second question. God's promise to David was the only foundation on which the later kings could stand.

In both Israel and Judah the prophets raised constant complaints against royal failings and abuses. The kings, of course, viewed their censures as rebellion and tried to silence them, as most governments would do. But this opposition, finely summarized in Deut. 17:14-20, could never be uprooted from Israel. The monarchy might not be totally condemned as such, but it was seen to entail great risks if the kings departed from the path that God had marked out for them.

(1) Saul is a first example. His faults after the battles against the Philistines and the Amalekites led to his rejection by God and his replacement by David (1 Sam. 15:28). He made offerings without waiting for the arrival of Samuel, who should have presented them (13:7b-14). He did not destroy all the spoil, as ordered, after defeating the Amalekites (15:1-35). The mistakes might seem formal and trivial enough compared to David's later adultery, deceit, and treachery. Indeed, Samuel protested against the Lord's decision to reject Saul (15:11). Later Saul became jealous, distrustful, and cruel. He turned his anger not only upon David but also upon the priests of Nob and the Gibeonites. An evil spirit seized him (16:14), so that, although responsible for his acts, he was hastened toward his tragic end.

Saul was not one-sidedly a bad king. But he was the king who bore the divine rejection and stood under the black shadow of the divine wrath. No more wicked than others, he makes it plain that every king falls short and merits only condemnation. The OT depiction does not especially blacken him. He was respected in both life and death, as the magnificent lament of David shows (2 Sam. 1:17-27). Where God condemns, no place is left for human condemnation. But the lesson is plain. None can be a true king of Israel on his own—only by divine grace and with divine help.

(2) David sinned astonishingly with Bathsheba. He had reached the peak of his power, received the promise of God (2 Sam. 7), defeated his enemies (ch. 8), shown mercy to Saul's descendants (ch. 9), and made it

apparent who the "beloved of God and man" truly is. But then he slept with another man's wife, tried to deceive her husband, had him killed, took the woman to wife, lost the child of the liaison, and repented bitterly when boldly accused by the prophet Nathan.

David did not openly deny his faith. He simply acted as a king who has property rights to the souls and bodies of his people. Some nations conceded such rights to their kings. But David had been raised to the throne by the Lord, the God of Israel, the King of the whole earth. He obviously did not see the implications of this. Committing adultery, deception, and murder, he broke the law that he should have upheld. Violating Israel's right, he violated the Lord's right. The illness and death of the child and the censure of Nathan the prophet made him aware of the heinousness of his sin. He then confessed his fault and received both forgiveness and the promise of another son, Solomon.

Astonishing are both the fact that David did so great a wrong and that when rebuked he did not stand on his royal dignity but admitted his sin and humbled himself. Astonishing, too, is the fact that while God rejected Saul he put away David's sin (2 Sam. 12:13 RSV) and renewed his love (12:24). Nevertheless, sad events would now pursue David to the day of his death. He had to bear the consequences of his fault. Deceit, vengeance, rebellion, and a coup d'état would shake his house until Solomon finally ascended to the throne. David lost three beloved sons (Amnon, Absalom, and Adonijah) and experienced painful humiliations. He fell to the temptation to conduct a census and brought down the Lord's anger on the people, thus proving himself to be the very opposite of a good king. Only by the Lord's grace and mercy could he finally benefit the people, buying land for an altar that would later become the site for the temple (2 Sam. 24:18ff.; 2 Chron. 3:1).

Clouds of anger and rejection thus overshadowed David's later life. He showed himself to be ambitious, arrogant, deceitful, and weak. If he had an advantage over Saul, it did not consist of moral superiority but of strength in times of trouble: when hunted by Saul, when confessing his sin with Bathsheba, when cursed by Shimei (2 Sam. 16:5-14), or when hearing of the death of Absalom (18:33–19:8). The very king who suffered under the divine judgment was the king whom the Lord loved more than any other of Israel's kings.

(3) Solomon, too, for all his glory as the "prince of peace," had his negative side. His reign began with intrigue. Not the will of God but the machinations of a few men at court—Nathan the prophet, Zadok the priest, and Benaiah the commander of David's bodyguard—secured his anointing as David's successor. Once on the throne, he was notorious for moral and religious laxity. He failed to retain dominion over Edom and Aram, and imposed a stern system of forced labor that probably led to the dangerous revolt of Jeroboam.

Solomon, too, might have been justly rejected and condemned by the Lord. Praised for his wisdom and clothed with the splendid role of glory, he was in a sense the forerunner of the messianic king. Yet in his real stature he merited little praise. By right the glory belonged to the grace of God alone which was so richly bestowed upon him.

In fact none of the three great kings of Israel was actually worthy to reign or genuinely able to discharge the high office of kingship. Sooner or later all of them fell. Yet their lots differed. Saul had a hard death (2 Sam. 31). David suffered for his faults and the people had to suffer with him. Solomon never had to bear serious misfortune as a sign of divine rejection, but judgment fell on his son Rehoboam and on all the house of David (1 Kgs. 11:11-13, 30-36). God exempted Solomon himself from punishment "for the sake of your father David" (1 Kgs. 11:11ff.). Like a mirror, Solomon reflected the light of God's own glory and kingship. But what a scratched mirror he proved to be!

(4) In the subsequent history of the two kingdoms there was little deserving of praise. Jeroboam, son of Nebat, began well. He championed a despotically exploited people (1 Kgs. 12:1-24; 14:21-31). But apart from rebelling against the Davidic dynasty he disregarded the unique claim of the Jerusalem temple by establishing new centers of worship at Bethel and Dan. He also offended the Lord's holiness by casting golden bull-calves as symbols of the Lord's presence (12:25-33). His fault was all the worse because he induced all the kings and the whole people of Israel to follow his example. Twenty times we read of the "sins of Jeroboam" that caused Israel to sin (14:16; 15:26, 30, 34; 16:13, 19, 26; etc.).

A second particularly wicked king was Ahab (871-852 B.C.). Ahab was not without good qualities. He faced the attacks of the Aramean king with wisdom and courage. He would take advice from the prophets and servants of God (1 Kgs. 20:13, 22, 28). He preferred a true but bitter word to the flattery of false prophets (22:15-16). Nevertheless, Ahab was a weak man. He was too much under the influence of his wife Jezebel, a Sidonian princess, who fanatically promoted the worship of Baal and "massacred the prophets of the Lord" (18:4), apart from Elijah, who went into hiding for three years (17:3; 18:1). In spite of Elijah's courageous protests, and the vacillating opinions of the people, Ahab sponsored Jezebel's program, himself erected a temple and altar to Baal at Samaria, and also set up "a sacred pole" (NEB) or "Asherah" (RSV; 16:31-33). In this way, although no doubt "limping with two different opinions" (18:21 RSV) like the people, he had to bear responsibility for rebellion against God and the seduction of Israel into idolatry. By his belated repentance he averted disaster from himself, but not from his family (21:27-29).

Manasseh, son of Hezekiah, who reigned 696-642 B.C. and Amon his son (641-640 B.C.), were among the very bad Davidic kings of Judah. The list of Manasseh's actions (2 Kgs. 21:2-9, 16) contains all imaginable crimes against the Lord. He reintroduced "hill-shrines" (NEB) or "high places" (RSV) outside Jerusalem, developed the worship of Baal and Asherah, built new altars for "all the host of heaven," and promoted magical practices, profaning "the two courts of the house of the Lord" and even the house itself. He not only encouraged syncretism but led the people actually to forsake the Lord in favor of the gods the Canaanites had worshiped at the time of the conquest. He also reigned arbitrarily, so that Jerusalem was full of innocent blood (21:16). God's Word to him by the prophets was one not of rebuke but of total rejection of both king and people (21:10-15). Amon followed in his father's footsteps and "forsook the Lord the God of his fathers" (21:20-22).

Worship of the host of heaven was apparently a condition that Assyria imposed on satellite powers such as Judah, and that Manasseh clearly accepted. Later, when imprisoned in Nineveh, Manasseh regretted what he had done, humbled himself before God, and back in Jerusalem improved his way (2 Chron. 33:10-20), so that he finally died in peace. In the mystery of the divine patience, not he himself but his son Amon and all Judah and Jerusalem had to suffer for his misdeeds, Amon being killed in a palace conspiracy (21:23; cf. 24:3).

Jehoiakim, son of Josiah, who reigned from 609 to 598 B.C., was king at a difficult time when the little kingdom of Judah was squeezed between the two great powers of Egypt and Babylon. Trying to play the strong and wealthy king, he exposed his country to great dangers. Toward the outspokenly critical Jeremiah he reacted partly with violence and partly with friendliness (Jer. 22:13-19; 26:1-24; 36). He did not openly rebel against God like Jeroboam, Ahab, or Manasseh, but he resisted the prophetic message and displayed both stubbornness and cruelty. He died in peace at the very time when enemy groups were already infiltrating the kingdom (24:6)—another sinful king who did not have to pay personally for his faults.

Jehoiachin, son of Jehoiakim, reigned only three months in 598 B.C. He did not worship idols as Manasseh did, nor shed innocent blood like his father. His only mistake was to continue the political machinations that Jehoiakim had initiated. But the hour was now too late. Judah was invaded, Jerusalem fell (598 B.C.), and Jehoiachin went into exile with ten thousand men and women of the upper class. Yet although Jehoiachin stood in the shadow of God's anger, a ray of hope shone on him, for the king of Babylon showed him favor (2 Kgs. 25:27-30; Jer. 52:31-34) and children were born to him in exile (1 Chron. 3:16-17). God's faithfulness stood fast even amid his wrath.

Zedekiah, son of Josiah, was the last of Israel's kings (597-586 B.C.). Like his brother Jehoiakim, he continued the policy of brinkmanship between Egypt and Babylon, ignoring the signs of the times to which the prophets called his attention (cf. Jer. 21:1-10; 28; 32; 37:1–39:7). When he broke his pledge to Babylon and rebelled (cf. Ezek. 17:1-24; 21:25-27), Jerusalem was taken again and destroyed. The king tried to escape but was seized and suffered cruel punishment at Riblah, his sons being slain before his eyes and he himself blinded and brought to Babylon, where he died without hope, in total darkness. This time there was no sign of patience. It was "the hour of final punishment" (Ezek. 21:25). The Lord had "banished them [Jerusalem and Judah] from his sight" (2 Kgs. 24:19-20), and Zedekiah had to suffer God's anger in his own body *with* his people, not *for* them. His faults were no worse than those of his predecessors. But like Saul he became a symbol of the divine rejection—in this case the definitive rejection of Israel's kings.

c. God's Aim with the Kings

It seems, then, that we have two divergent evaluations of the monarchy. The monarchy is good, but it is also bad. What, then, is the OT theology of kingship?

A simple answer might be that there are good kings of whom God approves and whom he rewards, and wicked kings of whom he disapproves and whom he punishes. We can indeed start at the justice of God in trying to understand history, but the concept of just retribution and recompense raises problems. Does it really accord with the witness of 1 and 2 Samuel and 1 and 2 Kings? Does God always reward each king according to his acts? This key hardly seems to fit in every case. Saul was certainly not a thoroughly bad king, and even the worst kings of Israel, like Jeroboam and Ahab, had their better qualities. Conversely, the kings on whom God bestowed abundant grace, like David and Solomon, were far from virtuous, David being notorious for his weakness, Solomon for his arrogance.

The element of retribution and recompense certainly exists. But God exercises justice according to his own wisdom, which does not always correspond to human ideas of distributive justice. Saul had to bear a heavy burden, while the faults of David and Solomon were dealt with more lightly. Was the Lord unjust, then, to Israel's kings? From the OT standpoint such a notion is absurd. The OT constantly extols the justice of God. But the justice it has in view is not simply distributive justice. It respects the mystery of the Lord's will and plan. This mystery cannot be decoded in terms of a simplistic principle of reward and retribution.

Again, we might appeal to the idea of divine predestination in history. Some kings are predestined to experience favor, others wrath, according to God's free decision. Does not God have the right to decide as he wills that this king will be blessed and that king will be punished? There is an element of truth here, too. David *had* to rise and Saul to fall and perish. Solomon, loved by God from birth, *had* to become king and know God's richest blessings. Jeroboam and his successors *had* to lead Israel to ruin. The last kings of Judah *had* to follow a similar pattern and run toward the ravine of destruction. There was no longer any help for them.

But is this the real key to an understanding of the OT? Is the OT simply proclaiming the absolute autonomy of God, his right and power to bless the one king and destroy the other? If this were so, might we not expect some kings to be absolutely good and others absolutely bad? Instead, they are all alike flesh and blood. God addresses them all and challenges them all as responsible persons. He leads them on different paths, but they are far from being mere puppets in his hand. What the OT essentially proclaims is not God's absolute autonomy but his plan of salvation for his people and the world. The concept of predestination alone does not solve the problem of the monarchy.

A third idea is that the development, decline, and fall of the monarchy in Israel might be viewed as an experiment that failed. God allowed the people to have the king they wanted, showed them the weaknesses of the system, and finally lost patience and shattered both kingdoms as useless earthen jars (Isa. 30:14; Jer. 18:1-6; 19:11-12). Yet this view has no real basis at all in the biblical witness itself. Like creation or the election of Israel, the raising up of the kings was not meant as a mere experiment. Certainly, when God enters into relations with nations and individuals, risks are entailed. But God takes the risks into account in promoting his ultimate plan of salvation. He might reject kings that fail, but precisely in so doing he confirms the institution that he sanctions.

A fourth thesis might be that the contradictory elements in the monarchy reflect two different tendencies in society, one supporting the monarchy, the other rejecting it in favor of theocracy, the kingship of God alone. On this view the monarchy enjoys favor so long as the king respects the people's interests, but anti-royalist sentiment grows if he begins to infringe on the people's rights. Government officials, court prophets, and the priests of the royal sanctuary naturally give their support to the king, but the prophets, local leaders, and people whom the king has offended form a critical opposition. The evaluations of the kings are simply an expression of these different approaches.

In fact, however, the OT offers little evidence in favor of this kind of thesis. What God did was often contrary to the general sentiment of the people or of leaders of any tendency whatever. He might stand for a king whom the people at large disliked or reject a king who enjoyed the broadest popular support. A sociological explanation does not solve the problem. God had his own aim and plan for the monarchy. But what was this aim or plan that seemed to go in two different directions? What might be the key to an understanding of the biblical witness to the royal period?

When preaching at Pisidian Antioch, the apostle Paul, once called Saul, discussed the royal period as the prehistory of the coming of Jesus (Acts 13:21-23). Himself of the tribe of Benjamin (Rom. 11:1; Phil. 3:5), Paul mentioned Saul as well as David—the two representative kings that are so near and yet so different, both chosen and loved by God, yet the one rejected, the other confirmed in his kingship. At Antioch Paul did not expressly raise our present problem, but he came back to it in a broader context in Rom. 9–11 when he considered the election and rejection of Israel and the nations in the light of God's dealings with Jacob and Esau or Moses and Pharaoh. The conclusion that he draws is that with steps to the right and to the left, God consistently follows his own just and gracious purpose.

Applying Paul's line of thinking to the monarchy, we acknowledge first that God's policy toward Israel's kings is a mystery. It is hard to discern God's just and merciful aim in the actual events as one king is accepted and another rejected. To the people it seems at times that God has broken his promise (cf. Ps. 77:7-10; 89:38ff.; Lam. 1:6; 2:9; 4:20). The prophets bring home the truth that kings and people have themselves broken the covenant and that God has thus to pursue his plan in longsuffering patience or in sharp rejection (cf. Neh. 9:6-37). Yet God's wisdom in his dealings with individual kings still remains an incomprehensible mystery.

It should be noted, however, that the stories of election and rejection, and the stories of the kingdoms of Israel and Judah, form an integrated whole. The account of David's ascent to the throne goes hand in hand with that of Saul's decline and fall. The histories of the kingdoms are separate yet not merely parallel, for they are also linked by specific events. The acts of God that might seem to be contradictory are in fact complementary. They are the two sides of a single aim and purpose.

Because the two sides of the divine policy are complementary, we can understand why kings that stand in the light of the divine favor are not in fact ideal kings. The light is not theirs alone, for it also falls to some degree on all the kings, even those who like Saul or Ahab are set at the left hand of God. Furthermore, those on whom the light shines brightest do not merit this privilege. They are not chosen by works, but "because of [God's] call" (Rom. 9:11 RSV). No effort is made to conceal their human weaknesses. They are vessels of mercy in the potter's hand (9:23), and as such they cannot boast against the vessels of wrath (11:18). The glory is God's alone.

The kings at God's left hand, who are under his wrath, can also be understood differently. How slight a difference separates them from the kings that are chosen! Only on the basis of God's decision are they vessels of wrath. Those at God's right hand might well have merited a similar fate. Yet even in ordaining their destiny, God remains the just and merciful God, tolerating them "with great patience" (Rom. 9:22 CB), and working out his saving purpose through his dealings with them.

Finally, although it seemed that the destruction of Judah had brought a final end to the monarchy, it is more or less plainly implied in the historical books of the OT, and expressly stated in the prophets, that the office of the royal shepherd, the liberator, the just ruler, the bringer of *šālôm*, was not definitively revoked. The Lord would fulfil his purpose for the Davidic monarchy by finally raising up a just king in whom his wider purpose of salvation for the race would also be fulfilled in a single act of rejection and election.

4. God Promised a Coming Just King

God raised up kings among his people for a limited span, and then rejected them. But his initiative in raising up kings still has meaning for the future.

THE GREAT ACTS OF GOD that we have studied thus far— creation, the election of the patriarchs, the liberation from Egypt, the leading through the wilderness, the revelation at Sinai, the giving of the land, and the raising up of kings— are all solidly rooted in history. Yet God and his revelation are not imprisoned in past history. God lives and moves, and his acts, too, are moving and living. Creation is constantly renewed. The liberation from Egypt is the model for many later liberations. The revelation at Sinai is the first of many revelations of God's will. The gift of the land is not a static, once-for-all event (Amos 9:13; Hos. 2:23; Exod. 20:42).

The same pattern holds true for the raising up of kings. Israel does not simply remember God's acts in the past. Recalling the joys of David's reign, Israel hopes for a confirmation and renewal of what God has done in the past. Giving thanks for just kings in former days, it hopes for a just king in the future. It expects God to act again and again to fulfil his promise. God himself gives rise to this expectation.

The main factors relating to the monarchy all have this orientation to the future. Rulers endowed with the Spirit of God were forerunners of the Servant of the Lord who would enjoy the fulness of the Spirit. Anointing by God, at first postulated of all the kings, then of a select few, would finally be applied only to the coming king. "Son of God" as a general royal title would also be restricted to the few and ultimately to the one alone. The same might be said of the description of the king as him "who sitteth at the right hand of God." Israel's kings never measured up to what was expected of them. The king had yet to come who would save, rule with justice, and establish true *šālôm.* Humanly speaking, it might seem that the judgment on Judah, Jerusalem, and the house of David had annulled this future. But there is still a future for Israel's kingdom if God himself will open it.

The OT texts relating to the coming king of justice, salvation, and peace fall into four categories, each with its own particular emphasis. (a) Some are for the purpose of confirming an existing reign, (b) some hope for radical change in a period of disaster, (c) others again look ahead to reestablishment, or (d) a new beginning, in the remote future.

a. Prophecies Strengthening the Ruling King

By raising up kings, God also gave rise to expectation of a savior king, a just king, a prince of peace. In some cases expression might be given to this expectation in connection with existing rulers, either at their enthronement or in the light of initial successes. Whether God was truly with the ruler had still to be demonstrated. Authoritative confirmation of the king's divine calling still lay in the future. The hope was, however, that this might be the king of promise.

Jacob's blessing of Judah (Gen. 49:8-12) might well have been used on such occasions. It claims that "the scepter shall not depart from Judah, nor the ruler's staff from between his feet, until he comes to whom it belongs; and to him shall be the obedience of the peoples" (RSV). Who is this man "to whom it belongs"? Obviously a powerful king whom foreign nations obey and who establishes the fulness of *šālôm.* As the Qumran sect saw it, this had to be the Messiah, the sprout of David (4Q Patriarchal Blessings). Primarily David himself might have been seen as this ruler, but when he and his successors failed to measure up to the prophetic hope, it became clear that the reference could be only to the messianic king.

The prophecy of Balaam in Num. 24:15-19 is also apposite: "I see him but not now . . . a star shall come forth out of Jacob, a comet [or scepter, RSV] arise from Israel. He shall smite the squadrons of Moab, and break down all the sons of strife [or Sheth, RSV]." The Hebrew of vv. 18-19 is so bad that translation can only be guesswork, but the occupation of Edom seems to be the point. Again, a reference to David and his victories over Moab and Edom makes sense, but the stress is on the deeds of God himself, and the ultimate application has to be to the messianic king.

The prophecy of Nathan in 2 Sam. 7 has usually been regarded as messianic. A Qumran text (4Q Florilegium I, 10-12) equates the "son" here with the sprout of David who will come in the end time. In the NT, Heb. 1:2, 5 proclaims that the last time has begun with the coming of the promised Son of God, Jesus. In the actual passage Nathan came to David at the peak of his power. David himself would not be allowed to build the temple but his son and successor (2 Sam. 7:1-7). Then came a confirmation of David's kingship and dynasty: "I will set up one of your family, one of your children, to succeed you and I will establish his kingdom. . . . Your throne shall be established for ever" (vv. 12, 16). In his prayer of thanksgiving David underscored the prophecy. His descendants would succeed one another on his throne (vv. 19, 25-29). Was this an unconditionally valid promise? Later generations knew better so far as the kings of Judah were concerned. If the kings did wrong they would be punished (v. 14). If they walked faithfully in God's sight, David would "never lack a successor on the throne of Israel" (1 Kgs. 2:4). In the first instance Nathan's prophecy obviously applied to David's royal successors, though only Solomon, the builder of the temple, was alluded to directly. The promise gained a new dimension, however, when the kings of Judah failed to walk in God's ways and the dynasty came to an end. The expectation now was that of a new son of David who would also be God's Son and who would fulfil the promise in a deeper sense. Nathan's prophecy, then, came to exert a very profound influence as the promise of a coming messianic king.

Another frequently quoted messianic prophecy is found in Ps. 2. The opening words have already a prophetic aspect. The nations are in turmoil. God's words have an even stronger prophetic dimension: "You are my son. . . . I will give you nations as your inheritance." As modern commentators like to think, the psalm might well have had royal ceremonies in Jerusalem as its background. Each new king became God's "son," receiving his office and authority from the Lord. The shattering of enemies with an iron rod might reflect the Egyptian custom whereby a new king shattered pots and figurines carrying the name of enemies of the state. With the end of the monarchy, however, this passage, too, was seen to have a broader sense. Qumran related it to the Messiah (4Q Florilegium I, 18-19). The NT viewed it as a prophecy of Christ. The conspiracy of kings pointed to the machinations of Herod, Pilate, and the Jewish leaders against "the holy servant of the Lord, whom he had anointed as Messiah" (Acts 4:25-28 CB). The coming and the resurrection of Jesus fulfilled v. 7 (Acts 13:32-33; Rom. 1:4). The saying about the Son lies behind the confirmation of the sonship of Jesus at his baptism (Mark 1:11 par.) and transfiguration (9:7 par.). In Revelation the psalm foretells the victory of Jesus and his church (2:26-27; 6:15; 11:15; 12:5; 17:18; 19:15, 19). The psalm might well have been used originally as an enthronement liturgy, but already it pointed ahead to the future, when the definitive Son of David would be the unique Son of God.

One might also quote Ps. 72:10ff. and 110:1ff., where again we find promises to living kings that also have a prophetic dimension. With the end of the Davidic dynasty the promises opened up a new future for Israel. God had an intention for Israel that far surpassed what the prophets of the age of the monarchy might themselves have envisioned, but which lay within the promises that they had made as God's Word to Israel's kings.

b. Prophecies of the Replacement of a Bad King

In this second group we have prophecies of the new king that God would raise up. This time the orientation was wholly to the future. A new king would be born and enthroned. He would rule with loyalty and justice. Since this king did not appear in the age of the monarchy, in course of time it was seen that he could be none other than the coming Messiah.

The texts in this group all come from the royal period. King succeeded king for two centuries in Israel and for over three in Judah. Prophets did not always side with them. There were independent prophets as well as court prophets. These, too, respected the king, but their primary allegiance was to God. They had visions. They were given strange messages. They had to speak God's Word against the ruling kings. They could not strengthen an unjust monarch in his office. Such a king had to make way for a better one.

Three famous prophecies—Isa. 7:10-17 (Immanuel), 9:2-7 (the Prince of Peace), and 11:1-10 (the just shoot of the stock of Jesse)—have a similar content and come from the same background, namely, Isaiah's ministry ca. 733 B.C. The message of Isaiah is striking because it seems to be contradictory: imminent judgment on the one hand, exhortation to repentance and hope of a future beyond the judgment on the other; the condemnation of David's house on the one hand, a message of salvation and restoration on the other. The two aspects complement one another.

A meeting between King Ahaz and Isaiah precedes the prophecy of 7:10-17. The prophet tells the king to choose between unbelief and invasion on the one side, faith and a firm stand on the other. When Ahaz refused, Isaiah spoke the puzzling word from God which expresses both condemnation and salvation. The house of David was to suffer a worse catastrophe than anything since the disruption (v. 13). An unnamed young woman would be pregnant and bear a son to be called Immanuel: God with us (v. 14). Was this son to be a child of the people, or the prophet's son, or a son of the royal house? No matter! His birth would shame Ahaz and his court, for the danger of war would disappear, and he would be a sign to the unbelieving court. Ultimately Judah would be destroyed, but before this happened God wanted to give a sign to the ruling king. Did Isaiah have in view a saving king who would replace Ahaz and inaugurate a new period in Israel's history? The prophecy certainly disturbed Ahaz, as the words of the wise men would disturb Herod (Matt. 2:2). In fact, Hezekiah became Ahaz's successor and the prophecy found partial fulfilment in him. Only in its messianic dimension, however, would it find complete and definitive fulfilment (Matt. 1:22-23).

The next passage (9:2-7) is well-known as a Christmas reading. It is not couched in the form of prophecy but in that of praise and thanksgiving: "For a boy has been born for us, a son given to us . . . and he shall be called in purpose wonderful [RSV Wonderful Counselor], in battle God-like [RSV Mighty God], Father for all time [RSV Everlasting Father], Prince of peace." Praise was given to God for liberation from oppression (vv. 2-5) and for raising up a just king who would establish peace (vv. 6-7). Had the liberation already taken place? The past tenses suggest this, but the closing sentence shows that it is all still future: "The zeal of the Lord of Hosts shall do this" (v. 7). This joyful prophecy of light is set in a dark context. Isaiah's message was not accepted. He could only wait for the day when God would bring judgment on Israel and Judah by the hand of the king of Assyria (7:18-20; 8:5-8; 10:27b-32). Unexpectedly, however, good news came amid the prophecies of condemnation. It did not relativize them. Judgment had to come before there would be room for the just king who would replace Ahaz. But did not the prophecy raise hopes too early for the just king who would bring boundless peace on David's throne? Generation after generation waited for his coming, and finally it came to be seen that this would have to be the messianic king. The reference according to the NT witness is to the Prince of Peace whose reign commenced with the birth of Jesus and will come to its full manifestation at his second coming.

The third passage (11:1-10) is similarly set against a troubled background. As we see from 10:27b-34, an Assyrian army was marching on Jerusalem. It already stood at Nob and the signal was given for an advance on Zion (11:32). The court, which was responsible for this dangerous attack, was shocked. Judah's leaders were like lofty trees, full of high-flown ambitions. God would hew them down (11:33-34). It was from the stock of Jesse, what was left when the tree was cut down, that the shoot—the just king— would then grow. First the tree of David's family had to be cut down. Then the new shoot would come—the king who "fears the Lord" because "the Spirit of the Lord rests upon him" (cf. 11:2-3). The prophecy offered great comfort for the future, but still judgment for its own time. The present kings had to be removed to make way for the new king. This new king would rule according to the norms of his office. He would be a just judge and "defend the humble" (vv. 3-4). He would be dedicated to the people's service. The Lord himself would raise him up and equip him with his Spirit. The message was a revolutionary one. It might easily be construed as treason. Yet it was also constructive at a time of disintegration. It carried a promise of liberation from evil (vv. 6-9) and hope even for other nations as well (v. 10). Only the end-time Messiah could finally bring this promise to fulfilment.

In Jeremiah, too, we find messianic prophecies. Jeremiah lived at the very end of the royal period. He brought God's Word in the form of reprimands to Judah, to Jerusalem, and to the last kings as they were heading for disaster. In the light of his bitter responsibility, it is surprising, perhaps, that Jeremiah was also called upon to comfort his people with revelations of the coming messianic king.

Ignoring Jer. 3:15, which is too general to be truly messianic, we turn first to 23:5-6: "The days are now coming . . . when I will make a righteous Branch spring from David's line, a king who shall rule wisely. . . . This is the name to be given to him: The Lord is our Righteousness." The context brings to light Jeremiah's disappointment as he looked at the contemporary kings (21:11– 23:8). After Josiah's death, no king "dealt justly and fairly" (22:15-16). The prophet perhaps hoped that Zedekiah would do better after the first capture of Jerusalem and the removal of Jehoiachin, but his hopes were quickly dashed. Zedekiah was easily led. The righteous branch would replace a branch that was to be cut away. A new king was promised who would enjoy the full support of God, but in the context of an attack on the existing ruler. The good news was far from cheap or shallow; it implied rebuke and challenge.

The prophecy, of course, did not find fulfilment in Jeremiah's day. The tree of David's house was cut down, but the shoot did not yet come. Yet Jeremiah's saying was remembered, and Qumran identified this righteous branch or shoot as the messianic king of the last days (4Q Patriarchal Blessings 3; Florilegium I, 11). A prophecy that might originally have had a king of Judah in view was again seen to have a larger meaning in messianic terms.

Also calling for attention are the sayings of Ezekiel in 17:22-24 and 21:25-27. This great prophet of the exile referred frequently to a future king or shepherd whom God would raise up after passing judgment on his people. In 17:22 he mentions a "slip from the lofty crown of the cedar" (cf. the shoot or branch of Isaiah and Jeremiah). The hailing of a new king means that the present king must fall, and Ezekiel strongly condemns the disloyalty of Zedekiah, the "impious and wicked prince of Israel" whose "hour of final punishment" has come and who must now yield to the "rightful sovereign"— "then I will give him all." To whom does the prophet refer in these final words of 21:25-27? To Jehoiachin, Nebuchadrezzar, the Messiah? Perhaps Ezekiel himself was not sure. What he knew was that God would destroy the existing system and give authority to another in accordance with his saving plan. The future course of events would bring to light the messianic implication.

c. Prophecies of the Reestablishment of David's Throne

Jerusalem fallen, the temple destroyed, David's dynasty ended, many of the people in exile—this was the bitter reality that shook God's people in 587 B.C. as reflected in Lamentations. But God still raised up prophets to speak his Word. Jeremiah disappeared shortly after 587 (Jer. 43–44), but Ezekiel continued his ministry until 571 (Ezek. 29:17). God's Word also came to the exiles in Isa. 40ff., and under the Persian occupation Haggai, Zechariah, and later Malachi were active. Surprisingly, the theme of raising up kings in Israel was still a burning issue for these later prophets. What was the point when Israel was under the dominion of foreign rulers? They could not strengthen ruling kings or rebuke them by announcing their replacement. Their only option was to kindle the hope that one day God would somehow renew the kingdom. We thus have prophecies of the reestablishment of David's throne.

This was not, of course, an immediate theme or expectation. The Lord was free. He was not tied to his promise to Nathan in the literal sense that might have been hitherto perceived. God had truly rejected Israel, Jerusalem, and David's house. The prophets viewed this rejection with awe. They did not dare to hope, or to raise the hope, for a speedy restoration.

Indeed, in Isa. 40ff. there was no reference at all to the reestablishment of the monarchy. Liberation would come, but no king to lead the people. The Lord himself would act as Israel's King (Isa. 43:15; cf. 41:21; 44:6). David's ministry as a witness to the peoples was now entrusted to the whole community (55:3ff.; cf. 43:10-12). Foreign rulers now held sway, and temporarily Israel must acknowledge their authority. There would be no simple or automatic restoration of David's throne.

A passage from Amos that had relevance to the exilic period carried the message of a Davidic restoration: "On that day I will restore David's fallen house . . ." (9:11-12). In part it found fulfilment in the Persian period when the city and temple were rebuilt, but even then David's kingdom was not reestablished. A Qumran fragment would later interpret "the house of David" as an image for the branch or shoot of David (4Q Florilegium I, 12-13). James quoted the passage to show that the prophets had foretold that foreign nations would become part of the people of God (Acts 15:15-17). Though the verses do not refer directly to the coming king of peace, this aspect came to play an important role later with the expectation of the restoration of David's throne in the end time.

Another relevant passage is Hos. 3:4-5: "after that they will again seek the Lord their God and David their king, and turn anxiously to the Lord for his bounty in days to come." The preceding period when Israel had no king or prince came when Israel fell prey to Assyria in 722 B.C. and Judah to Babylon a century or so later. It was then realized that the Lord's 8th-century promise still held good in the 6th century. Judah would turn back to the Lord and to David. The prophecy obviously had in view the reestablishment of the throne of David. It would take place, however, in the latter days. This fact shows how big a miracle was hoped for—the advent of the Messiah being the ultimate object of the promise.

One of the most familiar of all the prophecies with messianic relevance is to be found in Mic. 5:2-4. Matthew quotes this passage in connection with the coming of the wise men (2:5-6), John in connection with the visit of Jesus to the temple at the Feast of Tabernacles (7:42). The text is in poor shape, but the meaning seems to be: "You, Bethlehem in Ephrathah, small as you are to be among Judah's clans, out of you shall come forth a governor for Israel. . . . He shall appear and be their shepherd in the strength of the Lord, in the majesty of the name of the Lord his God." The passage comes after a series of texts prophesying the salvation of Jerusalem in the "latter days" (4:1 RSV). All nations will then come to Zion, the center of the kingdom of peace (4:1-5). Dispersed Israelites will be regathered on the hill of Zion and become a strong nation. Their former sovereignty will be restored (vv. 6-8), the exile will end (vv. 9-10), and the daughter of Zion will be prepared for the final struggle and victory (4:11–5:1). The power of foreign occupants will be broken and "our land" will be free (5:5-6). Those that are left of Jacob will be exalted above their foes (vv. 7-9) and the instruments of war and idolatry will be destroyed (vv. 10-15). Obviously the words of 5:2-4 are embedded in the context and we must understand them accordingly.

Taking the passage as a whole, we may start with the words "he shall give up Israel" (CB) in v. 3. The point here is that God has given Israel into the hands of its enemies. Jerusalem has been taken, the king and his counselors are no more, the people must go to Babylon, and Zion is like a woman "in labour." Yet the dreadful crisis will end, the woman will give birth, and "those that survive . . . shall rejoin their brethren" (v. 3), i.e., return from exile. When Jerusalem is saved, the kingdom will be reestablished and the king raised up again from Bethlehem, the place from which God raised up David long ago (v. 2). This king will rule as a good shepherd like David (Ps. 78:70-72), and "his power will reach to the ends of the earth" (Mic. 5:4 CB; cf. Ps. 72:8).

Once again the postexilic period saw a partial fulfilment. Jerusalem was rebuilt, but David's throne was not reestablished. Believers thus came to hope for a Davidic king from Bethlehem in the latter days. This king would be far more wonderful than any monarch of the royal period. The Gospels bear witness to the fulfilment of this hope when the end-time coming became a present-day fact: "Today in the city of David a deliverer has been born to you" (Luke 2:11; cf. v. 4).

Another relevant prophecy may be found in Jer. 30:8-9: "In that day . . . they shall serve the Lord their God and David their king, whom I will raise up for them." Some studies (cf. W. Rudolph, *Jeremia,* Handbuch zum Alten Testament [1968]) place Jer. 30–31 in the later 7th century B.C. under Josiah, when Assyrian power was declining and the king of Judah was able to liberate Samaria and Megiddo from foreign occupation, and even planned to restore all Israel to the Israelites. In this situation Jeremiah envisioned a return of all the people of Israel from the places to which they had been exiled in 722 B.C. He addressed them as "a remnant of Israel" (31:7), used ancient names like Jacob and Ephraim, invited them back to their cities (31:21), and promised them "a ruler . . . , one of themselves," who would govern them with the Lord's help (30:21). This restored kingdom, however, would not repeat the sin of Jeroboam; the people would go up to Zion to worship the Lord there (31:6).

If an immediate restoration was at first expected, things worked out differently, for Judah itself was destroyed and the Davidic kingdom ended. The words of 30:8-9 thus carried the same essential message, but Judah was now included as well as Israel, and the prophecy took on a messianic sense with the expectation that David their king would be raised up again and freedom fully restored for the service of God.

The prophecy of Jer. 33:14-16 belongs to a similar context: "at that time, I will make a Righteous Branch of David spring up; he shall maintain law and justice in the land. In those days Judah shall be kept safe and Jerusalem shall live undisturbed, and this shall be her name: The Lord is our Righteousness." In this case the "Righteous Branch," i.e., the ruler who establishes justice and righteousness, is related to the Lord's promise through Nathan. A king of David's posterity will reign, priests of the house of Levi will be in office, and Israel will still be God's chosen people. The Righteous Branch is an exponent of the peace and justice that will then be established. Since no fulfilment came with the postexilic period, the Righteous Branch naturally came to be seen as the Messiah (as at Qumran).

Two prophecies of Ezekiel (34:23-24 and 37:22ff.) are connected and complementary and may thus be treated together. In the first we read: "Then I will set over them one shepherd to take care of them, my servant David. . . . I, the Lord, will become their God, and my servant David shall be a prince among them." Then in 37:22-23 we read: "I will make them one single nation in the land . . . and they shall have one king. . . . My servant David shall become king over them, and they shall have one shepherd. . . . They shall live in the land which I gave my servant Jacob. . . . They and their descendants shall live there for ever, and my servant David shall for ever be their prince."

These passages both belong to the period after 587 B.C. Earlier Ezekiel had announced judgment; now he increasingly promised salvation. This salvation would not come automatically. The Lord was under no obligation to save his chosen people. Israel would have to be raised from the dead; only thus could there be new hope for it (ch. 37). The exiled would then come home to be the Lord's people again, with the Lord as their God. On their return the people would again be a single kingdom with David himself as the symbol of unity. The emphasis is not exactly the same in the two passages. In both, David is the good shepherd who cares for the flock that bad shepherds had for so long neglected. But in ch. 34 the stress is more on the replacement of evil kings than on the reestablishment of the throne of David, while in ch. 37 David is the symbol of a lasting unity. The common element—David's function as the good shepherd—was to exert a permanent influence even though historically the Davidic monarchy would never be restored. The prophecies came to be seen as messianic prophecies, as in the NT (cf. Matt. 9:36; John 10:11; 1 Pet. 2:25).

Haggai also offers a prophecy of the reestablishment of the throne of David. This prophet worked ca. 520-518 B.C. during the reign of Darius of Persia. He played a prominent role in stimulating the people to rebuild the temple. But he also had a vision of the restoration of Judah under a Davidic ruler: "On that day, says the Lord of Hosts, I will take you, Zerubbabel son of Shealtiel, my servant, and will wear you as a signet-ring; for you it is that I have chosen" (2:23). Zerubbabel, an officer under the Persian government, was a grandson of Jehoiachin. With Joshua the high priest he had taken the lead in the rebuilding of the Jerusalem temple (1:14; cf. Ezra 5:2). The obvious aim of the passage was to encourage the two leaders. But was Haggai also nominating Zerubbabel as the future king? Such an action would have meant open rebellion, and therefore Haggai's words are ambivalent. God had chosen Zerubbabel to be his servant and his signet ring (cf. Jer. 22:24). Indirectly a restoration of David's throne seemed to be promised, but it would in fact be neither immediate nor political. The use of Hag. 2:6 in Heb. 12:26 shows that this prophecy, too, was finally linked to the coming of the Messiah.

d. Prophecies of a New Savior

The texts examined thus far all deal with the coming of a just king by God's wonderful intervention. In some cases, with references to a ruling king, the Word of the Lord would so confirm his rule that the hope of a future Savior was kindled. In other cases the Word of the Lord foresaw the birth of a just king to replace a bad king, and as time went by the advent of this just king was expected in a distant future, the just king being identified as the Messiah. In other cases again the promise was given of a restoration of the eliminated throne of David with a Davidic king again enthroned in glory. All three groups agree in describing the future divinely given liberator as a king in a normal if idealized sense. A fourth group, however, no longer sees the coming liberator in the image of a king alone. Other functions of leadership begin to play a role. The royal function does not disappear but it is complemented and influenced by others, by that of the priest, the teacher, and the prophet. The prophecies of this fourth group speak more generally, then, of the coming Savior.

Zechariah, a prophet of priestly descent, a contemporary of Haggai, foretold the reestablishment of David's throne but divided the leadership between two persons. In one of his night visions (4:2-3) he saw a golden lampstand with an olive tree to the right and another to the left. He was told that "these two are the two consecrated with oil who attend the Lord of all the earth" (4:14).

The idea of a double leadership recurs in 6:12-13: "Here is a man named the Branch. . . . he who will assume royal dignity, will be seated on his throne and govern, with a priest at his right side, and concord shall prevail between them." Primarily Zerubbabel and Joshua are the two in view, but in fact these men would never set up independent rule for Israel. The temple and city would be rebuilt but David's throne would not be set up again. The prophecy of Zechariah remained a promise that still awaited fulfilment like that of Hag. 2:23. It came to be seen as a messianic prophecy, and the Messiah would unite in himself the twofold function. He would be priest as well as king.

The new interest in the priesthood reflected the situation under Persian rule when the temple was rebuilt. For centuries the king had been the focus of interest; now the priest came to the fore. If the restoration of David's throne was still hoped for, kingship could no longer be imagined without priesthood as its complement. In Jer. 33 there was already a balance between the king and priest, and Ezekiel's vision of the new Jerusalem gave more prominence to the priest than to the king (Ezek. 40–48). Along these lines the Qumran community could thus expect not one Messiah but two, a king of the line of David and a priest of the line of Levi.

Psalm 110:4 probably played an important part in this development: "You are a priest for ever, in the succession of Melchizedek." Addressed to David and his successors, this would be no more than a title of majesty. The newly anointed king was to have the name and honor of Salem's former king (Gen. 14:18). With the suppression of the royal office, however, the verse came to be seen as a messianic prophecy and the wording was seen to have the deeper significance that the coming Messiah would not be an ordinary king. He would also be a priest who could make reconciliation for his people.

Chapters 9–14 of Zechariah, ascribed by many scholars to a later period than chs. 1–8, also give evidence of a development of messianic expectation. The most famous passage, familiar to Christians from its liturgical use, is in Zech. 9:9-10: "Rejoice, rejoice, daughter of Zion . . . for see, your king is coming to you . . . humble and mounted on an ass, on a foal, the young of a she-ass. . . . He shall speak peaceably to every nations, and his rule shall extend from sea to sea, from the River to the ends of the earth." This saying is like a pearl in a difficult setting, for the context presents insoluble problems. The prophecy foresees the king's entry into Jerusalem in total triumph (cf. Ps. 21). His kingdom now covers all the earth. But he is a humble king. He rides on an ass like common folk. He is peaceful. He destroys all weapons. He announces šalôm to the nations. This is indeed an original saying. The king is still a strong head of state, but his strength lies not in brute force but in the Spirit of the Lord (Zech. 4:6). This new feature would have a great impact on messianic expectation and on the description of the Messiah's work (cf. Matt. 21:5 par. John 12:15).

In Zech. 12–14, which many scholars date even later than the rest of the book, we find yet another development. The complaints and hopes of the people come to expression in 12:8, 10: "On that day the Lord will shield the inhabitants of Jerusalem; on that day the very weakest of them shall be like David, and the line of David like God. . . . Then they shall look on me, on him whom they have pierced, and shall wail over him as over an only child." What the original reference of this saying might be, no commentator can say. Was some martyr in view who died to save the city? We do not know. The prophecy seems to confirm the ancient prophecy of a Davidic restoration, but the figure of the Savior-King is no longer unbroken. NT quotations (Matt. 24:30; John 19:37; Rev. 1:7) show what a deep influence this new vision exerted on the understanding of the expected Messiah.

It has always been a source of astonishment that there is no direct messianic prophecy in Isa. 40ff., which OT scholars often date in the exilic and postexilic period. The chapters obviously refer to the imminent liberation of the people from exile and to a wonderful future restoration, but they do not say specifically that a Davidic king will play a role in this liberation. They foresee instead two saviors for Israel: politically Cyrus, king of Persia, and spiritually the Servant of the Lord, who shows the features not of a king or priest but rather of a prophet. Has this mysterious Servant a truly messianic rank and quality? Many divergent answers have been given to this question, as may be seen from the commentaries on Isa. 42:1-4; 49:1-6; 50:4-9; 52:13–53. We will here content ourselves with the following observations.

First, the Servant is called, acts, and struggles as a prophet. He must transmit God's Word to Israel and the nations (42:1-4; 49:1-6; 50:4). In discharging this task, he meets opposition and humiliation (49:4; 50:5-9; 53:3, 5, 7-9) in much the same way as Jeremiah and Ezekiel. Yet his ministry also differs from a normal prophetic ministry. He announces liberation from oppression by bearing suffering personally. He willingly "exposed himself to face death" (53:12) and "made himself an offering for sin" (53:10 CB). Apart from Moses, no other prophet was ever said to have suffered for the salvation of his people.

Second, we also find some royal elements in the Servant Songs. Not a prophet but a judge or king was normally endowed with the Spirit and thus enabled to become his people's liberator or savior. "To restore the tribes of Jacob" (49:6) and to "make justice shine" (42:1, 3) "to earth's farthest bounds" (49:6)—these were the tasks of a mighty king. If the Servant was truly a prophet, at the very least his ministry also involved royal authority and power.

Third, no single answer can be given to the question who the Servant is (cf. Acts 8:34). Each of the different answers given contains an element of truth. The first reference might have been to a prophet, e.g., the author himself. But the texts could also apply to the people that God had chosen and sent (cf.

49:3). The Servant might also be seen as the coming Savior, as in the LXX version of the fourth song. From the 2nd century B.C. onward, apocryphal works increasingly identified the Servant as the coming messianic king (cf. W. Zimmerli and J. Jeremias, *The Servant of God,* Studies in Biblical Theology [1957], pp. 57-78). In the NT Jesus is the Servant, as he is also Messiah and King.

The message of the Servant Songs gave a new turn to messianic expectation. The image of the Messiah was now no longer so exclusively dominated by the royal elements. It was both enlarged and deepened. The people still expected a king who would establish justice, peace, and prosperity on earth. But they came to see that this goal could be achieved only through suffering, through the reconciliation that this king, the Servant of the Lord, would himself bring.

A prophecy in Malachi also emphasizes that the coming Savior would be a peacemaker when it tells of Elijah's end-time coming to "reconcile fathers to sons and sons to fathers" (4:5-6). The new feature here is that the prophet will come before the day of the Lord. In Sirach (Ecclesiasticus), written ca. 200 B.C., Elijah will restore the tribes of Israel (48:10). This new Elijah is obviously no less powerful than a king or savior. From John 6:14 we know that the Samaritan community in the days of Jesus awaited a prophet to liberate them. Elijah is mentioned 30 times in the NT, but here his end-time role is never more than that of a forerunner. He never attains to the stature of the Messiah himself.

Further development of the concept of the Messiah may be seen in Dan. 7:13-14: "I saw one like a man [RSV son of man] coming with the clouds of heaven; he approached the Ancient in Years and was presented to him. Sovereignty and glory and kingly power were given to him, so that all people and nations of every language should serve him; his sovereignty was to be an everlasting sovereignty which should not pass away." The context in ch. 7 is a vision of the last days when the kingdoms of this wicked world will be destroyed and God's kingdom will become a visible reality. What Daniel, a "man of visions" and "interpreter of visions," saw in vv. 13-14 bears some similarity to an anointing ceremony (cf. Ps. 2). It also reminds us of prophecies of a just king replacing a wicked one. A heavenly court will dethrone kings that act like wild beasts (Dan. 7:2-8). Then sovereignty will be given to a new king, who is like a son of man.

Who is this new sovereign? Many theories have been advanced. "One like a man" does not have to denote a specific man. It may mean "one who has a character like a man." As distinct from the wicked kings, this new king will be humane and kind. He is an earthly ruler, but he will not use his power to deprive people of their rights. Instead, he will establish "everlasting right" (9:24) among the nations. God himself will be the ultimate sovereign (7:17-27) and he will give power to "the servants of the Most High" (CB 7:18, 22, 27), i.e., his chosen people. Nowhere is any specific reference made to the Davidic king, the Branch, or the Messiah. The remnant that lives under oppression will eventually be given sovereignty and will exercise it forever.

On the other hand, Jewish writings of the 1st century A.D., and especially the Synoptic Gospels and Revelation, take the expression "son of man" to refer to a specific person, i.e., the messianic king. How the awaited Savior originally came to be called "son of man" we cannot say. There can hardly have been any specific relation to the Branch or the new David. But the vision of Dan. 7 shows that the idea of the Savior of David's line was being widened to that of a Savior for the whole world. A further step was taken when the son of man and the Servant of the Lord were brought together (cf. 1 Enoch 45–50). The foundation was thus laid for the NT understanding of the Messiah.

The amazing result of this development of the image of the coming Savior was that the image lost its original more definite character. The just king, the Branch of David's line, might be clear-cut, but was increasingly seen to be inadequate alone. New elements had to be added to achieve a fuller and deeper understanding. The pattern of the victorious king was challenged by that of the humble king, even of the Servant who would suffer humiliation and defeat before the final victory. The time of the Savior's coming also became more and more uncertain as immediate expectation faded. The diversity of imagery was so great, indeed, that the texts that spoke about the coming Savior never specifically equated him with the Messiah.

The apparent confusion is explicable, of course, for, as Peter says, "the prophets pondered and explored," trying "to find out what was the time, and what the circumstances" in which the grace of God would be manifest (1 Pet. 1:10-12). God was working out his saving purpose in the tangle of human events. Only intimated in the ancient prophecies, it would be brought to light, according to the NT witness, in the life and work of Jesus, Messiah King, Son of God, Priest, Reconciler, Prophet, Servant of the Lord, and Son of Man all in one. But the NT writers themselves, we must emphasize, could not have given this witness had they not received a key to the understanding of the mystery of Christ's person and work. This key was already there for them "in every part of the scriptures, beginning from Moses and all the prophets" (Luke 24:25-27 CB).

Chapter VIII

God Chose Jerusalem

"GOD ACTS IN HISTORY. He intervenes in the world. He manifests the power of his love." With these words we opened Chapter VI, which dealt with a specific country. We repeat them now that our concern is with a particular city, the city called Zion or Jerusalem, which plays an outstanding part in both the OT and the NT and which might be seen as the capital of the kingdom of God.

Neighboring nations (e.g., Egypt and Babylon) mention Jerusalem at least from the 15th and perhaps from the 18th century B.C. The normal form then was *Urusalim*. What the name meant is unknown. The first part (*yeru* or *uru*) might mean "town" *(uru)* or "possession" *(yeru)*, but another possibility is *ûr/îr*, "furnace" (cf. Ariel, "God's furnace," in Jer. 29:1-2). The second part is also obscure. One suggestion is that Salem or Salim was the name of a god worshiped there (cf. Ir-shemesh in Josh. 19:41, the town of Shemesh). But Salem might also be related to the similar-sounding *šālôm* (Akkadian *šalāmu*), meaning "peace" or "salvation."

The city was also known as Jebus, the town of the Jebusites (Josh. 15:8; Judg. 19:10-11). A central part of it went by the name of Zion, another word of unknown meaning, often used later for the city as a whole. On the ruins of the former city the Romans built a new town which they named Aelia Capitolina (A.D. 130) after the emperor Aelius Hadrianus and the temple of their supreme god Jupiter Capitolinus which adorned the city. When Muslim armies took the city (A.D. 638) they gave it yet another name, el-Quds, the "holy city." Jews and Christians continue to use the biblical name.

The changing names point to the main periods of the city's history. We can distinguish three main biblical periods. Little is known about the first period prior to David's seizure of the city from the Jebusites (ca. 1000 B.C.). We do not know who founded it. It was originally small, though ruling over a larger territory. In the second period (ca. 1000-586 B.C.) David and Solomon ruled the united nation from it, but with the disruption it lost importance as merely the capital of

Judah, the seat of the Davidic kings. The third period (586 B.C.–A.D. 70) is marked by foreign occupation: the Babylonians (586-539), the Persians (539-332), the Egyptian Ptolemies (300-200), the Syrian Seleucids (198-143), and finally the Romans (63), who destroyed the city in A.D. 70. Independence had been temporarily achieved under the Maccabeans (165-63 B.C.), but full liberation was expected only with the end-time coming of God's kingdom.

As regards the later history, Hadrian forbade Jews to enter his new city. They were readmitted when Constantine made Jerusalem the spiritual capital of the Christian world. This was a golden time for the city, but it ended in the early 7th century when Christians and Jews fought for control of the city. Then in A.D. 635 Arab armies under Caliph Omar took Jerusalem and made it the third spiritual center of Islam after Mecca and Medina. Arab hegemony lasted for nine centuries (638-1517) with only a brief interruption when Western armies set up the kingdom of Jerusalem as a result of the first Crusade (1100-1187). In the 16th century the Ottoman rulers of Turkey incorporated Palestine into their empire (1517-1917). Britain seized the country in 1917 and made it a protectorate with Jerusalem as the capital (1922). The new state of Israel took over the town in 1948, Jordan annexing the old city and the mosque of el-Ahram. Finally, in 1967 Israel occupied the whole city, making it the capital in 1980. Thus the foreign occupation that had begun in 586 B.C. came at last to an end.

Jerusalem is situated at the north end of the mountains of Judah on the watershed between the western slope, which descends smoothly to the Mediterranean, and the eastern slope, which drops steeply to the Dead Sea. Two mountain chains, 800 m. above sea level and 1,200 m. above the Dead Sea, enclose the town (Ps. 125:2), which is built on two parallel hills that are higher in the north and lower in the south, the eastern hill being narrower, the western broader. The deep valley of Kidron lies in the east, that of Hinnom in the south and southwest. A shallow valley runs through the city between the hills. The oldest part of the city lies to the south of the eastern hill. Jebus, the fortress of Zion, the city of David, is very small (about 400 by 100 m.). The temple court that stretches northward is sometimes seen as part of Mt. Zion, which looks steep and high from the Kidron Valley. Houses were built on the western hill from the royal period. It is not clear how large the city was when a new protective wall was built in the 5th century B.C.

1. The Witness of Scripture

God chose Jerusalem as his holy mountain, his dwelling place, the center of his kingdom on earth, in order to grant his people a strong

rock and safe shelter. God raised up his servant David and other kings
so as to make of his city a home of freedom, justice, and peace. It
pleased God to accept the Jerusalem temple as the place of his special
presence where he would hallow Israel as a community that worships
him alone. God condemned Jerusalem when it rebelled against him
in order to renew the city as the birthplace of his new people made
up of both Jews and Gentiles.

THE HOLY CITY has an important place in the witness of scripture and Israel's
faith. The OT mentions Jerusalem 669 times and Zion 200 times. No other
city or mountain figures as often. There were good reasons for this.

God chose Jerusalem as his own city, his holy city. Between God and
Jerusalem there was a bond of love as close as that between God and Israel
or God and Abraham and David as Israel's representatives. This city was "the
place which the Lord your God will choose" (Deut. 12:5, 11) or the city which
God "has chosen" (1 Kgs. 8:44; 2 Kgs. 21:7; Zech. 1:17). It was God's own
city in a very special way. The election of Jerusalem was thus one of the great
deeds of God that no survey of biblical theology may ignore.

God chose Zion. This act cannot be studied apart from the act by
which he raised up kings, especially David (cf. 2 Chron. 6:6). One of God's
aims in choosing Jerusalem was to raise up kings. Conversely, the vocation of
kings can be properly understood only in relation to God's intention for the
royal city. Some aspects of the king's personal ministry find analogies in the
calling and ministry of Zion.

At a first glance the link between the choice of Jerusalem and creation
might seem tenuous. Yet the themes are related. God is praised as King and
Creator in Jerusalem (Ps. 93). As we learn from Abraham's meeting with
Melchizedek of Salem (Gen. 14:18-20), the Creator of heaven and earth was
already extolled in this city long before Israel's day. From a very early time
it had been the dwelling place of the Most High, the center of the world.

Genesis 14 also shows a link between Zion and the election of the
patriarchs. Furthermore, Mt. Moriah, on which Abraham was to sacrifice Isaac,
was at one time identified as Mt. Zion on which God's house was later to be
built (Gen. 22:1, 19). The patriarchal promises were frequently recalled as well
when foreign occupation threw doubt on God's presence in Zion.

Links are not always apparent between Zion and the exodus, the
wilderness wandering, and the gift of Canaan. Isaiah never expressly refers to
these themes. But Jeremiah saw their importance. Perhaps the message of
northern prophets like Hosea had an influence in this regard. Some psalms,
too, show that the honor of Jerusalem rests on God's great saving acts at the
beginning of Israel's existence (Ps. 114; 76:2).

The revelation at Sinai also came into association with Zion. Mt. Sinai lies at a great distance from Mt. Zion, and God was present in the two places with widely different intentions. The main theme at Sinai—the revelation, hearing, and keeping of the Torah—had at first no specific role in relation to Zion. But after the rebuilding of the temple (Ezra and Nehemiah) Jerusalem became the center from which the Torah went forth and to which the nations would come for instruction (cf. Isa. 2:1-5).

A tenser relation connects the election of Zion to the sending of the prophets. As a royal city and sanctuary Zion had court prophets. Some of these simply praised and supported the kings and priests. Others like Nathan proclaimed God's positive purpose for the city. Independent prophets, however, condemned the pride and complacency connected with the city and sanctuary, though also holding out hope for renewal.

In discussing the divine choice of Zion, we shall focus on four main aspects. First, it pleased the Most High God to be present in a very special way in this city and on his holy mountain. Second, God raised up kings in Zion and made it the home of righteousness (Isa. 1:21), a place of wisdom and knowledge (33:6). Third, Zion was the site of God's house where Israel worshiped the Lord with prayers, praises, and offerings. Fourth, God had and fulfilled a special purpose for this chosen city.

2. God Chose Jerusalem as His Own City

Primarily Jerusalem was the city of God. God first chose Zion as his holy mountain, and only then did he also choose it as the city of David and the site of his house. The choice of Zion is just as hard to explain as the election of Israel, but it is an essential part of the biblical witness.

a. Biblical Data

MANY BIBLICAL EXPRESSIONS refer to the unique relation between the God of Israel and Zion or Jerusalem, the former Jebusite hill city. Being familiar, these expressions attract little attention. Yet they have important implications for our knowledge of God and our understanding of the faith of Israel.

The strongest and most concentrated expressions occur in the Psalms of Zion (46; 48; 76; etc.). Since most of the psalms originated in Jerusalem, we naturally find similar utterances in other psalms as well. Prophets who lived in the holy city, e.g., Isaiah, Jeremiah, Ezekiel, and Zechariah, also spoke in the same way.

(1) To be noted first are expressions that call Zion God's creation, possession, or dwelling place.

Thus Zion is "the mountain of the Lord" (Ps. 24:3) or God's "holy mountain" (2:6). The idea of possession is contained in the phrase "the city of God (or the Lord)" (46:4; 48:8; cf. Jer. 25:29). "The holy city" expresses the same idea, but without pronouncing the divine name (Neh. 11:1). Zion is *naḥᵃlat YHWH* in the sense of "the Lord's dwelling place" (Exod. 15:17; Ps. 79:1, NEB "domain," RSV "inheritance"). It is also the Lord's "throne" (Jer. 3:17) or "footstool" (Ps. 99:5; Lam. 2:1). God is enthroned in heaven, but heaven and earth meet in Jerusalem. In virtue of God's presence, Zion is also "the perfection of beauty" (Ps. 50:2 RSV; Lam. 2:15), "the very centre of the world" (Ezek. 38:12).

(2) Who is this God who possesses and is enthroned in Jerusalem? Many passages give God titles connected with Zion. Revealing his presence here, God introduces himself from a new angle.

Melchizedek had blessed Abraham by God Most High (*'el 'elyôn*), and the Psalms entitle God "the Most High" dozens of times. Jerusalem is "the city of God, which the Most High has made his dwelling" (Ps. 46:4). "The Most High himself" established it (87:5 RSV). As Creator, he is "the Most High over all the earth" (83:18). A similar title expressing God's worldwide sovereignty is "the Lord of all the earth" (*'ᵃdôn kol-hā'āreṣ*, Ps. 97:5; Zech. 4:14). "The Lord of Hosts" is even more common, notwithstanding the obscurity of the original *YHWH ṣᵉbāôt* (celestial or terrestrial armies? the hosts of Israel?). This title occurs frequently in the Psalms (24:10; 48:9 [Eng. 8]; etc.), and even more so in Isaiah (6:3 and 55 times) and Jeremiah (2:19 and 77 times).

The divine title "King" also stands closely related to Jerusalem. The "King of glory" enters his holy city, the people receive him in procession, the everlasting gates lift up their heads (Ps. 24:7-10 RSV). Jerusalem is "the city of the great King" (48:2 RSV). He is seated there on his "holy throne" (47:8; Jer. 3:17). Many psalms honor him as King (47:2; 93:7; 96:10; 99:1-2), and prophets swell the chorus of praise (Isa. 6:5; Jer. 10:7; Zeph. 3:15; Zech. 14:9).

The designation of God as Judge may also be connected with Zion. Many psalms call him "judge" (7:11; 9:4; 50:6; etc.). The Lord of all the earth is also Judge of all the earth. As we have seen, the king and the judge were one and the same.

(3) To the divine attributes we may add various nouns and adjectives related to God's presence in Zion.

Special stress falls on transcendence: the Lord's glory (*kābôd*, "weight," "honor"; Ps. 24:7ff.; Isa. 6:3; Jer. 17:12), might (*'ōz*, Ps. 29:1; 96:6), splendor (*hādār*, Ps. 29:3; 145:12; Isa. 2:19), majesty (*hôd*, Ps. 104:1; 145:5), and terror (*paḥad*, Isa. 2:10). As the Most High, God is great, fearful, mighty, holy, and strong. "Great" (*gādōl*) is often used to describe his name (Ps. 76:1), glory (21:5), or doings (111:2), but mostly it is used of God himself (47:2; 48:1; Jer. 10:6; Neh. 9:32). The same is true of "terrible" or "fearful" (*nôrā'*, Ps. 47:2; 99:3; 111:9), mighty (*'addîr*, 8:2; 76:5; 1 Sam. 4:8; Isa. 33:20), holy (*qādôš*, Ps. 99:4; Isa. 6:3; Jer. 32:18), and strong (*gibbôr*, Ps. 24:8; Jer. 32:18).

(4) Expressions that call Jerusalem a stronghold, rock, fortress, or shield also call for notice. People can feel safe there, but the city itself does not guarantee security. Safety is complete only because God by his wonderful presence makes himself known as "a tower of strength" (Ps. 48:3).

God is himself a rock (*ṣûr*) or stronghold (*sēlaʿ*) (Ps. 18:2; 19:14; 28:1; Isa. 26:1; 60:18). Christian hymns have taken up this thought: "On the rock of ages founded." The image is based on the rocky hill of Zion and the protection it offered. Its application to God, however, is broad. The same is true of "tower" (*miśgāb*), "refuge" (*mahʰseh, māʿôn, mᵉṣûdāh*), and "shield" (*māgēn*), which have also found abundant liturgical use.

b. God's Chosen Dwelling

How did Jerusalem ever come to be God's city? It is easy to see why it became David's city. Did he not capture it and make it his capital? It is also easy to see why it should be the city of God's house. Did not Solomon build the temple there and Josiah establish it as the center of worship? But why should it be God's city?

Before David's time Jerusalem was obviously known only as a Jebusite town. Israel showed no awareness of it as the city of God. A change came only when David transformed the Jebusite city into his capital and a center for worship. In terms of Israel's understanding, Jerusalem became God's city and holy dwelling only at a specific time and in consequence of specific historical developments.

At the same time the OT shows that Jerusalem had been the city of God even when Israel was not aware of it. From this standpoint Jerusalem enjoys an eternal glory that is independent of once-for-all events in Israel's history.

(1) Looking first at the historical events that brought the city to prominence, we note that Judah (Josh. 15:63) and Benjamin (Judg. 1:21) failed to dislodge the Jebusites from it. At one point the men of Judah set fire to it (Judg. 1:8) and it was listed as a Benjaminite city (Josh. 18:28), but it had not in fact been occupied. Even under Saul it was still a Jebusite stronghold, so that David must have carried Goliath's head there later (1 Sam. 17:54). An account of the final capture of the city is given in 2 Sam. 5:6-12. The proverb about the lame and the blind in vv. 6-8 is obscure, but David and his men

clearly managed to penetrate the city "up the water shaft" (v. 8 RSV). Having taken Zion, David made it his capital and built a house for himself in it (vv. 10-11). When he had defeated the Philistines he moved the ark there (ch. 6) and planned to build a temple (7:1-2). Though the execution of this plan was left to Solomon, Israel was already beginning to think of Jerusalem as the holy city, as God's own city.

David, of course, was an able commander and statesman. He saw the strategic value of Jerusalem, its advantageous political neutrality as a city that no one tribe had occupied, and its unifying force as a center of worship for all Israel. Nevertheless, we are not to conclude too hastily that David planned to make his capital a holy city and in this way to confer on it a new status. Here as always God took the initiative, though allowing David to participate in his work.

In his study *Jerusalems Aufstieg* (1925), Albrecht Alt offers an excellent appraisal of David's role. He extols his wise choice of Jerusalem, his use of his own men to make it a private possession, his locating of the ark there to give the new capital spiritual force and authority, and his association with priests and prophets (Zadok and Nathan) for the more effective realization of his ambitious goals. But Alt's account is far too one-sided to be true to the OT witness.

The biblical record in 1 and 2 Samuel undoubtedly finds a place for David's wisdom and merits. Ultimately, however, it was always the Lord and not David who so governed the march of events that Zion became the holy city. Before David ever had any such plan, the Lord had planned already to make Jerusalem his dwelling place among his people. David chose Jerusalem, but behind his choice stood God's prior choice. The account of the ark's migration to Jerusalem makes this unambiguously clear.

The ark was a symbol of God's presence. Wherever the ark stood visibly, the Lord of Hosts was present invisibly. When Samuel was called to be a prophet (1 Sam. 1–3), the ark was at Shiloh, a sacred town in Ephraimite territory. Israelites from all the tribes would meet there for the annual feasts. The migration began when sinful Israel was twice defeated by the Philistines (1 Sam. 4). On the second occasion the ark itself was present and was captured, thus leaving Shiloh and beginning its circuitous journey to Jerusalem.

With the capture of the ark it seemed as though the Lord himself had been led away into captivity (1 Sam. 5:1-2). But the very humiliation was quickly turned into victory as afflictions fell on the Philistine kings and people and on their god Dagon. Those who had thought they could play with the ark as a toy became afraid. They moved it from place to place, but to no avail. Eventually, in a repetition of the liberation of the people from Egypt, the ark came back to Israelite territory (1 Sam. 6–7). Under the compulsion of plagues the Philistines had to let the ark go, and it did not go empty or without a gift (6:3). It thus came first to Beth-shemesh (6:9, 12), then to Kiriath-jearim in the mountains of Judah (7:1-2), about 10 km. from Jerusalem.

The climax came twenty years later. Saul and Samuel had now passed from the scene. David had become king in Jerusalem and beaten the Philistines. The time had come to put the ark "in its place" (2 Sam. 6:17) in Jerusalem. Yet David could not carry out this pious plan as he wished. Uzzah's death vexed him and made him afraid (6:6ff.). The ark stayed three months at Obed-edom's house. Only when the Lord showed his willingness to let the ark be moved by blessing the Gittite's family did the king bring it up to the place that the Lord wanted (6:11-14). At last, then, the ark reached its destination.

The story of the ark stresses that God himself chose Jerusalem. He took the initiative in deciding where he would be present as he did in raising up kings in Israel. David simply carried out what the Lord had previously decided. The story of the ark is placed very conspicuously before that of the conquest and consolidation of Jerusalem as David's capital and the later building of the temple. The closing strophe of Ps. 78 drives home the lesson: "He forsook his home at Shiloh. . . . He despised the clan of Joseph. . . ; he chose the tribe of Judah and Mount Zion which he loved" (vv. 60, 67-68).

(2) The Bible testifies that at a specific time the Lord came to Jerusalem and made Zion his dwelling place. The attributes honoring Jerusalem support this conclusion. What was their origin? Why did Israel include them in their hymns and prayers?

When they took Jerusalem, the Israelites began to live there alongside Jebusites whom they had not driven out. In the interaction between the two groups, the Israelites received as well as gave. Jerusalem was "israelized," but the Israelites were also "jerusalemized." It might be, then, that historically many of the lofty terms for the city came from the treasury of ancient Jerusalem tradition.

Thus Jerusalem was praised as "the holy habitation of the Most High" (Ps. 46:4 RSV). Israel might well have adopted here an ancient title (Gen. 14:18ff.), but it equated the Most High with Yahweh. The same holds good for the designation of God as King. This was not a divine title used in the days of the patriarchs, the exodus, the desert wandering, or the Sinai revelation. But Israel saw again that properly it belongs to Yahweh alone.

The Israelites had good reason to use these titles. They did not do so as mere newcomers adapting to existing customs. They saw that God's greatness, glory, and holiness found expression in divine names of this kind. They thus confiscated the titles for the Lord and filled them with new meaning. Praising God's greatness and glory, they achieved a new and universal dimension of faith.

It was this great God who had chosen Jerusalem as his dwelling.

Israel, then, began to view the city differently. It found it normal to extol God's "holy habitation," the "city of the great King," the "center of the world," the capital of God's kingdom that encompasses both heaven and earth. Because the Creator is enthroned in Zion, Zion itself can be described in paradisal colors as the "perfection of beauty," the holy mountain that is the source of the rivers that irrigate the earth.

A river gladdens the city of God (Ps. 46:4). Pilgrims to Zion sing: "All my springs are in you" (87:7 RSV). "The river of God is full of water" (65:9 RSV). "He will drink from the torrent beside the path" (110:7). The future Zion is to be the source of blessings flowing as rivers of water (Ezek. 47:1-12). In it is "the fountain of life" (Ps. 36:9).

Israel did not adopt Jebusite culture uncritically. It "israelized" it. In his regal role as King and Most High, the God of Israel differed from Canaanite deities. The latter—El or Baal, Hadad or Asherah—symbolized natural forces that might fight as well as agree. How different was the Lord! He revealed himself in Israel's history. He freely bound himself to his people and led them to a future in keeping with his plan of salvation for them. He ruled as "the King of Israel" (Isa. 44:6 RSV), "our king" (Isa. 33:22), but as such he was "King of the whole earth."

The relation of the Lord to the world influenced Israel's concept of Jerusalem. Zion was primarily the center of God's kingship over his own people, and only as such the center of the earth. Israel loved Zion as God's headquarters in this world and in time. The Lord was present there to act in history, to do his saving work first for his own people, then for the nations, and even for nature itself. This conviction emerges clearly in Pss. 145–150.

c. The Rock That Cannot Be Shaken

"Those who trust in the Lord are like Mount Zion, which cannot be shaken but stands fast for ever" (Ps. 125:1). The holy city was the eternal city. Because the Lord was present there, it was a safe dwelling for his people. The Lord had founded it; how could it be shaken?

Jerusalem was safe, however, only insofar as the Lord was actually in it. Zion in itself was by no means unassailable. It might be called a rock or stronghold or refuge, but it never bore as such the titles *"my* rock," *"our* stronghold," or *"my* refuge." Designations of this kind were reserved for the Lord. Israel could believe in the safety of Jerusalem only because it believed in the Lord's presence there.

Nevertheless, the belief in Zion's safety was not just a dream or wishful thinking. It rested on events. God's presence was proved by his coming to the city, and on many occasions God proved to be "our shelter and our refuge; a timely help in trouble" (Ps. 46:1).

(1) As we read in Ps. 93, which reminds us of the victory over chaos at creation, God has given security to the world, so that even the threatening waters of the flood cannot overwhelm it (vv. 3-4; cf. 77:16; 104:5-9). At times these forces may be poetically represented as the "sea-serpent" or Rahab (Ps. 74:12-14; 89:9-10; Isa. 51:9). The point is that the whole world, including Jerusalem in particular, is endangered by natural forces, but the Lord has subdued them and has promised to continue to do so. Jerusalem, then, cannot be shaken or swallowed up by these forces so long as the Conqueror of cosmic powers extends his protection to it.

(2) Nations as well as natural forces threatened Jerusalem. The kings of the earth conspired to attack and destroy it. At such times the Lord would again be a powerful defender, defeating the enemy, slaying and scattering the attackers, and saving the city and its inhabitants.

God himself had to do this. Only when enemies saw and felt his tremendous presence would they abandon their attack (Ps. 48:4-6; 76:3, 7, 8, 12; 46:6-9). Unable to trust in themselves or the defenses of the city, in virtue of the Lord's presence and power the people could confidently say: "We are not afraid when the earth heaves . . . and the mountains quake" (Ps. 46:2-3), for God himself stilled both "the roaring of the waves" and "the tumult of the peoples" (65:7 RSV).

During the period after David and Solomon there were in fact frequent attacks on the city. In particular the armies of Assyria (2 Kgs. 18–19) and Babylon (chs. 24–25) assailed it. Many times Jerusalem was either saved from danger or rose again after a time of destruction. Exposed to repeated attacks, the people clung to the well-proven fact that God had already saved his dwelling place several times and would help it again in times of trouble. Prophets both before and after the exile promised safety to Jerusalem.

Israel did not believe in the absolute security of Jerusalem. The basis of its confidence was that God had many times proved his presence in his city and his readiness to save it. Whether against cosmic flood or human foe, God himself was the city's sure defense, but its only sure defense (Ps. 48:3 RSV).

d. A Place of Refuge and Joy

God chose Jerusalem in order to grant to his people a safe shelter. But in granting this refuge he expected his people to respond. It is to this aspect that we now turn.

A feature of the Zion psalms is the distinctive use of the pronoun "we" or "our" (cf. 46:1, 7, 11; 48:8). The collective voice of the congregation is heard here. It is the voice of God's people coming together in Zion and confessing their common faith. The confession is an echo, an answer to God's presence. The people do not remain silent when they experience God's help. They respond consciously and actively. The Lord is present in Zion as the fountain of life, and he expects the people to come and drink.

How did the people respond? They are said to "seek refuge" and to "believe." A study of these words shows how closely confessions of faith are linked to the Lord's presence in Zion.

Nearly every psalm of supplication, complaint, or thanksgiving speaks of taking refuge (*ḥāsāh*) with God or trusting (*bāṭaḥ*) in him. At times the confession is addressed to God: "In thee I find refuge" (Ps. 7:1; etc.), or: "In thee I trust" (25:2; etc.). At other times it is addressed to the community: "In the Lord I have found my refuge" (Ps. 11:1), or: "I have trusted in the Lord" (26:1 RSV). Sometimes in thanksgiving an invitation is given to the community: "Blessed is the man who trusts in thee" (84:12 RSV; cf. 40:4) or: "Blessed are all who take refuge in him" (2:12 RSV).

To take or find refuge and to trust mean much the same thing in this context. They also carry the implication of love (*'āhab*), holding fast (*dābaq*), and fear (*yārē'*). *TDOT* (II, 88ff.; V, 64ff.) finds three aspects in the two main verbs. First, there is witness to a changed situation, i.e., from affliction to security. Second, joy results, for even though there is still danger, there is also protection; the Lord is a refuge (*maḥ*ᵃ*seh*) and place of trust (*mibṭāh*). Third, a promise is given to serve the Lord, and the community is invited to do the same.

The Lord manifested himself, then, as a rock or unshakable stronghold. But where? In Zion. Jerusalem was where he had laid a strong foundation. This did not mean, of course, that there was no refuge outside Zion. But Zion was where Israel learned to experience and rejoice in it.

Trust was what the Lord demanded of his people in Isa. 1–39. They had a kind of trust, but "in devious and dishonest practices" (30:12), taking refuge "under Egypt's wing" (30:2). The women trusted "in nought," "living without a care" (cf. 32:9-11). During his prophetic ministry Isaiah lived through two foreign attacks (734 and 701 B.C.), and he summoned the people to trust in the Lord alone: "Have firm faith" (7:9); "he who has faith shall not waver" (28:16). In the account of the saving of Jerusalem in chs. 36–39 the root *bṭh* occurs no less than seven times (36:4-7, 9; NEB and RSV mostly "rely"). The invitation, of course, is not to trust in Jerusalem as such but to wait upon God. Even though through judgment (1:5-9; 5:14-17) Jerusalem will be preserved or restored as the city of God.

Jerusalem as the place where God had chosen to dwell was the place where the Israelites learned decisive and mature trust amid experiences of danger and liberation. God expected this response; he never enforced it.

The atmosphere of the Psalms, especially of the songs of Zion and the pilgrim hymns (Pss. 120–134), is one of happiness and joy: "Let Israel rejoice in his Maker, and let the sons of Zion exult in their king" (149:2; cf. 48:11; 47:1-2). What is the source of this joy? When a sick person is healed (30:12), a prisoner liberated or an oppressed person freed (35:9-10), an enemy defeated (21:2), a king anointed (1 Kgs. 1:40), or a feast celebrated, the people rejoice. Even in petitions and lamentations, joy is looked for in place of suffering. This joy is in most cases connected with a specific place, with Jerusalem. The mystery of God's presence there is its starting point. It is the response that the God who chose Israel awaited.

The various words used, e.g., *śāmah* ("to rejoice"), *rānan* ("to exult"), *śûś* ("to be glad"), *rûaʿ* ("to shout in triumph"), or *ṣāhal* ("to break into cries of joy"), all have basically the same meaning. They denote a visible and audible expression of joy. This joy is not just serenity of heart. It involves shouting, jumping (Jer. 50:11), stamping (Ezek. 25:6), clapping (Isa. 55:12), and dancing (2 Sam. 6:14). It also involves singing *(šîr)*, accompanied singing *(zāmar)*, praising *(hālal)*, and magnifying *(zākar)*.

Who is it that summons the people to give free rein to their happiness? Traditionally it is the people themselves through a leader: "Come! Let us raise a joyful song to the Lord" (Ps. 95:1); or it is an individual: "I will rejoice and exult in thee" (9:2). As individuals and the community trust in the Lord and find refuge in him, they rejoice and exult in him also in a free response to his presence.

Yet it is the Lord himself who makes this response possible. He not only hoped for the response but opened up the way to it. He was himself the host inviting the people to come and praise him. Rejoicing in the Lord meant sharing his own gladness when present with his people. As the fountain of life God was also the fountain of joy. The community experienced joy as his grace (Ps. 100:2).

This grace of gladness in the Lord liberated the community from sadness, fear, and hopelessness. A final day of deliverance would one day come (Zech. 3:14-18), but already here and now Zion could rejoice and invites the nations and all creation to join it in joyful praise.

3. God Chose Jerusalem as the City of David, Birthplace of a Just Society

God chose Jerusalem as a royal city in order that it might be a model for both Israel and the nations. He granted its kings the energy to erect magnificent buildings, but the building up of a society of

(a) freedom, (b) justice, (c) wisdom, happiness, and peace was his primary goal.

a. A Society of Free Men and Women

WAS JERUSALEM REALLY A FREE CITY, a community of free citizens? Hebrew has no direct equivalent for "free" and the Bible nowhere expressly calls Jerusalem a city of freedom. Indirectly, however, the biblical witness is clear. God liberated his people and raised up kings to share in the work of deliverance. How, then, could he leave his people in bondage?

(1) In the Psalms the laments, confessions, thanksgivings, meditations, and hymns of praise all reflect the experience of the inhabitants of Jerusalem, the pilgrims who came to worship there, the oppressed who sought refuge there, and the exiles who were driven away from it. Liberation is one of the central themes. Those under the assault of sickness, danger, adversity, or enemies all ask God to deliver them. Those who confess or give thanks do so because they have experienced deliverance. Oppressed by cruel rulers or threatened by powerful foes, Israel cries for deliverance. The kings themselves, though sharing in God's liberating acts, also stand in need of deliverance (cf. Ps. 3; 20:9; 84:9).

The idea of deliverance or liberation is expressed by many different Hebrew words, e.g., *pādāh* ("to redeem," 42 times in the OT), *yāšaʿ* ("to help," "to save," 184 times), *nāṣal* ("to deliver," 191 times), *ʿāzar* ("to help," 81 times), *gāʾal* ("to deliver," "to redeem," 59 times), and the corresponding nouns. The data show clearly that we have here a dominant theme. The prayers and praises may fall into a customary pattern in this regard, but they do so because the pattern corresponds to the needs and experiences of those who pray and praise. If Jerusalem was to live as a free city, it could do so only because the Lord himself freed it.

(2) The historical works also give evidence of the freedom of this society in the form of the free portrayal of the weaknesses and faults of the kings and their negative consequences. Criticism of the king is a striking expression of freedom. Davidic Jerusalem was a royal city. In the ancient Near East such cities usually had a totalitarian character. Critical historians would be treated as subversive and their works confiscated and destroyed. At Jerusalem, however, they escaped such a fate. The city of David provided an atmosphere of unusual tolerance in which freedom of speech was not stifled. With access to the royal archives, historians could write honestly about the failings and failures of the kings.

[246]

(3) The prophets ran into greater opposition. So long as they would proclaim "Peace, peace" (Jer. 6:14 RSV), no one disturbed them. But when they boldly prophesied against Jerusalem, the king, the court, and the people, they were hated and rejected (cf. Isaiah, Micah, Jeremiah, and Zephaniah). Jerusalem was a difficult place for God's prophetic servants (cf. Matt. 23:37). Yet there were also some bright spots in the dark picture. When Jeremiah was imprisoned and the leaders and people assembled to condemn him to death (26:11), some of the elders opposed his execution (v. 17) and he was acquitted. Victories for freedom in the royal period were perhaps rare (cf. the martyrdom of Uriah, Jer. 26:20-24), but Jerusalem did not in fact halt the free proclamation of God's Word. Indeed, the books of the prophets were collected and preserved there.

(4) A significant gesture of freedom was made when Judah was falling to the armies of Nebuchadrezzar and Jerusalem itself was under threat. The king and citizens proclaimed "an act of freedom for the slaves" (Jer. 34:8-9). Unfortunately this act of emancipation was no more than a gesture, for when the threat receded the citizens cancelled it (34:11). Nevertheless, great stress is laid on it in the OT. There was reason for pride that the gesture had been made, for shame at the backsliding which hastened the fall of the city (cf. 34:20-22).

Zion had wonderful opportunities as the royal city. All classes were called upon to be aware of their freedom and to realize it in mutual respect as free citizens. The king and his ministers, the priests and prophets, the elders and family heads, the whole people, rich and poor, high and low, men and women—all were challenged by the possibility that God had given them to live and grow as a society of free people.

b. A Stronghold of Righteousness and Justice

Jerusalem was also summoned to be a society that honors law and justice. As the city of David, it was granted an original endowment of law and justice that it was both to utilize and to increase. It had a vocation to become a just society. A concern for social justice was one of its distinctive features.

Four words commonly express the idea of righteousness and justice: the nouns *ṣedeq, ṣᵉdāqāh,* and *mišpāṭ,* and the adjective *ṣaddîq.* The terms occur most frequently in Isaiah, Jeremiah, Ezekiel, Psalms, and Proverbs. These books account, respectively, for 65%, 60%, 40%, and 75% of the 199, 157, 422, and 206 instances. We will consider the prophets first, then the Psalms.

(1) Isaiah, a son of Jerusalem, shocked his fellow citizens when he told them that destruction was imminent. The city had forgotten its calling:

"Once the home of justice where righteousness dwelt—but now murderers!" (1:21). The leaders bore a terrible responsibility: "Rebels, confederate with thieves," itching for gifts, not giving orphans and widows their rights (v. 23). God "looked for justice and found it denied" (5:7). He would judge the city but not totally reject it, for it was still to be "the home of righteousness, the faithful city" (1:26). He would finally fill it "with justice and righteousness" (33:5 RSV) when a king would come who would "reign in righteousness" (32:1-8). Less directly, perhaps, the calling of Jerusalem to be a just society is also a theme in Isaiah's contemporary, Micah. He, too, accuses the rulers and the wealthy of injustice, deceit, and violence, and he stresses that the clear requirement of the Lord is "to act justly" (6:8; cf. vv. 10ff., 16).

Jeremiah's message was no less plain. At first accusing the people only of infidelity in worship (Jer. 1–6), he then increasingly charged the kings with unjust rule, commanding them: "Deal justly and fairly, rescue the victim from his oppressor, do not ill-treat or do violence to the alien, the orphan or the widow, do not shed innocent blood in this place" (22:2-3). Only when disaster has first struck, however, will the words again be heard: "The Lord bless you, O home of righteousness, O holy mountain" (31:23 CB). Even in its best days Jerusalem was no model of social justice. Yet it was called upon to achieve this, and God continually sent the prophets to remind it of its calling.

(2) Justice is also a primary concern in the Psalms. It is true that this book is mainly an expression of Jerusalem's liturgical life. Too little attention has thus been paid to its interest in justice. We need, then, to examine the relevant texts, which we may classify in three groups.

Those in the first group deal with God's justice. God is Judge (5 times). He is just (8 times). He establishes law, justice, right (17 times). He owns justice (34 times). He acts righteously (31 times). He is the King who is coming to judge his people and the nations (cf. Ps. 50:4; 76:7-9; 96:10). His judgment will be fair; he is no respecter of persons. He will redress the balance for those deprived of their rights. He will "save all the oppressed of the earth" (76:9 RSV).

Texts in the second group deal with the people's justice. Those that pray are often called "the just" (42 times). They are not perfect. They have no righteousness of their own. They come with empty hands, in need of justification. But they do so because they love righteousness and seek it: "Give me justice, O Lord" (Ps. 26:1) is a common request. Those who have tried to live "without reproach" (26:1) are accused "without cause" (35:7 RSV). But there is confidence that God will deliver: "I know that the Lord will give their due to the needy and justice to the downtrodden" (140:12). Thanksgivings may even imply that justice has been secured in the court in which God himself is Judge (cf. 58:11).

Texts in the third group deal with the justice of the king in Zion. The king is expected to establish justice among his people. Prayer must be made for him with this in view: "O God, endow the king with thy own justice . . . that he may judge the people rightly and deal out justice to the poor and suffering" (72:1-2). The king must "love right and hate wrong" (cf. 45:7). He must "put all wicked men to silence and . . . rid the Lord's city of all evildoers" (101:8). He had himself to struggle for a just life like all others. He might also have to seek justice in his own life, like David (40:17). His primary task, however, was both to do justice and to require that justice be done.

Some psalms, then, are concerned with the justice of God as Judge, others with the question how sinners can appear before the heavenly Judge and be accepted as just. But many display a concern for just relations in the community. Ordinary folk—the poor and weak and oppressed—cry out in protest against calumny, lies, and violence. This was not just a matter of conventional phrasing. Defamation and oppression were rife in the city that was called upon to be a stronghold of righteousness and justice. A powerful protest is thus uttered in the Psalms against the shameful injustice that characterizes society. An appeal is made to God's justice. He will take the side of the oppressed, raise up his king in Zion to establish righteousness, and oppose those who trample on the rights of the poor. The ultimate hope is for a free and just society in which no one need fear discrimination or oppression.

c. A School of Wisdom

If the royal city of Jerusalem was called upon to achieve a free and just society, it was also to be a center where wisdom was sought and taught in the interests of both Israel and indirectly the nations. As we read in Isa. 2:3 (par. Mic. 4:2): "Instruction [*tôrāh*] issues from Zion, and out of Jerusalem comes the word of the Lord," for "wisdom [*ḥokmāh*] and knowledge [*daʿat*] are the assurance of salvation" (33:6). Jerusalem was to be the home of wisdom (Sir. 24:1, 10-11). Where did this vocation originate? What fruit did it bring? To what end was this city called to be a school of wisdom?

(1) Wisdom is a primary theme in the accounts of Solomon's reign. Solomon was given "a heart so wise and so understanding that there has been none like you before your time nor will be after you" (1 Kgs. 3:12). "All the world courted him, to hear the wisdom which God had put in his heart" (10:24). The Queen of Sheba came "to test him with hard questions," and he answered them all (10:1ff.). He was the king of wisdom as David was the king of the psalms and Moses the mediator of the law.

Jerusalem both admired Solomon's wisdom and preserved and developed it. It shared in the effort to seek and collect and teach wisdom on the foundation that God gave it with Solomon. We see this in the so-called wisdom literature.

Proverbs consists of collections of proverbs *(māšāl):* chs. 1–9, wisdom based on fear of the Lord; chs. 10–15, the difference between the wise and the foolish; 16:1–22:16, instructions of Solomon to civil servants; 22:17–24:34, advice of father to son; chs. 25–27 and 28–29, proverbs transcribed by the men of Hezekiah; and chs. 30–31, sayings of Agur and Lemuel.

Ecclesiastes consists of critical reflections on traditional wisdom. For this reason its canonical status was in doubt for a long period.

Job begins and ends with a prose story telling how Job was tested (chs. 1–2 and 42:7-17). A dialogue between Job and his friends is set within this story. Three poetic cycles reflect on Job's sufferings. Elihu's speeches follow Job's final survey and the climax with God's reply and Job's submission (38:1–42:6).

Psalms contains not a few samples of wisdom teaching. Sometimes this comes within thanksgivings (Pss. 32; 91). Some psalms reflect on wisdom (37; 73). Some show that those who fear the Lord are blessed (112; 127). Three Torah psalms (1; 19; 119) claim that obedience to the law is wisdom.

Various tales teach wisdom. The parable of Jotham (Judg. 9:7-15) carries the lesson that kingship invites oppression. The Joseph stories offer an illustration of wisdom in action. In the account of David's rise to the throne (1 Sam. 16–2 Sam. 5) the main characters are wise, i.e., honest, loyal, humble, patient, etc. The story of Ruth also describes Ruth and Naomi as wise, and in the story of Esther wisdom defeats Haman's foolish plot, Haman being an example of one who digs a pit and then falls into it (cf. Prov. 26:27; Ps. 9:15).

Not all the wisdom material was written in Jerusalem. The Jotham parable was told well before the Davidic period, and some works came after Jerusalem's destruction as a royal capital. Nevertheless, wisdom teaching originated in Jerusalem. Solomon was the first wisdom teacher and writer, and he appointed wise men as advisers and as teachers of the royal children. His court thus became a center of learning and teaching. Wisdom teaching then extended to all classes, and the Jerusalem community participated in a movement of renewal on the basis of wisdom teaching. The royal city also opened up the way for smaller towns and villages, for all Israel, and ultimately for the nations. By God's grace Jerusalem truly became the center of wisdom teaching.

(2) What was the nature and aim of this teaching? Generally speaking, wisdom was a science of education. Its aim was to produce good and happy citizens. Guidelines were sought and taught to help toward life mastery. The search for instruction *(tôrāh)* was at the core of wisdom (cf. especially Prov. 10–29). This wisdom exuded a special enthusiasm and confidence. The following features call for notice.

First, Israel's wisdom was international or universal. It reflected human experiences which did not typify Israel alone. It was open to the outside world, like Solomon's court. Foreign wisdom teachers, along with diplomats and artists and advisers, had no doubt come to the new capital. Israel profited from these contacts. The Sayings of the Wise (Prov. 22:17–24:22) even quote extensively from the Egyptian Instruction of Amenemopet (ca. 1000 B.C.; see Pritchard, ed., *Ancient Near Eastern Texts Relating to the Old Testament,* pp. 421ff.). Instruction could be gained from aliens even though the roots were deep in Israel's own faith (cf. 22:19, 23; 23:11).

The presence of Egyptian wisdom in Proverbs demands brief consideration. Wisdom sentences such as those of Prov. 11–29 are not without parallel in world literature. In both form and content we find similar sayings not only in Sumerian and Akkadian wisdom books but also in the written and oral traditions of all ages and continents. If the OT could tap such sources, there is no reason why Christians should not listen cheerfully to the religious and secular wisdom of the peoples among whom they live.

Second, wisdom teaching was addressed predominantly to individuals. Real persons, not just anonymous members of a community, were invited to live wisely, to use their minds, to have open eyes and ears (Prov. 20:12). Enrolled as students of wisdom, they were taught to "understand" *(bîn),* i.e., to know the difference between good and evil. In this way they could take up their responsibilities and decide on the right attitude and action in face of the ever new challenges of life.

A very high respect for human dignity stands behind this concept. G. von Rad was probably right to speak about the rise of a kind of "humanism" under Solomon *(OT Theology,* I, 55). Here in the city of David Israel ventured to think of little "sovereigns" determining their own destiny!

Third, wisdom teaching draws heavily on the difference between two attitudes: the one right, good, and wise, the other wrong, bad, and foolish. Proverbs does not offer a clear moral standard by which to know the good and the bad in any situation. It offers instead scores of observations and directions loosely assembled in no very recognizable order. Disciples must weigh the possibilities and draw their own conclusions. If no general definition of wise and foolish is presented, a few typical distinctions repeatedly emerge.

(a) The wise are humble and modest, the foolish are arrogant and presumptuous: "Pride will bring a man low; a man lowly in spirit wins honour" (Prov. 29:23; cf. 11:2; 16:18-19). The test is this: The wise will accept criticism and rebuke, the foolish will not—"He who loves correction loves knowledge, but he who hates reproof is a mere brute" (12:1; cf. 13:1; 19:18; 29:15). Many people view humility as a sign of weakness; the wise know better.

(b) Many proverbs praise diligence and condemn laziness: "Idle hands make a man poor; busy hands grow rich" (10:4; cf. 6:6ff.; 10:4; 21:5). Fools regard work as toil and slavery, but the wise know that "diligence brings a man to power, but laziness to forced labour" (12:24).

(c) The wise are honest, fair, and loyal, the foolish cheat and deceive, do not keep their word, and will even give false witness (11:1; 12:17; 13:5; 16:8). "The criminal's conduct is tortuous; straight dealing is a sign of integrity" (21:8). Honesty may be rare (20:6), but the way of honesty is the way of wisdom.

(d) The wise are open-minded, patient, and peace loving; the stupid are impatient, irascible, and quarrelsome (15:18; cf. 14:29; 29:22). A wise person refrains from saying, "I will requite him for what he has done" (24:29). The peace loving are generous to those in need (11:17, 24-25; 21:26; 28:27), patient with those who offend them (10:12; 16:6), and helpful to those in danger (24:11-12). Wisdom exacts a price.

(e) A distinctive feature of wisdom is the sparse use of words. In contrast, fools speak a great deal without first thinking what they should say. The importance given to this aspect of wisdom is astonishing. "When men talk too much, sin is never far away; common sense holds its tongue" (10:19; cf. 10:20-21; 11:9, 12-13; 12:6; 13:3; 15:1, 2, 4, 23, 28; 16:1; etc.). The truly wise will "speak plain truth" (23:16). "The tongue has power over life and death" (18:21). Words are thus of crucial importance. What is taken lightly may have the most serious consequences for good or ill.

Proverbs maps out a narrow and stony way. To search for wisdom is to leave the track of the majority. This is always hard. Wisdom cannot be bought. A person cannot "buy wisdom if he has no sense" (17:16). Wisdom demands struggle. Yet a wise heart is also a great gift.

A fourth general feature of wisdom is that it is always taught with authority and conviction. Its teachers do not speak in their own name or power. Nor do they discharge a task decreed by the king, for rulers themselves must follow wisdom (8:15). Oddly, there is not even an appeal to revelation in validation of wisdom sayings. It may be said at times that a course of action is "dear to the Lord's heart" or an "abomination to the Lord" (cf. 11:1, 20; 12:22; 15:8-9; 18:22), but no word or command of God is quoted. What, then, is the basis of this authority?

Those who seek wisdom are invited to look at the evidence of people around them. How great is the difference between the situation of the wise and that of fools! Whatever attitude we take, the consequences will show. Wisdom has happy consequences, folly bad ones. The evidence speaks for itself. We have simply to see it and to learn from it.

Proverbs presents this evidence in very simple terms. The situation is either black or white. The wise enjoy blessings. They prosper, eat their fill, and grow rich (Ps. 1:1; Prov. 10:3), while fools are poor and lack the necessities of life (Prov. 10:4; 13:11). In trials the wise are acquitted, the wicked condemned (Ps. 1:5). The wise are respected, shame comes upon fools (Prov. 12:8; 14:35). The good live securely, the bad come to grief (10:8; 11:3, 5; 12:7, 12, 19; 13:6; 14:32; 18:7). The good will rise again even though they fall, the bad will be brought down (24:16). The wise are granted life, the wicked earn death (10:21; 11:4, 19, 30; 13:14; 14:30; etc.).

In what sense is this distinction really evident? Are the good always happy, the bad unhappy? The wisdom teachers were well aware that it did not always work this way. The wise might suffer misfortune, fools enjoy good fortune. This reversal of the normal situation had to be faced with a cool head. But soon enough, it was believed, the abnormal situation would give way again to the normal.

Not for nothing the normal state is always put in the future tense. The wise *will be* blessed, saved from danger, brought to happiness. The stupid *will be* shamed, brought down. "A road may seem straightforward to a man, yet may end as the way to death" (Prov. 14:12; 16:25). Property piled up in haste "will bring you no blessing in the end" (20:21). The Hebrew word for "end" is ʾaḥᵃrît, "future" (cf. also 14:13; 23:18). ʾaḥᵃrît has the same root as the Arabic aḥirat ("end of times"), but it does not have an eschatological sense in Proverbs. The results of wisdom or folly will become apparent sooner or later in the lifetimes of those concerned. The balance will be kept.

This conviction does not merely rest on an optimistic worldview. Confidence is not placed in a world order in which justice prevails. Only because the Lord rules the world is good order maintained (23:11). Trust in the Lord is the foundation on which the wise build their view of the world (16:20; 28:25; 29:25-26). In keeping with the universal character of wisdom teaching, however, seldom is this root laid bare. At times even God's people have to speak in "worldly" terms!

(3) Other forms of wisdom teaching also developed. Various experiences, e.g., the rise of the prophets, the struggle against foreign powers, the influence of alien cultures, and finally the fall of Israel and Judah all brought a keener sense of the limitation of human wisdom. We shall now consider the main features of this distinctive form of OT wisdom.

First, an awareness appears that the human ability to choose is restricted. This point emerges already, though not so fully, in Prov. 10:1–22:16. We may have our own schemes, "but the Lord's purpose will prevail" (19:21). "A horse may be ready for the day of battle, but victory comes from the Lord" (21:31). For this reason the fear of the Lord is the foundation of wisdom (10:27; 14:26-27; 15:16; 16:6; 19:23), or the beginning of wisdom (1:7; Ps. 111:10; Job 28:28). In this context, of course, the fear is not fear of judgment. Those who fear God are those who honor him and realize their own limitations, not thinking themselves wise (Prov. 26:12; 28:11).

A sense of the limitation of human wisdom may perhaps be seen already in Gen. 3. God's intention was good when he forbade Adam and Eve to eat of the tree in the middle of the garden. They were to be protected against dangerous knowledge. Why was this knowledge dangerous? Is not knowledge (da'at) very close to wisdom (ḥokmāh) and understanding (bînāh, tᵉbûnāh), the ability to distinguish between good and evil? Yet even a good gift may be evil when divorced from the will of God. Did not transgression of God's prohibition bring a disruption of human relations and of trust in the Creator (Gen. 3:9-19)? This is the result of wisdom or knowledge when it is used without fear of the Lord.

Second, an awareness of the limitations of human wisdom grew as the prophets fulminated against purely human wisdom: "Shame on you! you who are wise in your own eyes" (Isa. 5:21). When God acts against his people, "the wisdom of their wise men shall vanish" (29:14; cf. 1 Cor. 1:19). As Jeremiah put it, "My people are fools . . . they are clever [ḥākām] only in wrongdoing" (Jer. 4:22). The time was coming when "the wise are put to shame. . . . They have spurned the word of the Lord, and what sort of wisdom is theirs?" (8:9). As God said, "I reverse what wise men say and make nonsense of their wisdom" (Isa. 44:25).

This criticism was aimed primarily at the court experts who in Judah, as in Egypt or Babylon, were responsible for government policy. The use of wisdom as such was not under attack, but the bad policy advocated. Instead of listening to God's Word, the political and religious advisers were simply consulting their own wisdom and thus putting the state on the road to destruction.

Third, wisdom had also to meet the challenge of the fact that many of the just did in fact suffer while the wicked prospered. One might argue that sooner or later things would change, but this was not true in every case. A new look was thus taken at the problem and a new answer sought in the wisdom poems in the Psalms and Job.

Psalm 37, an alphabetical poem, urges trust in the Lord. The promise of the land is renewed by way of consolation: "The righteous shall possess the land" (v. 29). No matter what occurs, the Lord is a "refuge in time of trouble" (v. 39).

Psalm 49 struggles more urgently with the question why the wicked grow rich and the righteous suffer want. One answer is that the wicked will suddenly lose their prosperity, at the latest when they die (vv. 7-14, 16-20). The righteous, however, may live without fear of death: "God will ransom my life, he will take me from the power of Sheol" (v. 15).

Psalm 73 faces the same riddle and acknowledges that wisdom cannot solve it (vv. 2, 16, 21-22). Although finding no help and suffering severely, the psalmist resists the temptation to doubt; knowing that God is near, he is strengthened (vv. 23, 28). Wisdom teaching merges here into a confession of trust. God's continuing presence is the consolation.

Job's friends all share the conviction that Job's sufferings must be due to some unconfessed sin. They do not wish to convict him, of course, but to help him to relief by way of a confession of guilt. If Job will only come back to God, God will forgive him and restore him. In his book *Wisdom in Israel* (Eng. tr. 1972; pp. 212-13) von Rad points out that this was the recommended course in Solomon's prayer at the consecration of the temple: Sin causes suffering, but if repentance and confession follow, there is pardon and restoration (1 Kgs. 8:33, 35, 45ff.). The same steps may be found in Pss. 32; 51; 130; 143, though cf. Pss. 6 and 30. The solution of Job's friends conformed to the liturgy of confession in the worship tradition of Israel. In many cases it was undoubtedly true, but it was of little help in Job's case.

From the days of Ezra the Torah became increasingly the basic element in the teaching given to the Jewish community. To be wise was to obey God's law. The three Torah Psalms (1; 19; 119) are witnesses to this type of wisdom. "Fear God and obey his commands" is the summary advice given in Eccl. 12:13. Wisdom is here an instrument of God's revelation (cf. Prov. 1–9). It is like a young woman who calls upon people to heed her injunctions (Prov. 3:1). In this context wisdom is theology. It does not just invite people to consult the evidence and then choose between good and evil. It presents God's law as the one and only option. The wise are not just responsible citizens. They are members of the believing community.

Fourth, the OT sets two strange wise men before us in Job and Ecclesiastes. Both stand on the soil of Israel's faith. Both confess the Lord. But both raise acutely the problems that can arise with both the practical wisdom of Prov. 1–10 and the more spiritual wisdom that is grounded in the fear of the Lord, the confession of sin, and obedience to the law of God.

In his speeches (Job 3; 6; 9–10; 12–14; 16–17; 19; 21; 23; 26–27; 29–31) Job vigorously protests against his fate, summarily rejects the insights and advice of his friends, and can see no special cause for repentance, even accusing God of depriving him of his rights. He does not see the reason for his sufferings as readers can from the initial prose narrative. In his special case suffering is a test of the sincerity of his faith. Satan (the accuser) doubts Job's authenticity, and God allows him to put Job to the test. Will Job serve God even though goods, family, and health itself are stripped from him? It seems as though Job might fail the test, for his sense of the injustice of his treatment raises serious questions as to God's goodness and righteousness. The idea of a test of faith that results in even greater blessing if successfully passed does not occur to him, though we find it already in the life of Abraham (Gen. 22:1) and it comes to expression in Dan. 11:35 and frequently in the NT (cf. *peirasmós*).

Job's protest must be heard, however, for it contains an element of truth as well as misunderstanding. The misunderstanding is that he presumed to speak without full knowledge of God's ways and rashly doubted God's mercy toward his creatures. The truth is that he had reason to complain about the disasters that befell him. Why did he specifically have to endure these excessive sufferings? Why did God refuse to answer him as if indifferent to his servant's distress? Similar complaints are commonly heard in the Psalms (cf. 6; 22; 38; 69; 88). The friends were no help with their accusation; the psalmists, too, had to deal with friends who behaved like enemies (27:10; 38:11; 88:8, 18). Job properly saw it as his right to appeal to God. Is not the Lord the God who defends the cause of the oppressed (cf. Job 16:19-21; 19:25)? Did not others appeal to God's faithfulness with no prior confession of sin (cf. Ps. 7:3-5; 17:2-4; 26:1-6; etc. with Job 23:10-12; 31:5-40)?

Behind the pious wisdom of his friends Job set a question mark that is not easily erased. His claim challenges a way of wisdom that transgresses its limits. Without Job's sharp criticism of hypocrisy: "No doubt you are perfect men and absolute wisdom is yours" (12:2), wisdom can easily become a lifeless theory which brushes aside the freedom of God, violates the right to human freedom, and forces both divine and human action into an unbreakable mold. Job did not understand the wisdom of God, but even in the depths of his distress he could not abandon his trust in God. For this reason he was finally vindicated and his friends, whose confident solutions were in his case even wider of the mark, came under condemnation.

Ecclesiastes presents a different criticism of human wisdom. If Job struggles with righteous suffering, Ecclesiastes calls all human life into question as it is lived "under the sun" (1:3; etc.). "For who can know what is good for a man in this life?" (6:12). For years the author has applied his mind to the study of wisdom, and failed (1:13). The traditional maxim that the good are happy and the wicked unhappy is not convincing (8:12-13). What use is a wise life if God predetermines all things (3:14)? One person is granted wisdom, another behaves stupidly (2:26). For everything there is a season, but what it is we do not know (3:1ff.). God has created both good days and bad and set them alongside one another, but in such a way that we cannot find out what will happen next (7:14). We cannot understand why the wicked should prosper and the righteous suffer (8:10-14). One day fools will meet their end, but so will the just: "One and the same fate overtakes them both" (2:14). In this respect we "have no advantage over beasts" (3:19). Nor do we know the hour (9:12). Again, we do not understand the constant rise of injustice and oppression (3:16; 4:1-3; 10:5-7).

Ecclesiastes grants that God made the world perfectly (3:11) but cannot grasp his intention for it. We have "no comprehension of God's work from beginning to end" (3:11). Life, then, seems to be without meaning. It is "vanity of vanities" (RSV), "emptiness," "chasing the wind" (1:2, 14; 2:26). We do not call it vain or empty in itself, but in its apparent meaninglessness.

These sayings are often seen as the expression of an exaggerated pessimism. But a positive kernel lies behind the negative husk. Attacking superficial and complacent optimism, the author proposes a new form of optimism. He rejects the results of human thinking (1:12-18) in order to praise the wisdom that the Lord gives (2:26; 7:11-12). Attacking human attempts to achieve satisfaction, e.g., by wealth or pleasure (2:1-11), he invites the reader to enjoy the good gift of God, however small, and to be thankful (2:24-26; 3:22; 5:18-20). Excessive piety is as stupid as wickedness (4:17; 5:1ff.). Both are contrary to true fear of God (3:14; 7:18; 8:12-13), which accepts human limitations with humility (7:20).

The path is narrow between stupidity on the one side and excessive wisdom on the other (7:16). We cannot of ourselves attain to the true wisdom (cf. Job 28). God alone knows where it is and what it is. As Matt. 11:25 would later say, it is hidden from the wise and learned. No sharper challenge could be hurled against the human search. Yet God gives his own wisdom to those who seek it in humility and faith.

Wisdom teaching, then, takes both a practical and a spiritual form. In this regard it resembles Jerusalem itself as both the city of David and the center of Israel's faith. Peripheral practical wisdom has a spiritual center, while spiritual wisdom has indispensable consequences on the practical plane. The two are not contradictory; they are complementary.

4. God Chose Jerusalem as the City of the Temple, Home of the Worshiping Community

God chose Jerusalem as his dwelling and allowed his house to be built there. In so doing he invited and moved the city to respond to the grace of his presence. Jerusalem and its inhabitants, led by the king, priests, and prophets, and in cooperation with all Israel, took up the call and began construction of the temple, worshiping God and fulfilling their calling.

a. The City Where the Temple Was Built

RELIGIONS OF EVERY PLACE AND TIME distinguish holy places from profane. As a religious community Israel was no exception. The patriarchs had already had holy places where they built altars and worshiped the Lord. The wilderness generation had the tent of meeting and the tabernacle. Houses or temples were built when Israel settled in Canaan. Jerusalem was already a holy place when David took it, and it was natural that it should become a holy place for Israel, too.

In many religions heroes or demigods are associated with holy places, but in the OT ordinary historical people play this role. In the case of Jerusalem, it was David who was led to the temple site and Solomon who was granted grace to do the building. Later, in Israel, Jeroboam became the symbol of human unworthiness to build any house for God. These three kings represent the whole community that God moved to worship him.

(1) Although Solomon actually built the temple, he did not choose the site. The long account in 1 Kgs. 5–8 makes no mention of this important decision. Obviously Solomon had no need to seek or buy or prepare a site. The place was already chosen. But how?

We learn the answer to this question in 2 Chron. 2–7, which tells us that "Solomon began to build the house of the Lord . . . on Mount Moriah, where the Lord had appeared to his father David, on the site which David had prepared on the threshing-floor of Ornan the Jebusite" (3:1). It was David who decided where the temple was to be built.

The choice relates to the story of the census which displeased God and led to a devastating pestilence that finally menaced Jerusalem itself. To stop the danger at the last moment David bought Ornan's threshing-floor, built an altar there, and brought an offering to God. In this way the pestilence was stayed, but the climax of the story came with the revelation to David that this was to be the site of the temple, "an altar of whole-offering for Israel" (1 Chron. 22:1). David then prepared the place, but in fact the real decision was not David's but God's. The fact that the site was on Mt. Moriah underscores the sovereignty of the divine decision. At the same time, once the choice was made, David threw himself wholeheartedly into preparations for the construction. His interest and crucial role in the project find additional expression in Ps. 132:2ff., in which David said that he would not sleep "until I find a sanctuary for the Lord, a dwelling for the Mighty One of Jacob."

(2) The two extensive reports of the building of the Jerusalem temple (1 Kgs. 5–8 and 2 Chron. 2–7) both ascribe the work to Solomon. It is clear, however, that many others participated in the work, kings and other leaders, qualified and unskilled workmen, and thousands of donors. The OT shows a deep interest in the human work involved in building the temple, as previously in that of the tabernacle (Exod. 25:8, 10; 35:10-19).

Solomon, of course, took the initiative, drawing up the plans, collecting the materials, raising the funds, directing the operations, and finally consecrating the finished building. But the whole community made an essential contribution. If David and Solomon are singled out for special mention, it is only finally as representatives of Israel as a whole.

The same emphasis on the community effort may be seen later in the building of the second temple on the same site as the first. The prophets Haggai and Zechariah then kindled the people's desire and the leaders initiated the work. Sheshbazzar had previously laid the foundations, and two Persian kings first permitted and then ordered the building at public expense (Ezra 1:1-4; 5:14-15; 6:1ff.). After some delay the prophets rekindled the people's interest and Joshua and Zerubbabel began to build, with the people behind them to add to the momentum and to make contributions. Thus "the elders of the Jews went on with the rebuilding. . . . and finished the rebuilding as commanded by the God of Israel and according to the decrees of Cyrus and Darius" (Ezra 6:14). God undoubtedly moved the people to do the work, but they did it of their own free will.

One of God's purposes in choosing Jerusalem was in fact to move the people to build him a house there. How glorious and happy a task it was to prepare for God a welcome at the place where it pleased him to be present! David and Solomon set the work in train, but only as members of the chosen people. Under God it was the community itself which was the true builder.

(3) The stress on the human activity is the more surprising in view of the repeated biblical denial that God needs a house erected by human hands. As Stephen would say, "the Most High does not dwell in houses made with hands" (Acts 7:48 RSV). Or as Paul would say, the "Lord of heaven and earth does not live in shrines made by man" (17:24). These sharp statements do not simply express a new situation in NT days. Stephen and Paul were in fact quoting the prophets (Isa. 66:1; 1 Kgs. 8:27). Just as the monarchy was not instituted without serious reservations, so was the idea of a temple for the God of Israel.

Opposition was partly due to the role of human purposes and interests in the construction of the temple. David's dynastic ambitions were probably one reason why his plan for a temple was abruptly rejected: "Are you the man to build me a house to dwell in?" (2 Sam. 7:5). The account of Solomon's temple (1 Kgs. 5-7) shows unmistakably that he intended this magnificent house of the Lord to be a royal temple serving political and dynastic as well as devotional and liturgical ends. Both the temple and the palace belonged to the same development plan for Jerusalem (1 Kgs. 7:1-12). God and the king, throne and altar, were to be indissolubly linked.

How dangerous this identification might be is evident from the story of the coming of Amos to Bethel, then the spiritual center of Israel (Amos 7:10-17). When Amos dared to prophesy even here against the king, state, and nation (7:10), it cost him his expulsion. This was "the king's sanctuary, and it is a temple of the kingdom" (7:13 RSV). Similarly, the words of Micah and Jeremiah against the Jerusalem temple (Mic. 3:12; Jer. 26:6) were seen by the authorities as involving conspiracy against both king and nation.

Israel had to learn a painful lesson when later both sanctuaries perished along with the kingdoms with which they were so deeply connected. The vision of a new temple in Ezek. 40–48 no longer sees the king as master of God's house. No special gate will directly link palace and temple. The ruler will have to enter from the east like every other worshiper (46:2).

The history books confirm this insight with their condemnations of the shrines at Dan and Bethel. The temples built by Jeroboam were decisive symptoms of the people's degeneracy. Jeroboam erected these sanctuaries outside Jerusalem for political reasons (1 Kgs. 12:26-31). It was in vain that he consecrated them to the Lord. In fact he had himself already turned to idolatry, worshiping the Lord only as one of many gods (12:28). Jeroboam thus became a representative of treachery not only to Jerusalem and Judah but to God himself, not only to his exclusive sanctuary but to his exclusive sanctity.

All human temples and not merely those at Dan and Bethel face the danger of abuse. The Jerusalem temple was no exception. Nevertheless, the OT clings to the wonderful fact that it did please God to dwell among his people and to be worshiped in the house they built for him. In so doing he made himself vulnerable. He exposed his holiness to our unholy possessiveness. This was the price of his engagement with Jerusalem.

b. The Place to Meet God

When Israel was moved to build a house for the Lord, it had to ask what kind of edifice would be adequate. The most beautiful temple would be useless were not God pleased to be graciously present in it. But what kind of sanctuary would meet this condition?

Contrary to what one might expect, the Israelites had no single answer to this question. The OT presents us with several different models. In pre-monarchy days there were various places at which God was worshiped. The patriarchs had built stone altars as the people of other nations had done (cf. Gen. 4:3ff.; 9:20; Deut. 12:3). Moses worshiped at an altar (Exod. 17:5), and so, too, did Joshua (Josh. 8:30ff.), Gideon (Judg. 6:25-28), Saul (1 Sam. 14:35), and David (2 Sam. 24:18-25).

We do not know what form these ancient altars had. A simple structure of unhewn stones seems to have met the need (Exod. 20:25). Sometimes a big stone was used (1 Sam. 6:14). Rocks or stone pillars could be set up (Gen. 28:15). Whatever the form, an altar was a symbol of God's presence. It was a simple "house of God" (Gen. 28:22). It was a place of meeting with God. Even the stone buildings of a later time had to have an altar in front of them.

(1) For a time in the desert days Israel then used a simple tent called the tent of the presence or the tent of meeting. This older tent was small and light. Moses, alone or with the help of Joshua, could carry it and "pitch it at a distance outside the camp" (Exod. 33:7). "When Moses entered it, the pillar of cloud came down, and stayed at the entrance to the tent while the Lord spoke with Moses" (33:9). This tent, however, was simply the place where God spoke his Word. There is no reference to an altar or to priestly ministrations. God's people would meet him there and ask for his decisions about various situations. The function was limited but indispensable and enduring.

The ark also had a liturgical aspect as an instrument of the divine presence. It was a chest which could be carried on long poles affixed to it. Its lid was adorned with cherubim. The Lord of Hosts invisibly sat there, "enthroned upon the cherubim" (1 Sam. 4:4; 2 Sam. 6:2; 2 Kgs. 19:15; Ps. 80:1). As he was present in the tent to speak, he was present above the ark to save (cf. Num. 10:35-36; 14:39-45; Josh. 3–4; 1 Sam. 4).

In addition to the construction of the tabernacle for worship during the long years of desert wandering, it seems that on entry into Canaan stone temples were built already prior to the royal period. Temples of this kind might be found on the mountains of Ephraim, at Shiloh, where the tabernacle found a resting place, at Nob, and elsewhere. Solomon's temple would be the greatest and the most magnificent of Israel's temples, but not the first.

In form, the ancient sanctuaries, like the tabernacle, were probably similar to Solomon's, being divided into three parts, one of which would contain a symbol of the divine presence, e.g., a sacred pillar. With the building of Solomon's temple, however, they lost their function, as did also the tent of meeting and the tabernacle. Finding within it a place for the ark and the tent, the Jerusalem sanctuary would combine all the previous functions in itself as the place of meeting with God.

(2) God's house at Jerusalem stood in all its glory for three and a half centuries before being destroyed by the Babylonian soldiers. Many changes took place during this period, but we must consider first its original purpose and function.

First, Solomon obviously built it as a royal sanctuary where God would be present and all the citizens of Israel could come together and worship him. The idea of a royal sanctuary was new in Israel. In this regard Solomon was following the example set by neighboring kingdoms. The foreign influence shows in the use of foreign workmen and expensive foreign materials (1 Kgs. 5). The walls were adorned with "carved figures of cherubim, palm-trees, and open flowers" (6:29) or paneled with images of "lions, oxen, and cherubim" (7:29)—all representing strength and fertility in Canaanite religion. The meaning of the bronze pillars and sea of cast metal before the temple gate (7:15-22, 23-26) is unknown, but they, too, might well have symbolized divine power.

At the same time Solomon incorporated into the temple the familiar features of Israel's sanctuaries. In front there was, of course, a large altar made of valuable materials (6:20-22). The ark was given a prominent place as David desired (2 Sam. 7:2). The consecration of the whole building could take place only when the ark was brought "to its place, the inner shrine of the house" (1 Kgs. 8:2-8). A place for the tent was also found (8:4).

Second, Solomon built his temple as a lasting habitation for the Lord: "Here I have built thee a lofty house, a habitation for thee to occupy for ever" (8:13). Jerusalem as a whole was "the city of God, which the Most High has made his dwelling" (Ps. 46:4), but it bore this name because the house of God lay visibly within it: "The Lord has chosen Zion and desired it for his home: 'This is my resting-place for ever'" (Ps. 132:13-14).

The term "resting-place" (*menûhāh*) suggests that a nomad has wandered from place to place and at last found somewhere to settle. God had now ended his own journey and would no longer need a tent (cf. 2 Sam. 7:6). The royal sanctuary was to be a permanent habitation. God had bound himself to this city and to the kings of David's line.

Third, although the biblical accounts tell us how long, broad, and high the temple was, what materials and techniques were used (1 Kgs. 6), what metals were cast (7:13-51), and how the building was consecrated (ch. 8), all this information does not really give us a clear picture of God's house. We know that it was rectangular. It was also divided into three parts: a vestibule open to the east, a main sanctuary in the middle, and a smaller inner shrine in the west, with a large inner court before the vestibule. But what was the point of this arrangement?

The inner shrine (*debîr*, later called "the Most Holy Place" or "Holy of Holies") was a block ten meters long, broad, and high. Two large cherubim of olive wood guarded the place of the Lord's presence, with the ark under their wings (6:19-28). The main room (*hêkāl*, literally, "palace") was 20 m. long, 10 broad, and 15 high. It contained the golden table for the bread of the presence and ten lampstands (7:48-50a). The vestibule (*'ûlām* or *'êlām*) was 5 m. long and 10 broad. Outside it were the two bronze pillars, Jachin and Boaz. The inner court was 50 m. long and broad. It held the altar of burnt offerings in the middle, a sea of cast metal on twelve oxen in the southeast, and ten trolleys of bronze with purification basins on the right and left side of the building.

The arrangement and furnishings suggest that the temple was meant to serve as a habitation for the Lord but also as a meeting place for the people. The inner shrine was open toward the middle room (the Holy Place) where the priests ministered, and the middle room toward the vestibule, the reception room, which in turn opened toward the court, where visitors came. The house and its furnishings provided a place where God and his people could meet.

As a royal temple, of course, the house of God was primarily the place where the king could meet God. The importance of the king's role may be seen from the fact that the temple and palace lay side by side as two parts of a single whole. The palace buildings were astonishingly luxurious, consisting of "the House of the Forest of Lebanon" (7:2-5), the king's own house (7:8), and "the Hall of Judgement" (7:7). God's house was modest in comparison. When the king as first citizen and people's representative entered the new house of God as the main priest (8:5, 62-63; 9:25), the aim of the building had already been achieved. Solomon's authority was evident when he installed Zadok as permanent high priest (2:35). Next to the king himself, only Zadokite priests might enter all three parts of the house. Kings and priests were the mediators between God and the people.

(3) After Solomon's death the temple stood for over three centuries. With the passing years it needed repairs and improvements. There was also at times a need for spiritual renewal. Various events—the disruption of the kingdoms, their decadence, and the sharp messages of the prophets—contributed to a reassessment of the meaning of the temple.

An important OT expression gives evidence of the new orientation. David wanted to build a house for the Lord (2 Sam. 7:13), but Solomon was allowed to build it only in honor of the *name of the Lord* (1 Kgs. 5:2; 2 Chron. 2:1). What was the origin of this phrase, and what was its point?

The phrase "the name of the Lord" was used already in connection with the worship of the patriarchs when they "built an altar to the Lord and invoked the Lord by name" (cf. Gen. 12:8; 13:4; 26:25). Then God promised that "wherever I cause my name to be invoked, I will come to you and bless you" (Exod. 20:24). The dwelling of God's name in a place or house is found in Deut. 12:26.

Use of the expression both earlier and in the royal period reflects a keen awareness of God's holiness. The people themselves did not always sense this. God's presence in the temple, as in earlier sanctuaries, tended to be taken for granted. But especially when Israel fell, when Judah was under threat, and when the prophets were announcing judgment, this confidence was badly shaken. It might please God to dwell among his people, but he was holy, glorious, and free, bound to no place or sanctuary. As Hosea put it, God is "the Holy One in your midst" (11:9). It was in the name of the Holy One of Israel that Isaiah prophesied (5:16, 19, 24; 10:20; 17:7; etc.). Jeremiah saw the futility of the cry: "This place is the temple of the Lord, the temple of the Lord, the temple of the Lord" (7:4). The Lord might have chosen the temple as his dwelling, but it was a free and sovereign choice.

The reference to the name of the Lord did not mean, of course, that God himself was not present, "only" his name. True, God himself is said to dwell in heaven (Deut. 26:15; cf. 1 Kgs. 8:23, 27, 30, 39, 43). He comes down to earth from heaven (Gen. 11:5; 19:24; Exod. 3:8). But his dwelling in heaven does not make impossible his presence in certain places on earth. Jacob's vision at Bethel offers a key to this duality. "How fearsome is this place! This is no other than the house of God, this is the gate of heaven" (Gen. 28:17). God's house on earth is the meeting place of heaven and earth.

The "name of the Lord," then, is none other than the Lord himself. The phrase "the dwelling of the name of the Lord" lays even greater stress on the presence of the Lord in his dreadful majesty. Where the name dwells, the Lord himself is present in holiness as the free, autonomous God of Israel who is above all the national deities extolled in royal sanctuaries.

This understanding of the temple as the dwelling place of the name goes hand in hand with an understanding of the function of the ark. This holy object was the throne of the invisible God, a symbol of his presence. But it was also the place where the tablets of the law were kept and as such it was the ark of the covenant (or ordinances) of the Lord. It was still a symbol of the Lord's presence but of his presence in the Word, in the laws and commandments by which he hallows and unites his people. Attention thus focused not so much on the blessing and protective strength of God but on the authority of his Word. The ark had the role that the Torah would play in the synagogue and the Bible in the church. The house of God as the place of his presence was the place where he spoke and revealed his promises and commands.

If the temple was truly the dwelling place of the Lord's name, there could be only one house. At first this conclusion did not seem self-evident to many Israelites. Had not the Lord in any case manifested himself to the fathers in many places? Had they not built altars at these places? Later generations, then, built sanctuaries at Dan and Bethel in spite of the centralizing of worship during the wilderness wandering. It was not perceived why the choice of Jerusalem should forbid pluralism and demand centralism. Gradually, however, the people came to realize that centralized worship at Jerusalem was in fact the divine will and not just a political decision. The prophets sharply criticized the many sanctuaries because there the people were in fact worshiping many gods (Amos 4–6). As Israel had only the one God, the Lord of heaven and earth, so it must worship the one God: "Hear, O Israel, the Lord is our God, one Lord" (Deut. 6:4). The uniqueness of God was the driving force behind the ultimate abandonment of the fatal pluralism. By the end of the royal period, especially with the destruction of Israel, it was being increasingly accepted that worship must be at the one house of God at Jerusalem, the one place that God had chosen to let his name dwell (Deut. 12).

Josiah's reform (2 Kgs. 22–23), which enforced centralization, was like a painful surgical operation both for the priests who served outside Jerusalem and for the worshipers. Yet for all the pain it was also felt as a liberation from the ambiguity that had been a burden for centuries. Cultic centralization opened the door to theological concentration. It offered a new opportunity of discovering the Lord who was pleased to let his name dwell in Jerusalem.

(4) The Lord's house underwent the most radical change when it was destroyed in the catastrophe of 586 B.C. The furnishings, the instruments, and the vessels of precious metal were carried away by the enemy. Even the ark was lost (cf. Jer. 3:16). It seemed that the history of the house, of God's dwelling among his people, had ended.

But this was not so. The remnant of Judah that came back from exile built a new temple on the ruins of the old (Ezra 3–6). Zerubbabel's temple was consecrated ca. 516 B.C. and stood for centuries until Herod built a bigger and finer one known to us from the writings of Josephus and many NT sayings.

Did Zerubbabel build the new temple after the model of the old? That was the intention, but the concept of a house in which God would dwell was not exactly the same. The fact that "the Lord spurned his own altar and laid a curse upon his sanctuary" (Lam. 2:7) was burnt into the consciousness of the community. Would the Lord be willing to dwell in a new house? How would he manifest his presence? There was still confidence that God would be faithful to his promise and that he would thus be present in his house. But it was seen more clearly that he would come of his own free will and manifest his presence as he chose.

In this regard, Ezekiel, the priest-prophet of the exile, calls for notice. In three visions of the existing temple (chs. 1–3, 8–11) and the future temple (chs. 40–48), he dealt with the question of the divine presence, which took on burning urgency when the first temple was destroyed. The visions take it for granted that God is pleased to dwell in his temple. But he is not anchored there permanently. Thus in the first vision, by the river Kebar (RSV Chebar), Ezekiel saw the glory of the Lord, accompanied by four cherubim, coming in a windstorm from its normal place to an unclean foreign country to call Ezekiel as a prophet (chs. 1–3). The point here is that although God's glory dwells at Jerusalem, it may move about at will.

In the second vision (chs. 8–11) Ezekiel saw God's judgment fall on the holy city, beginning with God's own sanctuary (9:6). As judgment fell, "the glory of the Lord rose high from above the cherubim and moved on to the terrace of the temple" (10:4), then "left the city" to the east, halting for a moment on the Mount of Olives" (11:23).

When the holy city and temple had lain in ruins for fifteen years, the prophet had his third vision (chs. 40–48). He "beheld the glory of the God of Israel coming from the east" (43:1) and entering the temple, so that "the glory of the Lord filled the temple" (43:4-5). The promise was then given that the

Lord "will dwell among the Israelites for ever" (43:7). Did this mean that God had come back to his temple home in Jerusalem?

Yes and no! As Ezekiel saw it, God does not tie himself by his own promise. He is free to be present or not. It is always a wonder when he manifests himself. His presence is not a constant and automatically secure state. God is constant in his love but free and holy in its manifestation. If Ezekiel was appalled when he saw God's glory leaving the temple, he was probably even more startled that the free and holy God would want to be present again in his new sanctuary.

At the time of rebuilding, the importance of the tabernacle as the original place of Israel's united worship also called for increasing attention. Nowhere do we expressly read that the tabernacle was a model for either the first temple or the second. The data show, however, that it did have something of this role. Thus the people were invited to bring contributions in cash or kind for the tabernacle (Exod. 25:2-7), and similar collections were made for both temples (2 Kgs. 12:4-16; Neh. 10:33). The tabernacle could also itself be described as a sanctuary for God (Exod. 25:8). The word used here *(miqdāš)* normally means a house with stone walls, so that the temple was ultimately in view. Again, when Moses was on the mountain, he was shown a heavenly design, pattern, or model *(tabnît)* that he was to follow carefully in making the tabernacle (25:9; 26:30; 27:8; Num. 8:4). Later, the tabernacle itself, constructed on the divine model, would become something of a pattern for sanctuaries.

Its plan, in fact, was the same as that followed by Solomon, Zerubbabel, and Herod. It was divided into three parts and oriented to the east, with the altar of burnt offerings in the inner court. Nevertheless, it had certain distinctive aspects which throw light on the proper way to understand the temple. Terms like *miqdāš* and *miškān* show that it was a house for the Lord, but it was also called the "tent of meeting" (RSV; NEB "Tent of the Presence") or the "tent of the testimony" (RSV; NEB "Tent of the Tokens," *'ōhel hā'ēdût*), i.e., the place where God freely meets his people either directly or through the mediation of Moses (Exod. 29:42-43; Num. 9:15). We thus find complementary roles that the temple had also to have. The temple, like the tabernacle, must be both a place where the Lord dwells and also the place where he meets his people and grants his living Word.

The fact that the glory of the Lord came down on the tent from time to time in the sight of all the people is of the utmost importance. The glory descended first on the simple tent of meeting (Exod. 33:7-11), then on the full-fledged tabernacle at the consecration (40:34-35), at the first offering (Lev. 9:23-24), and during the desert wanderings (Num. 14:10; 16:19; 20:6). Later it descended similarly on Solomon's temple when this was consecrated (1 Kgs. 8:11).

The fact that the tabernacle could be lifted up and carried from place to place was also significant. The sanctuary in Jerusalem would have to be a house, but it must also have something of the character of a tent. The focus could not be the site as such or the durability of the structure, but the willingness of the Lord actually to be present there.

A final point about the tabernacle was its location in the middle of the camp. The original tent had been "at a distance outside the camp" (Exod. 33:7). But the tabernacle was placed in such a way that the Lord could "dwell among the people" (25:8 CB; 29:45). Intimacy of relationship between God and his people was the point here. Protection might be needed against the divine glory (37:26, 28; 43:7), but Israel would enjoy close fellowship with God based on the gracious manifestation of his presence and his no less gracious provision of covering for its sins as signified by the cover of the ark, the *kapporet*, the mercy seat.

As distinct from the first temple, perhaps the greatest change in the second related to the Holy of Holies. The ark and the cherubim had been destroyed in the overthrow of Solomon's temple. They could not be replaced. Nevertheless, the temple would still be a place for the covering of sin by expiatory offerings. In meeting his people, God was pleased to take away their sin. The destruction of the first temple as a judgment on Israel's apostasy gave even added emphasis to Israel's sense of the necessity of God's atoning work.

Embedded in the second temple, then, were three essential beliefs. First, it still pleased God to dwell amidst his people and to have an intimate relationship with them. Second, God would be present according to his own free and sovereign will as the holy God who manifests his glory as it pleases him. Third, God would be present to take away the sin of the people that assembled to meet him.

c. The Place to Worship the Lord

God was present in the temple to meet the community that came to meet him and worship him. The temple was the meeting place between God and his people. The meeting could take place only if it pleased God to manifest his presence. The temple might have the best possible shape and satisfy every liturgical requirement, but it could not guarantee God's presence. We must keep this freedom of God in mind as we expound the main aspect of Israelite worship.

Set against the background of the temple, the Psalms are our most important source of information in this area. Other hymns that call for attention may be found in Exod. 15:1ff., 1 Sam. 2:1-10, Jon. 2:2-9, Isa. 38:10-20, and Lamentations. Liturgical ordinances make up much of Exodus, Leviticus, and Deuteronomy. These deal with the three main feasts, the altar and offerings, vows, the firstborn, the priests, and the blessing. Accounts of altars, the covenant ceremony, the first offerings presented by Aaron and his sons, Passover celebrations, and the consecration of the temple are also relevant. The prophets rebuke false worship (Hos. 3:4; Amos 4:4-5; Mic. 4:6-8; Isa. 1:10-20; Jer. 6:20; Hag. 2:14; etc.) and look ahead to the future renewal of worship (Isa. 30:28; Jer. 29:12-13; Ezek. 43:18-27).

Not all this material relates directly to worship at Jerusalem, but since Jerusalem became the main center of worship after the building of the temple there is usually an indirect relation, the more so as traditional practices were continued at Jerusalem. If it is true that there are differences between the worship of the early period and that of the monarchy, the many constant elements can serve as guidelines in our exposition. We will first consider Israel's worship in general, then as prayer, as thanksgiving, and as praise.

(1) As we have noted, worship was meeting. First, then, those who worship must move. They must leave the place where they live and go to the sanctuary. They must draw near and enter the place of worship. At a first glance this movement from one place to another might seem to be unimportant, yet its relevance appears at once when we consult the Hebrew terms.

Going (hālak), going up ('ālāh), coming (bô', 'ātāh), and entering (bô') all play a significant role (cf. Isa. 30:29). In the court of the Lord's house gather all "who come to worship there" (Jer. 26:2). Each "went up from his own town to worship" (1 Sam. 1:3 CB). The pilgrim songs set the mood (Ps. 122:1). People rejoice as they come to the holy court or enter into it (Ps. 5:7; 42:2; 86:9; 95:6; etc.). Coming near (qārēb) is an important category (Ps. 65:4 RSV; Lev. 9:5 RSV).

Going, coming, entering, and drawing near were not just steps preceding worship. By leaving their own ephemeral dwellings and entering into the presence of God the people passed from their own world to God's world. What a happy passage this was from the very outset! Worship itself began with moving toward God: "Enter his presence with songs of exultation" (Ps. 100:2).

Second, when people came thus to worship God, they always expressed their respect and allegiance. They could not enter God's house as they might a neighbor's. If respect must be shown when coming to a royal palace or the house of an important official, then especially so when entering the Lord's house. A vital part of worship was to give some acknowledgment of God's majesty and one's own lowliness, usually by calling on his name and bowing down in adoration.

The patriarchs had invoked the Lord by name at holy places in Canaan (Gen. 12:8; 13:4; etc.). In response to God's self-revelation at Sinai Moses had called on the name of the Lord (Exod. 33:19). To invoke God's name was the beginning and the heart of worship (Ps. 116:13; 80:18). Foreign nations "do not invoke thee by name" (79:6; Jer. 10:25). When Israel rebelled, there was "no one who invokes thee by name" (Isa. 64:7). The people will do this willingly again in the end time (Zeph. 3:9; Joel 2:32). To invoke God's name is to "ascribe to the Lord the glory due to his name" (Ps. 29:2), to glorify him, to do him honor (Isa. 29:13, Hebrew *kabbēd*).

Posture accompanied words: kneeling on the ground *(kāraʿ birkayim)*, bowing down *(hištaḥᵃweh)*, and standing *(ʿāmad)*, but not sitting. The Israelites used these ways of showing respect without inquiring into their origin. The actions themselves, the prophets taught, are not the important thing. They do not prove that a true sense of respect pervades the heart. Condemnation falls if "this people approach me with their mouths and honor me with their lips while their hearts are far from me" (Isa. 29:13). "Not every one who calls me 'Lord, Lord' will enter the kingdom of Heaven" (Matt. 7:21).

Third, when speaking about worship the OT often refers to the "face" of the Lord *(pānîm)*. The temple was the place where God and the people met. In worship, then, the congregation stood face to face with the Lord. The face of God is God himself graciously present among his people.

"To seek the face of God" (Ps. 24:6; Hos. 5:15 RSV) and "to see God's face" (cf. Ps. 17:15; 63:2) are familiar expressions. English translations tend to favor the rendering "to be in the presence of God" for "to see the face of God," which is what the Hebrew really means. But the phrase can also be translated literally, as in the dialogue between Moses and Pharaoh in Exod. 10:28-29.

The expression *lipnê YHWH* ("before the Lord," "in the presence of the Lord") also occurs constantly in connection with worship. People come, draw near, bow down, kneel, stand, bring offerings, cry out, pray, give thanks, praise, eat and drink, and are joyful *lipnê YHWH*. They direct all these actions or activities toward the Lord.

Can human creatures really see God's face? According to the OT they may indeed do so, though rarely. Moses and the elders saw God on Sinai (Exod. 24:9-11). Moses stood "face to face" with God (33:11). He was allowed to "see the very form of the Lord" (Num. 12:8). At the same time, it is still true that one cannot see God and live (Exod. 33:18; cf. John 1:18). The direct vision granted on special occasions was not the same as seeing God's face in normal worship. In worship the phrase has a general sense, simply denoting worship. On occasion, however, a sense of the great wonder of seeing the Lord finds expression: "I shall behold thy face in righteousness" (Ps. 17:15 RSV); "One thing I ask of the Lord . . . to gaze upon the beauty of the Lord" (27:4); "I come before thee in the sanctuary to gaze upon thy power and glory" (63:2). Did not Job long to see God himself with his own eyes (Job 19:26-27)?

Meeting the Lord in worship was a tremendous and even dangerous experience, yet one that was also joyful and intimate. Coming as guests to the Lord's house, the people faced the altar, the cherubim, and the ark, stood amid the multitude (Ps. 42:4 RSV), watched the priests and Levites discharge their office, and above all "saw" God's own face, entering into close contact with the invisible Host of the house. Overcoming their blindness, they met the holy and compassionate God. With soul and body they could "taste and see that the Lord is good" (Ps. 34:8 RSV). God let them experience his presence. This was how they saw his face.

Fourth, there could be no worship, of course, without offerings. "No one shall come into the presence of the Lord empty-handed"—this was a basic tenet (cf. Deut. 16:16-17; Exod. 23:15). The act of offering was obviously not the main element in worship. God had first to give himself to his people, to be their God (Gen. 17:7-8). This divine gift implicitly precedes and surpasses all human deeds. We must stress its priority before discussing the human offerings that are certainly an intrinsic part of Israel's worship. Did the Lord's unique presence and gift give a distinctive character to the offerings of Israel as compared to those of surrounding nations?

Worship is an act of service to God (*$^{a}bōdāh$*). Divine service is not now so familiar in English as worship, which comes from "worth" and implies recognition of worth. Yet we do well to understand worship along the lines of divine service, i.e., the rendering of our service to God.

At the exodus Israel was freed from bondage to serve God (Exod. 3:12; 4:22; etc.). Serving God here meant celebrating a feast to the Lord in the wilderness, and at the core of the celebration the people "offer sacrifice to the Lord" (3:18; 5:3, 8, 17; 10:24-26). To worship is to offer sacrifice.

Having focused already on other aspects of offerings in the OT, we will emphasize here the aspect of offering as a gift, as service to the Lord. When it is said that the people offered something, the term "to offer" stands for Hebrew terms that originally had a very specific meaning: *hēbî* (from *bô'*, "to come"; Gen. 4:3-4; Exod. 23:19), "to bring"; *hiqrîb* (from *qārab*, "to draw near"; Lev. 7:9; Num. 28:11), "to bring near"; *zābaḥ* (Exod. 20:24; Ps. 54:8 [Eng. 6]), "to slaughter" (hence *mizbēaḥ*, "place of slaughter, altar"); *he^{e}lāh* (from *'ālāh*, "to go up"; Lev. 14:20; Ps. 51:21 [Eng. 19]), "to lift up" (hence *'ôlāh*, "burnt offering"), and *hiqṭîr* (from *qāṭar*, "to smoke"; Lev. 9:13; Exod. 30:7-8), "to burn frankincense." Some offerings at least were meant as gifts of the congregation to the Lord. Noah offered whole offerings to "soothe" God (Gen. 8:20-21), and the Hebrews slaughtered for the Lord to prevent plague or sword (Exod. 5:3). Offerings could sometimes be called God's "food" (Lev. 21:6; 22:25; Num. 28:2, 7).

Were the offerings obligatory or free? They had to be presented according to valid ordinances. It would have been unthinkable for people to offer them as they pleased. The priests insisted on orderly offerings. Yet opportunity was also given for free-will offerings (Exod. 25:2; Lev. 7:16; 22:18). God did not want merely to bind people by commandments. He preferred to move their hearts and wills (Exod. 35:3; Ps. 54:6; 1 Chron. 29:5; Ezra 1:4).

Many different offerings—whole offerings, shared offerings, material goods, metals, and money—were brought in the Lord's service. The difference between the offerings of Israel and those of other nations lay, however, in the fact that offerings to the Lord, the glorious God who is above all other gods (Ps. 96:4), could have only limited value. The Lord did not need food or other gifts (Isa. 43:23-24; Ps. 40:6; 50:7-15). He abhorred those who brought offerings in order to secure a blessing or to buy his favor. Better no offerings at all than hypocritical offerings disguising an unjust and unholy life! The trenchant criticisms of the prophets (Amos 5:21-27; Hos. 6:6; Isa. 1:11-15) are unparalleled in world literature. They show us what is the right place of offerings if they are to be valid.

Fifth and finally, there were specific times and occasions for worship in the temple. Assemblies could not be held at random. The Lord would be present in the place he had chosen, but at times when it pleased him to meet with his people. The people might be invited to seek his face every day, or day and night (1 Kgs. 9:59), but he also hallowed specific times for common worship.

In addition to the sabbath and the three pilgrim feasts (Passover, Pentecost, and Tabernacles), we must mention the day of the new moon (Hos. 2:11), the day of the new year (Lev. 23:23-25), and the Day of Atonement (Lev. 16:1-11; 23:26-32). All these are called "days" *(yôm),* but we also find "appointed season" *(môʿēd),* "convocation" or "assembly" *(miqrāh* or *ʿaṣeret),* and "feast" *(hag)* with no discernible distinction.

A feast was a season especially owned by God and therefore holy. It was not holy in itself or by tradition or by royal appointment (1 Kgs. 12:32), but solely by the grace of God, who was and would be present on this special day.

A feast was also a season of extraordinary assembly. On it God's people came together in convocation. Individual worship had its own time, but only as a section of the time that God designated for the community.

Finally, a feast was above all a joyful event (Deut. 16:11, 14). Joy, as already noted, was a typical element in the cultic tradition of Jerusalem. The people assembled in a festive spirit.

Feasts, of course, were also subject to prophetic criticism. By celebrating them in the temple on the proper days and according to valid ordinances, Israel had no guarantee of the Lord's acceptance. "I hate, I despise your feasts, and I take no delight in your solemn assemblies" (Amos 5:21 RSV). "New moons and sabbaths and assemblies, sacred seasons and ceremonies, I cannot endure" (Isa. 1:13-14). What really counted was not mere observance but faithful devotion to God.

(2) Israel's worship, then, involved the five main steps of entering the sanctuary, invoking the Lord's name, standing before his face, presenting

offerings, and holding the appointed assemblies. Following these steps might seem to be simply performing a round of religious duties. But this was not so. The Israelites did not worship merely because they were commanded to do so. They did not seek God's face out of fear of condemnation should they refuse. Their worship was fundamentally spontaneous.

People came to the holy court to pray, to ask for something they badly needed. This was a first motive for worship. How many of the psalms are requests for help! How many texts are prayers offered either by individuals or the whole people! People could ask God's help in any place, but they especially did so at the place that he appointed for meeting with him, i.e., in his house at Jerusalem, which would "be called a house of prayer for all nations" (Isa. 56:7; Matt. 21:13).

(a) Sufferings and needs moved individuals to pray for help (cf. Hannah in 1 Sam. 1). The prayer might involve attitudes, acts, and ceremonies, but primarily it was a seeking of God's presence in a spontaneous unburdening of the heart according to a specific pattern involving five main elements: a cry invoking God's name; a complaint describing the need or suffering; a request for mercy, comfort, and help; praise of God and confession of faults; and confession of faith and a vow to the Lord. The order might vary, and there might be repetition, but these were the essential constituents.

Most prayers for help, whether from an individual or a congregation, begin "O Lord" or "O God" (Ps. 3:1; 4:1; 5:1; 6:1; 12:1; 44:1; etc.). The prayer is unambiguously addressed to Israel's God, not to many deities in the hope that one might hear (cf. Babylonian prayers). The close relation to God that underlies the prayers comes out even more clearly in the cry "O my God" ('^{e}lōhay, Ps. 3:7; 7:1; etc.; '$\bar{e}$lî, Ps. 18:2; 22:1; etc.) or "our God" ('^{e}lōhênû, Ps. 106:47; Dan. 9:15; Ezra 9:10; etc.), less commonly "my Father" (Ps. 89:26 RSV) or "our Father" (Isa. 63:16; 64:8 RSV). Even this confident address, of course, could not force God to hear, nor could unceasing calling (qārā'), crying (sā'aq), or crying for help (šāwa'). Whether God would hear and answer depended on God's free and faithful grace.

The sufferings might be described at length ("pouring out my heart," 1 Sam. 1:15). The complaints often seem to be exaggerated. Worshipers put their condition in the darkest colors: physical and mental pains (Ps. 6:2-3, 6-7; 22:14-15), almost unbearable distress (31:7; 71:20), alienation and isolation even from relatives and friends (27:10; 35:11-14; 41:9), the attacks of enemies, and apparent abandonment by God (13:1-2; 30:7; 42:9; 88:3ff.; Job 13:24). Community psalms offer similar descriptions of the catastrophic sufferings that befell the people (war, famine, defeat, etc.). With the request that God should act, a persistent question is raised. Why (lāmāh) have these things happened? By God's permission or even by his will? And how long will they last? Those who make the complaints obviously feel trapped. They can see no way out. They are thrown back totally on God.

At the heart of the prayer, then, there is supplication (t^{e}pillāh, 1 Sam. 1:10;

2 Kgs. 19:15; Ps. 5:1-2; Jon. 2:7). What is sought is deliverance, or at least a token of God's kindness (Ps. 86:17), or a promise of salvation. The request is an attempt to break through the wall of separation from God: "Listen" (Jer. 18:19 CB), "be merciful" (CB Ps. 4:1; 6:2; etc.), "answer me" (13:3; 102:2), "come back" (6:4; cf. 80:14), "make thy face shine" (31:16; 80:3).

To restore the relation to God when he hides his face, there is sometimes a confession of sin and a request for forgiveness. It is realized that sin might have caused the suffering (Ps. 38:3-4; 40:12; 51:4; etc.). Confession is thus made even though no specific fault might be mentioned (25:11; 32:5; 51:4-5). Confession of sin is parallel to giving honor to the Lord (Josh. 7:19; 1 Sam. 6:5) or confessing his name (1 Kgs. 8:33, 35). Congregational confession of sin became frequent after the exile (Ezra 9:1-15; Neh. 9:16-37).

Common requests are that God would heal (Ps. 6:2), give life (41:2), revive (80:19), restore (138:7), preserve (143:11), keep (16:1), defend (86:2), guard (140:4), help or save (3:7), bring out (25:17), set free (143:11), deliver (6:4), redeem (*pādāh*, 26:11), ransom (*gā'al*, 69:18), and give justice (7:8), or that enemies might be ashamed (6:10) or fall and perish (9:3).

Intercession is also made for others. Abraham (Gen. 20:7), Moses (Num. 11:2), Samuel (1 Sam. 7:5), Elisha (2 Kgs. 4:33), Amos (Amos 7:2, 5), Jeremiah (Jer. 7:16), and Job (Job 42:2, 10) all offered intercession. The congregation prayed for the king (Ps. 61:6-8) and the people later asked to pray for the places where they lived as exiles (Jer. 29:7).

The request was not a blind cry for help. Arguments were presented with which to convince God. Reasons were given for the hope that he would intervene. Appeal was made to his righteousness (*ṣedāqāh*, Ps. 5:9 [Eng. 8]), to his steadfast love (*ḥesed*, 6:5 [Eng. 4]), to his mercy or tender care (*raḥamîm*, 40:12 [Eng. 11]). How could God forget the glory of his own name? He surely recalls that the one who makes the prayer is a faithful servant (27:9). The worshipers are clinging to him, trusting in him, finding refuge in him, waiting for him, hoping in him. They can protest their honesty and innocence (7:10; 17:1ff.). Even before help is received a promise might be made to praise him (7:17). How could God ignore the prayer of those that so fully trust him that they can give thanks even as they suffer (22:22-31)?

(b) Gestures and actions might accompany the words in the plea for help. This does not mean that the words lacked efficacy or that God took notice only when actions strengthened them. The gestures had the same meaning as the words, but they enabled the whole person to join in the prayer, often in a mood of combined solemnity and expectancy.

Suppliants might stretch out their hands and arms (cf. Moses in Exod. 9:29; 29:33; Solomon in 1 Kgs. 8:22, 54; Ezra in Ezra 9:5; the whole people in 1 Kgs. 8:38). This gesture was useless, however, if there was "blood on the hands" (cf. Isa. 1:15). The unfaithful daughter of Zion would find no help even though "stretching out her hands" (Jer. 4:31 RSV).

Often, too, people would kneel down (1 Kgs. 8:54), bow down, or prostrate themselves when praying for help: Saul (1 Sam. 15:31), David (2 Sam. 12:20), the whole people (Neh. 9:3).

Mourning and anxiety might be expressed by rending clothing (1 Kgs. 21:27), tearing the hair or beard (Ezra 3), putting on sackcloth (Ps. 69:11), rolling in ashes (Jer. 6:26 RSV), sprinkling ashes on the head (Ezek. 27:30), wailing (Jer. 49:3 RSV), weeping (Judg. 20:23), and especially fasting (Judg. 20:26). On occasion, especially under accusation, the hands might be washed as a sign of innocence (Ps. 26:6; cf. Deut. 21:6), but the prophets sharply criticized misuse of this ceremony.

An offering might accompany the request for help (cf. Ps. 5:3). To offer, of course, was to present something. Did this mean that God might be influenced by human gifts? Entreating the Lord's favor (cf. 1 Sam. 13:12) by a burnt offering might seem to suggest this. So, too, might the presenting of a burnt offering as a "soothing odour," which in the story of Noah is followed at once by the declaration: "Never again will I curse the ground because of man" (Gen. 8:21; cf. the same phrase in Exodus, Leviticus, Numbers, and Ezekiel). Making expiation *(kappēr),* which occurs 67 times in Exodus, Leviticus, and Numbers, is parallel, yet it can hardly mean that the priests can secure forgiveness by their ministry, for it is God alone who decides whether the offering is acceptable. Offerings, in fact, do not sway God. It is of his own free grace alone that he responds either to the request or to the offering that accompanies it.

The acts and gestures had the role of strengthening the spoken plea. On their own they could easily assume a magical character. For this reason they had always to be linked to prayer. They took on the nature of enacted prayer. By means of them, along with the words, the people asked God for help and prayed for reconciliation with him.

A prayer for help, whether by word or deed, had to be honest. The house of the Lord was a place of help but it was also holy ground (Exod. 3:5). Integrity had to mark both the prayer and the accompanying acts and gestures. How could God accept the ceremony of expiation if there was no repentance or attempt at amendment (cf. Lev. 6:1-5)? How could expensive offerings, severe fasting, and endless prayers please the Lord so long as his people would not leave their wrong ways and come back to him (Lam. 3:40-42)? Prophecies like Isa. 1:15-16, Amos 5:21-22, and Isa. 58:6-12 remind Israel of the basic requirement of true worship, and God's people from the nations today would do well to take notice.

(3) Praying for help was not the only spontaneous way of worshiping the Lord. Another important way was that of thanksgiving. Asking for help and giving thanks for it complete one another. One without the other is like trying to clap with a single hand.

The context of thanksgiving is clear. God has answered the petition. He has healed, rescued, revived. The recipient of his help has made a vow and now goes to the sanctuary to give thanks. Many others are present when thanks are given, and so the private experience becomes a public one, a specific form of both individual and congregational worship.

In the OT thanksgivings occur mostly in the Psalms (cf. 18; 30; 32; 116; 118; 138) and the Prophets (Isa. 12:1-2; 38:10-20; Jon. 2:2-9). Several texts also express a vow or wish to give thanks, often in prayers for help (Ps. 22:22-31; 28:6-8; etc.). Ps. 107 is a thanksgiving liturgy. In Job 33:26-28 Elihu describes the experience of one who has just been healed of serious illness and saved from death.

It was customary to present a thanksgiving offering (Jon. 2:9; cf. Ps. 66:13-15; 116:17-19). Leviticus contains ordinances for shared-offerings as thank-offerings (*tôdāh,* 7:12), as votive offerings or free-will offerings (7:16; 22:18). Such offerings seem to have concluded with a thanksgiving meal (cf. Ps. 22:26).

(a) The thanksgiving prayer has a formal but decisive feature, namely, that it is prayed in the presence of God ("I will praise thee," Ps. 118:21) but also in witness to the congregation ("Come, listen, all who fear God, and I will tell you all that he has done for me," 66:16). The fact that God has saved his servant is the one reason for giving thanks, but thanks are given both vertically to God and horizontally to the congregation. This twofold expression of gratitude shows us the true character of this form of voluntary worship.

In the short prayer of Isa. 12:1-2, for example, v. 1 is addressed to God ("I will praise thee, O Lord") and v. 2 to fellow worshipers ("God is indeed my deliverer"). Ps. 118 first recites what God has done to the assembled people outside the temple (vv. 5-18), and then, after the psalmist enters "the gates of righteousness" (v. 19 RSV), God himself is praised (v. 21). In Ps. 66 the prayer of thanksgiving (vv. 13-20) begins with direct praise of God and then recounts what God has done to those who "fear God." Ps. 32 puts the thanksgiving to God in the middle (vv. 3-7) with witness to God's help both before (vv. 1-2) and after it (vv. 8-11). The same structure marks Hezekiah's prayer in Isa. 38:10-20. Ps. 34, an alphabetical psalm, has a purely instructional purpose and thus omits the prayer of thanksgiving to God.

In the traditional thanksgiving service, then, the praise of God, accompanied by an offering, is closely linked to witness, and perhaps to an invitation to a festive meal and other expressions of joy. The order may differ but the two elements are constant. It would be unthinkable either to praise God without inviting the congregation to join in the praise or to inform the congregation about God's help without thanking God himself.

(b) In thanking God believers use words and also present an offering. Words and offerings are like two sides of the same coin. Hebrew has the same word for both *(tôdāh).* They belong together. Thanks cannot be said to God with words alone. On the other hand, an offering cannot please God unless it springs from a true awareness of what he has done.

[275]

The words usually consist of a short but meaningful sentence (cf. Isa. 12:1; Ps. 30:1; 118:21; 138:1-2). The structure is normally as follows. First, the Lord is invoked by name, then thanks are expressed, and finally the event is reported, i.e., the reason given.

As regards the offering, we know the fact of it (Ps. 116:17-18; Jon. 2:9) but not the nature. A vow was usually made both to give thanks and to present an offering (Ps. 54:6). From Ps. 66:13-15 it seems that the two might go together, the offering accompanying the thanksgiving.

Both words and offering were simply an expression of gratitude, not the gratitude itself. Indeed, the traditional rite was not absolutely necessary. People might pay their vows and give thanks to God even without formal words and offerings, e.g., when temple worship was no longer possible. Gratitude could find expression in any form of true service to God. Dedication is at the core of true thankfulness (cf. Ps. 50:23; 51:16-19). This is the point made by Paul in Rom. 12:1.

(c) As noted, the service of thanksgiving involves an address to the congregation, again in the form of both words and acts. Having thanked God, the recipient of help turns to the people and gives direct information about the assistance received. This report usually follows the pattern of the prayer of thanks, but on a larger scale. Serious misfortune and great suffering had suddenly come upon the speaker, help was sought from God, God had granted the request, and help had come.

An interesting point is that a declaration of intent usually precedes the report. The recipient of help wants to tell the story, to make known or proclaim what has been experienced. The verbs used show that the aim is not just to give information but to bring good news to the congregation. The personal story of a servant of God is not a private story. It reflects the sufferings and liberation of all God's people, past, present, and future. This is why the congregation is invited to join in the thanksgiving (Ps. 118:1, 29 RSV; 30:4; 32:11).

The report may also become teaching, counseling, or even preaching (Ps. 32:8; 116:5; 118:8; 40:4). A humble believer who was downtrodden and distressed has now become a strong witness to God's mercy, an authoritative teacher, an evangelist.

An act completes the story of teaching. The guests are invited to join in a thanksgiving meal, to "eat and be satisfied" (Ps. 22:26). The words: "Taste and see that the Lord is good" (34:8 RSV), probably presuppose a thanksgiving meal in which the meat of the offering was shared. "I will take in my hands the cup of salvation" (116:13) suggests a libation and the serving of wine to the guests.

The thanksgiving celebrations of, e.g., Indonesian society form an interesting parallel. A Christian family will issue invitations at church, also individually to non-Christian relatives and neighbors. At worship the father or mother will say a prayer of thanks, the Bible will be read and explained, a hymn will be sung, and the guests will then share a meal to which all contribute, the family serving rice and tea.

(d) A special reason for thanks was salvation from death. God had brought back his servant from the grave, from *še'ôl*. In rescuing people from affliction, healing serious sickness, or saving from enemies, God truly raised them from the dead. The OT pays little attention to the problem of death except in prayers, which disclose the personal struggle of the Israelites with this ultimate enemy and the wonder of victory over it.

Sometimes we have cries for help from those in danger of death (Ps. 13:3). Sometimes death is felt to be a present reality (22:15; 31:12; 55:4; 143:3; cf. Lam. 3:54-55). The psalmist is already in the kingdom of death (Ps. 130:1; 61:2; 69:1-2). Yet surely the Lord cannot throw away his servant forever. Hence there may be confidence: "God will ransom my life, he will take me from the power of Sheol" (49:15; cf. 16:10).

The prayers of thanksgiving proclaim the great victory: liberation from death, rescue from the grave, passage from the world of the dead to that of the living. How are we to understand this? The answer is not easy. Many scholars think that the reference is not to literal death or resurrection. The statements about the grave and Sheol are to be seen as poetic. They are meant to stress the dreadful nature of the sufferings and the wonder of the divine help. The believer was *almost* dead, and the liberation thus amounted *almost* to a resurrection. When real death came, however, Israel, on this view, had no hope. The dead remained in *še'ôl*, their "eternal home" (Eccl. 12:5 RSV), "cut off from God's care" (cf. Ps. 88:5). Only in a few later texts, it is argued, do we find the hope of resurrection and eternal life as in the NT (Ps. 16:9-11; 17:15; 27:13; 49:15; 73:23-26; Isa. 26:19; Dan. 12:2).

Another possible explanation is that the victory over death was a real experience, but that death was seen as a two-sided reality: on the one hand as the boundary of life that God has fixed for each of us, on the other as the power of destruction that menaces us on our path through the world. This second aspect of death, it is thought, manifests itself in illness, persecution, and the other forms of suffering that endanger believers and against which they need God's help. Even though still living, they thus fall into the clutches of death. Their plea for liberation is a plea for freedom from death's invasion, not from the natural death that terminates life. When the plea is answered, the psalmists can praise the Lord who "brought them alive out of the pit of death" (107:19-20; cf. 30:3; 116:3; Isa. 38:17 RSV; Ps. 56:12-13).

A similar motif of defeating death may be found in other nations as well. Thus a 13th-century thanksgiving stela from the ruins of Thebes in Egypt carries the inscription:

[277]

"Thou art Amon-Re, Lord of Thebes, who rescues him who is in the underworld" (Pritchard, *Ancient Near Eastern Texts,* 3rd ed. [1969], p. 380). A parallel text from Babylon states that "Marduk is able to revive in the grave. Sarpanit knows how to deliver from destruction" (p. 437).

If death can be defeated in this life, this means, of course, that there can be liberation from the fear of death (cf. Heb. 2:14). Thus the OT people of God did not have to die in despair. They already had a share in victory over death—the victory that would be won definitively by Jesus, the suffering Servant of the Lord and Savior of the world, when God raised him from the dead (1 Cor. 15:3-4; Rom. 1:4).

(4) Praising God was yet another form of Israel's worship. Services glorifying God were in some way the climax of all other forms. Praise had priority, as we see from many psalms and hymns (cf. Psalms, Chronicles) in which the temple had almost no other function than that of the place where the Levites and all Israel praised God.

Services of praise were held regularly at the great feasts. People might ask for help and give thanks on special occasions, but services of praise were constant in response to God's invitation to Israel to come together and magnify his name.

The biblical material relating to this form of worship consists of over forty hymns (*teḥillāh,* Pss. 8; 19; 24; etc.), the songs of Moses (Exod. 15:1ff.), Miriam (15:21), Deborah (Judg. 5:2ff.), Hannah (1 Sam. 2:1ff.), and Habakkuk (Hab. 3:3ff.), and the briefer praises included in prayers for help (Ps. 5:11-12; 22:3-4; etc.) and the prophetic books (Isa. 6:3; Jer. 10:6-10; Amos 4:13; Isa. 42:10-13). References to praise are particularly prominent in Chronicles, Ezra, and Nehemiah.

(a) What specifically was Israel's aim in praising God? As noted, the aim of all worship was to honor the Lord. God was to be praised, exalted, magnified, glorified. In petition this took the form of invoking him by name and confessing one's sins to him. In thanksgiving it consisted of recognition of the benefits received. In praise, however, it was the precise aim of the whole service. The congregation came together to honor the Lord irrespective of needs or blessings.

The aim was always clearly stated. Worshipers were called upon to praise God at the outset and often in the middle and at the end as well. No less than 200 times we find the imperative (second person plural) "praise" (*halelû*), "sing," "sing psalms," "give thanks," etc. We also find the third person plural: "May they praise, sing, give thanks, rejoice," and the first person plural: "Let us praise, etc." At times a single individual calls upon himself: "Bless the Lord, my soul," or expresses an intention: "I shall praise." The call may be differently addressed. Normally it goes out to the congregation: "Come, bless the Lord, all you servants of the Lord" (Ps. 134:1). Sometimes it goes out to the "righteous ones," or "you who fear the Lord," or the "sons of Jacob" or "sons of Israel." A choir often led the praise, accompanied by an orchestra and dancers (cf. Ps. 118:1-3; 149; 150). The people might call upon each other (103; 104; 145; 146). Yet the invitation went out to others beyond God's own people: to "all the earth" (96:1 RSV), to "all the inhabitants of the world" (33:8 RSV), to "families of nations" (96:7), to "all thy creatures" (145:10, 21), even to the heavens, the seas, the earth (96:11-12), and to the heavenly hosts or angels (29:1).

What was meant by "praise"? In daily speech to praise a person or thing is to recognize the value and importance of the person or thing. That is also the meaning of the Hebrew verb *hālal, hillēl,* and the noun *t^ehillāh.* Yet there is a difference between praising a person or thing and praising the Lord. The many parallels to *hillēl* show this. First, we have words meaning "bless, give thanks, proclaim, make known, herald, tell, extol, glorify, honor, declare, exalt, sing, and sing psalms." Then we have those meaning "rejoice, jubilate, exult, shout for joy, shout in triumph, and make music." In the first case praise is expressed by words, in the second by spontaneous bodily actions: joyful shouts, music (Ps. 150), clapping of hands (47:1), and dances (Exod. 15:20). The two forms complement one another. Intelligible words alone could not express all the feelings that are indispensable to true praise. Conversely, wordless utterances for their part require direct proclamation of the reasons for praise.

The purpose of praise is to make God's magnificence known as joyful news to all creatures and at the same time to invite them to join freely in the praise and to share in the joy of God's goodness and mercy. Israel fulfilled its divinely ordained function by engaging in this ministry. It pleased the Lord to accept its praise. Indeed, he called upon his people to render it and thereby to discover the secret of true happiness for all creatures.

(b) What was the content of this praise? Why was the Lord to be praised? Many of the people, among them the priests and Levites, were well aware of God's majesty and mercy, but many others needed to be reminded of them or even taught them. All the hymns, apart from Ps. 150, which is simply a call to praise, serve this purpose of teaching or reminding. They give examples and make practical suggestions that can be taken up with variations and additions.

We refer first to the short Song of Miriam: "Sing to the Lord, *for* he has risen up in triumph; the horse and his rider he has hurled into the sea" (Exod. 15:21). With this we might compare the equally short hymn that is often used as a thanksgiving: "O give thanks to the Lord, *for* he is good; *for* his steadfast love endures for ever" (Ps. 106:1 RSV; 107:1; 136:1; 118:1-4, 29; Jer. 33:11). Here the "for" *(kî)* might be better rendered "surely" or "truly," and the RSV "O give thanks" is better than the NEB "It is good to give thanks." In both cases we probably have responsive singing. One group issues the call, the other gives the reason, either an act or a perfection of the Lord.

God's acts are usually celebrated in short sentences following the pattern "God has done." He is to be praised because "he spoke, and it was" (Ps. 33:9), "he founded it [the earth]" (24:2), etc. He is to be praised for his deeds in history: He has "chosen Jacob to be his own" (135:4), "brought Israel from among them [the Egyptians]" (136:11), "made us . . . his people" (100:3), etc. Nor are God's great acts limited to the past. It is right to praise God also for what he *is* doing or *will* do: "The Lord of hosts is with us" (Ps. 46:7, 11), he "brings out the prisoner safe and sound" (68:6), "he will judge the peoples justly" (96:10, 13; 98:9), he reigns as King (93:1; 97:1).

God is praised not only in simple indicative sentences but also in sentences headed by an active participle in the masculine singular standing as a divine attribute, e.g., *bôrē'*, "creating, having created," *šōmēr*, "preserving, having preserved," *nōtēn*, "giving, having given." This form indicates ongoing action from the very beginning, though unfortunately this cannot be brought out in English. Examples may be found in 1 Sam. 2:6-8; Ps. 33:5, 7, 15; 65:6-7; 113:6-9; 135:7; 145:14-16; Isa. 40:21-26; 42:5; 45:6-8; Jer. 31:35-36; 32:18; Amos 4:13; 5:8-9; 9:5-6.

These participial sentences are mostly used to praise God in specific fields, e.g., as the Creator of heaven and earth, the Upholder and Governor of the world, the Leader and Protector of kings and nations, or of all people and creatures, in righteousness and mercy. The references in such cases are always more generally to God, not specifically to Yahweh, "the Lord," and there is no mention of the great acts of salvation history. Sumerian, Babylonian, and Egyptian texts addressing Ea, Ishtar, Marduk, Amon-Re, and other deities suggest that Israel might have taken over the form from other nations. At the same time it often added the identifying formula "The Lord of Hosts is my name" (Isa. 51:15; Jer. 31:35), or "I am the Lord, there is no other" (Isa. 45:18; cf. 42:5; 45:6-7), to rule out any misconceptions.

Short sentences addressed to God himself are another form of praise: "Thou didst create, liberate, etc." This form occurs sometimes in individual hymns (Exod. 15:1ff.; Ps. 8:1-3; 104:8, 24, 26, 28-30; Hab. 3:13-15). It is more common in collective lamentations (Ps. 44:1-2; 74:12-17; 80:8-9; 85:1-3; 90:3, 5, 8) and in hymns proper (Ps. 65:5, 9-11; 66:3, 10-12; 68:18; 99:4, 8). Praise in this vertical form reminds us of the twofold direction seen already in thanksgiving. We praise God directly as well as singing his praises to others.

(c) Praise, too, includes the presentation of offerings. In this regard it resembles prayer and thanksgiving. The call is to "ascribe to the Lord the glory due to his name" and to "bring a gift and come into his courts" (Ps. 96:8). This invitation is in fact the only proof in the Psalms that offerings were presented in praise, but further evidence may be found in stories (Judg. 6:25-27; 2 Sam. 6:17-18; 1 Kgs. 8:62-64; Neh. 12:43) and in the liturgical ordinances (Exod. 23:14-19; Lev. 23; Num. 28–29; Deut. 16:16-17; Ezek. 45:21-25).

Various kinds of offerings are mentioned, but unfortunately we do not know how they were presented or what was their specific significance. They obviously had three aims which are closely linked but differently stressed.

In some early stories festive worship centered on the community's confession of the Lord as the only God. Jethro, Moses' father-in-law, "rejoiced at all the good the Lord had done for Israel," and his confession: "Now I know that the Lord is the greatest of all gods," was "sealed," as it were, with an offering (Exod. 18:9-12). Similarly, the offerings of Gideon (Judg. 6:25-27), David (2 Sam. 6:17-18), Solomon (1 Kgs. 8:62-64), and Elijah (18:36-38) were meant to confirm their confessions of faith.

Confession of the Lord meant dedication to the Lord. This commitment found expression in laying one's hand on the victim's head (Lev. 1:4; etc.). Identification with the sacrificed animal meant self-dedication to the Lord. The offering confirmed the confession: "The Lord is God, he has made us and we are his own" (Ps. 100:3). The congregation stood to its confession by consecrating itself to the Lord by a free and joyful sacrifice.

Would the Lord accept the gift? The Israelites realized that he was free to accept or refuse their gifts (cf. Gen. 4:1-16). The prophets often denied that he would in fact accept the people's offerings (Hos. 8:13; Amos 5:22; Mic. 6:7; Jer. 6:20; Mal. 1:10). The offering had to be worthy (Lev. 1:4; 22:21, 23, 26), but so, too, did those that presented it (7:18; 19:5; 22:19-20, 25, 29). With each offering, then, the request was made that the Lord would graciously accept his people's worship.

To praise the Lord was Israel's most important vocation and ministry, as it is also the church's. Praise is the core of all worship. When crying to God for help or thanking him for help received, the community is simply confessing and praising him in a specific situation. The Lord is "holy, enthroned on the praises of Israel" (Ps. 22:3 RSV). It is by growing into an awareness of the calling to praise the Lord, and fulfilling it, that believers in both Israel and the church become and are the people of God.

d. The Home in Which God's People Grew Up

In a sense God's people already existed as such long before capturing Jerusalem and building the temple there. In another sense, however, Israel was also born as God's people in the temple and grew up there.

This statement obviously needs explanation. It must be seen in the light of what the OT says about Israel's birth. This birth took place more than once! The election of the patriarchs was Israel's beginning. Israel was also born when God liberated it from Egypt. The desert wanderings, too, had to do with Israel's beginnings. The same goes for the Sinai revelation and the giving of the land.

[281]

Israel's birth as God's people was never a finished act. The people often forgot, or did not know, its true life as such. Israel had to receive it again from God. This happened when the people gathered in the Jerusalem temple to worship the Lord. Whatever its condition at the time, here it could again become God's people and achieve awareness of its calling. In Jerusalem it developed its specific concept of being the people of God.

(1) The Israelites gathered for worship as the people of the Lord. The relation between Israel and the Lord's people was so close that it is tempting to equate the two. Yet would the equation be really true? A study of the terms "people," "nation," and "community" might throw light on the matter.

(a) The Israelites were certainly a people or nation in the ordinary sense. The English word "people" might denote an indeterminate number of individuals, a related group ("my people"), or a nation. The last two meanings correspond roughly to the Hebrew words ʿam and gôy as used of Israel.

The noun ʿam originally meant a limited group, e.g., an extended family. Elisha did not have to defend the rights of the Shunammite woman because she stayed among her own ʿam (2 Kgs. 4:13). Jeremiah went to receive his patrimony among his ʿam (Jer. 37:13). The patriarchs were gathered to their fathers' kin (ʿam, Gen. 17:14). The same word was also used for each tribe (Gen. 48:4), then for all the inhabitants of a land (Isa. 6:9-10), but it was always assumed that those concerned were related, usually through a common ancestor.

The word gôy means "nation" with the emphasis on common language or culture rather than common descent. God promised Israel's ancestors that their offspring would become a "great and powerful nation" (gôy, Gen. 12:2; 18:18). Ezekiel had a vision of Israel and Judah united as single nation (gôy, Ezek. 37:22). After the exile the term took on a negative connotation and finally implied "pagan" or "infidel" (cf. gôyim in 2 Kgs. 17:8; Ezek. 20:32). Yet biblical Israel, for all its distinctiveness, clearly understood itself as a nation.

As a nation Israel had ordinary national characteristics: land, language, culture, state, and religion. To deny this in view of its status as God's people is contrary to the biblical evidence. Israel never lost its character as one nation among others.

(b) Nevertheless, without detriment to its quality as a nation, Israel was truly called, adopted, and born to be the Lord's own people, a holy people. It was not by nature holy. Its religious zeal was not so great that it could become so. God himself took this nation to make it his people. In its history God was pleased to do this freely whenever the people gathered for worship. At worship Israel was called by his name or named his own (Deut. 28:10; Jer. 14:9; Isa. 63:19; 2 Chron. 7:14). The nation that was "not my people" (Hos. 1:10) was again and again accepted as God's people.

[282]

The terms "people of the Lord" (*'am YHWH*), "assembly of the Lord" (*q^ehal YHWH*), "community of the Lord" (*'^adat YHWH*), and "holy people" (*'am qādôš*) show that Israel's greatness is rooted in the event of worship. N. Lohfink in a special study of *'am YHWH* ("Beobachtungen zur Geschichte des Ausdrucks *'m Jhwh*," in *Probleme biblischer Theologie* [1971], pp. 275-305) found a special link between this expression and worship. He counted only 10 instances of *'am YHWH* but nearly 350 of "my, thy, or his people," more than two-thirds being in either "words of God" (prophecies, exhortations, revelations) or liturgical responses (prayers, confessions). Both the saying: "You are my people" (cf. Exod. 6:6) and the acknowledgment: "We are thy people" (cf. Deut. 9:26, 29) have their origin in worship, in which God was pleased to meet and adopt his people.

The same might be said of the description of Israel as God's *qāhāl* or *'ēdāh*. These words might denote various assemblies or companies of people, so that the *q^ehal yiśrā'ēl* or *'^adat yiśrā'ēl* would not necessarily be the *q^ehal* or *'^adat YHWH*. The gradual limitation of the terms to the worshiping assembly is an indication that Israel's very existence as the Lord's people depended on the central event of worship in which God freely received it as such.

Of itself Israel was not a holy people or nation (*'am/gôy qādôš*). God alone is holy. He alone let Israel share in his holiness. As Moses says: "You are a people holy to the Lord your God; the Lord your God chose you . . . to be his special possession" (Deut. 7:6). Holiness is commanded: "You shall be holy, because I, the Lord your God, am holy" (Lev. 19:2). The promise of holiness is conditional on keeping the law: "If only you will now listen to me and keep my covenant . . . then you . . . shall be . . . my holy nation" (Exod. 19:5-6). Israel might fulfil this condition anywhere, but God's house was the chosen place where God repeatedly sanctified Israel (Exod. 37:28 RSV).

(c) The central event in worship was the revelation of God's Word by which Israel might become a holy nation, the Lord's people. God himself made true worship possible. How could Israel glorify him unless he would accept it as his people? Acceptance was normally by revelation, by the Word of God that could be heard and understood and taken to heart. To be sure, God manifested his presence in many ways. Yet wordless signs were not of themselves enough. Israel came to meet the living God, not a mute divinity fashioned by human hands. Only with and through his Word could God lead the people to become *his* people.

Psalms, the main liturgical collection, shows this plainly. Divine words of self-revelation often accompany human prayers and praises: "Learn that I am God" (Ps. 46:10); "I am God, your God" (50:7); "I am your deliverance" (35:3 RSV). So, too, do words of promise (12:5), confirmation (60:6-8), and reminder or rebuke (81:8-16).

Temple prophecies give even more evidence of the importance of God's Word as the central event in worship. Amos was expelled from Bethel (7:13), and Jeremiah was forbidden to speak in the Lord's house (26:9), but the message of the prophets was undoubtedly meant to be the core of Israel's worship. Did they not communicate the "call of God" (*qārā'*, Isa. 40:3, 6, some 15 times in Isa. 40–66)? Did they not invite those that had gone astray to come back to God?

The priests, too, had the task of transmitting God's Word to the assembled people. The Levites were to "observe thy word" and "teach thy precepts to Jacob, thy law to Israel" (Deut. 33:9-10). Teaching duties were no less important for priests than sacerdotal duties. In the latter days "instruction issues from Zion, and out of Jerusalem comes the word of the Lord" (Isa. 2:3). The fountain of the Torah, from which Israel alone could drink, was to be accessible to all peoples.

Speaking to his people, God challenged, renewed, and educated them to live as his people. He communicated his Word through prophets, priests, and other servants, even though they might be "of unclean lips" (Isa. 6:5). At times, of course, he might speak directly, whether from heaven, the mountain, or from "above the cover" of the ark (Exod. 25:22), but normally, to spare the people (cf. Deut. 5:23-27), he would use a human mediator whom he empowered for the task.

(2) Coming together for worship, the Israelites were united into a community. This was not just a national community. Even when divided, or when some were in exile, they would still think of themselves as one nation. But they also had a different unity as the unique community of God's people, linked not merely by a common land, language, or culture, but by a very different force. Three points call for notice in this regard.

(a) As the Lord's people the Israelites lived as a community because the Lord was pleased to be among them when they worshiped. It was thanks to his presence that they became his people. Their existence as a community was thus a gracious gift. Israel might be a nation, even a religious nation, but its unity as such had to be modified and hallowed and a new kind of community had to emerge as it came together for worship. The Israelites did not own or control this gift. They had to ask for it.

A question arises whether *'am YHWH* could be regarded as the family or relatives of the Lord. Lohfink takes this view, and in fact God is at times called the Father of the Israelites and they his children (Isa. 1:2; Exod. 4:22; Deut. 8:5; 32:6). He also played a kinsman's part in redeeming Israel. Prayer could thus be made to him as "our father" or "our Ransomer from of old" (Isa. 63:15-16). Yet God was not under any obligation to Israel nor did it have any claim upon him. He was always free either to help or to withhold his help.

Awareness of distance finds expression in the use of *'ēdāh* ("assembly") rather than *'am*. It has even been suggested (cf. L. Rost, "Die Bezeichnungen für Land und Volk im AT," in *Festschrift O. Procksch* [1934], pp. 125-48) that *'ēdāh* was a deliberate replacement, possibly because it comes from the root *y'd* ("meet"). The truth in this view is that the Israelites belonged together because they met for common worship and the Lord himself met them and spoke to them, hallowing their meeting, not merely in the temple, but already in the wilderness and later in exile.

(b) Israel could experience the communion of the Lord's people because it pleased the Lord to choose, hallow, and gather individuals and to unite them as his own people. A reality that we must not forget is that God deals not only with the people as a whole but with each of its members in particular. The whole people is chosen and accepted and sanctified when it assembles in God's presence, but so, too, is each individual. By his Word God states whom he accepts. He may also reject those who think themselves worthy in virtue of their position or merits. The Word distinguishes with full authority between those that belong to God's people and those that do not. Israel can thus meet as "the assembly of the holy ones" (Ps. 89:5 RSV).

The question arises: "O Lord, who shall sojourn in thy tent? Who shall dwell on thy holy hill?" (Ps. 15:1 RSV). "Who may go up the mountain of the Lord? And who may stand in his holy place?" (24:3). What we have here is a liturgical "entrance examination." All are invited, but certain practical conditions must be met for belonging to the assembly of the holy ones (cf. 81:8). Those that have heard the Word and have been accepted and sanctified by it are counted among the holy ones. Only on this basis is the church, too, the communion of saints.

The conditions for membership are stated in Deut. 12–26. Three groups are excluded in 23:1ff.: eunuchs in v. 1, bastards in v. 2, Moabites and Ammonites in v. 3. The door would later be opened to eunuchs (Isa. 56–57), and David could be Israel's greatest king in spite of his Moabite ancestry (Ruth 4:17). The time would come, indeed, when Edomites and Egyptians could be members of the Lord's assembly. The restrictions were not inflexible.

As a community of holy ones, Israel had limits that God alone could fix. He alone had the final right to decide who would belong to this community. He could freely confirm existing members but also add or subtract as he chose. Descent was outweighed by an openness in which the first might be last and the last first according to God's sovereign will.

(c) The quality of the community calls for notice. In common worship a form of communion arose that Israel could not know merely as a nation. The Israelites unquestionably knew solidarity and kinship as members of the same nation. A shared religious life strengthened the solidarity. But national and religious unity alone has little in common with the true fellowship that God had promised to Israel as his people.

Israel was born, or reborn, as the people of the holy God. It was thus a "brotherhood." This term (Hebrew *ah^awāh*) occurs in the OT only at Zech. 11:14, but the concept plays a basic role. Tribes and individuals treated one another as brothers (*'āh*), whether as children of the same father, descendants of a common ancestor, or simply kinsmen and compatriots. When the tribes became a nation (or two nations), each Israelite was a brother with the same status as any other Israelite (cf. Deut. 17:15 RSV).

Two other terms are relevant in this connection: *rēaʿ*, meaning "fellow," "friend," or "neighbor," and *ʿāmît*, meaning "fellow citizen" or "compatriot." All three words play an important role in legal ordinances, *ʾāḥ* in Deut. 12–26, *ʿāmît* in Lev. 17–26, and *rēaʿ* in Exod. 20:33–23:19 as well as Deut. 12–26 and Lev. 17–26. But what especially was distinctive about this form of solidarity in Israel?

The OT certainly makes no boast about an ideal communion in Israel. The people achieved no special depth of fellowship. Israelites often failed to develop or maintain good relations with their fellows. Brothers could be jealous of one another (cf. Gen. 4:1ff.). Psalms and Jeremiah complain about broken ties of family and friendship (cf. Ps. 27:10). Treason from within hurt more than hostility from without (69:9; 31:11; 41:9; Jer. 12:6; 20:20; Lam. 1:2). The Israelites did not constitute a close "company of good men" (Ps. 111:1). When they met in the Lord's presence, they were only too keenly aware of what they lacked.

Along these lines another specific feature is the use of "*your* brothers, neighbors, or fellows" in legal commandments (Exod. 20; Deut. 5; Lev. 17–26; Deut. 12:26). "Your brothers" occurs 9 times in Lev. 17–26 and 16 times in Deut. 12–26; "your neighbors" occurs 4 times in the Decalogue, 3 times in Lev. 17–26, and 6 times in Deut. 12–26; and "your fellows" occurs 6 times in Lev. 17–26. God himself reminded the Israelites to respect the interests of their compatriots. He guaranteed their rights as the foundation on which the community stood. Listening to his Word, the people learned to know others, not as insignificant or dangerous persons, but as brothers or sisters (cf. Gen. 4:9; 45:4). Because the Lord assembled them, they hoped in worship to grow into a people that would respect all others as members of a common family.

Another aspect of the Lord's people as a community is the deep concern that is shown for the weak, the poor, and the oppressed. Passages in the Prophets, the Law, and the Psalms all emphasize that the mystery of the community's strength lay in care for the needs of its smaller and weaker members.

The prophets often rebuked Israel for the oppression of widows and orphans (Isa. 1:17-23; Jer. 7:6; Ezek. 22:7) and exploitation of the weak (Amos 3:6-7; 5:11-12; Isa. 10:2). How could God's people grow into a mature society if it oppressed its weaker members under the guise of law and order? Zephaniah had a vision of the proud and arrogant being driven out so that only the afflicted and the poor would be left (3:11-12). The law specifically demands that justice be done to the poor and the weak (Exod. 22:21-27; Lev. 19:9-18; Deut. 15:1-11; etc.). God himself sides with the oppressed. He defends their rights and establishes justice for them. In the Psalms the humble and oppressed pray for help or give thanks for it (22:24; 25:16; 34:6; etc.). Many of God's people were poor and simple folk (cf. 1 Cor. 1:26-29). The strong had not only to deal justly with them. They must come down from their lofty seat and take their place among them (1 Sam. 2:7-8). Brotherhood could never be authentic so long as some behaved arrogantly. Nor had the humility and solidarity to be spiritual alone. It had to have political and social ramifications.

"Your neighbour" is the English rendering of *rēʿaka* (Exod. 20:16-17). But who is meant? First, of course, the fellow Israelite, but some laws had a wider reference to foreigners as well. The resident alien *(gēr)* also had rights (Lev. 19:33-34; Deut. 23:15-16). The Israelites had themselves lived as aliens in Egypt (Exod. 2:22; Deut. 10:19). How, then, could they refuse to keep company (Ps. 119:63), to celebrate the sabbath (Exod. 20:10), or to observe the Passover (12:49) with *their* aliens (cf. Deut. 1:16)?

The Lord's people find the specific communion they hope for when they gather for worship. Community has to be celebrated. Those that assemble in the Lord's presence receive the gift of helping (Deut. 22:1ff.), forgiving (Gen. 50:17), and loving one another (Lev. 19:18, 34). "How good it is and how pleasant . . . to live together!" (Ps. 133:1). With its own strength Israel could not achieve this kind of fellowship, but it was called and invited to celebrate it in concert. Thanks to the Lord's presence among his people, worship was a source of never-ending communion.

(3) Coming together in worship and confession, the Israelites were at God's disposal. They were ready to fulfil their calling in God's worldwide kingdom. They were chosen to be God's own people, enjoying true communion and receiving God's rich blessings (Ps. 133:3), but their election was part of a wider divine purpose in which the destiny of all nations depended on God's dealings with this one people. Only by fulfilling its wider vocation and function in God's plan of salvation could the Israelites be truly "happy" and discover the depths of the love of God.

(a) An assembly usually takes place by invitation or command. Israel assembled because the Lord commanded it to do so. The invitation might be issued in different ways, e.g., by blowing the trumpet, but behind the sign it was God's own voice that summoned the people to gather in his presence. It was assumed that a number of persons would come (at least 10 adult men by Jewish custom). God wanted men and women to come together in order that he might equip them to transmit his call to others. His chosen people was to be a sent people.

This missionary aspect may be seen in the description of God's people as *qāhāl*. Though some scholars trace this word back to the same root as *qôl* ("voice"), this is unlikely.

Like 'ēdāh, it might be used for any assembly (cf. Gen. 28:3; Ps. 26:5). It is often used in a military setting (Gen. 49:6; Jer. 50:9). But the OT uses it, too, for the assembly that meets to celebrate the great feasts (1 Kgs. 8:22), that listens to God's Word (Deut. 18:16), or that observes the service of expiation (Lev. 16:17, 33). Thus it is only in a spiritualized sense that Qumran saw itself as qᵉhal 'ēl ("God's host"; cf. Eph. 6:10-20).

The LXX uses *ekklēsía* nearly a hundred times for *qāhāl*. The expression *ekklēsía toú theoú* occurs nine times. The NT then takes up *ekklēsía* as the main term for God's people assembled out of every nation. The choice of the term reflects the conviction that the new community of the church is the fulfilment of the older *qāhāl*. Like the *qāhāl*, the *ekklēsía* is the assembly of the called, of those that have accepted the call and are ready to take up the responsibility of passing it on to others.

(b) The worship of Israel was meant to be a model for all nations. The services took place, of course, in their own context. Israel had been separated from the nations in order to worship the Lord. Yet as it worshiped the Lord in its own place and it own way, Israel worshiped the Lord publicly. Other nations might admire, ignore, or scoff. But Israel's prayers and thanksgivings and praises were not without significance for them.

The nations were invited, indeed, to join in the praises of Israel (Ps. 66:1-2; 98:2), along with all creatures. They were invited, too, to join in the thanksgivings (86:8-9) that glory might be adequately given to God's name and that the number of those that confess him as the only God and Savior might increase. Less commonly, they were invited to join in Israel's prayers. The nations might normally cry out to their god for help (Jon. 1:5), but even in OT days there were exceptions—Abimelech of Gerar (Gen. 20:3-5), Pharaoh (Exod. 12:32), and Naaman (2 Kgs. 5:1-19)—and the conviction is expressed that finally all nations will follow Israel's example (Isa. 45:22) and God's house will be "a house of prayer for all nations" (56:7). Paradoxically, the period of outward weakness was the period when the community became most conscious of the worldwide relevance of its worship.

(c) The importance of Israel's worship for the nations was due in no small measure to the role of their prophets in it. The prophets were sent with God's Word not only to Israel but to the nations. We recall, however, that their commissioning often took place during worship and that they would frequently deliver their messages in the temple court (cf. Isa. 6:1-13; Ezek. 1–3; Amos 1:2). Might it not be, then, that the sending of the prophets was representative of the sending of all Israel to be witnesses to God's Word? Israel was not always conscious of its prophetic vocation. A clear awareness developed only during the exile when the call of Isa. 40ff. came home that it should be a witness (Isa. 43:10), a servant, a messenger, divinely commissioned to testify to the nations (42:19), inviting them to acknowledge that the Lord is one and to focus their worship on him alone.

This message was not one of merely theoretical monotheism. It was the incomparably good news that brings freedom to Israel and every nation. Living increasingly in scattered groups among the peoples, Israelites willy-nilly became missionaries of the one God and Savior with a message for a world imprisoned in misery and oppression—a message that God's liberating acts for Israel itself already confirmed.

Israel had to proclaim this message by living as well as preaching. This would naturally entail fighting, resisting, and suffering for the sake of God's name: "In thy service I have suffered reproach" (Ps. 69:7). But the struggle was not without hope: "Those who sow in tears shall reap with songs of joy" (126:5). Worship had the function of guiding and equipping God's people for this prophetic ministry. Thanks to the worship that had Jerusalem as its center, the Israelites, for all their weaknesses and limitations, would have increasing influence outside their own nation and in this way play a role of immeasurable importance in the purpose of God and his kingdom.

5. God Promised the New Jerusalem

An aspect still calling for discussion is that of the renewal and con-summation of Jerusalem. Jerusalem became an (a) adulterous and (b) forsaken city, but God will (c) restore and perfect it as the heart of his new people in accordance with its initial vocation and function.

WE HAVE DISCUSSED JERUSALEM as the Lord's own city, the refuge of his people and center of the world, as the city of David, the birthplace of a just and sustainable society, and as the city of the temple, the place of God's presence and his people's worship. But the OT also presents Jerusalem as the focus of divine glory (Isa. 60:1-22) and the center of the new world that the Lord himself will create (65:17-25). As Revelation says in the NT, "I saw the holy city, new Jerusalem, coming down out of heaven from God" (21:1-2).

When we speak of the new Jerusalem, we recall that the prophets had to rebuke the old Jerusalem for its failure to live up to its vocation. The prophetic threats had finally come true with the capture and destruction of the city by the Babylonians. With this unparalleled disaster it seemed as though God's history with his chosen people and city had come to an end. The city was dead. Its life was past history. No hope could be seen for the future. It had become "old" Jerusalem in the ultimate meaning of the term. Without the failure and destruction of the old Jerusalem, however, we cannot understand the new. For the coming of the new would not have been possible without the death of the old. We need to look first, then, at the prophetic message, then at the destruction of the city, and finally at the prophecies of renewal.

a. The Adulterous City

God chose Jerusalem as his holy mountain, inspired David to make it his capital, and made the city the site of his holy house. These three divine acts gave Jerusalem its vocation. But did it live up to its vocation? Prophets like Isaiah, Micah, Zephaniah, Jeremiah, and Ezekiel boldly proclaimed from God that it did not. The chosen city that should have led Israel to the Lord led it instead in rebellion against him, to an abandonment of God like that of a husband by his wife. In consequence God would deliver up the city to dreadful judgment.

This message rang heavy in the ears of all those who heard it (Jer. 19:3). Leaders and people alike were shocked. We who already think of OT Jerusalem as sinful may find this hard to understand. A few examples might help us to realize how strange and startling the prophetic accusations must have been to the people of their own day who thought of their city as the city of God, of David, and of the temple.

(1) As the city of God, Jerusalem was meant to be the stronghold where Israel could live in security and prosperity. But did Israel really trust in God to provide it with protection? This became a burning issue when the city was assailed by the allied armies of Aram and Israel ca. 734 B.C. Instead of trusting in God, the court was panic-stricken. The problem arose again in 713 and 701 B.C. when Hezekiah had to defend his kingdom against the even more serious Assyrian menace. Instead of trusting in God, however, he was trying to secure protection from Egypt (Isa. 30:4). Isaiah's central accusation, then, was that the people did not really trust in God at all (30:1-2; cf. 28:14-15; 31:1ff.), even though this was the course of true wisdom. Lack of trust in God was for Isaiah the very core of Jerusalem's sin. There might be many other offenses, yet this was the stumbling stone (28:16), the life and death issue, the source of every other form of infidelity against God and his law.

(2) As the city of David, Jerusalem was called upon to be the model of a just and prosperous society. Its citizens were to live in freedom and justice, especially seeing to it that the weak received their rights. Instead, however, it had become a center of injustice and oppression, and for this reason God sent prophets from Micah to Ezekiel to remind it of its vocation and to rebuke it for its failure to live up to this vocation.

Micah complained sharply of bloodshed (3:9-10), the coveting and seizing of land and houses (2:1-2), robbery (2:7-8), and the perverting of justice by bribes (7:3). Isaiah castigated the city of justice as a home of murderers

(1:21) and complained of the heaping up of possessions (5:8), the acquitting of the guilty for money (5:23), and the despoiling of widows and orphans (10:2). A century later Jeremiah similarly criticized the shedding of innocent blood (2:34), the greed of the wealthy (5:27), the prevalence of fraud, and the depriving of workers of their wages (22:13). Ezekiel, while complaining primarily of idolatry, also censured the city for violence (7:23), the exploiting of aliens, the taking of usury, the oppression of orphans, and abhorrent sexual offenses (cf. 22:6ff.). Zephaniah was moved to say: "Shame on the tyrant city, filthy and foul" (3:1ff.). A city that did not trust God could no longer be a city of justice. The sacral and the social were closely interwoven.

(3) As the city where the house of the Lord stood, Jerusalem was called upon to lead Israel to true worship. But in this respect, too, it failed totally. So loud and numerous are the accusations of false worship that this more narrowly religious sin might seem to be the real sin of Jerusalem. The breaking of the first two commandments called for increasingly insistent prophetic criticism as the royal period came to its end.

Micah and Isaiah in the late 8th century B.C. did not specifically rebuke Jerusalem for idolatry as Hosea did Israel. Isaiah's complaint was that people ostentatiously celebrated the feasts but disregarded social justice (1:10-20). Micah, too, censured religious hypocrisy (6:6-8). It was Jeremiah who first compared Jerusalem to an adulteress (2:21ff.). In the first instance this charge might have applied to the North, but strictly it was Judah or Jerusalem that was playing the role of an adulterous wife, for instead of setting an example of the pure worship of God, it also found a place for idolatrous practices.

We see this clearly from Zephaniah, for whom syncretism was the primary offense, the mixture of religion that resulted from Judah's foreign policies (cf. 1:4-5). Ezekiel, too, was shocked at the defiling not only of the city but even of the temple itself "with all your vile and abominable rites" (5:11). Brought back to the temple courts in a vision, he saw there "the image of Lust" adored by the people (8:3-6). The beloved city had left the Lord and plunged into adulteries. She was even worse than her sister Samaria in shameless arrogance (ch. 16). Leaving the Lord, refusing to listen to the prophets, and offering to Baal and the host of heaven—these were the offenses that represented Jerusalem's most radical betrayal of its vocation and that would finally bring down upon it the divine condemnation (cf. Jer. 32:31; 33–34).

We thus reach the crushing conclusion. God had abundantly blessed Jerusalem. He had summoned it to a life in keeping with the gift that it had received. But the Jerusalemites refused. They did not accept their calling to be the city of God, the city of David, the city of the Lord's house. Thanks to the patience of God, there was a positive side to the picture. Some kings had attempted genuine reforms. In the main, however, God did not find the response that he expected and had a right to expect. That was the message of his servants the prophets.

b. The Forsaken City

In the summer of 586 B.C., Jerusalem fell. This was one of the most tragic events in Israel's history. Many OT passages mourn the death of the city. All Jewish writings recall it with sadness. The day of the fall is to this day a day of mourning.

In fact, of course, Jerusalem's fate was by no means exceptional. World history, and especially the history of the Middle East, knows many parallel events. The capitals of many small- and medium-sized kingdoms—Tyre and Sidon, Megiddo and Hazor, Rabbat-Ammon and Samaria—were all destroyed. Even such large and famous cities as Ur and Babylon, Asshur and Nineveh, Memphis and On, Ecbatana and Suza, were also laid in ruins. It could hardly be expected that Jerusalem would escape.

Many factors contributed to the city's fall. Its situation had grown more critical from the middle of the 8th century B.C. with attacks by Assyria first, then Babylon. The petty kings had tried in vain to secure some independence by paying tribute, offering sacrifices to alien gods, and allying with one another or with Egypt. These devices could not avert the growing threat. One after another the little kingdoms fell and were occupied, Israel in 722, Judah in 597 and 586. The kings of Judah and Israel had taken too great risks, underestimated the power of the enemy, and overestimated their own strength. Historically speaking, the fall of Jerusalem was inevitable.

The OT fully recognizes the political and military factors that led to the destruction of Jerusalem. The accounts in 2 Kgs. 23:31–25:21; Jer. 39:1-10; and 52:1-26 offer a realistic picture of the course of events. The resistance Judah put up to defend its independence may be admired but the miscalculations of the leaders are deplored. The focus of the OT witness, however, is not on the historical facts as such but on their place in God's involvement in human affairs. We shall look at this witness in three ways: first as a cry of pain and despair, then as a struggle to accept and understand the catastrophe, and finally as the acceptance of a new vocation.

(1) To understand what the fall of Jerusalem meant for the Lord's people we must listen first to those who experienced it. As groups gathered trying to come to terms with their fate, lamentations and prayers were raised both at home and in exile. Some of these have come down to us in Lamentations and Psalms.

There is lamentation for the city: "How solitary lies the city, once so full of people! Once great among nations, now become a widow; once queen among provinces, now put to forced labour!" (Lam. 1:1). This was no ordinary capital but the city once called "Perfect in beauty" (2:15), the "footstool" of the Lord (2:1), the "throne of [God's] glory" (Jer. 14:21), God's "home" (Ps. 74:2). God's city had now fallen into foreign hands, the land had lost its holiness, God's people had forfeited their right to live there.

Jerusalem had been David's city, but no king of David's house was left. "The Lord's anointed . . . was caught in their machinations; although we had thought to live among the nations, safe under his protection" (Lam. 4:20). The Lord himself had plainly rejected his anointed king, "spurned him and raged against him," "denounced the covenant" with him, and "laid his fortresses in ruin" (Ps. 89:38-40).

The outcry at the destruction of the city of God's temple is even louder. The Lord had "stripped his tabernacle as a vine is stripped" and "laid a curse upon his sanctuary" (Lam. 2:6-7). Enemies had set fire to the temple and polluted the sacred shrine (Ps. 74:3-7). Ruined beyond repair, the holy temple had been defiled (Ps. 79:1; cf. Lam. 1:10).

The destruction of the city and temple was obviously the work of foreign enemies, first Babylon, then neighboring states that had seized the occasion to humiliate the powerless city. Feelings of hatred and revenge find a place, then, in the laments (Ps. 137; 79:10-12; Lam. 1:22). Judgment will fall in turn upon these peoples (Ezek. 35; Obadiah). Yet the desolate community also realized that its enemies could have done nothing had not the Lord let them do it. Does not God rule the whole world? Had he, then, changed his mind? "It is my grief that the right hand of the Most High has changed" (Ps. 77:10 RSV). He who was Israel's keeper (12:4) now seemed not to care any more. "Bestir thyself, Lord; why dost thou sleep . . . heedless of our misery and our sufferings?" (44:23-24). The possibility that the Lord had forgotten Zion haunted the community like a nightmare (Lam. 2:1; Ps. 74:19).

Another possibility, of course, was that the Lord was angry with Zion: "Why art thou . . . so angry with the sheep of thy flock?" (Ps. 74:1). For how long? (79:5). Had he rejected Jerusalem forever? Did he no longer view Israel as his people? How could he ever cast off his people? Yet it seemed to have happened (44:10; Lam. 1:45; Jer. 14:19).

In their despair the people could even think that the Lord himself had become their enemy, destroyed the city, and killed and scattered its inhabitants (Lam. 2:2, 5, 8, 21; Ps. 89:39-41). The bitter realization struck that God had forsaken his city, his king, and his sanctuary. "Zion says, 'The Lord has forsaken me; my God has forgotten me'" (Isa. 49:14; Lam. 2:7; 5:20).

Why did the disaster happen? Why did it fall on Jerusalem? It is a question that Israel, like many another people, raised despairingly in its agony. To be forsaken by God is to be delivered up irrevocably to death. Jerusalem was cut off from the Lord. It had no hope. Its story had apparently ended, and with it the story of Israel as the Lord's chosen people.

But was the story truly finished? Amos had already said so: "The end has come upon my people Israel" (8:1-3 RSV). Ezekiel could say the same of Jerusalem: "The end is now upon you" (7:3). There could be no future indeed for the dead city. The survivors could only weep and mourn. Things could change only if the Lord himself would speak again and give new meaning to the event.

(2) As the community continued to struggle, it arrived at a new attitude to God's Word. Believers in their misery had felt severed from the Lord, as if no Word of God would ever be heard again (Lam. 2:9; Ps. 74:9). In the midst of this emptiness a new hunger arose for the Word. Keener attention was paid to prophecy. A new interest developed in Amos, Hosea, Micah, Isaiah, Jeremiah, and Zephaniah. The congregation began to see that far from forgetting his people, the Lord had already spoken and was still speaking.

During the exile worship had to be in the simplest form. Believers would come together in houses. The traditional offerings could not be made. Reading God's Word gained in importance, the Prophets as well as the Torah. This reading gave a new tone to the services. People might still complain. They might still express hatred of the enemy. But they also began to see their own responsibility for the catastrophe and to repent honestly and humbly.

The Lord had never been unfaithful or uncaring. It was the community itself that had shown no care for the Lord and broken faith with him. The Lord had indeed been silent. He had hidden his face and forsaken Zion for a brief moment (Isa. 54:7). Yet he still cared for his people. He was still faithful. Even in condemnation he was still speaking. For a long time the Israelites had closed their ears, but now in exile they were ready to listen. This revolutionary change came to expression in confessions of sin (Lam. 1:18; 2:14; 4:6).

"O Lord, turn us back to thyself, and we will come back; renew our days as in times long past" (Lam. 5:21). This petition shows clearly that the people longed for inward renewal even more than for outward restoration. They had acknowledged their sin (5:16); they were now oriented to the future. For any hope of continued life they had to turn around, to change their thoughts and words and deeds, to become a new people. But there could be such a renewal only if the Lord himself helped. Only by coming back to the Lord as the Lord turned them back could the people have real hope for the future.

The Hebrew verb *šûb* ("to turn back") often has the sense "to repent," i.e., to turn away from wickedness, but the verb as such is neutral. It might denote change for either the better or the worse. A wicked person can give up wicked ways, but a righteous person can also turn back from righteous ways (Ezek. 18:21, 24). God may turn in another direction (Jer. 4:28; 12:15; Hos. 11:9; Jon. 3:9), whether to punish or to pity his people. Different renderings of *šûb*, then, are needed as the context suggests.

Where did this desire for renewal come from (Lam. 5:21)? The mere fact of the destruction of Jerusalem and the foreign occupation and exile could never have produced it alone. Like the people's awareness of their own failings, it could come only from the impact of God's Word through the prophets. The people were now studying the prophetic admonitions and threats that they had hitherto ignored. Realizing that the prophetic message was true, they wished to come back to the Lord. They longed for a renewal of the very roots of their existence as a people.

Could they be persuaded that in the disaster God had not only passed judgment on his apostate people but also healed them of their apostasy? Had the will to resist God crumbled with the walls of Jerusalem? If so, the destruction of the city opened up a new possibility of life. God had to condemn the people, but by this very condemnation he had shown compassion on his people. He had invited them to let themselves be renewed. As the later prophets would proclaim, Jerusalem was not dead forever. It was about to begin a new life, to be rebuilt in a new glory.

c. Jerusalem, the Heart of the New People of God

The old Jerusalem symbolizes the Israel that had turned away from God and that God had thus left to its own devices. But the city is to rise from the dead and become the new and perfect community that it has been called to be from the very first. In itself Jerusalem is not the eternal city as cities like Rome or Istanbul proudly claim to be. Its only strength is that of the Lord acting with unexpected initiatives to fulfil his plan of salvation. We must now consider the divine promises of the coming new Jerusalem that will consummate God's involvement in the history of this city.

We shall develop the theme in three parts. First, we must look at the *content* of the biblical promises and try to distinguish the different categories. Second, we must discuss the *form* and *nature* of the new Jerusalem, asking whether its glory belongs only to the distant future or is already present in a hidden way. Third, we must meditate upon the *meaning* of the promises and their weight and authority for the people of God that heard and hears them.

(1) In previous sections we have considered three aspects of Jerusalem's election and vocation: Zion the city of God, Zion the city of David, and Zion the city of the temple. Elements of this threefold election and vocation are present again in the failure of Jerusalem and the ensuing disaster. It is to be expected, then, that we shall find them, too, in prophecies of the new

Jerusalem. This time, however, the three aspects are more closely linked and finally merge into a unity, so that we cannot treat them in isolation.

We begin with prophecies that refer generally to the renewal of the city. For a town that lies in ruins the first aspect of renewal is reconstruction. As we read in Mic. 7:11: "That will be a day for rebuilding your walls, a day when your frontiers will be extended." The Lord says of Jerusalem, " 'She shall be inhabited once more', and of the cities of Judah, 'They shall be rebuilt' " (Isa. 44:26). How splendid the new city will be (Isa. 54:11-12)! How strong and secure it will be! "We have a strong city; [God] sets up salvation as walls and bulwarks" (26:1-2 RSV).

New walls alone do not guarantee the promised renewal. The new Jerusalem will be truly erected only when it has again been elected. But this, too, is God's promise. He says to Zion: "You are my people" (51:16). He takes back the wife he had forsaken: "You shall wed him who rebuilds you" (62:4-5). The Lord "once again . . . will make Jerusalem the city of his choice" (Zech. 1:17).

It is not merely in a general sense, however, that Jerusalem will be renewed, restored, and perfected. It will again be the city of God, the place of his dwelling on earth, the place where his people find refuge and security. "Cry out . . . you that dwell in Zion, for the Holy One of Israel is among you in majesty" (Isa. 12:6). "The Lord your God is in your midst, like a warrior, to keep you safe . . . he will show you his love once more" (Zeph. 3:17). The Lord will come, or return, to his holy mountain (Isa. 40:10).

Coming to dwell in Jerusalem, God will shower blessings on its citizens: "Arise, Jerusalem . . . the glory of the Lord shines over you" (Isa. 60:1-3). The city will again be a place of refuge (54:14; Zech. 12:8; Joel 3:16). It will be like the garden of God (Isa. 51:30). Its inhabitants "shall draw water with joy from the springs of deliverance" (12:3; cf. Gen. 2:10; Isa. 33:21; Ezek. 47:1-12; Zech. 14:8). The population will increase sharply (Zech. 8:4-6), life expectancy will be high (Isa. 33:24; Jer. 33:6), and joyful sounds will be heard in the streets (Jer. 33:9-11).

In the city of God, the world's center, there will be blessings for foreign nations as well. Many of these were notorious enemies of Israel and at first their hostility might increase (Zech. 12:9). The Lord himself will intervene, however, and "all who survive of the nations which attacked Jerusalem shall come up . . . to worship the King, the Lord of Hosts" (Zech. 14:16; cf. 2:11; Isa. 56:6; 60:3-4; 66:18-21; Jer. 3:17; Isa. 2:2-4 par. Mic. 4:1-3).

As foreign nations share unexpectedly in blessing, Jerusalem itself will be richly blessed by their coming: "You shall possess the wealth of nations" (Isa. 60:5-7). The nation's tribute of gratitude will far exceed any former tribute paid to Israel's kings (1 Kgs. 10:10-11; Ps. 72:10-11). Erstwhile oppressors will be ready to serve Zion (Isa. 60:10; 61:6; 66:20). These people belong already to the people of God. They gather in God's city both to confess the Lord with their mouth and to serve him freely in personal dedication.

The renewal of Jerusalem means also that it will be restored in majesty as the city of David. As the city of God Jerusalem was chosen to be the capital of a kingdom, a *polis,* a political community, a society that enables all its members to live peacefully together in freedom, justice, and wisdom. The destruction of the city ended the story of its failure to build a just and sustainable society. But it also began a new history—for God does not abandon the work of his hands.

Many prophecies envision Jerusalem as again the capital of an independent, safe, just, and prosperous kingdom. "Then at length you shall be called the home of righteousness, the faithful city" (Isa. 1:26). "In righteousness you shall be established" (54:14 RSV). "I will make your government be peace and righteousness rule over you. The sound of violence shall be heard no longer in your land" (60:17-18, 21-22). As we read in Amos: "I will restore David's fallen house" (9:11-12), or in Micah: "The Lord shall be their king on Mount Zion . . . your former sovereignty shall come again" (4:7-8; cf. Isa. 33:5; Rev. 21:2).

But how will David's fallen house be restored? How will Jerusalem become the strong and perfect city of David? The answer lies in the righteous King of the future, the true descendant of David. It is the function of this just King to renew Jerusalem as the capital of a new kingdom, the center of a new world.

The new Jerusalem will become a reality with the enthronement of the son of Isa. 9:5-6: "Boundless [shall be] the peace bestowed on David's throne . . . to establish it and sustain it with justice and righteousness from now and for evermore" (9:7). Similarly, the reign of the shoot of Jesse will bring peace "in all my holy mountain" and to the whole land (11:1ff.), even the whole earth (RSV). Again, in the days of the righteous Branch "Judah shall be kept safe, and Israel shall live undisturbed" (Jer. 23:5-6). So strong will be the rule of justice that Jerusalem will even receive refugees from hostile Moab (Isa. 16:1-5). It might seem impossible that Jerusalem should shelter its enemies, but it will now be a stronghold of righteousness beyond all human possibilities and hence a place where refugees of every nation will find a welcome.

Jerusalem will be renewed, too, as the city of the temple. The best-known promise in this regard is to be found in the great vision of Ezek. 40–48, which has the return of the divine glory at its center (43:1-12). Cyrus ordered the building of the postexilic temple in 536 B.C. (Ezra 1:2), but the work was slow and the results were disappointing. Haggai, however, prophesied that "the glory of this latter house shall surpass the glory of the former" (2:8-10), and Zechariah promised that eventually the nations would come as pilgrims to

God's house at Jerusalem and even become part of God's people (2:10-11). The peoples will say: "Come, let us climb up on to the mountain of the Lord, to the house of the God of Jacob, that he may teach us his ways" (Isa. 2:2-4). God will give foreigners joy in his house of prayer (56:6-8). In this way, says God, "glory shall be added to glory in my temple" (60:3-7).

Naturally, worship in the new temple will be free of the hypocrisy that led to the destruction of the old. People will wholeheartedly pray, give thanks, present offerings, and keep the feasts, so that the Lord can delight in them (Ps. 51:18-19). The new congregation "shall be called a Holy People, the Ransomed of the Lord" (Isa. 62:12). Restoration of the temple building in material glory would be futile were there no new people of God to live up to its calling. When perfect worship is offered, then "you shall know that I am the Lord your God, dwelling in Zion my holy mountain" (Joel 3:17).

(2) A question arises: Where is this wonderful new Jerusalem? Have God's promises been fulfilled already? Or is the new Jerusalem only a future reality? What is the nature of the new Jerusalem?

It is easy to suppose that the holy city is no more than a fruit of human fantasy. Our 20th-century tendency is to discredit visions as unreal, as mere dreams. We respect religious traditions, but with growing modernization and secularization we view the promises of a new Jerusalem, and even of the coming kingdom of God, as no more than dreams of a utopia that can never become a reality.

The message of God's Word, however, is that God will renew and perfect his city. The fulfilment of the promise is not yet visible, but in God's eyes the content of his Word is already a reality. God's new world is even more real than the old world that we now see. His Word has the authority to convince us that the new and hidden reality does in truth exist. A brief discussion of biblical prophecy, vision, and promise might help us in our approach to the mystery of the reality of the new Jerusalem.

First, the relevant texts almost all have the form of divinely inspired prophecies. Prophets transmitted the word they had received from God, not their own wishes or dreams or opinions. The content of their message thus had the authority of God's own Word and was to be believed as such.

The Bible distinguishes, of course, between true and false prophecies. One test of false prophecy was when it was pleasing to the people. Those who prophesied good in the name of the Lord were suspect (cf. Micaiah and the false prophets in 1 Kgs. 22:1-28, or Jeremiah and Hananiah in Jer. 28:2ff.). How, then, could it be known that the promises of restoration for Jerusalem were true and not false?

Another test was that of facts. If a prophecy came to fulfilment, then it was obviously true, like the prophecy of judgment, not deliverance, for Israel and Judah. But this proof cannot be adduced at the time when the prophecy is uttered.

Another test was that of content relative to God. Does the prophecy confront the people with the living God who is always just and always merciful? An authoritative message of condemnation always contains an element of mercy, a message of love and salvation never lacks an element of judgment. False prophets predict deliverance for Jerusalem without the condemnation that falls on other nations. Dreams of this kind have no basis in reality. Prophets who are truly sent by God may announce that Jerusalem will one day be renewed and perfected, but first it must be destroyed. These prophets respect God's holiness. They may thus bring a message of mercy that is a true and authoritative Word from God.

Second, the glory of the new Jerusalem is described in images. This is not surprising, for the prophecies often take the form of visions, which can be communicated only with the help of a vivid imagination. Visions are sometimes taken literally, sometimes taken as poetry that we must demythologize, sometimes seen as an indication that the new Jerusalem will be totally heavenly and spiritual. Which of these possibilities of interpretation should we choose?

A few examples will perhaps help. We are told that the mountain of the Lord "shall be set over all other mountains" (Isa. 2:2). Jerusalem will be built of gold, silver, jewels, and precious stones (54:11-12). The sun and moon will fade before the glory of the Lord shining on his holy city (60:19-20). Jerusalem will be like Eden (51:3), a place of harmony and peace (11:6ff.; 35:9-10; 60:18). Its inhabitants will enjoy good health (33:24) and live to a ripe age (65:20-23). Death will be swallowed up forever (25:8). The city itself is compared to a bride (61:10), a woman giving birth (66:7ff.), also a fixed tent (33:20). The Lord is like "a wall of fire round her" (Zech. 2:4-5).

To understand these comparisons we must recall the old Jerusalem on the one side, the city that God chose but that he forsook when it betrayed him, and the new Jerusalem on the other, the city that he has chosen and will renew and perfect in glory. The reference in both cases is to the real city on the mountains of Judah with its streets, walls, and buildings, its people and cattle, and its three or four millennia of history. It is this real city that laments the present and looks ahead to the future. It will still be a real city when it is born anew and clothed in glory. The renewal will be at God's initiative. It will succeed in the power of his Spirit. But this does not mean that Jerusalem will become purely spiritual and celestial. It will still belong to this world.

The perfection to which God will bring the city will surpass anything that the human mind can imagine. The miracle of new creation (Isa. 65:17-18) can be described only with symbols. Visions and dreams point to facts that are beyond the reach of the mind. Comparisons serve as mirrors of an inconceivable perfection. The visions may not become reality in every detail. Nevertheless, they are not just an extravagant way of speaking, nor do they simply give expression to a purely spiritual reality. The point is the simple one that the new Jerusalem will be far more perfect and glorious than any human description can portray.

Third, the future glory of Jerusalem is a matter of promise. The fulfilment may come in either the near or the distant future. But this raises again the question of the concrete reality of the new Jerusalem. Normally a gift that we receive now has for us more value than a promised gift. We therefore tend to devalue the prophetic promises. This assessment might be justified if all we had were wishful thinking. In fact, however, the promises are promises of more than an unknown future.

The relevant prophecies are usually in the future tense: "Justice *shall* redeem Zion" (Isa. 1:27; cf. 16:5; 25:7; Jer. 3:17). When will this happen? The answer is vague: "At that time" (Jer. 3:17), "on that day" (Isa. 11:10), "that will be a day" (Mic. 7:11), "when that time comes" (Joel 3:1), "in days to come" (Isa. 2:2). We do not yet find the expressions "last day" or "end of time" (cf. 1 Thess. 5:1-2). The main point is that the promises will be fulfilled when the Lord will come, return, or be present in his glory (Isa. 2:2-4; 24:34; 27:13; Jer. 3:17; Ezek. 43:1ff.; Joel 3:16-17; Zeph. 3:15-17; Zech. 1:16; Ps. 102:16; etc.).

The future of Jerusalem is linked to the Lord's presence in it. At the time when it pleases him to come and stay in Jerusalem as its King and Protector, the city will be renewed and perfected. Renewal can take place only when the Lord is there. The two themes are so closely linked that they belong together. What is promised is identical to him who gives the promise. The Lord has promised this city a glorious future, but he himself is this future. He so shares in the city's life that he becomes its future. No imaginable future could be more perfect than the Lord's very presence.

Inasmuch as the renewal of Jerusalem is linked to the Lord's presence, the day of fulfilment cannot be pinned down to a calendar day. In past, present, or future, whenever the Lord is willing to come as King and Immanuel, the old Jerusalem begins to change into the new, the new heaven and earth begin to replace the world that is so full of disorder due to human faults. In Psalms we find clear witness to this work of renewal that is going on in the dark world. The new Jerusalem, the new earth, the new humanity, or, in NT terms, the kingdom of God or of heaven, is not yet consummated, but in God's eyes it is already a reality. For believers the renewal begins in their own lifetime insofar as the Lord manifests his presence. God's invisible presence is the renewing power.

(3) Why is the new Jerusalem still invisible apart from a few

glimpses? Why has the promise not yet been fulfilled? These questions point to an aspect of the promises that is often seen as their weakness but is ultimately their true strength. It *pleases* God to promise first. By so doing he gives those for whom he creates his city the time and opportunity to accept their vocation and share in his work. Because the new earth is still to come we have the chance to serve God as his officers, helpmates, and fellow workers.

This final point shows that what the promises bring is good news, gospel. They give us comfort. What kind of comfort?

The verb "to comfort" (*nāham;* cf. the names Menahem, Nahum, Nehemiah) is found in many of the promises to Zion: "Comfort, comfort my people" (Isa. 40:1-2; cf. 49:13; 52:9; 66:13-14); "Once again the Lord will comfort Zion, once again he will make Jerusalem the city of his choice" (Zech. 1:17).

These passages show first that when God comforts he takes away fear. Zion had lived in fear of enemies, of occupying powers, and of God himself, lest he might leave it forever. The fear was largely due to awareness of failure. Taking away fear, the word of comfort was thus a word of forgiveness: "Her penalty is paid" (Isa. 40:2; 12:1; 43:25). Forgiveness removes the fear of enemies, no matter how powerful or treacherous they may be (41:11-16; 51:12; 54:14). As Paul could later say: "If God is on our side, who is against us?" (Rom. 8:31). This is the confidence that comfort brings to God's people in every time and place.

When he comforts, God also takes away sorrow (Isa. 65:17; 66:10-11). It is a universal custom to visit the suffering and bereaved (2 Sam. 10:2-3; Jer. 16:7; Job 2:11) and to express sympathy by word or sign. But well-meant comfort of that kind cannot take away sorrow. When Jerusalem was destroyed no one gave her "the cup of consolation" (Jer. 16:7; cf. Lam. 1:2, 8, 16, 21; Isa. 54:11). There was no healing for so deep a sorrow, so dark a despair, so serious a wound. The Lord alone could comfort. He could comfort because he did not merely express his sympathy but suffered himself with the condemnation of his people. As H. W. Robinson shows in his book *The Cross in the Old Testament* (1955, pp. 181ff.), Jeremiah grasped this point. The Lord himself was disappointed, hurt, and wounded (Jer. 2:5ff.; 12:7ff.). His was a greater sorrow (Jer. 45). His sharing of the suffering lifted the burden. Joy and gladness replaced sorrow (Isa. 51:3; Zech. 2:10). Sorrow could be overcome and joy could flourish when God's solidarity with his people was understood and it was realized that forgiveness is the result of God's own struggle.

When he comforts, God also sets his people moving, so that they have a part themselves in the fulfilment of the promises. The comfort of the promises is not just that of soothing. The people with the promise of a glorious future have not just to sit back confidently and wait for it. God has liberated his people from fear and sorrow. He has taken away the burden of past iniquity. He has firmly promised total salvation. But with the word of liberation God also challenges, motivates, and even orders his people to act, to confront the disorder of the present. In comforting God challenges and in challenging he comforts. The cry goes out: "Awake, awake; rise up, Jerusalem" (Isa. 51:17; 52:1-2; 60:1). Giddy, lying in the dust, Jerusalem must rouse itself and stand and put on the waiting garment of glory. It has a glorious vision, but not one that it may just passively acknowledge. It must be up and doing. With this hope it is even to seek the welfare of the city in which it is exiled (Jer. 29:7, 11 RSV). Any constructive effort in any part of the world contributes indirectly to the building of the new Jerusalem. Jeremiah was to buy a field in Anathoth with a view to the future (32:6-15). Exiles were moved to go and "rebuild the house of the Lord . . . whose city is Jerusalem" (Ezra 1:1ff.). Haggai inspired Zerubbabel and Joshua to take the lead in this enterprise (Hag. 2:5-7). With God's help Nehemiah set the people to work "vigorously and to good purpose" to complete the city walls (Neh. 2:17-20). Having a word of hope, the people could act with discipline. Freed from fear, sorrow, and apathy, they could accept rules that are appropriate to the free (cf. Ezek. 45:9-12; Zech. 8:16-17). They had the motivation to lead a more just and cooperative social life, banning idolatry (Isa. 57:6-13), shunning marriages with foreign women (Ezra 9–10), and engaging in sincere fasting (Isa. 58:13-14). This discipline was the result of an inner renewal which was itself the work of the Spirit (Ezek. 36:24-28; Jer. 31:31ff.) through the word of divine comfort.

In comforting, God also gives his people orientation. He shows them that they are on the way to the day of fulfilment. There is present renewal, but the core of comfort lies in the future. The basis of hope, God himself in his glory, who alone can make all things new, transcends the reality that we can comprehend with the senses and lies beyond the boundary of our human lifetime. The gaze is thus lifted from the present to the future. As Balaam put it, "I see him, but not now; I behold him, but not near" (Num. 24:17). The comforted people do not cling to the present, good or bad. They see the present in the light of what will finally be manifest. Even when rebuilding Jerusalem, they keep in view the new Jerusalem that God himself builds (cf. Ps. 127:1-2). Reality has to be seen without illusions, but we must also raise our eyes, lift them up and look all around, and see the coming perfection (Isa. 49:18; 60:4), namely, the Lord himself, who will finish his work (Ps. 121:1; 123:1-2). Biblical realism (cf. Hendrik Kraemer) is the right term for this type of vision.

"O my enemies, do not exult over me; I have fallen, but shall rise again" (Mic. 7:8). These words echo Jerusalem's experience of defeat, failure, suffering, and struggle prior to the day of liberation (v. 11). More amazing than the grief, however, was the people's patience and constancy. The Lord's promise gave it strength and enabled it to stand firm until it won (Ps. 126:5-6).

Even under attack, it could prevail (129:1-2). It had a vision and could thus tell itself: "If it delays, wait for it; for when it comes will be no time to linger" (Hab. 2:3). In the words of Ps. 130:5: "I wait for the Lord with all my soul, I hope for the fulfilment of his word." Israel had to hope for the fulfilment of God's promises. But did it really hope with confidence and believe unafraid? Fundamentally, neither hope nor faith is ever a sure possession of God's people. God has to comfort them again and again with his promise, thus emboldening them to believe and hope from day to day as a pilgrim people on their way to the promised city. The Lord, the Creator of heaven and earth, keeps faith with this human earth of his. He does not give up what he has begun. He gives vigor to the tired, so that "they will run and not be weary, they will march on and never grow faint" (Isa. 40:28-31).

A final question is this: Who was this people that God comforted and liberated and set on its way with a strong hope? We Christians of every continent and century have to be reminded that the message was not for us first. The citizens of Jerusalem, Israelites according to the flesh, were the primary recipients of the promises of God (cf. Rom. 9:4-5). As a people that was called later, we may not step higher than those who preceded us nor than those who have not yet heard God's call but may still do so. The coming kingdom of God is but one, and the symbol and center of this kingdom is the new Jerusalem.

Chapter IX

God Sent His Prophets

Introduction

AS WE TAKE UP OUR FINAL TOPIC, the sending of the prophets, we must bear in mind that Israel was not the only people to have prophets. As most religions have deities, temples, gatherings for worship, and sacred rules, so many of them, and not merely the so-called prophetic religions (Judaism, Christianity, and Islam), refer also to prophets. The character and authority of prophets may differ, but formally they are always ordinary men or women who claim to have had a divine revelation or vision; who have been endowed with spiritual gifts enabling them to speak with authority, to see the future, or to work miracles; who have gone out as divine delegates proclaiming the divine will or judgment or promise to the community at large, notwithstanding opposition; and who have often shared their mission with disciples and thus formed the nucleus of a new believing community.

A constant problem that we have met already in the OT was that of distinguishing between true prophets and false. Meeting the formal criteria did not of itself guarantee authenticity. Anyone might claim to have a divine revelation or vision, but fact and claim do not necessarily converge. The OT itself speaks of false prophets who could not always be differentiated immediately from the prophets that had a real message from God. In the event, however, the OT bears witness to true prophets whom God sent to his people Israel. Our focus, then, must be on these prophets.

1. The Witness of Scripture

The Lord, the God of Israel and King of the world, acted always according to his own plan and purpose, but was also pleased to let

[304]

*his people know what he did by (a) sending them men and women to
speak his Word. (b) He himself sent the prophets as (c) one of his
great acts (d) in the context of all his other acts.*

IN DISCUSSING THE PROPHETS we must consider (a) the biblical material relating to their sending, (b) the biblical basis of the topic, (c) their sending as a
great act of God, and (d) the relation of this topic to others.

a. The Sending of the Prophets

The prophetic books contain information about the sending and experiences
of the prophets as well as the prophecies themselves. Additional relevant
material may be found in the historical books.

In the meeting between Abraham and Abimelech of Gerar (Gen. 20:1ff.), Abraham has
the role of a prophet (v. 8). Moses, too, has a prophetic mission (Exod. 3:1-4, 17).
Aaron fulfils the function of a prophet (7:1), and Miriam is called a prophetess (15:20).
In the wilderness the Spirit comes on seventy elders who then help Moses in his
prophetic office (Num. 11:16-17, 24-30). Balaam, the son of Beor, was an unwilling
prophet when three times he blessed Israel. Deborah, a leader against Sisera, was both
judge and prophetess (Judg. 4:4-5). A nameless prophet rebuked the tribes (6:11-24),
and a nameless man of God rebuked Eli and pronounced judgment on his sons (1 Sam.
2:27-36). Samuel was a prophet as well as a judge (1 Sam. 3:1–4:1). Nathan and Gad
were two prophets under David (2 Sam. 7:1ff.; 24:10-14). Ahijah of Shiloh rebuked
Jeroboam (1 Kgs. 14:1ff.; 15:29-30). Shemaiah forbade Rehoboam to wage war on
Israel (1 Kgs. 12:21-24). Jehu, the son of Hanani, spoke several oracles against Baasha
and Elah of Israel (16:1-4, 7, 12-13).
    We learn more about Elijah of Tishbe in Gilead (1 Kgs. 17–19; 21; 2 Kgs.
1–2). He rebuked Ahab and prophesied a drought (1 Kgs. 17:1ff.), helped the widow
and her son (17:7-24), met the civil servant Obadiah (18:1ff.), challenged and defeated
the prophets of Baal on Mt. Carmel (18:21-46), journeyed to Horeb (19:1ff.), called
Elisha (19:19-21), reprimanded Ahab for seizing Naboth's vineyard (21:1-29), rebuked
Ahaziah (2 Kgs. 1:1-17), and was finally taken up into heaven (2:1ff.).
    Elisha, who followed Elijah, purified the water at Jericho (2:19-22), cursed
the children who jeered at him (2:23-25), prophesied success for Jehoram and Jehoshaphat (3:4-27), helped a prophet's widow (4:1-7) and a woman of Shunem and her
son (4:8-37), made the food safe to eat and fed a hundred people (4:38ff.), healed
Naaman (5:1ff.), made iron float (6:1ff.), saved the king of Israel from the Aramaeans
and also saved Samaria (6:8ff.), prophesied in Damascus (8:7-15), called Jehu to be
king (9:1-13), foretold victory for Jehoash (13:14-19), and still worked wonders after
his death (13:20-21).
    Among other prophets Micaiah, the son of Imlah, opposed false prophets and
foretold Ahab's death (1 Kgs. 22:1ff.) and Jonah, the son of Amittai, prophesied the

victory of Jeroboam II of Israel (2 Kgs. 14:23-27). Isaiah, the son of Amoz, brought a message of salvation to Hezekiah (19:1ff.) and helped him when sick (20:1ff.), but later rebuked him for pride (20:12-19). Anonymous prophets foretold condemnation for the wrongdoings of Manasseh (21:1-15). Under Josiah the prophetess Huldah also prophesied disaster. Chronicles additionally mentions Heman, David's seer (1 Chron. 25:5); Azariah, the son of Oded, under King Asa (2 Chron. 15:1ff.); Zechariah, who suffered martyrdom under Joash (24:19-22); a nameless prophet (25:14-16); and Oded in Samaria (28:9-15). Jeremiah also refers to Uriah the son of Shemaiah, who was put to death in the reign of Jehoiakim (Jer. 26:20-24).

The biblical references to seers, servants or men of God, and prophets or prophetesses are truly impressive. Not for nothing did the Jews call the historical books the Former Prophets. The very existence of Israel as the Lord's people would in fact be inconceivable without the prophetic witness.

b. God Sent His Servants the Prophets

We stress first that God himself was acting. He took the initiative. He worked through the prophets. To say this is not to belittle human responsibility. The stories of the prophets are stories of action and suffering. The prophets were no passive tools. They were set in motion by God. Yet the OT shows clearly that it was God who made them prophets. He alone raises up true prophets (Deut. 18:15, 18).

God *sent* his servants the prophets. The verb "send" is chosen deliberately. Other verbs might be used. We could say that God revealed himself or spoke to the prophets, that he called them, that he put his Spirit on them. "Send," however, corresponds best to the total biblical witness.

Some examples will show that the verb "to send" *(šālaḥ)* was widely used with reference to the prophets. God said to Moses: "Come now; I will send you to Pharaoh. . . . This shall be the proof that it is I who have sent you" (Exod. 3:10, 12; cf. v. 15; Acts 7:34-35). Among the sent we might also mention the judges Gideon (Judg. 6:14), Jephthah, and Samuel (1 Sam. 12:11) and the prophets Nathan (2 Sam. 12:1), Gad (24:13), Ahijah (1 Kgs. 14:6), Isaiah (6:8), Jeremiah (1:7), and Ezekiel (2:3).

Another important term for a prophet is *mal'āk* ("messenger"). Though the OT can use this word for heavenly messengers, i.e., angels, it also uses it for the human messengers whom God sent. The "angel" of Judg. 13:3 is a "man of God" in v. 8. The noun *mal'āk* is from the root *l'k*, which means much the same as *šālaḥ*. Being sent, the prophet was a *mal'āk* (cf. Mal. 1:1; 3:1). The NT later gave the same designation to John the Baptist, and it is the background of the NT *apostéllō* and *apóstolos*.

Divine sending characterizes a prophet. Personal conviction and dedication may play a role, along with the ability to communicate and influence.

But the decisive factor lies beyond human gifts or feelings. It lies in the act of God who sends a person to be his prophet.

c. God's Sending as One of His Great Acts

Divine sending might be a constant and constitutive factor in prophecy, but are we right to see it as one of God's great acts? Is it true that the OT puts it on the same level as the acts by which God constituted Israel? Was it a saving act that retains its meaning and gives hope for the future? Is it a subject of confession, thanksgiving, and praise?

The Psalms seldom praise the sending of the prophets. Thanks are given for Moses and Aaron: "his mouthpiece to announce his signs" (Ps. 105:26-27; cf. 77:20; 103:7). Samuel is also mentioned among those who call on God's name (99:6). But the theme is hardly a traditional topic of praise.

Teaching formulations are more positive. Thus we read in Hos. 12:10: "I spoke through the prophets in parables," and in Amos 2:10-11: "I raised up prophets from your sons." In Jer. 6:16-17 God appointed watchmen to direct his people. Reminders of the prophets also occur in Nehemiah's confession (Neh. 9:26, 29-30) and Daniel's prayer: "the prophets, who spoke in thy name to our kings and princes" (Dan. 9:6).

In historical summaries Moses plays a prominent role: "I sent Moses and Aaron" is said in Josh. 24:5, and the sending of Moses, Aaron, Jerubbaal, Barak, Jephthah, and Samuel is recalled in 1 Sam. 12:8-10. Micah reminds Israel that God sent Moses, Aaron, and Miriam, and also Balaam (Mic. 6:2ff.). The sending of Moses is a proof of God's unfailing love in Isa. 63:7ff.

In passages such as these the sending of the prophets is indeed one of God's great acts. Through Moses, Aaron, and Miriam he delivered his people from Egyptian bondage. Through Deborah and Samuel he saved them from imminent destruction. Through prophet after prophet he proved his faithfulness to Israel. It was a sign of his grace when there was a prophet from the Lord in Israel (2 Kgs. 3:11). "Hunger . . . for hearing the word of the Lord" (Amos 8:11) gives indirect evidence of the great esteem in which the prophets were held, as does the work of writing down and preserving their prophecies.

d. Relation to Other Topics of Israel's Faith

If the sending of the prophets is a basic element in the witness of the OT, we must also ask what its relation is to the other topics of Israel's faith. Generally speaking, the relation is close. God's great acts are seldom mentioned without some reference to the contribution of a prophet sent by God. Conversely, God's sending of a prophet was almost always connected with one of his mighty deeds. The theological dimensions of the divine acts are often made clear only in the prophetic message, and conversely the preaching of the prophets makes sense only in the context of the acts.

Three topics are more loosely related to the sending of the prophets: creation, the raising up of kings, and the election of Jerusalem. Nevertheless, the prophets helped Israel to see that creation is not a myth but a saving act that God directs toward the new world that he purposes, that he raised up kings as servants responsible to himself for his people's welfare, and that the primary reason for the glorifying of Jerusalem is that God chose it to be his own city.

As regards the patriarchs, the prophets made it plain that they were not heroes but ordinary people whom God called and challenged and comforted. When it came to the liberation from Egypt, the wilderness journey, the Sinai revelation, and the gift of the land, the emphasis fell on God's own work of liberation, leading, and blessing through Moses the prophet, whether assisted by others or alone. By interpreting and applying God's acts for their own times, the prophets brought to light their enduring relevance for God's people in every concrete situation.

In sending the prophets, then, God both continued his work and broadened and deepened the witness to it. The sending of the prophets complemented the other topics. In so doing, it also became an article of Israel's faith in its own right.

2. God Called and Sent the Prophets

Before acting on behalf of his people, God would often call persons secretly and associate them with his work. (a) By words and visions God revealed to these persons that he was about to act and showed them why. (b) God entrusted his Word to these persons, and by their own words, attitudes, and acts they communicated it to the people that needed it. (c) Since these persons were unable to fulfil this task of themselves, God gave them the promise of his presence and other pledges of his assistance.

ALL THE BIBLICAL PROPHETS from Moses to Daniel had a commission from the Lord, the God of Israel. Even false prophets thought they had. No prophets ventured to speak without a true (or false) vision or revelation, a transforming spiritual experience. The OT lays great stress on this point. But how precisely did a person become a prophet?

Consulting the biblical data, we find that the stories of prophetic vocation fall into two groups: those told by the prophets themselves, and those told by others. We begin with the first group.

Amos refers to his vocation when on his expulsion from Bethel he says: "I am no prophet. . . , nor am I a prophet's son; I am a herdsman and a dresser of sycamore-figs. But the Lord took me as I followed the flock and said to me, 'Go and prophesy to my people Israel' " (7:14-15).

Isaiah's is the most familiar story. He experienced his decisive hour in the Jerusalem temple. The account consists of five scenes: (1) the vision of the Lord on his throne and the seraphim around him (6:1-2); (2) the audition: the praise of the divine choir, a model for all earthly praise (vv. 3-5); (3) the sanctification, the purifying of Isaiah's lips with a glowing coal (vv. 6-7); (4) the sending: Isaiah offers himself (v. 8); and (5) the commission: Isaiah is given his message.

Jeremiah's account of his calling forms the main part of the opening chapter (1:4-19). It can be divided into four smaller units: (1) Jeremiah is called, his objections are met, the Lord's Word is put in his mouth (vv. 4-10); (2) first vision: a blooming almond tree, the name of which indicates the substance of his future prophecy (vv. 11-12); (3) second vision: a boiling cauldron, the contents of which are about to be poured out on Judah (vv. 13-16); and (4) the commissioning (vv. 17-19).

Ezekiel bears witness to his calling in 1:1–3:15. The main elements in this passage give a clear picture of his call: (1) introduction: place and time (1:1, 3); (2) vision: the coming of the glory of the Lord on four creatures (1:4ff.); (3) audition: Ezekiel is called and given a scroll to eat (2:1–3:11); and (4) the withdrawing of the Lord's glory and Ezekiel's return to the exiles dumbfounded (4:12-15).

Among the stories of prophetic vocation told by others we refer first to the call of Moses in Exod. 3:1–4:17. Addressed by God, and sent to be his spokesman and the liberator of his people from Egypt, Moses hesitates (3:13; 4:1, 10). But the revelation of God's name, the miracles, and the naming of Aaron as a helper give him confidence.

The call of Gideon is not unlike that of the prophets (Judg. 6:11-18). The angel of the Lord comes to him unexpectedly (vv. 11-12), commissions him to deliver Israel (v. 14), meets his objections (vv. 13, 15), and gives him a sign (v. 18; cf. v. 21) as requested.

Vocation is the prominent concept in the story of 1 Sam. 3:1-14. Samuel is asleep and has had no previous experiences of revelation (v. 7). The Lord calls him, however, and sends him to Eli with a message of condemnation, then as a prophet to Israel as a whole (cf. 3:19-21; 4:1a).

Finally, when Ahab is being deceived by false prophets, Micaiah, the son of Imlah, tells him that in a vision he has seen the Lord on his throne with the host of heaven, and allowing lying spirits to enter the prophets so that they will induce Ahab to embark on his fatal campaign (1 Kgs. 22:8-28). Micaiah, too, is sent by the divine council but is granted the spirit of truth.

There are differences in the accounts. Some open with a divine vision while others put the main stress on the hearing of God's Word. More prominence is given in some than in others to the uncertainty and objections of the prophet. Nevertheless, the similarities are so great that many exegetes discern a common pattern in the stories.

According to N. Habel ("The Form and Significance of the Call Narratives," *Zeitschrift für die alttestamentliche Wissenschaft* 77 [1965] 297-323), the stories almost all include six elements: (1) divine confrontation: God reveals himself; (2) introductory word: God calls and addresses his servant; (3) commission: God entrusts to his servant a message that he is to communicate; (4) objection: the one who is called presents objections; (5) reassurance: God promises his presence; and (6) sign: God grants a miracle in visible proof. The presence of these common elements, of course, does not mean that the stories were written according to the same model or with an identical structure.

In the discussion that follows we shall not adopt any system but focus on three main aspects of the one and indivisible event of vocation. The first aspect is that the whole event has the character of a revelation, describing as it does the tremendous experience of the Lord's presence. The second aspect is that the whole event involves sending and commissioning. The third aspect is that the whole event includes a strengthening of the prophet for ministry.

a. God Reveals Himself

When a prophet emerges, a tremendous event has just taken place. God himself, the Lord, has revealed himself to a human creature. This divine manifestation is both the beginning and the basis of a prophetic life. "God has revealed himself to me" is a prophet's answer if his authority is questioned. Without the initial experience no one would dare act and speak as a prophet. Certain elements are almost always integral to the experience.

(1) God is suddenly present. God himself chooses the time and place and manner, just as he himself chooses whom to call. God always takes the initiative.

The fact that it pleases the Lord to come and meet a person is so extraordinary that proper description is hardly possible. The OT uses general expressions: "God came to Laban in a dream by night" (Gen. 31:24; cf. Num. 22:20). "The Lord came and stood there, and called, 'Samuel'" (1 Sam. 3:10). "The angel of the Lord came and sat under the terebinth at Ophrah" (Judg. 6:11a). The Lord also *appeared* (Gen. 12:7; 35:9; Exod. 3:2; 1 Kgs. 3:5) to his servants or *met* them (Exod. 3:18).

Did the Most High God really appear to ordinary folk? The OT says so. Nevertheless, the divine presence is concealed, as it were. No description can be given. He comes in a dream at night (Num. 22:20). Moses and Elijah see him passing by (Exod. 34:6; 1 Kgs. 19:11). Isaiah sees only the skirt of his robe (Isa. 6:1-2).

Often the angel of the Lord is said to come, not God (Gen. 16:7; Exod. 3:2; Josh. 5:13; Judg. 6:11-12; 1 Kgs. 19:5). Plainly it is God himself who meets Hagar, Moses, Balaam, Joshua, or Gideon, but he comes in the form of an angel, the angel himself being at times likened to a man (Gen. 18:2) or a servant of the Lord (Judg. 13:9). The impact of God's presence is enhanced rather than reduced when it is said that it pleases him to appear in human or angelic form.

God comes suddenly and unexpectedly. A person is at work or asleep and suddenly a mighty vision changes the whole course of life. Moses is keeping his father-in-law's sheep (Exod. 3:1). Gideon is threshing wheat (Judg. 6:11). Samuel is sleeping (1 Sam. 3:3). Saul is looking for his father's asses (9:3). Amos is following his flock (Amos 7:15). Isaiah is standing in the inner court of the temple either meditating or worshiping (Isa. 6:1). Ezekiel is busy by the river Kebar (Ezek. 1:1). None of them is looking for God's coming. None is ready or worthy to receive so overwhelming a grace. None holds a prophetic office. None has the required qualities, gifts, or spirituality. The free divine initiative decides everything. Those that have the experience, then, are deeply startled. As Ezekiel says, "the hand of the Lord came upon me" (Ezek. 3:22; cf. 1:3; Isa. 8:11). Jeremiah even feels duped and outwitted (Jer. 20:7). Nothing on the human side can account for what happens.

(2) God appears to certain persons in order to communicate with them. In showing them something, he also speaks a clear word. The vision, then, is no mere dream or fantasy.

Without visions there are no prophets. The stories of prophetic calling make this plain. Two verbs, *rā'āh* and *ḥāzāh,* with their derivatives, are normally used in this regard. They both mean "to see," though *rā'āh* is taken from everyday speech and *ḥāzāh* is a literary term, often translated "to contemplate."

On the one hand, many prophets begin their prophecies with the words: "I have seen" or "I see" (*rā'āh;* e.g., Balaam in Num. 23:9, Micaiah in 1 Kgs. 22:17, 19, Isaiah in Isa. 6:1, Amos in Amos 9:1). At times they may say: "The Lord has revealed (or shown) to me" (Elisha in 2 Kgs. 8:10, 13, Amos in Amos 7:1, Jeremiah in Jer. 24:1, Zechariah in Zech. 3:1). Samuel and Ezekiel are both said to have received a vision (*mar'āh).* We also recall that "seer" (*rō'ēh*) was the original term for a prophet.

On the other hand, *ḥāzāh* and derivatives are also common. Balaam, "the man whose sight is clear . . . sees in a trance the vision from the Almighty" (Num. 24:3-4, 15-16, *maḥ^{a}zēh*). In Eli's days, no vision was granted (1 Sam. 3:1, *ḥāzōn*). During the exile prophets "received no vision from the Lord" (Lam. 2:9). The early exiles ignored Ezekiel's vision (Ezek. 12:27). "The vision received by Isaiah" is a title (Isa. 1:1). The word *ḥōzeh* ("seer") could also be used for a prophet.

When granted by night, visions are like dreams (cf. Gen. 26:24; 1 Kgs. 3:5; Dan. 7:1). When God's Spirit is poured out and all prophesy, then "old men shall dream dreams and . . . young men see visions" (Joel 2:28). False prophets, however, often take pride in their dreams, so a warning has to be issued against being led astray by empty dreams (Deut. 13:1ff.; Mic. 3:3ff.; Jer. 23:25-32; Zech. 10:2).

What exactly did the prophets see? In some cases they saw God himself (Amos 9:1; Isa. 6:1; Ezek. 1:28). More often they saw a motionless object or person: a plumb line (Amos 7:8), a basket of summer fruit (8:2), a man on a bay horse (Zech. 1:8), a man with a measuring line (2:1), four horns (1:18). In other cases they saw all Israel scattered (1 Kgs. 22:17), Elijah carried up in a whirlwind (2 Kgs. 2:9ff.), the earth without form (Jer. 4:23ff.), Nineveh captured (Nah. 2:3ff.), the glory of the Lord leaving Jerusalem (Ezek. 10:1ff.), Babylon being destroyed (Isa. 21:1ff.), four beasts coming up out of the sea (Dan. 7:3).

In themselves the visions are not clear. The seer does not understand them. A word must accompany and explain them. God makes the meaning plain by speech. What the prophet sees is but the instrument of God's Word. It is never on the same level as the Word. Visions have authority only inasmuch as a word fills them with meaning and truth. Amos sees a basket of summer fruit *(qāyiṣ)* and the word explains its meaning: "The time is ripe [*qēṣ*] for my people Israel" (8:1-2).

In some verses word and vision are equated: "The word of the Lord was seldom heard, and no vision was granted" (1 Sam. 3:1); "Nathan recounted . . . all that had been said to him and all that had been revealed [*ḥizzāyôn*]" (2 Sam. 7:17); "I spoke to the prophets, it was I who gave vision after vision" (Hos. 12:10). The parallelism may still be felt in, e.g., Ps. 89:19 or Num. 12:6. Along these lines Eliphaz says to Job that "a word stole into my ear . . . in the anxious visions of the night" (Job 4:12-13). In Isaiah "the vision received by Isaiah" is the same as "the word which Isaiah . . . received in a vision" (1:1 and 2:1; cf. Amos 1:1; Hab. 1:1).

Nevertheless, a distinction may be made between prophets who tell dreams and those who speak God's word in truth (Jer. 23:28). Prophets have revelations but shrink from calling them visions or dreams. They prefer to say that the Word of the Lord comes to them (*hāyāh*, "happened"). We find this expression over 40 times in Jeremiah, 50 times in Ezekiel, and also in 1 Kgs. 12:22; 13:20; etc. "The word of the Lord which came to" is the title given to the books of Hosea, Joel, Micah, and Zephaniah (cf. also Mal. 1:1). At the same time, Zechariah, Joel, and Daniel speak boldly of dreams or visions.

(3) God reveals himself and speaks his Word in order to initiate an action that he is about to undertake, especially when evil and suffering go behind the limits that he has set. Critical situations that he finds intolerable

and incompatible with the sanctity of his name repeatedly move him to take action and to send prophets as the first witnesses to his word and deed.

Why did God send Amos from Tekoa to prophesy against Israel? "The Lord roars from Zion," he can no longer stand to see the spread of evil throughout Israel and the surrounding countries (Amos 1). Isaiah, too, was called in the year of Uzziah's death when wickedness had reached a peak in Jerusalem and its leaders neither trusted God nor respected civil rights. Jeremiah was called a century later to announce God's judgment on Judah and Jerusalem because of the people's infidelity.

In earlier times Moses had been called when Israel was oppressed in Egypt, Samuel when the leadership of Eli's sons was corrupt, Elijah when Ahab and Jezebel were promoting idolatry, and Elisha when Israel was endangered by Aram and Moab.

The prophets were sent as occasion demanded. They did not have an institutional function. For long periods God might be mute (1 Sam. 3:1). The coming of a prophet was always an unusual and astonishing event. In times of crisis it showed that God still cared even for an unfaithful people by intervening for it and by announcing his intervention through a weak servant of his own choosing.

b. God Entrusts His Word to the Prophets

If, as we read, the hand of the Lord came upon the prophets, God apparently coerced them. He chose and sent them to fulfil a task that they did not themselves choose. They were called and ordered to play a role that they might actually dislike. Willy-nilly they had to become "another man" (1 Sam. 10:6). God had decided to act on his people's behalf, and he began with one-sided action on these individuals.

Prophets like Jeremiah and Ezekiel both complained inwardly and protested outwardly against the violence done to them by their calling (Jer. 20:7-9; Ezek. 3:14). But were the human partners really coerced? Were they no more than chess pieces, instruments that God used as he pleased? To say this is to misread the situation. In reality God in no way lessened the dignity of those he called to be prophets. On the contrary, he enhanced it. Several factors show this.

(1) God entrusted his Word to those whom he called. He met them, granted them a vision, revealed to them his Word, and in this way elevated them, granting them more trust than any human being really merits.

In 1 Sam. 3:20 we read that "Samuel was confirmed as a prophet of the Lord." In fact the Hebrew (ne'ᵉmān) says that he was "trusted" as a prophet of the Lord. Earlier God had spoken to Moses face to face because he was a man "entrusted [*ne'eman*] with all my house" (Num. 12:7 RSV).

The verb "to trust" is not common in the stories of prophetic calling, but it is most apposite. God did not humble the prophets with his mighty power; he humbled himself by entrusting the mystery of his Word to mere creatures. Thanks to God's totally unexpected trust, a human creature was allowed to have been present "in the council of the Lord, seen him and heard his word" (Jer. 23:18). The content of the Word, the mystery of the divine action, was placed in a human being's hands. By doing this, God took a great risk. The human being might misuse the knowledge. But again and again God was willing to take the risk. He used his power to "force" the person to listen to his Word, but he simultaneously handed over his power to this person. He let a creature share responsibility for his own Word.

(2) God's wisdom in handing over his Word to a human creature is strange indeed. Revealed to a person, the Word goes through a tremendous transformation. It moves from the eternal world to the ephemeral. There is a change of language as well as place. The heavenly language has to be translated into human language. This is the astonishing transformation that has to take place when God's Word comes to and through his servants.

Eliphaz speaks of a "whisper," a "low voice" (Job 4:12, 16). Elijah at Horeb heard a "low murmuring sound" that later became clear speech (1 Kgs. 19:9ff.). Job reminds his friends: "How faint the whisper that we hear of him! Who could fathom the thunder of his might?" (Job 26:14). If God's speech takes the form of a whisper, it can also take that of thunder! As Amos says, "The lion has roared; who is not terrified? The Lord God has spoken; who will not prophesy?" (3:8). At Sinai "it thundered and the lightning flashed, . . . they heard the trumpet sound" (Exod. 20:18). Whether as a whisper or as thunder, however, the speech of God always strikes the listener with awe.

How does the audible or visible Word of God become a human word that people can understand? Who gives it the form of prophecies, exhortations, meditations, sermons, teachings, threats, consolations, complaints, satires, court dialogues, and other literary forms common to the culture of antiquity? All the prophetic material has this human form. Did God himself translate it into human speech, or did the prophets?

Our first reply must be that God himself revealed his Word in a form that humans can understand. What the prophets received, what they uttered, and what was then recorded, is wholly God's work. It is revelation. The prophets had only to listen, take in, and then transmit faithfully what they had received (cf. Deut. 4:2). They were called upon to be God's speakers. They were entrusted with the communication of God's own Word. Their prophecies begin and end with the formula: "Thus says the Lord" (RSV).

At the same time the prophets also transmitted God's Word in words of their own. Indeed, in many cases they did not even make the direct claim that what they said was God's Word. We are not to conclude, of course, that some parts of the prophetic message consist of God's own Word while other parts do not. Such a conclusion would pose an impossible task of differentiation. The truth seems to be that all the prophetic utterances are God's Word but all are also couched in human words. The prophets were not tape recorders on the one hand, nor did they add their own introductions or explanations to God's Word on the other hand. They transmitted God's Word faithfully as they had received it, but they had the task of shaping the language and the literary form in which it could reach the people. Theirs, then, was a heavy responsibility. This was the risk that God ran in entrusting his Word to them.

(3) The task of the prophets was not merely to speak God's Word but also to record it. God commanded them both to speak and to write his Word. Freezing it into written letters, words, and sentences would preserve it on the one hand but would also expose it to the possibility of damage and destruction on the other. Was not the written account of Jeremiah's prophecies thrown into the fire by the king of Judah (Jer. 36)?

In only a few cases are we specifically told that the prophets wrote down their own message. Isaiah wrote the name Maher-shalal-hash-baz and some other words on tablets so that they might be "there in future days, a testimony for all time" (Isa. 8:1ff.; 30:8). Isaiah was also told to "fasten up the message, seal the oracle" among his disciples (8:16). Jeremiah wrote down his message on a scroll with Baruch as his scribe (36:1ff.), and he then rewrote it with additions when Zedekiah destroyed the first copy (36:32; cf. also chs. 30–31). In the main, however, disciples probably collected most of the prophetic sayings and preserved them in this way for all future generations, God himself adding his own authentication.

c. God Equips His Prophets

The responsibility of communicating God's Word in human words was obviously too great to be carried by the prophets alone. But God was well aware of this. He also equipped and strengthened those whom he sent. He himself enabled them to do what they had to do.

(1) The prophets were fully conscious of their unfitness for the task entrusted to them. Isaiah might spontaneously answer God's question: "Whom shall I send?" with his "Here am I, send me" (6:8), but he also realized with

great anguish: "Woe is me! I am lost, for I am a man of unclean lips" (6:5), and when he heard what message he had to deliver he cried out again: "How long, O Lord?" (6:11). He did not even want to be the bearer of this message, and he could see no way of properly delivering it.

"I do not know how to speak; I am only a child," said Jeremiah (1:6). This was not just modesty. Jeremiah was actually afraid (cf. the "Be not afraid" of 1:8 RSV; cf. also v. 17). He felt totally inadequate to be "a prophet to the nations" (1:5). He did not think he could face the opposition his message was sure to arouse (1:7-8, 18-19).

Ezekiel, like Jeremiah, had to be told not to fear (3:14). He also had no taste for his mission. God had to say to him plainly: "You, man, must listen to what I say and not be rebellious" (2:8). His instinct was apparently to refuse the mission that God had for him. He had of himself neither the liking nor the ability for it.

The sense of inadequacy plays an important role especially in the call of Moses. Five times he tried to excuse himself: "But who am I, that I should go to Pharaoh, and that I should bring the Israelites out of Egypt?" (Exod. 3:11; cf. 3:13; 4:1, 10, 13). Moses was hesitant, abashed, afraid, unable to speak, unwilling to go, yet he was the greatest among the prophets!

Gideon, too, raised objections when he was called to be the deliverer of Israel: "But pray, my Lord . . ." (Judg. 6:13, 15). Saul, when chosen to be king, excused himself; his tribe and family were among the least in Israel (1 Sam. 9:21). Finally, we remember Jonah, who, when called to go to Nineveh, set out for Tarshish "to escape from the Lord" (1:1-2). Readers understand him only too well!

Both serious objections and artificial excuses are raised. Human beings are indeed unable, unworthy, and therefore unwilling. But it pleases God to call them, and therefore even their serious objections are null and void. Of themselves, those whom God calls certainly could not be prophets, but God himself overcomes all impediments. Entrusting a difficult ministry to the prophets, he also gives them the strength and willingness to execute it.

(2) God equipped the prophets. Those who felt too young became mature. Those who were slow of speech were enabled to speak with convincing authority. Those who felt weak were given the strength to face opposition. Those who were deaf had their ears unstopped. Those who were hesitant became willing. How? By receiving a most exceptional gift from God. God's Spirit, the Spirit of the Lord, was their decisive equipment.

In earlier times the Spirit would often grant miraculous power to do what is normally beyond all human possibility (cf. Gideon, Jephthah, and Samson in Judg. 6:34; 11:29; 13:25; 14:19; 15:14). The spirit of Elijah had clearly "settled on Elisha" when the latter miraculously crossed the Jordan (2 Kgs. 2:9, 13ff.). But prophetic rapture might also bear witness to the working of the Spirit, as in the case of the seventy elders in the desert (Num. 11:14ff.) or the "company of prophets" in the days of Saul (1 Sam. 10:5-6; cf. 1 Cor. 12:10). Along these lines the Spirit was already the instrument to reveal or communicate God's Word to the prophet or seer (Num. 24:2).

Strangely the writing prophets of the royal period (e.g., Hosea, Amos, or Isaiah) make no reference to the gift of the Spirit. Hosea was mocked as a "man of the spirit," i.e., a madman (Hos. 9:7 RSV), but he himself did not speak of the Spirit in relation to his task. Isaiah opposed the plan and guidance of the Spirit to human plans and devices (Isa. 30:1; 31:3) but he did not relate the saying to his own ministry. Micah is the only exception when in contrast to officially paid prophets who mislead the people he proudly states: "I am full of strength, the Spirit of the Lord, of justice and power, to denounce his crime to Jacob" (Mic. 3:8).

Why did not the great prophets speak about the role of the Spirit in their ministry? The clash between Micaiah and the court prophets may provide an answer. The central issue here was whether the Lord's Spirit was with the prophets. A common opinion seems to have been that the prophets had the Spirit in virtue of their office. Micaiah opposed this view and unmasked the false prophets. Not the Spirit of the Lord but a lying spirit inspired them (1 Kgs. 22:22-23). The prophets of the royal period, then, were probably avoiding a claim that had been sadly misused when they made no reference to empowerment by the Spirit. They did not wish to be identified with the court prophets.

During the exile, however, Ezekiel opened a new chapter in prophetic history. Having witnessed the coming of the Lord's glory to the banks of the Kebar, he felt restored, elevated, and transported by the Spirit (2:2; 3:14; 8:3; 11:1), like Elijah and Elisha before him (1 Kgs. 18:12; 2 Kgs. 2:16). The Spirit also sent him visions (Ezek. 11:24b) and words (11:5). It could then be stated afresh that both prophetic revelation and prophetic enabling come by the Spirit. Thus Zechariah refers to "all that the Lord of Hosts had taught them by his spirit through the prophets" (Zech. 7:12). Nehemiah in his long prayer says: "Thou didst warn them by thy spirit through thy prophets; but they would not listen" (Neh. 9:30). As Chronicles puts it, "the spirit of God came upon" his prophets (2 Chron. 15:1; 20:14; 24:20).

The Spirit, then, was the true equipment of the prophets, the mediator of revelation to them. The fact that some prophets do not mention this does not invalidate its truth. It reminds us, however, to be on guard against the misunderstandings that easily arise. God's Spirit is God himself, present with his prophets, enabling them to give authoritative witness to him. The Spirit cannot be a power that is external and inferior to God. He is the abundant grace of God, but grace that is free as God himself is free. No one can possess the Spirit of God. The Spirit communicates God's own Word. This is an astonishing and even startling Word. The Spirit cannot be mistaken, then, for an inoffensive power that is agreeable to both prophet and people.

The Spirit who works in the wonderful power of the holy God is the mystery that shines in the fire of God's Word, the force that overcomes all obstacles, first in the prophets themselves, then in their hearers.

(3) The stories of prophetic calling describe in other ways as well the mystery of God's equipping of the prophets to communicate his Word. We do not mean that the Spirit was one of many instruments that God used for this purpose. Our task is to consider other aspects of the one divine equipping.

God sent his servants as envoys to different groups, e.g., Moses to the elders (Exod. 3:16), Amos to "my people Israel" (Amos 7:15), Isaiah, Jeremiah, and Ezekiel to "this people" (Isa. 6:9; cf. Jer. 1:17; Ezek. 3:4, 11), Jonah to Nineveh (Jon. 1:2; 3:2). In sending them, however, he gave them the promise of his presence: "I am with you." He gave this promise to Moses (Exod. 3:12), Gideon (Judg. 6:16), and Jeremiah (Jer. 1:8, 19). In this regard the Hebrew uses the preposition 'im or 'ēt, "with," in close relation to the name of the Lord in Exod. 3:12-14.

"I am with you" implies that God will help and bless and empower his servants on the thorny path that they are to tread. This was God's promise to Israel in the wilderness. It had specific implications for Joshua (Josh. 1:9) and later for Gideon (Judg. 6:15) and the prophets. It might take the form of speech or the power to work miracles (Moses or Elisha). It might take the form of companions (Aaron for Moses, disciples for Isaiah [cf. Isa. 8:16], Baruch for Jeremiah). It also took the form of inner strength, the courage to face opposition, the wisdom to stand amid criticism, the enthusiasm and patience to overcome weakness. Of themselves the prophets did not have these qualities, but God promised them and gave them: "I will make you a match for them. . . . I will make your brow like adamant, harder than flint" (Ezek. 3:8-9). God's presence with his servants was their real strength.

"I am with you." Digging deeper, we see that God not only gave his servants strength when he sent them to communicate his Word. He was present in person. He did not himself stay at home, avoiding the risks of engagement. The Lord, the God of Israel, was really with his envoys. He went with those whom he sent. He spoke when they spoke. He carried the burden of a prophetic ministry that was too heavy for them.

The divine presence was a hidden reality. The prophets knew it but did not feel or see it. They apparently went out on their own and struggled on their own. Yet how could they dare to go if God did not go with them? Their boldness derived from the divine presence: "Fear none of them, for I am with you" (Jer. 1:7-8). This presence stopped Jonah from running away from his task. It guarded the prophets' tongues so that they could truly speak in God's name. Because of it God's Word was spoken through their word. To hear them

was to hear him, to reject them to reject him. As Bishop Eivind Berggrav of
Norway once said: "When you open the Bible, you are in the presence of
God." This certainly applies to the words of the prophets, both spoken and
written.

The prophets had to endure many conflicts and temptations. They
suffered severely as God's emissaries. Yet God himself was suffering with
them. Indeed, he was basically the first to suffer. The burden that the prophets
carried was not too heavy for them because the Lord himself carried it with
them. They triumphed in the power of his hidden presence.

The presence and the Spirit cannot be separated. They belong together.
The reference is to one and the same divine action. Some passages stress the
gift of the Spirit, others the presence of God, but all of them praise God for
his willingness to strengthen, enable, and equip his servants for their humanly
impossible ministry.

3. God Uproots: The First Message of the Prophets

*God sent many prophets—(a) Amos, (b) Hosea, (c) Isaiah, (d) Micah,
(e) Nahum, Habakkuk, and Zephaniah, (f) Jeremiah, and (g) Ezekiel—
to challenge his people and to announce imminent disaster. God
would first uproot Israel, then Judah, then the surrounding nations.*

OUR NEXT TASK is to unfold the message of the prophets. What did they have
to say to the people of their times? God sent them all to proclaim his Word,
his just and gracious decision. He himself did not change. But as generation
succeeded generation his Word was always new. It met each generation in its
own circumstances. Each prophet, then, had a distinctive message. What was
said was not simply a repetition of what had been said before. It is necessary,
then, that we pay attention to each of the sixteen canonical prophets, the four
major prophets (Isa. 1–39, Isa. 40–66, Jeremiah, Ezekiel) and the twelve minor
prophets.

In this discussion, however, we shall not simply follow the biblical
order but divide the prophetic messages into two groups, the first in which the
stress is on God's uprooting of his people, the second in which it is on his
rebuilding (cf. Jer. 1:10). In both cases, of course, we find the same judgment
and salvation, but the emphasis differs even though the divine love does not
change. We begin with the first group.

a. Amos of Tekoa

Amos is the first of the prophets whose words are recorded in a book. Working ca. 760 B.C., he was sent to Israel. He was not a professional prophet but a sheep-farmer and dresser of figs (1:1; 7:14). He belonged to Judah, and hence, apart from Jonah, he was the only prophet actually sent to another country where he might face added danger. Speaking out plainly against a society that oppressed the weak under the cover of religiosity, he became a model for the other prophets of the first group.

Amos was sent to Israel during the reign of Jeroboam II, the son of Jehoash (787-747 B.C.). It was a time of economic expansion that profited only the upper classes. In God's name the prophet from Tekoa had to face the aristocracy in Samaria, the priesthood at Bethel and Gilgal, and possibly the people who gathered for worship at these shrines. He had a message that could no longer be modified. God was now about to condemn Jeroboam and his whole kingdom. He did not want to doom his people, but so long as they did not turn away from their misdeeds his Word could be only one of accusation and threat. The sharp note of warning is a distinguishing mark of the message of Amos.

Chapters 1 and 2 contain the first collection of the prophet's sayings. He seems to have arrived at Bethel in the middle of a religious and national festival. The crowd expected a seer to bring a message of judgment on foreign nations and an oracle of blessing on Israel. Amos met the first expectation. The Lord would judge such kingdoms as Damascus (1:3-5), Gaza (1:6-8), Ammon (1:13-15), and Moab (2:1-3) because of their cruelties. But would there be blessing for Israel? On the contrary! Having received the greater mercy (2:9), Israel would experience the greater condemnation!

The main collection in the middle of the book opens with a saying that expresses the bitter disappointment of the loving God: "For you alone have I cared among all nations of the world; therefore will I punish you for all your iniquities" (3:2). Where did the prophet acquire the boldness to bring this message? His explanation takes the form of entertaining questions about ordinary events and their unavoidable consequences: "The lion has roared; who is not terrified? The Lord God has spoken; who will not prophesy?" (3:8). There then follow several sayings of Amos either in Samaria, the capital, or Bethel, the royal sanctuary (3:9–4:3; 6:1-14). Threats of coming judgment alternate with reproaches that explain the threats. A few warnings and praises are also interjected (4:13; 5:8-9; 9:5-6). The constant theme is that the kingdom of Israel is to come to an end. The Lord will bring a day of total darkness and overwhelming disaster, not a day of light as the people expected (5:18-20). A foreign enemy will attack Israel (3:11; 6:14) and reduce the proud city of Samaria to ruins (3:11, 12, 15; 6:8, 11). Many prominent citizens will either die or go into exile (4:2-3; 5:27; 6:7). The holy places will not be spared (3:14; 5:5; cf. 7:9).

Why will all this happen? The accusation of Amos is that the ruling class was oppressing the poor and exploiting the weak (3:9-10; 4:1; 5:10-12). He condemned the whole social structure: "You have turned into venom the process of law and justice itself into poison" (6:12; cf. 5:7). He attacked sharply the luxurious lifestyle (4:1; 6:3-6), the boasting about Israel's strength (6:13), the false innocence of those who claimed they had not been warned (4:6-13), and the hypocritical religiosity: "Come to Bethel—and rebel! Come to Gilgal—and rebel the more! Bring your sacrifices for the morning, your tithes within three days" (4:4-5).

In his warnings Amos pleads with the people: "Resort to the Lord" (5:4, 6), "seek good" and "enthrone justice in the courts" (vv. 14-15). True, the time for real change is past. The prophet can hardly promise that "the Lord the God of Hosts will be gracious to the survivors of Joseph" (v. 15). Yet he can still issue the challenge: "Let justice roll on like a river and righteousness like an ever-flowing stream" (v. 24).

The next collection (chs. 7–9) consists in the main of five visions: the locusts (7:1-3), the flame of fire (7:4-6), the plumb line (7:7-8), the basket of fruit (8:1-3), and the Lord standing by the altar (9:1-4). All these visions threaten Israel with catastrophe. When and how it will strike is open. Twice Amos asks God to relent (7:2, 5), but from the third vision onward Amos is convinced that Israel must fall (8:2). Further threats complete the series (7:9; 8:4-11; 9:7-8). Those against the sanctuaries and the house of Jeroboam (7:9) are linked to the expulsion of Amos from Bethel (7:10-17). The only ray of light (thought to be later by some scholars) is the promise that through judgment God will save his people (9:8b-10). God is a God of grace as well as judgment, and salvation is his ultimate goal (9:11-15).

Is the message of Amos still relevant for God's people today? To this question we must give a positive answer. To understand the message, however, we must enter into solidarity with God's people in Israel and see that the reproaches and threats of Amos apply no less to us. God may "hate our feasts," too, and take "no delight in our solemn assemblies" (cf. 5:21 RSV), for he rejects religious activity that is an end in itself and worship that has no concern for justice and righteousness. The lesson of Amos to the church is that it should examine itself, see its own faults, and again and again "seek the Lord."

b. Hosea, the Son of Beeri

A few years after Amos God sent another prophet to Israel, this time one of its own citizens. Hosea worked between 750 and 722 B.C., i.e., from the end of the reign of Jeroboam II to the fall of Samaria. We know very little about his life or background except that he was married to Gomer, that they had three children (Hos. 1:2ff.), and that he was not accepted but ridiculed (9:7-8; 11:5, 7; 12:1).

Hosea followed Amos, but what a difference between them! On the one hand, Amos would never have compared Israel to an unfaithful wife, as Hosea did. On the other hand, Hosea laid less stress on the lack of justice in Israel than did Amos. These two points throw light on Hosea's distinctive message.

Unfortunately, the Hebrew text of Hosea is in sad shape. It is the worst preserved of any OT text. Many sentences are hard to understand and translate. The reason is probably that many records were badly damaged in the disorder resulting from the Assyrian conquest. Several of the sayings seem to have been brought to Judah, either orally or in writing, and collected there in the form in which we now have them.

Hosea prophesied in Samaria and the royal sanctuaries while the country was still independent. He usually addressed the royal court, the priests, and the aristocracy. He referred at times to Judah (5:10ff.) but did not address it directly. He based his prophecy on the basic tenets of Israel's faith, the election of the fathers (Jacob), the liberation from Egypt, the leading through the wilderness, and the gift of a fertile land.

(1) The first chapters (1–3) stress the theme of Israel as an unfaithful wife. As we read in 1:2-9 and 3:1-5a, Hosea lived out the content of his message. He first took Gomer as his wife and gave their three children strange names expressing God's threats against Israel. When Gomer fell into adultery, he then bought the adulteress and shut her up in the house to show what God would do to his adulterous people.

Within the narrative are three series of sayings. The first (1:10–2:1) presents three promises that God's people, including Judah, will be restored. The second (2:2-13) reports what the Lord has to say as a husband in a suit against Israel, his unfaithful wife. The third (2:14-23) again promises restoration. The Lord calls Israel into the desert to woo her again (vv. 14-15). Though judgment is imminent, God does not give up his love. The husband's disappointment may be bitter, his rebuke of the wife who has become a prostitute severe, but how strong is the love that holds on and struggles to restore the initial relationship (vv. 18-19)! Hosea himself shares in the struggle.

(2) The second and main part of the book (chs. 4–14) gives broader and more pregnant expression to the same message. We find in it fourteen units, though these are hard to delimit and are not arranged in any easily explicable order. The charge in 4:1-3 is that "there is no good faith or mutual trust, no knowledge of God in the land." This charge is applied in 4:4-19 to

the adulterous worship into which the priests lead the people. Rebukes and threats are launched in 5:1-7 against leaders who are led by a "wanton spirit," possibly as a result of the affluence under Jeroboam II. Disorders in the war between Ephraim and Judah are highlighted in 5:8-15 and 6:1-6; Israel's rulers look in vain for help from either Assyria (5:13) or the Lord, whom they do not worship loyally (6:4). In 6:7-10 and 7:1-16 (a very difficult text) Ephraim is reproached for both political and religious disloyalty. Similar reproaches may be found in 8:1-14. The attacks on the king reflect the atmosphere of the last years of Israel. In 9:1-9, a famous passage, Hosea seems to be disturbing the crowd at a feast (vv. 1, 5), but the people reject his message (v. 7). In 9:10-13 Ephraim is threatened in a passage that alludes to Israel's desert origins. Attacks on Samaria's altars and idols occur in 9:14–10:8. Threats against Ephraim are the theme in 10:9-15. In 11:1-11 we find an astonishing expression of disappointment that Israel has rejected all God's bounties since the days in Egypt, but also the promise that even in judgment the Lord will again have mercy on his people. A comparison is made with Jacob in 11:12–12:14 (vv. 2-5, 12). In 13:1–14:1 no hope of pardon can be expected in view of the seriousness of the offenses. Nevertheless, in 14:2-9 Ephraim is invited to repent (vv. 2-4) and restoration is then promised (vv. 5-9).

Hosea consists mostly of threats and accusations but also includes words of invitation and consolation. How can we best sum up these categories, and what is the relation between them?

First, the message is the startling one that overwhelming disaster will fall on Israel. Ephraim will be destroyed. The land will be laid waste. The cities will be in ruins. The people, poor or powerful, old or young, will perish. The kingdom will disappear forever. Hosea's message is one of total rejection. Sentence of death is passed even though it may be the death of exile (8:13; 9:3; 11:5). The people are now "Not my people," "Not my wife."

Second, Hosea explains why the Lord rejects Ephraim. Ephraim is not faithful. It commits adultery. It is guilty of deceit and revolt. Disloyalty prevails everywhere. Dishonesty pervades both national and international relations. Worship of the Lord is mixed with worship of Baal. The government outwardly respects religious ideals but in fact fosters trickery and robbery. The courts do nothing to prevent exploitation and oppression. Foreign policy is no more than a fierce struggle for power. If Ephraim is no more wicked than Judah or other peoples, judgment is the ineluctable consequence of its offenses.

Third, Hosea issues invitations to repent, but they are comparatively rare. The people's "misdeeds have barred their way back to their God" (5:4). The Lord cannot be found by those who have forgotten him (2:13; 4:6; 8:14), who "care nothing for" him (5:4, 6). Loyalty is what God wants (6:6). Hosea still hopes that all will "turn back" and "wait upon" their God (12:6), that Jacob will "sow . . . in justice" (10:11-12), but he has a strong sense that the time for repentance is coming to an end. Ephraim must first "pay the penalty" (cf. 10:2 RSV; 14:1). Only then will the people "look earnestly for [God] in their distress" (5:15). There is thus little point in constant invitations to repent.

Fourth, Hosea cannot bring much consolation to Israel. How can he speak of salvation to a people that rejects God and that God has thus rejected, so that now it is "Not my people"? Yet Hosea does have a promise for those who go through judgment and come to an awareness of their faults. Not the judgment or suffering itself, but God's free mercy will make possible a new beginning and open up a new future (1:10; 2:21-23; 11:9-11; 14:5). Bought back from its life of adultery, Israel will be God's wife again—a message which the NT applies to the people of God that is the bride of Christ, the Son whom God called out of Egypt and through whose life and death and resurrection he manifested his love and achieved salvation for a rebellious race (cf. Rom. 9:24-25; Eph. 5:25ff.; Matt. 2:19ff.; 1 Cor. 15:55).

c. Isaiah, the Son of Amoz

God also sent prophets to Judah. Isaiah was the first of the writing prophets to work there. He began to speak in Jerusalem ca. 740 B.C., only a few years after Hosea began his ministry in Israel. Isaiah himself records his call in the years of Uzziah's death (6:1). He was married (8:3) and his two sons, like Hosea's children, were given symbolic names, both implying fright (7:3; 8:3, 18). Isaiah was active off and on for about forty years under three kings: Jotham (740-733 B.C.), Ahaz (733-714), and Hezekiah (714-696). The war with Israel (733), the fall of Samaria (722), and the growing pressure of Assyrian expansion all marked his lifetime and left an echo in his message. He obviously had close relations with the ruling class and probably belonged to an influential Jerusalemite family. His relation to Ahaz was tense, but he acted as an appreciated adviser to Hezekiah.

(1) Like Amos and Hosea, Isaiah was sent by God to proclaim judgment on his people. In chs. 1–39 we can distinguish five parts: prophecies against Judah and Jerusalem in chs. 1–12, oracles against foreign nations in chs. 13–23 (Jerusalem in ch. 22), oracles and hymns on the last days in chs. 24–27, and prophecies relative to Judah and Jerusalem in chs. 28–35, with historical material similar to that of 2 Kgs. 18ff. in chs. 36–39.

We shall take a closer look at the first, second, and fourth parts.

In chs. 1–12 four sequences of threats and reproaches close with a promise of salvation, and the whole collection ends with a hymn of praise (12:1-6). The Lord first accuses his rebellious people (1:2-3). He reminds his people of the devastation of Judah by Sennacherib in 701 B.C. (1:4-9). He condemns hypocritical worship (1:10-17). He threatens Jerusalem, the citadel of injustice (1:18-20, 21-26). A promise of end-time renewal is added (2:2-5).

In 2:6–4:6 the focus is on the impending day of the Lord. God rebukes his proud people (2:6-22) and reprimands the leaders (3:1-15) and the women who live in luxury (3:16ff.). Another promise of renewal follows (4:2-6).

In 6:1–9:7 Isaiah describes his experiences at the time of the attack on Judah by Israel and Aram (733 B.C.): his call (6:1-13); his meeting with Ahaz and the promise of Immanuel's birth (7:1-25); the name given to Isaiah's second son as a sign (8:1-4); an oracle on the Assyrian attack (8:5-8); a divine reminder to prophet and people (8:11-15); the interruption of his prophecy (8:16-18); the people in darkness (8:19-22); finally, the promise of liberation and the birth of the Prince of peace (9:1-7).

The fourth collection consists of threats. Some scholars place here the satirical song on the Lord's vineyard (5:1-7) and the seven oracles beginning with the words: "Shame on you" (5:8-24; 10:1-4a). In 9:8–11:16 we have a series of oracles ending with the refrain: "For all this his anger has not turned back" (9:8-21), a threat beginning: "Woe on Assyria!" (10:5-9 CB; cf. vv. 13-15), a promise of salvation for Israel (10:20-27a), a threat against Jerusalem (10:27b-34), the promise of the Prince of peace (11:1-10), and the promise of a remnant's return (11:11-16).

The second part (chs. 13–23) contains an oracle on Aram and Israel during their war with Judah (17:1-6), a threat against the Philistines (14:28-32), an address to the Ethiopian envoys (18:1-7), a sign against the pact with Egypt (20:1-6), an oracle on Jerusalem (22:1-14), the saying about court officials (22:15-25), two oracles on the miraculous defeat of the Assyrians (14:24-27; 17:12-14), and prophecies against Babylon (13:1ff.; 21:1ff.), Egypt (19:1ff.), Tyre (23:1ff.), and Moab (chs. 15–16).

The fourth part (chs. 28–35) has as its background the Assyrian crisis, which affected all the states in the region. The theme of condemnation is stressed by repetition of *hôy*, "Alas for" (CB) or "Woe to" (RSV) (28:1; 29:1; 30:1; 31:1, all with reference to God's own people, and 33:1). An oracle against Samaria and Ephraim (28:1-4) is followed by a threat against Jerusalem (28:7ff.), which includes the famous words on the cornerstone in v. 16, and which gives instruction about the wisdom of divine punishment (vv. 23ff.). It is then prophesied that Ariel (Jerusalem) will be overrun (29:1ff.), and there is a rebuke for God's blind and deaf people (29:9-10) whose worship is but a human precept (29:13-14) and who think they are cleverer than God (29:15-16). Criticism of Hezekiah's policies follows: Judah rebels against Assyria, prepares for war, and looks to Egypt for help. But Rahab (Egypt) cannot help (30:6-7) and the people are foolishly refusing to listen (30:8-11), relying on evil practices (30:12-14), and refusing to heed God's call to stay quiet and trust in the Lord (30:15-17). Yet the Lord will intervene. Jerusalem will be attacked but it will escape destruction (31:4ff.). The last threat sounds a gloomy note (32:9-14), but words of comfort and promise follow.

(2) Isaiah spoke with a characteristic voice. His was a fluent, beautiful, and powerful language. He could attract attention, attack, rebuke, but then unexpectedly raise new hope. He might transmit God's Word in satire (5:1ff.). He might also juxtapose words of similar sound but opposite meaning: "Your very rulers are rebels" (1:23; cf. 5:9; 30:16). The names of his sons predict catastrophe, yet the related sayings carry a promise of salvation (7:7-9; 8:4). The name Ariel ("furnace [or altar] of God") is given a reverse meaning: "I will make her . . . a flame of devouring fire" (29:2, 5 CB). The name Immanuel holds no cheap promise of security in virtue of the divine presence. Only amid and beyond disaster and destruction does the sign hold good: "God with us."

(3) Isaiah presented many distinctive theological concepts. He probably initiated the divine designation "the Holy One of Israel" (1:4; 5:19, 24; etc.). The adjective "holy" had ancient roots, but Isaiah gave it a challenging edge as a term that denotes both the glory of God and the love of God. The Lord shows himself to be holy in his righteousness as the Judge who defends the poor (11:4) and who demands justice from rulers (3:14) and people (1:17) alike. God has a purpose for Israel and the world (5:19; 30:1); how wonderful it is, and how strange his work (28:21, 29)! Yet he acts freely; hence his purpose is not fate or a blueprint. The people must not trust instead in their own plans but trust in the Lord. This does not mean that they may view the Lord's help as guaranteed. Those who do this, like those who rely on armaments (31:1), do not really trust the Lord and what may often seem to be his inexplicable purpose.

(4) What was the core of Isaiah's message? First, he had to rebuke and threaten. God had heaped blessings on his people but it reacted with indifference and rebellion. Jerusalem had become a center of injustice and unbelief. Pride rather than idolatry was its cardinal sin. It served God, but hypocritically. Like Samaria, then, it faced imminent disaster, though Assyria, God's instrument of destruction, would also come into judgment.

Second, Isaiah also proclaimed God's faithfulness. If his wrath had to find expression in punishment, he could be so wrathful precisely because he loved his "cherished plant" (cf. 5:7). Through judgment he aimed to refine (1:25), not to destroy. Jerusalem would yet again be a righteous city (1:26) and stand fast (1:19) under the rule of a just king. The message of hope, however, always went hand in hand with that of judgment. The light of salvation arises above the darkness of destruction. Isaiah focused on the mystery of God's faithfulness and he extolled the divine purpose, not the future greatness of Judah or Jerusalem.

Third, Isaiah did not find a friendly welcome for his strange message. He confidently put himself at God's disposal but enjoyed no great honor among his fellow citizens. Had he failed? Sometimes he nearly despaired (8:16ff.; 22:4). His oracles were not only ignored but they actually seemed to dull and deafen the people so that they could not "turn and be healed" (6:10). He could only trust that through judgment the Lord himself would heal his people.

His message is no less relevant for us today than for its first hearers. It comes home to us as the members of a community that professes faith in the Lord and is called to work for a just society and to contribute to international reconciliation. It challenges us to have confidence in the divine purpose, to see the significance of the divine election of Jerusalem, and to rest in the promise of the coming Messiah.

d. Micah of Moresheth

Micah was another 8th-century prophet of whom we know little more than that he came from Moresheth, a small town in the mountains of Judah close to the Philistine cities on the coastal plain. We do not know the name of Micah's father, nor if he was married, nor how he received his vocation. Perhaps, as H. W. Wolff has suggested (*Micah the Prophet* [Eng. tr. 1981], pp. 18ff.), he was one of the "elders of the land" (Jer. 26:17), the elite concerned with the general well-being of society (Mic. 3:1).

Micah was sent to the people of Judah in the late 8th century B.C. He was more or less a contemporary of Isaiah. He saw Samaria about to be taken by the Assyrians (1:6) and prophesied the same fate for the towns of Judah and even for Jerusalem itself (2:9; 3:12). He worked during the reigns of Jotham, Ahaz, and Hezekiah. With his rural background, he did not greatly admire the capital as the center of the nation's power but viewed it critically. Like Isaiah, he met with opposition and rejection (3:6, 11). The authorities preferred favorable oracles to bitter words (3:5, 11). He can hardly have had an easy life as a prophet.

(1) Micah's prophecy opens with an announcement of judgment on Samaria: "So I will make Samaria a heap of ruins in open country" (1:6-7). Nor will Judah escape: "Her wound cannot be healed; for the stroke has bitten deeply into Judah; it has fallen . . . upon Jerusalem itself" (1:8-9). Injustice, avarice, and oppression are the reasons for God's wrath (2:1-2, 8-9 RSV). "Listen, you leaders of Jacob . . . you devour the flesh of my people" (3:1ff.). "Her rulers sell justice, her priests give direction in return for a bribe, her prophets take money for their divination" (3:9-11). Jerusalem itself is not immune: "Therefore, on your account Zion shall become a ploughed field, Jerusalem a heap of ruins, and the temple hill rough heath" (3:12).

Later passages contain words of comfort (4:9; 5:6), an attack upon idolatry (5:12-13), an exhortation (6:2-8), a lament (7:1-7), and a prophetic liturgy (7:8ff.). Interspersed are prophecies of the restoration of Jerusalem (2:12-13) and of the pilgrimage of all nations to Zion (4:1-5).

(2) The core of Micah's message lies in the first three chapters. A storm is coming that will sweep away Samaria and burst over Judah. Jerusalem and the temple can no longer guarantee security. The people will either be destroyed or will go into exile. This is the Lord's doing and it seems to spell doom for his whole people.

Micah states very clearly why God was passing judgment in this way on Israel, Judah, and Jerusalem. Like Amos and Isaiah, he held the rulers primarily responsible. They so disappointed the Lord that he would abandon his people to their enemies. In this regard Micah made little reference to idolatry. He primarily condemned the blatant evils of injustice and exploitation. The rulers were called upon to establish justice but they loved evil. They might use pious words, but they were corrupt at heart and overripe for destruction.

Most impressively Micah not only reproached and threatened but also himself suffered and lamented, even going "stripped and naked" (RSV) because of the stroke that had "fallen on the gate of my people" (1:8-9). Micah mourned for his people even as the Lord did, not only because the weak and the poor were oppressed but also because destruction was about to fall. This people was still "my people," the Lord's chosen people (2:4, 9; 3:3), and for this reason there could also be exhortation and promise, stern though the message of condemnation might be.

(3) Although it earned authority enough to save Jeremiah a hundred years later (Jer. 26:16ff.), Micah's prophecy was largely disregarded in his own day. Yet it still carries a timely and relevant message. God's people constantly need to achieve an awareness of their high vocation. The God with whom we meet still sides with the victims of injustice and oppression. To stand by them with spiritual weapons is at the heart of our calling as his people. This can never be a secondary task, a mere addendum to the church's ministry. If it must not crowd out other essential activities, it must have its vital place if the church is genuinely to be what it is called upon to be, the people of God.

e. Nahum, Habakkuk, and Zephaniah

(1) Nahum came from the Judean mountains and prophesied against Assyria between 633 B.C., when Assurbanipal's armies defeated the Egyptians and took Thebes (No-amon, 3:8), and 612 B.C., when Nineveh fell to the Babylonians. He had only the one theme: "Nineveh is laid waste; who will console her?" (3:7). He compared Assyria (represented by Nineveh, its capital) to two lions taking away food to feed their cubs (2:11-13). It had numerous spies and secret agents (3:16-17). Nineveh was a "blood-stained city, steeped in deceit, full of pillage" (3:1), "a mistress of sorcery" (3:4). The Lord himself, against whom it plotted evil, was against it (2:13). He would bring judgment upon it but care

for those who sought his protection and bring "them safely through the sweeping flood" (1:8). In spite of their many allies, the Assyrians would be "cut off" (1:12 RSV), and there would be no further need for the tribute that had been exacted from Manasseh (1:12-13). Judah could give thanks, for in a world that seemed to be dominated by might, the Lord was still in control, and the fall of Assyria could thus be awaited with confidence.

(2) When Assyria was broken at the end of the 7th century B.C. and the Babylonians and Egyptians were fighting for power, the society of the ancient Near East was in turmoil. Law was no longer respected, princes struggled to enlarge their dominions, and the powerful planned to enrich themselves at the expense of the rest. During this upheaval a prophet emerged who embodied the Jerusalem tradition at its best. Rooted in temple worship, he felt the impact of its liturgical phrases. He had a mastery of pre-Israelite myths and used them in praise of God (3:3ff.). He was imbued with the wisdom that shows how nations can be justly ruled so that both peoples and environment may prosper. He was also deeply concerned with the central problem: Why do the just suffer? (1:2ff.; 2:1ff.).

The book of Habakkuk can be divided into two parts: the first dealing with the struggle for a just society (chs. 1–2), the second consisting of a psalm in praise of God (ch. 3). We know the prophet only through his message and can presume that he had a similar background to that of Isaiah and was possibly influenced by him. He was a contemporary of Jeremiah.

Habakkuk felt God's presence in a way that shaped his whole life (3:16). The call to prayer: "The Lord is in his holy temple; let all the earth be hushed in his presence" (2:20), is the lively experience of the one who alone in the OT calls God "my Holy One" (1:12 RSV). The revelation of God is described in the words of a theophany (3:3-4). Before the holy God the prophet shivers as in a fever, the nations tremble, the earth is shaken, the sea thunders (3:5ff.). Habakkuk has heard of God's deeds and seen his work (3:2) and this gives him joy: "yet I will exult in the Lord" (3:18). Out of his intimate communion with God, "whose eyes are too pure to look upon evil" (1:13), he cries out: "How long, O Lord" (1:2ff.).

God's answer shocked the prophet. He raised up the Chaldeans, a "savage and impetuous nation" that made its own rules (1:5ff.). The prophet asked again why God was silent when the wicked devoured "men more righteous than they" (1:13ff.), and violence was done even to nature (cf. 2:17). Until he received a satisfactory answer the prophet would keep watch: "I will stand at my post, . . . I will watch to learn what he will say through me" (2:1). The answer he finally received was twofold: first, a call for patience (2:4), then the assurance that God would judge the nations that enriched themselves at the expense of others, that founded their cities on injustice, and that abused nature and worshiped their own works (2:6-19).

Habakkuk's message retains its relevance amid the turmoil of nations when little individuals and peoples suffer from a sense of their own impotence. The need is to have faith in the God who will himself work and to live righteously to his praise. But this faith can have an even deeper and broader dimension as the faith which casts itself upon God's saving work in Christ in face of the final judgment in which no human work can help (Rom. 1:17; Gal. 3:11; Heb. 10:33).

(3) Zephaniah prophesied in Jerusalem ca. 630 B.C. when Josiah was still underage and the ruling class was under Assyrian influence. He helped to prepare public opinion for the renewal that Josiah would attempt when he came of age (cf. 2 Kgs. 22–23). Looking at Judah almost a century after the fall of Samaria, he proclaimed that God was about to condemn it without any appeal (Zeph. 1:4ff.). "The great day of the Lord is near. . . . That day is a day of wrath" (1:14-15). "Shame on the tyrant city, filthy and foul" (3:1-2).

Zephaniah took up the message of Amos and Isaiah. He addressed his message to those who also worshiped Baal, the host of heaven, and Milcom (1:3ff.); to the aristocracy; to the royal house; and to the government officials who aped foreign ways, competed for influence, and filled "their master's house with crimes of violence and fraud" (1:7-10). Josiah's father, Amon, was killed by his own officers, and the rulers of Judean towns favored Josiah and held up the ideals of David's kingship, so that power games were naturally the rule during Josiah's minority (cf. 2 Kgs. 21:23-24).

The inhabitants of Jerusalem would be condemned because they looked only for their own advantage. The Lord would "search Jerusalem with a lantern and punish all who sit in stupor over the dregs of their wine, who say to themselves, 'The Lord will do nothing, good or bad.' Their wealth shall be plundered, their houses laid waste" (1:10-13). The ruling classes, both civil and religious, who betrayed God, desecrated his sanctuary, and did violence to his law, would be uprooted: "Then I will rid you of your proud and arrogant citizens. . . . But I will leave in you a people afflicted and poor" (3:11-12).

To the words of judgment, however, were also appended words of hope and salvation. God's people will be renewed as a humble people living by God's laws and seeking his righteousness. All nations, after universal judgment, will "be given pure lips that they may invoke the Lord by name" (3:9-10).

f. Jeremiah, the Son of Hilkiah, of Anathoth

Among all the prophets whom God sent to his people, Jeremiah is in many ways the most attractive and the most challenging. His book has been studied for centuries, but the more it is considered, the greater the riddles that face us.

Jeremiah was a prophet of great authority, but often in his writings he seemed to have doubts about his calling and to come near to abandoning it. He was a major preacher and poet, but often, surprisingly, he expressed uncertainty about what he should do. He was a prophet of doom, predicting condemnation, yet he was always ready to defend those who were about to be condemned, and to bring consolation and hope when condemnation had fallen. Who, then, was this Jeremiah?

We know little about his life. He belonged to Anathoth, a little Benjaminite town less than 5 km. northeast of Jerusalem. His father was a priest (1:1). His family possessed land as a patrimony (32:6ff.; 37:12). They were very critical of Jeremiah when he became a prophet (12:6). He did his work in Jerusalem and ran into increasing difficulty there as a man with no influential connections (16:1-2) who performed strange signs (e.g., 18:1ff.) and brought a stern and unpopular message. He suffered expulsion, torture, and imprisonment, and at the end he had to flee the disorder in Judah and take refuge in Egypt, where we lose all trace of him.

The historical background of his mission is of special interest. During his lifetime, at the end of the 7th and the beginning of the 6th century B.C., great changes took place in the Middle East. Assyria, which had ruled with great cruelty, was in retreat. The smaller kingdoms took the opportunity to throw off foreign dominion. But their independence did not last. As Babylon grew stronger, it inherited Assyria's power, though ruling with greater humanity. In vain the little kingdoms of Syria and Palestine tried to form alliances and to seek Egyptian help. They fell one by one to Babylon, Judah being no exception. Jeremiah, who had foreseen the disaster, witnessed the destruction of Jerusalem (586) and the beginning of the exile.

The time of Jeremiah's activity as a prophet can be divided into three periods corresponding roughly to the reigns of Josiah (627-609), Jehoiakim (608-598), and Zedekiah (597-586). During the first period Assyrian power was ebbing and Josiah was able to bring parts of Israel under his rule. During the second period Babylonian power was growing and Jehoiakim wavered between the pro-Egyptian and pro-Babylonian lobbies at court. During the last, Babylon extended its dominion, Zedekiah rebelled, and Jerusalem was attacked and taken.

(1) New Hope for Ephraim. Astonishingly, in Jer. 2:2–4:2 and 30:2–31:22 we find oracles that are addressed not to Jerusalem and Judah but to Israel, to which Jeremiah had been commissioned to proclaim this message (3:12). The content is even more astounding, for instead of pronouncing new judgment God invited his people back to himself (3:12, 22) and granted them a compassionate promise of salvation (30:2ff.). Israel, or Jacob, still lived on as a remnant, and it still had a future. This was an almost unbelievable message for the people of Israel.

To be sure, the people had to be reminded of their infidelity and of the need for a radical change: "I brought you into a fruitful land . . . but . . . you defiled it" (2:5ff.). The Israelites had behaved like children denying their father (2:27), like oxen breaking the yoke (2:20a), like a choice vine that has become worthless (2:21), or like a stupid farmer preferring a cracked cistern to a spring (2:23ff.). This was why the cities had been "razed to the ground and abandoned" (2:14-15). But the remnant could still come back to the Lord. The Lord himself was inviting them: "Come back to me, apostate Israel" (3:12-13). Nor did the invitation go unheeded: "Hark, a sound of weeping on the bare places, Israel's people pleading for mercy" (3:21). Hence the good news could be proclaimed: "Cease your loud weeping. . . . There is hope for your future" (31:16 NEB, 17 RSV); "I have dearly loved you from of old" (31:3).

Though this message was primarily directed to Israel, it was no less relevant to Judah when disaster struck. It would give hope to the Judeans, too, during the dark days of occupation and exile.

(2) Catastrophe from the North. In a vision Jeremiah saw a cauldron on a wind-fanned fire tilted away from the north. He then heard God say: "From the north disaster shall flare up" (1:13-15). This was a message for Judah, and as Jeremiah had had words of comfort, so now he had to speak words of menace.

Two contemporary events formed the background. Josiah had fallen at Megiddo in 609 B.C. and the hope of rebuilding greater Israel had vanished. Nebuchadrezzar had defeated Egypt at Carchemish in 605 B.C. and was now poised to oust Assyria as ruler of the Middle East. The two events brought Judah and God's people into imminent danger. In vision after vision Jeremiah had to alert his fellow citizens to approaching disaster.

First, he had to make the people aware of the danger and to prevent them from feeling secure. He thus described the expected attack as so powerful that resistance would be useless and total destruction might result. The holy land was about to return to the state of *tōhû wābōhû* ("without form and void," 4:23). The God of Israel was himself bringing the catastrophe from the north (4:6, 11-12; 5:15-17). Could he really act as an enemy and bring death to his own people? Yes, was the prophet's strange and startling message.

Second, Jeremiah had to call the people to account. Israel must understand why disaster was about to befall it. The threat of death must produce alarm at sin. To this end Jeremiah emphasized that the people had forsaken the Lord, had been unfaithful to him (5:7, 11), had forgotten him (13:25). Fraud, lies, and treachery called for condemnation (5:31; 6:13; 7:4; etc.). No harm was seen by the people in perjury, adultery, or exploitation.

There was no readiness for conversion (8:5; 9:5). Evil had become the people's very nature. How could the Lord welcome sacrifice, fasting, or worship (6:20; 7:21)? No longer the Lord's people, the Judeans were about to be punished (5:9), spurned (6:30), abandoned (7:29), and handed over to the enemy for destruction (12:7). The prophet's aim, however, was to challenge people to awareness of the situation, to repentance and salvation (4:14; 13:15-17; 21:12).

Third, Jeremiah accompanied his message by strange acts pointing to the coming disaster. He cut off his hair, threw it away, and raised a lament (7:29). He was forbidden to have a wife or family (16:2). He could take part in neither mourning nor feasting (16:5, 8). He was to put a linen girdle around his waist, then hide it in a crevice, and later retrieve it "spoilt, and no good for anything" (13:1ff.). He bought a jar and publicly shattered it (19:1ff.). He put a yoke around his neck, and when this was broken replaced it with a bar of iron (27:2ff.). By these strange acts he caused the people to sense that the disaster which seemed remote in his words was already a reality. He also showed that the reality had a deeper dimension. In the mirror of the acts we see that the people's suffering is the judgment of the Lord on its unfaithfulness to him.

(3) Jeremiah's Struggle. In seven passages generally known as the confessions of Jeremiah the prophet offers unique insight into his personal struggle. The confessions are not confessions of sin or of faith but of feeling as Jeremiah wrestles with his calling. He is, as it were, thinking aloud in poetic prayers (12:1-6), in accounts of his experiences (11:18-23), or in complaints at the harshness of God's Word and the people's refusal to listen to it (4:19ff.; 6:10-11). The confessions are intensely personal, but in three ways they are connected with Jeremiah's message.

(a) Jeremiah shares his people's fate. He is thus torn between two loyalties. He wants to serve God even though God's Word nearly crushes him. The Word that had once been his delight has now become bitter as he sees the imminent doom of his people. This is no shallow sympathy. The disaster strikes the prophet, too: "I am wounded at the sight of my people's wound" (8:21-22). He shares the bitter suffering (4:19ff.). He cannot desire "this day of despair" (17:16). He must boldly stand up for the people and make intercession (15:11; 18:20). The double pressure almost breaks him.

(b) Jeremiah also suffers rejection by the people. The suffering of rejection exacerbates the suffering caused by the Word. Initial disappointment at the people's indifference (6:10) and ridicule (17:15) is succeeded by complaint at his lot as the Lord's messenger. Forced to live a life of isolation, he feels duped (20:7-8). Even his relatives and friends humiliate him and try to kill him (11:19, 21; 15:15; 18:18-20; 20:10). His only apparent recourse is to seek God's help and the overthrow of his enemies (12:3; 17:14), even though he has just interceded for them (18:20). His own survival and that of his mission are at stake.

(c) Jeremiah struggles with God himself. The Lord does not ignore his servant's complaints. He renews the initial promise: "I am with you" (1:18-19; 11:21-23; 15:20-21). He encourages the prophet to struggle on to success (12:5). Yet Jeremiah is not always sure of his help: "Thou art to me like a brook that is not to be trusted, whose waters fail" (15:18; cf. 20:7). A laughingstock of the people and apparently abandoned by God, he will not "speak in his name again" (20:9). He even curses the day of his birth (20:14ff.). Hopelessness cannot be his final word, for strength continually comes to him from God, but his ministry is one of constant wrestling as God seems to have laid upon him an impossible and thankless task.

(4) The Impact of Jeremiah's Message. Included in the book of Jeremiah are accounts of his experiences under Jehoiakim and Zedekiah. In addition to telling us something about his life and sufferings, these stories also show us what was the impact of his ministry on the people.

First, of course, the stories confirm the fact that the people rejected his message. The kings, the prophets (Hananiah, ch. 28), the other leaders, and the people as a whole regarded his oracles as offensive to ruler, nation, and religion alike (ch. 26). Nevertheless, this rejection could not suppress the message. Unexpectedly a few individuals took Jeremiah's side: some elders of the land (26:17), Ahikam the son of Shaphan (26:24), other members of Shaphan's family (36:10, 25), and Ebed-melech the Cushite eunuch. As a result the prophet was able to continue his disturbing ministry.

Second, the disaster that Jeremiah prophesied finally came and the people felt the concrete impact of God's Word: The Lord brought down on the inhabitants of Judah "all the calamities with which I threatened them, and to which they turned a deaf ear" (36:31). Jerusalem fell, the temple was destroyed, Judah ceased to exist as a nation, many of the people were killed or exiled, the new beginning came to a swift end with the murder of Gedaliah, and Jeremiah himself became a victim when he was finally forced to take refuge in Egypt.

Third, Jeremiah's message deeply influenced those who faced the problem of Israel's future after the disaster of 586. Jeremiah had foreseen a future—not a glorious restoration but a modest start (29:4-7). The Lord would build up again after uprooting (1:10; 12:14-15). But reconstruction could begin only after radical spiritual renewal (31:31ff.). The people must give up their dreams of glory and be ready to live humbly as the Lord's people, whether in exile or in their own land (7:1-15; 22:1ff.; 42:10-17). Their calling was to be a witness to powerful nations which would themselves fall under judgment for injustice, cruelty, and oppression. In this sense Jeremiah would finally be indeed a "prophet to the nations" (1:5).

g. Ezekiel, the Son of Buzi

Ezekiel was a prophet of the stature of Isaiah and Jeremiah, yet he remains comparatively little known, his book is seldom read, and his message is largely ignored by both Jews and Christians. (Muslims have usually never even heard of him, since the Koran does not mention him.) With its strange visions, its unusual signs, and its sharp threats, the book is not immediately attractive, but it will well repay us to savor the sweet kernel (3:3) under the hard shell.

Facts about Ezekiel are sparse. He was a priest, or at least the son of a priest (1:3). His sacerdotal origins make themselves felt in his interest in the temple and his concern for its holiness. When Jerusalem first fell in 597 B.C., he had gone into exile with Jehoiakim and thousands of the upper class. In 593 he was called to be a prophet by the river Kebar (1:1, 3), i.e., in Tel-abib in Babylonia (3:15). He was married but lost his wife at the very time when Jerusalem fell again in 586 B.C. He probably died in exile sometime after 571 B.C. (cf. 29:17), long before the promised restoration. Though contemporary with Jeremiah, he ministered against a different background.

The book of Ezekiel is clearly arranged in three main parts: the condemnation of Judah and Jerusalem (chs. 1–24), oracles concerning the nations (chs. 25–32), and prophecies of renewal and restoration (chs. 33–48). Distinctive features are that God's Word came to the prophet directly (1:3; 3:6), that he received impressive visions at decisive moments (1–3; 8–11; 40–48), that he was addressed as "son of man" (ben-'ādām, 2:1; 3:8; etc. RSV), and that the knowledge and the glory of God are here the declared purpose of the divine acts (6:13; 7:9; 36:9).

(1) Against the Optimism of the Exiles. Ezekiel's mission began with his calling by the Kebar in 593 B.C. Four years had elapsed since the Babylonians took Jerusalem (2 Kgs. 24:8ff.). The situation in Judah was normal again. The elites in exile expected that they would soon be allowed to return home. They did not see the event of 597 as a stern summons from God to repentance but as a mere accident of history. Ezekiel was sent by God to oppose this optimism, primarily among his fellow exiles.

The story of his call (1:1–3:15) merits our attention from three angles. First, the heavens were opened and the prophet had a tremendous vision of the Lord seated above the heavenly vault (1:22, 26). God himself had to take the initiative to break through the wall separating him from the creaturely world. He had to come personally, by way of an unworthy "son of man" called Ezekiel, to an unclean foreign land to visit the very people he had thrown away from his presence. Second, the people to whom the message is to come were negatively described as "a nation of rebels" from the very first (2:3). God's grace was unfathomable that he should send the prophet to such a nation! Third, Ezekiel was charged to speak God's Word firmly "whether they listen or whether they refuse to listen" (2:5, 7; 3:11). Does this mean that Ezekiel did not really care about the people's negative attitude and its painful consequences? His preaching was marked indeed by a certain harshness. It was for the people's good, however, that he was to speak so sternly. There would come a time when his firmness would command respect: "They will know that they have a prophet among them" (2:5), and some at least would pay heed to him.

The sharpness of Ezekiel's message may be seen especially in what he says about the day of the Lord. Traditionally Israel looked forward to a great day when the Lord would punish its enemies (Isa. 13:6), but Amos and Isaiah had already shown that the day of the Lord would be a day when God punished his own people (Amos 5:18-20; Isa. 2:12-17). Ezekiel pressed home the point: "Behold, the day! the doom is here, it has burst upon them" (7:10ff.). The day of the Lord would be indeed the last day for Israel. The whole people now faced divine judgment. It could no longer be evaded. Instead of indulging in optimistic dreams, the people must face the terrifying reality.

Ezekiel illustrated his sharp message by symbolical acts that must have astonished those who witnessed them. He traced out a road crossing which would set the king of Babylon on the way to Jerusalem (21:18-23). He depicted the siege of the city on a brick (4:1-3). He baked bread of different kinds of flour and ate it in daily rations as in a period of famine (4:9ff.). He left the city in a hurry at dusk (12:1ff.). He groaned (21:6-7), shaved his hair and beard (5:1-2), remained shut up in his house (3:25-27), and was forbidden to mourn when his beloved wife died (24:15-18). Many people no doubt regarded him as mad, but his actions clearly illustrated his message for those who made the connection.

In 592 B.C., a year after his call, Ezekiel had a vision. The Spirit transported him to Jerusalem, to the vicinity of the temple. He saw there the unfaithfulness of both priests and people. Judgment would begin in the temple itself. At the climax of the vision he saw the $k^e b \hat{o} d$ $YHWH$, the glory of the Lord, leaving the temple (chs. 10–11). Behind all the visible disasters, God's abandonment of his people was the supreme judgment. Of all the prophets Ezekiel grasped most fully the awful meaning of the approaching end.

(2) Opposing the Rebellious People. What were the sins, transgressions, infidelities, and rebellious acts that led to so severe a judgment?

First, Israel rebelled against the Lord in its worship. Inheriting a priestly tradition, Ezekiel laid emphasis on false worship. The people had set up hill altars and offered sacrifices to idols (ch. 6). They had practiced "monstrous abominations" (8:13) even in the temple itself, venerating the image of lust (8:3), erecting idols in the form of reptiles, beasts, and vermin (8:1), carrying out ceremonies for Tammuz (8:14), and prostrating themselves before the sun-god (8:16). The Judeans no longer had a divided heart; they openly provoked the Lord. They had become a defiled people. The whole land was defiled, and the Lord's name was profaned. Spiritually, Israel had become a harlot (chs. 16; 23).

Nor was the rebellion limited to the field of worship. Ezekiel sharply criticized the injustice and lawlessness that resulted from unfaithfulness to God. All classes—led by the king, the nobles, the priests, and the prophets—had revolted against God. Their sins (22:6-12) showed the close link between offenses against God (vv. 8-9) and acts of oppression that show disregard for human dignity (vv. 6ff.). They had trampled on the law of God that was designed to ensure the people's welfare.

In addition to religious and social rebellion, there was also political rebellion. Three chapters (17; 19; 23) use different literary forms to show how stupid and futile was the game of power politics that the kings of Israel and Judah had tried to play. A lament in 19:1ff. recalls the fate of Jehoahaz and Jehoiachin and warns Zedekiah against falling into the same trap. A riddle or parable in 17:1ff. makes it plain that if Jehoiachin, the very top of the cedar, had come to grief, Zedekiah, the vine that prospered in lowliness but schemed to grow bigger, would also be destroyed. The problem of power politics is also the issue in the vision of the two harlot sisters, Oholah and Oholibah, in ch. 23. Judgment has passed already on the former (Israel), but Judah stubbornly persists in its wicked course and will also be condemned. In this case the "whoring" consists of seeking alliances with alien peoples (cf. 23:30), especially Egypt, instead of trusting firmly in God alone.

Idolatry, injustice, and power politics were simply different aspects of one and the same revolt or rebellion against the Lord, the people's true and only Husband, Ruler, and Protector. All the Israelites were rebels. They always had been.

One of the best examples of this negative view of Israel and its history occurs in ch. 20. Certain elders consulted Ezekiel, hoping he would give them the promise of a quick return from exile. But Ezekiel had for them only a word of divine rebuke: "Tell them of the abominations of their forefathers" (20:4). All Jacob's descendants, in Egypt, at the liberation, at Sinai, and in the desert, had broken faith with God in spite of his many mercies. Nor had the rebellion ended in the land of promise. How, then, could the elders hope for a word of salvation?

Equally sharp condemnation may be found in ch. 16, where Jerusalem, representing Israel as a whole, is compared to a harlot. The Lord had adopted this proud city in pure mercy (vv. 6-14), but her shameless deceit (vv. 15, 24-25) would bring judgment upon her (vv. 35ff.). For all that, God was still wooing his people!

Ezekiel also compared Jerusalem to an unfruitful vine, no better than any other tree (15:1ff.). What good was it except for burning? This was the bitter reality that the prophet had to face. The people's proud self-delusion had to be broken. Only after judgment could there be a new beginning.

(3) Kindling a New Hope. Up to the destruction of Jerusalem Ezekiel's message was consistently one of rebuke and condemnation. But as soon as the city fell, his message changed. Zedekiah had revolted against Babylon. The Babylonians besieged the city. Ezekiel was incited to utter even sharper rebukes. He then fell mute in face of the disaster that was about to fall (3:26). But when news of the capture of Jerusalem came, he recovered "the power of speech" (24:27). Now that the prophecy of judgment had come true, he had the freedom to speak God's Word again.

Between the message of condemnation and that of salvation he pronounced condemnation on the nations. As Judah and Jerusalem had been judged, so would their neighbors, especially Tyre (chs. 26–28) and Egypt (chs. 29–32), though not yet Babylon. The nations would not be able to scorn God's people and in this way bring the name of God himself into disrepute (cf. 28:24).

A theme that links the two phases of Ezekiel's ministry is that of the watchman: "Son of man, I have made you a watchman for the house of Israel" (3:17; 33:7 RSV). In a protective role the watchman had to give warning of approaching danger. This Ezekiel had already done. But a watchman had to be on the lookout for approaching good as well as evil. He must prepare the people for its future destiny. This was what Ezekiel had now to do.

Another connecting theme was that of individual responsibility. The new generation did not have to suffer for the sins of the old. As the old generation might have averted judgment by repentance, so the new can find God's forgiveness if it turns from wicked ways. God's Word to Israel was ultimately one of hope: "I have no desire for the death of the wicked. I would rather that a wicked man should mend his ways and live" (33:11; cf. 18:32).

Ezekiel did not himself decide to exchange his message of death for a message of life. God himself granted the prophet a vision of life (37:1-14) that would replace the vision of death (chs. 8–11). Ezekiel saw a plain full of dry bones symbolizing the victory of death (37:1-3). But he must now prophesy to these bones. When he did, they came together, covered with flesh, but still lifeless (vv. 4-8). He had then to call upon God's Spirit to bring the slain to life again (vv. 9-10). In the same way the Lord would restore life to his dead people and bring it back to its own land (vv. 11-14). In this regard four points are to be noted.

(a) Israel's future after 586 had to be a new and radical beginning, a miracle. Israel had now come to an end. It lay in the grave. It could not live on as though it were a wounded or ailing people. Its only hope was new creation by the Lord, a new exodus, a new leading into the land of promise.

(b) This promise of a new beginning rested on God's free and unilateral act. Repentance was required, yet not as a precondition but as a challenge to which the Israelites had to respond. The exiles and those that remained in the land were invited to lead a new life, to turn to a new way, to take what God offered them, to step out of the pit into which their rebellion had plunged them. This was the challenge of Ezek. 18:1ff. and 33:10-20.

(c) Ezekiel spoke of the new beginning with a striking simplicity. He stressed the first steps. He insisted on a new obedience to God's laws, not on the coming glory of Israel. The reunification of the tribes, the emergence of a Davidic ruler, the rebuilding of the city and the temple, and the renewal of the covenant would then follow. Above all the temple would be rebuilt (chs. 40ff.). God's presence among his people (43:1-12) was the very basis of its restoration.

(d) Ezekiel emphasized the high price of the grace that he announced. God was not reviving Israel out of mere compassion. His concern was for his holy name (36:22). The profanation of the divine name had caused God himself to suffer but it had also incited him again to create a people for himself. This people would have the mission of confessing the holiness of the name of the Lord, and in this way of leading the nations to confess it too.

(4) Impact of Ezekiel's Ministry. Whether Ezekiel enjoyed success or not, his primary purpose—that the people would "know that they have a prophet among them" (2:5; 33:33)—was unquestionably achieved. Indeed, even if he was ignored individually, without his prophecy the people would have had little chance of preservation from death and little hope of a new future enabling them to face the challenge of life in exile or under foreign occupation.

Ezekiel also had a great influence later on the NT community. Revelation quotes him no fewer than 60 times. Paul's indictment in Rom. 1:21 (cf. Rev. 16:9) takes up a specific aspect of his message. The first petition of the Lord's Prayer echoes God's promise through him: "I will hallow my great name" (Ezek. 36:23). In later Christian history Calvin was one of his most illustrious disciples, insisting similarly on the holiness and glory of God, on human rebellion, and on the divine sovereignty in reconciliation and renewal. The nut again is hard, but in it is a sweet kernel, the praise of God's burning love.

4. God Builds Up: The Second Message of the Prophets

God also sent prophets to give new hope to survivors of the catastrophic judgment, (a) declaring that salvation is at hand and issuing a challenge of (b) freedom, (c) compassion, and (d) renewal.

THE BIBLE MAKES NO DISTINCTION between the prophets or their prophecies. The fifteen prophetic books of the Hebrew canon form a single series, beginning with Isaiah and ending with Malachi. The prophets of judgment are also prophets of salvation. The prophets of hope are also fierce challengers of God's people. God's Word is one of both rooting up and building up. The close relation between the two elements will direct our thoughts as we now focus specifically on the prophecy of rebuilding.

The exile brought a brief interruption of prophecy. Ezekiel was mute for a time. Jeremiah's voice was silenced. The prophets "received no vision from the Lord" (Lam. 2:9). As Ps. 74:9 sadly states: "We have no prophet now." But quickly God sent a prophetic message again to his people, and this time it was primarily a message of salvation.

a. Salvation at Hand

(1) Isaiah 40–55: Good News for Exiles. Whether or not these chapters are seen as Isaiah's work, the reference of their message is obviously to the exilic period. The prophet receives a special vocation in 40:1ff. to bring comfort to Jerusalem. A heavenly voice entrusts to him a message of salvation. God will bring his people back from exile notwithstanding all opposition (vv. 6-8). Whether the reference is also to the prophet's own mission in 42:1, 6 is debatable. Possibly Israel is in mind here, or the ultimate Servant of the Lord. The prophet's own function, however, is clear. He is a herald of unconditional salvation. These chapters have rightly been called the gospel in the OT. Without restriction they announce salvation both for Israel and the nations. God has set aside his wrath. He has forgiven the sin of his people. He has decided that the exiles will go free and return to their own land, which will itself be restored with Jerusalem as its center.

This good news is told with a beauty of style that readers can appreciate even in translation. The adopted form is in no way less attractive. The prophet speaks here like a priest communicating divine oracles to the people. The people come with complaints, and they are given oracles of salvation as Hannah was by Eli (1 Sam. 1:17). Specific features of these oracles of salvation, of which J. Begrich ("Das priesterliche Heilsorakel," *Zeitschrift für die alttestamentliche Wissenschaft* 11 [1934] 81-92) finds at least twenty, are the designation of those addressed as the Lord's servants, the self-disclosure of God, the stating of the reason for the oracle, its purpose, and the promise of divine presence and help, often introduced by the words: "Do not fear."

The miserable condition of the exiles is clear enough. They are called "Jacob you worm and Israel poor louse" (Isa. 41:14). They are wretched and poor (41:17). They are a "remnant" (46:3). They are "prisoners" and "in darkness" (49:9). They are "taunted" (cf. 51:7). They are like a "deserted wife" (cf. 54:6). They are still stubborn and "far from deliverance" (46:12 RSV). Yet unexpectedly God is now calling them by name. They are "my people" (51:16), "my servant . . . whom I have chosen" (41:8-9). He has fashioned them and they are his own (43:1-2).

The element of self-disclosure by God gains a new dimension when we remember that the exiles had left God. The identity of God is stressed: "I, the Lord your God" (41:13). He is "the Lord of Hosts" (54:5), "the Mighty One of Jacob" (49:26), "the Holy One of Israel" (41:14). The God who has manifested his holiness by wrath now speaks as "your creator" (43:1), "your Redeemer" (41:14 RSV), "your deliverer" or "Savior" (RSV) (43:3). From the very first God has been faithful (49:7) and has loved Israel (43:4), but he does so freely and unexpectedly.

The core of oracles of salvation is the promise of divine help. This comes in the form of the pledge: "I am with you. . . . I help you" (41:10, 13, 14; 43:1, 5; 44:2; 51:12; 54:4). The call not to remember former things perhaps explains the exhortation not to fear; the people are not to dwell on "days gone by" (51:9 NEB). The Lord had once freed the people from Egypt, led them through the wilderness to Canaan, and chosen Jerusalem, but now the time has come for a reenactment of these events which is all the more wonderful against a background that is so gloomy: "I will bring your children" (43:5); "I will make a way even through the wilderness" (43:19); "I will lead the blind" (42:16 RSV); "I will grant deliverance in Zion" (46:13).

The promise of this new exodus is unconditional but it is not without a purpose. At the end of salvation oracles we often find an injunction to proclaim God's works so that his name may be praised not only by his own people (41:16) but by nations that have thus far not yet known him (41:20), and even by heaven and earth (49:13). Promising to pour down his Spirit (44:3), the Lord shows that this salvation will make possible a wholly new way of life.

Though the whole of Isa. 40–55 has salvation as its message, only a few texts are in fact salvation oracles. Most of the material consists of discussions or questions and answers that expound the message of liberation and adduce reasons and proofs to convince those who hear it. Obviously there is an unwillingness on the part of the recipients of the message. They are dumb (unwilling to listen) and blind (unable to see the signs of the times). The prophet thus engages in a debate in which people bring their questions to God and hear his answers.

Two literary forms have been distinguished (cf. H. Gunkel and J. Begrich): the legal debate in which prosecutor, accused, defense attorney, witness, and judge speak in turn (41:1-5, 21-29; 43:8-13, 22-28; 44:6-8), and the discussion in which the partners speak to a certain theme (40:12-31; 44:24-28; 45:9-13). Since the theme is always the same, however, we may take both forms together.

The Lord promises to deliver his people from foreign nations so that the latter may recognize his majesty. But has he really the power to keep his promise? Is his "arm too short to redeem" (50:2)? The exiles found the power of Babylon so great that they might be tempted to think Babylon's gods were stronger than the Lord. The prophet thus reminded them that the Lord alone is in charge, and that no one in heaven or earth can be compared to him: "I am the Lord, there is no other" (45:5). If proof is needed, then "lift up your eyes to the heavens; consider who created it all" (40:26). The Lord also created Israel, and if he liberated it once, why could he not do so again? In contrast to him the gods are mere idols, the work of human hands (40:18-20; 41:6-7). Only stupid people trust in an "image" (42:17), in "a god that cannot save" (45:20).

The Lord will save Israel in his "love which never fails" (54:8). But where was this loving God when catastrophe struck? Was Israel's plight "hidden from the Lord" (40:27)? "No; it was through your own wickedness that you were sold" (50:1). The Lord was purifying his people "in the furnace of affliction" (48:10), but even in the worst hours "my love shall be immovable . . . and my covenant of peace shall not be shaken" (54:10).

The Lord made known this good news through his Word, but after many deceptive promises given by false prophets the people were hesitant. Did not this Word stand in sharp contrast to the bitter reality? Did not Babylonian power reign unchallenged? In answer, the prophet argued that past oracles had come true (42:9) in spite of their apparent impossibility: "For my thoughts are not your thoughts, and your ways are not my ways" (55:8-9). The power that now oppressed the exiles was only temporary. Kingdoms rise and fall (40:15-17, 23-24). God's Word can shape reality unexpectedly. The rise of Cyrus after 546 B.C. was proof enough. This ruler could be hailed as the chosen instrument by which God would deliver his people (41:2-5; 42:25; 44:28; 45:1ff.; 46:11; 48:14-16).

Among the compositions telling of Israel's approaching deliverance are four strange poems centering on the mysterious person of the "Servant of the Lord."

In 42:1-4 the Lord introduces his servant as a representative to the nations, though it is not wholly clear how he will establish justice or quietly bring his message. In vv. 5-9 the Lord gives him the task of bringing light to the nations and delivering them from the prison of blindness.

In 49:1-6 the servant acknowledges that the Lord has called him to be an instrument of revelation, that the Lord sustains him in his prophetic struggle, and that the Lord confirms him as a messenger of salvation for both Israel and the nations.

In 50:4-9 the Lord leads his servant day by day and teaches him how to stand firm against oppression. Those who suffer injustice are invited to follow the servant's example, and those who violate justice are severely censured.

In 52:13–53:12 it is God's faithful people who speak. They have seen the servant's suffering and death and they acknowledge the significance of these events for their salvation. The servant's victory is affirmed and his suffering is interpreted as a sacrifice for the forgiveness of the sins of "many nations" (52:13-15; 53:11-12).

These poems are new elements in the chapters. Elsewhere all Israel is called God's servant (41:8-9), but here the servant is a single individual. Elsewhere the stress is on the deliverance and restoration of God's people, but here the central reference is to the mission and struggle of the servant. Elsewhere the nations will lose their power and be ashamed, but here they have the promise that they, too, will be saved by the servant.

Who is this servant? He is obviously a prophet. He is called and sent and endowed with the Spirit (42:1). His mouth is like a sharp sword (49:2 RSV). His message is one of liberation for Israel and the nations. But he also sharply challenges his hearers. In fulfilment of his mission he meets with constant opposition and rejection. He was perhaps imprisoned or suffered from poor health. He finally died as a martyr and was "assigned a grave with the wicked" (53:8-9). Yet he willingly accepted his sufferings (50:5-6). He even "made himself a sacrifice for sin" (53:10). He suffered for no faults of his own. By the Lord's commission and as the Lord's deputy he bore the sin of many. His defeat, then, was turned into victory (53:10-12).

Exegetes differ widely in their attempts to identify the servant. Some argue that Israel itself is the servant, some the author, some an unknown prophet. Irrespective of any contemporary reference, however, the NT has no difficulty in finding in Jesus the true and definitive Servant of the Lord, and in his vicarious passion, death, and resurrection the fulfilment of the Servant's mission (Acts 3:13, 26; 4:27, 30; 8:27ff.; 1 Pet. 2:21ff.).

(2) Other Passages. Many passages in the older prophets, regarded by some scholars as exilic additions, also held out the hope of restoration for Israel. Thus in Amos 9:11-12, 13ff. David's house will be built up again and the Israelites will return to their own land. Again, in Hos. 1:7ff.; 2:14-23 there is a promise of compassion for Judah, and in Hos. 14:4-8 the hope of restoration after catastrophe. Similar promises occur in Isaiah (e.g., 2:2ff.; 11:11ff.; 12:1ff.; 28:5-6), Micah (2:12-15), Jeremiah (3:14-18; 5:18-19; 16:14-15; 23:3ff.), Zephaniah (3:9-20), and Ezekiel (11:14-21; 17:22-24; 36:1ff.; 37:20ff.).

A common theme in these prophecies is that of a new exodus. Thus we read in Isa. 11:11ff. that God will "extend his hand again to recover the remnant of his people" (CB) and that there will be a "causeway" for them as when "they came up out of Egypt." Micah, too, speaks of a gathering of "the whole house of Jacob," the Lord himself leading the way (Mic. 2:12-13). The people's prayer to God is this: "Show us miracles as in the days when thou camest out of Egypt" (7:15). The famous oracle in Jeremiah 31:31-32 links the exodus out of Egypt to the coming exodus out of Babylon, yet with the difference that God will now make a new covenant with his people.

Another common theme is that of abundant blessing in the ancestral land. Although the land has suffered devastation, it will now yield bountiful crops (Amos 9:13-15; Hos. 2:20; Isa. 30:23-24). The ruined towns and villages will be rebuilt (Amos 9:11; Mic. 7:11; Jer. 31:38-40). God will be present among his people as their King (Mic. 4:7; Isa. 4:5-6). David's throne will be restored (Amos 9:11; Jer. 23:5; Ezek. 34:23-24), and under this strong rule the people will be reunited (Hos. 1:11; Isa. 11:13-14; Jer. 3:18; Ezek. 37:22), justice will reign (Isa. 28:5-6; Jer. 3:15), and there will be lasting peace and security (Hos. 2:17-19; Isa. 11:6ff.; Mic. 4:3-4; Zeph. 3:13).

Spiritual renewal is another important theme. As we read in Ezek. 11:19-20: "I will give them a different heart and put a new spirit into them." As the Spirit is poured upon the people (Isa. 32:15; Ezek. 39:29), they will repent of their wickedness, know and do God's will, and hallow the name of God (Isa. 29:23; Jer. 31:33-34; Ezek. 20:43-44). Pure worship will again be possible (Hos. 14:2-4; Ezek. 16:63) and idolatry will be banished (Hos. 2:14-16; Isa. 30:22). God's law will be in the people's hearts in fulfilment of the covenant: "I will become their God and they shall become my people" (Jer. 31:31ff.; cf. Ezek. 37:26-27).

With the restoration, the wrath of God will judge the nations that oppressed Israel (Amos 9:12; Isa. 11:4; Mic. 3:13; Zeph. 3:19; Ezek. 35; 38). Yet the nations will not be totally destroyed. There is a future for them, too. They will come as pilgrims to the holy mountain to worship the Lord (Zeph. 3:9; Isa. 2:2-4 par. Mic. 4:1-3; Isa. 11:30). The Lord rebukes the peoples only to show that they are included in his care and to turn them from their evil ways. He will finally heal them with great compassion (Isa. 19:22; Jon. 4:11).

b. The Challenge of Freedom

(1) Haggai. When Cyrus allowed the Babylonian exiles to go home in 538 B.C. (Ezra 6:3-5) at first only a few returned to Jerusalem, and when there they could do no more than erect an altar for worship. Around 521 a larger group came under the leadership of Zerubbabel, a grandson of Jehoiachin, who had died in Babylon, and of Joshua, the exiled high priest. This company apparently returned at a time when the throne of the new king Darius was endangered by various revolts.

To these returned exiles the prophet Haggai brought a message from God on August 29, 520: "Go up into the hills, fetch timber, and build a house acceptable to me" (Hag. 1:8). This challenge came to people who believed that the economic situation was still too bad to make rebuilding of the temple possible, their concern being primarily for their own houses. But Haggai told them that neglect of the temple is in fact the reason for the poor economy: "You look for much and get little. . . . Why? . . . Because my house lies in ruins, while each of you has a house that he can run to" (1:9-10). Haggai's words moved the people and persuaded the two leaders, Zerubbabel and Joshua, to initiate work immediately on the Lord's house (1:13-14). The temple site was cleared (cf. Zech. 4:7), and by the middle of September 520 rebuilding began with the laying of the foundation stone. Perhaps Haggai then gave the promise: "From this day on I will bless you" (Hag. 2:19; cf. 2:1, 15-18).

A month later people were comparing their efforts with the glorious temple of Solomon, bemoaning the insignificance of the new structure, but Haggai encouraged them: "Take heart. . . . Begin the work, for I am with you" (2:4). For all the paltriness of the house from a human standpoint, God would himself see to it that "the splendor of the latter house will surpass the splendor of the former" (2:8-9 CB).

A further saying of Haggai is difficult to interpret. The prophet asks the priests for a ruling whether consecrated meat can sanctify other food if a fold of the robe in which it is carried touches it. The answer is in the negative. But if someone who is defiled by contact with a corpse touches any food, that food is defiled. The meaning might be that existing sacrifices cannot sanctify a people that is defiled by death, or that the unclean Samaritans must not share in rebuilding the temple as they desired (Ezra 4:1ff.), or that those who put their own interests above the Lord's cannot bring acceptable offerings. In any case, blessing will come with the concerted effort to rebuild the Lord's house (Hag. 2:18-19).

Finally, Haggai in God's name recognized Zerubbabel as the Lord's servant, the "signet-ring" replacing that lost in the person of his grandfather Jehoiachin (cf. Jer. 22:24). Amid the turmoil of nations God will establish his own chosen ruler, prefiguring the Prince of peace (Isa. 9:6) who will finally inaugurate God's own reign of righteousness for all nations.

(2) Zechariah. Zechariah took up the same call as Haggai. He was the son or grandson of the priest Iddo (Ezra 5:1), and since he used images taken from Babylonian culture he had probably returned from exile. He began to prophesy in October 520, shortly after Haggai. His primary message may be found in chs. 1–8 and it falls into two main parts: first, a series of visions unfolding God's plan of salvation, along with oracles on Joshua and the Branch (chs. 1–6), then, on the basis of the visions, oracles on the coming salvation and its moral implications (chs. 7–8).

Like Haggai, Zechariah proclaimed the Lord's return to his house: "I have come back to Jerusalem with compassion, and my house shall be rebuilt in her" (Zech. 1:16). Zion was again the chosen city. To touch it was to touch the apple of God's eye (2:8), for God had made his dwelling there (2:10). The exile had been a judgment on the people's defiance (7:11-14), but if the people will come back to God, "I will come back to you" (1:3; cf. 8:14). In virtue of God's presence there was no reason to fear, but the people must "speak the truth to each other, administer true and sound justice" in the courts (8:16).

In the first vision Zechariah saw riders who had visited the whole world and heard the report that the world was "still and at peace" (Zech. 1:11; Darius in 519 B.C. had quenched the revolts). Though Jerusalem was disappointed at the Lord's lack of compassion for it, the assurance was given that the Lord burned with love for his chosen city and would see to its restoration (1:7-17). The second vision portrays the scattering of the nations that had afflicted God's people as four smiths destroy the horns that dealt so harshly with Judah (1:18-21). The third vision relates to the rebuilding of Jerusalem. A surveyor is measuring out the length and breadth of the new city with a line, but an angel stops him, saying that "Jerusalem shall be a city without walls," the promise of God being: "I will be a wall of fire round her," even "a glory in the midst of her" (2:1ff.).

The divine presence is the theme of the central vision (4:1ff.), that of a golden lampstand with seven lamps, each with seven pipes, and two "sons of oil" (NEB "consecrated with oil," RSV "anointed") standing before it (4:11-14). Zerubbabel, who had laid the foundation of the new house, would also finish it, yet "neither by force of arms nor by brute strength, but by my spirit! says the Lord of Hosts" (v. 6). The vision of the flying scroll then proclaims the cleansing of the city from theft and perjury. Those who have seized the land of exiled families and sworn it was their own stand under the curse of the scroll (5:1-4). In a sixth vision the wickedness of Jerusalem is put in a great barrel which is then rammed shut and taken to Babylon (5:5-11). In a final vision God sends four chariots to the four corners of the world. The one that went north (to Babylon) brought rest there, though the exact meaning of the original text is not wholly clear (6:1-8).

What were the offices of the two "sons of oil" of 4:14? According to 3:1ff. Joshua stood before the Lord wearing filthy clothes and accused by Satan. The filthy clothes were taken off as the guilt of the people was removed. Joshua received clean vestments, a turban, and a precious stone. These signified his investiture as high priest—"an omen of things to come" (3:8).

In 6:9ff. the prophet was to collect offerings of gold and silver from the returned exiles and to make a crown for the man called "the Branch" who would build the Lord's house. This man would "assume royal dignity . . . and govern, with a priest at his right side, and concord shall prevail between them" (v. 13). Obviously meant for Zerubbabel, the crown at his death would become "a memorial in the temple of the Lord" (v. 14), a symbol of hope for the coming messianic King (cf. Isa. 33:15; Zech. 3:8).

Zechariah occupied a position of influence. When a group came to the priests to ask if they should fast in memory of the fall of Jerusalem, Zechariah was the one who replied. First, they were to "administer true justice, show loyalty and compassion to one another, . . . not oppress the orphan and the widow, the alien and the poor, . . . not contrive any evil one against another" (7:9), but second, the time for fasting had gone and "festivals of joy and gladness" had come for the house of Judah in the love of truth and peace (8:18-19).

Zechariah described these new and happy days in seven short oracles. Though it might not seem possible, God in his fierce love for Zion would rescue his people and renew his covenant (8:6-7). Jerusalem would thus be granted a new identity as the "City of Truth" and the "mountain of the Lord of Hosts" (8:3). People would live there in peace, the elderly sitting in the streets and watching their grandchildren at play (8:4-5). Israel and Judah, once the symbol of a curse, would now "become the symbol of a blessing" (8:13). The new salvation would flow out from Jerusalem to Judah and then to all peoples, making God known as "the Lord of the whole earth" (4:14 RSV; 6:5; 8:20ff.).

The final invitation to the nations to come and be saved was to find fulfilment when God was present in Jerusalem as Immanuel, incarnate in Jesus Christ. The promise of blessing issued through Zechariah is thus an ongoing incentive in Christ's name to preach the good news of salvation to every people.

c. The Challenge of Compassion

(1) Isaiah 56–66. The hopes raised by Isa. 40–55 and the promises made through Haggai and Zechariah were not wholly met. Many Jews in the post-exilic period suffered from poverty; only a few lived in affluence. The Jews readily worshiped God, but showed no great concern for neighboring countries. Some still looked for security both from the Lord and from other deities. In this sad situation the message of Isa. 56–66 proved especially relevant.

As in Isa. 43:1ff. the prophet claims here that he has a servant ministry, the announcing of good news: "The spirit of the Lord God is upon me, . . . to bring good news to the humble . . . to proclaim a year of the Lord's favour" (61:1-3). The Lord has sent his servant to proclaim the jubilee year when debts are remitted and lands restored (Lev. 25:25ff.; Jer. 34:8ff.). Since this proclamation is a legal decision (*mišpāṭ*), it is stressed that the Lord loves justice (*mišpāṭ*) (cf. Isa. 42:1ff.; Ps. 37:8). By this decision God secures the rights of the poor. He promotes just social relations by taking the part of the oppressed (Isa. 57:15). He gives the simple a chance (65:21, 23). Healing his people and giving them relief (57:18), he makes them like "a well-watered garden, like a spring whose waters never fail" (58:11). Caring for the needy, he demands that those who worship him share in liberating the oppressed and see to the basic needs of their fellow citizens: "Is not this what I require of you as a fast: to loose the fetters of injustice . . . to snap every yoke? . . . Is it not sharing your food with the hungry, taking the homeless poor into your house, clothing the naked . . . and never evading a duty to your kinsfolk?" (58:6ff.). The whole message rings out already in 56:1: "Maintain justice [*mišpāṭ*], do the right; for my deliverance is close at hand, and my righteousness will show itself victorious."

Those who conform to God's justice and worship him, keeping the sabbath undefiled, are saved, even though they might be aliens who give allegiance to the Lord (56:6), or eunuchs who are now given "a memorial and a name" in the house of the Lord (56:5). Yet the year of grace is also a year of recompense. The Lord was "displeased. . . . and put on garments of vengeance" (59:15ff. RSV) when he found no justice, righteousness, or honesty. Iniquity raised a barrier between the people and their God (59:20). Repentance was demanded (59:20). In the case of Edom, judgment was inevitable, for Edom had taken the opportunity to humiliate and oppress its neighbor when Jerusalem fell (63:1ff.).

The good news was addressed first to Jerusalem. Its inhabitants had been in darkness for a long time (59:10; cf. 9:2), but it could now arise: "Your light has come and the glory of the Lord shines over you" (60:1). The Lord's coming opened up unknown possibilities: "The Lord shall be your everlasting light" (60:19). Foreign nations were to assist the Jews to return and serve them (61:15). The Jews were to become "priests of the Lord," "a Holy People, the Ransomed of the Lord" (61:6; 62:12), so that "all who see them will acknowledge in them a race whom the Lord has blessed" (61:9).

Nor is salvation limited to Israel alone. "So shall the Lord God make righteousness and praise blossom before all the nations" (61:11). God will liberate all the oppressed. There must be constant expectation until God "makes Jerusalem a theme of endless praise on earth" (62:6-7). As the NT sees it, these final hopes, echoed in Ruth and Jonah, will find fulfilment later in Jesus Christ, whose good news of the kingdom of God is also proclamation of the year of the Lord's favor (Luke 4:18-19). Jesus comes to dwell among the broken, to free them from all fetters, and to invite them to live in the light of God.

(2) Ruth. Although Ruth describes events in the time of the judges, the book was no less applicable under the Persian occupation, when many people suffered hunger (Neh. 1:3; Ruth 1:1), were forced to sell their lands (Neh. 5:5; Ruth 1:1; 4:3), and had either to work for food or wages (Neh. 5:5; Ruth 2:13) or to make their way in a foreign land like Elimelech (Ruth 1:2). Only good landlords respected the right to glean loose ears and pick fallen grapes (Ruth 2:3ff.), which offered some protection to the poor (Lev. 19:9-10). The head of a clan redeemed the field of an impoverished relative only if it

offered some hope of gain, not to provide for needy family members (Ruth 4:4ff.; Neh. 5:1ff.). There was widespread disregard for God's law.

In a situation of this kind, Naomi, a widow who had lost both her husband and her sons, was representative of God's people suffering the full bitterness of poverty. She could ask to be called, not Naomi ("she who pleases"), but Mara ("the bitter one," Ruth 1:20). Yet she sought the Lord. Before returning to Bethlehem, she tried to send away her daughters-in-law with her blessing, since she could no longer guarantee their future. But Ruth ("friend") showed lovingkindness to her mother-in-law as she had formerly done to her husband— lovingkindness (hesed) is a key word in the story, though this is lost in translation (cf. 1:8; 2:20; 3:10). Ruth accompanied Naomi through the desert to a foreign land and accepted her God. Lovingkindness from Boaz was her reward. He not only let her glean but staunchly defended her rights before the elders, and although not himself the brother of Elimelech or Mahlon, redeemed the land that would belong to Elimelech's grandchild (yet to be born). The fact that "the Lord keeps faith with the living and the dead" (cf. 1:9) was the ground on which Ruth and Naomi stood. It enabled them to show solidarity to one another and to experience the truth that the Lord is with the broken, and also with those who help to liberate the crushed (Isa. 57:15; 58:6, 8).

The book shows, too, that God blesses all who give their allegiance to him. Foreign wives might be a danger (Ezra 9:1-2; Neh. 13:22ff.), but they did not have to be. Ruth the Moabitess was more precious to Naomi than seven sons could be (Ruth 4:15), and God himself chose her to be the grandmother of Jesse, the father of David. Indirectly but strikingly, then, the book shows that blessing does not have to come solely from temple worship. It can be found in the lovingkindness that Ruth, Naomi, and Boaz showed to one another, and that all of them experienced from God.

(3) Jonah. Like Ruth, Jonah is a short story set in the past. When Jeroboam II reigned over Israel in the 8th century B.C., Jonah, the son of Amittai, stood up and prophesied (2 Kgs. 14:25). According to the story God also gave Jonah a mission to Nineveh. Whether historical or fictional, what happened carried an important lesson for the postexilic period.

When given his commission, Jonah tried to evade it. Instead of going east, he took ship to Tarshish, where he hoped to be "out of reach of the Lord" (Jon. 1:3). But God did not let him escape. He sent a fierce storm, and when the sailors could not save the ship from sinking they ordered Jonah, who had taken refuge below deck and fallen asleep, to pray to his God. Still in extreme peril, they then cast lots to see who was to blame, and the lot fell on Jonah (1:7). Asked where he came from and what his business was, Jonah replied: "I am a Hebrew, and I worship the Lord the God of heaven, who made both sea and land" (1:9). Yet in spite of this confession he showed no sign of repentance; he wished only to die. The sailors, indeed, displayed more genuine fear of God than Jonah did. When hard rowing still failed to bring them to shore, it was only with reluctance that they threw Jonah overboard: "O Lord, . . . do not charge us with the death of an innocent man" (1:14). In the calm that followed, they also offered a sacrifice and made vows to the Lord (1:16). Even in trying to escape from God, Jonah had in fact been made a witness to the pagan sailors.

Jonah himself, it seemed, would evade his mission by death, but again God did not let him escape. He ordained that a great fish should swallow Jonah and then vomit him up again after three days and nights, eliciting from the prophet a psalm of trust and thanksgiving (ch. 2). Then the Lord gave Jonah exactly the same commission as he had given him before, and this time Jonah had no option but to go to Nineveh and give its inhabitants the short and terrible message of its approaching overthrow (3:4). The people, however, believed the warning, repented of their wickedness, engaged in a total fast, and hoped that God might relent (3:5ff.). The way that the Israelites repeatedly shunned was taken by pagan Nineveh!

Instead of welcoming the success of his warning, however, Jonah was angry. He had no concern for this alien people. He wanted God's judgment to fall upon it. He did not like it that the Lord was "a God gracious and compassionate, long-suffering and ever constant, and always willing to repent" (4:2). Instead of praising God as the God of grace, he wanted God to bring death to the great city. When he saw God's mercy, he angrily asked God to take away his own life: "I should be better dead than alive" (4:3).

Yet the Lord did not let his servant die. As he had ordered the fish to come, so he ordered a gourd to grow over Jonah's head to shelter him from the sun. But then with a fine sense of humor he ordered a worm to attack the gourd. When Jonah complained, he showed him how absurd was this complaint. Jonah could not suffer a little discomfort, but could look with indifference on the destruction of a great metropolis.

Playing with recurring and contrasting words and situations, the story masterfully ridicules supposedly pious but in reality self-centered Israelites who were not really dedicated to the Lord's service but concerned only for their own well-being. In contrast, it emphasizes God's overflowing compassion not only for his own people but for all peoples and all creatures. In addition, it finds in so-called pagans a greater willingness to respond to God's Word than is found among those to whom it is primarily addressed.

d. The Challenge of Renewal

(1) Joel. No record has come down to us of the life and times of Joel, the son of Pethuel. The book has been dated as early as the royal period and as late

as the Persian period. Though always relevant, its message was especially so for the postexilic community.

Joel opened his ministry with the startling challenge: "Alas! the day is near, the day of the Lord . . . a mighty destruction from the Almighty" (Joel 1:15). In this regard he took up a familiar prophetic theme, that of the day of the Lord as darkness and not light (Amos 5:18, 20). Locusts and a drought had already wasted the land, and a host from the north threatened even greater devastation: "Great is the day of the Lord and terrible, who can endure it?" (Joel 2:11; cf. vv. 1ff.).

Under this threat Joel summoned the people to repentance: "Turn back to me with your whole heart. . . . Rend your hearts and not your garments" (2:12ff.). The people responded, coming before God with solemn prayer and fasting, and God in his love and compassion answered their prayer, turning the famine into plenty (2:18-19).

The point here is that although God is a God of both justice and love, his ultimate purpose is the positive one of renewal. Restoration, not destruction, is his "proud deed" (2:21) or "wonder" (2:26). God enjoys giving life in all its fulness. He has as his primary aim: "You shall know that I am present in Israel" (2:27). To know God is not simply to have knowledge about him or to know his law. It is to live in an intimate relation with him (2:28-29).

As Ezekiel had promised a "new spirit" (Ezek. 11:19) and Jeremiah a new covenant (Jer. 31:33-34), so Joel promised a new relation in which all, by oracle, dream, or vision, will know God's plans and requirements. Nobody will have to depend on a priest to know God's will. All will be equal before him. His presence by the Spirit is freedom (cf. 2 Cor. 3:17), for no one is above others and "everyone who invokes the Lord by name shall be saved" (Joel 2:32). A dynamic community of this kind in which there is neither discrimination nor hierarchy, since all partake of the same enabling Spirit, has not yet been definitively achieved. It is the community of the future for which we long and toward which we strive.

(2) Malachi. In the difficult conditions of postexilic reconstruction, many Jews began to wonder if God still loved his people (Mal. 1:2). Many argued, too, that serving God is useless since evildoers are more successful than the righteous (3:14-15). To meet this situation, probably around the mid-5th century B.C., a prophet arose under the name "my messenger" (mal'ākî). He came with both a challenge and a promise to "clear a path before" the Lord (3:1).

The priests of Malachi's day did not honor God nor respect the people they were supposed to teach. They "set at nought the covenant with the Levites" (2:8). Despising God's name, they thought that any animals would do for sacrifice (1:6). Instead of rejoicing in their temple ministry they found it irksome: a mere business instead of joyous worship (1:6ff.). Instead of giving true teaching, they "made many stumble with [their] instruction" (2:8). Hence God would turn their blessing into a curse and abase them before the people, purifying the Levites and refining them like gold and silver (2:2ff.; 3:3-4).

Not the priests alone but all the people were violating the covenant by "being faithless to one another" (2:10). They were divorcing the wives of their youth in favor of foreign wives who could bring land or riches but who also worshiped alien gods (2:10ff.). They were prone to sorcery, wronged their workers, cheated widows, orphans, and aliens, and had no fear of God (3:5). Indeed, they even cheated God (3:8-9; cf. Acts 5:1ff.). But again God issued his call: "Return to me, and I will return to you" (3:7 RSV; cf. Zech. 1:4). If they responded, theirs would be a "favoured land" (3:6ff.).

Was this renewal possible? We do not know. What we do know is that God will send the messenger of the covenant to testify against all breaches of this covenant, and "who can endure the day of his coming?" (2:17–3:3). The coming judgment will separate "all the arrogant and the evil-doers," who will be like chaff, from those "who fear [the Lord's] name," of whom a record is kept and upon whom "the sun of righteousness shall rise with healing in his wings" (4:1-2). This judgment can only be the final act of human history.

Malachi closes with an injunction to remember the law of Moses (4:4) and an announcement that Elijah will come before the day of the Lord to reconcile fathers and sons. As Christians see it, John the Baptist played the role of Elijah, but implementing the reconciliation of generations which he initiated, and which Jesus consummated by his reconciling work, remains an ongoing task of prophetic ministry.

5. God Revealed His Ultimate Salvation

As God created heaven and earth and chose Abraham as his friend and Israel as his people that through them blessing might overflow to all nations, so (a) he revealed that (b) through Zechariah 9–14, (c) Isaiah 24–27, 35, and (d) Daniel that he will bring world history to an end (eschaton) and establish his kingdom of righteousness and peace.

a. The Meaning of Apocalyptic

GOD LED HIS PEOPLE INTO FREEDOM in order that they might live in responsibility both to him and to one another. Instead, they sought security in other gods, in wealth or power. They thus dishonored God and wronged their fellows. He passed judgment on them to bring them back to himself. In so doing he promised salvation to a faithful remnant. It became increasingly clear, however, that his coming would have to mean something totally new, and when under prolonged occupation and oppression the people began to ask whether he still cared for them, and why he let them suffer, he revealed his plans to seers, enabling them to see behind current events, and disclosing *(apokalýptō)* to them the true situation.

The true situation is that the Lord himself is about to come. He will free the oppressed and grant them fulness of life. He will put an end to the wicked powers that rule the world. He will end history itself and usher in his own kingdom. Judge of the mighty and Defender of the poor, he will make all things new. This reality is still hidden, but believers share already in the life of the coming kingdom and live according to its rule. The apocalyptic message thus has a subversive character. It shows that power structures must crumble, and it gives the poor and oppressed the courage to resist evil in the name of God their Defender.

Apocalyptic has three aspects. The old age is ending, the new age is coming. Those who know the mystery of God's coming live by the strength of this coming. Their realism is thus the decisive event of history. They are the link between the past and the future. To those who do not know the mystery they may seem to be the victims of wishful thinking, but they are not. If God is more patient with the world than they expect, they still stand directly before him who judges, liberates, and creates anew. Each generation of God's people stands before the coming Lord and lives with his kingdom on the horizon. The call of apocalyptic seers is that they should resist the structures of power that God has condemned and live already in terms of the coming *šalôm*.

Like the prophets, the apocalyptic seers were told of God's coming action, though not in detail. They differed from the prophets only by using the latter as a basis, often quoting their words but giving them a different context to express a different aspect of the truth, e.g., individual believers in Dan. 12:1 instead of the nations in Jer. 30:7. They also described symbolic visions instead of performing symbolic actions—visions which were not meant, of course, to be taken literally, but which give intimation of the divine action.

b. Zechariah 9–14

Although the later chapters of Zechariah are spoken as prophecy, they have many of the features of apocalyptic. They open with an oracle similar to that of Mal. 1:2-5. The Lord's greatness reaches beyond Israel. He calls a hero from the north, takes Syria, lays siege to Tyre and Sidon, invests the Philistine cities, and posts a garrison for his own house (Zech. 9:8).

The relation between Zech. 9–14 and specific historical developments is unclear, but in the vicissitudes of the times the people are like a flock for slaughter that false leaders, whose concern is only for their own interests, buy and sell. Hence God raises up a shepherd with two staffs, the one called "Favour" symbolizing God's covenant with all nations, the other called "Union" symbolizing the close relation between Judah and Israel. Yet this servant of God was rejected, the staffs were broken, his wages were put in the treasury, and the flock was handed over to a wicked shepherd who came under a curse (13:4ff.).

In these critical times divine revelation will come to an end. If idols are removed, so, too, are prophets. If any claim to be prophets, they will be accused of falsehood. Like Amos, a true prophet will disclaim the title: "I am no prophet, I am a tiller of the soil" (13:2ff.).

Yet the Lord does not withdraw from history. On the appointed day he will blow the trumpet and march to battle with Judah and Ephraim as his weapons. Judgment will fall on his enemies and blessing on his flock, so that young men and maidens will rejoice in the land (9:11-12). The cry of the dispersed will be heard; they will enjoy a more wonderful liberation than the original exodus. The Nile will be dried up and the pride of Assyria and Egypt shattered. The Lord will gather his people and they will spread to Gilead and Lebanon. "Israel's strength shall be in the Lord" (10:12; cf. vv. 1ff.).

On that day Jerusalem will be a cup that inebriates those who drink it, a rock that injures those who try to lift it. Panic, blindness, and madness will strike the enemy. Judah will be like a devouring brazier. A greater victory will be given than David's (12:1ff.). Though Jerusalem will fall first, the Lord will come, the Mount of Olives will be split, a road will be opened up for "all who survive of the nations" (14:16; cf. Isa. 45:20, 22), and they shall come to Jerusalem, which is renewed like the garden of Eden, and celebrate there the great Feast of Tabernacles, praising the Lord as King of the whole earth (14:1ff.).

The precise relation between the one who is pierced in 12:10 and the smitten shepherd of 13:7-8 is hard to determine. The message is clear, however, that after suffering the people will call on God's name. In a renewal of the age-long covenant God will reply: "They are my people," and they in turn will answer: "The Lord is our God" (13:9).

c. Isaiah 24–27 and 35

Chapters 24–27 of Isaiah, which follow the oracles of judgment on the nations, also deal with the last judgment and the ultimate salvation. Because of violations of the eternal covenant, judgment falls on evildoers (24:4-6). God is a righteous God. He cannot let evil go unrequited. He also cannot let those who trust in him be finally destroyed. "They that sleep in the earth will awake and shout for joy" (26:19ff.). On his holy mountain God will "show his glory" (24:21ff.) and "prepare a banquet" for all the peoples, wiping away all tears (25:6-8). It will then be said: "See, this is our God for whom we have waited . . . let us rejoice and exult in his deliverance" (25:9-10). The proud city that is the symbol of opposition to Zion will be crushed, and the Lord himself will be a "refuge to the needy" (25:1ff.). Israel, formerly the unfruitful vine, will now become a pleasant vineyard (5:1ff. and 27:2-3), and the scattered people will be gathered and "worship the Lord on the holy mountain" (27:12-13).

The aim of ch. 35 was to strengthen the feeble arms and steady the tottering knees, i.e., to confirm the people's trust that God will redeem them. God is indeed coming to save, and then the blind will see, the deaf hear, the lame walk, the dumb speak, the waters flow, and a pilgrim way of holiness be opened up on which the dispersed may come home, shouting for joy (35:4ff.). The imagery here is pushed to the limit. Against a dark background those who trust in the Lord are granted from heaven a vision of the new world that God will create. So, too, against the background of Golgotha, Christians walk in the light of Christ's resurrection, in which God's future is our present and our present is God's future.

d. Daniel

(1) A Varied Book. Daniel is a book of astonishing variety. It first presents Daniel as an exemplary believer in a religiously pluralistic society. Then Daniel himself describes his visions, which an angel has to interpret for him, and which all look ahead to the coming reign of God.

Daniel lived in the 6th century B.C. at the Babylonian court under Nebuchadnezzar, Belshazzar, Darius the Mede, and Cyrus. He followed the advice of Jeremiah in Jer. 29:7, bearing witness by assuming civic duties as well as by faithful worship. He had a message, then, for the later Hellenistic period when with greater economic and cultural intermingling Judah came under severe Hellenizing pressure. The message is to resist, for God will set up his own kingdom and strengthen those who already seek it.

Daniel did not claim specifically to be a prophet. He never stated: "Thus says the Lord." The Jews did not place the book among the Prophets but in the Writings. Daniel was a seer. A man greatly loved (Dan. 10:11), he prepared himself by prayer and fasting (9:3ff.) to receive God's revelation. Of himself he might be weak (10:8-10), but the heavenly messenger gave him strength (12:6-7) and showed him when God would end the period of affliction. Gabriel also interpreted his last visions. The book is in two languages: Hebrew in 1:1–2:3 and 8:1–12:13, Aramaic in 2:4–7:28.

(2) Daniel an Example. The first six chapters present Daniel as a man of faith. He was one of four young Jews of noble birth who were trained for government administration at the Babylonian court. Though grasping the opportunity, the four maintained their Jewish identity by politely refusing unclean food and asking simply for cereals, vegetables, and water. As a result God blessed them both physically and mentally, thus encouraging others to accept public responsibilities but without giving up their identity as God's people.

The king then had a dream which so burdened him that he could not tell its content but wanted an interpretation. As God had showed his plan for Egypt to Joseph (Gen. 41), so he revealed the secret of Nebuchadnezzar's dream to Daniel (Dan. 2:19, 28). Daniel took the opportunity to show the king that God's power limits all earthly power, so that praise belongs by right to him alone. A second dream followed in ch. 4, that of a lofty tree which God's watcher cuts down, leaving only a stump (cf. Gen. 11:1ff.; Ezek. 31:2ff.). The king is then humbled, suffering from mental alienation until he recognizes that "the Most High is sovereign . . . he gives [the kingdom] to whom he will" (Dan. 4:25). The powerful who do not recognize their limits become crazy for more power. Power corrupts, and absolute power corrupts absolutely.

The problem of power is the theme again in chs. 3 and 6. A single cult centered on a state symbol unifies a pluralistic society. But the demand is that this symbol alone be worshiped. Prayer must not be made to any other power (6:7). Those who believe in the one God, however, cannot accept this situation (3:12; 6:10). They thus bring the "sentence of death upon themselves" and can only entrust their lives to the God who is able to save them (3:17). In ch. 3 the king passes judgment in great anger (3:19), but in ch. 6 he realizes that he will lose one of his best counselors. There is here an "unalterable ordinance" even though it may harm the state (6:8). In ch. 3 the believers are thrown into a burning furnace and are joined by one like a god (3:24). In ch. 6 Daniel is thrown into the lions' den, and "God sent his angel to shut the lions' mouths" (6:22), thus justifying the king's confidence that Daniel's God would save him (6:16). Men and women of this type who "obey God rather than men" (Acts 5:29) are needed constantly to prevent states from pressing totalitarian claims.

In Dan. 5 the king transgresses the limits of lawful power by using the sacred vessels in a drunken feast and thus asserting that he may do as he pleases with what is holy to God (whether it be liturgical vessels or basic rights). A mysterious inscription on the wall challenges the king. Daniel alone can interpret it, and it intimates the end of Belshazzar's rule (5:26ff.); that he has "set [himself] up against the Lord of heaven" (5:23).

Daniel exemplifies a life of obedience to God. He also shows what is the prophetic ministry of God's people vis-à-vis the state. Appropriately, then, the church has placed his book among the Prophets.

(3) Daniel the Seer. At the center of power in his time, Daniel saw that those in power work constantly both to maintain and increase it. Their interest is not primarily in the welfare of those whom God has entrusted to their care. Hence the Lord himself has to take action.

In the vision of 2:31ff. Daniel saw a huge image symbolizing four kingdoms. The head of fine gold probably stood for Babylon, the breast of bronze for Persia, the belly of bronze for Media, and the feet of iron for the kingdoms of the Ptolemies and Seleucids (cf. Hesiod's division of history into four periods of gold, silver, bronze, and iron). At the climax of the vision "a stone was hewn from a mountain, not by human hands; it struck the image . . . and shattered" it (2:34). This stone had been ignored, but once God set it in motion, it destroyed the powers and became "a great mountain filling the whole earth" (2:35). The stone symbolized God's kingdom coming into the world (2:44; cf. 7:18; Luke 20:17-18, which relates the stone to Ps. 118:22 and Isa. 8:14-15 and interprets it messianically). God's kingdom is not set up by human hands; God himself sets it up to liberate the oppressed.

The night vision of Dan. 7 explores the same theme more deeply. Four beasts rise up out of the sea: a lion (Babylon), a bear (Persia), a leopard (Media), and horns (the Hellenic kingdoms). The Lord gives them power, but within limits. In a change of scene God himself comes in judgment. Thrones are set up and the Ancient in Years appears in flaming fire, arrayed in the white robe of purity and with the white hair of wisdom. Thousands attend him. Judgment begins, and power is given to "one like a man" who has come "with the clouds of heaven" like God himself (7:13-14). The power misused by the first man is now given to the "son of man," God's representative, who will care for God's earth and who, as King, will share God's eternal government. The "saints of the Most High" accompany him, i.e., God's faithful people (7:18, 22, 27). The aim of God's history with the race is not the kingdom of beasts but the kingdom of one who is responsible to God and who lives in communion with him. Solid hope is thus given to those who suffer from political and judicial oppression.

Daniel then had the vision of the he-goat trampling down the ram and the little horn that makes a prodigious show of strength, aspiring "to be as great as the host of heaven" and destroying "true religion" (8:3ff.). This "master of stratagem" (8:23) will even challenge the "Prince of princes" but will "be broken, but not by human hands" (8:25; cf. 2:34).

In ch. 11 it is said again that the blasphemous king "will meet his end with no one to help him" (11:45). Deliverance will then come to "every one who is written in the book" (12:1), i.e., individuals, not a collective. But when will deliverance come? First, there will be a time of unparalleled distress, then an equally incomparable liberation, and soon after that "the time of the end" (8:17; "the end of wrath," 8:19; "the latter days," 10:14 RSV). The ultimate liberation is too wonderful to be described.

To receive revelation, Daniel prepared himself by mourning, fasting, praying, and meditating on scripture (cf. 9:2ff.). Gabriel came to him (8:16; 9:21) and enlightened his understanding so that he might comprehend God's plan of salvation (9:22). He had the intimate fellowship with God that typified "wise leaders . . . [who] give guidance to the common people" (11:33; cf. 9:22) and tell them "what will happen . . . in days to come" (10:14). These wise leaders "shall shine like the bright vault of heaven, and . . . be like the stars for ever" (12:3). Eternal life is granted to all those "who sleep in the dust of the earth" (12:2). The Lord is righteous, and therefore those who trust him and are faithful to him will be raised up to share in his victory. The wicked will awake, too, but "to the reproach of eternal abhorrence" (12:2).

In 8:16 Daniel heard a voice telling Gabriel to help him understand the visions. The speaker stood before Daniel in the resemblance of a man but with gleaming body, shining face, flaming eyes, sparkling arms and feet, and a mighty voice (10:5-6). Was this the "son of man," or Gabriel, or God himself? The man raised Daniel up (10:9-10), touched his lips (10:16), and encouraged him: "Do not be afraid, man greatly loved . . . be strong, be strong" (10:19).

Enabled to speak like Isaiah (cf. Isa. 6:7), entrusted with an oracle of salvation, and told "what is written in the Book of Truth" (Dan. 10:21), Daniel occupied a place between the prophets and the later servants of God. From him we learn to see that God's kingdom is on the horizon of our own time and to look and work for it with a single mind. We cannot tell God, however, when the time has come for him to consummate his saving work. He himself decides this in his own freedom. His ways are not our ways. They are always so totally new that we can only marvel and give him the glory.

Conclusion

As THE WITNESS OF THE NT has it, God sent not only the prophets. John the Baptist was also "sent from God" (John 1:6), sent "to baptize in water" (1:33), charged with the message: "Repent; for the kingdom of Heaven is upon you" (Matt. 3:2ff.). John was preparing a way for the Lord (Matt. 3:3; cf. Isa. 40:3). He was the forerunner of the Messiah (John 3:28; cf. Matt. 11:13).

In the parable of the disloyal vinegrowers, the landowner sent his servants one by one and they were thrashed, stoned, and killed. At last, he sent his son, whom they conspired to kill so as to seize the vineyard for themselves (Matt. 21:33ff.). The servants were obviously the persecuted prophets (Matt. 5:12) who preceded Jesus, the Son of man. The Son was Jesus himself, coming "to give up his life as a ransom for many" (Mark 10:45).

Among his disciples, as among the people, Jesus was recognized to be "a prophet powerful in speech and action before God and the whole people" (Luke 24:19), but Peter saw that he was more than this; he was "the Son of the living God" (Matt. 16:16). John the Evangelist offered the same insight in his distinction between the Baptist and Jesus: "The Word became flesh . . . and we saw his glory, such glory as befits the Father's only Son" (John 1:14-15). By way of conclusion we may thus take note of the distinctiveness of Jesus, especially as it emerges in John's Gospel.

His teaching, he said, "is the teaching of him who sent me" (John 7:16). Like the prophets, whom God also sent, he communicated truthfully to his generation the message that God entrusted to him. He could do this because God was with him. Like the prophets, he had the gift of the Spirit, but in his case with unparalleled fulness (3:34). "All authority" was thus given to him, so that those who put their faith in the Son have eternal life (3:35). Like the prophets, Jesus transmitted God's words, but unlike the prophets, he is himself God's Word (1:1-2, 14). He did not act, of course, on his own initiative. Like the prophets, his aim was "the will of him who sent me" (5:30). But unlike the prophets, who went through times of silence, he always knew God's will; it was his "meat and drink" to do it, and to do it without delay (4:34; 9:4). In the work of salvation God and his messenger were one. They acted with the same authority and no differentiation could be made between their deeds.

It is true that the words and work of Jesus can be questioned. No absolute demonstration of their truth is possible. They can be genuinely understood only by those who believe in God and are open to his action. In this regard there is no difference between Jesus and the prophets. The religious leaders, wanting to defend their own ideology or position, and refusing to be challenged by the living God, accused the prophets of being false prophets instead of listening to them. Similarly, Jesus came under the charge of blasphemy (10:36). The testimony had been given by the Father (5:37), and no one can come to Jesus "unless he is drawn by the Father who sent me" (6:44). It is by faith that Jesus is seen to be the authentic messenger of God who is himself the eternal Son (5:24; 6:29; 11:42). Faith is the key to true knowledge of God (17:3, 8, 25).

God sent the Son not only to teach the world, and certainly not to judge it, but to save it (3:16-17). Jesus grants eternal life to all who trust in him (10:28). He gives himself as the bread of life (5:35) received in faith (5:24). He came that people might have life, and have it in its fulness, not as a private possession, but like an ever-flowing spring (10:10; 4:14).

In sharing his life with those who believe in him, Jesus gave himself for them. He was the good shepherd who lays down his life for his sheep (10:10-11). He showed the fulness of love by laying down his life for his friends (15:13). He died not only as a prophet bearing witness to the truth, but as "the Lamb of God, who takes away the sin of the world" (1:29 RSV). He took to himself the judgment that rightly falls on human sin. He thus effected definitive salvation for believers of every age and race. He inaugurated the ultimate salvation which prophets and seers perceived and prefigured, and which awaits its consummation with the manifestation of his hidden kingdom, which is the eternal kingdom of God.

Index of Subjects

235, 243, 254, 278, 292, 293, 312, 325, 331, 338, 342, 344, 346, 357; king of, 336; Babylonia, Babylonians, 19, 27, 39, 75, 261, 272, 280, 289, 328, 329, 335, 345, 355, 356; Pan-Babylonianism, 4

Balaam, 221, 302, 305, 307, 311

Belief, 14, 15, 42-43, 62, 64, 72, 79, 81, 88, 89, 96, 112, 255. *See also* Faith

Bethel, 45, 46, 47, 48, 259, 264, 309, 320, 321; and Dan, 215, 260, 264

Bless, blessing, God's, 29-30, 31, 43, 109, 180, 268, 287, 318, 326, 344, 349, 354, 356; of Adam and Eve, 27; and the ark, 241; in covenant, 120, 123, 127, 128, 129, 347; and curse, 347, 352; and fear of the Lord, 250; and heaven, 16, 17; illegitmate request for, 271; individual, 165; on Jerusalem, 291, 296, on the king, 196, 204, 207, 213, 218; of land, 184; through Moses, 308, to the nations, 54, 148, 186, 187, 204; oracle of, 320; of patriarchs, 52, 53, 55, 57; people ask for in tent, 149, 152; power as, 26; promised, 178, 263; on rebuilding temple, 345; and preservation, 100; and trust, 244; withheld, 34; and wisdom, 252

Blood, 159; of Abel, 34, 36; of the covenant, 124, 153, 179; on the hands, 273; innocent, 216; kinship, 129; life/soul in, 22; and offerings, 107, 161, 163, 164; of Passover lamb, 65; plague of, 74

Body, 21, 27; and soul, 65, 270. *See also* Soul

Cain, 29, 30, 31, 32, 35, 36, 47, 155, 160

Canaan, Canaanites, 7, 19, 39, 40, 43, 45, 48, 50, 53, 54, 58, 71, 73, 86, 87, 90, 94, 102, 103, 108, 109, 110, 111, 113, 114, 117, 120, 135, 136, 138, 143, 148, 157, 166-87, 189, 204, 216, 236, 242, 258, 261, 268

Chaos, 14-15, 29, 243

Circumcision, 50, 54, 112, 132

Community: as builder of temple, 259; built up by God's Word, 127; created by God, 63; human need for, 10, 28, 113-14; Israel as, 57, 64, 144, 257, 285; and Jerusalem, 295; Joshua as head of, 112; justice in, 249, 327; originally without king, 189; priests as representatives of, 143, 155; and serving God, 244; and Torah, 136, 137, 147-48, 255; trust in God, 245; united by God, 139; and worship, 160, 184-85, 186, 267, 281, 283, 284

Compassion, God's, 33, 35, 41, 101, 129, 137, 270, 350, 351

Complain, 90, 91, 95, 97, 108, 272

Condemnation, 76, 137, 207, 223, 224, 269, 291, 295, 299, 301, 309, 320, 321, 325, 328, 330, 331, 332, 335, 338, 353

Confession: of Abraham, 41, 57, 73; confessional summaries, 5-6, 102, 124; of faith, 80, 86, 92, 94, 95, 101, 136, 140, 167, 177, 244, 255, 281, 283, 287, 288; of guilt, sin, 30, 31, 91, 92, 97, 255, 256, 272, 273, 278, 294; of Jeremiah, 117, 333; of Jonah, 349; of law, 133; of trust, 255

Conquest, 50, 167-87, 216

Covenant: ceremony, 268; confirmation of, 150, 182; of David with Judah, 195, 197; eternal, 354; law, 116, 130-48; with the nations, 354; new, 344; with the patriarchs, 38, 40, 49-52, 53, 57; with the people, 87, 92, 93, 117, 118-30, 149, 159, 173, 177, 219, 344; with priests and Levites, 153; renewal of, 102-3, 339, 347; violated, 352. *See also* Ark

Creation, 9-37; Creator, 100, 176, 236, 238, 242, 280, 303; in creeds, preceding election, 39; and fathers, 47, 89; and gift of land, 168; and God's acts, 113; of heaven and earth, 15-20; of humanity, 20-28; and Jerusalem, 236; and kingship, 191; as miracle, 11-15; and myth, 308; new, 299, 338; OT witness to, 57; perfect, 15; and preservation, 28-37; renewed, 220; and sabbath, 96, 132; and the Word, 13; victory over chaos, 14-15, 77, 243

Creedal summaries, creeds: Christian, 6, 73, 199; OT, 5, 9, 10-11, 16, 18, 38, 39, 40, 57, 67, 81, 86, 117, 118, 167, 168

Curse, 16, 26, 35, 110, 120, 123, 127, 128, 132, 137, 141, 334, 347, 352, 354

Cyrus, 197, 202, 231, 297, 342, 344, 355

Dan, and Bethel, 215, 260, 264

Daniel, 17, 232, 308, 355-58

Darius, 344, 346, 355

David, 21, 189-233; and altar, 214, 260; anointing of, 195-97; and ark, 262; branch of, 226, 228, 233; election of, 198; family of, 155, 224; God's promise to, 213, 222; and grace, 217; hero, 170; house of, 202, 221, 223, 225, 343; ideals of kingship, 330; and Jerusalem, 171, 208-9, 239-40, 241, 246, 258, 293; and justice, 203-4; kingdom of, 179, 189; line of, 230, 231,

233, 293; loved by God, 207; and messianic king, 206, 221; Moabite ancestry of, 285, 349; model king, 206, 210, 220, 228; and Nathan, 221; and patriarchs, 191; prophets under, 305; and Psalms, 190, 249; rise of, 217, 219, 227, 250; and Saul, 207-8, 213, 217, 219; as savior, 201; as shepherd, 228; sin of, 213-14; and Solomon, 187, 222, 234, 258-59; and Spirit, 193-94; suffering of, 208, 215; throne of, 199-200, 209, 226, 229, 230; throne restored, 344; victory of, 354; and war, 200, 208

Day of the Lord, 325, 336, 351, 352

Death, 34, 122, 168, 293, 299; and curse, 110; and disease, 143, 275; and exile, 323; and the fall, 21, 35, 36; fear of, 254; God brings, 332; Israel preserved from, 93; and the law, 145, 146; and life, 16, 75, 80, 112, 127, 148, 252, 253, 277-78, 338; penalty, 147-48; salvation from, 277-78; and sin, 62, 104, 163, 253. *See also* Life

Deborah, 24, 193, 202, 278, 305, 307; Song of, 185

Decalogue, Ten Commandments, 56, 116, 123, 124, 132, 134, 139, 140, 141, 145, 286

Deliver, deliverance: of Canaanites to Israelites, 170; to death, 293; false prediction for Jerusalem, 299; and Gideon, 316; and God's righteousness, 51; of Israel from Egypt, 57, 75, 80; and kings, 246; and Psalms, 248, 273. *See also* Salvation

Deuteronomy, 63, 113

Ecclesiastes, 6, 250, 255, 256-57

Egypt, Egyptians, 12, 17, 19, 27, 39, 43, 56, 57, 58, 59, 60, 64, 65, 67, 69, 71, 72, 74, 75, 76, 77, 79, 80, 82, 83, 84, 86, 87, 88, 91, 92, 94, 96, 101, 108, 113, 115, 117, 120, 124, 136, 138, 141, 144, 148, 154, 166, 168, 170, 178, 181, 185, 191, 197, 198, 216, 222, 234, 235, 240, 254, 277, 280, 281, 285, 287, 290, 292, 308, 309, 313, 322, 323, 324, 325, 328, 329, 331, 332, 334, 337, 338, 354, 356

El, 12, 48, 70, 183, 184, 197, 198, 242

Elders: at anointing of king, 192, 195; in Ezekiel's time, 337; and Joshua, 171; of the land, 327; and Moses, 69, 70, 74, 80, 81, 82, 83, 93, 121, 122, 128, 132, 269, 305, 317, 318; and Ruth, 349

Elect, election: of David, 198; of the fathers,

38, 48, 53, 57, 61, 115, 117, 124, 168, 281, 322; of God's people, 7, 40-44, 87, 88, 90, 127, 219, 287; of Jerusalem, 236, 327; of kings, 212; and preservation, 93; of priests, 152, 154, 158; and rejection, 220; of Zion, 169

Elijah, 19, 22, 116, 170, 172, 184, 215, 232, 305, 311, 312, 313, 314, 316, 317, 352

Elisha, 282, 305, 313, 316, 317

Elohim, 47, 48, 184

El-Shaddai, 48, 50

Enoch, 36, 47

Ephod, 154, 155

Esther, 250

Eve, 30, 31, 32, 33, 34, 35, 254

Evil, 15, 18, 33, 77, 91, 254, 312, 325, 328, 333; people resist, 353; powers, 14, 162; spirits, 87. *See also* Good and evil; Wicked

Exile, 10, 40, 73, 107, 177, 187, 189, 216, 225, 231, 243, 265, 273, 282, 284, 285, 288, 292, 294, 295, 311, 317, 328, 331, 332, 335, 340, 346

Exodus (event), 7, 39, 40, 55, 56-85, 270, 354; as beginning of Israel, 62, 63, 69; and covenant, 50; importance of, 57, 61; and law, 60; leaders of, 80, 81, 82, 83; new, 338, 341, 343-44, 354; and Passover, 64-65; pharaoh of, 77; and promised land, 168; and revelation, 44, 47, 66, 67, 69, 100; and wilderness wandering, 86, 89; and Zion, 236

Expiation, 107, 132, 150, 151, 152, 153, 154, 155, 156, 158, 161, 163, 164, 267, 274, 288. *See also* Atonement

Ezekiel, 72, 225, 228-29, 230, 231, 265-66, 282, 290, 306, 309, 311, 313, 317, 318, 335-39

Ezra, 70, 155, 237, 255

Faith, faithfulness, 181, 271, 327; of Abraham, 255, birth of, 63; of Daniel, 356; of David, 214; and David's reign, 206; and the exodus, 57, 65, 67, 68, 73, 80; of God, 51, 52, 71, 86, 87, 95, 98, 99, 216, 256, 265, 303, 307, 326, 341; Israel's inability for, 89; and Jerusalem, 237, 241; in Jesus Christ, 359; and promised land, 167, 168, 173, 182; and God's promises, 179; and prophets, 307, 308, 322, 330; role of creation in Israel's, 9, 10, 39; and Sinai revelation, 117, 211; and the wilderness wandering, 85, 86, 95, 102, 110; and wisdom, 251, 255, 257. *See also* Belief

ugees from, 297; judgment of, 248, 320, 344; kings of, 200; laws of, 135, 147; Moses passes revelation to, 69; offerings of, 271; oracles concerning, 324, 335; and peace, 204; pilgrimage to Zion, 327; praise God, 341; and promise, 180; promise of deliverance of Israel from, 342; salvation for, 242, 340, 347; and sex, 143; threaten Jerusalem, 243; turmoil of, 330, 345; and wisdom, 249-50

Nebuchadnezzar, 77, 113, 225, 247, 332, 355, 356

Nehemiah, 70, 237, 302, 307, 317

Nineveh, 35, 216, 292, 312, 316, 318, 328, 349, 350

Noah, 29, 31, 36, 270, 274

Obedience, obey, 19, 42, 43, 50, 89, 90, 120, 124, 138, 168, 171, 181, 205, 207, 255, 339, 356

Offering, 46, 47, 54, 65, 105, 106, 107, 116, 121, 129, 132, 138, 149, 150, 151, 152, 153, 154, 157, 158, 159, 160, 161, 162, 163, 164, 165, 196, 258, 266, 267, 268, 270, 271, 272, 274, 275, 276, 280-81, 294, 298, 345, 346. *See also* Sacrifice

Oppression, 59, 342, 344, 353

Passover, 57, 64, 65, 74, 83, 94, 132, 138, 148, 159, 161, 268, 287. *See also* Feast

Patriarchs. *See* Fathers

Patrimony, 86, 88, 109, 111, 113, 132, 174-80, 331

Paul, 15, 36, 38, 74, 79, 85, 135-36, 162, 190, 219, 259, 276, 301, 339

Peace, 114, 172, 173, 180, 204, 205, 209, 211, 216, 221, 224, 227, 228, 230, 232, 234, 252, 297, 344, 347; king of, 226; Prince of, 205, 223, 224, 325, 345

People, God's, 7, 56; and adoption, 89, 90, 91, 124, 126, 140, 142, 152, 153; and blessings, 180, 356; called God's son, 198; and Canaan, 166, 172, 173; and church, 281; community to serve God, 64; and covenant, 87, 117, 131, 159; creation of, 10, 57; and death, 278; degeneracy of, 260; defiance of, 346; and doom, 320; and Egypt, 77; election of, 65, 88, 91, 92, 93; exodus as birth of, 62, 63, 69, 120, 282; faithful, 343, 357; and fall of Jerusalem, 292; freed by God, 60-65, 82, 84, 91, 115, 144, 301-2; God loves, 13, 351; God's compassion for, 295; God's presence with,

101-7, 284-85, 339; God's solidarity with, 301; and God's Word, 127, 283, 284; healing of, 327, 328; holy, 125, 141, 143, 283; in image of God, 27; infidelity of, 332, 336; and judges, 186; judgment on, 324; judgment and mercy, 97; and kingship, 189, 191, 199; and land of rest, 108-14; and laws, 118, 130-31, 133, 135-36, 138, 144, 147, 157; live in communion with God, 119, 285, 286, 287; mediators for, 263; and mercy, 323; and nations, 296-97, 298; nations scorn, 338; new, 2, 206; oppressed, 73; as pilgrims, 109-14, 303; poor, 287; and praise, 279; prayers of, 272; and priesthood, 153, 352; and prophets, 304, 306, 308, 340; protected by God, 93; purified, 342; and reconciliation, 149, 165; and remnant, 331; renewal of, 133, 161; represented by Aaron and Moses, 84; responsive, 351; restored, 343; and revelation, 123; and sabbath, 96; salvation of, 211, 228, 242; stubborn, 92, 96, 97, 100; and suffering, represented by Naomi, 349; and temple, 262, 265, 267; unity of, 157; and worship, 270

Pharaoh, 14-15, 60, 64, 66, 68, 69, 73, 74, 75, 76, 77, 78, 79, 80, 81, 82, 83, 166, 197, 198, 219, 269, 288, 316

Philistia, Philistines, 43, 75, 177, 185, 240, 241, 325, 327, 353

Pilgrim people, 109-14, 303

Plan, of God, 21, 41, 44, 45, 47, 49, 52, 53, 76, 80, 118-19, 205, 225, 242; of salvation, 287, 295, 345, 358. *See also* Aim; Intention; Purpose; Will

Power: of darkness, 14, 77; divine, 10, 13, 16, 22, 27, 47, 68, 69, 73, 81, 119, 122, 123, 125, 128, 139, 159, 166, 179, 243, 261, 299, 300, 314, 316, 318, 319, 342, 356; human, 17, 25, 26, 28, 31, 76, 77, 356; of other gods, 19, 68; of Torah, 144

Praise, of God, 10, 11, 13, 15, 18, 23, 27, 28, 30, 31, 37, 42, 47, 56, 57, 58, 61, 66, 67, 68, 69, 72, 78, 79, 80, 84, 88, 90, 92, 95, 96, 97, 99, 100, 107, 110, 117, 118, 119, 121, 126, 128, 139, 149, 150, 157, 171, 180, 190, 199, 209, 223, 224, 238, 241, 245, 246, 268, 272, 273, 275, 278, 279, 280, 281, 283, 288, 320, 324, 329, 330, 339, 341, 350, 354, 356

Pray, prayer, 5, 35, 107, 119, 121, 151, 176, 196, 203, 222, 241, 246, 249, 255, 268, 272, 273-74, 275, 276, 277, 278, 280,

Remnant, 184, 227, 325, 331, 332, 340, 353

Repentance, 215, 223, 255, 274, 294, 323-24, 333, 335, 338, 344, 348, 349, 350, 351

Rest, God's, 10; for people, 96, 107, 109, 112; place or land of, 86, 108, 111, 112, 113-14, 180, 204

Revelation, 2, 33, 39, 40, 49, 52, 57, 86, 103, 160, 168, 169, 224, 236-37, 252, 255, 258, 281, 283, 304, 308, 329, 342, 354, 355, 358; of God's name, 73, 78, 88, 100, 309; God's self-, 1, 7, 13, 17, 20, 29, 40, 44-49, 53, 66, 67, 68, 69, 71, 78, 102, 115-65, 166, 306, 310-13, 341

Righteous, righteousness, 52, 144, 145, 228, 247, 248, 249, 254, 255, 256, 273, 280, 294, 297, 321, 326, 330, 345, 351, 354, 358

Ruth, 59, 191, 250, 348-49

Sabbath, 65, 96, 106, 114, 132, 138, 139, 140, 142, 143, 145, 148, 271, 348

Sacrifice, 50, 59, 94, 106, 116, 119, 128, 129, 132, 141, 142, 143, 148, 149, 152, 153, 154, 155, 211, 236, 333, 336, 343, 350, 351. *See also* Offering

Salvation, save, saving act, 2, 7, 37, 59, 87, 171, 236, 302, 333, 343, 355; and calling of people, 5; common need of, 20; creation as salvific, 9, 10, 14, 15; from death, 275, 277; of Jerusalem, 227; and judgment, 319, 321, 330; message of, 76, 223, 299, 338, 340; oracles of, 340, 341, 345, 358; plan of, 218, 225, 242, 287, 295, 345, 358; promise of, 228, 273, 324, 325, 326, 331; prophet suffers for, 231; prophets of, 339-52; and righteousness, 51; savior, 83, 200, 201, 229, 231, 233, 278, 341; ultimate, 354; work of, 360; of world, 26, 220, 348. *See also* Deliverance

Samaria, 35, 215, 227, 291, 292, 320, 322, 323, 324, 325, 326, 327, 328, 330

Samuel, 134, 193, 201, 202, 207, 208, 213, 240, 241, 305, 306, 307, 309, 311, 313

Sarah (Sarai), 43, 46, 76, 191

Satan, 255, 346

Saul, 76, 189, 192-233, 239, 241, 260, 311, 316, 317

Scripture, 1-5, 6, 117, 358

Servant of the Lord, 43, 61, 112, 277; angel as, 311; Cyrus as, 231; and helper, 24; Jesus as, 114, 233, 278; kings as, 191; Moses as, 134, 171; priest as, 158; prophets as, 191, 306, 310, 314, 319, 333, 343,

347, 350, 358; rejected, 354; Saul as, 207; Servant Songs, 231-32; ultimate, 220, 340, 342-43; Zerubbabel as, 345

Serve, service, 60, 64, 73, 78, 80, 89, 91, 137, 139, 144, 147, 153, 154, 155, 156, 171, 189, 270, 271, 275, 276, 284, 288

Sheba, Queen of, 199, 209, 249

Shechem, 43, 45, 48, 123, 128, 132, 134, 157, 175, 177, 181, 182, 183, 186, 195, 212

Sheol, 100, 254, 277

Sin, sinners, 2, 21, 31, 32, 33, 35, 62, 65, 91, 92, 104, 118, 150, 151, 152, 153, 154, 159, 162, 163, 164, 172, 207, 212, 214, 215, 249, 252, 255, 267, 273, 278, 290, 291, 302, 326, 332, 336, 337, 338, 340, 343, 360

Sinai, 20, 44, 45, 50, 57, 71, 82, 86, 87, 102, 103, 113, 115-65, 166, 168, 169, 170, 177, 181, 185, 236-37, 268, 281, 308, 314

Slavery, 26, 58, 59, 60, 61, 62, 63, 65, 66, 75, 77, 84, 86, 125, 136, 140, 144, 146, 148, 168, 180

Sodom, 32, 35, 46; and Gomorrah, 172

Solomon, 46, 71, 76, 155, 176, 187, 189, 191, 192-233, 234, 239, 240, 249, 255, 258-59, 261-63, 266, 273

Sons of God, 17, 27, 68, 197-98, 220, 222, 233

Soul, 21, 22; and body, 21, 22, 27, 65

Spirit: of God, 186, 193-95, 207, 220, 224, 299, 302, 305, 306, 312, 316-18, 336, 338, 341, 343, 344, 351, 359; human, 22

Stubbornness, 80, 86, 89, 92, 95, 96, 97, 98, 100

Suffering: call on God's name, 354; of David, 208, 215; end to human, 36; and evil, 312; and fear, 63; of God, 34, 301, 339; for God's name, 82, 289; and hardness of heart, 78; human, 37; of Jeremiah, 333, 334; of Jerusalem, 302; of Job, 250, 254-56; and joy, 245; and judgment, 324; of just, 254, 329; and king, 249; of Micah, 328; of Moses, 112; of Moses and Aaron, 98; of Naomi, 349; and oppression, 59, 63, 75; people ask why God allows, 353; and prayer, 272; of prophets, 306, 319; and psalms, 276-77; of servant, 231, 278, 343; as slaves, 66, 87; in wilderness, 91, 110

Sumer, Sumerians, 4, 27, 120, 197, 251, 280

Syria, Syrians, 12, 39, 43, 48, 49, 75, 166, 331, 353

Index of Scripture References